A HISTORY OF THE ENGLISH PEOPLE
IN THE NINETEENTH CENTURY

A HISTORY OF THE ENGLISH PEOPLE IN THE NINETEENTH CENTURY

JOSEPH CHAMBERLAIN
H. von Herkomer
(*National Portrait Gallery*)

A HISTORY OF THE ENGLISH PEOPLE
IN THE NINETEENTH CENTURY — V

IMPERIALISM
AND THE
RISE OF LABOUR

by

ELIE HALEVY

Translated from the French by
E. I. WATKIN

ERNEST BENN LIMITED
LONDON

First published in French 1926
First published in English 1929
Second (revised) Edition 1951

Published by Ernest Benn Limited
Bouverie House, Fleet Street, London.
Printed in Great Britain by
STAPLES PRINTERS LIMITED
at their Rochester, Kent, establishment

Translator's Note

THE TRANSLATOR wishes to point out that the present volume embodies certain modifications and amplifications made by the Author in consequence of additional information made public since the French original appeared—particularly the publication of *British Documents*.

Introduction

WHEN, twenty years ago, I undertook the task of writing a general history of the English people during the nineteenth century I did not find it easy to decide where I should end my narrative. At Queen Victoria's death? But her death, which occurred in the middle of the Boer War, was in no sense a turning-point in English history. With the conclusion of the Boer War in June 1902? But the peace of Vereeniging was at least the apparent victory of Chamberlain's imperialism, and could such a victory be considered the natural conclusion of a century which had given England a Robert Peel and a Gladstone, a Cobden and a Herbert Spencer? Or ought I perhaps to conclude with the election of 1906 and treat the downfall of the party which had linked its fortunes with those of an aggressive imperialism, and the revival of Liberalism or rather the advent of a new and more democratic Liberalism, as marking for Great Britain the real end of the nineteenth century? The years passed, the centenary of Waterloo was approaching and my indecision had not been dispelled when the commencement of a great European war, in many respects comparable to that which had stained with blood the opening of the century, seemed to provide the natural conclusion of my work. But more than ten years have passed since then, and I have come to another decision. I will conclude my narrative about the year 1895—that is to say, about the time when Gladstone disappeared from political life. Neither Chamberlain with his exploitation of the warlike passions of the democracy, nor Lloyd George, author of the budget of 1909, the Insurance Act of 1911, and the programme of land reform of 1912 were men of the Victorian age. The period between 1895 and 1914 does not belong to the British nineteenth century, as I understand it. It is at most the epilogue of that century, as it is the prologue of the century which opened with those four years of tremendous upheaval, both military and social.

Must I therefore abandon the idea of writing the history of those nineteen years? I could not face without regret the prospect of leaving unused the mass of material I had accumulated when preparing the lectures which for almost thirty years I have given at the *Ecole libre des sciences politiques*. Or must I postpone writing it until I had completed my history of the nineteenth century? Life is too short for plans so remote to be safely formed. So I decided to write immediately the history of this epilogue of the nineteenth century in two volumes.

I will not, however, deny that the treatment of this period presents special difficulties to an historian like myself who has in a sense specialized in the history of the nineteenth century. Having approached the study of that epoch with a determination to treat it in a spirit of critical sympathy, and convinced that it was the culmination, or to speak less dogmatically, one of the culminations of British culture, it is difficult for me not to regard the subsequent period as, by comparison with its predecessor, a period of 'decadence'. But decadence is a dangerous word. It can be applied without qualification only to a period marked by a general decay of culture and a general decline of prosperity. But we find nothing of the sort in Great Britain during the years which I am studying. The country was becoming more civilized every day. Am I then prepared to maintain the paradox that 'civilization' and 'decadence' are synonymous, and that England was suffering from over-civilization? I must explain the special sense in which the term 'decadence' is applicable to the period whose history I am about to relate.

On the one hand, whatever the improvements made in her national institutions, England felt an increasingly powerful conviction that her vitality was less than that of certain other nations, and that if she was progressing, her rate of progress was less rapid than theirs—that is to say, if not absolutely, at least relatively to her rivals, she was declining. It was this loss of confidence which explains the far-reaching change in her foreign policy which took place towards the end of the nineteenth century. The British Government, no longer certain that the country was sufficiently powerful to stand by herself, abandoned the policy of 'isolation', and sought external support in some system of alliances. I shall tell the story of the deliberate *rapprochement* with the United States of America, also of the advances made towards Germany and their ignominious failure, and I shall then describe the advances made to the enemies of Germany. I shall recount the developments which imperceptibly conducted Europe along the fatal path, hidden from so many contemporary observers, which led to the great war of 1914. In relating this history I shall make England the centre of my perspective, but I shall adopt a method possibly somewhat different from that often adopted. I shall not plead against or in favour of any Government. In 1914, the aims respectively pursued by the different Governments and which each regarded as legitimate proved incompatible with the maintenance of peace. Moreover the aims of the German Government proved irreconcilable with the aims pursued by all the great nations, and in that sense Germany 'deserved' the alliance which was formed against her. But I do not intend to discuss in its usual form the question of the 'moral' responsibility for the war. I hope the day has already gone by for the literature of war propaganda, and equally for that propaganda against war, which is itself a form of war propaganda.

We also witness the decline, if not of England herself, at least of the ideal which she had pursued for an entire century and which she had come to regard as the secret of her greatness—the decline of that individualist form of Christianity in which Protestantism essentially consists—and a revival of Catholicism, or, more generally, of the Catholic forms of Christianity. I shall mark the limits of that revival. I shall inquire whether it was not accompanied by a phenomenon of far deeper significance, a decline of the Christian faith, and should not be regarded as in certain respects its 'euthanasia'. But I shall not on that account deny its reality, but shall relate its progress in the objective spirit of the historian, leaving to the reader to decide how far the progress of this Catholic movement should be considered a phenomenon of senescence, fostered by the panic which dare not face the difficulties of inquiry and the dangers of doubt, by moral weariness and intellectual timidity.

The simultaneous decline of economic individualism, the growth of Socialism, I shall relate as an historian, not as a propagandist, and shall present Socialism as a movement of the working class rather than the diffusion of a creed. I shall study with all the sympathy it deserves this effort of a class to achieve its emancipation. But my sympathy will be accompanied by a certain scepticism. The British workmen found fault with the employers for their lack of initiative, attachment to routine, and slowness in adopting technical improvements, as compared with the employers in countries which were truly progressive, and on these grounds sought to get rid of them. But the employers returned against the working class the charges they brought. They denounced the routine of the trade unions and the obstacles systematically erected by the unions to hamper the expansion of British industry. The impartial observer will be disposed to conclude that both classes had formed an unconscious alliance against that appetite for work, that zeal for production by which British industry had conquered the markets of the world. An irrational appetite? A blind zeal? Possibly. But on the other hand this prudent philosophy is perhaps the philosophy of the aged. Reserving our judgment on this point we will be content to show that, in spite of all claims to the contrary, the spirit which inspires what we may term in the most general sense Socialism, is opposed to the spirit of production.

Both Neo-Catholicism and Socialism are phenomena common to the entire western world. But we must not forget the extent to which England differs from the rest of Europe. Too many people conclude from the progress which Socialism has made in England that a 'social revolution' is imminent, similar to those which have taken place on the Continent. They forget that Socialism in Great Britain, confining its aims to the satisfaction of purely economic demands, and adapting itself to the traditional forms of party government, has assumed the constitutional and moderate form of 'Labour'. Too many Catholics cherish the hope that the day is at hand when the majority of Englishmen will once more accept the authority of the Pope. They forget not only that popular Protestantism presents an obstacle to the spread of Catholicism in England which will certainly not be overcome, but also that the characteristic form taken by Neo-Catholicism in England is the insular compromise known as 'Anglo-Catholicism'. Though the historian is compelled by the nature of his work to emphasize the changing aspects in the life of a people, he fails in his task if he does not also call attention to the permanent foundation which underlies these superficial changes. Today as in the past everything in England is instinctive groping, mutual tolerance and compromise, the effects of that moral and religious constitution whose factors we have analysed elsewhere. That constitution persists in its main lines unchanged and is still the source of those admirable political manners, abused, but all the while secretly envied, by those who, on the Continent, whether they belong to the parties of the right or of the left, profess the creed of violence.

My thanks are due to M. Emile Bourgeois, Sir Valentine Chirol, and Messrs. Graham Wallas, Cloudesley Brereton, and G. P.

Gooch who on particular points have kindly given me the benefit of their learning and personal experience; also to M. Paul Vaucher and Mr. C. M. Everett for the most valuable assistance which they rendered in acceding to my request to read through my book in proof and make suggestions, and finally to Baron de Meyendorff, who kindly placed at my disposal the correspondence of Baron de Staal, Russian ambassador in London during the closing years of the nineteenth century.

E. H.

August, 1926.

Contents

PART I

IMPERIALISM

CHAPTER I

Chamberlain and Lord Salisbury

I IMPERIALISM

I

IN June 1895, the Liberal Cabinet, which for the past three years
had dragged out a precarious existence, took the opportunity
afforded by a defeat in the Commons on a clause in the army
estimates to resign and thus transfer to the Opposition the responsibility of making a new appeal to the country. The Cabinet,
formed a few days later by Lord Salisbury, was not, like the
Government produced by the Conservative victory of 1886, a
Conservative Cabinet enjoying the support from outside of the
group of recalcitrant liberals led by Chamberlain which had refused to accept Gladstone's programme of Irish Home Rule. It
was a Coalition Government in which these rebels, now in the
strict sense deserters to the opposite camp, took their seats with
the representatives of traditional Conservatism. The formation of
the Cabinet was followed speedily by dissolution, and the General
Election, which began on July 12 and finished on August 10,
proved a brilliant victory for the Conservative Party, or, to use
the term current since 1886, the Unionists—that is to say, the party
which wished to maintain the Parliamentary union between
Great Britain and Ireland. The Election of 1892 had returned to
the House of Commons 274 Liberals and 81 Irish Nationalists as
against 269 Unionists and 46 Liberal Unionists. The Government
therefore had a majority of 40, if supported by all the Irish
Nationalists, and a series of unfavourable by-elections had since
reduced that majority by almost half. The election of 1895 returned to Parliament 340 Unionists and 71 Liberal Unionists as
against 177 Liberals and 82 Irish Nationalists. That is to say, there
was a Unionist majority of 152; 411 members supported Lord
Salisbury's government against a Liberal and Irish Opposition of
259. The Liberals did their best to minimize the significance of
the returns. The alliance between the Conservative and Liberal
Unionists, between Lord Salisbury and Chamberlain, was, they
argued, artificial and precarious. And if it had for the nonce won
a victory at the polls, it was because the temperance legislation of

the late Government had alarmed the brewing interest, and the Bill which had passed the Commons to disestablish the Church in Wales was a direct attack upon the Anglican Church. The great brewers, they explained, had placed immense sums of money at the disposition of the Conservative agents, and in every constituency the Anglican clergymen had worked hard in the same cause. And after all, the Conservative victory assumed very different proportions when account was taken not of the seats won but the votes cast for either party. Out of a total electorate of 6,300,000 less than 4,800,000 had polled, and of those 4,800,000 voters, 2,412,000 had voted for the Unionists, 2,380,000 for the Liberals and their Irish allies. That is to say, the Unionist majority amounted to little more than 31,000 votes. There could be no doubt that within the next five or six years the Unionists, now placed in office, would have lost the allegiance of 30,000.

But these arguments and figures produced little impression on public opinion. It was generally felt—and the writer bases this assertion not on the evidence of documents which he has consulted but on his personal reminiscences—that the election of 1895 marked a turning-point in the moral and political history of the British people.

In the first place, even if we take the most favourable view of the situation from the Liberal standpoint, it appeared certain— they would have admitted it themselves—that the Liberals would never again see those glorious days when for close on half a century they might have fairly claimed to be the regular Government of the nation. In those days Freedom—intellectual freedom, civil freedom, freedom of production and trade, freedom of nationalities, had been the magic formula which was expected to solve in the immediate future every political and social problem. In those days the Conservative party had been excluded from office because its very title branded it as the foe of liberty. If it had occasionally succeeded in forming a Cabinet, and on one occasion, in 1841, had even won an election, those successes were only temporary accidents, and the political balance was speedily redressed in favour of the Liberals. Unfortunately, since the Reform Bills of 1867 and 1884, which without actually introducing universal suffrage had given the country an extremely democratic constitution, new problems had arisen for which Cobden's disciples and Gladstone's followers had either no solutions, or solutions to

4

which the electorate was not prepared to accord an unreserved assent. The two parties had held office in turn, and the utmost the Liberals could hope after each defeat was, as everyone agreed, a new swing of the electoral pendulum which would restore them to power with the certainty of being turned out at no distant interval. But there was a widespread disposition to regard their defeat in the summer of 1895 in a more serious light and to believe that for the renovated Conservative party it might well prove the beginning of an epoch of continuous rule comparable to the rule of the Liberals throughout the middle of the century.

It was all very well for the Liberals to denounce the coalition between the traditional Conservatives and the deserters from Gladstone's party. Although the Liberal Unionists had decided to maintain an electoral organization distinct from the Conservative, at Westminster the two groups were a single party receiving one whip, and the Liberal Unionists expelled from the great National Liberal Federation were admitted without opposition to all the Conservative clubs in London and the provinces. Both groups obviously composed a homogeneous party. This could not be said of the new Opposition. In the first place it contained the Irish Nationalists, on whom for the last three years the Liberals had depended for their majority in the House, but who for that very reason had enormously contributed to their unpopularity. For in England the Nationalists were hated for their unpatriotic language, despised for their intestine squabbles. They were divided into two or three warring factions, which attacked each other unsparingly. Wales, where, moreover, the Conservatives had just begun to make a little headway, was beginning to cause similar anxieties though to a far slighter degree. For the example of Irish Nationalism had called a Welsh Nationalism into being, and the Welsh Radicals formed at Westminster a distinct group which demanded a modicum of Home Rule for the Principality. It was indeed to satisfy their wishes that the Liberal Cabinet had reluctantly placed upon its programme the Welsh Disestablishment, which had just contributed to its defeat. And in Scotland, where the Conservatives had won almost half the seats, and in England itself, where the Conservative majority was overwhelming, the Liberal party was obviously suffering from a profound internal disintegration.

2

The definite retirement of the aged Gladstone in 1894 at the venerable age of eighty-five possessed, as everyone agreed, a deep significance. He had realized—possibly too late—that times had changed. Two reasons had decided the step; his second Irish Home Rule Bill had been thrown out by the Lords with the obvious approval of the entire country, and his colleagues had demanded an extensive programme of naval construction that contradicted the principles which throughout his career had inspired his finance and his political objectives. His retirement left the leaders of his party a prey to disunion. On one side were those who remained faithful to his tradition, convinced opponents of expenditure and war, of bureaucracy and state socialism. On the other were the younger men, who vied with the Conservatives in their zeal for the consolidation of the Empire and who at the same time, as though with the deliberate intention to appear, in contrast with the old-fashioned Gladstonians, progressive, displayed leanings towards collectivism, of an indefinite and very moderate character it is true. The destinies of the old Liberal party were therefore in the hands of leaders at issue among themselves, and their disagreement was reflected in the party as a whole by a double crisis effecting respectively its organization and its voting strength. In the first place the party machine was passing through a crisis. Not only in the boroughs but also in the counties, the local organization of the party had gradually come under the exclusive, or almost exclusive, control of artisans and labourers. The workmen who came forward as Liberal electioneering agents or candidates were the secretaries of the great trade unions, whose membership grew every year. It might have been expected that the unions would have worked for the return to Parliament of representatives of their own class and have created a Labour party to take the place of the Liberals. But although within the last twenty years a certain number of working men had been returned to Parliament, they were a tiny and unpretentious group, content, indeed almost proud, to be merged in the organization of Gladstonian Liberalism. And on the whole, the trade unions were not eager to grasp political power. They preferred to employ their money for other than electoral purposes, extend their organizations for mutual assistance, and accumulate the funds necessary to finance a strike.

Politically they remained loyal to the aristocratic traditions of the country, and sought above their own ranks in the governing classes the only candidates they considered worthy to represent their interests in the government of the nation. Their search was seldom successful. Among the great landowners and leading manufacturers there were only a few who, more from family tradition than personal inclination, remained faithful to the Liberal creed. Even among the gentry, manufacturers, bankers and traders of the middle class an uninterrupted stream of defections thinned the party ranks. The party was obliged to be content with second-rate candidates, cranks, and men inspired by personal ambitions—political adventurers greedy of spoils and honours. But it was a costly business to stand as a Liberal candidate in an English constituency. For as the number of wealthy Liberals decreased, the heavier became the demands made by the local electorate upon the purse of the few who remained. If in the August of 1895 the Liberal agents had been asked what in their opinion was the immediate cause of the Liberal defeat, they would all have replied without the least hesitation that it was lack of funds and lack of candidates. The Liberals had indeed surrendered to the Conservatives without a contest no less than 124 seats as against the ten in which a Liberal was returned unopposed.[1]

If the organization of the party was passing through a crisis, its position as regards numbers was no less critical. The electors were abandoning a party unable to offer either sufficiently respectable candidates or a definite programme. The lack of programme was indeed the direct result of the dissension which prevailed among the party leaders. A programme of social reform had, it is true, been adopted: state regulation of the conditions of labour in factories; compensation for accidents to workmen in the course of their employment; restriction of the hours of work in mines. All these seemed calculated to satisfy an electorate in which labour was the predominant element. But it was public knowledge that a considerable section of the leaders had accepted these items of the Liberal programme only with extreme reluctance. And moreover, no one could fail to notice that the proposals for social reform put forward by many Liberal candidates were for all practical purposes indistinguishable from those presented by a considerable

---

[1] *Annual Register*, 1895, p. 153. Cf. the *Fortnightly Review*, June 1898 (vol. lxiii, pp. 910 sqq.): An unsigned article entitled 'The present State of the Liberal Party'.

number of Unionists loyal to the tradition of Beaconsfield or friends of Chamberlain. And finally it was clear that certain of the proposed reforms—in the first place, the restriction of the miners' day—would be opposed by a section of the working class, which at this date had not yet been widely affected by the socialist propaganda. Should the Liberals then return to their old programme of uncompromising hostility to war and militarism, colonial expansion and armaments? No decided opposition to a policy of that kind was anywhere discernible among the electorate. For militarism was hardly felt by the masses of a nation which knew nothing of conscription, and the British budget was so arranged that the burden of expenditure on the army and navy was not borne by the working class. Moreover, as we have already pointed out, an entire section of the Liberal leaders, the followers of Lord Rosebery, were imperialists, and during the three years of Liberal government the Foreign Office had pursued an imperialist policy. But if a policy of imperialism must in any case be adopted, the imperialism of Lord Salisbury and Chamberlain was preferable. It was perfectly frank, and was not compromised by an alliance either with the supporters of peace at any price or, and this was the decisive factor, with the partisans of Irish Home Rule, the would-be disrupters of the United Kingdom.

3

The jingoism which at the close of the nineteenth century prevailed in the large towns was a phenomenon of transition. The great mass of electors were disgusted with middle-class Liberalism. They had not yet discovered Socialism. But at the time no one appears to have clearly perceived that the Conservative victory was essentially a passing phase. Alike at home and abroad everyone expected that many decades must elapse before a popular party would arise rejuvenated from the ruins of the old Liberalism. For the moment it was the Tory party which boasted its rejuvenation and claimed to be in the strictest sense a popular party. It was no longer an obscure country party whose opposition to the interests of the large towns went unheeded by the nation at large. Not only in the counties but in the boroughs also the Tories and their Liberal Unionist allies had won an overwhelming victory. Lancashire, the home of Cobden and Bright, only a few years before the citadel of free trade and Liberal ideals, returned 48 Unionists as against only 7 Liberals and an Irish Nationalist who represented an Irish division of Liverpool. In London 54 Conservatives were returned for 8 members of the new Opposition. In the music-halls bellicose sentiments received as much applause from the pit and gallery as from the stalls and dress circle. And it was the Conservative party which, at the very time when both in London and the provinces it was extending its control over the Press, created a new type of newspaper to meet the needs of a public more extensive and less educated than that which journalism had hitherto addressed. On May 4, 1896, the young Alfred Charles William Harmsworth—the future Lord Northcliffe—brought out the first number of the *Daily Mail*, a paper of reduced size and costing only a halfpenny.[1] The new paper contained no feature which resembled the carefully accurate information and well-informed argument which for over a century had been the glory of British journalism. There were illustrations, serial stories, political articles of extreme brevity, and large headlines which dispensed a hurried reader from the perusal of the text. And there was an abundant supply of sensational news items to tickle the popular palate—crimes, catastrophes, royal marriages and funerals, sport, naval and military reviews and wars.[2] Harmsworth's venture was immediately rewarded by an unprecedented success. At the end of the first three months the *Daily Mail* had reached a circulation of over 200,000 copies, at the end of three years the circulation approached 550,000. The handful of democrats who protested against the exploitation of warlike feelings presented the aspect of a select group of aristocrats, distinguished but powerless. When the Liberals had taken office fifteen years before, their policy had been a reaction against Lord Beaconsfield's imperialism.

[1] Two morning papers were indeed already published in London at a halfpenny—*The Morning* and *The Morning Leader* (the latter a Radical organ)—but they were not very successful. There were also two halfpenny evening papers—*The Star* (since 1888) and *The Evening News*, which Alfred Harmsworth had purchased in August 1894, to prepare the ground in London for the Conservative candidates at the election which was felt to be imminent. In 1897 the Radical *Morning Herald*, and in 1900 the *Daily Express*, followed. But it is from the brilliant success of the *Daily Mail* that we must date the real beginnings of the halfpenny Press (Kennedy Jones, *Fleet Street and Downing Street*, 1919, pp. 117 sqq.).

[2] 'What sells a newspaper? is a question asked me. The first answer is "War". . . . War apart, a State Funeral sells more papers than anything else. The public takes a livelier interest in funerals than in weddings. . . . Next to a State Funeral comes a First-class Murder. . . . After a First-class Murder, any big public pageant or ceremony will swell a paper's sales' (Kennedy Jones, *Fleet Street and Downing Street*, 1919, p. 200). Kennedy Jones was one of the original editors of the *Daily Mail*.

They had evacuated Afghanistan and the Transvaal, and had abandoned Gordon at Khartoum to a death they refused to avenge. They had gone further and attempted to break up the Empire. They wished to consolidate the Empire by granting the Irish Home Rule. Now the imperialists, once more masters of Parliament and public opinion, reacted in their turn against these pacific tendencies. They called upon the British to forget party quarrels and unite in a firm front against the Irishman and the foreigner. And their appeal was not addressed to the mother country alone, but to Britons in every part of the Empire. They wished to consolidate the Empire by establishing a federal bond between the Mother Country and her Colonies, and to extend it by foreign conquest. This might seem a sufficient explanation of an aggressive policy which, practised with a brutal ostentation, would in a short time arouse the hostility of the entire world. If, however, we examine the new imperialism more closely, we shall discover that, if the British were aggressive, it was because they believed themselves threatened. A peaceful nation the English had undoubtedly been in the period around 1860, possibly more peace-loving than any nation in the entire course of history. But these peaceable dispositions masked a profound disdain. Sure of her command of the seas and proud of her vast wealth, England scornfully abandoned the Continent to its dissensions. Unfortunately, the situation, not only on the Continent, where peace had prevailed for twenty-five years, but throughout the world, had radically altered during the last half century to the disadvantage of Britain.

In 1851, if France was poorer, her population still exceeded that of Great Britain; 35,700,000 Frenchmen as against only 27,000,000 British. But the population of the United States was only 23,000,000, Germany did not exist as a State, and the power of Russia, whose population was not exactly known, was shortly to be weakened on the Bosphorus and in Asia by the Crimean War. Twenty years later, on the morrow of the Franco-German War, the population of Great Britain exceeded 31,800,000 and was thus on the way to overtake the French figure of 36,500,000. But the population of the newly created German Empire in the very first year of its existence was nearly 41,000,000 and the population of the United States, 38,600,000, also exceeded that of Britain. At the end of another twenty years, in 1891, the populations of Great Britain and France were almost equal—each slightly above 38,000,000—and the former would soon exceed the latter. But on the other hand Britain was left far behind by Germany with a population of 50,000,000, and by the United States with a population of 63,000,000, and the population of Russia was estimated at 100,000,000. Britain was and knew herself to be threatened by 'empires'. How could she recover the advantage? She must pursue the programme already laid down by Lord Beaconsfield and assert her position, not as a nation like her rivals, but as an empire. No doubt the population of Great Britain barely exceeded 38,000,000, but there were nearly 2,000,000 British subjects in Cape Colony and Natal, over 600,000 in New Zealand, over 3,000,000 in Australia, and 5,000,000 in Canada. Add to these figures the Indian subjects of Great Britain, almost 300,000,000, and a further 46,000,000 in the remaining territories under some form of British rule or influence and the total amounted to 394,600,000. What other State could hope to rival such a figure? Moreover, the number of British subjects was on the increase, and optimists could entertain the hope that within two generations, if not one, the population of the self-governing colonies alone would be four times its present figure and equal the population of the Mother Country.[1] The area of the Empire was also on the increase: in September 1896, a statesman calculated that in twelve years 2,600,000 square miles had been added to it—that is to say twenty-four times the area of Great Britain.[2] In 1895, it was 11,335,000 square miles.[3] A few more annexations and it

[1] 'The British Empire must stand and fall together, and in twenty years' time the larger part of Britain will be outside of Great Britain' (speech by the Canadian, G. E. Foster; *Report . . . on the Colonial Conference at Ottawa with the Proceedings of the Conference*, 1894, p. 203). 'At the present rate of increase the inhabitants of Australia at or before the close of the next century will number about 190,000,000, and constitute no inconsiderable part of the population of the world' (David A. Wells, *Recent Economic Changes and Their Effect on the Production and Distribution of Wealth and the Well-being of Society*, 1890, p. 454).

[2] Lord Rosebery. Edinburgh speech, October 9, 1896: '. . . The British Empire is in truth—as Napoleon III said quite falsely of his empire—the British Empire is peace. It means peace and it needs peace.' He immediately added: 'For the last twenty years, still more during the last twelve, you have been laying your hands, with almost frantic eagerness, on every tract of territory adjacent to your own or desirable in any point of view which you thought it desirable to take.'

[3] In this total Egypt is not included. Cf. Sir Robert Giffen, *The Relative Growth of the Component Parts of the Empire*, read at a meeting of the Royal Colonial Institute, February 1899: 'The increase in area and population in this Empire, excluding Egypt and the Sudan, amounts since 1871 to 2,854,000 square miles of the area, or more than one-fourth of the whole, and to 125,000,000 of population, which is also more than one-fourth of the whole. The increase of the ruling race included in this population amounts to about 12,500,000, or about one-fourth of the number in 1897; and the increase in the subject races is 112,000,000, or nearly one-third the numbers in 1897. The increase in the subject races is largely, but by no means exclusively, due to annexation' (*Economic Inquiries and Studies*, vol. ii, p. 223).

would amount to a quarter of the entire land surface of the globe.

4

This was the object which the convinced imperialists deliberately pursued—to extend indefinitely the area of the Empire until it became impossible for any rival nation to entertain the hope of equalling its magnitude. But when they spoke of extending the Empire they had in view not only, as the foregoing considerations might lead the reader to suppose, an increase of area and population, but also, perhaps most of all, an increase of the national wealth, an improvement of the nation's economic position. For, if for some years previously a vague feeling of pessimism and anxiety had prevailed in England, it was because a number of symptoms—decrease of exports and unemployment—had led the English to ask themselves whether their country had not entered upon an era of industrial stagnation, possibly of actual decline.

The British could still contemplate with pride the vast size of their mercantile marine, whose tonnage equalled that of all foreign merchantmen together.[1] But what of the goods carried by these innumerable vessels? British exports for the year preceding the return of the Conservatives to power in 1895 did not so far exceed in value American, French, or German as in former years.[2] Comfort might be derived from the consideration that, if the national

[1] Dr. V. Juraschek (*Uebersichten der Weitwirtschaft*) credits Great Britain with the ownership of 42.7 per cent of tonnage of the world, and, taking steam tonnage as equivalent in carrying-power to three times as much sailing tonnage, with just over 50 per cent of the carrying-power of the world (A. W. Flux, 'British Trade and German Competition'; *Economical Journal*, vol. vii, p. 43-4).

[2] Export figures for 1894: United Kingdom £216,000,000, United States £181,100,000, Germany £148,100,000, France £123,100,000. In 1892, American exports had reached the figure of £211,600,000, as against the £227,000,000 of British exports. (See the Tables and Diagrams in: *Memoranda, Statistical Tables, and Charts prepared in the Board of Trade with reference to various matters bearing on British and Foreign Trade and Industrial Conditions*, 1903, pp. 5 sqq.) It should be added that if the British imagination was disagreeably impressed by the increase of American exports, the latter did not, speaking generally, compete with British industries. On the contrary, they provided British manufacture with the cheap bread and cheap cotton it required. (*Foreign Trade. Statistical Tables relating to the Progress of the Foreign Trade of the United Kingdom and of other Countries in recent years, with report to the Board of Trade thereon*, 1894, p. 4.) But the United States was also exporting manufactured articles, and in greater numbers every year. Out of her total exports in 1880, about 10 per cent were manufactures, and about 90 per cent food and raw materials; in 1899, about 29 per cent were manufactures, and about 71 per cent food and raw materials. These percentages say something; and the absolute figures say more. The value of her manufactures exported in 1880 was £17,165,000, in 1899 £75,798,000; of food and raw materials in 1880 £154,490,000, in 1899 £185,329,000. (Sir Vincent H. P. Caillard, *Imperial Fiscal Reform*, 1903, pp. 19-20.)

production were to be fairly estimated on the basis of these figures. they must not be taken simply, but the value of the exports must be divided by the number of the population. It would then be seen that Great Britain still far outstripped her competitors. The value of British exports per head of the population was more than double the value of American.[1] But even estimated by this standard it must be admitted that the value of British exports had during the past twenty-five years steadily declined. The exports of the United States and Germany on the other hand showed a steady increase, and it seemed possible to predict with an almost mathematical certainty the day when Britain would be overtaken by these two nations. French competition did not inspire the same anxiety; like the population, the value of French exports remained almost stationary. Russian competition gave even less grounds for uneasiness. Nevertheless, Russia and France were extending their colonial empire in Asia and Africa and every area occupied by a foreign power was immediately closed to British imports by a customs barrier. The dissatisfaction inspired by the unfavourable economic situation had without doubt contributed to the Conservative victory at the polls. How did the Conservatives propose to remedy ills for which the Liberal policy had no cure? Their prescription was imperialism, the opening of new markets to British exports by the annexation of new colonies.

However, if Britain had lost her former confidence that she would always remain the greatest exporter of goods, she enjoyed a unique position, which moreover improved every year, among the nations of the world as the exporter of capital. At the date with which our history opens an economist estimated that the amount of British capital invested abroad, or in the colonies, had risen from £144,000,000 in 1842, to £600,000,000 in 1877, £875,000,000 in 1882, and £1,698,000,000 in 1893, and represented 15 per cent of the entire capital of the nation.[2] A few years later the Treasury estimated that the income from foreign investments subject to income tax had risen between 1884 and 1900 from

[1] For the period 1895-9, £5 19s. 5d. per head for Great Britain, £2 18s. 4d. for the United States. Twenty-five years earlier (1870-4) the figures had been £7 7s. 3d. for Great Britain, £2 9s. 2d. United States. France remained stationary: £3 15s. for the first five-year period, £3 14s. 8d. for the second. The German figure rose from £2 16s. 7d. to £3 7s. 9d. (*Memorandum on the Comparative Statistics of Population, Industry, and Commerce of the United Kingdom and some Leading Countries*, 1902, p. 11.)

[2] Michael G. Mulhall, *The Dictionary of Statistics*, 4th ed., 1899. Capital.

£33,829,124 to £60,266,886.[1] To this we must add the interest, not easy to distinguish, earned abroad or in the colonies by British companies, insurance companies, for example, or building societies. Statisticians who took into account every possible source estimated the total annual interest from foreign investments at about £100,000,000.[2]

Britain could well afford to import far more than she exported. Since she was receiving at the same time the interest of capital invested abroad, the balance of commerce remained favourable and the country grew wealthier. But several disquieting factors detracted from the comfort to be derived from this consideration. The great banking houses which controlled in London the investment of British capital were slipping out of British hands. Since the disappearance in 1890 of the celebrated firm of Baring, they all bore German, German-Jewish or American names.[3] What use would they make of the sums entrusted to them by British capitalists? It was no matter for indifference if this capital was absorbed without return in some remote Argentine, as had actually happened during the previous decade or went to nourish the newborn industries of rival nations, Germany, for example, or the United States. Ought it not rather to be employed in developing the resources of the Empire, the Indian cotton mills, the large scale agriculture of Australia, the gold and diamond mines of South Africa and the Canadian foundries? The imperialists wished to guide British capital into the latter channels while at the same time

---

[1] C. K. Hobson, *The Export of Capital*, 1914, pp. 200–1. The same writer (p. 207) gives the following statistics showing the export of capital at three different dates, separated by intervals of ten years:

	Capital Invested in the United Kingdom	Capital Invested Abroad	Total
1885	..	£8,735,000,000	£1,302,000,000	£10,037,000,000
1895	..	£9,063,000,000	£1,600,000,000	£10,663,000,000
1905	..	£11,009,000,000	£2,025,000,000	£13,036,000,000

[2] Sir Robert Giffen, 'The Excess of Imports' (*Journal of the Royal Statistical Society*, March 1899, vol. lxii, p. 81).

[3] 'In the City of London today there is not a single English firm among what may be called the *haute finance*. If a large financial operation has to be concluded we first go to Messrs. Rothschild, then to Messrs. Raphael, both German Jews; then to Messrs. S. S. Morgan & Co., an American house; after that, probably, to Messrs. Speyer or Messrs. Seligmann or Messrs. Stern, also German Jews; then perhaps to Messrs. Hambro, a Danish firm; then to houses like Messrs. Frühling & Goschen, and so on, all foreign houses and mostly Jews; but there is no strictly English name among them since the unlimited Barings ceased to exist in 1890; and the period during which the Barings' business was best managed was while it was under the direction of Mr. Joshua Bates, an American.' (J. W. Cross, 'British Trade in 1898. A Warning Note', *Nineteenth Century*, May 1899, p. 854.)

making an outlet in the same direction for the surplus population of the country.[1] In this way the capital of Great Britain would foster the development of lands which should be regarded as England overseas, Greater Britain. By contact with her young colonies the old country would renew her youth.

In those distant days when England was at war with the armies of revolutionary and imperial France, it was the fashion in Paris to declaim against the nation of shopkeepers, the insular Carthage which presumed to oppose the modern Rome. In reality the nation of shopkeepers at that period returned only a handful of business men to Parliament: it was represented and ruled by an aristocracy whose ample revenues derived from the rental of their estates raised them to a position of supremacy over the representatives of business. When therefore that aristocracy fostered on every sea the development of British commerce, its position as the defender of the national interests was the stronger, because it was impossible to suspect the ministers of defending their private interests or even the immediate interest of their class. What changes a century had brought! Business men of every description—manufacturers and merchants, directors of companies, mine owners, brewers, bankers—made up 250 members of the House of Commons returned in 1895,[2] and the remaining members,

[1] 'Between 1845 and 1870 4,000,000 British subjects emigrated from the United Kingdom to the United States, between 1870 and 1890, 3,000,000. Between 1879 and 1899 only 1,250,000 Englishmen emigrated to the colonies.' (Alleyne Ireland, *Tropical Civilization*, pp. 14, 15, 16.)

[2] To be exact, according to my calculations, 244 out of 670 members. But even this figure does not convey an adequate notion of the political power wielded by business men in each of the countries which together composed the United Kingdom. If we take into consideration England alone and also leave out of account the representatives of Universities, the Scottish, Welsh (Monmouthshire being here reckoned with Wales, of which it may fairly be regarded as a part) and Irish members, we find that out of 456 members, 189 were business men. Among the 70 Scottish members were 26 business men. Of the 34 seats for Wales and Monmouthshire, 9 were held by business men. Of 101 Irish members, 20 were business men. Moreover, the exact position occupied by these 20 members requires examination. Hotel-keepers, drapers, cornchandlers, they were, presumably, petty tradesmen, parish-pump politicians. Ireland differed entirely from England both in social organization and intellectual atmosphere. The following classification by parties as well as by districts affords further information of interest. England (exclusive of Monmouthshire)—Liberals: 30 business men out of 65 members in the counties, in the boroughs 19 out of 42, in London 2 out of 7. Conservatives: In the counties 35 out of 141, in the boroughs 33 out of 99, in London 22 out of 50. Liberal Unionists: In the counties 3 out of 5, in the boroughs 4 out of 16. Wales (and Monmouthshire)—Liberals: In the counties 5 out of 20, in the boroughs 3 out of 6. Conservatives: Of the 2 county and 5 borough members returned none were business men. Liberal Unionists: 1 (the only representative of the party in Wales). We notice the large proportion of business men among the Liberal Unionists, which reveals the true character of the revolt. In England, the proportion of business men is even greater among the Liberals than among the Conservatives, still in

barristers, officers, and gentlemen of leisure, were bound to the business world by ties almost as close. The gentry in particular, still well represented on the Conservative benches, could not dream of living on the rents of their estates. The fall in the price of all food stuffs had hastened the decay of British agriculture, and now landowners visited the country only to spend the money they had made in the cities. How did they make it? The enormous growth of limited liability companies enabled the old ruling class to maintain on the whole its position in a country thoroughly industrialized. It was estimated that since the statute of 1862, which had placed their legal position beyond dispute, joint stock companies had issued shares representing a capital value of £1,500,000,000, an amount, it was calculated, double that invested in French and German companies together.[1] And this calculation took no account of the capital of the colonial and Indian companies. Every Member of Parliament was identified to some extent by his annual dividends with the interests of the great financiers by whom all these companies had been floated, and the latter did their best to tighten the bond by offering Members of Parliament a place on the boards of directors which managed their companies and even by appointing them Chairmen of the boards.[2] What could look better on a prospectus than the name of a Peer, or of the head of some great family? When in 1896 the Chinese Li-Hung-Chang visited Europe, and in every country was welcomed with open arms in the hope of valuable concessions, the Duke of Devonshire did not deem it disrespectful to his guest to receive him at the great foundry where he was Chairman of the Board of Directors. The Duke of Fife, whose marriage had made him a

the country districts the party of the landed gentry. But this does not apply to London, where almost half the Unionist members were business men. If we examine these figures from a slightly different point of view we discover that the Unionist Party was the party of the bankers (among the Liberal members there was not a single banker), of the brewers and wine and spirit merchants (far better represented on the Conservative than on the Liberal benches), whereas manufacturers were proportionately more numerous on the Liberal side of the House, merchants and mine owners in an actual majority. After the election of 1900 the proportion of business men of every description appears to have increased, if we can trust the statistics of the *Constitutional Year Book* for 1896, p. 125: and for 1902, p. 136 (statistics, however, which for the Parliament of 1895 give slightly different figures from those at which I have arrived by my own calculations. In 1900 there were 139 business men on the Unionist side of the House as against 101 in 1895, and 94 on the Liberal as against 76 in 1895).

[1] *Quarterly Review*, April 1900, 'The Reform of Company Law' (vol. cxci, p. 374).

[2] After the election of 1900 270 members of the House of Commons sat on boards of directors, of whom 164 were Unionists, 22 Liberal Unionists, 76 Liberals and 8 Irish Nationalists (*Constitutional Year Book*, 1902, p. 136).

member of the royal family, was a director of the Chartered Company, founded to exploit the gold mines of the Northern Transvaal and Cape Colony, which played such an important part in the national policy. An even closer relative of the Queen, the Duke of Connaught, was considered by public opinion to have been compromised by the disgraceful failure in 1903 of the London and Globe Society, which cast a shadow over the death-bed of Lord Dufferin, a former Viceroy of India.

The scandal was the culmination of a series of scandals which, during the previous decade, had from time to time filled the columns of the newspapers. In 1893 there was the colossal fraud of the Liberator Building Society; in 1894 the failure of the New Zealand Loan Company, which had compelled the resignation from the Cabinet of the minister Mundella: and in 1898 the bankruptcy of the financier Hooley, who had made an enormous fortune by floating industrial and trading companies. To attract shareholders Hooley had needed titled directors; he was proved to have bought for a cash payment the names of several noblemen. The unbridled speculation on the Transvaal gold mines constituted another scandal on account of its too obvious influence on British colonial policy. This undisguised determination of policy by financial interests[1] might have been expected to excite public disapproval, and provoke an organized campaign of protest in the Press and heckling in the House. There was nothing of the sort. Both parties agreed not to exploit a particular scandal against its opponent, and their silent pact was obviously approved by the general public. The effect upon the public mind produced by the protests of a Stead or an Arnold White cannot be compared with the enormous popularity enjoyed in very different times by such a pamphleteer as William Cobbett. In the course of the century public life had obviously become increasingly impervious to the appeal of the agitator, as political institutions became more democratic. No one desired to invest party strife with the bitterness and passion it possessed in contemporary France, and no one con-

---

[1] *The Economist*, August 12, 1899: 'It is undeniable that during the session just ended there has been an atmosphere of money in the lobby and precincts of the House of Commons scarcely known before. All manner of interests have gathered there, as they gather in Washington and in the various State Legislatures in America. More attempts to influence the votes of members have been made than has been known before, or, at any rate, than members can recollect since the days of railway construction. Incidents connected with the Telephone Bill, the Petroleum Bill, and the Clerical Rates' Bill point to a closer connection between finance and legislation than is desirable or safe.'

sidered that the riotous scenes provoked in Paris some two or three years earlier by the Panama scandal were likely to raise the tone of French public life. Moreover, when all has been said, and the imperialist trend of public opinion which placed the Conservatives in office has been considered in its most commercial aspect, justice demands that we should regard it from another aspect, equally real. Not for a single moment could the imperialism of the government programme have awakened the enthusiasm of the masses, if it had been nothing more than a manifestation of commercial greed, and had not contained a very considerable element of idealism. This aggressive and martial ideal now demands brief analysis.

5

One thing at least is beyond dispute. At the very time when we are witnessing what might appear at first sight nothing more than the expression of a purely commercial policy, we also witness in the realm of ideas the decline of the 'morality of self-interest' or 'utilitarianism' which had been so widely accepted as the philosophy of British Liberalism at the epoch of its supremacy. The great missionary of Free Trade, Cobden, had professed the ethics of self-interest, and Herbert Spencer had embodied this ethical and political creed in a vast system of sociology based on the principle of an identity, or at least a progressive identification, during the historical period through which humanity is actually passing, of individual self-interest with the interest of society. But it was precisely the historic inevitability of this identification which in Herbert Spencer's native country was being questioned more and more widely thirty or forty years after his popularity had reached its zenith. The English neo-Hegelians, influenced by German metaphysics, refused to regard society as a mere collection of individuals. Far from it being true that society existed in virtue of individuals and for their sake, individuals existed only in virtue of society and for the sake of society—that is to say, in so far as society was the embodiment of the ideal ends—science, art, religion, whose pursuit alone gave value to the individual. Society, in Hegel's terminology, the State, depository of all the moral traditions of the nation, the real State, closed to all interference from without, and admitting no society superior to itself, a veritable

earthly god: this was the philosophy which in 1899 found powerful expression in a book by Professor Bosanquet, which soon took
its place as a classic.[1] Moreover, the English neo-Darwinians drew
from the doctrine of evolution conclusions very different from
those drawn by Herbert Spencer. In a book whose success testified
to the degree in which it reflected the temper of the period[2] Benjamin Kidd, a self-educated writer, developed the thesis that the
quality which gives superiority to a species or race and ensures its
victory over its rivals, is not reason, a critical and destructive
faculty, but faith, the willingness to subordinate immediate to
remote interests, the interest of the individual to the interest of
society. Reason becomes useful to the race only when it has been
brought into the service of faith. It was not to their intellectual
but to their religious and moral superiority that the Teutonic
races, the English and Germans, owed the ascendancy they had
achieved over the Latin races, victims of their intelligence and
individualism, for example Renaissance Italy and Revolutionary
France.

[1] Bernard Bosanquet, *The Philosophical Theory of the State*, 1899. See especially p. 320.
'The Nation-State . . . is recognized as absolute in power over the individual, and as his
representative and champion in the affairs of the world outside.' See further on the
question 'whether State action is to be judged by the same moral tests as private action',
pp. 322 sqq., especially p. 323. 'The State, as such, certainly cannot be guilty of personal
immorality'; p. 324: 'Promises and treaties . . . are acts which embody public ends. And
here the State on its side is bound to maintain good faith; but still its agent is likely to go
wrong if he mixes up the obligations of the State with his private honour. The question
for him, if he has to keep or break a public undertaking, is—to what is the State substantially bound, not to what extent would he be bound, if he had made the promise or
engagement in question in his private capacity.' Also p. 326: 'A public act which inflicts
loss, such as war, confiscation, the repudiation of a debt, is wholly different from murder
or theft. It is not the act of a private person. It is not a violation of law. . . . It is the act
of a supreme power, which has ultimate responsibility for protecting the form of life of
which it is the guardian, and which is not itself protected by any scheme of functions or
relations, such as prescribes a course for the reconciliation of rights and secures its effectiveness.' See further on the France of the Dreyfus case the note on p. 321: 'The dangers
besetting the French Republic today (December 1898) are, in essence, tests applied to the
strength of a national idea. If the idea cannot maintain itself, we must reluctantly suppose
that it ought not—that the common life has not the necessary depth.'

[2] Benjamin Kidd, *Social Evolution*, 1894. In four years the book went into 19 editions.
'The Divine mission and special duties of a nation, the right of Success and Force, such
formulas irritate the reader who comes to them for the first time. But when we discover
how naturally these ideas have . . . taken root and grown into the permanent structure of
men's minds, until their truth has become an unconscious presupposition, and realized the
ardent conviction with which everyone here regards them as binding the conscience with
a religious sanction, we must admit that we have to do with a genuine moral code.'
(André Chevrillon, *Etudes Anglaises*, 1901, p. 332.) For other contemporary French witnesses see E. Boutmy, *Essai d'une psychologie politique du peuple Anglais*, 1901; also J.
Bardoux, *Essai d'une psychologie de l'Angleterre contemporaine*. *Les crises belliqueuses*, 1906,
and in P. Mantoux, *A travers l'Angleterre contemporaine*, 1909, the essay entitled, 'Du
Jingoisme et de la guerre Sud Africaine', originally written in 1902.

19

From this point of view, however, men of letters are perhaps more significant than professional philosophers. They address a wider circle of readers, and are, therefore, more representative of their period. What then was the tendency which prevailed in English literature at this time when the great Victorian epoch must be regarded as already past, even before the death of the Queen by whose name it would be known to the historian? English literature had indeed felt the influence of the pessimistic French realism. But the importer of this foreign 'manner', George Moore, would not become a great artist until he had discarded it. And the far more British realism of Thomas Hardy as yet worked only below the surface; it was not until later that he would be recognized as the forerunner of an entire generation of revolutionary realists. Need we mention here those tragic young writers —the eldest in 1895 was not forty years old and only one of the group was destined to outlive the age of fifty—who had been fascinated by the literature and philosophy of the French 'decadents', Oscar Wilde, Aubrey Beardsley, the editors of the *Yellow Book*? They were nothing more than a coterie of eccentrics proud of their isolation, and the thunderbolt launched in 1895 by Puritan morality when Wilde was sentenced to five years' imprisonment for homosexual vice broke up the confraternity. Very different from these were the authors read by the general public, who must be regarded as the authentic interpreters of the prevalent outlook.

That fascinating writer Robert Louis Stevenson, who had settled in an island of the Pacific to die in voluntary exile, was amusing children and delighting adults by his stories of adventure and heroism in the South Seas. Joseph Conrad, a smaller artist despite his loftier pretensions, a naturalized alien of Polish extraction who had served for many years in the British merchant service, was beginning to make a name by his novels, which almost invariably told the story at once sublime, sordid, and pathetic of the white man in the Tropics at grips with the hostility of nature and the aborigines. The unfortunate Henley on a bed of sickness and pain dreamed of battles, glory, and conquest, and, if his poems were too 'select'—both in quality and quantity—to reach the masses, this was by no means the case with the works of another writer, the literary mouthpiece of the period. Young Rudyard Kipling, the son of an artist who was curator of an Indian museum, had begun his literary career by imitating the French novel, and had dreamed of becoming an English—or Anglo-Colonial—Maupassant. But soon, as he celebrated the melancholy of the British Tommy on garrison in Asia and hymned the greatness of an empire washed by 'seven seas', he became by universal consent the unofficial poet laureate of British imperialism. And now he wrote—for children, was it, or for adults?—his 'Jungle Book'. He set his hero, the little Mowgli, in the world of beasts, and the beasts taught Mowgli the law of the jungle, which maintains the balance of species at the cost of a never-ending struggle, a truceless war. Must this struggle, this war, be condemned as evil? Not when it is the law of the world. The spirit of conquest and aggrandisement must not be confused with the spirit of hatred, greed, and delight in doing mischief for its own sake; it is the courage ready to hazard all risks which gives the victory to the better man. A species of Darwinian philosophy expressed in a mythical form was the foundation of a moral code, chaste, brutal, heroic, and childlike.

We now see the exponent of imperialism under an entirely different aspect. Far from appealing to the self-interest of their audience, they call upon them to sacrifice their private interests, even their very lives, in pursuit of a lofty national ideal. Can we in a few words define more precisely the nature of this ideal, as it was understood by the British imperialists at the close of the nineteenth century? It was, in the first place, the consolidation—if possible, the federal union—of the British of the United Kingdom with the British in Canada, South Africa, and the Pacific, of one democracy with its fellows. In many respects this ideal was Liberal, almost Republican, humanitarian, and its pursuit was not ignoble. In the second place, it was the forcible annexation of a large portion of the globe neither inhabited nor habitable by white men. But experience had apparently proved—and on this point about the year 1900 few Liberals disagreed with the Imperialists[1]—that

---

[1] In a little book published in 1900 under the title *Liberalism and the Empire* and written in collaboration with F. W. Hirst and J. L. Hammond, Gilbert Murray devoted a chapter to the study of the exploitation of inferior races in ancient and modern times. After describing the abuses, indeed the atrocities, which have accompanied the system, and the evil effects it has invariably produced, he nevertheless concludes: 'The coloured races whose land we invade cannot remain free men. The white man who lives among them, do what we will to control him from Westminster—and those who wish to control are a small and perhaps a diminishing party—will either force the coloured men to serve him or else sweep them from his path. Let us help him, in order that we may control him' (p. 155). For a study of the problem from the strictly economic standpoint of trade, see Benjamin Kidd, *The Control of the Tropics*, 1898, and for an account of the system of

tropical conditions did not admit of the spontaneous development of great independent civilizations of the European type. Where England did not install herself by annexation, other European nations would occupy the empty place. To stand aside was not, as the Gladstonians maintained, to refuse from moral scruples to share the spoils, it was a cowardly refusal to fulfil to the utmost of the national ability the noble mission of the European races to civilize the world, to refuse to bear what Kipling called the White Man's Burden.

II THE NEW GOVERNMENT: TWO YEARS OF DISILLUSIONMENT

I

Such was the current of public opinion which had borne the new cabinet into office. Lord Salisbury, Premier and Foreign Secretary; Arthur Balfour, First Lord of the Treasury and leader of the Commons; Sir Michael-Hicks Beach, Chancellor of the Exchequer; the celebrated Joseph Chamberlain, Colonial Secretary; Goschen, a deserter from the Liberals who already in Lord Salisbury's first ministry had acquitted himself brilliantly at the Exchequer, First Lord of the Admiralty; Lord Lansdowne at the War Office, and the Duke of Devonshire, President of the Privy Council—these were the outstanding members of a huge Cabinet of twenty-seven which bore every appearance of a strong government. Should the critic find fault with its composition as too aristocratic—there were eight peers, of whom three were the heads of great families? The objection would betray ignorance of the times. The peerage had never enjoyed a more solid popularity. It was significant that a very large number of municipal bodies had

native labour, the more fundamental work by Alleyne Ireland, *Tropical Colonization. An Introduction to the Study of the Subject*, 1899, especially Chapters Four—The Earlier Aspects of the Labour Problem in the Tropics; Five—The Indentured Labour System; and Six —Solution of Labour Problems by the Dutch. See further, L. C. A. Knowles, *The Economic Development of the British Overseas Empire*, 1924, Book Two, *The British Tropics*; also the extensive and useful compilation published in 1903 by the American Government under the title, *Colonial Administration, 1800–1900* (*House Documents*, vol. xli, No. 15, pts. 7–9. *Commerce and Finance*, January–March 1903; 57th Congress, 2nd Session, 1902– 3). The works of Howard Hensman, *A History of Rhodesia Compiled from Official Sources*, 1900 (a defence), and H. C. Thomson, *Rhodesia and Its Government*, 1898 (a criticism), contain interesting observations on the treatment of the natives in a particular colony.

lately made a custom of choosing as their honorary president the bearer of some great name.[1] Was it a matter for uneasiness that the Cabinet contained too many statesmen of the first rank? Among the members of the Cabinet, the *Spectator* pointed to four, possibly five, ministers fitted to become Prime Minister,[2] and it was beyond dispute that the Cabinet contained two eminent statesmen, differing so profoundly from each other in origin, character, and temperament that friction seemed inevitable, the one regarded by public opinion and regarding himself as the great man of the Cabinet, the other its official head—Chamberlain and Lord Salisbury.

Joseph Chamberlain's age in 1895 was almost sixty. Thirty years had gone by since as a young Radical manufacturer in Birmingham he had led the campaign which finally resulted in the great statute of 1870 establishing primary education, the imperfect realization of Chamberlain's democratic and secular ideal. It was twenty years since he had launched that other campaign, a reaction against Lord Beaconsfield's imperialism, which returned Gladstone to power at the election of 1880. President of the Board of Trade in the Cabinet which Gladstone had formed on taking office, the recognized leader of the Radical section of the Liberal party, and famous for the democratic methods, at times even verging on Socialism, by which he had conducted the local government of Birmingham, he had outraged Conservative sentiment by his violent diatribes against the aristocracy and the plutocrats. He was waiting for Gladstone to retire to become the official 'leader' of an ultra-democratic Liberal party. But Gladstone refused to grow old, and in 1885 disconcerted the nation by his sudden conversion to the programme of Irish Home Rule. Chamberlain thereupon broke with his chief and took with him a group of malcontents.

Was it chimerical to entertain the hope of a reconciliation between this group of seceders and the old Gladstonian party? As the years passed and Gladstone clung to office it became increasingly plain that the rupture was incurable. Chamberlain was sent

[1] See the striking list of these aristocratic chairmen in an interesting article in the *Quarterly Review*, vol. clxxxiv, pp. 270 sqq, 'The Citizenship of the British Nobility'.

[2] *Spectator*, June 29, 1895: 'The four statesmen were the Duke of Devonshire, Arthur Balfour, Joseph Chamberlain and Edward Goschen'—to whom the article added Lord Lansdowne, less familiar indeed to the public, but in the opinion of the *Spectator*, 'one of those Anglo-Irishmen who can rule by a sort of instinct'.

to Washington by Lord Salisbury to settle certain matters at issue between the United States and Canada. He there learnt to interest himself in colonial questions and, without abandoning all his democratic opinions, became a missionary of British imperialism. It was not surprising. The British Empire, at least in one of its aspects, was a free confederation of democracies, already at the end of the nineteenth century far more democratic than the Mother Country, and Chamberlain himself,[1] a self-made man of the middle class, a former screw manufacturer, had far more in common with politicians like Seddon of New Zealand and Reid of Australia than with the Duke of Devonshire and the Marquis of Salisbury. No one was astonished that when offered the choice between the War Office, which would involve an enormous task of administrative reform, and the Colonial Office, he chose the latter. At a period when Colonial questions had assumed such importance, and Colonial conflicts between the Powers were becoming so frequent and so serious, the day might well come when the Colonial Office would be the real Foreign Office. If there was ever a man to enlarge the scope of his commission, that man was Chamberlain, whose ambition was the more insatiable, because it had been so long unsatisfied and who had reached the age of sixty when at last he found himself in a position to play the part in his country's history of which he felt himself capable. Everyone in England or on the Continent knew that pallid face, those pursed lips, that faultless frock-coat, that orchid in his buttonhole, and that eloquence at once cold and vehement which infuriated his opponent. By nature a firebrand, his words and actions alike kindled a conflagration.

It was only to be expected that Lord Salisbury, who combined the functions of Prime Minister and Foreign Secretary, should feel uneasy at the entrance of this outsider into his Cabinet. What points of contact could exist between an uneducated manufacturer who had never been at Oxford or Cambridge, and was not even a member of the Church of England, and the head of such an old family as the Cecils, on which he had conferred a high repute for culture and traditional piety? Destined from youth, by his birth

[1] Human memory is short and in 1895 it was widely forgotten how intense, fifteen years earlier, had been Chamberlain's opposition to imperialism. See *Standard*, July 1, 1895. 'There are Radicals who scarce seem to be patriots. But no one will affirm that Mr. Chamberlain was not, at every period of his career, a thorough-going Englishman, and an ardent champion of the Imperial idea.'

as much as by his tastes and capacity, to fill the highest offices of State, at a period when he still occupied a subordinate position, he had offered a stubborn resistance to the democratic, and later to the imperialist, projects of Disraeli. Between 1886 and 1892 as Prime Minister in an administration which was perhaps one of the best England had ever known, he had contrived to extend the Empire without the bloodshed and expense of military enterprises, by friendly compacts with foreign Powers, and at the same time by a series of domestic reforms had satisfied the demands of Chamberlain and his followers. But Chamberlain was then an external ally with whom it was the easier to treat because his position in the House was weaker. Relations between the two statesmen were likely to be far more difficult when they disputed within the same Cabinet the control of British foreign policy. The difference of age indeed was not very great. But the one was all impatience to cover in the few remaining years of active life the ground he had failed to traverse during a career as slow as it had been lengthy. The other, the elder by five years, when he returned in 1895 to the Foreign Office may possibly have entertained sweeping ambitions. But he was very quick to realize their futility and thought only of a peaceful close to a career long since crowned with success. He was ailing and obliged to nurse his health by wintering every year in the south of France. He was a lover of solitude, never so happy as when he could pass long hours in the chemical laboratory he had installed at Hatfield. From a philosophic nonchalance rather than from deliberate haughtiness, he kept his colleagues at a distance—the story went round that he did not even know by sight one of his fellow ministers. His language was brutally outspoken and he had a reputation for disconcerting sallies. But they did not display the violent temper of a man of action, they were merely the cynical frankness of a sage, and moreover, of a sage now far advanced in years. One day a Chinese statesman laid before him a project of intervention in Northern China. Lord Salisbury refused to entertain it, the risks were too great. 'I understand,' replied the Chinaman; 'we govern, you and I, two Empires on the decline.' Lord Salisbury loved to repeat this story as a good joke. And, after all, the Chinaman was possibly right. He was right if he meant that Lord Salisbury, with the weariness of old age, felt that his country was old like himself and equally in need of rest.

These two statesmen were indeed strange yokefellows! 'There had been', said a speaker of the Opposition, 'conjunctions in our history which needed a great War Minister and there had been conjunctions which needed a great Peace Minister. Chatham was a War Minister. Walpole was a Peace Minister. But what they never wanted was a Minister half Chatham and half Walpole.'[1] The difficult task of maintaining communications between the Chatham and the Walpole of the Cabinet fell to Lord Salisbury's nephew, the leader of the Commons. Arthur Balfour, declared a political opponent, is 'one of the rare men who make public life tolerable and even respectable'.[2] He was a metaphysician who refused to take seriously the claim of the outer world to be real. And if he regarded the world as an enigma, it paid him back in his own coin. It was indeed to the enigmatic aspect of his personality that he owed so much of his power to impress and charm. Was he never to be anything more than the youthful sceptic and æsthete who, fifteen years before, had first attracted notice by the publication of his *Defence of Philosophic Doubt*, and who, lolling carelessly beside Lord Randolph Churchill in the House of Commons, amused himself by turning into ridicule the leaders of both the historic parties? Or had he revealed his true nature when in 1886 Lord Salisbury gave him a seat in the Cabinet as Irish Secretary and for the next six years, an autocrat without mis-givings, he had bullied the Irish for their own good? The return of the Conservatives to office in 1895 revealed him in yet another guise, ripened by experience. A second philosophical essay, *The Foundations of Belief*, discovered a convinced traditionalist behind the sceptic's mask, and revealed that a sincere attachment to the faith in which he had been brought up by his mother, the charm-ing Lady Blanche Balfour, was the firm foundation on which his imperturbability and irony reposed. Indolent he always remained and throughout an entire session seemed to take pleasure in annoy-ing his fellow Conservatives and even his opponents by the spectacle of his nonchalance. Then all of a sudden he would shake off his lethargy and meet the attacks of the Opposition or defend some important and complicated measure with an untiring energy and a sovereign command of dialectic. In defending the indefen-

---

[1] John Morley's speech at Leeds, June 8, 1898.
[2] Sir William Harcourt to John Morley, about the end of December 1898. A. G. Gardiner, *The Life of Sir William Harcourt*, vol. ii, p. 478.

sible, reconciling the irreconcilable and in removing by his skill in verbal manœuvres the bad effect produced by some intemperate outburst of his redoubtable colleague, he knew no rival. The Opposition contrasted him with Chamberlain to his advantage and liked him. The old Tories, to whom Chamberlain's methods were often distasteful, and who would never have consented to serve under his orders, were willing to work with him under the leadership of Balfour, a man who was never put out by anything and was disposed to derive amusement from everything. Was such a sorry affair as the world worth taking tragically? Balfour was now a finished Parliamentary leader, indeed the model Parliamentary leader, the darling and spoilt child of Parliament, as Chamberlain was its *enfant terrible*, and if his popularity was less obvious than Chamberlain's, it was perhaps more firmly established with a nation which has, so to speak, the Parliamentary system in its blood.

2

The new Government had hardly been in office six months when a sensational event revealed to the world the methods which Chamberlain's imperialism would pursue. There had lived for years in South Africa one of the great men of the Empire, the most typical representative of that imperialism whose outlines we have sketched, with its characteristic blend of commercialism and idealism.[1] Still quite a young man, Cecil Rhodes, the fourth son of a clergyman, had settled in South Africa for his health. There he had amassed a very large fortune. He was the King of Kimberley, the diamond City. Unlike the business men of his entourage, he nourished lofty ambitions and used his wealth in the spirit of a Napoleon. He was the Prime Minister of Cape Colony. He was chairman of the great chartered Company which as far north as the Zambesi developed the territory called after his name, Rhodesia. He was planning to construct a railway which would serve Rhodesia, and when complete would traverse Africa as far as Cairo and seal the hegemony of Great Britain over the entire continent. He looked further still, and dreamed of binding the Empire together by a federal constitution. His imperialism was

[1] For his career, see among a host of authorities Vindex, *Cecil Rhodes, His Political Life, Speeches, 1881–1900*, 1900, an interesting collection of documents (letters, speeches), and especially Basil Williams' excellent book, *Cecil Rhodes*, 1921.

coloured by a vague Liberalism. In Cape Colony he governed with the unreserved goodwill of those Dutch colonists who had originally brought European civilization to South Africa, and it was by reconciling the two races that he sought to secure British rule. In England he subscribed to the funds of the Liberal party.[1] Formerly a friend of Parnell's, he contributed to his party funds and one of his intimate friends was a member of the group.[2] In his ideal of imperial federation there was room for the Irish nation. A bachelor and a woman-hater, he belonged entirely to his work, and was never weary of tinkering at his strange will—the testament of a dreamer—which bequeathed his entire fortune to found a species of knighthood, which should spread his ideal throughout the Anglo-Saxon world and assure to the English-speaking peoples the dominion of the world.[3]

But an obstacle stood in the way of his plans for immediate annexation. In the very middle of British South Africa were two Boer republics—that is to say, republics inhabited by Dutch colonists. Annexed under Lord Beaconsfield's Government, they had regained their independence when Gladstone was in office. Five years earlier, gold had been discovered in the more northerly of these two states, the Transvaal, and a British population had grown up around the Johannesburg mines, more numerous and more discontented every year. Financiers, engineers, traders, labourers, and barristers, the Uitlanders chafed against their treatment as a floating mob of aliens without political rights. The Transvaal Boers, on the other hand, had elected as their President the aged

[1] This subscription was at first kept secret and the circumstances connected with it made a sensation when they became public. See *Spectator*, August 3, 10, 17; October 12, 1901; also the correction (which was not a disclaimer) in the *Daily Chronicle*, August 19, 24; October 12, 1901.

[2] For the relations between Cecil Rhodes and Parnell see R. Barry O'Brien, *The Life of Charles Stewart Parnell, 1846–91*, 1898, vol. ii, pp. 184 sqq.; also Vindex, *Cecil Rhodes*, appendix iv: the correspondence between Rhodes and Parnell, on the gift of £10,000 to the Irish Party, pp. 839 sqq.

[3] For the history of the will and the successive forms which it assumed between 1877 and 1899, see *The Last Will and Testament of Cecil John Rhodes*, with elucidatory notes, to which are added some chapters describing the Political and Religious Ideas of the Testator, edited by W. T. Stead, 1902. See especially p. 59: 'After recalling how the Roman Church utilizes enthusiasm, he suggests the formation of a kind of secular Church for the extension of the British Empire.' For the curious mixture of mysticism and Darwinism which constituted Cecil Rhodes' 'religion', see pp. 85 sqq. See also (p. 64) his letter to Stead of August 13–September 3, 1891: 'Please remember the key of my Idea discussed with you is a Society copied from the Jesuits as to organization.' The object of this society was to be the establishment of world peace by the union of Great Britain and the United States. 'The only thing feasible to carry this idea out is a secret society gradually absorbing the wealth of the world to be devoted to such an object.'

Kruger, an uncompromising foe of British influence. It was certain that he would never grant the Uitlanders the rights they demanded. Nor would he allow the Transvaal to be incorporated into a federation dominated by the British. To overcome his opposition Rhodes plotted a stroke of armed violence.

The directors of the chartered Company delegated to Rhodes, by formal deed, the full powers which by their charter of incorporation they had received and were under an obligation to employ—that is to say, Rhodes was invested with nothing short of a dictatorship within the Company's territory.

At this juncture, the Colonial Secretary transferred to the Company the extensive territory of Bechuanaland, hitherto a Protectorate, which on the west[1] bordered the Transvaal Republic, and the bodies of police already established in the country were ordered to assemble at Mafeking, where an agent of Rhodes, Dr. Jameson, would form out of their number the nucleus of a new police force in the Company's service. Thus Jameson found himself in command of a small army on the Transvaal border.

Meanwhile, Rhodes was engineering a rebellion at Johannesburg. He and his friend Beit, a German by birth who had made a fortune out of the gold mines, spent together £260,000 on organizing the plot. They were convinced that the rebellion would be immediately successful and would not even involve bloodshed. What they feared was that the victors of the Johannesburg rebellion would be attacked by the Boers from the country districts. Then the moment would arrive when Jameson and his band could effectively intervene. Rhodes would persuade the home government to sanction the *fait accompli* and if not as in 1877, to annex the entire Transvaal, at least to set up a system of local self-government for Johannesburg and the Rand.

But the plot was bungled. In the first place, the malcontents in Johannesburg wasted valuable time. Many among them were

[1] Bechuanaland comprised two parts, a crown colony whose annexation to Cape Colony had been practically completed when Chamberlain became Secretary, and a protectorate, whose future annexation had been promised without, however, any particular date being fixed. In this decision the partisans of annexation were embarrassed by the opposition of three native chiefs, who complained that their rights had been violated, and whose cause was espoused with considerable warmth by philanthropists in London. (See Rev. Edwin Lloyd, *Three great African Chiefs, Khama, Sebele and Bathong*, 1895.) The difficulty delayed Chamberlain, but not for long. For he took office during the closing days of June and the annexation was effected on November 6. (*Second Report from the Select Committee on British South Africa.* Together with the proceedings of the Committee and *Minutes of Evidence*, 1897, pp. 336–8.)

Germans, who took alarm at the suggestion of joining a distinctively British movement. They denounced the plot to Berlin, and
Berlin made diplomatic representations in London. Then Jameson
lost patience and acted too soon. On December 27, 1895, without
waiting for a summons, he invaded the territory of the Republic
at the head of some four or five hundred men. This rash move lost
everything.

To what extent was Chamberlain informed of the plot by
Rhodes' agents in London? How far was he guilty, though not a
formal accomplice, of conniving at it? Must we conclude that he
deliberately refused to be told plans of whose nature he was well
aware?[1] In any case, it is unthinkable that a statesman of such
acute intelligence should have begun his ministerial career as an
unsuspecting dupe. But when, instead of a revolt breaking out
spontaneously on Boer territory, as Rhodes had planned, a military raid was attempted—that is to say, a hostile invasion of the
Transvaal by British troops without a preliminary declaration of

[1] This conclusion is certainly suggested by Dr. Rutherford Harris's account of his interview with Chamberlain in London on August 1, 1895: 'I referred to the unrest at Johannesburg and added a guarded allusion to the desirability of there being a police force near the
border. Mr. Chamberlain at once demurred to the turn the conversation had taken', also
Chamberlain's own version a little later of the same interview: . . . 'It was in the course
of this conversation that he (Dr. Harris) made the remark, the exact words of which I
could not possibly pledge my memory to at this distance of time, but it was to the effect
"I could tell you something in confidence", or "I could give you some confidential information". I stopped him at once. I said: "I do not want to hear any confidential information; I am here in an official capacity. I can only hear information of which I can make
official use".' (*Second Report from the Select Committee on British South Africa*; together with
the *Proceedings of the Committee and Minutes of Evidence*, 1897, pp. 337, 339.) It is amazing
that these two documents, which in my opinion prove Chamberlain's connivance, are
understood by many Englishmen—and not only by Chamberlain's political sympathisers
—as acquitting him of all responsibility. Must we go still further—and speak not merely
of connivance, but of actual complicity? Chamberlain's obstinate refusal in 1897 to permit
the production of certain documents, the untruthful evidence given by Miss Flora Shaw,
and the extraordinary excuses trumped up to clear Edward Fairfield, leave very little
doubt on the point. See for the text of the Hawkesley documents, William T. Stead,
*Joseph Chamberlain, Conspirator or Statesman? An Examination of the Evidence as to his
Complicity in the Jameson conspiracy, together with the newly published letters of the Hawkesley
dossier*, 2nd ed., 1900. The additional documents published by *l'Independence Belge* on
January 6, 1900, under the title *Les Dessous d'une Guerre: Chamberlain et Jameson*, are
however all later than the raid and when read after twenty-five years' interval do not
seem to warrant the sensation caused by their original publication. Edmund Garrett and
E. J. Edwards, two journalists at the Cape, in a work fully documented, and most carefully weighed, entitled *The Story of an African Crisis: Being the Truth about the Jameson
Raid and the Johannesburg Revolt of 1896: Told with the Assistance of the Leading Actors of the
Drama*, 1897, admit that the project of collecting the Bechuanaland police on the Transvaal border for the purpose of assisting the Uitlanders was already known to the Liberal
Cabinet in 1894, and C. Ian Colvin (*The Life of Jameson*, vol. ii, pp. 166 sqq.) hints that
this was the explanation of the surprising weakness displayed by the representatives of
the Liberal Opposition on the Committee of Enquiry in 1897.

war, he had no option, in spite of Rhodes' telegrams imploring a few days' delay, but to yield to the demands of the German Government[1] and disavow Jameson. Kruger, meanwhile, entertained the Johannesburg malcontents with insincere negotiations, until the Boers, hastily summoned to the field, surrounded Jameson's troop at Krugersdorp and compelled it to surrender.

The abortive attempt provoked keen indignation throughout Europe. The German Emperor sent President Kruger a telegram of congratulation. On the other hand, British feeling was dangerously excited, and to satisfy the public the Government despatched two regiments to Africa and mobilized a flying squadron. To understand the universal hostility of Continental opinion, the Emperor William's interference, and the British nervousness, we must understand the relations which obtained between Great Britain and the Powers about the date when the Unionists took office.

3

Europe was divided between two rival groups of powers—the Triple Alliance of Germany, Austria, and Italy, and the Dual Alliance of Russia and France. But if in its inception the Franco-Russian Alliance was aimed at Germany, it had possessed from the outset another aspect, hostility towards Great Britain. For the Russian Government was steadily losing interest in the Balkans, where its victories of 1878 had brought only a series of disappointments, and cherished ambitious designs of Asiatic conquest both in Persia and Afghanistan, and in China. In these regions, therefore, Russian imperialism clashed with British. Nothing could have been further from the thoughts of the statesmen who followed each other in the government of France than to provoke a war with Germany, even if they could have obtained a guarantee of Russian intervention. They also were occupied in the pursuit of an ambitious scheme of colonial expansion in China and Indo-China and above all in Africa, which at every turn brought them into conflict with the British policy of annexation. In consequence, the British Government inevitably drew closer to the Triple Alliance which opposed France and Russia. The *rapproche-*

[1] For these demands see *Second Report of South African Committee* . . . Appendix, p. 459. Translation of Documents presented in the Reichstag, February 12, 1896; also, *Die Grosse Politik der europaischen Kabinette*, 1871–1914, vol. xi, pp. 15 sqq.

ment had already begun between 1886 and 1892 when Lord Salisbury was at the Foreign Office. Not only was there an avowed friendship, almost an understanding, between the British and German Governments, but a formal agreement, whose object was confined to the maintenance of the *status quo* in the Mediterranean and which, though not termed an alliance, was in effect an alliance against France, had been secretly concluded between England, Austria and Italy. The same policy had been followed by Lord Rosebery both as Foreign Secretary and later as Prime Minister in the Liberal Cabinet. And, indeed, there existed many ties of a sentimental nature which were calculated to facilitate a political *rapprochement* between England and Germany. The British royal family was closely related to several of the ruling houses of Germany, and to the Prussian in particular. Young Englishmen in large numbers went to finish their education at German universities, to return imbued with respect for their professors, and friendship for their fellow students. There was no rivalry at sea. As yet Germany had no navy. Between the two armies there was nothing but the memory of victories won in common against France, during the Seven Years War, in 1814 and in 1815, and every year in both countries certain regiments celebrated the anniversary of Waterloo. But, to the advances made by Great Britain, the German Government had failed to respond. Not only did the Franco-Russian alliance, as it became anti-British, cease to alarm Germany, but the Emperor William and the officials of the Wilhelmstrasse, encouraged by the excellent relations which had prevailed between the courts of Berlin and Petersburg since the accession of Nicholas II, were beginning to entertain the project of a general alliance of the Continental powers against England under German leadership. During the last two or three centuries every great military power had been seduced in turn by this ambitious dream: Spain first, then France, and now it was the turn of Germany. In Russia, an entire party was pledged to this policy; and French anglophobia had become of late very acute. The Emperor William believed that his project was on the eve of being realized, when, in 1895, after the Japanese rout of the Chinese army and the cession to Japan by the treaty of Shimonoseki, of the Liao-Tung peninsula, the united intervention of the German, Russian, and French Governments compelled Japan to abandon her conquest. England found herself alone in support of Japan against this Triple Alliance of the Far East, as it was called in Germany. Might not the new Triple Alliance find further spheres of action in other parts of the globe, even in European waters?

Such was the unfavourable diplomatic situation bequeathed in the summer of 1895 by the Liberal Cabinet to its Unionist successor. It is likely enough that Lord Salisbury was inclined to lay the blame upon Lord Rosebery. Throughout his former ministry the relations between England and Germany had been excellent. Why should they not be so once more? The situation in the Near East seemed to him an opportunity to effect a reconciliation. The Turkish authorities had suppressed a rebellion of the Armenians in Asia Minor by a general massacre. The British consuls had denounced the barbarity which had marked the suppression of the revolt; the Christianity and humanitarianism of the British public had been deeply shocked, and the convention of 1878 had invested Great Britain with a species of moral protectorate in regard to the Armenians. Lord Salisbury had never been a friend of the Turk and his indignation was, perhaps, fanned by the reports of Turkish atrocities put before him by his two sons, Lord Robert and Lord Hugh Cecil, both devout Anglicans of the High Church party. He was persuaded that the hour of dissolution had at last struck for the Ottoman Empire, shaken by this latest crisis. The crowning achievement of his last ministry had been the peaceful partition of Africa. Why should not Turkey be divided among the Powers, with the prospect perhaps of a future partition of China? The wisest procedure was to make a bid for German support. Italy, which was endeavouring to establish a colony on the coast of the Red Sea, saw her efforts frustrated by the formidable opposition of King Menelik of Abyssinia, who was openly supported by France and Russia. Might it not be possible to compensate Italy from the pickings of the Turkish Empire, for example in Albania? And since Italy was the ally both of Germany and of England, she provided a common ground on which both powers might meet. Conversations were begun between the Foreign Office and the German Embassy in London. They were continued between Lord Salisbury and the Emperor William in person, when on August 5 the Emperor attended the Cowes Regatta.

But the Kaiser proved decidedly adverse to Lord Salisbury's proposals. He regarded himself as officially pledged to protect the integrity of the Turkish Empire. Moreover, in his defence of the Ottoman Empire he had the full support of the Russian Government, for Russia had too many Armenian subjects to be willing to establish an independent Greater Armenia at its very gates. France accepted the Russian standpoint. There was thus formed at Constantinople against the threatened British intervention a Triple Alliance of Germany, Russia, and France, a Triple Alliance of the Near East, a replica of that Triple Alliance of the Far East which was thwarting British policy in the Yellow Sea. The interview at Cowes, far from restoring good relations between the two Governments, made them far worse than before. The Emperor left England at variance with the British Court, and four years would pass before he repeated his visit. He had also quarrelled with Lord Salisbury, leaving him thoroughly disabused of ambitious foreign policies and in particular of the policy of an understanding with Germany.[1]

This diplomatic embroglio, long kept secret, explains the Kaiser's telegram to President Kruger. Though his action took the public by surprise, it could not have surprised the Cabinet after what had passed at Cowes in August. It was evident that the Emperor was pursuing with his ministers' full approval a policy of persistent hostility to British imperialism. At Pekin first and later at Constantinople he had formed an alliance of the powers to oppose it. He now attempted to do the same in South Africa. In January, on the very morrow of the Jameson raid, he sounded the French and Russian Governments as to the possibility of a joint intervention to protect the independence of the Transvaal. But the Radical Government then in office in France declined the suggestion. Was it because the loss of Alsace-Lorraine was still too recent a memory? Or was it because the Radical complexion of the Cabinet rendered the ministers less amenable to Russian influence than their predecessors? Or did they shrink from a direct challenge to British sea power? Against the British navy, German

---

[1] For the details of these abortive negotiations, see 'Hermann Freiherr von Eckardstein', *Lebenserinnerungen und politische Denkwurdigkeiten*, vol. i (1919), pp. 211 sqq., vol. ii, p. 284, vol. iii (1921), pp. 121 sqq. There are numerous inaccuracies in Baron von Eckardstein's account; nevertheless, he must receive the credit of having been the first to reveal this important episode. For further details, see Sir Valentine Chirol, *Ex-Kaiser and England. A New Chapter of Diplomacy* (*The Times*, September 11 and 13, 1902), in its turn completed and corrected by *Die Grosse Politik* . . . chap. lx (vol. x, pp. 1 sqq.). Despite its importance the incident is not mentioned either in vol. iii of the *Cambridge History of British Foreign Policy*, 1923, or in the *History of Modern Europe, 1878–1919*, by G. P. Gooch, 1923.

support, even had they thought of asking for it, would have been worthless. For at this date the German navy did not count.[1]

<h1 style="text-align:center">4</h1>

The defeat sustained by German diplomacy at Paris in January 1896, although less public, was no less damaging to German imperialism than the failure of the Jameson raid to British. In consequence, the policy of both Governments during the months which followed became extremely confused. The Emperor William attempted a diplomatic *rapprochement* with England by a step for which the colonial difficulties of Italy again provided the occasion, though this time the overtures were made by Germany, not by Great Britain. The Italian army, after a sanguinary defeat, had just been driven back upon the coast of the Red Sea. There was now no question, as in the previous July, of offering her territorial compensation in the Mediterranean. But might not England ease the position of the Italian army in Africa by effecting a diversion? Over ten years had passed since she had refused, after Gordon's death, to proceed with the invasion of the Egyptian Sudan, either in her own name or as the representative of the Khedive. Why not resume the design then abandoned and despatch an expedition to Khartoum on the rear of the Italian army.[2] The British Cabinet jumped at the suggestion. The victory would recover the prestige lost by Jameson's humiliating defeat. The expedition, arranged in haste, proved an arduous task; thirty per cent of the officers perished. But it was successful. Sir Herbert Kitchener, who left Wady Halfa about the end of April, defeated the enemy on June 7 at Ferkeh and on September 19 at Hafir. On September 23 Dongola was occupied. The first stage had been covered on the road to Khartoum.

The expedition was regarded by the entire world as a reply to French designs upon Abyssinia and the Upper Nile. It is not easy

[1] If vessels of every description are taken into account, already in 1895 Germany, with 201, enjoyed a superiority, if not over France (439) or Italy (224), at least over Russia (189). But this was due to the large number of her torpedo boats (114 to 85 British). If, however, we take into account only first-class ironclads (vessels with a minimum speed of 11 knots, a minimum tonnage of 6,000, and less than 12 years old in 1894), Germany possessed only 5 as against 8 Italian, 17 Russian, 21 French and 29 British. Or again, if we consider only first-class cruisers (15 knots, 5,000 tons and above, together with a few old ironclads), Germany possessed only 1 to 5 Italian, 7 Russian, 6 French and 29 British.

[2] Prince Hohenlohe to Count von Hatzfeldt, March 4, 1896 (*Die Grosse Politik*, vol. xi, p. 235).

to understand why the step was taken at the very moment when Lord Salisbury, aware for the past six months of the dispositions of the German Government, was doing his utmost to improve British relations with France and was concluding an agreement about Siam, whose provisions were censured by Lord Rosebery as inspired by an excessive anxiety to placate the French.[1] Indeed, before embarking on the Sudanese expedition, perhaps he had yielded reluctantly to the Italian and German suggestions and his colleagues'[2] views, but had attempted to obtain the approval of France. The British army, he had proposed, should advance beyond Dongola only if an agreement had been previously reached with the French Government. But although the French Minister for Foreign Affairs, the famous scientist Berthelot, received Lord Salisbury's overtures favourably, he found himself opposed by the majority of his colleagues and by the Russian embassy. He resigned. The expedition was despatched in spite of French opposition, and since the hostility of France and Russia made it impossible to finance the expedition from the reserve of the Egyptian Debt, the Khedive opened a loan, which, being entirely subscribed in England, strengthened the British hold upon Egypt.[3]

The Foreign Office, however, did not lose heart but continued to do its utmost to improve relations with France. It felt that in pursuing this policy it was supported by public feeling, just then acutely inflamed against the Emperor William and his people, and further exasperated by the disclosures of German policy published in October 1896 by the Bismarckian Press. The negotiations already engaged between the two Governments for the demarcation of their respective boundaries in the Niger zone were pushed

[1] H. of L., February 11, 1896 (*Parliamentary Debates*, 4th Ser., vol. xxxvii, pp. 35–6).

[2] M. de Staal to Prince Lobanov, March 20, April 11, 1896: 'Lord Salisbury hotly defended his point of view though admitting a certain measure of truth in my argument so far as Italy was concerned. He spoke with particular warmth when he argued that military necessity had compelled the decision of the Cabinet. He was, perhaps, inspired by the zeal of the convert, if the story is true that he was one of the last to be won over to the suggestion of an expedition in the Soudan . . .' (*Archives of the Russian Embassy in London*). He had written to the same correspondent a fortnight before (March 4–16, 1896): 'Her (Britain's) interests will always make her seek a good understanding with Italy. She will do her best to assist that Power in her present difficulties. But it is doubtful whether she will so readily return to her former orientation towards the Triple Alliance. . . . In my opinion British sympathies are rather with Russia and France than the Central Powers. . . . M. de Courcel who, in a very short time, has achieved an important position here, is of opinion that the solution of the many Colonial questions outstanding between the two countries cannot fail to improve the relations between their respective governments, and it is for this that he is working, in his opinion, with marked success.'

[3] *Die Grosse Politik*, vol. xi, pp. 158 sqq.

on with the sincere intention of bringing them to a successful issue, and although they broke down, at least an agreement about Tunis was concluded on September 18, 1897, which enabled France, in return for certain concessions, to revoke the commercial treaty the British had made with the Bey of Tunis before the French occupation. We may conjecture that Lord Salisbury hoped by these demonstrations of friendship to obtain French support for his Armenian policy. For at the close of 1895 the Sultan, encouraged by the inaction of the Powers, had given the signal for massacres, which on the lowest estimate made 80,000 victims in a single year. They stirred the British public. There was an outbreak of indignation on humanitarian grounds, led by the Churches. Patriotic sentiment also played its part. What a disgraceful spectacle of weakness Britain was displaying in the Levant! Punch and Gladstone united to deplore the fate of the unhappy Armenians. Never had a more unanimous movement of public opinion pushed the Government to energetic intervention. But what could be done against the solid combination of Germany and Russia which France, now governed by a Cabinet of moderates, supported more firmly than ever? Lord Rosebery, the official leader of the Liberal Opposition, refused to associate himself with the agitation on behalf of the Armenians. 'Against the policy of solitary interference in the affairs of the East I am prepared to fight tooth and nail. . . . I am convinced that there was a fixed and resolute agreement on the part of the Great Powers of Europe, all of them, or nearly all of them, to resist by force any single-handed intervention by England in the affairs of the East. . . . Isolated action by Great Britain means a European war.'[1] And when the old Gladstonians found fault with his timid language he resigned his leadership of the party, which remained without a recognized head.

Then the disturbances in Crete, complicated as they were by Greek intervention, distracted attention from the conditions in Armenia, and, although the attitude of the Russian Government was more favourable to the Cretan rebels than it had been to the Armenian, the Sultan, relying on German and Austrian support, declared war on Greece in April 1897. In Greek territory his army inflicted a crushing defeat on the Greek army, and the war ended in September with a victorious peace imposed by Turkey. This

[1] Edinburgh speech, October 9, 1896.

Turkish victory was a final humiliation for the British Foreign
Office.

Such in the Levant were the more than unsatisfactory fruits of
British policy. Sir Herbert Kitchener's march to Dongola—
already a year old—had done nothing to nullify at the other end
of Africa the bad effects of the Jameson raid. And finally, each of
the three Powers which had formed in 1895 the Triple Alliance of
the Far East was attempting to secure the highest possible return
for the assistance then given to China. Railway construction was
beginning in China and many politicians in London urged that
England should take her share in it. Among them was Lord
Charles Beresford, a member of one of the most important families of the Anglo-Irish nobility, whose chequered career included
the command of a naval squadron, active participation in the
House of Commons, and a journey through China in the role of
a diplomatic commercial traveller on behalf of British manufacturers and merchants.[1] But, if by a treaty concluded with China
on June 5, 1897, the British secured concessions to the South of
the Yang-Tse-Kiang, in the north they were obtained by Russia,
financed by French capital, and served by Belgian engineers.
Russian also concluded an agreement with Japan for the demarcation of their respective spheres of influence in Korea, and, at the
same time, the report was current that a secret treaty had been
signed by which she was empowered to extend the Trans-
Siberian Railway through Manchuria and received the lease of a
Chinese port, Kiao-Chau or Port Arthur. In reality, it was Germany which, in November, first effected a military occupation of
the Shan-Tung peninsula and took over the port of Kiao-Chau
on a 99 years' lease. The Russian Government replied to this step
in December by despatching a squadron to Port Arthur. The control which England had so long been accustomed to exercise over
the whole of China was a thing of the past.

[1] For the Chinese question at this period, see the Hon. George N. Curzon (Lord
Curzon), *Problems of the Far East*, 1894; (Sir) Valentine Chirol, *The Far Eastern Question*,
1896; Lord Charles Beresford, *The Break-up of China, With an account of its present Com-
merce-Currency, Waterways, Armies, Railways, Politics, and Future Prospects*, 1899; also, the
American publication by P. S. Reinsch, *World Politics at the End of the Nineteenth Century
as influenced by the Oriental Situation*, 1900.

5

How could this series of mistakes and failures be retrieved? When Jameson and five of his lieutenants, surrendered by the Transvaal Government to the British authorities, had been tried in the London courts and sentenced to several months' imprisonment, a Parliamentary Committee was appointed to probe the conspiracy to the bottom. It reported in July 1897. The members of the committee, both Conservatives and Liberals, were unanimous. Only an insignificant minority of two, a Radical and an Irishman, dissented from the report. The conduct of Rhodes and several of his accomplices was censured, but no punishment was suggested, not even the removal of Rhodes' name from the list of Privy Councillors. The Colonial Secretary was acquitted of all knowledge of the plot, but no steps had been taken to procure the documents which alone could have decisively proved whether or not his ignorance was genuine. It was only with considerable difficulty that the Radical opponents of imperialism secured the appointment of a special sitting for the discussion of the Report by the House. And when on July 26 the issue was put to the vote, their motion obtained only 77 votes as against 304 in favour of the Government, and the sitting concluded with a speech by Chamberlain which was not so much a defence of his own conduct as a panegyric of Rhodes, rebel and patriot. Was his intention when he spoke in these terms merely to satisfy public opinion, which for the past eighteen months had regarded Rhodes as a hero and a martyr? Or was it rather to signify his intention, now the path had been cleared, to revive at the first opportunity his aggressive policy in South Africa after its temporary check?

The Committee reported immediately after the splendid Jubilee Celebrations with which Great Britain kept the sixtieth anniversary of the Queen's accession. Once more, as at the former Jubilee in 1887, the ministers of the self-governing colonies met in conference in London. They discussed, though with the utmost caution, what steps could be taken towards a federal union of the Empire. But the festival was itself a manifesto. No longer, as in 1887, was it simply an act of almost religious homage paid to the person of the aged Queen, it was an act of homage to the Empire. In the long procession, which started from Buckingham Palace, visited the centre of the City, crossed London Bridge, and regaled the slums of Southwark with the spectacle, figured the premiers of the great self-governing colonies, the vassal princes of India, the governors of crown colonies, representatives of every military or naval force in the Empire, mounted infantry from Australia, Canada and the Cape, Sepoys, and specimens of a hundred different races in their native costumes. From this point of view, the Jubilee was a gesture of defiance flung by England to the nations of the world. Possibly she was isolated; her isolation, as Sir Wilfrid Laurier expressed it in a phrase which caught on immediately, was 'splendid'.[1] The world might hate Britain. Britain was a world by herself.

If, however, the Jubilee celebrations were a 'splendid' answer to the German Emperor's unsuccessful attempt eighteen months before to unite the Continent in an active league against England, the German occupation of Shan-Tung was a reply to the Jubilee, which England was obliged in her turn to leave unanswered. Public opinion was still uneasy, even at the moment when the British were seeking to persuade the world, perhaps to persuade themselves, of their imperturbable self-confidence, and it was symptomatic of the state of public feeling that Kipling's Jubilee poem was a solemn meditation on the mortality of empires.

> Far-called, our navies melt away;
> On dune and headland sinks the fire:
> Lo, all our pomp of yesterday
> Is one with Nineveh and Tyre!
> Judge of the Nations, spare us yet,
> Lest we forget—lest we forget!

No one could charge the Government with injuring the material prosperity of the nation. For the past two years there had been a brisk recovery of trade by which the Treasury and industry alike profited. Nor could they be charged with neglect of imperial defence: the big naval programme which Goschen laid before

[1] The phrase seems to have been first used by a Member of the Canadian Parliament, G. E. Foster, when in their Lower House he spoke on January 16, 1896, of: 'These troublesome days when the great Mother Empire stands splendidly isolated in Europe.' Three weeks later Sir Wilfred Laurier gave it currency: 'Whether splendidly isolated or dangerously isolated, I will not now debate; but for my part I think splendidly isolated, because this isolation of England comes from her superiority' (House of Assembly, February 5, 1896). Three weeks after this the British First Lord of the Admiralty, Goschen, naturalized the phrase in England: 'We have stood alone in that which is called isolation—our splendid isolation, as one of our Colonial friends was good enough to call it' (speech at Lewes, February 26, 1896).

Parliament in 1896 had received the almost unanimous approval of both parties. And if, on the other hand, the Cabinet's domestic policy, biased in favour of agriculture and the Anglican Church, had aroused discontent in a few urban constituencies, Radical politicians deceived their audiences or themselves when they predicted for the next election a reversal of the verdict given in 1895. For the Opposition continued to be weakened by profound internal dissensions. When imperialists like Lord Rosebery or Sir Edward Grey criticized the conciliatory spirit which Lord Salisbury displayed toward the French colonial movement, the Gladstonian section of the party, still powerful in the National Liberal Federation and among the party leaders in the Commons, refused to follow them. They praised persistently and pointedly Lord Salisbury's policy of moderation, delighted it would seem to embarrass by their praise, even more than Chamberlain, the man who a year ago had been their official chief and who perhaps cherished hopes of recovering that position. Both parties alike were suffering from anæmia. Never had the debates obeyed with such docility the strict ruling of the Speaker, never had they been so lifeless, and never had the public taken so little interest in the proceedings at Westminster. It was evident that the Unionist coalition had failed to give the national pride the satisfaction which had been expected and which no other party could give. Just then an event took place, if not in England, at least in an English-speaking country, which with a dramatic suddenness awoke British imperialism to new life.

III UNION OF THE TEUTONIC PEOPLES

I

Since 1895 the large island of Cuba had been in revolt against Spain, and the rebels were receiving from the American continent not only encouragement, but money and arms. In 1896 they were recognized as belligerents by the Government of the United States, which in 1897 made representations on their behalf at Madrid. On February 15, 1898, the *Maine*, an American man-of-war, was sunk by an explosion in the harbour of Havana. The preposterous tale was immediately circulated in the United States, and confirmed by an official despatch, that the Spaniards had deliberately destroyed the *Maine*. At once a formidable wave of patriotic enthusiasm swept the country; humanitarian zeal on behalf of the oppressed Cubans, lust of conquest, desire to avenge a slight upon the national honour were blent in one powerful movement of public feeling, which President McKinley was unable to resist. On April 20 war was declared; on July 3 the entire Spanish fleet was wiped out off Santiago; and on August 2 Spain asked for the peace—concluded on December 10—which abolished the last vestiges of her colonial empire. It was an important date in the history of imperialism throughout the world. America had reacted to the stimulus of European example, abandoned the peaceful isolation which Washington had laid down as the fundamental principle of her foreign policy, and become in her turn a conqueror. And, unlike the European empires up to the present, she had aggrandized herself at the expense of a European and a Christian nation. She had acquired a colonial empire by expelling the Spaniard.

How was her action regarded by British public opinion? Three years before, at the very moment when the Unionists took office, American imperialism had clashed with British. A frontier dispute had arisen between British Guiana and the Republic of Venezuela. President Cleveland had intervened and, taking his stand on the doctrine laid down in 1823 by President Monroe which denied the right of foreign powers to interfere in the affairs of the New World, had offered his arbitration. When Lord Salisbury in disdainful terms refused to entertain the offer, Cleveland, on December 17, 1895, invited Congress to appoint a commission to inquire into the Anglo-Venezuelan dispute. When it had reported, it would, he maintained, be the duty of the United States to resist by every means at its disposal, as a deliberate attack on its rights and interests, the occupation by Great Britain of territory adjudged after due inquiry to Venezuela. On the appointment of the commission the British Cabinet retreated and accepted the arbitration which in November it had rejected in principle.

No doubt the threat of war between the two great English-speaking nations had at the time occasioned lively protests on both sides of the Atlantic. British holders of American bonds sold out. There was a panic in Wall Street, and financial circles both in England and America realized how close was the community of interests between the two countries. Nor was it merely a community of interests; there was also a community of sentiment. The leaders of thought,[1] the clergy of every Protestant denomination, indignantly denounced the suggestion of a fratricidal war. It must also be admitted that, as a result of these demonstrations, the Government of the United States finally carried out the arbitration in such a fashion as to spare to some extent British susceptibilities. Nevertheless, the entire episode added another to the long list of defeats suffered by the Unionist Cabinet. And the American politicians completed the humiliation of Great Britain and baffled the attempts at *rapprochement* made by the two Governments. When a treaty of universal arbitration had been signed by the Secretary of State, Olney, and the British Ambassador, Sir Julian Pauncefote, the Senate after long debates refused to ratify it. After all this, it is not surprising that at the beginning of 1898 the Unionist Press as a whole was frankly hostile to the American point of view, and favourable to Spain. Nor is it surprising that Sir Julian, who had been humiliated in 1895 by the arrogant attitude of America and a second time in 1897 by the rejection of his arbitration treaty, attempted at the beginning of April to revive the project of arbitration, to be proposed this time to the United States by the joint intervention of all the European powers.[2] Certain Tories, descendants of the seventeenth-century Cavaliers, had always cherished a traditional affection for the Catholic and Latin nations. And men with the temperament and outlook of Lord Salisbury and Arthur Balfour could hardly fail to prefer the Spanish crown to the business men of Chicago?

But the attitude of the Radical Press was very different. The

[1] It is curious to compare the language of the American philosopher, William James, about the Venezuela affair with his language two years later during the Spanish-American War. Then he expressed indignation: 'Cleveland, in my opinion, by his explicit allusion to war, has committed the biggest political crime I have ever seen here.' (Letter to F. W. H. Myers, January 1, 1896. *The Letters of William James*, vol. ii, p. 31.) In 1898 his tone is utterly different and while lamenting that 'at the least temptation all the old military passions rise and sweep everything before them', he writes: 'The European nations of the Continent cannot believe that our pretence of humanity and our disclaiming of all ideas of conquest is sincere. It has been *absolutely* sincere! The self-conscious feeling of our people has been entirely based on a sense of philanthropic duty, without which not a step would have been taken.' (Letter to François Pillon, June 15, 1898; ibid., p. 74.)

[2] *Die Grosse Politik* . . . vol. xv, pp. 23-4, 28, 29. It must be added that when the story of this proposal leaked out in the early part of 1902, it was categorically denied by Lord Cranborne, a son of Lord Salisbury and Under-Secretary for Foreign Affairs (H. of C., February 11, 1902; *Parliamentary Debates*, 4th Ser., vol. cii, p. 992). The German evidence seems, however, decisive. In fact, the German documents prove, if their evidence is reliable, that Sir Julian Pauncefote's attitude was the attitude of all the leading Conservative organs in London until the middle of April. The Cuban War is not mentioned in vol. i of the *British Documents on the Origins of the War, 1898-1914*.

intellectual circles and the religious organizations which constituted the backbone of the party shared to the full the American
outlook and sentiments. How could they do otherwise than
champion the United States against Spain, even if, from the
standpoint of international law, the latter was in the right? From
March onwards the *Speaker*, the *Daily News*, and the *Daily
Chronicle* were demanding the conclusion of an Anglo-Saxon
alliance,[1] and the Nonconformist bodies expressed the wish that
every effort should be made to bring the two peoples together.[2]
No doubt the outbreak of Jingoism in the United States was em-
barrassing to those Liberals who were professed opponents of
militarism. They escaped the difficulty by the reflection that this
was a war of liberation, undertaken to free the Cubans from the
Spanish yoke, or again, that since American civilization was commercial and peaceful, the defeat of Spanish militarism was, in fact,
the victory of peace. And if the editors of the *Manchester Guardian*
felt some difficulty in solving the problem, it was otherwise with
the *Daily Chronicle*, at that time the most popular of the important
London dailies. The reader is given the impression that the entire
Anglo-Saxon world was at war with Spain, and that the Englishman was almost guilty of treason who refused to take part, mentally, if not as a soldier, in a war which was nothing less than a
crusade waged against a barbarous and corrupt foe.

It was not long before it became clear that the Liberal attitude
on this question corresponded better than the Tory with the interests of the nation. What was it that made the British so uneasy?
The spectacle of a virtual combination of the great Powers of
Europe against their country. Now, in every Continental capital,
from Petersburg to Berlin and Paris, the same combination was,
it appeared, being formed against the United States. Was England
to condone all the injuries she had received and unite with the
European Governments in the defence of Spain? Should she not
rather espouse the cause of the United States and as her ally take
up the gauntlet which the old world seemed desirous of throwing
down, not to the United States alone but to the entire English-
speaking world? Before the end of April, the Conservative Press

[1] *Daily News*, March 16, 1898; *Daily Chronicle*, March 18, April 15, 1898; *Speaker*,
March 19, 1898.
[2] See the telegram of sympathy despatched on April 27 to President McKinley by the
Spring Meeting of the Baptist Union of Great Britain and Ireland (*Daily Chronicle*, April
28, 1898).

had altered its standpoint and, with the solitary exception of the eccentric *Saturday Review*, had taken the side of the United States. It was a turning-point in British foreign policy. The British Press, like the British Government, has never since departed from the attitude, now definitely adopted, of deliberately courting the friendship of the American Government and people.

2

It is not easy to say with certainty how far the Unionist Press yielded to the spontaneous pressure of public opinion, or how far the Government dictated the policy of the party organs. It is, however, worth remark that throughout the whole of April Lord Salisbury was convalescing in the South of France after influenza and that, in consequence, Chamberlain's influence in the Cabinet lacked the usual makeweight. Chamberlain was entirely devoid of the prejudice against the Yankee usual among the Tories. For he was a newcomer, a man of the Colonial or American stamp. The sentiments which led the Radical Press to espouse the American cause were native to the society into which he had been born, and in which he had made his political apprenticeship. The Radical Jingoism of the *Daily Chronicle* was his own. Was the agreement at this juncture between himself and the great Radical daily a mere coincidence? Or is there reason to suspect a secret understanding? I could call attention to a significant fact. On March 8, the *Daily Chronicle* was demanding not only an understanding with America, but an understanding, even a military alliance, with Germany. On the 14th it repeated the demand, and on the 18th united both suggestions in the single grandiose project of a Triple Alliance. 'The world is coming to be ruled by great forces or combinations of forces. The huge Russian empire and the vast strength of the French Republic—that is one union. All German-speaking people will be under one flag before the next century is very old.' At the very time when the *Daily Chronicle* was elaborating this ambitious scheme, Chamberlain was working hard to realize it by secret negotiations with the diplomatic representatives of Germany, negotiations whose details were long kept secret but whose results were soon apparent.

In the course of the winter the suggestion had often been mooted that the underground league of the Powers against Great

Britain, which seemed on the way to become universal, might be broken by specific negotiations with one or other of them. Many symptoms pointed to a weakening of the alliance between Russia and Germany in the Far East now that the time had come for the allies to divide the spoils of their common victory. In October, Russia had watched with an unfavourable eye the German occupation of Shantung and, in December, Germany had been chagrined by the Russian counter-move, the military occupation of Port Arthur and the Liao-Tung peninsula. Under these circumstances was it impracticable to negotiate with Russia a partition of spheres of influence between the two nations, both in China and in Turkey, by which Northern China would be definitely abandoned to Russia? Negotiations were, in fact, carried on between London and Petersburg until the end of March,[1] on the very eve of the Russian occupation of Port Arthur. Or was the alternative policy, an understanding with Germany, impossible? In January, Sir Herbert Kitchener resumed his advance up the Nile and began his conquest of the Soudan. Every day witnessed a further step on that route from Cairo to the Cape which was now the dearly-cherished ideal of the Chamberlain school of imperialism. It was common knowledge that the French colonials had replied by an ambitious counter-initiative. In the summer of 1896, Captain Marchand had left the Congo with a commission to forestall the British on the Upper Nile and bar their advance by setting up a cordon of French posts between Brazzaville and Djibouti—that is to say, a conflict between France and Great Britain was imminent. Moreover, the relations between the British and the Boers in South Africa were becoming strained. The problem of the legal status of the Uitlanders in the Transvaal was still unsolved. There also, any day, matters might reach a crisis. Prudence suggested that in view of the difficulties likely to arise at any moment in North or in South Africa steps should be taken to prevent further demonstrations of hostility by the Emperor William, such as had embarrassed the British Government towards the end of 1895, and, by timely concessions to the German

[1] See *British Documents*, vol. i, pp. 5 sqq., in particular the Marquis of Salisbury to Sir N. O'Connor, January 25, 1898. See also the apprehensions expressed by Graf von Hatzfeldt in a letter of March 25: 'The conviction prevails in the City that the situation as regards China is at present very critical and that at the meeting of the Cabinet today important decisions will be taken. It is believed in many quarters that the Cabinet will attempt to reach an understanding with Russia, disarm her enmity and prevent her from actively supporting the French demands' (*Die Grosse Politik*, vol. xiv, p. 196).

colonial movement, secure in advance the diplomatic isolation of France and the South African Republics. Ever since November 1897, Lord Salisbury's language in his weekly conversations with the German ambassador had assumed a conciliatory tone which his interlocutor regarded as significant, and there can be no doubt that it was with the backing of both Governments that a group of English and German financiers, having first secured the rejection of a rival offer from Russia, advanced China in February the amount of her war indemnity to Japan.[1] But when Lord Salisbury expressed his desire for an understanding between the two countries he had been careful to explain that he did not mean an understanding directed against any third party. In Parliament he continued to speak the language of peace, protested against the current belief that it was a duty to grab whatever Britain could lay her hands upon, stand up to the entire world, and turn every dispute into a *casus belli*, and lamented the discredit which had overtaken the Cobdenism of his youth.[2] On the other hand, no indications at the beginning of 1898 pointed to Chamberlain as the man who would give a new orientation to British foreign policy. The German ambassador looked to Lord Salisbury, not to Chamberlain, to improve the relations between the two countries. At the end of December, Chamberlain told the Russian ambassador 'that the only sound policy for Great Britain was an understanding with Russia and consequently with France'.[3] For England was involved in colonial disputes with Germany, as with other countries, and a settlement was no easier to reach. His high-handed methods made Chamberlain intensely unpopular in Berlin.[4] That

[1] Graf von Hatzfeldt to the German Foreign Office, November 20, 1897 (*Die Grosse Politik*, vol. xiii, p. 43).

[2] H. of L., February 8, 1898 (*Parliamentary Debates*, 4th Ser., vol. liii, p. 45).

[3] M. de Staal to Count Mouravieff (December 10–22, 1897). Cf. M. de Staal to Prince Lobanov (February 7–19, 1896): 'Many indications combine to show that British public opinion is taking a direction favourable to our country. The other day at a social function I met Mr. Chamberlain, the leading statesman of the moment. He took me aside and spoke very warmly in that sense.' A little later, when Chamberlain in a violent speech had thrown down the gage to Russia (see below, p. 51), Lord Salisbury could apologize to the Russian ambassador for the incident and add: 'That his astonishment when he read the speech was the greater because in the Cabinet Mr. Chamberlain had consistently pleaded for an understanding with Russia.' M. de Staal confirms Lord Salisbury's evidence on this point (M. de Staal to Count Mouravieff, May 13–25, 1898, *Archives of the Russian Embassy in London*).

[4] Graf von Hatzfeldt to Prince von Hohenlohe, December 2, 1897: 'When I seek to discover the motives of the unreasonable demands of the English and the obstinacy with which they adhere to them, I am led to the conclusion that Mr. Chamberlain's personal ambition is primarily responsible, *possibly also his lack of sympathy with Germany*' (*Die Grosse Politik*, vol. xiv, p. 108). And on December 18, when Lord Salisbury had explained

was the Chamberlain touch. He mistook it for strength. But he was also and, for the same reason, addicted to rapid and sensational decisions. The Russian occupation of Port Arthur produced an outburst of anti-Russian feeling in England which rendered a diplomatic understanding between the two countries impossible. Under these circumstances, he espoused the policy of an understanding with Germany. At once he went further than Lord Salisbury was prepared to go; indeed, he would very soon alarm his chief. It was his deliberate design to give the understanding a more theatrical setting and consequently a less pacific character than it had possessed in Lord Salisbury's intention.

It would seem that the discussions which he proceeded to initiate were undertaken on his personal responsibility, without previous consultation with the Premier. The agents were: on the German side, a certain Baron von Eckardstein, a former secretary to the embassy, who, in consequence of his marriage to a wealthy London heiress—daughter of the well-known furnisher, Sir John Blundell Maple—had left the diplomatic service and lived in London as a private gentleman of means; on the English side, Lord Rothschild, a member of the group of Liberal Unionists whose nominal head was the Duke of Devonshire, but which was, in fact, led by Chamberlain. The Duke of Devonshire had married a German wife, as Eckardstein an Englishwoman, and Devonshire House played an important part in the negotiations. The discussions apparently began about the end of February but no active steps were taken until Lord Salisbury fell ill, ceased to attend the meetings of the Cabinet, and finally, on March 15, left for a month's holiday in the South of France. Chamberlain was now for practical purposes Prime Minister, and his authority was enhanced by the violent protest of certain English newspapers[1]

to the ambassador that the Cabinet could not with safety attempt to influence public opinion too strongly in favour of Germany, the Emperor wrote against the passage of his report in which von Hatzfeldt repeated the Premier's words: '*Das ist von einem Cabinett mit Chamberlain darinnen nicht zu befürchten*—A Cabinet of which Chamberlain is a member need have no fear on that score' (*Die Grosse Politik*, vol. xiii, p. 47).

[1] *The Times*, March 28, 31. *Morning Post*, same dates—cf. *Fortnightly Review*, April 1 (vol. lxiii, pp. 513 sqq.), the article entitled 'Where Lord Salisbury has Failed', by Diplomaticus. (The writer, however, at the conclusion of his article, declared that it was not his intention to demand Lord Salisbury's resignation of the Foreign Office.) See also H. of C., March 30: Sir Charles Dilke's motion condemning the union in a single hand of the Foreign Office and the duties of a Prime Minister (*Parliamentary Debates*, 4th Ser., vol. lv, p. 1360). The *Daily Chronicle* supported the motion, but, very characteristically, the official organ of the Radical Party, the *Daily News* (March 31) warmly espoused the defence of Lord Salisbury.

against the virtual resignation at such a critical moment of the statesman who, in spite of his advanced age, attempted to combine the duties of a Prime Minister with those of a Foreign Secretary.[1] Throughout the entire month, both inside and outside the House, the language employed by certain ministers was calculated to prepare public opinion for grave eventualities.[2] Finally, Chamberlain arranged for March 26 a dinner at Lord Rothschild's at which Balfour and himself were to meet the German ambassador. Balfour would seem to have been afraid of committing himself too deeply to Chamberlain's schemes; he pleaded an engagement for the 26th and on the 25th called on the ambassador. At the interview he was content to express in general terms the opinion that an understanding between England and Germany, in China and elsewhere, seemed to him practicable in the interest of both countries. But on the following day, Chamberlain had a conversation with the ambassador in which he frankly admitted that England could not remain any longer isolated, and proposed then and there that the Triple Alliance should be transformed into a Quadruple Alliance, of which England should be a member.[3]

The Emperor William rejected the proposal, almost naïve in its suddenness. But it was no slight matter for congratulation that at the very time when his personal policy was at last victorious at Berlin, and the Reichstag, by passing the first law of naval construction, had recognized the necessity of equipping Germany

[1] Was it really his inactivity which the Press blamed and not rather the active resistance which, even when invalided abroad, he opposed to his colleagues' imperialism? See (Sir) W. S. Blunt's account in his diary of a conversation with George Wyndham on March 24: 'George . . . walks home most nights with Arthur Balfour from the House, and hears a good deal of what is going on. He tells me Lord Salisbury does not intend resigning, and though he has made over the Foreign Office temporarily to Balfour, he still keeps interfering with affairs there not altogether to Arthur's pleasure' (*My Diaries*, 1888-1914, vol. l, p. 357).

[2] See the speech delivered on March 2 at Bradford by Lord Selborne, Under-Secretary for the Colonies: 'He thought that the majority of his countrymen would agree that the one trite rule of conduct in the real interests of the country was peace, but not peace at any price. It was the responsibility of the elector to make up his mind as to the exact point at which the price became too much.' Sir Michael Hicks-Beach, the Chancellor of the Exchequer, had already spoken in bellicose terms on January 17 at Swansea and on January 19 at Bristol. Lord Salisbury's pacific utterance in the House of Lords on February 8 was a reply to these speeches of his colleague.

[3] The first account of Anglo-German negotiations to be made public appeared in the *Daily Telegraph* of April 15, 19, 26 and September 3, 7, 10 and 11, 1912. It does not seem to have made much impression on the public. The story was retold in Baron von Eckardstein's book, *Lebenserrinerungen und Politische Denkwürdigkeiten*, 1919 (see especially vol. i, pp. 291 sqq.). *Die Grosse Politik*, vol. xiv, pp. 191 sqq., corrects in certain details and completes on many points but on the whole confirms in its essentials Eckardstein's account.

with a fleet worthy of a first-class power, he had won abroad a diplomatic success, almost equally important. England, which only two years before he had so seriously insulted, was now invoking his assistance. He did not altogether reject the British advances, and many signs warned the public that a new era in foreign policy was about to open. When, on March 27, Russia signed the public treaty with China which guaranteed her possession of Port Arthur, Britain replied by occupying Wei-Hai-Wei with the entire approval of the Berlin Government, and when, on April 5, he justified the step in the House of Commons, Balfour was at pains to lay stress on the common interests in China of England and Germany, which must be jointly defended against Russia. On April 8, Sir Herbert Kitchener, as he advanced victoriously on Khartoum, received a public letter of congratulation from the German Emperor. As though in obedience to an official command[1] the British Press desisted from the attacks, common since 1896, on Germany and even on the Emperor's person. This was the position when during the first half of May two speeches delivered, one by Lord Salisbury three days after his return from the Continent, the other by Chamberlain, carried public excitement to the highest pitch.

3

Addressing the Primrose League on May 4, Lord Salisbury, after a few remarks on current questions of domestic politics, enlarged on the foreign situation. Events in Northern China served as a pretext for inviting his audience to consider the state of the world as a whole. There were 'living' nations. There were also 'dying' nations. It was 'inevitable' that the former should expand at the cost of the latter. And that expansion could be effected only by war. Not that the Prime Minister was eager for war—far from

[1] Prince von Radolin to Prince von Hohenlohe, August 2, 1898: 'Even in England where the Press is completely free, a hint from headquarters has sufficed to recall, at least all the respectable newspapers, to a correct attitude' (*Die Grosse Politik*, vol. xiii, p. 186). The Emperor William to the Emperor Nicholas, May 30, 1898: 'In the beginning of April the attacks on my country and person, till then showered on us by the British Press and people, suddenly fell off. . . . This rather astonished us at home and we were at a loss for an explanation. In a private enquiry I found out that H.M. the Queen herself, through a friend of hers, had sent word to the British papers that she wished this ignoble and false game to cease. This is the land of the "free Press".' (The Kaiser's letters to the Tsar, pp. 52–3.) On Chamberlain's relations with the Press, see Kennedy Jones, *Fleet Street and Downing Street*, 1917, p. 95.

it. The entire speech was a mournful jeremiad rather than a call to arms. In a somewhat ambiguous sentence Lord Salisbury urged the British people not to squander the resources of the Empire before the day arrived when the fate of the world would be settled, on 'matters which, if at the moment they appeared serious, would be dwarfed to insignificance in the perspective of the future'. While claiming for England her share of the spoils, he explained that his country would bear no grudge against other nations, if they extended their dominion over regions 'where the British grasp was unable to reach'. He pleaded for a policy of isolation, and warned the country of the dangers of 'a policy of prestige'. Very different in tone was the speech which Chamberlain delivered at Birmingham and which had the appearance of a deliberate reply to his chief. From beginning to end it breathed war. He began by denouncing 'the mysteries and the reticences' of the traditional diplomacy. He claimed for a democratic government like the British the right to take the nation into its confidence and conduct its foreign policy in public under the eyes of the world. He then declared himself unable to be content, as Lord Salisbury appeared to be, with the policy of isolation to which England had proudly adhered ever since the Crimean War. So long as other countries were isolated, that policy was defensible, but now, when the Continental nations were grouped in powerful alliances, England must find friends. War was no doubt a horrible thing, but 'even war itself would be cheaply purchased, if, in a great and noble cause, the Stars and Stripes and the Union Jack should wave together over an Anglo-Saxon alliance'. He proceeded to attack Russia, which in his Primrose League speech Lord Salisbury had been careful to spare. He denounced the treacherous intrigues by which Russia had contrived to obtain possession of Port Arthur and Talienwan. That treachery might indeed have been foreseen— 'who sups with the devil must have a long spoon'. But war with Russia was out of the question except in concert with an allied Power. Once more he condemned the policy of isolation and refused to 'reject the idea of an Alliance with those Powers whose interests most nearly approximate to our own'. The concluding portion of the speech, in which everyone saw an advance to Germany, was ill received on the other side of the North Sea. On the other hand, the suggestion of a possible 'Anglo-American alliance' was welcomed in the United States, and flags were hoisted at New York on the Queen's birthday, as in London on Independence Day. For the Americans, who were at war with Spain, were delighted to find, in England at least, sympathy with their cause, and even entertained the pleasing hope that they might yet win German sympathy through the good offices of Great Britain. When the American ambassador in Germany was invited to speak at Leipzig on July 4, he refused to begin his speech until a German flag had been added to the American and British flags which adorned the hall, and made his discourse a panegyric of Germany 'the second Mother-country' of the United States.[1]

These two speeches in which both speakers, one minister in a tone of anxiety, the other in accents of delight, seemed to agree in pronouncing war imminent, quite naturally kept the public for several days in a state of alarm. When the tension subsided it was evident that the Colonial Secretary had the nation behind him. The imperialist policy, which, since 1895, had been the unavowed policy of the Cabinet, had received from Chamberlain an expression calculated to strike the imagination of the country, indeed of the entire world.

Six days after the Birmingham speech the aged Gladstone died in his eighty-ninth year. The country with one consent paid his memory the tribute she is wont to pay without distinction of party to great statesmen who have had the privilege to serve her. Nevertheless, his disappearance from the scene at this particular moment was symbolic. His funeral, so soon after Chamberlain's war cry, seemed the funeral of the political tradition which bore his name. The old Liberal orthodoxy was dead.

The struggle between Liberalism and despotism, industrialism and militarism, during which in any country the British Liberals were prepared to champion the former against the latter by naval support or active intervention, was a thing of the past. What meaning was there now in the opposition when the youthful and growing German nation was the perfect embodiment alike of industrialism and of militarism? There were progressive nations, and stagnating or decadent nations, 'living' nations and 'dying' nations. Which were the progressive and living nations?—preeminently the United States and Germany. But were not these two nations united with England by deep-rooted affinities?—in

---

[1] *Die Grosse Politik*, vol. xv, p. 54 note . . . *Autobiography of A. D. White*, vol. ii, pp. 168 sqq.

the first place by community of religion? All three countries were predominantly Protestant. Nevertheless, the advocates of an understanding between them did not stress their common Protestantism. And, if on occasion they brought it forward, it was not as a matter of theological truth but inasmuch as Protestantism in contrast with Latin Catholicism could be presented as the form of Christianity best adapted to the 'Saxon', 'Germanic', or 'Teutonic' temperament. For race had become the keystone of the current sociological systems. The progress of civilization had brought the European nations into contact with peoples at once less civilized than themselves and very different in racial character. The inevitable result was to establish a very close association between the two concepts of 'civilization' and 'race'. But were there not among the Europeans themselves racial distinctions, less marked no doubt, but real nevertheless, and differing only in degree from the distinction between the black races and the white, the white and the yellow races? And in particular, was there not a 'Teutonic' race, which throughout the North-West of Europe expressed Christian civilization in its most consummate form and, overflowing its European boundaries, had created beyond the seas, on the one hand the British Empire, on the other the United States of America? How powerless the rest of the world must prove in face of an alliance between the three great representatives of a race manifestly designated by its innate qualities to assume the empire of the globe?[1]

[1] For an even more definite formulation of Chamberlain's system, see his speech at Wakefield, December 8, 1898. If his allusions to Russia are more restrained, he adopts a hectoring tone towards France. 'As a moment's reflection will show that there is no part of the globe in which British and German interests conflict in any serious way, I think we may hope that in the future the two nations—the greatest naval nation in the world and the greatest military nation—may come more frequently together, and our joint influence may be used on behalf of peace and of unrestricted trade, in which case it will certainly be more potent than would be the influence of either Power taken alone.' He also advocated a tightening of the bonds which united England and her Colonies and a *rapprochement* with the United States. 'If we are assured of the friendship of the Anglo-Saxon race, whether they abide under the Stars and Stripes or under the Union Jack, there is no other combination that can make us afraid.' A few passages taken from writers of widely different provenance will prove the extent to which British imagination was possessed by the ideal of a panteutonic alliance. Annie Besant, *Ancient Ideals in Modern Life*, 1901, pp. 8–9: 'There is dawning now on the vision of the earth a vast Teutonic world-empire, formed by the English and their Colonies, with their huge offshoot, the United States, bound in close alliance. Their world-empire will be the next to dominate humanity.' *The Life of Hugh Price Hughes*, by his daughter, 1905, pp. 291–2: 'His attitude to Germany was that of unloving admiration, but he thought that the Emperor and Mr. Chamberlain were the two cleverest men in Europe. . . . The German people did not take his fancy, but England must increasingly ally herself with them. . . . Germany, like England, had accepted the Reformation, and stood for the future and for progress. France,

The Slavonic race was flooding Asia. Should England inaugurate her new policy by erecting in the East a dyke to stem the rising tide? But at the close of the nineteenth century Russia was far from being regarded as a 'dying nation', and very few at that time took seriously the revolutionaries who proclaimed the imminent collapse of the Czarist régime. On the contrary, public opinion was inclined to regard the Russian advance in Asia as something inevitable, irresistible as a force of nature. It was in another direction that the Anglo-Saxon race must take, had indeed already taken, the initiative. Spain, humbled by the United States, had apparently exhausted all her old vitality and power of expansion. Little Portugal stagnated, forgotten by the world, though still in possession of an extensive colonial empire. Italy, having achieved her unity, was attempting to raise herself to the position of a great power. But her attempts were a series of blunders, almost ridiculous: Crispi's megalomania had resulted in the fiasco of Adowa. France cherished the memory of a great past, still by no means remote, but, if the prospect of a military dictatorship was a constant source of anxiety, the inglorious Government, which for the past quarter of a century had managed to avert the danger, was an object of contempt. The Reactionaries in alliance with the Revolutionaries had exploited the Panama scandal against the Parliament. And now the Dreyfus affair was begin-

on the contrary, had not done so, and was declining daily and in that he loved that country he incessantly belaboured her'; pp. 552-3 (during the Boer War): 'When his opponents said, "You, an advocate of peace, and a member of the Peace Society, uphold this iniquity?" he thought: "Yes, indeed, and a vaster Peace Society than you wot of, my dear brother. Our Society ranges the earth, and sends men to their deaths so that thousands unborn may have some chance of enjoying what you and I do." This Peace Society, moreover, was distinctly Teutonic in character and friendly to the Teutonic peoples, because they had accepted the principles of the Reformation.' The Rev. Hugh Price Hughes, a distinguished Wesleyan, was an imperialist. And the language of the Congregationalist minister R. Horton, whose imperialism was less pronounced, if not pro-German, is at any rate, anti-Latin. See *The Awe of the New Century*, 1900, p. 51: 'The signs do not point to unity of that kind' (Catholic unity), 'the despotic kind. Popes and Caesars and Czars are merely survivals where the life of the new age is not yet felt. They have nothing to do with the everlasting Gospel; they have no point of contact with Christ. They are in the circle of ideas which made the Roman Empire, the Latin races, the Latin religion.' Sometimes panteutonism assumed a Liberal aspect. See Bernard Holland, *Imperium et Libertas, A Study in History and Politics*, 1901, pp. 8-9: 'In France . . . the Revolution and Napoleonic régime . . . did but put the last touches to the work of Louis XI, Richelieu, and Louis XIV. But in countries inhabited by races of the Teutonic breed—Germans, English, Swiss, Dutch—centralization has never been so complete, and liberties of all kinds, individual, municipal, and provincial, have been better maintained throughout history against the central power. In these countries the principle of division of power, which was at the bottom of the mediaeval social order, now asserts itself with better chance of success, because we are enlightened by the teaching of history, or experience.'

ning. Would a combination of the Republicans and the Revolutionaries take their revenge and utilize this new scandal to the detriment of the Army? Or, as the majority of Englishmen expected, would the unstable and scandalous political conditions enable a soldier of mediocre qualities to establish a precarious dictatorship? The colonial undertakings of France seemed disproportionate to her stationary population, and subordinate position in the markets of the world. Unpleasant rumours were current to the effect that the hastily organized expedition to Madagascar had been on the verge of disaster. This was evidently the quarter where the Teutonic attack must be delivered. No doubt, the turn of the Slavonic barbarian would come sooner or later, but the decadent Latin races must be the immediate victims.

4

Portugal was the first to suffer from the Anglo-German understanding. About the beginning of June, the report spread that Portugal was raising a loan in London on the security of the customs of her South African Colonies. Great Britain, no doubt, expected to secure in this indirect fashion a control over Delagoa Bay, sufficient to prevent the Transvaal Republic obtaining supplies by that route should there be a recrudescence of the conflict between President Kruger and the British Government. The German Government at once protested, pleaded previous engagements between the Portuguese Government and itself and demanded a share in the bargain. The plea was allowed and negotiations began. It was with Lord Salisbury that Graf von Hatzfeldt had to deal at first, and the discussions dragged on for over two months. But on August 9, the Prime Minister took a holiday of several weeks and left Balfour in temporary charge of the Foreign Office. No doubt Balfour had as little taste as his uncle, the Premier, for Chamberlain's spectacular foreign policy, but his dislike did not blind him to the fact that an understanding between England and Germany might serve the immediate interest of his country. Two agreements were signed in London on August 30. Though the first was not explicitly declared secret, the text was not published. In the accepted phraseology the two Governments agreed to guarantee 'the integrity and independence of Portugal'. If Portugal were in need of money, England and

Germany would jointly advance the necessary loan. The colonial customs of Portugal would be pledged to both creditors. In case of non-payment England would be entitled to the customs levied in that part of Mozambique which lay to the South of the Zambesi and throughout Central Angola, Germany to the customs levied in Mozambique to the North of the Zambesi and in the North and South of Angola. The second agreement, which was strictly secret, provided that if 'unfortunately' it should prove impossible to preserve the integrity of the Portuguese Empire, both the contracting powers should have entire liberty of action in the respective customs areas defined by the first convention. In short, Portugal, a European nation, and, moreover, an ally of Great Britain, was treated as the European powers were accustomed to treat Turkey, Persia, or China. As a first step, her colonies were divided into two spheres of influence, British and German respectively, and provision was made for their eventual partition between the two Powers.[1]

These negotiations concerning the Portuguese colonies were kept secret, as also were those begun in August by the British ambassador in Madrid, Sir Henry Drummond Wolff, for the conclusion of a convention[2] which would in practice have amounted to the establishment of a military protectorate or quasi-protectorate of England over Spain. Spain would agree not to erect fortifications within a radius of seven miles round Gibraltar. She would also promise her help to England in the event of war, and

[1] The territorial arrangements made by the two conventions are rather more complicated, and include important dispositions relating to the Portuguese colony of Timor in the Pacific. See for the full history of the negotiations, *Die Grosse Politik*, vol. xiv, pp. 257 sqq.; *British Documents*, vol. l, pp. 44 sqq. One point, however, after both publications, remains obscure, and that is the exact part played by Chamberlain. It would seem that afraid of giving offence at the Cape, and even in Australia, by too extensive concessions, he chose to remain in the background and leave to Lord Salisbury and Balfour the invidious task of arranging the deal. Reference is made to the Anglo-German agreement of 1898 in Baron von Eckardstein's *Lebenserrinerungen*, vol. ii, pp. 205–6. When the negotiations for a Portuguese loan finally broke down, the agreement of August 1898 was rendered inoperative, and it was even arguable that it had lapsed. When the conflict between Great Britain and the South African Republic became acute, and an unfriendly Portugal which permitted the free importation of arms into the Transvaal might have proved very awkward, Lord Salisbury seized the opportunity to conclude a treaty of friendship with Portugal, which had the air of a protest against the bargaining of the previous year (*British Documents*, vol. i, pp. 88 sqq.).

[2] The draft of this Convention which was never signed was confidentially shown by the Spanish Government to the Russian ambassador at Madrid, who later on communicated it to his French colleague. It has, apparently, left no trace in the Archives of the Foreign Office, but is referred to in the most explicit terms in a telegram from Sir H. D. Wolff to the Marquis of Salisbury, March 10, 1899 (ibid., vol. II, p. 255).

England would make herself responsible for the military and naval defence not only of the bay of Algeciras, but also of the Balearic and Canary Islands. But who was the enemy whose influence England was fighting in the Peninsula, and against whom she wanted to make sure of the help—voluntary or otherwise—of Spain? It was with another Latin nation, with France, that the tension had become more acute for several months previously; and there was nothing secret about the relations between the two countries.

The matter at issue was the settlement of the frontier between the French possessions in Western Africa and the British Colonies of the Gold Coast and Nigeria. When, in 1897, Lord Salisbury re-opened negotiations with this object he no doubt hoped to reach without much delay a friendly solution, such as had just been achieved in Siam and Tunisia. But the affair dragged on interminably. In February, the report became current that French officers had occupied certain of the disputed areas with the object of presenting England with a *fait accompli*. In consequence of an alarmist speech by Chamberlain in the Commons and a representation by Sir Edward Monson to the Quay D'Orsay the French minister of Foreign Affairs, Hanotaux, denied, or at least disavowed, the expedition.[1] In May, Chamberlain's warlike speech was at once understood—although the name of France had not been pronounced—as aimed immediately at France. On May 19th, four days after the Birmingham speech, a meeting of the Cabinet was held, a stormy meeting, if report be true. Chamberlain, it was rumoured, had demanded that the negotiations with France should be brought to a conclusion by the threat of an ultimatum. Faced by his colleagues' refusal, he had actually tendered his resignation. And he had finally prevailed. One thing at any rate is certain, that from this moment the negotiations progressed rapidly and on June 14 the agreement was signed.

Was it a humiliation for France? If she renounced her claim to Bussa and the entire navigable waters of the Niger, she secured in compensation the use of two ports on the Niger for the free transit of her goods. And if she abandoned the entire Sokoto, she kept Nikki in the Borgo region. Moreover, the frontier of the

---

[1] For the entire incident, see the debate between Chamberlain, John Dillon, and Labouchere, H. of C., February 24, 1898 (*Parliamentary Debates*, 4th Ser., vol. lxiii, pp. 1605 sqq.).

Gold Coast was rectified to her advantage. It is possible, therefore, to see in the agreement a compromise satisfactory to both countries, and in this instance, also, to detect Lord Salisbury's moderating influence. The fact remains that the British Cabinet believed—and not without foundation[1]—that it had been the intention of the French Foreign Office to protract the discussion, unite the question of the Niger with the question of the Upper Nile, and, by thus postponing the settlement of the former until the latter had reached a critical stage, secure that all the questions outstanding in Africa between the two Governments—including the Egyptian—should be the object of a general agreement, which would, they hoped, be more favourable to France. The speedy conclusion of the agreement was, therefore, in itself a diplomatic success for Great Britain. The settlement of the Niger question left the question of the Upper Nile where it was before.

5

While the British Government was hastening the settlement of the Niger frontier, Kitchener continued his advance on the Upper Nile. On September 2, he was before Omdurman, and his 23,000 men found themselves faced by the Khalifa's army of 50,000. That evening the victory was won. It was a massacre rather than a battle. On the Anglo-Egyptian side fifty were killed and 300 wounded. Of the Dervishes 30,000 were killed and only 4,000 wounded. Kitchener had, it would seem, given the order that no prisoners were to be taken. The same evening, the Sirdar's troops entered Omdurman and the ruins of Khartoum. The Mahdi's corpse was taken from its coffin, his head, severed from the trunk,

[1] 'The aim of the British representatives was, it may be truly said, to reduce the object of the negotiations within the narrowest limits, to confine them to the discussion of particular cases, and the demarcation of local boundaries. The French Government, which never lost sight of its wider aim, attempted to give them a more general scope, and sought to include the whole of Africa. This was the crucial issue which revealed the radical divergence of standpoint between the two parties. We believed that our object might be attained if only we could contrive to embrace in the same agreement, not only the right bank of the Niger, but its left bank, Lake Chad and the territories which extended as far as the Nile valley' (Gabriel Hanotaux, *Fachode*, p. 118). It is difficult to understand how after this admission M. Hanotaux can present the agreement as a victory for his policy: The Yellow Book, published in 1899, by the French Foreign Office under the title *Documents diplomatiques, Correspondance, et Documents relatifs à la Convention franco-anglaise du 14 Juin, 1898*, 1890–1898, contains no documents later than January 20, 1898, and therefore concludes at a date before the relations between the two Governments had become strained.

was sent as a present to a nephew of General Gordon, and the officers of the expeditionary force made souvenirs of his nails.[1] These were the orgies with which imperialism avenged Gordon's death.

Had Marchand outstripped the Anglo-Egyptian army on the Upper Nile and established himself above Khartoum? That was the question. On September 19, Kitchener continued his march up-stream, met Marchand at Fashoda and, ignoring his presence, annexed the country in the name of the British and Egyptian Governments. A serious conflict had begun between France and England. The British Government pointed out that in 1895 Sir Edward Grey, Under Secretary at the Foreign Office under the Liberal Government, had warned the French Government that any interference in the Valley of the Upper Nile would be regarded by Britain as an unfriendly act.[2] The French Government replied that Lord Kimberley, then Foreign Secretary, had repudiated his subordinate's speech by his subsequent declarations. The British Government further claimed to represent the Egyptian and maintained that, since the Sudan was the lawful possession of Egypt, Marchand had no status at Fashoda. The French Government replied that in the equatorial regions, and in one instance, even on the Nile, the British Government had recognized the rights of Belgium. Why then should not France assert her rights in those regions? Who, moreover, had conferred on England the mandate to represent Egypt? The Khedive? Or his suzerain, the Sultan? The French Government even went so far as to deny the existence, in the strict sense, of a Marchand mission, and proposed to wait for his official report before discussing the question. But the legal arguments were only preliminary fencing in the duel between Paris and London. It was obvious that between Kitchener and Marchand, force was the sole arbiter. It was equally obvious that force was on the side of Kitchener. Marchand and the handful of Sudanese under his command were cut off from all communication with the outside world by Kitchener's army of twenty thousand. Was France prepared to redress the balance by risking a naval war? What could the French fleet do against the British? And, after all, who in France wanted war?

[1] H. of C., June 5, 1899. John Morley's speech (*Parliamentary Debates*, 4th Ser., vol. lxxii, pp. 337 sqq.).
[2] H. of C., March 28, 1895 ibid., vol. xxxii, pp. 405-6).

The Dreyfus case was still dragging on and the situation was becoming more critical. As the scandal proceeded, it undermined the influence of the Nationalist and Colonial party. Delcassé had replaced Hanotaux at the Quai d'Orsay immediately after the conclusion of the Niger agreement, and had lost no time in showing his desire to restore friendly relations between France and England, which in the opinion of many had been compromised by the fault of his predecessor. He declared his readiness to evacuate Fashoda. He asked only that the evacuation should be effected under conditions which would, as far as possible, spare the honour of France. He proposed that, simultaneously with Marchand's retirement, negotiations should be begun to provide the African possessions of France with an outlet on the Upper Nile. Lord Salisbury, it seems, was not unfavourable to the proposal. He did not reject it in principle and replied that he should refer it to the Cabinet.[1]

But he found himself powerless. Since May, not he but Chamberlain had been the real Foreign Secretary, and Chamberlain's programme was to reconquer for England the prestige which in the eyes of the public had been jeopardized in every quarter of the globe by Lord Salisbury's weakness, his 'squeezability'. In the Far East no action could be taken against Russia without the active support of Germany, which up to the present had not been forthcoming. But in Africa, England enjoyed a free hand and could avenge at the cost of France the defeats she had been obliged to suffer in China. To secure the unconditional recall of the Marchand mission was now the slogan of the entire Press, practically without exception. Only one or two Radical organs, such as the *Daily News* and the *Manchester Guardian*, attempted to oppose the current of public opinion. And even their protest was made, so to speak, merely for the sake of principle: the outburst of anti-Semitism in Paris had done much to estrange Liberal sympathy from France. Lord Rosebery left his retirement, and on October 12 delivered a warlike speech in which he blamed the

---

[1] Baron de Courcel to M. Delcassé, October 5, 1898 (*Documents diplomatiques. Affaires du Haut-Nil et du Bahr-el-Ghazel*, 1897, p. 20). The same to the same, October 12, 1898 (ibid., pp. 25-6). To remove the bad effect produced in England by the publication of the *Yellow Book*, the Foreign Office immediately published a *White Book* giving an account of the same interviews. But on the point with which we are concerned the *White Book* does not, we believe, contradict M. de Courcel's two reports. (The Marquess of Salisbury to Sir E. Monson, October 12, 1898: 'Egypt No. 3' (1898): *Further Correspondence respecting the Valley of the Upper Nile*, pp. 8-9.)

Unionist Government for having adopted during the past three years a policy of conciliation towards France. On the following day, Asquith spoke in the same sense. Even in the Liberal camp, the Imperialists had gained the ascendancy.

Throughout the second half of October the situation seemed to become graver every day. England ostentatiously armed. A powerful reserve squadron was stationed in the Channel, and it was said that the Admiralty had forbidden the dockyards to undertake any repairs likely to require more than twenty-four hours to complete. After a Cabinet Meeting held in London on October 27 both countries were prepared for the issue of a British ultimatum. The same day, the first Lord of the Admiralty, Goschen, declined to preside at a dinner which had been arranged in his honour at Sheffield on the ground that under the present circumstances it was impossible for him to leave the Admiralty.

On November 3, the French Government gave way, and the dispute was settled by the recall of Marchand. And the settlement was complete when on March 21, 1899, an agreement was concluded which left the Wadai to France but reserved to Britain the Nile Valley and the region of Darfur. For the first time since 1895, a Colonial dispute between Britain and France had been settled neither by a victory for the latter nor by a compromise; France had capitulated unconditionally.

6

There is good evidence that in the Foreign Office Lord Salisbury continued to oppose Chamberlain's influence. Possibly he was encouraged in his resistance by the fact that, even during the year 1898, on the whole so favourable to his rival, he had succeeded in settling the difficult question of Crete in agreement with France and Russia and in opposition to Germany and Austria. And on several occasions during the following year he was able to win substantial successes. He concluded an agreement with Russia, which laid down two distinct spheres of influence for the construction of Chinese railways by the contracting powers. It was an apology to Russia for Chamberlain's insults of the previous spring. When further colonial negotiations were opened with Germany, circumstances enabled Lord Salisbury to delay their conclusion. For Rhodes, when he visited Berlin and made his peace with the German Government,[1] had promised, that if Germany would favour his great transafrican scheme, she should receive substantial concessions in the Samoan Islands. But the Colonial Office refused his urgent requests: the Australians did not favour an extension of German territory in their neighbourhood. By April, it was evident that the Anglo-German negotiations for the partition of the Samoan Islands had broken down. And towards France there was no doubt that Lord Salisbury's personal dispositions were as friendly as ever. Perhaps on this point he could count on royal support. It was rumoured that the aged Queen Victoria, who had persisted in wintering as usual in the South of France, had obtained from him a promise to spare her the horrors of a war during the few years she might still hope to live.

At the distance of a quarter of a century, it is easy to notice these minor matters which combine to show how artificial after all was the imposing system constructed in 1898 by the British Imperialists. But at the time, if they interested the embassies of Europe, they passed almost unobserved by the public. Relations with France continued to be strained. Between the Press of both countries there was open war. The French Press would not forgive England Fashoda; British journalists made the most of the opportunity for indignant comment furnished by the Dreyfus scandals. Moreover, it was in vain that Paul Cambon, who had just succeeded the Baron de Courcel at the embassy in London, continuing his predecessor's policy, proposed a general settlement of all the questions outstanding between the two countries, not only in Africa, but in Madagascar, Newfoundland, Siam, Shanghai, and the New Hebrides. However friendly his personal dispositions, Lord Salisbury always refused, and in January and March the questions, first of Madagascar, then of the port of Muscat in the Persian Gulf, occasioned further diplomatic conflicts between the two Governments. For in the intention of the French ambassador a general settlement meant the re-opening of the Egyptian question, which the British Government was determined to exclude from discussion. And, further, it would inevitably be a compromise reached by mutual concessions. That,

[1] Two years later he added a codicil to his will providing for the foundation of fifteen scholarships of £250 at Oxford, to be held by German students chosen by the Emperor. For, he added, 'a good understanding between England, Germany, and the United States of America will secure the peace of the world, and educational relations form the strongest tie'.

however, was no longer desired in London. The British wished to
raise in turn all the questions in dispute and settle each unfavourably to France. Without war? Yes, if France gave way all along
the line. But if at last she decided to stand firm, was another
'Cuban War' such an alarming prospect? Within two months the
American navy had wiped out the Spanish. Would it take the British
navy very much longer to destroy the French?[1] There was no
doubt a party in London in favour of war. And it was not confined
to Unionists but included members of the Liberal Opposition. In
December, Sir William Harcourt, leader of the Opposition in
the House of Commons, resigned. A few days later John
Morley, a loyal defender of Gladstonian principles, broke off all
political relations with the official leaders of the Liberal party.
Like Lord Salisbury among the Conservatives, Harcourt and
Morley had been swamped by the rising flood of imperialism.
Their isolation must have been brought home to them when they
read the speech delivered to his constituents by the Socialist, John
Burns: 'Recent events had taught them the duties and responsibilities of empire and shown that the dream of peace in which the
Manchester school indulged was based on delusion. . . . The Latin
and other races were beginning to see that the world-wide supremacy of the Anglo-Saxon race was imminent, if it had not already
arrived.'[2]

[1] We may call attention to certain imaginary forecasts published about this time, which
throw light on the attitude of the public. *National Review*, vol. xxxi, pp. 502 sqq., June
1898; J. N. Hampson, 'Great Britain against France and Russia': 'It is a picture of the
next war which except for England's loss of Egypt would be confined to the white
nations. All the belligerents would be exhausted and the sole result of the war would be
the aggrandisement of Germany against which we could no longer count upon the support
of Russia and France. The United States might come to our assistance, but we certainly
could not depend upon her doing so. Our best hope lay in the fact that in the course of
history no Power had ever attained military and maritime supremacy at the same time,
a fact illustrated in particular by the careers of Louis XIV and Napoleon. Assuming that
it was beyond the capacity of any Power to achieve the two objects at once, we might
conclude that Germany, being at the present moment undoubtedly the first military
Power in Europe would, if she tried to gain possession of maritime supremacy also, be
preparing her own downfall.' In short, the writer, while fearing the results, foresees a
war between England and the Dual Alliance. *How the Jubilee Fleet escaped Destruction; and
the Battle of Ushant: or two Episodes in the Career of a Naval Officer*, by P. L. Stevenson,
1899 (2nd ed.) (the letter prefaced to the 2nd ed. is dated January 1903): It is a brief
account of a war waged by England against a combination of Russia, Germany and
France, with no ally except Italy. The result is an overwhelming victory. The battle of
the Ushant Islands fought on December 1, 1902, is a second Trafalgar, more glorious than
the first. B***, *The New Battle of Dorking*, 1900, describes the invasion of England by a
French army. To prevent the danger the author demands the entire reorganization of the
British army, so as to make it possible to invade France and dictate peace in Paris.
[2] Speech at Battersea, November 13, 1898.

Suddenly a curious incident occurred, calculated, it might seem, to bring to a temporary halt the advance not only of British imperialism but of imperialism throughout the world. On May 18, on the initiative of the Emperor of Russia, the Peace Conference opened at The Hague.[1]

On August 24, 1898, the Czar Nicholas, taking by surprise every foreign government including the French, had issued a public document proposing that an international conference should be summoned to consult upon the best methods of securing to all nations 'the advantages of a genuine and lasting peace' and 'to fix a limit to the continually increasing growth of armaments.' The delegates accredited by the various nations, civil, military, and naval, entered upon the conference, for the most part sceptical, and in a very bad humour. Vice-Admiral Sir John Fisher communicated in private to the German naval delegate his views, which were those of the British Admiralty. 'The sole principle he admitted was that might is right and he had made it quite clear to Goschen that in the event of war he should regard any agreements that might be concluded at The Hague as null and void, if they were opposed in any way to the political and military interests of his country.'[2] But, on the other hand, the Czar's appeal had roused from their torpor the pacifists throughout Europe. 'The Conference', Count Münster reported to Berlin, 'has brought here the political riffraff of the entire world, journalists of the worst type, such as Stead, baptized Jews like Bloch, and female peace fanatics like Madame de Suttner, who yesterday again

[1] For The Hague Conference, see *Autobiography of Andrew Dickson White*, 1908 (part v, vol. ii, pp. 250 sqq.), also *Die Grosse Politik . . . Kapital C.* (vol. xv, pp. 139 sqq.).
[2] Report of Captain Siegel (of the German merchant service), one of the technical advisers appointed by the German Government. June 28, 1899 (*Die Grosse Politik*, vol. xv, p. 230). In a conversation with the American delegate, the American ambassador, Andrew White, he expressed himself in less bellicose terms, but his remarks were equally revealing: 'To my regret I found him using the same arguments as regards the sea that Count Münster had made regarding the land. He said that the navy of Great Britain was and would remain in a state of complete preparation for war; that a vast deal depended on prompt action by the navy and that the truce afforded by arbitration proceedings would give other Powers time, which they would otherwise not have, to put themselves into complete readiness. He seemed uncertain whether it was best for Great Britain, under these circumstances, to support a thoroughgoing plan of arbitration, but on the whole seemed inclined to try it to some extent. Clearly what Great Britain wants is a permanent system of arbitration with the United States; but she does not care much, I think, for such a provision as regards other Powers' (Andrew White, *Autobiography*, vol. ii, pp. 267–8). For the truculent speeches with which it amused him to frighten the professional diplomatists at The Hague, see W. P. Stead, 'Admiral Fisher' (*Review of Reviews*, February 1910; vol. li, pp. 117–18), also Lord Fisher's own *Records*, p. 55.

entertained the Russian delegation at a large banquet, Madame Salenko, etc. All this rabble (actively supported by the young Turks, the Armenians, and the Socialists into the bargain) are working in the open under the ægis of Russia.'[1] But in the existing situation the 'rabble' was able to exercise a species of moral influence on the Governments of the West.[2] Moreover, since none of the delegates wished to inflict a snub on the Russian Government, all united to prevent the failure which no doubt the vast majority secretly desired.

Limitation of armaments was rejected by a vote, unanimous except for the Russian delegates. But the British delegate, Sir Julian Pauncefote, was successful in introducing a scheme of organized arbitration. We have already seen how often during the past four years he had come into contact with the idea in Washington. It is true that, owing to the action of the German Government, a proposal for compulsory arbitration was rejected, and it was decided that only those international disputes should be submitted to arbitration which did not concern the honour or vital interests of the parties. In fact, it often happened during the course of the discussions that Germany found herself isolated, or on the verge of isolation, against a combination of all the great powers of Europe. But Germany had no desire to break with Russia, and the French delegates, Léon Bourgeois and d'Estournelles de Constant, found the formulas of agreement of which everyone was in search. A permanent Court of Arbitration was set up at The Hague, whose constitution, procedure, and powers were laid down in detail by a convention signed on July 29.

Where are we to look for the origin of this demonstration? Are we to believe that it was suggested to Petersburg by the desire to put an end to the competition in armaments with neighbouring nations, which Russia was already beginning to find a crushing

[1] Count Münster to Graf von Bülow, June 26, 1899 (*Die Grosse Politik*, vol. xv, p. 313).
[2] Andrew White, *Autobiography*, vol. ii, p. 285 (under the date of June 2, 1899): 'The shoals of telegrams, reports of proceedings of societies, hortatory letters, crankish proposals, and peace pamphlets from America continue' (ibid., June 14). 'In the course of our breakfast, Baron d'Estournelles made a statement which, I think, impressed every person present. It was that, as he was leaving Paris, Jaurès the famous Socialist, whom he knows well, said to him: "Go on; do all you can at The Hague, but you will labour in vain; you can accomplish nothing there, your schemes will fail, and we shall triumph!" or words to that effect. So clear an indication as this of the effect which a failure of the conference to produce a good scheme of arbitration will have in promoting the designs of the great international Socialist and Anarchist combinations cannot fail to impress every thinking man' (cf. pp. 304, 307, 312).

burden on her resources? It is certain that Count Witte had about this time become convinced that neither the financial nor the political system of Russia was sufficiently firm to support the burden of a war or even of an aggressive foreign policy. Or did the imperial project dissimulate a hostile intention towards England, and was the ulterior purpose to enable the great Powers by the reduction of their land armaments to concentrate their efforts on the construction of battleships and conspire to shake off the naval despotism of Great Britain? There is no doubt that the dream of a great Continental alliance against England haunted the imagination of many Russians, and it was the misfortune of the Chamberlain imperialism that any active campaign for peace must, in 1899, necessarily wear the semblance of an engine directed against Britain. But we must also admit that it was no mere historical accident that the founder of The Hague Court of Arbitration was the grandson of the emancipator of the serfs and the great-great-nephew of the author of the Holy Alliance, and that Slavonic mysticism played a part, indeed a large part, in the Emperor's decision. It was rumoured that he had been influenced by Ivan Bloch's great book on war.[1] The work has been prevented by its very size from attaining a wide circulation, but the movement of ideas which followed The Hague Conference made known at least its existence and title, and it has since inspired a host of writers more readable, if also more superficial, than Bloch. The journalist, Stead, immediately published an abridged translation for the use of the British public.[2] Disciple and literary executor of Rhodes, his imagination—Utopian though it was—had not crossed hitherto the frontiers of the Pax Britannica. Now he became the apostle of peace between men of all nations and all races. The 'pacifist'[3] movement was born in 1899.

Its birth, therefore, coincided with the date when British, or more correctly Anglo-Saxon, imperialism—for it was common

[1] I. Bloch, *The War of the Future, in its Technical, Economic, and Political Aspects* (Russian Original, 6 vols., 1898).

[2] *Is War now Impossible? Being an Abridgement of The War of the Future in its Technical, Economic, and Political Relations, by Ivan Bloch.* With a prefatory conversation with the author by W. T. Stead.

[3] The term, of course, is an anachronism at this date. My friend Th. Ruyssen informs me that it was coined by the Frenchman, Emile Arnaud, President of the International League of Peace and Liberty, who used it for the first time at the Glasgow Peace Congress of 1901. Severely criticized at first for its incorrect formation, it does not appear to have become current in France till about 1905, and in England still later. (At first the English insisted on the term 'pacifist'.)

to Chamberlain and Roosevelt—burst upon the world. Nor is the coincidence surprising. Pacifism took shape and grew, as the friends of peace saw the danger of a world war drawing nearer. The dread of it had lain heavy on Europe ever since the last upheaval had ended in 1815, but as that upheaval had been of a revolutionary as well as a warlike character, overthrowing churches and thrones, fear of revolution had long prevailed with the rulers of Europe to prefer peaceful solutions to indulging the lust of conquest. After forty years of peace a new era of wars had opened; but it was by a succession of short wars waged over limited areas, not by a general war, that the map of Europe had been re-arranged between 1850 and 1870. After the latter date, Colonial expeditions and the exploitation of Africa and Asia had provided the appetite of the Great Powers for conquest with sufficient satisfaction outside Europe. But now the globe was becoming too small for their greed, and the Spanish-American War threatened to prove the prelude to that world war whose menace had for many a long year been almost forgotten. What world war? The war whose programme Chamberlain had laid down in May 1898.

Chamberlain had found an accredited interpreter of his policy in the American writer named Mahan, a naval captain and professor at the Naval War College of his country. Mahan's utterances were invested with a double authority. To naval men he was a learned historian, to historians a man with personal experience of naval matters. His thesis which he was never weary of reiterating was that political supremacy belonged to the nation, and to that nation alone, which could keep the command of the seas. Naturally, his message was addressed in the first place to his compatriots. He wished to persuade them to form a navy proportionate to their economic power and thus win the hegemony of the world. But the examples he adduced to enforce his thesis were taken most often from the history of British achievement,[1] and it was in no jealous spirit that he told its story. For he did not conceive the American hegemony as won at the cost of the British. He desired not an exclusively American, but an Anglo-Saxon hegemony, and it was for the two fleets, the British and the American, united,

---

[1] *The Influence of Sea-power upon History, 1660–1783*, 1890. *The Influence of Sea-power upon the French Revolution and Empire, 1793–1812*, 1892. *The Life of Nelson, The Embodiment of the Sea-power of Great Britain*, 1897. For his biography, see Charles Carlisle Taylor, *The Life of Admiral Mahan, Naval Philosopher*, 1920.

that he claimed the command of the seas.[1] Was it surprising that his books were extremely popular in Great Britain? His thesis was that of Lord Rosebery and Chamberlain; it was the racial imperialism which had taken possession of the two great English-speaking nations on the occasion of the Cuban war.

In a work entitled *The Problem of Asia and its Effect upon International Policies* Mahan drew a picture of the imminent and inevitable war. The combatants were, it could not be otherwise, the two great races which would shortly dispute, had indeed disputed already, the government of Asia, the Anglo-Saxons and the Slavs. Against Russia, the Anglo-Saxons would be assisted by the alliance of Germany and Japan, and the four allied fleets would be supreme at sea. They would also enjoy the support of the German and Japanese armies which would attack Russia on her western and eastern fronts respectively. France would remain Russia's ally, and in the Mediterranean the combined Russian-French fleets might occasion some difficulty to their Anglo-American foes. But the latter could count on the alliance of Italy, also on the moral instability of the French, more Celtic perhaps than Latin. War was inevitable, the victory of the Anglo-Saxons equally inevitable.[2]

But at the very moment when, in 1900, *The Problem of Asia* was published, British imperialism was taking another direction.

[1] *The Interest of America in Sea-power, Present and Future*, 1897. See especially in this volume the study entitled 'Possibilities of an Anglo-American Reunion', which first appeared in July 1894 in the *North-American Review*, where it made one of a series of articles commissioned by Andrew Carnegie to promote a *rapprochement* between the two nations; 'Lessons of the War with Spain and other Articles', 1899.

[2] Admiral Mahan died December 1, 1914.

CHAPTER II

The Boer War

I THE WAR

I

IF, in the spring of 1899, the tension between Great Britain and France became less acute and the British Government adopted the conciliatory methods of the Foreign Office in preference to the aggressive methods of the Colonial Office, it was because Chamberlain's attention was turned elsewhere. The moment, he thought, had arrived to settle the South African question, which had been left pending for the last three years.

With feverish haste, President Kruger was arming the Transvaal Republic. No objection could be raised, for the Jameson Raid had placed his Government in a position of legitimate defence and by one of the ironies of history had provided him with the necessary funds to defray the cost. He had arrested the principal leaders of the plot, organized at Johannesburg in concert with Rhodes, and had allowed them to be sentenced to death by the tribunals. But he had then commuted the death penalty into the payment of enormous fines, and the money thus obtained was applied, together with other revenues, to the purchase of artillery, Maxim guns, rifles, and ammunition. Two large armoured forts were erected near Johannesburg, and their guns kept permanently trained on the mass of suspected Uitlanders. And besides these public preparations, it was rumoured that Kruger was making many others in secret, and that in a never-ceasing stream, cannons, rifles, and ammunition were pouring into the country through Delagoa Bay—more rifles, it was confidently reported, than would suffice to arm the entire population of the Republic. No doubt preparations were being made to distribute the surplus wholesale to the malcontents in Cape Colony, who were only awaiting the signal to throw off British rule. Moreover, Kruger's Government was rapidly becoming a naked dictatorship, and every Boer, whatever his position, judge, politician, or private citizen, who dared to contest his absolute rule was promptly ruined. Kruger made the serious mistake of neglecting to conciliate those among the Johannesburg capitalists who cared more for wealth than for political independence, and were still prepared to come to a friendly understanding with his Government. A commission of inquiry appointed by himself, and composed exclusively of Boers, had admitted in 1897 that the protests made by the Chamber of Mines against the reckless exploitation of the gold diggers by the dynamite monopoly and the Dutch Railway Company were fully justified. But he either ignored these grievances entirely or granted only the most trifling redress. It was clear that the exploitation was his deliberate policy. His object was not to develop the mining industry but simply to draw from it a revenue sufficient to hold down by armed force the foreign diggers on the Rand.

The President was faced at Cape Town by a formidable adversary. He was not Rhodes. Since the Jameson Raid, Rhodes had been on the shelf. He was no longer Prime Minister at the Cape, which was henceforward governed by the intransigents of that Afrikander Bond in concert with which he had ruled so long. Between the Bond and Rhodes there was now a complete rupture, and Rhodes was now exclusively occupied in the far north with the development of Rhodesia. But since February 1897, the young Sir Alfred Milner had been Governor of the Cape and High Commissioner for South Africa. As an undergraduate at Balliol, the new Governor had won a brilliant reputation for intellectual ability, and on leaving Oxford had completed his education at the German universities. Under-Secretary of Finance in the Egyptian administration, on his return to England he had published the results achieved by the years of British occupation in Egypt in a book which very soon became a standard authority. When the Government decided to send him to the Cape, he was in London as Chairman of the Board of Inland Revenue. Since he was regarded as one of the most distinguished representatives of the new imperialist school, his choice, a year after the Jameson fiasco, was highly significant. The aged and infirm Lord Rosmead, whom he succeeded, had made himself unpopular with the British population in South Africa by his scrupulous adherence to constitutional procedure—his weakness his critics called it. They were satisfied when they learned the name of his successor. It was obvious that Milner had not been sent out to the Cape to play the part of a vice-regal puppet, or be the long-suffering diplomat in his relations with Kruger. He was sent to speak the language of a master, to govern effectively, and assert British supremacy.

During the first months of his governorship he was quietly making himself master of a host of questions, political and social, with which hitherto he had been wholly unacquainted, and the self-respect of the Afrikanders was flattered when he learned the Taal, the debased Dutch which was the local idiom. It would indeed have been imprudent to display his colours within a few months after the Raid, when in London the Parliamentary Committee of Enquiry was engaged in clearing up an episode so damaging to British credit. But only a year after his arrival, in a public speech delivered in March 1898, he spoke a language novel in the mouth of a governor of the Cape. After explaining that the British Government wished to avoid even the appearance of interfering in the domestic affairs of the Transvaal, he suddenly, without, it would seem, feeling the least awkwardness in the contradiction, made an attack upon Kruger. For the tension which prevailed in South Africa he denounced and blamed what he termed 'the unprogressiveness—he would not say the retrogressiveness—of the Government of the Transvaal'. That Government was mistaken in fearing danger from without. The evil from which it was suffering must be sought within its own borders. The date of this speech is not without significance. It was delivered at the very time when Chamberlain, shaking off Lord Salisbury's yoke, attempted to make himself for all practical purposes Foreign Secretary and to bestow at last on the foreign policy of the Unionist Administration that firmness it should have possessed for the past two years and would have displayed had Lord Salisbury been less aged, less peace-loving, and less fearful of failure.

The following winter, the native 'boys' employed in the Rand mines complained of ill-treatment at the hands of the Transvaal police. The diplomatic representative of the British Government at Pretoria received their complaints, which were by no means novel, and transmitted them to the Cape. Milner was then on holiday in London; and the commanding officer of the British forces in South Africa, Sir William Butler, who was acting governor, refused to take cognizance of the matter. Then an English resident at Johannesburg, who had killed a man in a brawl, was himself killed by the policeman who was arresting him. The incident, in itself insignificant, provoked an explosion of resentment among the Uitlanders. A petition asking for the protection of the British Queen was sent to the Cape. Sir William Butler refused to transmit it. A second petition was then drawn up, signed by over 22,000 British subjects, placed in the hands of the British representative at Pretoria, despatched by him to the Cape, and transmitted to London by Milner, who had returned from England. It reached the Colonial Office on April 14. Once more the date is significant. Three weeks earlier, the question of the Upper Nile had been settled. The moment had come to settle—at as little cost it was hoped—the Transvaal question. Both well out of the way, the great undertaking of the Cape to Cairo railway could be begun from both ends.[1]

We are loath to relate in detail the legal debate between the two Governments which began towards the close of spring and continued until autumn, so umimportant does it appear in the perspective of the past. Were the arguments bandied between the parties the sincere expression of their convictions? The British maintained, and no doubt believed, that the majority of the Transvaal population was now composed of foreigners. The Boers denied it: the future would prove them right. But they recognized that, as the mining industry developed, the day might well come, and in a not distant future, when the British contention, if untrue at present, would be realized by the force of circumstances. Kruger contemplated with alarm the sudden overthrow of his entire policy, which would be entailed by the wholesale admission of the Uitlanders to citizen rights. The Transvaal would no longer be the citadel of all those Dutchmen in the Orange Free State and in Cape Colony who looked to him as their leader and cherished the design of shaking off the British yoke and founding in South Africa a vast Dutch-speaking republic, which should extend from the Cape to the Zambesi. Milner, on the other hand, when he supported the claims, to a certain extent legitimate, of the Uitlanders, was no doubt eager to alter

[1] For the preliminaries of the Boer War, the negotiations at Bloemfontein and Pretoria, see J. P. Fitzpatrick, *The Transvaal from Within. A Private Record of Public Affairs*, 1899. (The author represents the imperialist standpoint. He was an accomplice in the Jameson Raid. The latter portion of the book, p. 285 onwards, deals with the period 1895–1899.) Edward T. Cook, *Rights and Wrongs of the Transvaal War*, 1901 (Liberal imperialist). Though the book was written in support of the British contention, the attitude of the Government is often criticized by a journalist who, though an imperialist, belonged to the Liberal Opposition. It is also a work of painstaking research; see at the end of the book, pp. 376–8, the list of official publications dealing with the origin of the war. *Sir William Butler, An Autobiography by Lieut.-Gen. the Right Hon.* Edited by his daughter, Eileen Butler. Sir William Butler was Commander-in-Chief of the British Army in South Africa. His opposition to Milner's policy lost him the post.

suddenly in favour of England the existing balance of power in South Africa. He wished the Transvaal to furnish a political base for the British colonists at the Cape against the Dutch majority, which was organized in the Afrikander Bond and threatened in the near future to endanger the prospects of British imperialism in Cape Colony itself. Steyn, President of the Orange Free State, declared in 1898 the formation of a United States of South Africa impracticable, because the two Boer Republics would demand a republican constitution for the Union, the British colonists its incorporation in the Empire. If by impracticable he meant impracticable by peaceful methods, he was right. The conflict which now opened in South Africa was not a conflict of interests. Between conflicting interests compromise is always attainable. It was the conflict of two nationalities, two faiths, two passions, two absolutes. Between absolutes, force is the sole arbiter.

Neither the High Commissioner, however, nor the Boer President could enunciate their respective positions in these frank terms. Both were obliged to put forward legal arguments. And, unfortunately for England, Kruger's legal position was unassailable.

Milner declared himself the defender of the rights of the British residents in the Transvaal and in adopting this attitude he did not exceed his province as a diplomatist. But instead of losing time in a series of protests, renewed from day to day, against denials of justice indefinitely repeated, he adopted a more daring procedure. He called upon the Transvaal Government to change the political status of the Uitlanders and, by admitting them to full citizenship, enable them to defend their rights themselves on a footing of equality with the original Burghers. In his own striking phraseology he demanded that the British subjects in Johannesburg should, to safeguard their rights, be permitted to be British subjects no longer. The demand was a glaring interference in the internal affairs of the Republic. By what right did he interfere? In virtue, he alleged, of the suzerainty which Britain claimed over the Transvaal. The claim was not new; eighteen months before, in the course of a protracted diplomatic correspondence, Chamberlain had upheld it against the repudiation of the Boer Government. To what legal document could its upholders appeal? To the preamble of the Convention of 1881 by which England renounced her annexation of the Transvaal? It was certainly true that the word suzerainty was used in that document. But the Boer Governments had protested and secured its omission from the Convention of 1884. In place of an extremely vague and general declaration of British suzerainty they had obtained the substitution of a definite clause, reserving to Great Britain a right of control over the relations between the Government of the Transvaal and foreign powers.[1] With that one definite reservation the Transvaal could, therefore, claim to have possessed since 1884 the status of an independent sovereign state. To evade the force of this argument the Colonial Office now argued that the purpose of the Convention of 1884 had not been to annul, but merely to complete, the Convention of 1881, that the relations between England and the Transvaal Republic were determined not by the former alone, but by both conjointly, and that if by the latter, Kruger's foreign policy was made subject to British control, England in virtue of the former was still suzerain in the widest possible extension of the term. The contention could not be sustained but, to escape from a sheer *impasse*, England was obliged to maintain it.

2

On May 31 Milner and Kruger met at Bloemfontein, the capital of the Orange Free State. President Steyn had arranged the interview, which had Chamberlain's approval. Milner, urged by Kruger to state his case, first proposed that the complete franchise should be conferred on everyone who had resided in the Transvaal for five years and possessed a pecuniary qualification to be fixed later, and further that a number of new constituencies should be created on the Rand, so that the Uitlanders who were concentrated in that district might receive their just share of representation. Kruger replied by a counter-proposal. Naturalization would be granted after two years' residence, the franchise at the expiration of five more years—that is to say, after a residence of seven years, instead of the five proposed by Milner. Moreover, the measure would be but partially retrospective. It was only after

---

[1] With the exception of the Orange Free State—with which Kruger had concluded in 1897 an offensive and defensive alliance. Chamberlain had already appealed to the Convention of 1884 against certain legislation passed by the Transvaal Volksraad, but he had invoked definite clauses of the Convention (E. T. Cook, *Rights and Wrongs of the Transvaal War*, pp. 79 sqq.), and until the present crisis the general question of suzerainty had not been raised.

considerable discussion that Kruger consented to create three new constituencies on the Rand. And his concession was restricted by a number of very strict conditions which would render naturalization and the subsequent franchise more difficult to obtain. In principle these conditions were fully justified—it was impossible to enfranchise without rigid safeguards a heterogeneous, cosmopolitan, and floating population—'Monte Carlo superimposed upon Sodom and Gomorrah'[1]—men who too often had come out to draw high salaries and earn large profits, to return home, as soon as their fortunes had been made. But, on the other hand, it cannot be denied that Kruger, an adept at intrigue, might very well have manipulated the details of his franchise so as to render its concession nugatory. On this point, therefore, there was matter for discussion between the two negotiators. Milner, however, refused to allow the discussion even to begin. He demanded that his proposal, not Kruger's alternative, should be taken as the basis of negotiation. Kruger's proposal contained a number of very important concessions to the British point of view. But Milner was determined to make it clear from the outset that he was not treating with Kruger as with an equal, but had come to dictate to a vassal the terms on which friendly relations might continue. Kruger refused to yield. On June 6 the negotiations were broken off.

Kruger then took a bold step. He announced his intention to bring before the Volksraad the counter-proposal which Milner had refused even to discuss and make it the basis of a law to amend the franchise. It was in vain that Chamberlain protested from London, asked for a copy of the measure proposed and expressed his desire that the Transvaal Government should not proceed with the Bill before receiving the observations of the British Government. On July 23, the Franchise Bill was passed at Pretoria by the Volksraad. The British Government was placed in a difficult position. How could it reply to the passage of a Boer law which, taken as a whole, constituted a very considerable concession to the Uitlanders' demands by breaking off diplomatic relations with Kruger? Much against the grain it re-opened negotiations with the object of improving the new law by means of an enquiry to

---

[1] ' "It is Monte Carlo superimposed upon Sodom and Gomorrah," a well-known Cape politician had recently described it to me' (*Sir William Butler, An Autobiography by Lieut.- Gen. the Right Hon.*, 2nd ed., 1913, p. 415).

be conducted jointly by both Governments. This time the conversations were held at Pretoria between the British representative and the Secretary of State, Reitz. The former requested that the law should be revised on the basis of the proposals formulated by Milner at Bloemfontein. The request, however, was a mere form. The real object of the discussions was to agree on the best procedure to adopt for the amicable revision of the law of July.

It was Kruger who, on August 14, after the discussions had proceeded for two days, disconcerted the British representative by suddenly acceding to the request made by the British Government. He accepted the principle of five years' residence which Milner had put forward at Bloemfontein. He further declared his readiness to set up eight new constituencies on the Rand. Moreover, the new citizens should enjoy precisely the same rights as the original citizens, might even take part in the election of the President. But in return he asked that this interference of the British Government in the domestic affairs of the Transvaal should be expressly declared to be final, that Britain should renounce her claim to suzerainty as far as the internal administration was concerned, and finally, that a system of arbitration should be established to settle all future disputes between the two Governments.

The proposal for arbitration had been already made by Kruger at Bloemfontein. He thought, no doubt, that it would be difficult for the British Government to reject it at a time when The Hague Conference was in session, particularly since it was the British delegate who had proposed that the Conference should devote its efforts to organizing a regular procedure of international arbitration. But Milner, like the thorough-going imperialist he was, had refused to entertain the proposal. Arbitration, according to him, was out of the question, even between two friendly States on an equal footing, if the issue to be submitted to arbitration was the treatment of the subjects of one State by the government of the other. Milner had, however, conceded that once the question actually pending had been settled by a formal agreement between the Governments of London and Pretoria, the interpretation of its articles, should any question arise as to their meaning, should be submitted to a regular and automatic procedure of arbitration, provided only that the tribunal should contain no foreign element. In August, Kruger accepted this demand of Sir Alfred. He merely asked that not only Englishmen, citizens of the British colonies, and citizens of the Transvaal should be eligible for seats on the proposed arbitration tribunal, but also citizens of the Orange Free State. It was an important concession for it amounted to a partial incorporation of the South African Republic in the British Empire.

What was the British Government's reply to these advances? It was in the first instance a speech delivered by Chamberlain on August 26 to his followers at Birmingham. He accused President Kruger of 'procrastinating in his replies', of 'dribbling out reforms like water from a squeezed sponge'. The proposals which Milner had made at Bloemfontein had been moderate, so moderate indeed that many people charged them with weakness. 'We cannot ask less, and we cannot take less. The issues of peace and war are in the hands of President Kruger and of his admirers. . . . Will he speak the necessary words? The sands are running down the glass. The situation is too fraught with danger, it is too strained, for any indefinite postponement. The knot must be loosened . . . or else we shall have to find some other ways of untying it.' The speech was a significant preface to the note which the British Government despatched on the following day to the Government of the Transvaal. It insisted that no preliminary conditions, such as the Boer Government persisted in requiring, should be attached to the grant of the franchise—since they were likely to nullify the concessions granted by the proposed reform—refused to give any undertaking to abstain in future from interference in the affairs of the Republic, and concluded by pointing out that the franchise was not the only question which concerned the Uitlanders and demanding for the first time that all questions which affected their status should be settled at the same time as the franchise.

That is to say, every concession made by Kruger provoked a further demand from the British Government; and the latter thus proclaimed to the entire world that in its view the Transvaal was a sponge it intended to squeeze to the last drop. Kruger was faced with the alternative of refusal or unconditional surrender. He chose the former and withdrew the proposals he had made in August. Would the British Government reply by the immediate issue of an ultimatum? There can be little doubt that an ultimatum was proposed by Chamberlain at the Cabinet meeting held in London on September 8. But Lord Salisbury's conciliatory influence can be detected in the note despatched to Pretoria the same day, which was couched in polite language, once more asked the Transvaal Government not to withdraw its proposals, and was content with reserving the right to take more energetic measures in the event of refusal. It is true that the note raised a further issue. Britain asked that the representatives of the Rand in the Pretoria Parliament should have the right to speak English as well as Dutch. Nothing could have been more just. In the Parliament of Cape Town the Dutch had the right to use their own language. Kruger would have been well advised, if he had accepted the demand or, at least, had left it to the decision of the Volksraad to be elected under the new franchise. Instead he returned a blunt refusal and let it be clearly seen that he opposed to British intransigence an equal intransigence of his own. It would serve no useful purpose to follow in detail the subsequent exchange of notes between the two Governments. Everyone now knew that war was inevitable. On October 9, Kruger issued an ultimatum which was equivalent to a declaration of war. And the declaration of war by the Transvaal Republic was followed by a similar declaration on the part of the Orange Free State. Hostilities had, therefore, begun between the British Empire and the entire white population of South Africa not yet subject to British rule. By a strange irony the first war to follow the adoption by Great Britain of the methods of Chamberlain's 'new diplomacy' was waged against a small people of Teutonic race, indeed of a far purer Teutonic stock than the English. The proclamation in which the Secretary of State, Reitz, called to arms, not only the Burghers of the Transvaal but the Afrikanders generally was couched in the style of William the Silent: 'As once Spain at the height of her power with her bloodthirsty Duke of Alva and her invincible armies was compelled to drink the bitter chalice of defeat, so today the same God shall deliver our enemies into our hands.'[1]

[1] October 11. See the full text in the *Blue Book* entitled 'Further Correspondence Relating to Affairs in South Africa', 1900, p. 139. This community of race did in fact disturb many British imperialists, even when they were endeavouring to incorporate the Boers of the Transvaal and Orange Free State in the British Empire. See Lord Wolseley to Sir Gordon Sprigg, Prime Minister at the Cape, April 1896: 'When . . . I hear of the Boers arming and building forts and blustering and knowing how little it would all be worth, if we took the matter up seriously, I feel sorry for England and sorry for a race very kindred with our own and possessing some of our best characteristics. I grieve to think that two peoples that ought to live together in peace and unity are being set against one another' (Sir F. Maurice and Sir George Arthur, *The Life of Lord Wolseley*, 1924, p. 314). See further H. A. Conan Doyle, *The Great Boer War* (1st ed., p. 79): 'It was pitiable that it should come to this. These people were as near akin to us as any race which is not our own. They were of the same Frisian stock which peopled our own shores.

I was in London. I remember seeing the troops on their way to the front marching through the streets amid the cheers of the crowd. I remember a few days later watching in the halls of clubs and in hotels the tape unroll its tidings of defeat. I can still see the old gentleman—obviously a retired army officer of superior rank —who threw himself on me, while I was reading the news, to ask in anxious tones 'Have they come to blows?' And in the porch of the old War Office in Pall Mall I remember the little group whose composition was continually renewed, standing in front of the official list of dead and wounded. One evening when I was there it divided to let a carriage pass, at the back of which we caught a glimpse of Balfour, wearing a look of profound dejection; he was coming, like everyone else, in search of news.

3

The military preparations for the war had not been made.[1] At first sight the omission must appear surprising when we remember that the immediate cause of the fall of the Liberal Cabinet in June 1895 had been the mismanagement which prevailed at the War Office. And in fact when the new ministry took office it gave reason to believe that it intended to adopt strong measures in this department. The Liberals had just compelled the Commander-in-Chief, the Duke of Cambridge, the Queen's first cousin, to resign, and now that the Unionists had succeeded them in office, the Queen hoped that another Royal Prince, for example his brother, the Duke of Connaught, might take his place.

In habit of mind, in religion, in respect for law, they were as ourselves. Brave, too, they were, and hospitable, with those sporting instincts which are dear to the Anglo-Celtic race. There were no people in the world who had more qualities which we might admire, and not the least of them that love of independence which it is our proudest boast that we have encouraged in others as well as exercised ourselves.' Even Chamberlain, when hostilities began, declared his conviction: 'That one great Teutonic people cannot hold another Teutonic people in subjection . . . Does anybody imagine, whatever may be the result of the war . . . that we shall refuse as an ultimate settlement that equality of rights to the Dutch of the Transvaal which the Dutch in the Transvaal have denied to us?' (*Parliamentary Debates*, 4th Ser., vol. lxxvii, pp. 656).

[1] For the military policy of England before the war, see the debates which took place in the House of Lords at the beginning of 1901, between Lord Lansdowne, the Secretary of State for War, and Lord Wolseley, the retired Commander-in-Chief (H. of L., March 4, 15, 1901, ibid., 4th Ser., vol. xc, pp. 317 sqq.; vol. xci, pp. 6 sqq.). *Report of H.M. Commissioners appointed to inquire into the Military Preparations and other Matters concerned with the War in South Africa*, 1903. *The Times' History of the War in South Africa, 1899–1902*, vol. i (by L. S. Amery). See also the extremely interesting *Life of Lord Wolseley* by Sir Frederick Maurice and Sir George Compton Archibald Arthur, 1924.

But Lord Salisbury and Lord Lansdowne were firm and insisted on the appointment of Lord Wolseley, an experienced soldier who was regarded in the army as the leader of the reformers.[1] Unfortunately, he did little to realize the general expectation.

He purchased Salisbury Plain as a permanent ground for manœuvres. He reorganized the procedure of mobilization, and, three years after his appointment, boasted that he could mobilize two army corps in less time than the Admiralty would require to provide the necessary ships for their transport. But he did nothing whatever to reform the organization of the army. The system of linked battalions, introduced thirty years earlier by the Secretary for War, Cardwell, was retained. Each regiment was composed of two battalions, one stationed abroad, the other in barracks in London where it served as a depot for the former. The entire army consisted of 124,000 men serving abroad (of which 73,000 were in India, 51,000 in the Colonies and in Egypt) and 125,000 in the home battalions. To these 125,000 we must add 90,000 in the Reserve, 130,000 militia men, 265,000 volunteers and 12,000 in the Yeomanry (mounted volunteers). Together they composed a total of some 625,000 men in the United Kingdom. These 600,000 were not divided permanently and in time of peace into army corps. The army corps were temporary formations which existed only during war and were improvized as circumstances required. No steps were taken to improve the organization and quality of the Reserves; no doubt Lord Wolseley shared the prejudice against them, entertained by every member of the regular army. As for the Regulars, the terms of enlistment were so unattractive that there was a scarcity of recruits (especially when employment was plentiful) and it had been found necessary to create a new category of service, called special enlistments, for men of inferior physique and health, who could be brought up to the necessary standard by training in barracks after enlistment. In 1899, it was estimated that the 'specials' in some cases comprised over half the strength of the home battalions. In a case of emergency the recruits were despatched to the front, almost immediately after they had been called up. The 'specials' remained at home and became the real reserve to be sent out to the front, as they became fit for service. Four years after his appointment the

---

[1] Maurice and Arthur, *The Life of Lord Wolseley*, pp. 274 sqq.: The Liberals had wished to appoint General Sir Redvers Buller over his head.

Commander-in-Chief was in a position to mobilize in a fortnight only two army corps and two brigades of cavalry—that is to say, only 85,000 troops, by no means all of the best quality.

Why had Lord Wolseley, of whom so much had been expected, not accomplished more? Was he too old when he was appointed? Or, was it, perhaps, that at the very time, when in 1895 he became Commander-in-Chief, his powers had been strangely restricted by the introduction of a new system of army administration? The Commander-in-Chief would in future be no more than a high military official having the right of access to the Secretary for War on a footing of equality with a number of other officials whose functions he had formerly controlled. He was moreover placed, not only in a position of strict subordination to the War Office, but also under the control of a Council of Defence over which the Prime Minister presided and which was composed entirely of civilians. These changes the Liberal Cabinet had been preparing to make in the summer of 1895, that the proposals of an important commission of inquiry might be carried out,[1] and the Conservative Government had decided—whether willingly or not—to conform to its recommendations.[2] What was the result of the new system? The Commander-in-Chief, Lord Wolseley, and his defenders complained, was paralysed by the inertia of government departments whose torpor was never disturbed by a breath of public opinion in a country which took only naval questions seriously and in which the Army Estimates were passed every year by an almost empty House, whereas the debate on the Naval Estimates was among the outstanding features of the Session.

But if Lord Wolseley's complaints had been justified, the four years from 1895 to 1899 should have witnessed a continual series of disputes, between the Commander-in-Chief, pressing for reforms, and the War Office, refusing to make them. In fact, so far as the reform of the army as a whole is concerned, there is no evidence of a single dispute, nor have Lord Wolseley's papers disclosed any of those plans of military reorganization which a few

[1] *Preliminary and further Reports of the Royal Commissioners appointed to inquire into the Civil and Professional Administration of the Naval and Military Departments and the Relations of those Departments to each other and to the Treasury*, 1890. The Commission is usually known from the name of its Chairman as the Hartington Commission.

[2] Lord Lansdowne to Lord Salisbury, August 1895: 'We must try to follow, or seem to follow, the main recommendations of the Hartington Commission' (*The Life of Lord Wolseley*, by Major-General Sir F. Maurice and Sir George Arthur, p. 274).

years later would engage public attention. As regards the rein-
forcement of the British Army in South Africa, it is no doubt true
that Lord Wolseley, with Chamberlain's support, had persistently
pressed the Government ever since the Jameson Raid to send out
more troops. He was, however, faced by the opposition of the
Chancellor of the Exchequer and the Secretary for War. Twice
only did he obtain any satisfaction, at the beginning of 1896,
when war with Germany was threatened, and again at the end of
1898, when a war with France seemed imminent. And, even so,
his success had amounted to very little. In the summer of 1895
there were 2,100 British troops at the Cape and 2,800 in Natal—
in all, 4,900 men and six field guns. Two years later there were
3,800 troops at the Cape, 4,300 in Natal, in all 8,100 with twenty-
four field guns. And at the end of another two years, when the
Bloemfontein negotiations began, there were no more than 4,500
troops at the Cape, and 5,800 in Natal: a total force of 10,300.
And the field guns were still only twenty-four.[1]

When the negotiations inaugurated a new phase in British relations with the Boers, Lord Wolseley renewed his demand for
adequate military preparations. At the beginning of July, he proposed the immediate mobilization in England of an army corps
and a cavalry division. The mobilized troops would be kept in
readiness to be sent to the front in case of need, and even if they were
never required, the mobilization would in itself be a demonstration
which must strengthen the position of the British negotiators
at Bloemfontein. At the same time he proposed the immediate
despatch to South Africa of an additional force of 10,000.
But in the Cabinet he was opposed, not only by the party in
favour of conciliation, but even by the majority, led by Chamberlain. Everybody expected to be victorious at Bloemfontein
without the cost of a war. Paris had capitulated in 1898, why
should not Pretoria do the same in 1899? Only two thousand
troops were sent to Natal, and it was not until September that
with feverish haste, the steps were taken which the imminence of
war rendered necessary. But when this is admitted in exculpation
of Lord Wolseley, and he has been given full credit for perceiving
that the attitude adopted by the British Government must lead to

---

[1] *Report of H.M. Commissioners*, 1903, pp. 18 sqq. Maurice and Arthur, *The Life of Lord Wolseley*, pp. 315 sqq. See especially pp. 327 sqq., 'Précis of Letters and Minutes from the Commander-in-Chief to the Secretary of State'.

war, it is impossible to claim that the measures he advised would have been sufficient to overcome the resistance of the Boers. Moreover, there was no plan of campaign. On this point the neglect of the Commander-in-Chief was equalled only by the neglect of the War Office, and Lord Lansdowne was for once in entire agreement with Lord Wolseley when, called upon later by a commission of inquiry to account for the omission, he refused to admit that the general in supreme command of an expeditionary force ought as a matter of course to be 'furnished with full and precise instructions'.[1] Later, the advocates of the British Government appealed to this absence of preparation as a proof that Britain had not wished to go to war: Kruger, they argued, who was prepared for war, had deliberately taken England unawares by his ultimatum. The truth of the matter was that the British, misinformed by Rhodes and his followers, and misled by a long succession of colonial expeditions in which their opponents had been hordes of savages without discipline or courage, had miscalculated not the numbers, but the morale and the military capacity of the Boers. Both Government and nation expected either unconditional acceptance of the British terms or, at the worst, a rapid march of the British army, barely retarded by a few easily won skirmishes, to Johannesburg and Pretoria. It was quite possible that everything would be over before Christmas. They had not long to wait for a rude awakening.

4

Sir George White was in command of the British army in Natal,[2] a force of some 12,000 men stationed in the acute angle of

[1] *Minutes of Evidence taken before the Royal Commission on the War in South Africa*, 1904 (vol. ii, p. 514).

[2] For the history of the military operations, see in the first place *The Times' History of the War in South Africa, 1899–1902*, 7 vols., 1900–1907—an excellent work (General Editor, L. S. Amery). Vol. i (which deals with the preliminaries of the war), vol. ii and vol. iii are by L. S. Amery, vol. iv by Basil Williams, and vol. v by Erskine Childers. Vol. vi deals with the administrative problems which followed the restoration of peace. Vol. vii, Index and Appendices. See also *History of the War in South Africa, 1899–1902*, compiled by direction of His Majesty's Government by Major-General Sir Frederick Maurice with the assistance of a staff of officers, 4 vols., 1906–1910. (Vol. iii is anonymous; vol. iv by Captain Maurice Harold Grant.) A. Conan Doyle's *The Great Boer War* is a popular work contemporary with the events it records (the first edition appeared before the conclusion of the war). It ran into several editions. See further *The War in South Africa, prepared in the historical section of the Great General Staff, Berlin*; authorized translation by Col. W. H. H. Waters and Col. H. Dulcane, 2 vols., 1904–6; and two French works: Capitaine G. Gilbert, *La Guerre sud-africaine*, 1 vol., 1902, and Capitaine Fournier, *La*

British territory thrust between the Transvaal and the Orange Free State. He marched boldly towards the northern frontier. But hard pressed on either flank, he was soon driven back after a series of hard fights, one of which amounted to a minor disaster, on the town of Ladysmith. It was not long before he was surrounded in Ladysmith, and cut off from all communication by rail or telegraph with the capital of Natal. The Boers, advancing unchecked, reached by November 10 the town of Colenso and the Tugela river. The entire district of Ladysmith was then formally annexed to the Orange Free State and the Boers, crossing the Tugela, began to spread out in small bands in the direction of the capital of Natal, the seaport of Durban. In the west they invaded Bechuanaland, proclaimed its annexation to the Transvaal, and besieged Colonel Baden-Powell in Mafeking. They surrounded Kimberley, the metropolis of the diamond fields. Rhodes threw himself into the town and assumed charge of its defence, in co-operation, and often in collision, with the military authorities.[1] They crossed the Orange River at two points and scattered in different directions in eastern Cape Colony endeavouring, not unsuccessfully, to kindle revolt.

Meanwhile the British were obtaining reinforcements both from home and from India. Sir Redvers Buller landed at Durban on November 15 to take command of operations. He had presently over 20,000 troops under his orders. Lord Methuen landed at the Cape, and received from Sir Redvers Buller a detachment of 7,000 men for the relief of Kimberley. General Gatacre was despatched at the head of 4,000 men to drive back the Boers who were invading the east of Cape Colony. After defeating the Boers in a series of hard fights, Lord Methuen was finally defeated himself on December 9 at the bloody battle of Magersfontein. He retreated and asked for reinforcements. The following day, to the east of Lord Methuen's army, Gatacre was defeated at Stormberg. And five days later General Buller suffered a crushing disaster in what was regarded at the time as the principal theatre of opera-

Guerre sud-africaine, 3 vols., 1902–4. All three end with the capture of Pretoria. The student may also consult the *Life of General Sir Redvers Buller* by Col. C. H. Melville (a defence of the General containing very little new information) and the interesting *Life of Lord Kitchener* by Sir George Arthur.

[1] For the difficulties the military command endured from the headstrong arrogance of this megalomaniac, see *Kekewich in Kimberley; being an Account of the Defence of the Diamond Fields, October 14, 1899–February 15, 1900,* by Lieut.-Col. W. A. J. O'Meara, with a foreword by Lieut.-Gen. Sir R. Baden-Powell, 1926.

tions. His 20,000 men supported by thirty field guns and sixteen large naval guns attacked the Boer positions on the banks of the Tugela. They were defeated. A loss of 150 killed, 720 wounded, and 250 missing was the price of this ill-conceived frontal attack, which Buller never attempted to repeat. The same evening, he sent a despatch to warn Sir George White, besieged at Ladysmith, not to expect any further advance on his part for another month. If Sir George could not hold out so long, he advised him to surrender.

Thus, for the second time, and in a more serious encounter, the Boers had won. Alike in the number and quality of pieces their artillery was superior to the British. They possessed Krupp cannons and Creusot's heavy artillery, and their gunners were sometimes Frenchmen, more often Germans, or, if Boers, had received an expert training from European instructors. All their men were riders, and the British infantrymen, unaccustomed to fighting of this kind, found themselves suddenly faced by a host of 'mounted infantry'. They had the advantage of numbers. Though exact figures were unavailable the Boer troops were estimated at 40,000 or even 50,000. And these 50,000 were soldiers of fine quality. The British had to deal with redoubtable adversaries—intrepid hunters, excellent shots, hardy peasants of the Biblical stamp, who after two centuries revived Cromwell's Ironsides. Nevertheless, though the events of the 'black week' which witnessed the British defeats at Magersfontein, Stormberg, and the Tugela produced a deep impression both in England and throughout the world, a clear-sighted observer would even at that time have felt grave doubts as to the future of the Boers. As a matter of policy, was it wise to transform their war of independence into a war of aggression, to invade British territories, and annex them on the morrow of invasion? This, surely, was to oppose imperialism with a counter-imperialism and justify all the charges brought against Kruger by Chamberlain and his followers. And, on the other hand, having decided to take the offensive, had they not given a striking proof of military inferiority by failing to follow up their first successes? Why not march on Durban? Why leave unattacked, to the south of the Orange Free State, the enormous and undefended depot of provisions and munitions at De Aar? Their army, adapted for guerilla warfare in small bands, shrank from the risks of a war of positions in the open field, from the necessity of collective sacrifices on a large scale and the severe discipline of an organized command. To overcome their disconcertingly stubborn resistance England had only to meet it by a proportionate effort, an effort for which she was amply provided both with money and men. The Cabinet sent for Lord Roberts and made him Commander-in-Chief of the army in South Africa. Lord Roberts was the famous general who, twenty years earlier, had marched an army of 10,000 men 300 miles through the heart of Afghanistan to relieve a British force besieged in Kandahar. Kitchener was appointed Chief of Staff under his command. The reconquest of the Soudan had revealed a talent for organization more brilliant even than his skill as a tactician and strategist. While Lord Roberts was relieving Kimberley and Ladysmith, and occupying Bloemfontein and Pretoria, Kitchener's task would be to equip with the necessary organization the large army now being hastily created three months too late. All the Reservists, not yet summoned, were called to the colours, the seventh division, already in process of mobilization, and special detachments of artillery, were sent out immediately. Twelve militia battalions were authorized to volunteer for foreign service. The Government declared themselves prepared to enlist a sufficient number of volunteers to add a company to every battalion of troops already on active service. To supply the lack of mounted infantry, appeal was made to the Yeomanry at home, and offers received from Canada, Australia, and Cape Colony were gladly accepted.[1] Obviously these rough riders from the Colonies were the men best fitted to cope with the Boer horsemen. All the vessels required for the transport of these reinforcements were supplied by the large mercantile marine. By the beginning of February 1900, there were nearly 200,000 men ready to take the field. In the United Kingdom over 400,000 men were under arms, of whom 215,000 were volunteers.

Lord Roberts, whose immediate object was the relief of Kimberley, made no frontal attack on the lines at Magersfontein.

---

[1] This colonial support of which much was heard—and the popular enthusiasm contributed to draw closer the bonds which united the mother country and the self-governing colonies—amounted in reality to very little—from the commencement to the end of hostilities 30,000 men out of the ten million British subjects in Australasia and Canada. The terms of enlistment were for a year, or, the duration of the war, but when the year expired and the war was still unfinished almost all applied for their discharge and received it (*The Times' History of the Boer War*, vol. vi, p. 279; *Report of the Royal Commission on the War in South Africa*, vol. ii, p. 35).

5,000 cavalry under the command of General French made their way unmolested to the left of the Boer lines. On February 15, they reached Kimberley, which they relieved without striking a blow. The Boers fell back to the north and re-formed under the command of General Cronje. Lord Roberts sent his cavalry forward and, by occupying the fords of the Modder, cut Cronje's communications with Bloemfontein. He then made the mistake of a frontal attack on Cronje's army, just as Lord Methuen at Magersfontein and Sir Redvers Buller on the Tugela had attacked the enemy's front. Like them he paid the penalty and, unwilling to risk a second defeat, was content for the future to surround the Boer commandos with the far larger forces under his command, until at last, after a week's resistance, Cronje was starved out and surrendered; 4,000 prisoners and six cannons were the prize of the conqueror. The surrender was made on February 27. On March 13, Lord Roberts entered Bloemfontein. Ten days earlier, after a series of hard fights, not all victorious, Sir Redvers Buller had entered Ladysmith, and the Boers of the Orange Free State who had spread into the eastern districts of Cape Colony had evacuated them once more. Such were the results of the great strategic march planned by Lord Roberts from the banks of the Orange River to Bloemfontein by way of Kimberley and the Modder.

His operations were now brought to a temporary standstill. The pause is to be explained in part by the fact that, in the east of the Orange Free State, he encountered difficulties for which he was apparently unprepared. A new leader arose in the Boer camp, General Christian De Wet, who in the very neighbourhood of Bloemfontein inflicted losses on the British army and captured their convoys and guns. It was a guerilla war which could not lead to a decision, but which, as it developed, proved a permanent embarrassment to the attacking army. It was in vain that the Commander-in-Chief urged Buller, now master of Ladysmith, to bring up his troops and clear the district of the enemy. Sir Redvers who, no doubt, cherished a secret rancour against the great general who had replaced him in the command, refused to obey. He wished to win independent victories in Natal and undertake a direct invasion of the Transvaal in sole command of his army. Moreover, the very speed of his march had made Lord Roberts' position at Bloemfontein difficult. How could he keep 34,000 men and 11,000 horses supplied with food, when the only line of communication with his base, over 910 miles away, was a single line of railway? And besides food he needed reinforcements. The British camp was devastated by a violent outbreak of enteric fever. Within ten days of the British entrance into Bloemfontein 1,000 soldiers were in hospital, three weeks later the number had doubled, and, when Lord Roberts continued his advance, he left behind him no less than 4,500 incapacitated by sickness.

Nevertheless, at the date of his advance—May 1—his strength was greater than it had been when the campaign opened. When he left the Orange River he had been in command of 34,000 men and 113 guns; now the troops under his command amounted to 70,000 men supported by 178 guns. If we add the 55,000 troops under Buller's command, the British numbers considerably exceeded 100,000, as against some 50,000 Boer troops. Lord Roberts continued his advance with a force of 38,000. If ever the Boers made an attempt to block his advance along the railway from Bloemfontein to Pretoria, the British front was so extensive that their front was outflanked on both wings. To prevent their flanks being turned and their army surrounded, as Cronje's had been at Paardeberg, the Boers hastily retreated. Lord Roberts was thus enabled to advance unopposed—without striking a blow on the way; he entered Johannesburg on May 31, and Pretoria on June 5. Mafeking had been relieved on May 17. At the end of June, Buller forced the passes still occupied by the Boers and effected a junction with the main body. A month later the Orange general Prinsloo surrendered to the north-east of Bloemfontein with 4,000 men and three guns. Yet another month, and the British army held the entire railway which linked Pretoria with the Indian Ocean, as far as the frontier station of Komati-Poort. Kruger was a fugitive and had sailed for Europe from Lorenzo-Marques. Lord Roberts had proclaimed the British annexation of the Orange Free State and the Transvaal.

The Commander-in-Chief believed that the war was already over and that the only task remaining to be done in South Africa was to police and administer the conquered territory. He convinced the British Government. At the end of September, the Cabinet decided to recall him to England to succeed Lord Wolseley in the command of the British army. Kitchener was appointed his successor. The Cabinet also decided to exploit for their political advantage a victory, believed to be complete, and dissolved

Parliament. The General Election was held in October and resulted
in a Unionist majority, slightly reduced but substantial—134
instead of 152. The Government had thus provided against future
political risks by obtaining from the country a renewed lease of
power for six years.

5

Unfortunately the war was not finished. On December 1, Lord
Roberts left South Africa to take up in London the duties of the
post he had already held for two months. On December 13, at
Nooitgedacht, 43 miles from Pretoria, four companies were
trapped in a Boer ambush and only succeeded in effecting their
retreat with a loss of sixty killed, 180 wounded, and 315 prisoners.
This was the beginning of a long series of isolated conflicts which,
if devoid of real importance, continued almost eighteen months
and made the British army ridiculous in the eyes of the entire
world. Lord Roberts was charged with having bungled his work.
He had neglected, his critics complained, to observe the classic
rule of strategy that the enemy's army must be destroyed, before
his capital is occupied. They forgot that the rule was inapplicable
to the present case and that, if Lord Roberts had not destroyed the
enemy's army, it was for the simple reason that there was no army
to destroy.[1] Because the Boers were not in the strict sense an army,
they were never a danger to the British forces occupying Bloemfontein and Pretoria. The difficulty was of a different kind. It was
impossible to capture the Boer commandos, which were in a
position to continue over the vast stretches of the veldt an endless
guerilla war. The British enjoyed a superiority of numbers, organization, and strategy. But what strategy could deal successfully
with this swarm of tiny bands? The very superiority of the British
organization proved in certain respects a disadvantage to the
victorious army. A highly organized army required a degree of
comfort and an orderly routine which necessitated an extensive
system of auxiliary services. Moreover, owing to the size of the
occupied territory, the British were obliged to guard lines of
communication extending for thousands of miles. Therefore,
when Kitchener, who commanded an army of 200,000, despatched

[1] For the military organization of the Boers see *The Times' History of the Great War*,
vol. i, p. 66 sqq., vol. iv, pp. 476, 513; Sir Frederick Maurice, *History of the War in South
Africa*, vol. i, p. 68; also *Dix mois de campagne chez les Boers*, by a former Lieutenant-
Colonel De Villebois-Mareuil, 1900.

in any direction a body of troops to round up a Boer commando whose activities were reported to him, the pursuers were often no more numerous than their foes.

Can it be said that this long-drawn war taught valuable lessons of tactics and strategy? Here for the first time smokeless powder was employed, and its use threw considerable light on the conditions of attack in modern warfare; the danger of bright uniforms, the need of invisibility, and the impossibility of attacking after the old fashion in serried columns. And, on the other hand, the Boers taught European staffs that heavy artillery could be employed not only to defend forts, but in a war of movement over the open country. But that was all. The long duration of hostilities and the strength of the British forces engaged must not deceive us as to the character of the South African War. It was nothing but a guerilla war on a large scale and, after the lapse of a quarter of a century, it is amusing to find the British Press, indeed the European Press generally, treating as important battles skirmishes in which the casualties were counted by the dozen and the number of prisoners did not reach 1,000.

Nevertheless, this type of warfare presented far greater difficulties than the Continental critics of British strategy understood, and Kitchener employed the only possible methods at his disposal to wear down his elusive adversaries. His first problem was to secure his communications over railways which traversed a vast stretch of country in which every farmer was an armed foe or a spy. Blockhouses of stone and iron, pierced with loopholes and planted at intervals of two thousand yards, secured the railways from attack.[1] The generals were also authorized to demolish farms and private houses whenever in their judgment military interests demanded it. Their inmates, of whatever sex or age, were to be interned in vast concentration camps, where they could be supported and supervised by the British authorities, until the Boers were prepared to sue for peace. These demolitions were actually carried out, if a farmer were proved to have given armed assistance to the enemy, and even when his conduct afforded no ground for suspicion, if his farm, owing to its proximity to the railway, could be used by the Boers, with or without his consent, to shelter an attack upon the line. Finally, to capture an enemy

[1] For the blockhouse system see *The Times' History of the Boer War*, vol. v, pp. 256 sqq., 324 sqq., 396 sqq.

who could so easily make his escape after a surprise attack, Kitchener devised what were known as 'drives'.[1] A cordon of mounted infantry, spread over some hundreds of miles, drove whatever armed Boers might be contained within a given area into a vast network of barbed wire entanglements which by rendering escape impossible left the captives the alternative of surrender or death.

Scarcely a week passed in which the British public were not informed of the capture of some 400 or 500 prisoners. Even on the supposition that the Boers continued the struggle, until the last Boer had been slain or taken prisoner, the day of British victory could be calculated with an almost mathematical precision. It was simply a matter of money and time. But this method of warfare was far from heroic. The Boer defence made a very different appeal to the imagination. Kruger was in Europe doing everything in his power to excite the sympathy of the Continental nations. To the end, the Boers cherished the hope that one or other of the great Powers would make an offer of mediation, and there can be no doubt that this hope encouraged them to prolong their resistance beyond all military justification. President Steyn of the Orange Free State had remained in South Africa to support the determination of his people in their struggle with the British. For two years he was reduced to live as an armed outlaw in the country which not long before he had governed in peace. The two Generals of the first period had disappeared from the scene; Joubert was dead, Cronje a prisoner. But new men had taken their place. Louis Botha in the east of the Transvaal, Delarey in the west, and the indefatigable Christian De Wet, well-nigh everywhere, amazed the world by an unbroken series of minor successes. Twice the Boers invaded Cape Colony, twice the population of Cape Town learned that the presence of the enemy had been signalled on the Atlantic coast. On March 6, 1902—twenty-nine months after the declaration of war—General Methuen was surprised by Delarey's troops, 180 miles from Pretoria, and compelled to surrender with all his men who had not found safety in flight.

We must not be deceived by the charges which the combatants during the course of hostilities bandied in the usual fashion—the use of dumdum bullets, the slaughter of wounded soldiers, the

[1] *The Times' History of the Boer War*, vol. v, pp. 467 sqq.

ill-treatment of prisoners. In reality no war has been freer from
'atrocities'. Should we, like certain English historians, explain the
fact by the community of race which made the soldiers on both
sides too closely akin to cherish implacable hate? Or is not the
true explanation that both combatants belonged to a race whose
temperament is neither excitable nor cruel, a race peaceful and
calculating even in war, and, moreover, that they were preparing
by an instinctive moderation for the day when the war would be
at an end and they would be obliged willy-nilly to work side by
side at a common task, the development of the agriculture and
mines of South Africa. Moreover, the belligerents were fighting
in the presence of a couple of million Kaffir and Hottentot spectators who, if they took no active part, cherished a secret antipathy
to the whites on either side. It would obviously be an act of mad-
ness to carry the struggle to such a pitch that it amounted to the
collective suicide of the white race in South Africa. Vast numbers
of Dutch colonists from British territory came to the assistance of
the sister republics. Technically, they were rebels, liable to the
death penalty. But the British Government treated them with a
systematic leniency. Only in a very small number of extreme
cases did Sir Alfred Milner shoot these 'rebels'. It might have been
expected the operations in the field would be accompanied by a
species of civil war between two hostile populations, waged by
the methods with which the Irish had made the British only too
familiar, secret societies making armed attacks on private persons
unarmed. But nothing of the kind occurred. The entire contest
was confined to the two armies and waged according to the
accepted laws of war, with considerable obstinacy, no doubt, but
with very little savagery.

The Boers fought like hunters, the British like sportsmen. The
lion hunter does not strike an heroic attitude. He kills his lion or
takes to flight. A man who wages war as a form of sport is well
aware that he is engaged in the most dangerous of sports. He is
therefore, quite legitimately, anxious to restrict the danger by
rules, arranged between the opponents. On both sides, officers and
men, the moment they saw themselves defeated put up their
hands and the firing ceased. The British soldiers knew that, if
taken prisoner, they would be disarmed and set at liberty and the
surrenders became so numerous and the imperial Parliament was
alarmed for the reputation of British courage. Hence this insigni-

ficant guerilla war became a tournament, almost a child's game,
and it is noteworthy that it has in fact bequeathed to England and
modern Europe an institution for children. Colonel Baden-
Powell had become a popular hero on account of the courage and
resource he had displayed for months in his defence of the little
town of Mafeking on the Transvaal border against the Boers who
beleaguered it. Already known before the war by a little treatise
on the art of scouting, he conceived the idea of employing the
methods which he advocated, for the moral education of children. Today, his Boy Scouts are known and copied throughout
the world. Is the organization civil or military? Is its object to
train citizens or soldiers? To this question nobody in the most
opportunist nation on earth will ever return a definite answer.
'Scouting', wrote Baden-Powell, 'is like a game of football. . . .
Football is a good game, but better than it, better than any other
game, is that of man-hunting.'[1]

II PRO-BOERS AND LIBERAL IMPERIALISTS

I

As the war proceeded, what currents prevailed in public opinion
at home? At the close of 1899, as a year earlier during the diplomatic struggle with France, the Government had the general support of the nation. When, in December and January, the Cabinet
called upon the country to reply to the first defeats by a military
effort on a vast and unprecedented scale, they found behind them
its silent unanimity. Not only did recruits pour in—200,000 in
two months—but the cost of their equipment was often offered
besides: the City of London furnished 1,400 men, of whom 611
were mounted infantry, for service in South Africa. While the
Continent was practically unanimous in regarding England as a
powerful bully abusing her strength to enrich herself by robbing
two little Republics of their freedom, the British were practically
unanimous in the belief that they were waging a just war to
liberate their fellow countrymen, oppressed by an oligarchy of
corrupt and stupid peasants: if Europe believed otherwise, it was
because it was deceived by its Press and the Press had been bribed
by the Boers. But what need to say more? To attempt to analyse

[1] *Aids to Scouting*, 1st ed., 1899, p. 156.

a fit of patriotic frenzy would be a thankless task. The reader is likely to find more interest in following during the years of war the changing fortunes and sentiments of the parliamentary Opposition. It is easy to understand that in the opening days of the struggle, when the country was passing through the acute crisis of war fever, it was reduced to silence. But when the annexation of the Boer republics, Lord Roberts' return to England, and the October election were followed by a further series of disappointments, we might have expected that the repeated defeats of the British army would have improved its position. This was not the case. In war-time the lot of an opposition is hard. We shall find that the internal dissensions which had afflicted the Liberal Party ever since 1895 were accentuated by the war and that, contrary to what might have been anticipated, the prolongation of hostilities seemed at first to weaken instead of strengthening it.

Out of the vast body of Liberals we shall consider first the small group which professed an unqualified opposition to the war. They were the surviving stalwarts of Gladstonian orthodoxy, in whose eyes the maintenance of peace was the principal, one is sometimes inclined to say the sole, article of the Liberal creed. In support of their views they appealed to Cobden, Bright, and Gladstone. To be sure, they had suffered of recent years many rebuffs even at the hands of their fellow Liberals. But at the very time when Milner was negotiating with Kruger at Bloemfontein, their hopes had been unexpectedly revived by the meeting of the Peace Conference at The Hague. During the early days of October, when events were hurrying to the fatal issue, an emergency committee secured nearly 54,000 signatures to a National Memorial against War with the Transvaal. When war was declared, the canvass for signatures was discontinued. But the agitation was maintained by the methods traditional in England. There was a Stop the War Committee. There was a South African Conciliation Committee to prevent public opinion from being blinded by hatred of the Boers and to work for the restoration of friendly relations between the British and the Dutch in South Africa. Moreover, public meetings were held or, to speak more truly, were attempted, in London and the provinces.

But they were attacked and broken up by hostile crowds, and in the provinces the houses of their organizers were often sacked by the mob. With the exception of the *Manchester Guardian* and the *Westminster Gazette*, an evening paper, which, with amazing adroitness, contrived to preserve a certain freedom of criticism without damaging its sale, the entire Press was swamped by the wave of patriotic enthusiasm. Even before war was declared, the official organ of the Liberal party, the *Daily News*, had been converted to the imperialist standpoint on the question of South Africa, and the *Daily Chronicle*, which until October had trenchantly criticized the diplomacy of Milner and Chamberlain, changed its attitude in November and dismissed all those members of its staff who—headed by the well-known journalist, Massingham—persisted in opposing the war. The sole comfort left to the pacifist leaders was the bitter and proud satisfaction of feeling themselves to be a chosen few, sane men scattered amidst a mob of lunatics. If Sir William Harcourt and John Morley expressed their views so freely, it was because their words committed only themselves. For the past year they had been for practical purposes in retirement. 'I follow with languid interest', Harcourt wrote in June, 'the triumph of our arms and the dissolution of our Party.'[1] John Burns, who, a year before, had almost capitulated to Chamberlain's imperialism, returned to his pacifist opinions. In his opinion, British jingoism resembled too closely the Parisian chauvinism against which a year ago he had been prepared to preach a crusade. The night when London celebrated the relief of Mafeking by an orgy of rowdyism a friend met him returning home pensive and alone. He expressed his surprise at Burns' downcast air. 'How can I help feeling sad,' replied Burns. 'Don't you see England is falling to the level of France?'

But by no means all the members of the group to whom the soubriquet Pro-Boers was insultingly applied[2] abandoned themselves to despair. When the young politician David Lloyd George threw himself into the fray, he did not endanger an established position, but, on the contrary, by the notoriety he acquired, laid the foundations of his future popularity. Only thirty-seven years of age, he was the noisiest of those Welsh Radicals who had formed in Parliament for several years past an independent

[1] Sir William Harcourt to John Morley, June 1900 (A. G. Gardiner, *The Life of Sir William Harcourt*, vol. ii, p. 517).

[2] 'The first use of terms of political slang is often a subject of inquiry. The earliest instance of the term Pro-Boer, that I have come across, is in the *Daily News* of April 22, 1896: "If it were indeed a necessity of the situation to be pro-Boer or pro-British—the one to the exclusion of the other—then as Britons we should be for the British, we admit." ' (E. T. Cook, *Rights and Wrongs of the Transvaal War*, p. 78.)

group within the Liberal party and sold their support to the Government for measures in which Wales had a peculiar interest. For the example of Parnell and the Irish Home Rulers had aroused the national consciousness of the Principality and though they did not ask for complete separation, the Welsh were beginning to demand a species of modified home rule. In race were they not closer related to the Irish than to the Saxon English? And although between their religion and the dominant creed of England there was not the gulf which yawned between Irish Catholicism and English Protestantism, their Protestantism was not of the same shade. In Wales, only a minority belonged to the Anglican Church, the vast majority to the Evangelical and Calvinistic sects. Moreover, Welsh was spoken throughout the greater part of the Principality, was indeed far more living than Gaelic on the other side of St. George's Channel. It was as the mouthpiece of his little country that Lloyd George delighted to preach political morality to England. 'While England and Scotland are drunk with blood the Welsh continue sane; they are walking along the road of progress and liberty.'

He was a man of very humble origin. His father, an elementary schoolmaster, died in poverty when his son was still an infant. He had been adopted and educated by his uncle, a shoemaker and a Baptist lay preacher. By dint of hard work he passed the necessary examinations and became a solicitor in a little Welsh town, where he immediately plunged into the squabbles of local politics. In 1890, at the age of twenty-seven, he had been returned to Parliament as Radical member for Carnarvon, for which he had since been twice re-elected with increased majorities. Once or twice he had attracted the attention of the Press by intervening violently in debate. But it was the Boer War which brought into prominence this meteoric young man, a born politician, debater, and orator. In the House of Commons he had barely risen to his feet, before he stirred to fury the jingoes of the Conservative party and the moderates of his own. Throughout the country, he stood in the limelight as the most notorious advocate of the Boer cause. Once, at the risk of his life, he bearded Chamberlain in his Birmingham dependency. 'A brave and clever little man', wrote Sir William Harcourt, 'who ought to have a good future.'[1]

[1] Sir William Harcourt to John Morley, October 13, 1900 (A. G. Gardiner, *The Life o Sir William Harcourt*, vol. ii, p. 524).

What form did the opposition to the war assume? In the first place, the Pro-Boers attacked the character of those who had made it inevitable and were profiting by it. If the war disgraced England in the eyes of the world, it was not only because it presented the spectacle of the strong crushing the weak, but still more because it seemed to be waged for the possession of the gold mines at the instigation and for the profit of the Johannesburg capitalists and the City financiers, those wealthy upstarts, whose sumptuous mansions in Park Lane outraged public decency. Chamberlain's person was not spared. In 1899, considerable scandal had been caused when, a year after the dispute with France had been settled, Parliament authorized the purchase of the Niger Company's administrative rights for the sum of £865,000 and it became known that Chamberlain was one of the principal shareholders of the Company with a personal interest in maintaining its interests against France in the first place and now against Great Britain.[1] In December 1900, Lloyd George charged Chamberlain, his brother, and his son with being shareholders in a number of firms which supplied the Admiralty and the War Office.[2] Their critics, it is true, did not accuse them in so many words of making the war to fill their pockets. But the fact remained that the war filled them.

These attacks, hotly pursued during the first year of the war, and in which not only the Radical extremists, but the moderate Liberals, and even a number of Unionists, took part, do not appear to have affected public opinion. A great mercantile nation like England has little fondness for the public exposure of pecuniary scandals in which politics are mixed up with business. It was as though the Press and the political parties had entered into a tacit agreement to hush them up. The Pro-Boers accordingly turned their efforts in another direction and appealed with far better success to British humanitarianism. We have already remarked on the freedom from atrocities which distinguished the South African War, and have pointed out how often the army authorities mitigated or abandoned the repressive measures they had adopted. But the question remains whether this reluctance to employ severe measures was not chiefly due to the strength of the

---

[1] *Daily Chronicle*, July 6, 1899; also Chamberlain's defence, H. of C., July 6, 1899 (*Parliamentary Debates*, 4th Ser., vol. lxxiv, pp. 40–1).
[2] H. of C., December 10, 1900 (ibid., vol. lxxxviii, pp. 397 sqq.).

humanitarian opposition. In October 1900, a large number of farms were burned by order of Lord Roberts. The burnings aroused a tempest of indignation in England and in November he issued a second order defining with the utmost strictness the conditions in which a farm might be destroyed.[1] The concentration camps in which about the middle of 1901 some 60,000 Boers were interned suffered terribly from the effects of bad food, bad sanitation, and overcrowding. The average mortality was almost 117 per thousand, at the Bloemfontein camp as high as 383.15 per thousand, and among the children it approached 500 per thousand. This provided the Stop the War Committee and the Conciliation Committee with an opportunity to renew their agitation. A relief fund was organized for the victims of the concentration camps. An inquiry was opened on the spot. Finally, an important debate was held in Parliament, and the Secretary for War, while defending the system and pleading extenuating circumstances to excuse the bad organization of the camps, undertook to carry out the necessary reforms. He was even prepared to accept the assistance of the philanthropists who had denounced the scandal. Thus, at the very time when the opponents of the concentration camps were the object of public hostility and the anathemas of the Press, they were treated with a tolerance from which in the end the country benefited. A number of Englishmen entered into friendly relations with some of their South African foes and the friendship would make reconciliation easier when peace was restored.

The supporters of the Government charged the Pro-Boers with prolonging the war by the encouragement their protests gave to the enemies of Britain and by their continual interference with the action of the military authorities in South Africa. They stoutly denied the charge. According to them, the only way to shorten the war was to enter into negotiations as speedily as possible either with the Boer leaders in South Africa or with President Kruger. On what basis? The extremists persisted in demanding that the independence of both Republics should be conceded. Among them were Labouchere, the veteran Radical journalist, Sir Wilfrid Lawson, the patriarch of Puritan Radicalism, and Sir Leonard Courtney, a sturdy free-lance of eccentric views who, after quarrelling with the Liberals fifteen years earlier on the

[1] *The Times' History of the War in South Africa*, vol. iv (by B. Williams), p. 493.

question of Irish Home Rule, now quarrelled with the Unionists on the question of the Boer War. Few, however, were prepared to go so far. Lloyd George, in particular, was careful not to commit himself to so compromising a demand.[1] But all agreed in repudiating the attitude of Lord Roberts who, after the occupation of Pretoria, had rejected Botha's overtures and demanded unconditional surrender, or of Milner, who let it be understood that a treaty of peace was perhaps unnecessary; since the two Republics had been annexed to the Empire in 1900, the Boers had only to accept the situation.[2] Indeed, in the opinion of the Pro-Boers neither Milner nor Chamberlain was worthy, or rather, capable of concluding that peace of conciliation with the Boers which should assure them with the least possible delay self-government such as the French Canadians enjoyed under the British flag.

2

Within the ranks of the Opposition the Pro-Boers were opposed by those who, since the end of 1899, had been known as Liberal Imperialists. The appellation was coined at that date[3] by the statesman who became the unofficial leader of the new group, Lord Rosebery, the former Prime Minister, a man proud of his vast estates, proud of his colossal fortune (he had married a daughter of Lord Rothschild), proud of his magnificent racing stud (he was the king of the Epsom race-course and had twice won the Derby[4]), and proud of his scholarship; in the academic manner, an excellent writer and a fine speaker. Driven in 1896 from his leadership of the Liberal party by the Gladstonian veterans of the

[1] H. of C., July 4, 1901, Lloyd George's speech (*Parliamentary Debates*, 4th Ser., vol. xciv, pp. 891–2): 'I ask (him) to point to a single speech delivered by any Liberal Member of Parliament, sitting for a British constituency . . . in which there has been put forward a claim for absolute surrender to the Boers or for the restoration of absolute independence.'

[2] Lord Milner's speech, *Cape Times*, November 1, 1901: 'He wished he could congratulate them that the war was over, but he had come to the conclusion that it was no use waiting till the war was over. In a formal sense it might never be over, but it might just slowly burn itself out, as it was now doing.'

[3] Or rather revived; fifteen years earlier it had been applied to Lord Rosebery and accepted by him. See his Sheffield speech, October 20, 1885: 'The other day I was described as a Liberal Imperialist. So far as I understand these two words that is a perfectly accurate description. If a Liberal Imperialist means that I am a Liberal passionately attached to the Empire . . . if it means that I am a Liberal who believes that the Empire is best maintained on the basis of the widest democracy, and that its voice is powerful in proportion to the number of contented subjects that it represents . . . if these be accurate descriptions of what a Liberal Imperialist is, then I am a Liberal Imperialist.'

[4] A third time in 1900.

National Liberal Federation, he had lived in retirement for two years and returned to public life at the time of the Fashoda crisis to give Chamberlain's policy his unqualified support. During the Boer War he delivered with unflagging energy an entire series of speeches in which he expounded his programme in full.[1]

There was, he insisted, a fact whose reality and importance it was imperative that the Liberal party should recognize—the existence of the Empire. England was no longer the 'little England'—two islands lying off the north-western coast of Europe—to which half a century earlier a Liberal statesman might safely have confined his attention. Twelve million square miles, a population of 400 million, constituted at the opening of the 20th century 'Greater Britain'. But the peoples of the Empire united under a single sceptre were exposed to constant danger from the rivalry of other European nations eager to found empires of their own. One thing could be predicted with certainty of the coming century. It would be a century of keen, intelligent, even fierce, international competition 'which, moreover, would manifest itself more probably in the arts of peace even than in the arts of war'.[2] There was no cause for indignation. Was not the law of competition the law of progress? How then could the Liberal party, which prided itself on being the party of progress, attempt to evade it? It was for the British nation to consider whether its organization corresponded to the size of its empire, whether it possessed a sufficiently numerous and competent body of administrators to govern it. This raised the question of national education: the education given to the British people must be extended and brought up to date. And the nation must also ask itself whether the constitution of the race was sufficiently vigorous, its physique sufficiently robust, to bear the heavy burden it was called upon to carry. This was a question of public health which could be solved only by State action. In short, the aim which Lord Rosebery set before a rejuvenated Liberal party was to increase what he termed 'national efficiency'. If the Liberals were to be true to themselves, they must be the party of methodical and scientific progress.[3]

[1] Speech at Bath, October 27, 1899; at Chatham, January 23, 1900. 'Questions of Empire,' a Rectorial Address delivered before the students of the University of Glasgow, November 16, 1900. Speech at Chesterfield, December 16, 1901; at Glasgow, March 16, 1902.

[2] Glasgow speech, November 16, 1900.

[3] Chesterfield speech, December 16, 1901. See also the speech delivered earlier at Chatham, January 23, 1900: 'Another great advantage they ought to get out of the war

The Gladstonian stalwarts were, therefore, proceeding on the wrong lines when they endeavoured to arouse the pity of the public against the rigours of martial law and the horrors of the concentration camps, when they opposed the war as such and insisted that the Liberal party should be a party of peace at any price. It had not always been so, and Lord Rosebery, placing a rhetorical tribute on Lord Chatham's grave, hailed him as the founder of 'Liberal Imperialism'.[1] The charge which the Opposition might justly bring against the Conservatives was not that they had made an unnecessary war, but that they had made so little preparation for it, and when it came, they mismanaged it so grossly. Arthur Balfour, leader of the Commons, seemed to take a delight in making himself unpopular even with his own party by his attitude of ironical calm, his air of detachment, and the calculated pose with which he spoke of events as a disinterested spectator, not as a minister responsible for their conduct. Lord Lansdowne and Lord Wolseley within a few weeks of their respective dismissals at the end of 1900 from the War Office and the position of Commander-in-Chief, scandalized the House of Lords by their mutual recriminations, as they bandied in debate the charges of incompetence and want of foresight. Brodrick, who replaced Lord Lansdowne, lost no time in preparing an extensive scheme for the reorganization of the army. But it was soon abandoned and, in his turn, Brodrick became the object of the attacks which had been made upon Lord Lansdowne.

What method, then, did the exponents of Liberal Imperialism suggest to provide the British Empire with the military organization of which it was in need? The increase of parliamentary control? By no means. Lord Rosebery and his political allies were instinctively disposed to champion the executive against the criticisms of an incompetent Parliament, and Milner had no better friends in London than the group of Liberal Imperialists. Lord Rosebery proposed that the Commander-in-Chief should have the right to criticize government measures freely in the House of Lords, complained that since 1895 his authority had

would be the learning of some important lessons. In this country we lived a great deal too much from hand to mouth. In an age of science, we did not proceed by scientific methods, or profit as other nations did by them. Great as the task before us in the field was at this moment, a greater task would remain after the war was completed—the putting the Empire on a business footing—a task which, he believed, might occupy many governments.'

[1] Bath speech, November 21, 1899.

been controlled too narrowly by the civil power, and suggested that it would be a good thing if the War Office, Admiralty, and Foreign Office could be entrusted to permanent officials belonging to no party.[1] He was even prepared, in direct opposition to the traditional creed of the Liberal party, to contemplate the introduction of a system of conscription.[2] 'Take', he said, 'the example of Prussia, for I know no other so striking, of the necessity of constant vigilance in the strict maintenance of a State.' And he invited his countrymen to study and admire the Russian system of government. 'It is practically unaffected by the life of man or the lapse of time—it moves on, as it were, by its own impetus: it is silent, concentrated, perpetual, and unbroken: it is, therefore, successful.'[3] The two great military monarchies of nineteenth-century Europe were held up as examples to constitutional and parliamentary Britain by Lord Rosebery's imperialism, which called itself Liberal.

What was the immediate aim of this campaign of oratory? Did Lord Rosebery entertain at times the dream of effecting a reconciliation with Chamberlain's Liberal Unionists and forming, in conjunction with them, a centre party sufficiently strong to defy the combined opposition of the old Tory party and the old Liberal party? There were those who, sincerely or not, professed to believe it; but nothing in the behaviour either of the Liberal Imperialists or the Liberal Unionists permits us to take the suggestion seriously. Or was it his object to transform the Liberal party and reassume its leadership, from which he had been dismissed by the Gladstonians four years before? Was it without significance that at the first election of the London County Council the Radicals had christened their party the 'progressives', and that this 'progressive' party whose programme was throughout one of administrative reform and municipal socialism, had at every election maintained itself in power, though at the General Elections of 1895 and 1900 London had returned an overwhelming majority

---

[1] H. of L., August 3, 1900: 'I confess that, if my wish were to be carried out, I should have more officers non-political and less officers political than is now the case. So far from wishing to make the Commander-in-Chief political, I would gladly see the War Office non-political, and I would gladly see the Admiralty non-political, and if it were possible—I know none of these things are possible, I am only speaking of a Utopia—I would have the Foreign Office also non-political' (*Parliamentary Debates*, 4th Ser., vol. lxxxvii, p. 596).

[2] H. of L., January 20, 1900 (ibid., vol. lxxxviii, pp. 38–9).

[3] Glasgow speech, November 16, 1900.

of Unionists? It is possible that Lord Rosebery who had once been elected chairman by the progressive majority of the London County Council, impressed by its success, had conceived the project of remodelling Parliamentary Liberalism after the pattern of the municipal progressives. But was he, in fact, so anxious to return to office? Once already he had been Prime Minister, and the experiment had not succeeded. More, much more, attractive was the position he now occupied, popular, applauded, urged by a host of admirers to respond to his country's desire and hold himself at her disposal, ready to take the reins of government whenever she should invite him, but persistently evading their importunities, and deliberately taking his stand above the fray, content to play the easy part of adviser and umpire.[1]

3

Nevertheless, the Liberal statesmen who supported Lord Rosebery were active politicians, the ablest and most brilliant men on the front bench of the Opposition. They had held important positions in the last Liberal Cabinet. Sir Henry Fowler had been President of the Local Government Board, Henry Asquith, Home Secretary, Sir Edward Grey, Under-Secretary at the Foreign Office. Anxious to retain the leadership of their party against the day, whose speedy advent they desired, when the Liberals would return to power, they found it no easy task, in the circumstances, to decide on the best tactics to pursue. They were sure that the vast majority of the nation and probably the majority of Liberal voters approved of the support which they gave to the war policy of the Unionist Government. But were they so certain that they had the approval of the local leaders of the party through-

[1] When he spoke at Glasgow on March 10, 1902, he addressed an audience of 5,000, and 32,000 people asked for tickets. See Sir William Harcourt's letter to his son, November 1, 1899: '. . . *The Times* will get tired of puffing him and his hold on our people is limited. I doubt whether even in ten years he will be capable of leading a party. He is too selfish, too trivial, too much a *poseur*, and I fancy what he admires in Chatham was his isolation, which ended in his choosing to act with no one, till no one would act with him. . . . He will never take the rough and tumble of party warfare, but keep himself for the *réclame* of safe displays at intervals. . . .' Notice the contempt with which Lord Rosebery in his Glasgow speech (November 16, 1900) speaks of party government: 'The development and expansion of the empire have produced a corresponding demand for first-rate men, but the supply has remained, at best, stationary. Of course we do not employ all those that we have; for, by the balance of our constitution, while one half of our capable statesmen is in full work, the other half is, by that fact, standing idle in the market-place, with no one to hire them. This used to be on a five years' shift, but all that is now altered. Anyhow, it is a terrible waste.'

out the country? If not, what could they do to win them over?

Foremost among these local leaders and organizers were the officers—the ministers and lay preachers—of the Free Churches, the hereditary enemies of the Church of England and, consequently, of the Tory party. For the past five or six years, Lord Rosebery had been persistently courting the Free Churches. An inveterate foe of Home Rule, he had, since 1895, made the most of the conflicts which had occurred on the question of education between the Irish Catholics and the British Nonconformists. When the Irish Nationalists defeated a Bill to provide for the erection at the public expense of a statue of Cromwell in the House of Commons, it was Lord Rosebery who paid for its erection outside, at the entrance of the building, and on November 14, 1899, when the South African War had just begun, as though to remind the Nonconformists that their hero had been a great soldier, as well as a great statesman, he spoke at the unveiling. One of his principal supporters, Sir Henry Fowler, was a Wesleyan. The most active of the Wesleyan leaders, the Rev. Hugh Price Hughes, made his weekly organ, the *Methodist Times*, an imperialist newspaper whose jingoism was not surpassed by any Conservative paper. Even among the other sects—the Baptists and Congregationalists—Lord Rosebery had contrived to gain adherents—for example, the Rev. Robert Forman Horton, the Congregationalist. Nevertheless, though we can hardly doubt that the Nonconformist squadrons during these troubled years lost their cohesion, and many a chapel-goer voted for the imperialists and even for the Conservatives, the vast majority of the Dissenting ministers remained true to the traditional policy of peace handed down from Bright and Gladstone. The Rev. C. Silvester Horne and the celebrated Dr. Clifford were the natural allies of Lloyd George, himself an active member of the Baptist community as well as a Radical politician.

On the extreme left the leaders of Trade Unionism provided the Radical party with a further staff of workers. Some years previously they had been converted to the tenets of Socialism, and Socialism was a system from every point of view the antithesis of the economic individualism cherished by the supporters of Gladstone. Could not the new creed be turned to the profit of Liberal Imperialism? Was it impossible to persuade the working man that imperialism was more favourable to active measures of social reform than the orthodox Liberalism of the Gladstonians could possibly be? And, in fact, there were in the Socialist ranks thinkers who advocated an alliance between the Socialists and the more progressive section of Imperialists against the Gladstonian Liberals, now obviously discredited.

For the past fifteen years the Fabian group had preached a Socialism from which the romantic dreams of a revolutionary Utopia were rigorously excluded. Its two leaders, Sidney and Beatrice Webb, were in close relations with the group of Liberal Imperialists. Sidney Webb had often come into contact with Lord Rosebery when the latter was Chairman of the London County Council, of which the young Fabian was a member, and among the intimate friends of the Webbs was Richard Burton Haldane, a young Scotch barrister, a metaphysician, steeped in German philosophy, and already an active member of the group led by Lord Rosebery and Sir Edward Grey. Early in 1900, the faithful ally of the Webbs, the dramatist, Bernard Shaw, heralded their imperialist propaganda by a speech in which he declared war on the doctrine that small nations had the right to determine their own government. His Socialism repudiated such national individualism. He declared his conviction 'that the most governed state over the largest area is preferable to a number of warring units with undisciplined ideals. . .. The world is to the big and powerful states by necessity: and the little ones must come within their borders or be crushed out of existence.'[1] Eighteen months later, Sidney Webb maintained the same thesis in an article which attracted considerable attention.[2] He congratulated Lord Rose-

[1] Speech delivered at a meeting of the Fabian Society, Clifford's Inn Hall, February 23, 1900. The thesis is developed in detail in *Fabianism and the Empire: A Manifesto by the Fabian Society*. Edited by Bernard Shaw, 1900.

[2] 'Lord Rosebery's Escape from Houndsditch' (*Nineteenth Century*, September, 1901, vol. iv, pp. 366 sqq.). Reprinted later with important alterations as *Fabian Tract No. 108. Twentieth Century Politics. A Policy of National Efficiency. A Lecture to the Fabian Society*, November 8, 1901. For Sidney Webb's influence on Lord Rosebery, see a letter from Sir Henry Campbell-Bannerman to Herbert Gladstone, September 12, 1901: '. . . In our little political world at home things appear to have been quiet on the surface, whatever movement there may have been underneath. We have had the benefit of instruction by Mr. Sidney Webb and have survived it. I recognise in his lucubration admirable sentiments which I have heard enunciated by other and greater men: which may be master and which scholar I do not know. I fear I am too old to join that Academy.' To the same correspondent, December 18, 1901: '. . . All that he (Lord Rosebery) said about the clean slate and efficiency was an affront to Liberalism and was pure claptrap. Efficiency as a watchword! Who is against it? This is all a mere *réchauffé* of Mr. Sidney Webb, who is evidently the chief instructor of the whole faction.' (J. A. Spender, *The Life of the Right Hon. Sir Henry Campbell-Bannerman*, vol. ii, pp. 4–14.)

bery on having freed himself from slavery to the traditional
Liberal formulas and, three months before the Chesterfield speech,
urged him to place himself at the head of a reconstituted Opposition which should take for its programme National Efficiency.
But this was no more than the dream of a handful of theorists,
who addressed their propaganda to the middle-class intelligentsia
rather than to the labouring masses. What, meanwhile, was the
attitude of the militant trade unionists? Obviously there could be
no question of capturing such a vast movement for the pacifist
agitation. When the Trade Unions held their annual congress
they were too prudent to risk the unity of their organizations by
adopting an attitude of open opposition to the war. In 1900, a
Pro-Boer motion was passed only by an insignificant majority
and in 1901 the congress refused by a large majority to adopt a
similar motion. Nevertheless, among the secretaries of the Unions,
who were often devout Nonconformists, sometimes lay preachers, the vast majority—whether they had been converted to
Socialism or were still opposed to the novel creed—remained
loyal to the traditional humanitarianism of the Gladstonians.

What has just been said of the Nonconformist bodies and trade
unions is applicable for the same reason to the official organizations of the Liberal party—the Front Bench of the Opposition in
the House, the National Liberal Federation in the country. If the
Liberal party was to be kept together, there must be no breach
with either wing. But by the operation of what may be termed
the natural law of parties and owing to the fact that the Pro-Boers
represented the maximum of opposition to the policy of the
Government, the balance inevitably shifted by imperceptible
degrees towards what is termed in French politics the left.

4

Sir Henry Campbell-Bannerman, since Sir William Harcourt's
resignation the official leader of the party, had formerly been
Secretary for War. It was over a provision in his estimates that
the Liberal Cabinet had been defeated. A wealthy member of the
Scottish middle class, an excellent fellow, a fine specimen of the
normal, healthy citizen of average ability, liked by everyone for
his hearty and quiet good humour, everything pointed to him as
the man who in January 1899 could best keep the party together

and prevent a definite split in its ranks. Throughout the war, he made this his sole object. But the conditions were far from easy. In the first place, during those critical weeks which preceded the commencement of hostilities, he offended the Gladstonians by his lukewarmness, and their opponents by his anxiety to avoid a breach with Sir William Harcourt, John Morley, and their friends. When the National Liberal Federation met at Nottingham in March 1900, its chairman was not Sir Henry Campbell-Bannerman, but Sir Edward Grey, who might be regarded as, after Lord Rosebery, the leader of the Liberal Imperialists. When in July the Pro-Boers forced a division on a motion hostile to the ministry they mustered only 31 votes as against 40 Liberal Imperialists who voted with the Government. Sir Henry Campbell-Bannerman and 35 Liberal members abstained from voting. The Liberal Imperialists believed that the moment had come to get rid of a leader unable to assert his authority. They founded an Imperial Liberal Council, which at the General Election put forward 56 candidates whose unimpeachable patriotism it guaranteed, and declared that, as soon as the Election was over, the party must be purged of those members whose opinions rendered them unworthy to manage the affairs of a great empire. At a Council dinner held on November 12, R. W. Perks, a Wesleyan and as ardent an imperialist as Lord Rosebery himself, maintained that out of the 186 Liberal members of the new Parliament, 152 were 'virtually' Liberal Imperialists.[1]

But for all this, the Liberal Imperialists remained in political communion with their opponents, and the Unionists had just won a decisive victory at the polls by persuading the electorate 'that every seat won by the Liberals was a seat won by the Boers'. And three months after the Election it was the turn of the Liberal 'Pro-Boers' to gain a striking success at the expense of the Imperialists. Since the war began they had suffered from the disadvantage that they were totally unrepresented in the London Press. How could they obtain a newspaper? The prudent and the aged shook their heads at the suggestion. It would cost too much —£250,000—and where could they raise so large a sum?[2] The

[1] *Annual Register*, 1900, p. 223. Cf. J. A. Spender, *The Life of the Right Hon. Sir Henry Campbell-Bannerman*, vol. ii, pp. 295-6, and J. Saxon Mills, *Sir Edward Cook, a Biography*, p. 182.

[2] John Morley to Sir William Harcourt, December 3, 1899 (A. G. Gardiner, *The Life of Sir William Harcourt*, vol. ii, p. 512).

young Lloyd George did not lose heart. He went to Birmingham and sought the assistance of George Cadbury, a wealthy chocolate manufacturer, and a prominent member of the small sect of Quakers whose ardent piety had been fertile in missionary enterprise and works of social reform. At first Cadbury hesitated. He had always refused to take part in political strife. But Lloyd George pointed out that at the present juncture there was more at stake than a mere party question, the sacred cause of peace must be upheld. Cadbury provided £20,000, Thomasson of Bolton followed his example and contributed a further £20,000. No new paper was founded; the *Daily News* was purchased, its imperialist staff dismissed, and their places taken by a staff of Radicals. The new staff was Puritan as well as Radical. Two characteristic decisions were made. The paper would not publish racing tips or results and would refuse advertisements of alcoholic drinks.[1]

The first campaign fought by the newspaper after its change of ownership was on the subject of the concentration camps. It caused a sensation and drove Sir Henry Campbell-Bannerman to take action. Speaking on June 14 at a political banquet he denounced the 'methods of barbarism' employed by the British in South Africa. Three days later, he supported a motion by Lloyd George calling the attention of the Commons to the question. Fifty Liberals, though they did not actually vote against the Pro-Boer motion, as on the previous occasion a year before, abstained from voting. Seventy voted for it. The centre, under the leadership of Sir Henry Campbell-Bannerman, joined forces with the left. In future, Sir Henry would be considered a Pro-Boer.

Six months later, in December, the committee of the National Liberal Federation adopted a resolution calling upon the Government to state plainly the conditions on which it was prepared to make peace and demanding the immediate despatch to South Africa of a special body of commissioners to open the negotiations which Milner refused even to consider. At the same time, the committee rejected an amendment, proposed by the imperialists, asking that the necessary military measures should be taken to bring hostilities to an end. This success emboldened the

---

[1] A. G. Gardiner, *Life of George Cadbury*, pp. 215 sqq. J. Saxon Mills, *Sir Edward Cook, a Biography*, 1921, who in chapter xi gives extracts from the diary of Sir Edward Cook, the editor dismissed when the paper changed hands.

Pro-Boers, and in January 1902, when Sir Henry Campbell-Bannerman couched an amendment to the royal address in terms sufficiently vague to preserve the unity of the party, he was severely taken to task by Lloyd George.[1]

Lord Rosebery, on his side, threw off his inertia at last and consented to become the president of an important league in which the Imperial Council of 1900 was merged. Sir Henry Fowler, Sir Edward Grey, and Henry Asquith were the three vice-presidents of the Liberal League, founded in February 1902, to propagate the creed of Liberal Imperialism. But the situation when the League was founded was very different from what it had been when the Council had been founded in 1900. Then the imperialists had hoped to capture the leadership of the party. Now they admitted that they were a dissentient minority in a party the majority of which remained faithful to the Gladstonian tradition, as continued by Sir Henry Campbell-Bannerman.

Indeed, the politicians who controlled the Liberal League repudiated any intention of splitting the party, and it was within the party organization to which they still belonged that they proposed to spread their views. They borrowed from their Fabian friend, Sidney Webb, one of his pet phrases and explained that their aim was to 'permeate' the Liberal Party with their ideas. What, moreover, was the exact point at issue between the opposing groups in the spring of 1902? Was it as to the best method of bringing the war to an end? There can be no doubt that if, on this point, any divergence of opinion remained, it was very slight. Ever since the beginning of the war Sir Henry Campbell-Bannerman had declared himself in favour of annexing the Boer republics and Lloyd George had never opposed annexation. All that either statesman asked was that negotiations should not be delayed and that the peace should be a peace of conciliation which should admit at the earliest moment possible the citizens of the Transvaal and the Orange Territory to full political and civil rights. But in December Lord Rosebery had spoken to the same effect.[2] The question on which at the opening of 1902 Lord Rosebery and Sir Henry Campbell-Bannerman ostensibly differed had nothing to do with the Boer War. It was the question of Home Rule. And although for the past two years the Irish had exasperated patriotic

[1] H. of C., January 21, 1902 (*Parliamentary Debates*, 4th Ser., vol. ci, pp. 537 sqq.).
[2] Chesterfield speech, December 16, 1901.

Englishmen by the delight with which they hailed every British defeat, it was universally admitted that Home Rule at the moment was not a question of practical politics. At bottom the issue which divided the two groups was neither the Boer War nor Irish Home Rule. It was—and we must bear this well in mind, if we are to understand the history of the Liberal Party during the next few years—the question of the foreign policy to be pursued by the Liberals after the restoration of peace. Was it to be the policy the party had adopted half a century before, after the Crimean War? A profound loathing of war, a determination to avoid any commitment which might lead to war, an attitude of systematic indifference to all questions of foreign policy? Such was the desire of the group labelled Pro-Boers. Or had conditions changed too profoundly to permit the Liberals to continue the Gladstonian tradition and yet, as in the fifties, maintain their position as a great national party? That was the belief of Lord Rosebery, Sir Edward Grey and their supporters. They were convinced that if the Liberals returned to office they would be compelled to solve the problems of imperial defence in the same spirit and by the same methods as Chamberlain and his followers.

III ENGLAND AND EUROPE: THE GERMAN QUESTION

I

We must not imagine that the attention of the British public was so entirely absorbed by the war that it lost interest in the preservation of the balance of power on the Continent and throughout the world. Britain had seen every foreign nation, with the exception of one or two Mediterranean states dependent on her protection, espouse enthusiastically the Boer cause and welcome in common the British defeats of November and December 1899. She had felt once more the anxiety she had experienced at the opening of 1895, when the Emperor William had launched against her the Triple Alliance of the Far East, and at the end of the same year, when he had sent Kruger his telegram of congratulation. But if the English had at first been afraid that the universal anglophobia might issue in some diplomatic and military combination against their empire, and alarmed by the projects of invasion which certain French and German officers had indiscreetly made public they had been speedily reassured. Events had taken another turn equally, it must be admitted, disturbing to the British public. The Powers took advantage of the fact that Britain's hands were tied by the South African War to pursue unchecked in different quarters of the globe their schemes of colonial expansion. Russia acquired a financial hold over Persia, and worked hard to strengthen her influence in Manchuria and at Peking. The Latin nations began to think of parcelling out whatever remained to be annexed in North Africa. Italy might get Tripoli, France and Spain cast their eyes on Morocco. This would be the revenge of Italy, Spain, and France for Adowa, Cuba, and Fashoda. And what of Germany?

Germany acted like the rest. She had just acquired the Caroline Islands in the Pacific, was consolidating her influence in China, and pushing forward the project of the Bagdad railway for which she succeeded in obtaining a concession, formally guaranteed by two treaties. But at the same time the German Government was putting into execution a systematic and comprehensive foreign policy. There was no longer any question of a European combination against Britain. The scheme had definitely failed in January 1896. The policy pursued at present by the Kaiser and his Chancellor, von Bülow, was a policy of balance, whose principle may be defined as follows. Friendly relations with every foreign power, alliance with none. England was to be assured of Germany's benevolent neutrality in her struggle with the Boers, but Germany would not accept any alliance or understanding which might alarm France or Russia. If Austria drew closer to Russia and Italy to France, Germany would raise no objection, would indeed publicly profess her approval. So long as the interests of Great Britain continued to clash with those of France and Russia, a better understanding between those Continental powers could not have any very serious consequences for Germany. While England and France, and England and Russia were at variance, the German Empire was safe.

This policy was in the main that formerly practised by Bismarck. But there was a difference between Bismarck's foreign policy and the Emperor William's. Bismarck had intended his policy to be permanent, the Emperor's was provisional. At the beginning of 1896 William II had discovered that French public opinion was not yet prepared to accept the friendship of Germany. But the time would, he hoped, arrive, hastened by colonial disputes with Britain, when the French would consent to forget that Alsace and Lorraine had been part of France. 'Fashoda', wrote the Emperor, 'is doing wonders.'[1] William II had further realized that he did not possess the equipment necessary, if he was to put himself at the head of an anti-British coalition. For that he would require a navy at least equal to the French or the Russian. But in 1896 the German navy was still in its infancy. Henceforward, the Emperor never relaxed his efforts to obtain from the Reichstag a navy adequate to the greatness of Germany. That is the refrain which recurs throughout his correspondence with his ministers. 'If I had a navy . . . When I shall have a navy.' 'The British navy is strong enough to defy any hostile combination, Germany has practically speaking no navy. I am therefore compelled to observe the strictest neutrality. Before everything else I must provide myself with a navy. In twenty years' time when the navy will be ready, I shall speak a very different language.'[2]

What language? Did William II deliberately contemplate a war with England? No. He was perhaps a megalomaniac, but a megalomaniac who preferred a safe prestige to the hazard of battle. He was fond of parading troops, but he shrank from war. Nevertheless, this policy of bluff and display was calculated to alarm foreign powers and in particular constituted a menace to the position of England. The German attitude was the more disquieting because, whenever the Kaiser by some action he took showed his determination to remain on friendly terms with Great Britain, it was badly received by his people and the Emperor risked his popularity. But whenever in the course of his campaign for a big navy he delivered a boastful and sabre-rattling speech he seemed rather to follow than to lead public opinion. Sooner or

[1] Remark appended to a letter from Count von Bülow, of July 4, 1899 (*Die Grosse Politik*, vol. xiv, p. 560 n.).

[2] William II to Count von Bulow, Minister for Foreign Affairs, October 29, 1899 (ibid., vol. xv, pp. 407–8). Cf. the Emperor's note written on a despatch from Graf von Hatzfeldt, the German Ambassador in London, December 20, 1899: 'If we possessed a navy, Chamberlain would never have dared to act in this way' (ibid., vol. xv, p. 427). William II to his Chancellor Count von Bülow, March 5, 1901: 'Your report of yesterday about the situation in China has surprised me enormously and interested me very much. What an exciting situation! And what a fine thing it would be if only we had two squadrons of men-of-war ready to send out' (ibid., vol. xvi, pp. 333–4). William II to the Chancellor, Count von Bülow, November 12, 1902: 'Be careful! They have 53 ironclads in commission, we have 8! And in 1905 England will have 196 new ironclads, cruisers and armoured cruisers ready for service, for 46 of our own' (ibid., vol. xvii, p. 117).

later the British people must become aware of the German attitude towards their country. Throughout the period of the Boer War the decisive factor determining British foreign policy was the relationship which obtained between the two Courts, the two Governments, and the two peoples.

2

Since the summer of 1895 the Emperor William had not set foot in England. Official relations between the two Governments having improved, Queen Victoria decided in the spring of 1899 that the time had come to seal the diplomatic *rapprochement* by a reconciliation between the two Courts. She invited her grandson. But he did not even condescend to reply, and, when pressed to explain his insulting silence, demanded as a preliminary condition that the negotiations for the partition of Samoa should be reopened. When the condition was accepted—for the situation in the Transvaal was becoming steadily worse, and the British Government found it necessary to conciliate Germany—he promised to pay a visit in autumn, but postponed his arrival, not wishing to come over until the question of Samoa had been settled to his satisfaction.[1] A treaty signed on November 14 gave him all he asked. A fortnight earlier, Rhodes had concluded an arrangement with the German Government for the establishment of a system of telegraphs in East Africa. On November 20 the Emperor William, accompanied by his wife and two of his sons, landed in England on his way to Windsor.

The moral effect of his visit, made at this particular moment, was very great. It was a little over a month since the declaration of war, bad news was beginning to arrive from the theatre of operations, and England felt herself hated by the entire world. From France in particular rose a volume of bitter abuse. The Nationalists took their revenge for the insults heaped upon them during the Dreyfus case, the Republicans could not fail to sympathize with the protest of the British Radicals against a war waged upon a weak people by a strong for the possession of the gold fields, and what Frenchman would not rejoice that his country was

[1] *Die Grosse Politik*, vol. xiv, pp. 615, 620, 623, 625, 627; vol. xv, p. 410. Baron von Eckardstein's account, though containing additional information which must not be neglected, is inaccurate on several points (*Lebenserinnerungen und Politische Denkwürdigkeiten*, vol. ii, chs. i, ii, and iii).

avenged for the humiliations she had suffered a year before during the Fashoda crisis? Moreover, French invective took the obtrusive form of picture and caricature, and the caricatures did not spare the Queen herself. The British Ambassador at Paris warned the Quai d'Orsay that, if the attacks in the French Press continued, he would ask for his passport. This was the moment chosen by the German Emperor to testify by his visit his goodwill towards Great Britain. Britain was not, after all, a moral outcast among the nations of the world. The imperial visit effaced the memory of the Kruger telegram. And it covered the diatribes of the German Press.

But was it nothing more than an expression of goodwill? The Emperor had brought with him his Minister for Foreign Affairs, Count von Bülow. They did not, it is true, see the Prime Minister. Lady Salisbury had died two days before the Emperor's arrival and Lord Salisbury made his mourning an excuse to shut himself up at Hatfield. But William II and von Bülow had long interviews with Balfour, who represented Lord Salisbury, and above all with Chamberlain. What was the subject of these interviews? The nature of the proposals made by the British to the German Government may be guessed from the panteutonic sermon preached before the Emperor by Bishop Creighton in Sandring-ham Church at the express command of the Prince of Wales,[1] and from the sensational speech which Chamberlain delivered at Leicester on November 30, two days after William II set out on his return to Germany. After a sharp passage of arms with France Chamberlain expressed himself in favour of a policy of 'alliance' or at least 'understanding', if not with 'the German Press' at any rate with 'the German people' and, moreover, hoped that the Anglo-German alliance might be completed by 'a triple-alliance of the Teutonic race' between England, Germany and the United States of America.[2] The effect produced by the speech was disas-

---

[1] *Life and Letters of Mandell Creighton, Sometime Bishop of London.* By his wife, vol. ii, p. 417.

[2] If we can believe the German evidence (*Die Grosse Politik*, vol. xv, pp. 413 sqq.: Report of Count von Bülow drawn up at Windsor, November 24, 1899) all the proposals, which, moreover, are of a very definite nature, were made by Balfour, Chamberlain and the British royal family. The Emperor and Bülow had either passed them over in silence or discouraged them. This certainly was the impression which prevailed at the French embassy. 'The confidences I have been able to gather', wrote M. Paul Cambon from London on December 1, 'make it certain that with his usual impulsiveness and want of restraint, Mr. Chamberlain has spoken of the common interests of Great Britain and Germany throughout the world and proposed to the Emperor an alliance or at least a

trous; it provoked a storm of protest in the Press of the three countries concerned. In Germany, von Bülow took fright at the attitude of German opinion. Speaking in the Reichstag on December 10 he made no allusion to the Anglo-German alliance for which Chamberlain hoped, declared his intention to remain on friendly terms with the neighbouring powers both on the eastern and western frontiers and concluded by asking the Reichstag to sanction the naval programme which had been prepared by von Tirpitz. This was the prelude to the law of naval construction passed shortly afterwards by which the German Government undertook to devote to the construction of men-of-war during the next sixteen years the sum of £74,000,000, and thus, since the programme of 1900 was in addition to that of 1898, to equip Germany with the largest navy of any Continental power. It was evident to the entire world that Chamberlain's egregious blunder had undone the good effect of the imperial visit, and that the German Government was replying to his clumsy advances by a blunt refusal.

Six months passed. A popular rising broke out in the north of China. Though directed principally against the Germans and Russians, it became an indiscriminate attack on the foreigners who had begun the piecemeal dismemberment of the Chinese empire. The German minister was murdered. The legations were besieged in Peking. An expedition despatched to their assistance under the command of a British admiral failed to force its way through and retreated on Tien-Tsin. What steps would the European powers take to retrieve the initial defeat? England, fully occupied with the Boer War and obliged to maintain in South Africa an army of 200,000, could play only a minor part in the Far East. She supported the suggestion of a Japanese expedition, to which Russia would not agree, while Japan, on her part, would not agree to a Russian expedition. The German Government took

general agreement on all questions which concern the two countries. The Emperor has listened to his proposals, paid him compliments, excited his hopes and made promises, but has not, it seems, committed himself.' (E. Bourgeois and G. Pagè's *Les Origines et les Responsabilités de la Grande Guerre*, p. 284.) The British documents are silent as to the conversations which took place at Windsor between Balfour and Chamberlain and the Emperor and von Bülow. An appendix, not paginated, published at the end of vol. iii gives only a memorandum drawn up on November 26 by Sir Francis Bertie after a conversation he had held that day with von Bülow at the Foreign Office. 'In the course of conversation Bülow happened to say *en passant* that he knew that alliances are not in vogue in England.' That is the sole allusion, if it be an allusion, made during the interview to a British offer of alliance.

advantage of the undisguised hostility between the Anglo-Japanese and the Franco-Russian groups to enter the field. It secured from Russia first, then from Japan, an invitation to take control of the operations. The French Government yielded to the wishes of the Russian. The British Government, completely isolated, could only bow with an ill grace[1] to the will of other powers. The command of the international force sent to the relief of the legations was given to Feldmarschall von Waldersee. Not Feldmarschall but Weltmarschall—not Field-Marshal but World Marshal, a German diplomatist jestingly remarked.

No sooner had the legations been relieved than the friction recommenced. The agreement of October 16 by which England and Germany covenanted to maintain in China the principle of the open door might have been expected to satisfy the demands of British commerce. The Emperor, employing the language of the panteutonic alliance, spoke of the pact concluded 'with the greatest Teutonic people after ourselves'. But it soon became evident that in the opinion of the German Government, the agreement did not apply to Northern China, where Russia was left free to mark out a sphere of influence reserved exclusively for herself. And, on the other hand, Germany insisted on the speedy evacuation of Shanghai, which had been occupied during the rising by the international force and where the British, whose contingent was particularly large, seemed inclined to remain permanently. Military supremacy and diplomatic supremacy: never had the Emperor William's position been so strong. His hands held the balance of power.

Von Bülow wrote from Windsor on November 14, 1899, 'There can be no doubt that, taken as a whole, public opinion in England is far less anti-German than German opinion is anti-English', and added, 'If the British public were aware of the state

---

[1] Von Derenthall to the German Ambassador in London, Graf von Hatzfeldt, July 31, 1900: 'Yesterday Sir Frank Lascelles paid his first visit after his return from London. His conversation confirmed your Excellency's reports. He spoke of the disappointment and dismay with which British statesmen view the German attitude in the far eastern question, even those who like Mr. Chamberlain are friends of Germany. . . . The ambassador also referred to the question of the supreme command and let it be known that in Lord Salisbury's opinion, unity of command is unnecessary.' (*Die Grosse Politik*, vol. xvi, p. 75.) Graf von Hatzfeldt to the German Foreign Office, July 31, 1900: '. . . Lord Salisbury referred to the question of the supreme command and repeated what Lascelles has already said in Berlin. He merely added that it was a British characteristic, even if, perhaps, an unreasonable one, not to endure the command of a foreigner and that he was obliged to reckon with it.' (Ibid., vol. xvi, p. 76.)

of feeling which at present prevails in Germany, a great change would come over its view of the relations between England and Germany.'[1] There was in fact, as von Bülow admits in the same despatch, at least one newspaper, a newspaper, moreover, of the first importance, which was doing its best to enlighten the British public. When Valentine Chirol, *The Times* correspondent in Berlin, took up his post at the end of 1895 he was wholeheartedly in favour of an Anglo-German understanding.[2] But he had soon realized that in the present temper of the German Government and people it was quite out of the question, and did everything in his power to acquaint his readers with the true state of affairs.[3] And was *The Times* after all completely isolated? In all probability the German Chancellor did not realize the extent to which British opinion had already taken alarm at the German attitude. There can be no doubt that the novelist, Conan Doyle, in the popular history of the South African War, which he published in 1900 and which enjoyed a very wide circulation, voiced the sentiments of a considerable section of the public, when he excused the violent anglophobia of France and Russia. The naval supremacy of England had been built on the ruin of the French empire and the French might well be forgiven if they bore England a grudge. Russia was a barbarous country, and it was only natural that she should hate the most civilized nation in the world. But Germany, so deeply indebted to England for the assistance she had received in her struggle to throw off the French yoke! 'Never again on any pretext will a British soldier or sailor shed his blood for such allies.'[4]

Nevertheless, however galling the arrogant tone in which the Emperor William dictated to England—the word is scarcely too strong—the conditions of his friendship, his attitude towards the Boer Republics could not fail to give pleasure in London. Negotiations had scarcely begun between Milner and Kruger when he advised the President to compromise. And when, in August, a rupture seemed imminent, he had warned him not to count on

---

[1] *Die Grosse Politik*, vol. xv, p. 419.

[2] See his work, *The Far Eastern Question*, which appeared in 1896, p. 194.

[3] From the end of 1899 the German Government was disturbed by the attitude of *The Times*. See Count von Bülow letters of November 15 and 24, 1899 (*Die Grosse Politik*, vol. xv, pp. 412, 419). On two occasions at least it made an attempt to change it. (Letter from Count Metternich to the Chancellor, March 24, 1900, ibid., vol. xv, pp. 496–7.) Holstein's note on October 31, 1901 (ibid., vol. xvii, pp. 101 sqq.).

[4] *The Great Boer War* (1st ed., 1900, pp. 195–6).

the intervention of Germany. The outbreak of war occasioned many difficulties, the presence in the Boer ranks of a very large number of German volunteers, and the inevitable incidents arising out of the question of contraband. But the German Government persisted in observing an attitude of neutrality, almost of benevolent neutrality. When conversations were begun between Petersburg and Berlin as to the possibility of European intervention between the belligerents, it was the German Emperor who broke them off and informed the British Government of his action.[1] When in April 1900, an attempt was made by a Pro-Boer to assassinate the Prince of Wales as he passed through Brussels, the Kaiser, anxious to give the Prince a public mark of his sympathy, hastened to find him and met him unexpectedly at the port of Altona, as he was re-embarking for England. At the end of 1900, when Kruger fled to Europe, he wished to visit every capital in turn to solicit the sympathy of the civilized world. In Paris he was loudly applauded and received at the Elysée; but the German Emperor refused to give him a similar welcome, and he did not visit Berlin.

[1] Who began the negotiations? The Russian or the German Government? If we are to rely exclusively on the German evidence it was the Russian Government (*Die Grosse Politik*, vol. xv, pp. 501 sqq.). But the archives of the Russian embassy in London (utilized by Sir Sidney Lee in his *Biography of King Edward VII*, pp. 761 sqq.) throw suspicion on the German documents. It is certainly true that from January 27 until the end of February the initiative was taken by Mouravieff (cf. E. Bourgeois and G. Pagè's, *Les Origines et les Responsabilités de la Grande Guerre*, p. 280). But he made his proposals with the encouragement of the Russian Ambassador at Berlin, Count Osten-Sacken, who believed that he was carrying out the wishes of the Emperor William. And the interviews which took place between Osten-Sacken and the Emperor from the New Year until January 22 have either been reported in the German publication in a form extraordinarily different from that which they assume in the Russian or have been altogether omitted. In particular, the German publication says nothing of the conversation which the Emperor held with the Russian Ambassador on January 21, in which the Emperor informed the Ambassador of his anxiety as to the persistent rumours that England contemplated handing Egypt over to Italy. A few days later (January 28-31, 1900) M. Nelidow wrote from Rome: 'It is not easy to discover the source of the rumour that Italian troops are to be sent to Egypt or who started it. But there are indications that Germany has encouraged the report in Rome, with the object, it would seem, of creating an atmosphere of suspicion between England and Italy on the one side, and France on the other.' In this connection it is worth remark that the Duke of Mecklenburg, in an interview with the editor of *L'Eclair* (an organ hostile to England and friendly to Germany) made an allusion to reports of the same nature. But this was at the beginning of February (*Die Grosse Politik*, vol. xv, p. 511).—See again: Sir F. Lascelles to the Marquess of Salisbury, Berlin, February 9, 1900 (*British Documents*, vol. I, pp. 250-1).

On January 18, 1901, the British Press issued the official announcement that the Queen's health had been impaired by the anxieties of the past year and her doctors had ordered a complete rest. Four days later she died, mourned by the entire nation. 'As to her Majesty,' wrote a clear-headed and cynical contemporary, 'personally one does not like to say all one thinks, even in one's journal. By all I have ever heard of her, she was in her old age a dignified but rather commonplace good soul, like how many of our dowagers, narrow-minded in her view of things, without taste in art or literature, fond of money, having a certain industry and business capacity in politics, but easily flattered and expecting to be flattered, quite convinced of her own providential position in the world and always ready to do anything to extend and augment it.' But, adds Wilfrid Blunt, 'the public has got to look upon the old lady as a kind of fetish or idol, and nobody, even now she is dead, will dare print a word not to her glorification'.[1]

The days were distant when the Queen, still almost a child, and a devoted Whig, had been the object of violent diatribes in the Tory Press, when later her husband's persistent interference in politics had been warmly criticized by the newspapers, or when, later still, left a widow at the age of forty-two she had made herself unpopular by withdrawing from the duties of her position and her people's affection and making her widowhood a retreat from public life. For many years she had conscientiously performed all state functions. At the two Jubilees of 1887 and 1897 the nation had venerated in her person the embodiment of its own greatness. The very length of her reign was impressive, a symbol of the stability and immortality of British power. She was the grandmother of the Emperor of Germany and the Empress of Russia. During her reign three monarchs had succeeded each other on the throne of Italy, four on the throne of Spain, and two dynasties had fallen in France. And she disappeared from the scene at the moment when the embers of the South African War, which in September had been considered as finished, had been rekindled, and no end was in sight, and when the entire Continent with little attempt at disguise was expressing its eager hope that Bismarck's

[1] W. S. Blunt, *My Diaries*, vol. ii, p. 2.

prediction would be fulfilled and the British Empire find its grave in South Africa. A pall of gloom overcast the British horizon.

The Emperor William did not wait for the news of his grandmother's death to visit England. The moment he heard of her illness, he started, defying the customary etiquette and breaking off the preparations which were being made to celebrate the bicentenary of the Prussian monarchy. His haste produced a very favourable impression on public opinion. By the bedside of the dying Queen he was the loving and respectful grandson, to her mourning family the affectionate nephew and cousin. In the Isle of Wight, through the streets of London, and at the final scene at Windsor, he followed her funeral on foot or on horseback by the side of the new King of England. The day after the funeral he left England after a fortnight's visit, amidst the cheers of the crowd.

There could be no doubt that the new sovereign would be very different from the old Queen, whose long reign had at last ended. She had wished him to be known as Albert I, in memory of her husband. But when he ascended the throne, he dropped the name Albert with its hateful recollections of a Puritan education and chose among his other names the old Saxon name of Edward. We are told that he at once ordered the demolition of the cairn Victoria had erected to the notorious and absurd memory of John Brown, her favourite servant. Already nearly sixty years old, King Edward was a man of pleasure, with the thick face, protruding eyes, and violent passions of his race; wherever society takes its amusement, he was a well-known figure, at casinos where the play is for high stakes, at race meetings, and at those international watering places, where he was the arbiter of fashion. There were complaints that he had admitted into his circle of intimates, otherwise very exclusive, a number of wealthy financiers, often Jews, who no doubt had brought weighty arguments in support of their claims. Moreover, his conduct had caused at times an undesirable amount of scandal. At the time, the middle classes, highly sensitive to anything which might bring discredit upon the established institutions of the country, had been shocked, but for the same reason they were now prepared to bury the past and took for granted that, once on the throne, the new King would deserve the respect which no one would refuse the sovereign. And after all was there no excuse for the youthful indiscretions of the man who, for so many years, had been regarded as essentially the Prince of

Wales? The old Queen, a born despot, prevented by the firm barrier of British institutions and customs from exercising control over public affairs, had taken her revenge by bullying her entire entourage, her family, her guests, her servants. Was it surprising that her son sought elsewhere the money his mother refused him, and, excluded from public affairs and treated like a child at the age of forty and fifty, had indulged in the irresponsible pranks of a boy?

In any case, he was now King. In the past, his sympathies had been with France and Russia against Germany. But that was in the days of his youth; of recent years, his attitude had changed. Always a professed Liberal, he made it clear that he belonged to the group of Liberal Imperialists. His great friend, the statesman whom he valued most highly, was Lord Rosebery, the most determined opponent of France among the British politicians. Between 1895 and 1899 there had been a complete rupture between the Emperor William and himself. But they had been reconciled during William's visit to Windsor in November 1899, and, if in the course of the following year, the Emperor annoyed his uncle by the military advice he lavished upon him in a tone of condescending pity, his visit of January 1901 consolidated the friendship revived a year before. King Edward had long private conversations with the Emperor, who for a time was more popular at Windsor than he had ever been. A worthy descendant of the Great Elector and Frederick II, he made, we are told, suggestions which were adopted, for the reform on the Prussian model, of certain details in the British uniform.

There was, therefore, nothing in the change of sovereign to jeopardize the good relations between England and Germany. And there were other circumstances which may well have helped to improve them. If, at the time of the Queen's death, Lord Salisbury was still Prime Minister, he was no longer Foreign Secretary. The Cabinet had been remodelled in the previous autumn and Lord Lansdowne had exchanged the War Office for the Foreign Office. It was a double triumph for the partisans of an understanding with Germany. For since 1895 Lord Salisbury had been a stubborn opponent of the policy; Lord Lansdowne, on the contrary, who belonged to the same group of Liberal Unionists as Chamberlain and the Duke of Devonshire, had no sooner reached the Foreign Office than he made it known that he wished to re-open

negotiations with the German Government for a better understanding. The negotiations had already begun when the German
Emperor landed in England on January 20.[1] They were continued
after his departure. Their primary object was the settlement of
the Morocco question, which had been raised already in 1899,
and the terms of a partition were discussed. England might have
Tangiers and the control of the Mediterranean sea-board, Germany receiving Rabat, Casablanca and Mogador. In addition, the
possibility was explored of a formal treaty of alliance on the
following terms. If Germany were at war with a single foreign
Power, England would not intervene, but if she were at war with
two Powers, England would come to her assistance.[2] Berlin put
forward demands which the British Government found impossible and which were probably made in the expectation that they
would be rejected. The negotiations were, therefore, finally
broken off. But, with the encouragement of the German Government, the preliminary discussions had been accompanied by
similar negotiations with the Japanese Government, and it was
not with Germany, but with Japan, that England signed a treaty
of alliance on February 12, 1902.[3] It was framed on the model of
the draft treaty with Germany of the previous summer, and the
Anglo-Japanese alliance cannot have been regarded unfavourably
at Berlin, for it irretrievably embroiled England with the Franco-
Russian group of powers. In fact, the Russian Government
began once more to sound the German as to the possibility of
a great Continental alliance against Britain.[4] Germany refused, as
she had always done since 1896.

4

But in the interval between the failure of the negotiations with
Germany and the conclusion of the Anglo-Japanese alliance, an
incident, in itself absurdly unimportant, suddenly opened the eyes

[1] Freiherr von Eckardstein, *Lebenserrinerungen und Politische Denkwürdigkeiten*, vol. ii,
pp. 235 sqq.

[2] Ibid., pp. 274 sqq. *Die Grosse Politik*, vol. xvii, pp. 1 sqq.

[3] For the circumstances under which the negotiations with Japan were grafted into the
negotiations with Germany, see Freiherr von Eckardstein, *Lebenserrinerungen und Politische
Denkwürdigkeiten*, vol. ii, pp. 360 sqq. *The Secret Memoirs of Count Tadasu Hayashi*, 1915,
chs. iv and v (pp. 114 sqq.). Also Memorandum by Mr. Bertie, November 9, 1901
(*British Documents*, vol. ii, p. 73 sqq.)—Cf. vol. i, p. 260: Sir F. Lascelles to the Marquess
of Lansdowne, August 20, 1901.

[4] *Die Grosse Politik*, vol. xvii, pp. 152 sqq. See especially Holstein's note March 15, 1902
(ibid., pp. 175 sqq.).

of the British public to the intensity of German anglophobia. In a speech at Edinburgh on October 23 Chamberlain had informed his audience that, to put an end to the guerilla warfare in South Africa, England might possibly find herself compelled to have recourse to severer measures of repression. 'If that time comes, we can find precedents for anything we may do in the action of those nations who now criticize our "barbarity" and "cruelty", but whose example in Poland, in the Caucasus, in Algeria, in Tongking, in Borneo, in the Franco-German war—whose example we have never even approached !' The French and Russian Press appear to have received with a philosophic indifference attacks to which they had become accustomed, but the inclusion of Germany in the same condemnation as the other Continental Powers aroused such a violent outcry[1] on the other side of the North Sea that to satisfy public opinion, von Bülow judged it necessary to intervene. Speaking in the Reichstag on January 8, 1902, he replied to Chamberlain with the words of Frederick the Great, 'Leave this man alone, he is biting granite.' 'I do not give lessons to a Foreign Minister,' retorted Chamberlain, 'and I will not accept any at his hands.'[2]

The episode produced a strange effect on British opinion. Undercurrents of mistrust which the German policy had aroused, but which, hitherto, had been submerged by incompatible or contradictory sentiments, rose suddenly to the surface. It is no doubt curious that the incident had been occasioned and von Bülow's rejoinder provoked by the statesman who had conceived the ambitious project of a panteutonic alliance. Henceforward, the isolation of Germany became a favourite topic of the British Press. Sometimes the writer was content to state it as a fact[3] and explain it as the natural result of the blunders and insolence of German foreign policy. But it was also presented as the object which

[1] *Prima facie.* It is difficult to understand why the German Government took up so warmly an attack which equally concerned the other Powers. But Chamberlain's speech had followed a campaign in *The Times* against the atrocities committed by Germany in 1870–1. See the letters in the issue of September 3 and 6, signed 'Memor', which had provoked replies from the German Press.

[2] Speech at Birmingham, January 11, 1902.

[3] See the cartoon in *Punch*, December 25, 1901. It depicts a ball-room. The Czar Nicholas is dancing with Madame France, 'Britannia with her Colonies'. Alone and leaning against a door-post the Emperor William is twisting his moustache. He is annoyed that he cannot find a partner. Underneath are the words: *Britannia*: After all, my dear, we needn't trouble ourselves about the others. *Colonies*: No, we can always dance together, you and I.

British policy should deliberately pursue. The *National Review* under the vigorous editorship of Leo Maxse, whose tendencies hitherto had been anti-French, now began to advocate a radical change in British policy towards France. It would be interesting to know the names of the contributors, obviously well-informed, who, writing under the signatures A.B.C., etc., opened the campaign in November and December. They advocated, in opposition to Germany, a *rapprochement* with Russia and, indirectly, with France.[1] 'Great Britain is confronted with the development of a new sea power, founded on the same economic basis as herself and impelled by a desire to be supreme. But *l'ocean ne comporte qu'un seul maître.* We have secured in the past the sovereignty of the seas and our sceptre cannot be wrested from us without a desperate and bloody struggle.' On the whole—we shall return to the question later[2]—the evidence points to the group of Liberal

[1] 'British Foreign Policy' by 'A.B.C., etc.' 'Some Consequences of an Anglo-Russian Understanding', by 'A.B.C., etc.' (*National Review*, vol. xxxviii, pp. 343 sqq., 513 sqq.). Cf. in the January number the article entitled 'A Plea for the Isolation of Germany', signed C.P. (ibid., vol. xxxviii, pp. 703 sqq.). See especially p. 713: 'Combat . . . German Anglophobia, I would say, by working all round at the isolation of Germany. Bring home to her perils of her detestable geographical position between France, watching for a *revanche*, and Russia at the head of irreconilable Slavism.' Ogniben, 'Great Britain and Germany' (*Contemporary Review*, February, 1902, vol. lxxi, pp. 153 sqq.), an anti-German article. The writer's conclusion, however, is not easy to follow: 'Because Germany is resolved to be our enemy, it does not follow that any other European State is suitable or needful as an ally. The truth is—and it takes a long time to dawn on the minds of British politicians—that a World-Power like ours should be able to treat the question of friendships and alliances on the mainland of Europe as devoid of actuality. Having duly shaped our relations with other World-Powers, Russia and the United States, courtesy, firmness and aloofness should mark our dealings with all the other States. Self-sufficiency is an essential characteristic of a World Empire. Much, very much, remains to be done before that stage of "spendid isolation can be reached".' Cf. the article by Archibald Ross Colquhoun entitled 'Our German Ally' (*Monthly Review*, January, 1902, vol. vi, pp. 73 sqq.). Chalcas who for the past eighteen months had conducted in the *Fortnightly Review* an anti-German and pro-Russian campaign, 'Crux of Foreign Policy' (August 1900)—'Why not a treaty with Russia?' (October, 1900)—'Will England Last the Century?' (January, 1901)—'Will Germany Fail?' (May, 1901)— 'Russia and Her Problems' (June and July, 1901), was encouraged by the article in the *National Review* to go further in the same direction. See his article entitled 'The Crisis with Germany—and its Results' (December 1, 1901, vol. lxx, pp. 934 sqq.). And when certain French journalists complained that Chalcas had omitted their country from his calculations, he wrote to satisfy them, an article entitled 'The Revival of France' (May 1, 1902, vol. lxxi, pp. 785 sqq.) in which he advocated a *rapprochement* with France at the same time as a *rapprochement* with Russia. The historian would give a good deal to discover the identity of these pseudonymous writers. See also on this Press campaign, Jacques Bardoux, *Essai d'une psychologie de l'Angleterre contemporaine. Les Crises politiques. Protectionisme et Radicalisme*, pp. 106 sqq.

[2] See below p. 135. Lord Grey of Falloden in his *Reminiscences* (*Twenty-five Years, 1892–1916*, 2 vols, 1925) says nothing of any steps he may have taken during the Boer War to advocate a better understanding with France. But he relates (vol. i, p. 53) a sarcastic remark by Lord Rosebery about his French 'friends', which is extremely significant. Lord Rosebery must be excepted from the conclusion reached in the text. He remained to the

Imperialists as responsible for the conception of this new policy—the reversal of the policy pursued since 1898. What else should we expect from the operation of the party system? In their zeal for imperial expansion the Liberal Imperialists vied with Chamberlain's followers. On what point then could they oppose the policy of the Government? They could not, like the political heirs of Gladstone, renounce entirely a policy of alliances. They must therefore devise a new alignment directed against a different Power.

We do not, of course, mean to ascribe the formation of this body of opinion hostile to Germany to the Edinburgh speech and the explosion it produced. The incident could provoke an explosion only because the train had already been laid. In fact, five or six years before, public opinion had begun to take alarm at the threat to British manufacture and commerce from German competition, and it was obvious that the new German naval programme must completely transform the balance of power. Of these two factors, which exercised the more powerful influence over the public mind at the opening of 1902?

In the first place, we must remember that the competition between German and British trade was not so menacing to the latter in 1902, as it had been six years earlier when the Unionists took office. In Britain, the depression of the previous years had been followed by a boom, whereas the forced growth of German industry had produced a very serious crisis. Moreover, public opinion had fully supported the persistent attempt which the Government had made during the interval to conclude a military alliance with Germany. And if there was a country whose industrial competition was calculated to alarm the British, it was not Germany but the United States.[1] The formation of the gigantic

end in favour of an understanding with Germany. Nevertheless, even he was disagreeably impressed about this time by the account which his son, who had gone to Germany to finish his education, gave him of the state of feeling which prevailed there. (Count von Bülow to Count Metternich, March 13, 1902; Die Grosse Politik, vol. xvii, p. 151 and footnote.)

[1] W. J. Ashley, The Tariff Problem, 1903, pp. 197 sqq.: 'The question of the future is not German and English competition so much as American competition with both countries. Germany and England are naturally marked out to be friends by their position in face of the United States and Russia. And if Germany seeks to secure an outlet for her population in distant possessions worth having, e.g., in Mesopotamia—if she seeks to secure by treaty a permanent trade with the German people of Southern Brazil, it is difficult to see why this country should not watch her efforts with benevolent neutrality.' This, however, is the opinion of a solitary individual, and it is most significant that his contention, though from the purely economic standpoint extremely plausible, was not shared by any other British writer of the period.

Steel Trust and its absorption of an important British steamship company and several minor companies was of ill-omen for the future of British trade. However, the anxiety it caused did not betray itself by any outbreak of hostility to America in the Press, and the Government could pursue without opposition from public opinion its policy of friendship and benevolence towards the United States. In 1901, Great Britain, after discussions which lasted a year and in which the attitude of the American Senate had been as disagreeable as ever, left the United States complete liberty to dig and administer the projected Panama Canal and gave up all the safeguards America had accepted by a formal treaty fifty years earlier. The historian must be careful not to exaggerate the economic explanation of history.

It was very different with the naval question. This was beyond all doubt the decisive factor which determined the breach between Germany and Britain. In 1895, Germany had possessed only a third-class navy. The great naval law of 1901 proclaimed her intention to provide herself with a fleet inferior only to the British and capable of proving a match even for the British navy, if not all over the world, at least in the North Sea. Her latest men-of-war, though as yet few in number, but whose rapid increase in the near future had been announced to the world, were remarkable for the excellence of their construction and the quality of their crews. So long as the Boer War continued, the army, for once, eclipsed the navy in the interest of Parliament and Press, but now when the war was approaching its end we are not surprised to find an entire group of naval experts—Lord Charles Beresford, Arnold White, and Archibald Hurd[1]—drawing the attention of the public to the new threat to Great Britain constituted by the German navy. They demanded more modern methods of training for the officers, the establishment of a naval base in the North Sea, and a better distribution of the squadrons. If fewer ships were stationed in the Mediterranean, a larger number could be concentrated in home waters.[2] Did these experts also advocate an under-

[1] Archibald S. Hurd, *The British Fleet. Is it sufficient and efficient?* With an introduction by Admiral the Hon. Sir Edmund R. Fremantle, 1901. Archibald S. Hurd, *Naval Efficiency: The War Readiness of the Fleet—Lists and Particulars of effective ships of the World's Navies*, 1902. Arnold White, *Efficiency and Empire*, 1901, pp. 294 sqq. *The Memoirs of Admiral Lord Charles Beresford*, written by himself, 1914, vol. ii, p. 479.

[2] Already the Admiralty had quietly taken the following measures to protect the coast. 1. The reserve squadron had been transformed into a real squadron, in which every ship was ready to go into action. 2. The four training-ships had been, or would shortly be,

standing with Russia and France as a counterpoise to the naval power of Germany? On this point the state of public opinion about the end of the Boer War is difficult to analyse. Although it was obviously impossible to continue for very long to maintain, as in 1902, a navy costing as much, or almost as much, as the four navies of France, Russia, Germany and Italy,[1] there is no evidence that anybody in professional circles had as yet faced the inevitable. Both the French and the Russian Governments were speeding up their programme of naval construction, the French invention of the submarine was beginning to disturb the Admiralty, and the colonial policy of the two allies remained the same. Under these circumstances how was it possible to abandon the principle that the navy must be kept at a sufficient strength to be a match for the combined French and Russian fleets?[2] And if the principle were to be maintained, the most reasonable policy was clearly an understanding with the German Government, if not with the German people, provided the former was sufficiently enlightened to understand the value of British friendship and keep in check its subjects' anti-British feeling? Under these circumstances, we can well believe that neither the Foreign Office nor the Admiralty encouraged this outbreak of hostility towards Germany; that, on the contrary, Chamberlain's quarrel with Berlin embarrassed the Foreign Office, as much as his attacks on other Powers a few years before. The change of feeling which occurred during the winter months of 1901-2, and whose fundamental cause was undoubtedly the threat offered to British naval supremacy by the German navy, took place outside official or professional circles. It was a reaction of that vague entity called public opinion, a reply of British feeling to German, a revolt of the public against the caution of the Government departments.

replaced by six armoured cruisers which in an emergency could be employed as a squadron on active service (Archibald S. Hurd, *Naval Efficiency*, 1902, pp. 78–9).

[1] H. of C., March 21, 1901, February 26, 1902, E. Robertson's speech (*Parliamentary Debates*, 4th Ser., vol. xci, p. 779, vol. ciii, p. 925).

[2] Arnold White, *Efficiency and Empire*, 1901, p. 275: 'German efficiency has already secured a formidable and homogeneous fleet . . . Germany has already stretched out the trident. Neither France nor Russia is impatient to assist us to recover the supremacy which we have listlessly allowed to slip from our hands.' Archibald S. Hurd, *The British Fleet*, 1901, pp. 62–3, is content to remark that 'While the first importance attaches to the navies of the French and the Russians, it is impossible to ignore the vast sums which are being laid out in Germany and in the United States.'

5

On June 1, 1902, peace was concluded with the Boers. The first attempt at negotiation had begun long before, when, immediately after the occupation of Pretoria, Louis Botha had approached Lord Roberts. But the latter, who believed that the Boers could not possibly hold out any longer, had demanded unconditional surrender and the war had continued. In 1901, official conversations had been held. But they failed and on August 7th the Commander-in-Chief issued a proclamation sentencing to perpetual banishment from South Africa any Boer officer of whatever rank who had failed to surrender by September 15. The proclamation seemed a final barrier to further negotiations. Nevertheless, when in the spring of 1902, the Queen of Holland proposed that they should be re-opened, not only were preliminary discussions begun between the representatives of the British Government—Sir Alfred, now Lord, Milner and Sir Herbert, now Lord, Kitchener —and the accredited representatives of the Boer Republics, but the readiness with which the suggestion was welcomed was a guarantee that this time the negotiations would not break down.

Have we good grounds for concluding that when Chamberlain agreed to re-open the discussions he yielded to pressure from King Edward? In default of evidence, we are not entitled to affirm it. But we may well believe that, on the one hand, the King was anxious that peace should be concluded before his approaching coronation, and, on the other, that in his previous attitude Chamberlain had been influenced by the avowed representative of his policy in South Africa, Lord Milner. The latter, an administrator rather than a diplomat, who put his faith in force, had welcomed the idea that the Boers were rebels not belligerents and that any negotiations with them were therefore legally inadmissible. Kitchener, on the other hand, had long been eager to finish with the war. He had no love for the vast army of amateurs, hastily improvised, of which he had been compelled to take command.[1] He was annoyed by the way in which Lord Roberts, having plucked the laurels of an easy victory, had left him to do the dirty

[1] To Lady Cranborne, March, 1900: 'We are still here [at Bloemfontein]. It is very disappointing, but it is quite impossible to calculate on anything in this army. I must say, I like having the whole thing cut and dried and worked out; but people here do not seem to look upon the war sufficiently seriously. It is considered too much like a game of polo with intervals for afternoon tea' (Sir George Arthur, *Life of Lord Kitchener*, vol. i, pp. 312-3).

work, a thankless task and the more so because no one in Europe appeared to understand its difficulty. He blamed Milner for the failure of the negotiations of the previous spring[1] and was determined this time to overcome his opposition. His success was the easier because he had behind him the practically unanimous opinion of the British nation. The peace of Vereeniging was a typically English peace, inspired from beginning to end by the spirit which buries old scores.[2]

The Boers of the Orange and the Transvaal renounced their independence. But an undertaking was given that those burghers who should surrender or were already prisoners should return to their farms and be left in full possession of their property and personal freedom. They would not even be obliged to surrender their arms. The Boers were guaranteed the use of Dutch in the schools and courts of law. At the earliest possible date, the military was to be replaced by a civil administration and, as soon as circumstances permitted, representative government set up. Many in England had hoped that the cost of the war would be defrayed by a tithe on the produce of the gold fields. These expectations were not realized by the treaty of Vereeniging. Not only did a clause in the treaty formally provide that no tax on real estate should be levied either in the Transvaal or the Orange River Colony to defray the cost of the war, but the British agreed to pay £3,000,000 for the restoration of the farms destroyed in the course of hostilities, and if that amount should prove too little, a loan was promised on extremely generous terms. When, in August, the three Boer generals Botha, Delarey, and De Wet visited London to settle further questions connected with the restoration of peace they were welcomed by the noisy cheers of the crowd.

The little war, begun so light-heartedly, had lasted thirty-one

[1] A. Brodrick, March 22, 1901: 'I did all in my power to urge Milner to change his views, which on this subject' (the question of an amnesty) 'seem to me very narrow. Milner's views may be strictly just, but they are to my mind vindictive.' (Sir George Arthur, *Life of Lord Kitchener*, vol. ii, pp. 21–2.)

[2] For a good account of the Vereeniging negotiations, see ibid., pp. 90 sqq. See especially pp. 93 sqq.: Lord Kitchener's despatch of May 21 in which he sets out his differences with Milner on the financial clauses of the treaty. See also J. D. Kestell, *Through Shot and Flame. The Adventures and Experiences of ——, Chaplain to President Steyn and General Christian De Wet*, 1903, pp. 273 sqq. See also in Lord Shaw of Dunfermline's *Letters to Isabel*, 1921, pp. 202–3, the account of a remarkable interview between Kitchener and General Smuts which seems to have decided the Boers to sign the treaty, and in Henry W. Nevinson's *Changes and Chances*, pp. 318–9, the story of an equally remarkable interview with Milner on May 27.

months. It had cost £250,000,000. It had been found necessary to send out to the other end of the world 450,000 troops, of whom 22,000 never returned.[1] Nevertheless, the final victory seemed enough to save the credit of a Cabinet which, during the last year of the war, had made itself unpopular by its carelessness and sloth and by the manner, too cool in all conscience, in which it counted on patience and time to supply the admitted lack of method and ability. The internal dissensions which weakened the Liberal party, and which the war had only aggravated, encouraged the Government in the belief that in spite of the difficulties which several serious problems of domestic policy were likely to cause, it would be a long time yet before the Opposition was ready to take their place. And for the next three months a succession of excitements blinded the public to the weariness left by a strain of almost three years.

The coronation had been fixed for June 26; but the King's health was bad. It was believed, indeed he believed himself, that he was suffering from a cancer, and he looked forward with dread to the terrible fate of his brother-in-law, the Emperor Frederick. On the eve of June 26th the arrangements were countermanded, since an immediate operation had been declared necessary. It was performed; the disease was found not to be of the malignant nature which had been feared and King Edward's recovery was so rapid that the coronation could take place on August 9 with the customary ceremonial. It was a brilliant pageant which revived the imperial pomps of 1887 and 1897, and its effect on the spectators was enhanced by the fact that, owing to the length of the previous reign, only octogenarians could remember the last coronation. Edward VII was proclaimed King not only 'of the United Kingdom and Ireland' but also 'of the British dominions over the seas' and not only King but Emperor—'Emperor of India'. An imperial style, calculated to impress the world. But the diplomatic situation continued to give cause for anxiety. When a great naval review was held in Portsmouth Harbour in which a hundred ships manned by 30,000 sailors took part, only four foreign men-

[1] Official figures. Total number of troops on service in South Africa: 448,725, classified as follows: Regular Army 256,340. Militia of the United Kingdom, Yeomanry, Volunteers 109,048. Colonial contingents 30,333. Troops raised in South Africa 52,414. Slain 5,774. Deaths from wounds or sickness 16,168. Wounded 22,829. Sent back to the base 75,430. (*Times' History of the War in South Africa*, vol. vi, p. 279.) Cf. *Report of the Royal Commission on the War in South Africa*, p. 35 (where a different method of classification is adopted).

of-war came to pay their respects to the new King—two Japanese, one Italian and one Portuguese.

A colonial conference followed. The number of colonial premiers present had been reduced by the union of the six Australian Governments in a single confederation—the Commonwealth of Australia. The same questions were discussed which had always come up since 1887. How far was it possible to obtain from the colonies a formal agreement by which they bound themselves to take their share in imperial defence? Canada refused to make any financial contribution towards the increase of the British navy, and the contributions offered by the other self-governing colonies were very small. Not a single colony would consent to incorporate any portion of its forces in the imperial army. How far, moreover, was it possible to unite Great Britain and her colonies in an imperial federation? The colonies undertook to make certain reductions in their tariffs in favour of British imports. They declined to make any further concessions so long as England, bound by the dogma of absolute free trade, refused their imports a reciprocal preference.

6

Meanwhile, the Foreign Office continued to struggle against the Russian penetration of Persia and the French penetration of Morocco. In July, Lord Salisbury had definitely resigned. Arthur Balfour succeeded him as Prime Minister. The Duke of Devonshire had been passed over. Was this a deliberate rebuff to the partisans of an understanding with Germany? There is no proof of it. If the tension between the two peoples was more acute than ever, diplomatic relations between the two Governments continued to be extremely friendly and a series of official gestures showed the intention of both parties that they should remain so. The Prince of Wales' visit to Germany in January was followed in April by a visit of the Duke of Cambridge to Hamburg to be present at the unveiling of a statue of the Emperor Frederick, and in September the Secretary for War, St.-John Brodrick, and the Commander-in-Chief, Lord Roberts, who, a year before, had been decorated with the Black Eagle by William II, attended officially the great German manœuvres. Then William proposed a visit to Edward VII. He landed in England on November 8.

The following day he was at Sandringham. He stayed there until the 15th, engaged in the customary ritual of a royal visit. He shot wild duck, pheasants, and partridges; planted trees to commemorate his visit; was present at the performance of a little drama by Conan Doyle called 'A Story of Waterloo'. On this occasion his Chancellor, Bülow, did not accompany him, but Count von Eulenburg was with him, and he had conversations with the Prime Minister, Chamberlain, and Lord Lansdowne. On November 15, he left for the North, where he was Lord Lonsdale's guest at Lowther Castle for four days, and spent some hours with Lord Rosebery at Dalmeny. On the 20th, he sailed from Queensferry. Meanwhile, the King of Portugal had arrived at Windsor on the 19th, where he stayed until the 24th.

The Emperor's official reception had been brilliant; the attitude of the public extremely hostile. It was very different now from what it had been during his two earlier visits, when England was passing through difficult times. Even before he landed a chorus of protest had been raised in the Press.

Among the Unionist papers, the *Daily Telegraph*, which was supposed to reflect the views of the Chamberlainites, was polite, and the *Saturday Review* conspicuous for its moderate language. But the *Standard*, the organ of the old Tory party, addressed severe warnings to the Emperor, and the violence of *The Times*, *Morning Post*, *Daily Mail* and *Globe* knew no bounds. No one, it is true, contested the high personal merit of the royal visitor. At this period he was universally regarded as a man of outstanding ability. But what were his intentions? Was there to be further talk of an alliance? The principle of the balance of power forbade England ever to tie her hands by a treaty. She must keep herself free to crush whatever nation appeared at that particular juncture 'the greater menace to Europe'.[1]

On the Liberal side, the *Westminster Gazette*, it is true, uttered a warning against exchanging the Gallophobia of the preceding years for a hatred of Germany equally dangerous to the peace of the world.[2] But the *Daily Chronicle*, the mouthpiece of the Liberal Imperialists, surpassed all the other newspapers in the violence of its attacks, delivered at the very moment when the Emperor William was the guest of their leader, Lord Rosebery, at Dal-

---

[1] *Morning Post*, October 31, 1902.
[2] *Westminster Gazette*, November 10, 1902.

meny. It was not satisfied with political arguments to prove the danger of a German alliance: it entertained its readers[1] with ludicrous stories of all the Emperor's previous visits to the British Court, beginning with the long forgotten occasion when, at the mature age of four, the mischievous 'imp' bit the calves of the little Princes Arthur and Leopold in the Royal Chapel at Windsor. The *Daily News*, the semi-official organ of the Opposition, claimed to know every detail of the plot being hatched between the British and German Governments. It connected the Emperor's visit to Sandringham with the King of Portugal's visit to Windsor, and asserted that the British Government wished to obtain German assent to an agreement it was making with Portugal in regard to Delagoa Bay. It was rumoured that Germany with French support was asking in return for the evacuation of Shanghai. Was this, it asked, the result of Chamberlain's policy? It was high time that Balfour made up his mind to shake off the yoke.[2]

Disconcerted by the outcry, the Government thought it necessary to reassure the public. Speaking on November 10 at the Guildhall banquet Balfour protested against the 'fantastic inventions' occasioned by the imperial visit. The interview, he assured his hearers, had not been in any way concerned with politics. The Emperor's visit had been merely an unofficial visit to 'his nearest relatives'. But if the public were relieved of their fears for the moment, their indignation was the greater when, on December 7, they were informed that England and Germany, after sending a fruitless ultimatum to the Republic of Venezuela, were establishing a joint blockade of the Venezuelan coast, and that British and German cruisers were actually capturing or sinking Venezuelan gun boats.

We remember that seven years before, when the Unionists took office, there had been a Venezuelan question. We remember also that it had been finally settled by arbitration, and that, ever since, Britain had been determined to avoid even the semblance of a conflict with the United States, and that during the Spanish-American War the British Press had been unanimous in hailing

---

[1] *Daily Chronicle*, November 7.

[2] *Daily News*, November 10. For the *Daily News* Chamberlain is the object of suspicion, and *The Times*, though throwing doubt on the *Daily News* revelations, relates a very animated discussion between the Emperor and Chamberlain on the morning of the 9th. For the interview, which bore very little resemblance to the imaginations of the Press, see William's letter to Bülow of November 12, 1902 (*Die Grosse Politik*, vol. xvii, pp. 115–6).

the victories of the United States, as being not so much American victories as victories of the Anglo-Saxon race. This attitude was a bid in advance for American sympathy with any successes British imperialism might achieve elsewhere. And now Balfour and Lord Lansdowne were upsetting the delicate balance of this mighty combination, a combination not so much political as sentimental. Though President Roosevelt's attitude was far more moderate than Cleveland's had been in 1895, the mere shadow of danger to the country's good relations with the United States was sufficient to arouse general alarm. Moreover, what were the circumstances under which the naval demonstration had been made? France, Italy, and the United States had grievances against President Castro similar to those of England and Germany. But Germany was the only power which had taken part in the demonstration —Germany, whose grievances seemed less solid than those of any other nation; Germany, which was widely believed—and especially in the United States—to entertain the design of planting a colony somewhere on the South American coast; Germany, eager to display her new navy to the world. Was it well done of England to help her, and moreover, before the eyes of the whole world, to realize her desire? The outcry in the Press was even louder than it had been in November. *The Times* published a letter from Sir Robert Giffen whose heading 'The Venezuelan Mess' caught the public fancy. 'Germany', he wrote, 'is a false partner, as Austria-Hungary found out in the Schleswig-Holstein business. Our own experience in China lately has been by no means satisfactory. Germany is also our deadly rival and means an attack upon England at a convenient opportunity'.[1] And the same paper published a poem, more violent than even Sir Robert's letter, in which Kipling charged the Government with lying, almost with treason:

> Last night, ye wrote, our voyage was done
> But seaward still we go;
> And ye tell us now of a secret vow
> Ye have made with an open foe![2]

---

[1] *The Times*, December 20, 1902.
[2] Ibid., December 22, 1902. In the lines which follow, the poet unburdens himself of the bitterness accumulated during the three years of the Boer War:

The previous month, certain Liberal organs had attempted to restrain public feeling by protesting, as we have seen, against the excessive hatred towards Germany displayed by the remainder of the Press. This time they swelled the chorus. Nowhere was the cause of Anglo-American friendship held more sacred than among the pacifist intelligentsia which led the Liberal party, and, if it would not support even a war against Germany was still more opposed to a war waged, in central America or elsewhere, as her ally. And the Liberal Imperialists, delighted to find the Party for once united on a matter of foreign policy after long years of dissension, were unwearied in their attacks upon the Cabinet. Foremost among the politicians who were demanding that the understanding with Germany should be brought to an end were Sir Edward Grey and Haldane.

On February 6, Grey, addressing a public meeting, declared himself unable to attach unreserved credit to the assurance given by the Government that there existed no alliance or secret understanding with the German Government. Had not such a pact been quite recently Chamberlain's avowed policy? Though he wished England to remain on friendly terms with Germany, it must not be at the cost of good relations with France or Russia, and still less with the United States. Ten days later, on the very eve of the new session, Haldane took the chair at a meeting at which members of every party were on the platform, among them Leo Maxse, the editor of the *National Review*. The object of the meeting was to demand a squadron in the North Sea and a naval base on the East Coast. When the session opened, it was plain that the ponderous administrative machine had at last been set in motion. The Cabinet, disavowed by its own supporters and attacked by the Opposition, adopted several new measures. A Council of Defence was formed composed of four Cabinet ministers and four mem-

> That we must lie off a lightless coast
>   And haul and tack and veer,
> At the will of the breed that have wronged us most,
>   For a year and a year and a year.
>
> The dead they mocked are scarcely cold,
>   Our wounds are bleeding yet,
> And ye tell us now that our strength is sold
>   To help them press for a debt!

It is a curious fact that both Sir Robert Giffen's letter and Kipling's poem were printed by *The Times* in small type, as though the Conservative organ were afraid the expression of public resentment might endanger the Government.

bers holding high command in the Army and Navy: the Council had as a matter of fact been promised for more than six months. The Budget provided for an enormous expenditure on the navy. As *The Times* pointed out, never before, either in peace or during war, had the naval estimates been so high. What did these preparations portend? They were bound up with a further measure, in conformity, as we have just seen, with the unanimous wish of the House, which occasioned no debate in Parliament, no comment in the Press. On the eve of the day when the naval estimates came before Parliament Balfour announced the Government's intention to establish a new naval base on the North Sea at the entrance of the Firth of Forth. It was obvious that in the opinion of the Admiralty the threat to British naval supremacy no longer came from the traditional foe, to be met in the Channel. It was on the Norfolk coast that an invasion was now feared, and under cover of a fleet which would not be French.

PART II

THE INTERNAL POLICY OF THE UNIONIST CABINET

CHAPTER I

Educational and Religious Problems

I THE PROBLEM OF NATIONAL EDUCATION

I

THOUGH events in the Near and the Far East, the victories in the Sudan, the friction with France, and the South African War seemed to engross the attention of the public, the Cabinet could not wholly neglect meanwhile the problems of domestic policy, which had been so acute during the period which had preceded their advent to power and which, as we shall see, as soon as the Boer war was at end, would prove as urgent as ever and cost the Government their present overwhelming majority. In fact, the Conservative party, as reconstituted under the dual leadership of the aristocratic faction of the Cecils and the Birmingham group, had at its disposal—should it desire to carry it out— an entire programme of administrative reform, the work of the great statesman, who on a former occasion, thirty years earlier, had revived the Tory party after twenty-five years of complete impotence.

It was a programme of social reform. It had been Disraeli's hope that the Tories would improve the material conditions of the masses by an active intervention of the legislature, forbidden to the Liberals by the dogma of *laisser-faire*. And he could say with truth that the promises which he made to the working classes at the election of 1874 had been given long before when, about 1840, as the leader of the eccentric Young England group, he championed Chartism in the House of Commons and wrote *Sybil*. But since then his zeal for social reform had often cooled. It did not revive until an important historical event had taken place, shortly before the last quarter of the nineteenth century opened, of a nature to encourage Conservative social reformers—namely, the sudden advent and rapid rise of the German Empire under the leadership of Prussia.

The most 'progressive' State in the whole of Europe from whatever point of view it was regarded—scientific or military, industrial or social—was the democratic absolutism on the Cæsarian pattern of which Disraeli had dreamed, based on the double foundation of an hereditary monarchy and a democratic Parliament; and every other nation was attempting, more or less clumsily, to imitate in every sphere what he may call the Prussian model; and not only the Continental nations, as at the period when they feared and copied the monarchy of Louis XIV. Even the British nation, which two centuries earlier had been impervious to the charm of French absolutism, now seemed to be yielding to the spell of the Prussian model. Liberals of the old school were at a loss when the young Socialists refuted their timidity by the example of Bismarck, who, during the last ten years of his long career, carried through the Reichstag his comprehensive and celebrated system of compulsory insurance against workmen's risks.

In Germany, one great name dominated the entire history of this political and social development, the name of Hegel. It now seemed that Carlyle who, throughout his career, had regarded himself as an apostle of German metaphysics to the British had given proof of profound insight when he celebrated the praises of Germany and Prussia and sought the source of their excellence in the systems of their philosophers. If England was vaguely apprehensive that the success of the Prussian model might degrade her to the position of a second-rate power, it was perhaps because she had not paid sufficient heed to Carlyle and had taken Bentham too seriously. But Carlyle had made disciples. Hutcheson Stirling, a fellow-Scotchman, who had adopted his deliberately obscure style, had followed him in the attempt to initiate the British public into 'The Secret of Hegel'. Then Thomas Hill Green, at Oxford, as he studied the works of Kant had rediscovered for himself the road of post-Kantian philosophy, and at the moment when the Prussians were victorious at Sadowa and Sedan had inaugurated in the Anglo-Saxon Universities the tradition of what was known as Hegelian 'Neo-Kantism'. We have referred to this group already. At the close of the nineteenth century, Hegel possessed a larger number of avowed followers in England than in Germany.

This 'Neo-Kantism', which provided the Anglican clergy with a species of theology, was the fashion at Oxford, where the heterodox Bradley was even more successful than Green had been in raising the level of metaphysical speculation. It enjoyed an equal vogue in Scotland where it reigned supreme under the ægis of the Cairds and Seths. And in the person of the young MacTaggart it even attempted to force an entrance into Cambridge. Bernard

Bosanquet drew out the full social implications of the new doctrines when, in 1899, he published the work whose teaching we
have resumed above, *The Philosophical Theory of the State*, in which
the state is presented as the instrument and realization of human
personality. Nor was this state some ideal state yet to be born, and
dimly envisaged through the mists of futurity as one with the
entire human race. It was the state, as it actually existed here and
now, the absolute society to which all social values on earth are
subordinate. How distant were the days when young Englishmen
swore by John Stuart Mill, Buckle, and Herbert Spencer? If many
of the neo-Hegelians persisted in calling themselves Liberals, their
Prussianized Liberalism was a different thing altogether—how
could it be otherwise?—from the old British variety. Liberty was
conceived as an organic internal development of the personality,
not as an absence of external restraint, not as a means but as an end.
Therefore, when politicians of the school of Chamberlain or Lord
Rosebery sought to effect a political understanding, even an
alliance, with the German Government, their work was made
easier by the alliance already concluded with German culture by a
school which contained the flower of the rising generation of
thinkers. 'The name', wrote Haldane in 1895, 'of the little territory which encloses Weimar and Jena stirs the imagination of
thousands of our youth of both sexes, even as the name of Jerusa-
lem moved the hearts of men in the centuries behind us.'[1]

Needless to say, German influence was not confined to the
restricted world of metaphysicians. Those numerous Englishmen
who were actuated by the desire to improve social institutions
could not fail to be attracted by the success and efficiency of
German State-Socialism. Among those who came under its spell,
the two heads of the Fabian Society, Sidney and Beatrice Webb,
in virtue of the profound influence which they exercised over the
formation of public opinion during this period of English history,
hold the first place. Eleven years before 1895 this group of students and propagandists had been founded to divert English
Socialism from the paths of revolution and Utopia, and create an
opportunist Socialism which should take concrete shape as a
system of practical legislation, such as Parliament could be invited
to pass without further delay. At first, it would seem, the young
Sidney Webb, who belonged by his birth to a London family of

[1] R. B. Haldane, 'Hegel' (*Contemporary Review*, February, 1895, vol. lxvii, pp. 232 sqq.).

the lower middle class, had hoped to influence the Radical party and transform it into a party of moderate Socialists. But his attitude soon altered. We may conjecture that the change dated from his marriage to Beatrice Potter, the daughter of a wealthy railway director, who had been brought up in the individualist creed but, disgusted by the anarchy and fumbling improvisation inseparable from individualism, had been converted to a scientific Socialism by her passion for order and planning. For it was indeed with a feminine vehemence that the pair of inseparable fellow-workers did their utmost to widen the gulf which separated their social creed from the creed of Liberalism, and to make any compromise, or halfway house, impossible. They did not, however, dream of founding a Socialist party independent of the two traditional parties; they were obviously fascinated by the success of the Bismarckian State-Socialism.

We have seen them already during the Boer War uniting with the imperialists to deride the anti-militarist principles of the Radical party. We shall see them look to Chamberlain to copy the Prussian model in England and carry out a programme of social reform, conceived in a spirit, not revolutionary, but, to use a term then coming into use, 'constructive'. In their *History of Trade Unionism*, which appeared in 1895, they made a point of bringing into relief the part taken by the Tories in the teeth of opposition from the Liberal middle classes in building up a code of industrial legislation to protect the workers in the factories and mines. In their *Industrial Democracy*, published two years later, a work which is one long panegyric of State Control, an inconspicuous footnote calls the reader's attention to 'the increasing incapacity of the House of Commons to cope with its work' and suggests that England would 'be saved by the Royal Prerogative'.[1] Did the Fabian group swallow blindly the entire philosophy of the Webbs? There were no doubt a large number of Fabians who either failed to perceive where the Webbs wished to lead them, or, if they did, felt uneasy. But they were too English to be disloyal to their chiefs, especially since the group had good cause to be proud of two such eminent leaders. Willy-nilly they caught the infection of their ideas and so came indirectly under the spell of the Prussian model.

[1] *Industrial Democracy*, p. 800.

2

To the question what was the aspect in which, more than in any other, the Prussian model invited the imitation of the whole of Europe—what was the particular German institution to which, by the unanimous consent of all enlightened men, the German victories of 1866 and 1870 were due—the answer is not in doubt. Long since, many years before the foundation of the Empire, Prussia had decided that the State must take possession of every child at its birth and follow him to the elementary school, the secondary school, and the University to form the fully developed man, the perfect servant of society; and her present supremacy was the reward merited by her excellent system of education. What steps had England taken to raise her educational standard to the Prussian level? And what still remained to be done?[1]

For many years England had been satisfied with making grants to schools established by private initiative—voluntary schools. The State had also set up schools for the children of the paupers in the workhouses. And a statute had been passed by which children under thirteen years of age employed in factories were obliged to receive a rudimentary education. It was not until 1870, four years after Sadowa, and the year of Sedan, that Parliament extended elementary education to every child in the country. The Act passed in that year was intended, not to supersede, but merely to complete, previous enactments. It provided that in any locality in which there were not enough schools to meet the needs of the children, schools must be erected and maintained at the ratepayers' cost. For educational purposes it set up administrative areas in each of which a school board was to be elected by the ratepayers. All schools built under the provisions of the Act were placed under the management of the boards, which were empowered to levy the necessary rate.[2] At first it was left to the boards to decide whether the education given in their schools should be compulsory (between the ages of five and thirteen) or optional. But compulsory attendance at school, extended by an

[1] For the state of primary education in England about 1895 see *First Report of the Royal Commissioners* appointed to inquire into the *Elementary Education Acts*, 1886; *Second Report* 1887; *Third Report* 1887; *Final Report* 1888.
[2] 33 & 34 Vict., Cap. 75: An Act to provide for public Elementary Education in England and Wales (*Elementary Education Act*, 1870).

Act of 1876,[1] was made universal in 1880[2] and enforced in all cases in which attendance had been optional under the statue of 1870—that is to say, from the age of five until the child had reached a certain standard of knowledge, which, however, was not everywhere the same. Each school board was empowered to fix the age at which the obligation to attend school should cease, though it might not be extended beyond the completion of the 13th year. When once education had been made compulsory, it was very difficult not to make it free. An Act passed by a Conservative Government in 1891 provided that every school,[3] whether it were a voluntary school or a board school, should be entitled to a grant of ten shillings a year for every child, subject to the following conditions. If the school charged a fee of over ten shillings, it must be reduced to ten shillings. If the fee was not more than ten shillings, the school must become free. The effect of the Act of 1891 was to increase indefinitely the number of free schools, and by 1895 all, or practically all, elementary schools were free.

But the system of elementary education which these statutes had established in Great Britain was still defective. At the international congress held in Berlin in 1890 the British Government had promised to make compulsory education universal up to the age of twelve, but Parliament had taken no steps to redeem the promise. What indeed could be done, so long as it was legal by the Factory Acts, which the statute of 1870 had not repealed, to employ children in factories from the age of eleven,[4] provided a few hours every day were set apart for education? And how could the Factory Acts be touched without arousing the opposition, not only of the employers, but, what was more formidable, of the entire working class throughout Lancashire and Yorkshire? Admittedly the quality of the teachers left very much to be desired; only a minority had been through the training colleges, and

[1] 39 & 40 Vict., Cap. 79: An Act to make further provision for Elementary Education (*Elementary Education Act*, 1876). The Act (1) forbade the employment of a child who had not fulfilled the provisions of the statute of 1870, (2) set up wherever there were no School Boards, School Attendance Committees to enforce this provision and the provisions of the Act of 1870.

[2] 43 & 44 Vict., Cap. 23: An Act to make further provision as to Bye-laws respecting the attendance of children at school under the *Elementary Education Acts* (*Elementary Education Act*, 1880).

[3] 54 & 55 Vict., Cap. 56: An Act to make further provision for assisting Education in Public Elementary Schools in England and Wales (*Elementary Education Act*, 1891).

[4] The Factory Acts fixed the age at ten, but in 1893 an Act had been passed (56 & 57 Vict., Cap. 51) raising to eleven the age below which the obligation of attendance at school admitted of no exceptions.

the remainder who had picked up their education as best they could, learning to teach by actually teaching, taught very badly. And it was common knowledge that the obligation of attendance was very laxly enforced in many districts, especially in the country. Nevertheless, it could not be denied that the standard of education given in the elementary schools, especially in the board schools, was steadily improving, since many who had at first regarded them as beneath their social position—farmers in the country, shopkeepers in the towns—were no longer ashamed to send their children. Moreover, statistics showed a progressive decline in the numbers of the illiterate. The percentage of men and women unable to sign their names in the marriage register had fallen between 1873 and 1893 from 18.8 per cent to 5 per cent of the men, and from 25.4 per cent to 5.7 per cent of the women.[1] Something still remained to be done—but it was only the finishing touches—to bring primary education up to the German standard.

3

We will now consider, at the other extremity of the educational ladder, the institutions for higher education. The Universities of Oxford and Cambridge might have appeared at first sight not to have undergone the least change since the beginning of the modern period. They were still, what they had always been, groups of independent colleges, foundations of venerable antiquity, where teachers and students lived under the same roof, more ready to teach and learn the art of social intercourse than to work side by side for the advancement of knowledge. But this was already to a very large extent a deceptive appearance. Ever since the nineteenth century began the Universities had equipped with a solid erudition a select group of serious students.[2] Since the middle of the

[1] *Statesman's Year Book*, 1895, p. 33. Percentage of persons in England and Wales who signed by mark in the marriage register (1843–93) gives the following figures: The most illiterate counties for men in 1893 were Monmouth, 8.8, Buckingham, 8.4, Cornwall, 8.4, North Wales, 8.4, Cambridge, 8.0, Suffolk, 7.8 per cent. The Scotch figures were very satisfactory. The proportion of illiterates in 1892 was 3.23 per cent of men, and 4.97 of women. In 1857, the proportion had been 12.11 per cent of males and 24.66 females. In Kinross-shire all males and all females and in Orkney and Peeblesshire all males signed their names. In all the divisions except the North West, West Midland and South West the proportion was comparatively low. The most illiterate counties by this test are Sutherland 3.28 per cent males and 11.48 females, Ross and Cromarty 10.41 of males and 30.28 of females, and Inverness with 9.86 and 20.89 per cent.

[2] See my *History of the English People in the Nineteenth Century*, vol. i, *England in 1815*, pp. 543–51.

century progress had been more rapid. That the education given at the Universities might no longer be of a purely literary and abstract nature, the number of subjects in which examinations were held had been increased. At Oxford[1] to the two traditional schools, the Classical School, the School of Literae Humaniores, and the School of Mathematics, two new schools had been added, one for the natural sciences, the other for law and modern history. At Cambridge, two new triposes (public examinations) had been provided: one for the moral sciences, moral philosophy and political economy, modern history, jurisprudence and English law; the other for the natural sciences, anatomy, physiology, chemistry, botany, and geology. About the same period, the reform of the old constitution of the colleges was taken in hand and inquiries by royal commissions[2] had been followed in 1854[3] and again in 1877[4] by Acts of Parliament, the former still very conservative, the latter sweeping in its reforms, which had radically altered the character of both Universities.

A Royal Commission had been appointed, furnished with very wide powers, to revise the constitution of the colleges and the University and to make new statutes. To make possible the foundation of new chairs, the colleges had been obliged to contribute, in proportion to their wealth, to the funds of the University. Their finances had been inspected and set in order. The conditions of entrance had been rendered uniform. And though to the majority of college fellowships active duties of teaching or administration were attached, a certain number of temporary fellowships were retained, sinecures which provided their holders with the necessary leisure for disinterested research. Steps had been taken to break down the barriers which divided the colleges, to make it possible for undergraduates to attend lectures outside their own college and thus to lay the foundation of a division of

---

[1] For an account of the progress achieved see Hon. G. C. Brodrick, *A History of the University of Oxford*, 1886; J. Bass Mullinger, *A History of the University of Cambridge*, 1888.

[2] A Royal Commission appointed for the purpose of holding an inquiry into the state, discipline, studies, and revenues of the University and Colleges of Oxford (1850)—of Cambridge (1851).

[3] 17 & 18 Vict., Cap. 81: An Act to make further provision for the good Government and Extension of the University of Oxford, of the Colleges therein, and of the College of Saint Mary, Winchester (1854).

[4] 40 & 41 Vict., Cap. 48: An Act to make further Provision respecting the Universities of Oxford and Cambridge, and the Colleges therein (*Universities of Oxford and Cambridge Act*, 1877).

labour between the colleges. An attempt had even been made to enable a student who was not a member of any college to follow the University course and attend college lectures. Moreover, in 1895, a quarter of a century had passed since membership of the Universities had been thrown open to those who did not belong to the Anglican church,[1] and the obligation of the fellows to celibacy had been abolished at the great reform of 1877. The Universities were being modernized. At Oxford the change was more striking, because it had been more badly needed. But Cambridge followed the same path as her sister University.

Not to speak of the Scottish Universities, England possessed other institutions for higher education. Twelve provincial towns had their University Colleges.[2] Three of these—the Colleges of the great industrial centres of the North, Manchester, Liverpool and Leeds—were incorporated in a single University situated in Manchester, which conferred degrees on the students of the three colleges.[3] Durham already possessed a University.[4] And in the near future the Colleges of Manchester, Liverpool, Leeds and Birmingham would become independent Universities. In the final term of 1894 over 20,000 students were attending the institutions for higher education in Great Britain. No doubt these provincial colleges bore little resemblance to the two ancient Universities. If certain branches of technical instruction flourished, they could not claim to be centres of culture. But they were capable of turning out students fit to complete their education at Oxford or Cambridge, among the 3,000 undergraduates of either University.[5] One thing at any rate was beyond dispute—the high esteem in which the study of the natural sciences was held in England at the close of the nineteenth century. The discovery of new elements in the atmosphere—argon, helium, neon—attracted public attention. Of less popular interest, but far more revolutionary in its significance, was the electro-magnetic theory of matter, outlined by Maxwell and Lord Kelvin and worked out in detail by J. J. Thom-

[1] 34 & 35 Vict., Cap. 26: An Act to alter the law respecting Religious Tests in the Universities of Oxford, Cambridge, and Durham and in the Halls and Colleges of these Universities (*Universities Tests Act*, 1871).
[2] Aberystwyth 330 students; Bangor 162; Manchester 891; Newcastle 2,164; Nottingham 442; Sheffield 290; Birmingham 607; Bristol 403; Cardiff 308; Lampeter 129; Leeds 705; Liverpool 386 (*Statesman's Year Book*, 1895, p. 34).
[3] A. Lawrence Lowell, *The Government of England*, 1908, p. 349.
[4] Since 1880: 196 students in 1894.
[5] In the final term of 1894, Oxford had 3,256 undergraduates, Cambridge 2,839. (*Statesman's Year Book*, 1895, p. 34.)

son. The position had changed, vastly, since those early days of the century when the pioneers of modern chemistry and physics were elf-educated men outside the official centres of learning. Today, all the leaders of science were University professors, savants duly provided with the official diploma. Lord Rayleigh and Ramsay in London, J. J. Thomson and James Dewar at Cambridge, Ray Lankester at Oxford, Oliver Lodge at Liverpool, Lord Kelvin at Glasgow, P. G. Yait at Edinburgh, what country in Europe could boast of more famous names than these? Nothing, therefore, was needed except to encourage the foundation of new colleges in the provinces by local initiative and allow the system of education at the older Universities to develop freely along the lines laid down by the new constitution which the Act of 1877 had enabled them to adopt. If Oxford and Cambridge retained many of the advantages of the old system, so much the better. They were the better suited to the needs of that vast majority of their students who were neither scholars nor savants. Great Britain could claim with truth that by the end of the nineteenth century her system of higher education had borrowed from the Continent everything worth borrowing and had attained the standard of the German model.

4

When we turn our attention to the secondary education which bridges the gap between primary and higher education, and ask what had been done to introduce into the native chaos of the British secondary schools some degree of the order which prevailed on the Continent, and in Germany in particular, the question is not at all easy to answer in a few words. Here, as in the case of higher education, there had been no apparent change during the past century. The State still stood aside. Everything was still left to the same foundations of ancestral piety, the endowed schools. These were the public schools where the children of the gentry and upper middle class received their education and the grammar schools attended by the children of the lower middle class. Around these venerable institutions, and some more recent foundations which strove to imitate them, was the same old welter of private schools, whose headmaster might occasionally be an enthusiastic and disinterested educational reformer, but was more often a tradesman, intent on making his profit out of his customers. On the other hand, here, as in the sphere of higher education, something had been done to regulate the system and bring it up to date. But it must be added that no one felt, as they felt in the case of the Universities, that the reforms which had been carried out satisfied at any point the needs of the age and that enough had been done to realize the ideal put forward by Matthew Arnold, when, about the time of the Second Reform Bill, he contrasted the mediocrity of the public schools with the efficient education given in the French lycées and the German gymnasiums. We must try to explain what had been accomplished and what remained to be done.[1]

About the middle of the nineteenth century a number of schoolmasters in the west of England had conceived the idea of instituting what they termed middle-class examinations, that is to say, examinations for the benefit of those children of the lower middle class who did not go to the public schools. They hoped in this way to raise the educational standard and social position of the second-class schools which these children attended. When the scheme proved a brilliant success in Devonshire and had been adopted in several of the neighbouring counties, the founders asked the Universities of Oxford and Cambridge to take control of the movement and organize throughout the country a uniform system of examinations. They granted the request and instituted for the benefit of every town that desired to present for examination the pupils in its secondary schools, a system of certificates, and the two ancient Universities gave proof that they were in touch with the spirit of the age by including among the subjects for examination English literature, modern history and languages, physics, and other branches of natural science—subjects hitherto despised by the secondary schools. This system of examinations, which was shortly completed by a system of inspections, was received with general approval; about 1895 some 15,000 children

---

[1] For the condition of secondary education in England about the end of the 19th century see in the first place the extensive official report issued in 1895. *Royal Commission on Secondary Education*, vol. i. *Report of the Commissioners*, 1895, part i. *Historical Sketch*, part ii, *The Present Condition of Secondary Education in England*. See also *Studies in Secondary Education*, edited by Arthur H. D. Acland and H. Llewellyn Smith, with an introduction by James Bryce, 1892; the description by an American observer, Isaac Sharpless, *English Education in the Elementary and Secondary Schools*, 1892, and a French description by Max Leclerc, *L'Education des classes moyennes et dirigeantes en Angleterre*, 1894. See finally, Prof. Sadler, *Syllabus of a Course on the History of Education in England, 1800–1911*, 1911.

of both sexes took the annual examination. And a system closely similar had been introduced in the public schools.[1]

The Universities had not been satisfied with raising the standard of the secondary schools by acquiring a control over their curriculum. They also sent lecturers into the provinces to supply the deficiencies of the existing institutions. In this case also the invitation had come from the provinces. The isolated lectures given at first soon became continuous courses. Then the lecturers began to publish text books to assist their lectures. They corrected papers and transformed their courses into classes in which the student worked under the lecturer's supervision, until finally a system of education had been organized extending over several years, a certificate being granted at the end of each year to any student who passed an examination. It was Cambridge which in 1871 had taken the initiative in organizing this 'University Extension'.[2] In 1877 Oxford followed the example of Cambridge and in their turn London and the new Universities of northern England were drawn into the movement. In 1895, these missionaries from the Universities had been lecturing up and down the country for fifteen years. It was as though the zeal which a century before had sent the Methodist preachers to the remotest corners

[1] So rapid indeed had been the growth of the examination system that certain teachers took alarm: See *Secondary Education Report*, 1895, pp. 60, 134-5, 181. Cf. Sharpless, *English Education* . . . p. 69, who however adds: 'It' (the system of examination) 'however, suits the present temper of the English people. They have a security against shams. Good work of a certain sort has recognition, and undoubtedly poor work is mercilessly exposed.' Certain Continental students of British life whose admiration for British institutions was measured by their unlikeness to their own were filled with dismay. See E. Boutmy's preface to Max Leclerc's *L'Education en Angleterre*, pp. 13-14: 'I admit that the local examinations by which Oxford, Cambridge, and London control the curriculum in all schools taking the examinations leaves me with very mixed feelings. I seem to see the examination disease, the certificate fever, more deadly, I am inclined to believe, than any of the plagues of Egypt, infecting the entire country.'

[2] For an account of the movement see *University Extension Past, Present, and Future*, by H. J. MacKinder and M. E. Sadler, ed. 3, 1891; *Eighteen Years of University Extension*, by R. D. Roberts, 1891; *Secondary Education Report*, 1894. Memoranda on the University Extension Movement (vol. v, pp. 285 sqq.). Max Leclerc, *L'Education des classes moyennes et dirigeantes en Angleterre*, 1894, pp. 277 sqq. H. J. MacKinder and M. E. Sadler (*University Extension Past, Present and Future*, 1891, p. 44) give the following statistics of the growth of the movment:

Courses of Lectures	Oxford	Cambridge	London	Total
1885-1886	27	82	63	172
1890-1891	192	135	130	457
Average Attendance				
1885-1886	3,000	8,557	5,195	16,752
1890-1891	20,248	10,947	12,923	44,118

of England had donned secular garb. But these new missionaries addressed their audience of 50,000 on subjects very different from justification by faith. They lectured on Shakespeare, the Italian Renaissance, the French Revolution, and Greek Art. Sometimes, with their students' assistance, they staged the translation of a drama by Æschylus or Sophocles. The majority of their audiences were adults who in later life wished to fill gaps in their education. But children from secondary schools often attended the courses.[1] The University Extension movement was completed by the foundation of two Extension Colleges, one at Reading, the other at Exeter, foundations due respectively to the action of Oxford and Cambridge, permanent institutions[2] intended to link University education with the admittedly insufficient education given in the secondary schools.

5

Upon the action of the Universities was superimposed the intervention of the State. We may even wonder whether, when Oxford and Cambridge assumed the responsibility of regulating

[1] 'Most of the courses arranged by the Delegacy [of Oxford] are attended by some scholars from secondary schools. To provide instruction for such scholars is not the primary aim of the delegacy. On the contrary, it actually discourages the attendance of younger scholars by refusing to admit to the final examinations any candidate under fifteen years of age. Nevertheless, a large number of the elder pupils in the secondary schools attend the courses given under the superintendence of the delegacy. If the ordinary centres are taken, it appears that about 11 per cent of the audiences are elder pupils from secondary schools.' (*Memorandum from the Oxford University Extension Delegacy*, *Secondary Education Report*, 1894, vol. v, p. 289.) And the memorandum suggests that the University Extension movement might be regularly utilized (1) to complete the education of the staff of the secondary schools, (2) to supplement their curriculum. Evidence to the same effect is contained in the report presented by the University of Cambridge Local Examinations and Lectures Syndicate (ibid., pp. 296 sqq.) and in the Report of the London Society for the Extension of University Teaching (ibid., p. 300). The testimony of the latter is the more valuable because the writer of the report is frankly opposed to this 'secondary' utilization of the University Extension courses.

[2] For the clientèle of the Reading college see *Secondary Education Report*, vol. v, pp. 302 sqq.: The Memorandum from the Principal of the University Extension College, Reading: 'Some come from the elementary or the evening school at the age of fourteeen, others from the second-grade school at sixteen, and yet others from the first-grade school at eighteen. . . . It should be added that the College is the pupil teacher centre for the district, and thus carries on what is essentially a piece of secondary education, though outside the regular scheme, and with peculiariy intimate bearing on elementary education.' For the Exeter college see ibid., p. 304, the Memorandum by Miss Montgomery, Hon. Sec. of the Technical and University Extension College, Exeter: 'By far the larger portion of children leave the elementary and secondary schools at an early age with no idea of going to the high schools, where they do not find precisely such teaching in Latin, modern languages, English, geography, history, and mathematics, as would fit them for commercial life, clerkships, civil service appointments, etc. There was, in fact, great want of such teaching as is given in the German Real Schulen. This want our College supplies.'

and developing the institutions for secondary education, it was because they were alarmed by the disposition the State had shown to take up the matter and hoped to prove by the activity they displayed that its intervention was superfluous. A Royal Commission had been appointed in 1861 to inquire into the nine principal endowed schools in the kingdom.[1] The inquiry resulted in the passing in 1868 of a statute which reformed the government of seven of these schools.[2] Thus Parliament, adopting the policy for which Brougham had contended at the beginning of the century, claimed the right to supervise the management of these old charitable foundations and to intervene, if it was proved that the founders' intentions were not being properly carried out. A second Commission, appointed in 1864, had investigated the manner in which the schools omitted from the former inquiry were being conducted,[3] and it was in consequence of a recommendation made by the Commission that a permanent body of Commissioners had been set up,[4] incorporated in 1874 in the Board of Charity Commissioners,[5] to control the endowed schools. The board was empowered not only to exercise a very extensive control over the management of institutions for secondary education, but to issue syllabuses prescribing the subjects of study with a view to adapting the education given in these schools to the new needs of the age. It was given a right of inspection, which was systematized in 1887.[6] In every school under the control of the Charity Commissioners an examination must be held annually, and the Commissioners reserved the right to order a special examination to be held, whenever it seemed to them desirable. In 1895, of the 1,448 endowed schools, 902 had been already reformed in accordance with their instructions.[7] We should, therefore, be wrong, if we regar-

[1] *Report of H.M.'s Commissioners on Revenues and Management of Certain Colleges and Schools, Studies pursued, and Instruction given*, 1864.

[2] 31 & 32 Vict., Cap. 118: An Act to make further Provision for the good Government and Extension of certain Public Schools in England (*Public Schools Act*, 1868).

[3] *Report of Commissioners on Education in Schools in England, not comprised. within her Majesty's two recent Commissions on Popular Education and Public Schools*, 1867-8.

[4] 32 & 33 Vict., Cap. 56: An Act to amend the Law relating to Endowed Schools and other Educational Endowments in England, and otherwise to provide for the Advancement of Education (*Endowed Schools Act*, 1869).

[5] 37 & 38 Vict., Cap. 87: An Act to amend the Endowed Schools Acts (*Endowed Schools Act*, 1874).

[6] *Secondary Education Report*, 1895, p. 59: A Select Committee of the House of Commons on the Endowed Schools Acts, 1887, had advised that the work of inspection might be more efficiently carried out by the appointment of a number of supernumerary Assistant Commissioners.

[7] Ibid., pp. 8-9.

ded the endowed schools about the year 1895 as representing nothing more than the haphazard operation of uncontrolled private initiative. They were an organization placed under the permanent control of government officials and liable to their constant interference.

The Report of 1864 had gone further. If all its recommendations had been carried out, bodies of officials, constituting a special department of the public services, would have been created to control public education, both in the capital and in the local government areas. A Central Council of Education would have been set up to regulate the conditions of examination and appoint examiners. And the towns and parishes would have received the right to levy a rate for the erection and maintenance of schools.[1] On all these points it might seem that nothing had been done to give effect to the recommendations of the Commission. The statute of 1870 which set up the school boards was concerned only with the elementary schools. But it is significant that a corresponding statute for Scotland, passed two years later, placed not only primary but also secondary education under the control of the school boards,[2] and, moreover, that even in England the line of demarcation between elementary and secondary schools was so indefinite, that the school boards were tempted to extend their authority to schools not in the strict sense elementary. The Education Department had been left free to determine the limits of its jurisdiction by administrative regulations[3] and had made use of its discretion to extend its powers and permit the school boards to establish higher-grade schools which provided an education to

[1] Schools Inquiry Commission, vol. i, *Report of the Commissioners*, 1868, pp. 629 sqq.

[2] 35 & 36 Vict., Cap. 62: An Act to amend and extend the provisions of the Law of Scotland on the subject of Education (*Education (Scotland) Act*, 1872), sec. 62: 'With respect to such schools existing at the passing of this Act, in which the education given does not consist chiefly of elementary instruction in reading, writing, and arithmetic, but of instruction in Latin, Greek, modern languages, mathematics, natural science, and generally of the higher branches of knowledge, the following provisions shall have effect: (1) Such Schools shall be deemed to be higher class public schools, and shall be managed by the school boards accordingly, with a view to promote the higher education of the country.'

[3] The Act of 1870 (33 & 34 Vict., Cap. 75, sec. 1) defined 'elementary school' as 'a school or department of a school at which elementary education is the principal part of the education there given, and does not include any school or department of a school at which the ordinary payment in respect of the instruction, from each scholar, exceeds ninepence a week'. This clause made it possible to define elementary education not by the subjects taught but by the cost. For the manner in which the boards took advantage of this ambiguity of definition, see the remarks contained in the *Final Report of the Commissioners, appointed to inquire into the Elementary Education Acts (England and Wales)*, 1888, pp. 145–6, 164 sqq.

which the term elementary could not possibly be applied. Further, the school boards had become accustomed to utilize their school buildings for classes of every description, and there was no pretence that the instruction given at these classes was elementary. Evening classes had been arranged. They were confined at first to pupils under fifteen. But the age limit was later raised to twenty-one[1] and finally in 1893 abolished altogether.[2] At these evening classes all sorts of subjects were taught—drawing from nature, the differential and integral calculus, spherical trigonometry! The cost of this extensive curriculum of higher education in the elementary schools was defrayed from the most varied sources, both private and public. One of these was the rates which had been imposed by the statute of 1870 to provide for elementary education and for that alone. In this way, by devices of somewhat doubtful legality,[3] the State elementary education invaded the sphere of secondary education which the indifference of Parliament had left vacant.

The difference, however, had not been complete. During the years which immediately preceded the Election of 1895 Parliament had shown itself anxious to fulfil the duties of a democratic State in the matter of education. The opportunity was provided by the important Act passed in 1888 to remodel the system of local government.[4] Hitherto, on every occasion during the previous half-century when Parliament wished to institute some new branch of public service, its administration had been committed to elected bodies (boards they were called) specially set up for the purpose. There were Boards of Poor Law Guardians, Public

[1] *Education Department, Minute of the 31st May, 1892, establishing a Code of Regulations for Evening Schools*. By the Right Hon. the Lords of the Committee of the Privy Council on Education, 1892.

[2] *Education Department. Minute of the 18th May, 1893*, by the Right Honourable the Lords of the Committee of the Privy Council on Education, establishing a Code of Regulations for evening continuation schools, with explanatory Memorandum, schedule and appendix. The following were the objects which the evening classes had in view: (1) To supply the deficiencies of elementary education; (2) To continue the pupil's general education; (3) To prepare pupils for 'the special studies directed by the Science and Art Department, or for lectures established by the County Councils, University Extension Lectures, or other forms of secondary or higher education.'

[3] For the extremely complicated question how far these various encroachments by the School Boards into the domain of secondary education were illegal, see Sir John Gorst's very clear speech, H. of C., March 5, 1901 (*Parliamentary Debates*, 4th Ser., vol. xc, pp. 609–10).

[4] 51 & 52 Vict., Cap. 41: An Act to amend the Laws relating to Local Government in England and Wales and for other purposes connected therewith (*Local Government Act*, 1888).

Health Boards, and, since 1870, School Boards. Now, in every county, a Council was established, elected by the inhabitants—the County Council—intended in principle to provide for all the needs of the district. Why not hand over to these Councils the functions performed since 1870 by the School Boards? And why not at the same time deal with the problem left untouched in 1870 by giving the County Councils authority, for which the School Boards had been thought unfit, to organize not only elementary, but secondary education, as a department of the public service? A recommendation to this effect had been made in the report, issued in 1884, of a Royal Commission appointed to inquire into 'Technical Instruction'.[1]

The proposal was not carried out. Those who were responsible for its defeat did not trust the new Councils to display the requisite interest in the education of the lower and middle classes. They recognized that in the country districts the school boards performed their duties none too efficiently. But would the rural county councils show any greater zeal? In the towns, on the other hand, the school boards were justly proud of the work they had accomplished during the last twenty years. Should such active bodies be sacrificed to a pedantic desire for administrative unification? Moreover, throughout the country, the school boards were Radical strongholds. At a time when the election of 1886 had placed in office a coalition of the old Conservatives and the Liberal Unionists would the Opposition tamely stand by and allow their enemies to destroy the finest piece of work accomplished by the Liberal party, under the conditions created by the Reform Bill of 1867? It was finally realized that the opposition to the new proposal was insuperable. The County Councils, created by the Act of 1888, received no authority over education.

Nevertheless, the failure was not total. As after 1870 a special Act effected in Scotland what could not be done in England, and conferred on the school boards authority to organize a system of

---

[1] *Second Report of the Royal Commissioners on Technical Instruction*, 1884, vol. i, p. 517: 'The existing endowments are very unevenly distributed over the country: in many of the large manufacturing centres no resources of the kind exist; private enterprise is clearly inadequate to do all that is required in establishing such schools, and we must look to some public measure to supply this, the greatest defect of our educational system. It is to be desired that in the proposed reorganization of local government, power should be given to important local bodies like the proposed County Boards and the municipal corporations, to originate and support secondary and technical schools in conformity with the public opinion, for the time being, of their constituents.'

secondary education,[1] so now a special Act did for Wales what the Act of 1888 had failed to do for England. An Act of 1889[2] transferred to Education Committees, the majority of whose members were elected by the County Councils, the control over secondary schools hitherto vested in the Charity Commissioners, and at the same time empowered these committees to levy, with the sanction of the County Council, a special rate to provide for their maintenance. Even in England the County Councils soon received educational powers not conferred by the statute of 1888. By an Act passed in 1889[3] they (in common with certain other local authorities) were authorized to levy a rate for the promotion of 'technical or manual instruction'. It must not exceed one penny for every pound of the total rate. But in 1890 more considerable funds were placed at the disposal of the Councils. The duty on beer and spirits had produced a large surplus, and an Act was passed[4] by which a part of this surplus—£743,200 in 1890—which came to be called the whisky money was assigned to the Councils to facilitate the operation of the Technical Instruction Act of 1889.[5]

6

The language of these statutes is worth notice. Though concerned with an education above the elementary standard, they speak not of secondary but of technical education. Hitherto we have investigated the measures taken in England to provide a cer-

---

[1] See above, p. 153 and note[1].
[2] 52 & 53 Vict., Cap. 40: An Act to promote Intermediate Education in Wales (*Welsh Intermediate Education Act*, 1889).
[3] 52 & 53 Vict., Cap. 76: An Act to facilitate the Provision of Technical Instruction (*Technical Instruction Act*, 1889).
[4] 53 & 54 Vict., Cap. 60: An Act for the Distribution and Application of certain Duties of Customs and Excise, and for other purposes connected therewith (*Local Taxation [Customs and Excise] Act*, 1890, sec. 1, (2) (3) (4)).
[5] For the results achieved by these measures see the statistics furnished by the *Secondary Education Report* of 1894 (p. 32): 'In England, of 48 county councils, 42 were in 1894 devoting the whole amount of their local taxation money to technical education, and 6 county councils were devoting a part of it. The power of rating for technical education has not yet been used by any English county as a whole. But in 6 counties such a rate has been levied by urban sanitary authorities, most of which have received from the county council a grant equal in amount to the rates so levied. In 1893–4 the rate was levied by 42 urban sanitary authorities and the aggregate amount so raised was £6,044. In the period of four years, ended March 31, 1894, the aggregate amount received by the 48 county councils out of the residue of the Local Taxation (Customs and Excise) Duties was £1,684,288. Of this sum £1,025,583 was in that period expended on education under the Technical Instruction Acts, and an additional sum of £438,635 was appropriated to the same purpose and carried forward.'

tain number of children with an education which would enable
them to enter what we may call the governing class or, more
strictly, the liberal professions, the teaching profession, medicine,
the Bar. But a further question arose. Was the knowledge acquired
by regular practice a sufficient equipment for the exercise of any
trade, the management of any business, whatever its position in
the industrial hierarchy? Was it even a sufficient education for
commerce or banking? The persuasion to that effect which had
once prevailed in England had been weakening for many years
past. It was in 1852, at the very period when the liberal faith in un-
tutored skill was most confident, that a Department of Practical
Arts, transformed the following year into a Department of Science
and Arts, had been established at South Kensington, to provide
museums of science and art and promote artistic and technical
education.[1] Twenty-five years later, the International Exhibition
at Paris once more drew the attention of Englishmen to the defects
of their industrial and commercial organization and the need to
improve it, as was done on the Continent, by making full use of
the resources of science. A Royal Commission was appointed,[2]
and an unofficial association 'for the advancement of technical
instruction' formed to press the Government to implement its
report. After two Bills, one introduced by the Government, the
other 'private',[3] had been rejected, the Technical Instruction Act
was finally passed in 1889, and in 1890 the Government provided
the Local Authorities with the funds necessary to work it. But
the provision made by these Acts of 1889 and 1890 was far from
satisfying the demands of public opinion; the complaints were
even louder and more insistent than they had been in 1851 and
in 1878. For more clearly than ever the English perceived the
dangers which threatened their industrial supremacy. At the very
time when theoretical science was achieving its brilliant victories,
and the Cambridge school was astonishing the world by the
boldness of its hypotheses, England seemed to have lost that gift

[1] First Report of the Department of Practical Arts, 1853. First Report of the Department
of Science and Arts, 1854.
[2] A Royal Commission to inquire into the Instruction of the Industrial Classes of
certain Foreign Countries in technical and other subjects for the purpose of comparison
with that of corresponding classes in this country; and into the influence of such Instruction on manufacturing and other industries at home and abroad. First Report, 1882;
Second Report, 1884.
[3] H. of C., July 19, 1887: Sir William Hart Dykes' speech (*Parliamentary Debates*, 3rd
Ser., vol. cccxvii, pp. 1465 sqq.), also February 10, 1888: Sir William Roscoe's Bill
(ibid., vol. ccxxii, p. 236).

of technical invention which till lately had been her boast. An Italian, profiting by discoveries made in Germany and France, invented wireless telegraphy.[1] Despised France had invented and perfected the bicycle, invented a method of cold storage for meat, invented artificial silk, made the first experiments in transmitting power by electricity and made use of the German invention of the internal combustion engine to solve the triple problem of automatic locomotion on the roads, under the sea, and in the air. With the one exception of the motor turbine England produced no new invention during the last ten or fifteen years of the century to set beside these creations of foreign genius. It must certainly be admitted that the French did not show a gift of organization equal to their genius for invention. But here the palm belonged not to England, but to Germany. What a brilliant contribution British scientists and engineers had made in former days to the technical development of electricity ! How inestimable the debt of synthetic chemistry to the discoveries of Faraday and Perkins ![2] But England had failed to take advantage of these inventions and discoveries, which already belonged to the past. The centre both of the electrical and chemical industries was situated on the other side of the North Sea. This decline, or at least stagnation, of British industrialism was ascribed by some to hampering legislation[3] and the progress of State Socialism, practised by

---

[1] [Marconi, however, also made use of important work done by the Welsh scientist, Sir William Preece.—*Trans. Note.*]

[2] 'There was a period, not more than thirty or thirty-five years ago, when England led the way in applied chemistry. A new era was opened by the researches into the products of coal tar carried out by the celebrated chemist Hofmann when he was teaching in London. His pupil, Mr. Perkins (now Fellow of the Royal Society), discovered the first aniline dye. Why has the benefit of this new branch of applied science been reaped by Germany? Simply because Professor Hofmann, meeting with no encouragement in England, returned to Germany and took with him his band of assistants. The coal-tar industry, Professor Ramsay has said, left us with Hofmann. Had he remained in this country, the industry would have remained with him, and he would have remained, if a suitable position had been found for him.' (Th. Rothstein, 'La Crise Industrielle en Angleterre', *Le Mouvement Socialiste*, December 15, 1903, pp. 503–4). It is surprising that at a time when the economic interpretation of history is so fashionable, a general history of the progress of modern technology during the age of electricity is still entirely wanting. We may however mention a few books which our researches brought to light and which others might find it worth their while to consult: *Science and the Nation*, by Cambridge Graduates, 1917; *The British Coal-tar Industry, its Origin, Development and Decline*, by Prof. W. M. Gardiner, 1915; the *Reports* (from 1916) *of the Committee of the Privy Council cıScientific and Industrial Research*. See further, for the period with which we are immediately concerned, the excellent article by Kropotkin, entitled 'Recent Science' (*Nineteenth Century*, August, 1898, vol. xliv, pp. 248 sqq.).

[3] It was not until 1896 that mechanical locomotion on the roads was released from restrictions practically equivalent to prohibition by 59 & 60 Vict., Cap. 36. To benefit by the provisions of the statute a 'vehicle propelled by mechanical power must be under three

the municipal bodies to the detriment of private enterprise.[1] But the majority were agreed in laying the blame on an unsound theory of technical education, and called upon the State not to stand aloof any longer but to take such vigorous action as should destroy once for all the tradition of unscientific improvisation and rule of thumb which had formerly been the national boast, but was now regarded as unintelligent routine.[2]

7

In the reformers' opinion the aim of English education must be radically altered. Hitherto, the schoolmaster's object had been to form by games and the study of the classics an élite of gentle-men, and in spite of the attempts recently made to stimulate intellectual rivalry between pupils and schools by competitive examinations and to modernize the curriculum, the public schools clung to their traditions, and all those schools of lesser rank which modelled themselves on the public schools were equally conservative. But schools of this kind could not provide the staff of scientific experts which the new industrial civilizatior so sorely needed to meet the threat from German competition. It was no longer possible to discount the fact that a young English-man on leaving school was intellectually two years behind a German of the same age by the consoling reflection that he made up in character what he lacked in information, and that, if more ignorant, he was better equipped for practical life. How was it

tons in weight unladen, and not used for the purpose of drawing more than one vehicle (such vehicle with its locomotive not to exceed in weight unladen four tons), and so constructed that no smoke or visible vapour is emitted therefrom except from any temporary or accidental cause.' It was only in 1903 (3 Edw. 7, Cap. 36) that the weight unladen was raised from three tons to six tons and a half and that an entire code of regulations was enacted for motor traffic, the term 'light locomotive' being replaced by the term 'motor-car.'

[1] This was possibly true of the electrical industry. See F. Garcke, *The Progress of Electrical Enterprise*. Reprints of Articles from the Engineering Supplement of *The Times* on the British Electrical Industries (1907)—Cf. The Earl of Albemarle, 'Electrical Transmission of Power' (*Nineteenth Century*, January, 1892, vol. xxxi, p. 88). Also Leonard Darwin, *Municipal Ownership*, p. 18.

[2] 'Whereas six of the leading German firms employed on research work staffs of expert chemists, some 300 in all, the entire number engaged in similar work in England was not estimated at above thirty or forty. We are, therefore, not surprised that during the five years 1896–1901 the number of patents taken out by these six German firms for new dyes and other products of coal tar amounted to 946, whereas the six leading British firms only took out 86 patents for similar discoveries' (Th. Rothstein, 'La Crise Industrielle en Angleterre', *Le Mouvement Socialiste*, December 15, 1903, p. 50). Cf. the interesting observations by A. Marshall in his *Industry and Trade* (p. 96).

that in London itself the business houses of the city employed a host of Germans whose presence was unwelcome but whose industry compelled admiration? If English bankers and merchants preferred them to their fellow countrymen, it was because they found them less devoted to sport, more industrious, more methodical, and better educated. Victorian England was beginning to lose confidence in herself. A nation of amateurs was being forced to recognize that it could not compete with a nation of professionals.

The reformers also complained that sufficient provision was not made for secondary education; there were not enough secondary schools, and in those schools there were not enough free places. The extent of the need could not be easily gauged by statistics, for everything depended on the number of children for whom, in the interest of the community, a secondary education was deemed necessary. When, in 1894, the needs of secondary education were investigated by a Commission whose inquiries covered a very wide area, one witness expressed the opinion that a twentieth of the available accommodation should be reserved for holders of scholarships, another asked for a third.[1] How are we to choose between these two opinions? We can only observe that the more radical opinion was gaining ground every day and it was becoming more widely recognized that every position, however subordinate, in industry or commerce, demanded not only natural aptitude but a considerable amount of acquired knowledge and method. Three witnesses before the Commission were even prepared to express the view that secondary education should be as free as primary.[2] One fact, at any rate, had been disclosed by the inquiry—the extremely unequal distribution of educational facilities. In Bedfordshire, the scholarships at secondary schools amounted to 13.5 per cent of the population; in Warwickshire, only to 5.2 per cent. In the manufacturing districts the proportion was lower still: 2.1 per cent in Yorkshire, 1.1 per cent in Lancashire.[3] It could not be reasonably argued that it was impossible to do for Yorkshire what had been done for Bedfordshire, or that to promote the advancement of education in the interest of her industrial development England could not make

[1] *Secondary Education Report*, 1895, p. 167.
[2] Ibid., p. 183.
[3] Ibid., p. 48.

the pecuniary sacrifices she had made in 1870 for the primary education of her people.

If the reforms so widely demanded were to be carried out, and secondary education modernized, industrialized, and improved both in quality and quantity, the first requisite was to put an end to the chaos which prevailed throughout every branch of the educational services, and which had been aggravated by the piecemeal reforms of the last two or three decades.

At the top of the system there was chaos. The Charity Commissioners, who, besides their other duties, had administered since 1874 the Endowed Schools Act, were an independent body unconnected with any government department. The Department of Science and Arts, which for a time had been subject to the Board of Trade, had been placed in 1856, together with the Education Department, under the jurisdiction of the Lord President of the Privy Council and the Vice-Chairman of the Committee of the Council of Education. Nevertheless, without consulting the Education Department, it made grants not only to the technical schools established by the county councils, but to the school boards under the immediate control of the latter. Since 1889[1] the Board of Agriculture had possessed the power to make grants in aid of agricultural education. What functions remained for the Education Department to perform in the sphere of secondary education? We have seen how, by what was little short of an administrative trick, the Department provided in the board schools instruction in a vast number of subjects which were certainly not elementary. Moreover, it possessed the right to control, and make grants to, the provincial University Colleges which, despite their imposing name, were nothing more than secondary schools, and the Training Colleges whose pupils often became, after a period of teaching in the elementary schools, secondary school teachers. But these were makeshifts. In principle, the Education Department, which should have been, as its name suggested, a Department controlling the entire system of national education, had no authority to grant financial aid to secondary schools, or control their management.

At the base of the system there was the same chaos. Since in England the action of the central government was confined to

[1] 52 & 53 Vict., Cap. 30: An Act for establishing a Board of Agriculture for Great Britain (*Board of Agriculture Act*, 1889).

collaboration with the local authorities, it was scandalous that there did not exist in every administrative area a single body, chosen by election, and invested with control over every class of public education. The school boards, it was true, were usually prepared to exceed their legal powers, and whenever the opportunity arose, permit secondary education to be given in their schools. And it would not be difficult for the County Councils, which possessed the right to establish technical schools, to transform them by imperceptible degrees into secondary schools in the full sense. But these attempts to provide secondary education were neither strictly legal nor co-ordinated. Would it be argued on the other side that this competition between rival authorities acted as a stimulus? That anything was preferable to the deadening uniformity of the Continental system? At the period in their history which we have now reached, the English were obviously less impressed than formerly by these 'insular' arguments. They were tired of the waste, the superfluous machinery, and, above all, the restrictions which this system of administrative anarchy involved.

About this time the educational reformers gained a valuable recruit in the young Fabian, Sidney Webb. In 1892 he had been elected to the London County Council with five of his fellow Fabians. He had been immediately appointed chairman of the Technical Education Board—that is to say, had become the minister of public education for London, in so far as it was under the control of the County Council. His province was, it is true, confined to technical education. But if, to use his own words, technical education meant 'all instruction above the level of the elementary school with the exception of Greek and literature',[1] 'technical' became to a very great extent synonymous with 'secondary'. Moreover, there was nothing to prevent the provision of technical education above the secondary standard. Just about this time,

[1] Paper on *Technical Education* read at the Socialist and Labour Congress at Leeds, April 1, 1899 (*The Times*, April 3, 1899). See also the definition in the Act, 52 & 53 Vict., Cap. 76, Sec. 8: 'The expression "technical instruction" shall mean instruction in the principles of science and art applicable to industries, and in the application of special branches of science and art to specific industries or employments. It shall not include teaching the practice of any trade or industry or employment, but, save as aforesaid, shall include instruction in the branches of science and art with respect to which grants are for the time being made by the Department of Science and Art, and any other form of instruction (including modern languages and commercial and agricultural subjects), which may for the time being be sanctioned by that Department by a minute laid before Parliament and made on the representation of a local authority that such a form of instruction is required by the circumstances of its district.'

the Fabians were showing the way. With funds left to the society by a wealthy philanthropist to be spent at its discretion, they established, in a small apartment in the Adelphi, the London School of Economics and Political Science to teach political economy on more modern and more 'socialist' lines than those on which it had been taught hitherto, and to serve at the same time as a school of higher commercial education. The Fabians had also secured a footing in the other public body which controlled the public education of the metropolis. On the London School Board the Fabian Graham Wallas was supreme. But what purpose was served by two bodies in place of a single educational authority? Why this superfluous multiplication of elections calculated to discredit democracy by disgusting the electors? Installed in command of the two educational departments of the largest city in Europe, and at the very door of Parliament, Sidney Webb, Graham Wallas, and their friends decided to make an attempt to unify the entire system of public education of whatever class under the sole authority of the County Councils.[1] If they succeeded, their success both in winning Parliament to their views and in seeing that were carried out would demonstrate the effectiveness of Fabian methods. They would have helped to change the old chaotic society of *laisser faire* into a modern progressive state in which the welfare of the greatest number would be methodically realized by an entire code of laws and administrative regulations.

II THE RELIGIOUS PROBLEM

I

A complete reorganization of the system of public education and, as part of it, of the system of secondary education, at the cost and under the control of the State: that and nothing less was the demand of educational reformers about 1895. But it was not a demand to arouse party feeling. It was quite otherwise with another problem which concerned elementary education: a prob-

[1] See, in so far as it bears upon secondary education, Sidney Webb's evidence before the Royal Commission, *Minutes of Evidence taken before the Royal Commissioners on Secondary Education*, vol. i, pp. 254 sqq., also his paper at the Socialist and Labour Conference at Leeds, April 1, 1899.

lem moreover not peculiar to England, but a standing source of difficulty to the statesmen of all western countries. Could the education, even the elementary education with which society judged it necessary to equip its members, be considered complete, if it were not based on a theological foundation? Or, to state the question from a slightly different point of view, was an efficient moral education conceivable without any sanction drawn from traditional religion? How many Europeans, even agnostics, dared return an affirmative answer? In England, very few indeed—so few that the problem in this radical form never arose.

In the first place, the primary schools set up under the Act of 1870 were not secular schools in the full sense of the term. They were intended by Parliament to be Christian, though undenominational. Every morning, class was opened by half an hour devoted to religion, prayers, and the reading of a chapter of the Bible. But this religious instruction was given by the schoolmaster himself, and a clause of the Act—the celebrated Cowper-Temple clause, as it was named after the member who had moved it—expressly forbade the catechism or any other distinctive formulary of the Church of England to be taught in a board school.[1] In 1870, the clause had aroused considerable protest, and the vast majority of the objectors were not freethinkers. They were Nonconformists who were afraid lest, in spite of every precaution, the Anglican clergy should gain control over the religious instruction given in the State schools. But their fears were gradually allayed. The Nonconformists discovered that the undenominational instruction prescribed by the Cowper-Temple clause was precisely that purely Biblical Protestant Christianity which was their religion. The Anglican Church, on the other hand, seemed to regard

[1] 33 & 34 Vict., Cap. 75 St. Sec. 14 (2). Strictly speaking, the statute did not oblige the school boards to introduce any religious instruction into their curriculum. But the number of school boards which made use of this power to establish a purely secular education in their schools was negligible. See *Final Report of the Royal Commissioners appointed to inquire into the Elementary Education Acts*, 1888, p. 113: 'Out of 2,225 School Boards representing the judgment of more than 16,000,000 of our population, only seven in England and fifty in Wales, according to the Parliamentary Returns of 1879, 1884, and 1886, have dispensed entirely with Religious teaching or Observances. . . . Of the School Boards of large Towns, one alone dispenses with reading the Bible, and one alone dispenses with prayers and hymns, while those small boards which shut out direct religious teaching from their day schools are, for the most part, in Wales, where the Sunday School system powerfully affects the whole population.' The statute of 1870 (sec. 7) also made provision for parents who might wish to withdraw their children from the religious instruction. But the number of parents who took advantage of it was practically nil.

the board schools with as much, or almost as much, disfavour, as if they had been completely 'agnostic'. In England, therefore, the battle over education was not fought, as in France, between Catholics and freethinkers, but between the adherents of the sects and the members of the Established Church, though, as we shall see, the latter in their struggle against the Protestantism of the sects were supported by the Catholic minority.

The Anglicans, however, did not ask for the abolition of the board schools or the provision of a more dogmatic type of religious teaching. To understand the nature of their opposition we must refer once more to the Act of 1870. It had not set up school boards in every locality throughout the country. Its sole object had been to provide for needs hitherto unsupplied, and school boards were to be introduced only where the schools founded by private initiative were insufficient to meet the wants of the population. Long before 1870 the State had made grants to the voluntary schools. It continued to grant them after 1870. The situation about the year 1895 is best described by a formula, seemingly paradoxical, but a paradox only to those who are ignorant of the conditions of our western world. Two classes of school were competing against each other: State schools favoured by the Free Churches; free schools favoured by the State Church. We have now to explain the claims and counter-claims of the contending parties.

The Nonconformists refused to acquiesce in a system by which the board schools, with whose teaching they were on the whole satisfied, were available only for a minority of the children. In 1895, 2,446,000 children attended the voluntary schools, only 1,848,000 attended the board schools, and the vast majority of the voluntary schools were Anglican. And even these figures give too favourable a picture of the Nonconformists' position. For if in the large towns and the densely-populated manufacturing districts the co-existence of voluntary schools and undenominational board schools sufficed to protect parents against an Anglican monopoly, this was by no means the case in the country parishes. In these there was usually only one school and that a voluntary school. It was impossible to ask for a school board, for the free school provided ample accommodation. But did it provide the religious and moral teaching the parents desired? These country parishes contained a considerable population of Dissenters, people of modest position, traders, farmers, and artisans, who were delighted to have their place of worship to themselves and thus escape on Sunday the control of the squire and the parson. But they now found themselves obliged to submit to their authority all the week in the school. For the school had been built with the squire's money and taught the parson's catechism. And woe to the Wesleyan or Baptist child who refused to attend the religious lesson.[1] The representatives of the governing class could employ many forms of silent and intangible persecution against people of humble station. To escape this tyranny the Nonconformists demanded a new Education Act which should not be content with providing schools supported by the rates where the voluntary schools did not suffice for the population. They demanded that in every place, without exception, undenominational schools should, as in Scotland, be provided by the public authority for the use of poor children.

We may, at first, feel surprise that the Anglicans should have found cause for complaint. Two and a half million children attended the voluntary schools and of those two and a half million almost two million attended Church schools. This surely was a matter for congratulation twenty-five years after the statute had been passed which at the time they had contested so bitterly. But there was another side to the picture. In the country they reigned supreme, but what of the large towns? In London 513,000 children attended the board schools, only 224,000 voluntary schools.[2] And if, taking the country as a whole, more children were being educated in the voluntary than in the board schools, how much longer would this be the case? Since 1870, when not a single board school was in existence, the number of children attending the voluntary schools had more than doubled, but during the same period the number of children in the board schools had risen from nothing to almost two million. During the past five years the number of board school children had increased by 422,000,

---

[1] For the tyranny exercised by the Anglican Church in the country districts see the speeches by Samuel Smith and Lloyd George (H. of C., May 28, 1900. *Parliamentary Debates*, 4th Ser., vol. lxxxiii, pp. 1525 sqq., pp. 1543 sqq.).

[2] H. of C. June 17, 1898, Sir John Gorst's speech (ibid., vol. lxi. p. 597). A few years later the position of the voluntary schools was still weaker. Only 226,000 children attended voluntary schools in London, as against 752,000 in the board schools. (*Education in the Nineteenth Century. Lectures delivered in the Education Section of the Cambridge University Extension Summer Meeting in August, 1900*, 1901, p. 41. Paper by Sir Joshua Fitch, *Primary Education in the Nineteenth Century*.)

whereas the increase in the number of children attending the voluntary schools had been only 185,000.[1] It was easy to calculate the date when the board schools would educate more children than the voluntary if indeed the number of voluntary schools and children attending them did not begin positively to decrease. For the maintenance of their schools placed a heavy financial burden upon the Anglicans. During the period which immediately followed the statue of 1870 eagerness to compete with the new State schools had stimulated their generosity. But for some time past it had been evident that their funds were no longer sufficient.

The Anglicans, therefore, complained that, under the system established by the Act of 1870, the balance was deliberately weighted against their schools. For in every district where there was a school board—and their number could be indefinitely increased but could never be diminished—it was the school board which in the first instance decided whether more school accommodation was required, and, if necessary, ordered the erection of a new board school.[2] They further complained that the system by which both classes of schools received grants from the State was unfair, since besides the grant the school boards were in receipt of a school rate levied on the local ratepayers. In this unequal contest the voluntary schools could survive only by making economies in the school buildings and furniture—to be condemned by the inspectors of the Education Department—or by cutting down their teachers' salaries, with the result that they could obtain the services only of inferior teachers, and parents preferred to send their children to the board schools. Sometimes the Anglicans were content to ask that the grants made to their schools should be raised. Since 1871 every school had a right to a minimum grant of seventeen shillings and sixpence per child: any additional grant must be earned by a corresponding increase in the revenue derived from other sources. The Anglicans asked that the minimum grant should be raised, or even that no maximum should be fixed. Sometimes they ventured further and asked that no difference should be made between the voluntary and the board schools and that, equally with the latter, the former should receive assistance

[1] For these figures see *The Annual Report of the Committee of the Privy Council on Education to the Queen's Most Excellent Majesty in Council for the year.* . . .
[2] *Final Report of the Commissioners appointed to inquire into the Elementary Education Acts,* 1888, p. 55.

from the local rates in addition to the grant received from the central government.[1]

2

If, as we have just seen, both the Nonconformists and the Anglicans had their grievances and their claims at the end of 1895, of the two parties the Anglicans were by far the more urgent in pressing their demands. For the Liberal party had just placed the Disestablishment of the Welsh Church on its programme, and in consequence the Anglican clergy had played a very active part in canvassing for the Unionists, and when the latter won the election, claimed their reward. Would the new Cabinet act prudently in acceding to their request? Or would it on the contrary, imperil a victory, due not to the support of the clergy, but to causes of an entirely different order? The rapid progress of democracy had, indeed, produced an effect on the position of religion in the country which was beginning to attract notice. Before the Reform Bill of 1832, indeed until the Reform Bill of 1867, the number of Englishmen who practised some definite form of Christianity—Anglicans, Nonconformists or Catholics—was probably twice or three times the number of the electorate. But since 1867, and still more since 1884, the proportion had been reversed and the number of voters, the active members of the political community, far exceeded the number of active members of the Christian denominations. Thus the growth of democracy compelled the English, inclined, as they were, to regard themselves as the most religious nation in the world, to take cognizance of a fact which hitherto in their contempt for the lower orders they had deliberately ignored, that English piety after all was no more than a superficial phenomenon, the appurtenance of a select few. The Quaker, George Cadbury, of whose ardent zeal in the cause of international peace we have already had occasion to speak, had undertaken in 1892 a religious census of his native city of Birmingham.[2] His original intention had been to compare the respective activity of the Church and the sects. But he had reached conclusions

---

[1] For a statement of the Anglican grievances see the report laid before Convocation by the Archbishops' Committee in 1895. (A summary is given in the *Annual Register* for 1895, p. 44.)

[2] *Birmingham News*, December 3–10, 1892. Cf. A. G. Gardiner, *Life of George Cadbury*, p. 274.

equally disturbing to both; in Birmingham the total accommodation in all places of worship—Anglican and Catholic churches and Nonconformist chapels—sufficed for little more than a quarter of the population. Could it be said that the case of Birmingham was unique? Listen to Hall Caine's description, in a novel which enjoyed an enormous sale, of the spiritual and material destitution of London. 'Of the five millions of people in this vast city, not one million cross the threshold of church or chapel. And then remember their condition. A hundred thousand live in constant want, slowly starving to death every day and hour, and a quarter of the old people of London die as paupers.'[1] Charles Booth, the statistician and philanthropist, would shortly provide a scientific verification of the novelist's picture.[2]

It is true, no doubt, that there was little positive hostility to religion among the working classes. They were indifferent to it and content to be represented in Parliament by members of the middle class who paid homage to the traditional beliefs. Nevertheless, this indifference could not fail to cause considerable heartsearchings at a period when the lower classes had obtained political rights. Anglicans and Nonconformists were quarrelling before the eyes of a public uninterested in religion of any kind, and the question arises which of the two parties had more to fear from the irreligion of the masses, combined, as it was, with the growth of democratic institutions.

At first sight it might seem that the Establishment was in the greater peril. In consequence of the decay of the old aristocracy of landowners and the invasion of its ranks by wealthy men of every class, the governing class was becoming less rural, its members spent more time in London or abroad. The clerical profession was, therefore, ceasing to be an apanage of the landed gentry, a career in which their younger sons, if they had leisured tastes and liked to live in the neighbourhood of the family seat, could enhance the moral influence of their cloth by the social influence of their rank. In ever increasing numbers men of humbler station, members of the middle class, farmers, were sending their sons into the Church. Did they hope to see them take their place in this way among the gentry? If this was their ambition,

[1] *The Christian*, 1897.
[2] *Life and Labour of the People in London*, by Charles Booth. Third Series: *Religious Influences*, 7 vols., 1902–3.

it was doomed to bitter disappointment. A clergyman of humble origin found himself condemned to a life of isolation in his vicarage or rectory. He no longer cared to mix with the class from which he sprang, and at the country houses of the neighbourhood he was not received, as a clergyman of the old type had been received, as a friend and an equal. He was badly paid—a full half of the parochial clergy were obliged to live on a stipend of less than £200[1]—and the position of the curates was far worse.[2] No wonder the supply of candidates for ordination fell off. For the last ten years the number of ordinations had been steadily declining,[3] and the position would not improve in the succeeding period.

One fact, to be sure, eased the difficulty which the Church experienced in obtaining a sufficient number of clergy. But it was by no means consoling; for it was the constant increase in the number of posts which as a result of the progressive secularization of British institutions were ceasing to be the monopoly of the Anglican clergy. Thus, while there were fewer candidates to fill

[1] 'Quite half the parochial clergy, beneficed and non-beneficed, have an income of under £200 a year. There are at any rate 6,000 benefices of under £200 a year. What position can a man without private resources be in who accepted twenty years ago, when tithe was at £112, a living of £200 a year, then worth £224, now worth £136 and certain to fall lower? Out of this come (besides the initial first fruits) rates, land tax, house duty, synodals, procurations, tenths, dilapidations, and school subscriptions, amounting probably to £45 or £50. Or worse still, it is glebe and unlet.' (Douglas Maclean, 'The Church as a Profession', *National Review*, vol. xxxiii, pp. 952-3.)

[2] 'The initial stipend of an assistant curate has steadily risen. But this rise is confined to the earlier period of clerical life. The senior men get less and less. While the average income of all the assistant clergy is £130 a year, that of those who have been more than 25 years in the priesthood is but £118, their stipends thereafter decreasing at the rate of a pound a twelvemonth. So much greater is the value set by the public upon juvenile freshness and aptitude for serving tables, for "running" boys' clubs, and so forth, than upon experience and proved ability.' (Douglas Maclean, ibid., pp. 945 sqq.)

[3] The number of persons admitted to the diaconate fell from a maximum of 814 in 1886 to 638 in 1898. (Douglas Maclean, ibid., p. 947.) The following figures are given by the Rev. Anthony C. Deane in an article entitled 'The Falling off in the Quantity of the Clergy' (*Nineteenth Century*, vol. xlc, pp. 1023 sqq.).

1894	1,428	candidates for ordination, of whom 62 per cent were graduates of Oxford or Cambridge.		
1895	1,420	Ditto	60.0	ditto.
1896	1,321	Ditto	58.4	ditto.
1897	1,296	Ditto	58.7	ditto.
1898	1,276	Ditto	57.9	ditto.

The writer continues: 'At the Lent Ordination of this year, the number of men ordained was only 102 (per centage of graduates of Oxford and Cambridge 43). At the corresponding ordination in 1898 it was 113.' And the article concludes with the significant words: 'We want to induce the best class of men to take Holy Orders, and not those who properly would have been failures in any other profession.'

vacancies, there were also fewer vacancies to fill. The Anglican clergy were losing their control of the Universities. In 1891, if the vast majority of heads of colleges were still clergymen (eighteen to five), all the University professors were laymen, and out of the 391 'resident fellows', only 150 were in orders.[1] In the sphere of secondary education law and custom still required that the head-masters of the great public schools should be clergymen of the Established Church. But it was not the same with the large day schools, and the number of clergy on the staff of the endowed schools was rapidly declining.[2] It had been the custom at first to appoint clergymen inspectors of secondary schools. But by the present rule they must be laymen and the few surviving clerical inspectors would soon be extinct.[3] And finally, the great Education Act of 1870 had called into existence an entire new profession, at once secular and intellectual.[4] Perhaps teachers' salaries were still lower than the stipends of the clergy. But teachers had not the same social position to keep up as clergymen; the teacher's wife and himself were not obliged to spend so much on 'appearances'. And, moreover, their salaries were constantly rising under the pressure of a powerful trade union, the National Union of Teachers.[5] The day would come when, their social position rising with their salaries, and the barrier between primary and secondary education broken down, 'many a good schoolmaster would make quite as good an income as a parish clergyman and be in as good a position and would be bringing some of the best possible

[1] F. Prat, *Oxford L'Université* (*Etudes religieuses, philosophiques, historiques et littéraires*, Novembre 1892, vol. lvii, p. 489).

[2] *Secondary Education Report*, 1895, p. 15.

[3] Sharpless, *English Education in the Elementary and Secondary Schools*, 1892, p. 24.

[4] The results of the censuses of 1891 and 1901 are difficult to compare. But the census of 1911 gives exact figures on this point which we are perhaps entitled to use, since the statistical curve between 1901 and 1911 continues a movement begun in the previous decades. Between 1901 and 1911 the number of Anglican clergy fell from 25,235 to 24,859, a decrease of 1.5 per cent. During the same period the number of teachers rose from 230,345 (of whom 171,670 were women) to 251,968 (of whom 183,298 were women) an increase of 17 per cent and 6.8 per cent for either sex respectively. Attention is moreover called to the fact that many pupil-teachers, classified in former returns as 'teachers', are classified in 1911 as 'students'. When due allowance is made for this, we reach the conclusion that the increase for both sexes between 1901 and 1911 was 30.4 per cent and 33.6 per cent.

[5] I. Sharpless' *English Education in the Elementary and Secondary Schools*, 1892, p. 73. 'In 1857 the average salary of certificated masters in the public elementary schools was £65; in 1868 £91; in 1877 £115; while in 1890 it had risen to £120. The average of certificated mistresses received in 1869 £58, and in 1890 £77. The number of masters who were in receipt of salaries of £300 and over was 449. Considering the cost of rent, service and clothing in England, these salaries, while no more than they ought to be, are very respectable and are higher than those of any other nation for similar work.'

influences to bear upon all classes of children'.[1] Dangerous rivals for the Anglican clergy! It was only natural that the latter should complain that the number of candidates for ordination was declining—and at the same time ordained clergymen were left without employment. It is not surprising that to save the voluntary schools from the ruin which threatened them they called upon the State to come to their aid.

3

If, leaving the Church of England, we inquire what dangers threatened Nonconformist pietism from this growth of democracy and secularization of society it might seem at first sight that the Nonconformist bodies had made better provision than the Establishment to cope with the situation and had given proof of a remarkable vitality in the steps they had taken to meet the peril. About the year 1880 the Salvation Army had come into existence. From the historical standpoint it may be regarded as the last of the Evangelical sects; but it was intended to be something very different. It arose as a protest against the excessive multiplication of sects in English Protestantism. Why all these rival sects, when all should be united in a common war against infidelity? The Salvation Army was a corps of missionaries whose sole aim was to teach the doctrine of justification by faith in its simplest form, who refused to distinguish between Christians and opened their preaching halls—their Forts—to all indiscriminately. Their message was addressed primarily to the poor, to working men and women, and their attitude was a tribute to the Socialist feeling just coming to birth. They reproached English Puritanism with its middle-class respectability and a culpable failure to understand that a man of the lower classes was inevitably blinded to religion by the conditions of his lot. His spiritual and bodily welfare could not be separated. To win a sympathetic hearing, you must relieve his bodily needs.

The influence of the Salvation Army soon affected the small sect of 'Friends', the Quakers. Among the Free Churches, the Quakers constituted an aristocracy, practically speaking hereditary, a little church, silent, almost devoid of dogma or cult, but a church in which their very absence threatened to degenerate into

[1] *Secondary Education Report*, 1895, p. 155.

a rigid formalism. The manœuvres of General Booth's army, the blare of his bands and the shouts of his preachers roused the Quakers from their slumber. Wealthy Quaker manufacturers of Birmingham and York, the Cadburys and Rowntrees, felt the selfishness of their secluded piety and were ashamed of the isolation of which their co-religionists were so proud. They determined, like the Salvation Army, to go to the people. Extremely enlightened, and very well informed, their philanthropy, unlike that of the Army, was methodical and scientific. But these modern Quakers no longer prided themselves on being a unique body divided from the other sects by a spiritual gulf. They sought the fellowship of all who were inspired by the same zeal as themselves to combat evil in every form.

About the same date, the Wesleyans came under the same influence. Like the Quakers, though on very different grounds, they regarded themselves as an aristocracy among the Nonconformist sects, the High Church of Dissent. But by maintaining this aristocratic position did they not condemn themselves to extinction? It was against this aristocracy that so many revolts had taken place, to the left of the parent society, which had resulted in the foundation by the rebels of more democratic Methodist groups. And this aristocracy seemed likely to render the Socialist movement a dangerous rival of Christianity among that working class over whom a century earlier the preaching of Wesley and his immediate followers had exercised such a powerful spell. One of the leaders of the Wesleyan body, an organizer and a man of action, rather than a theologian or devotional preacher, Hugh Price Hughes, put himself at the head of what was known as the Forward Movement.[1] The Movement sought to reform the traditional organization of the Society. Its founders had laid down a general rule that no Wesleyan minister might remain more than three years in the same place. Their object in making the rule was to prevent him becoming the moral slave of his flock, and ensure that he always retained the spirit of the missionary and the loyal servant of the Wesleyan hierarchy. But experience had proved that this continual change of place tended to diminish a minister's interest in his work and make him an official, rather than the missionary the rule had been intended to produce. Hugh Price

[1] *The Life of Hugh Price Hughes*, by his daughter, 1905, pp. 190 sqq.

Hughes and his friends were successful[1] in obtaining the establishment in the working-class districts of the large towns of Wesleyan missions where the ministers in charge were encouraged to gain a personal influence over the people by the prospect of remaining indefinitely at their post, if the authorities of the sect thought it advisable. Like the Salvation Army and the Quakers, the Wesleyans also went to the people.

As in the case of the Salvation Army and the Quakers this zeal for social work brought them into co-operation with the other sects. Hitherto the Wesleyans had scrupulously kept aloof from their fellow Nonconformists and had made it clear that in several respects they were closer akin to the Church. Congregationalists and Baptists might be content that their children should receive the undenominational instruction given by the school boards; a section, at least, of the Wesleyans desired a more dogmatic form of religious education and pointed with pride to the special schools which they maintained like the Anglicans and Roman Catholics. At the annual Conference the adherents of the Forward Movement fought this exclusive attitude.[2] They made friendly advances to the other Methodist sects who had seceded from the Wesleyan body fifty or more than fifty years earlier, and began to raise the question of reunion.[3] They made similar advances to the older sects and sought to effect in co-operation with them a Federation of the Free Churches on the broad basis of Evangelical Christianity.

Between 1881 and 1884 in the Midlands, at Worcester and Stafford, the first local councils had been formed at which members of the different Free Churches met for friendly conference. But the movement did not become national and permanent until

---

[1] Not without hard struggles with the Wesleyan church authorities. Under the aegis of the Movement, the laity continued to improve their position in the annual Conference at the expense of the ministers. In 1901, the Conference was jointly opened by ministers and laymen though the ministers still retained the sole right to elect the President. (*The Life of Hugh Price Hughes*, by his daughter, pp. 526 sqq.)

[2] *Manchester Tracts on Education* by James A. Newbold, Tract vi: 'The Rev. Hugh Price Hughes, M.A., and Wesleyan Methodist Educational Policy', 1889.

[3] Reunion had been already effected in Canada, in 1874, and 1882 (W. J. Townsend, H. B. Workman, George Eayrs, *A New History of Methodism*, vol. ii, pp. 220-1), and in Australia negotiations for reunion were in progress (1894-1904. Ibid. pp. 264-5). And in England a tendency not only towards federation but actual union had shown itself in other branches of Nonconformity besides the Methodist. In 1876 the Presbyterian Church in England had united with the English congregations of the United Presbyterian Church of Scotland. (Rev. A. H. Drysdale, *History of the Presbyterians in England: Their Rise, Decline and Revival*, pp. 625 sqq.) In 1891 the General and Particular Baptists had united under the auspices of Dr. Clifford.

the Wesleyans in 1891, and George Cadbury and his friends in 1893 gave it their support. From 1892 a congress of the Free Churches was held annually and at Nottingham in 1893 the National Council of the Evangelical Free Churches took definite shape.[1] Henceforward the Nonconformists could oppose to the Anglican Church Congress the congress of their own federation. They reviewed their numbers and dared to claim that their membership was larger than that of the Establishment. The six leading Nonconformist denominations provided accommodation in their places of worship for 7,610,003, the Church of England only for 6,718,288, and there were 1,807,023 Nonconformist Communicants as against 1,778,351 Anglican: 3,103,285 children attended the Nonconformist Sunday Schools, only 2,329,813 the Anglican.[2] And the superiority became greater still, if, as was only natural in those days of imperialism and world politics, to the Nonconformists of the United Kingdom were added the members of the same denominations in the colonies and in the United States. A few years later the Nonconformists claimed over 21,000,000 'communicant' members in the British Empire and the States, as against 3,500,000 Anglican 'communicants'.[3]

4

These facts were disturbing for the Anglicans and encouraging for the Dissenters on the morrow of the defeat which the latter, in common with the Liberals, had sustained at the polls. But they must be squared with another fact, the universal impression at the same period that all was not well with Nonconformity, the impression conveyed by the current phrase, the decline of Dissent. It was in vain that the Nonconformist authorities brought forward an array of proofs that Dissent was making headway; they did

[1] Hugh Price Hughes, *Free Church Unity: The New Movement* (*Contemporary Review*, March, 1897, vol. lxxi, pp. 348 sqq.). C. Silvester Horne, *Nonconformity in the Nineteenth Century*, 1907, pp. 50 sqq. J. C. Carlile Alexander Maclaren, *The Man and His Message, A Character Sketch*, 1901, pp. 135–6.

[2] For these and many other interesting statistics see two articles by Howard Evans, 'Religious Statistics of England and Wales' (*Contemporary Review*, February, 1897, vol. lxxi, pp. 276 sqq.), also 'The Sects' (ibid., September, 1897, vol. lxxii, pp. 417 sqq.).

[3] C. Silvester Horne, *Nonconformity in the Nineteenth Century*, 1907, p. 159. Fifteen years before, the Methodists, multiplying the number of their communicants by four, claimed a total membership of 30 million (Rev. Hugh Price Hughes, 'John Wesley', *Nineteenth Century*, March, 1891, vol. xxix, p. 478). *Methodist Recorder*, October 22, 1891. But their estimate was contested (*Whitaker's Almanack*, pp. 626 sqq., *The Wesley Centenary and Modern Methodism*).

little to shake the prevailing belief that, if other aspects of the situation were taken into account, it was on the whole more favourable to the Anglicans than to the Nonconformists.

In the first place, that administrative secularization of which we were just now speaking, and from which the Establishment was naturally the first to suffer, was accompanied by a moral secularization, difficult to define precisely, but nevertheless as evident as the former, and more dangerous to the sects than to the Church. As a result of the increasing indifference to religion of the general public, the social position of the Nonconformists was improving every year, and this indifference and tolerance endangered the old Puritan tradition of Dissent. How much easier it had been for the Nonconformists, those Stoics of Christianity, to protest against the lax morality of the upper classes, when a rigid social barrier excluded them from their amusements! Now, a conscience clause admitted their children to all the elementary schools in receipt of grants from the Education Department, and to all the endowed schools, and they could even enter the Universities, once the citadels of Anglicanism. No one took offence at a Nonconformist member of the Cabinet. Indeed, the leading figure in the present Unionist ministry, Chamberlain, was a Unitarian. But these Puritans, softened by the easygoing morality of the new world to which they had been admitted, were becoming ashamed of the rigid code of their sects, played cards, attended races, no longer refused to go to the theatre.[1] In the war which for two centuries had been waged between the Puritans and the drama, the advantage once more lay with the latter. Every year more theatres and music halls sprang up in London and in the provincial towns, and England once more produced dramatists. The spirit most powerful at present was the spirit neither of traditional Protestantism nor of traditional Catholicism. It was the pagan spirit, the spirit of the Renaissance. It would shortly unfold its full strength and display an intense earnestness, hardly comprehensible to nations which have not passed through a century of Evangelical Protes-

[1] Bishop Creighton to Charles Roundell, July 21, 1896: 'Men are living on a moral sense, transmitted and inherited, while they are restive under the discipline and claims of the systems which generated that moral sense. . . . This is especially visible in the decay of Nonconformity. Originally it was a system of rigid discipline founded on the theology of Calvin. The theology decayed and Nonconformity tried to keep its spirit by identifying itself with Liberalism. It was frankly ready to say and do what the most enlightened people wished to have said and done. The result has been disaster.' (*Life*, by his Wife, vol. ii, p. 191.)

tantism. The nineteenth century had not run its course before everyone was vaguely aware that a new spirit was abroad.

When the faith of the laity decays, yet leaves behind it among large numbers what we may call the need of faith, the more sacerdotal varieties of religion prosper to the detriment of those in which the layman plays a larger part and which, to use Luther's formula, invite every adherent to regard himself as a priest. It was, therefore, to be expected that the Church of England should gain ground at the expense of the sects, and that, within the Anglican church, the High Church party should prevail over the Evangelicals, who had hitherto been the dominant party in a church which had caught the infection of Wesleyan enthusiasm. The Anglican clergyman who saw with apprehension the lower classes, now placed by the vote in the possession of political power, escaping from the influence of religion and asked himself what he could do to win their confidence, was driven to the conclusion that, since the emotional methods of Nonconformity were not at his disposal, he must fall back upon the attractions of Catholicism, the scent of incense, splendid ritual, veneration of Mary and the Saints. The clergyman of humble origin who recognized that the country-folk did not regard him with the respect they felt for the parson, when he was a member of the upper classes, found in his situation every inducement, coming, as he did, from theological colleges where his training had been more clerical than the education received at Oxford and Cambridge by parsons of the older generation, to emphasize the sacramental and sacerdotal nature of his office. The layman whose Protestant convictions had weakened lent a willing ear to the new teaching. Since I need a religion, give me one in which the priests relieve me from the effort of thinking for myself. Since I need a religion, give me one whose ceremonial pleases my ears and eyes.

Nor is it so certain that the movement among the Nonconformists which had brought about the federation of all the free churches was after all a symptom of vigorous life. At an earlier period the Wesleyan revival had given birth to a swarm of new sects, and during the first half of the nineteenth century this multiplication of sects had been the form naturally assumed by Anglo-Saxon Protestantism, as it developed. Was not the present movement towards reunion, however its leaders attempted to give it the appearance of a 'revival', a symptom, on the contrary, of failing vitality?[1] And those statistics which, as we have just seen, the Nonconformists produced so triumphantly against their opponents, were they not after all deceptive? No doubt the number of Nonconformists was very great, but were they increasing very rapidly? And if their numbers were still growing, did the growth keep pace with the increase of the population? This at any rate is certain; the sects about this time awoke to the fact that in their mutual competition they had saddled themselves with a heavy burden of debt by building too many chapels. When they proceeded to consider how best to remedy what amounted to a crisis of over-production they decided to adapt the supply to the demand by forming, if not a trust, at least a cartel. They were thus led to emphasize ideas which a more thorough-going Protestantism had hitherto discouraged: the very title 'free churches' which they assumed at this time was significant, and Hugh Price Hughes accurately presented the attitude which underlay the new movement when he wrote, 'We must be positive and constructive. In our own time we are known mainly by three names— Protestant, Nonconformist, Dissenter. We are proud of all three. ... But they are all negative. ... We now agree to say in the first place that we are "Churchmen". . . . The unit of this movement is not the individual Christian but the Church.'[2] The new tenden-

[1] The closing years of the nineteenth century produced only one new sect, the fancy religion of Christian Science. Christian Science has no connection with the Evangelical sects, and its unqualified denial of physical evil, which it regards as an illusion, might seem an offshoot of theosophy, did we not know its purely American origin. For the tenets of the new Church see *Science and Health with Key to the Scriptures*, by Mary Baker Eddy (1st ed., 1875). For its beginnings see Sibyl Wilbur, *The Life of Mary Baker Eddy* (1st ed., 1907) (an encomium), and Georgina Milmine, *The Life of Mary Baker G. Eddy and the History of Christian Science*, 1909 (satirical). The foundation stone (a block of granite brought from the United States) of the first church of 'Christ Scientist' opened in London, was laid in Sloane Square, November 26, 1900.

[2] *Contemporary Review*, March, 1897, vol. lxxi, p. 449. See also in the same article, p. 456: 'The numerous, totally distinct, and often inevitably hostile Orders of the Latin Church are all one in the Pope. Why should not our various denominations, which are not so separated from one another as the various Latin orders, and are not necessarily hostile to one another, as some of these organizations are—why should not our denominations realize their unity in Christ, and form, as Dr. Guinness Rogers said five years ago, a Catholic Church, securing all the legitimate objects of Christian Union, both internally and externally, without crushing any man's conscience, and without impairing the spontaneity and the freedom of Christian thought and Christian action?' Cf. Rev. John Watson (Ian Maclaren): 'One of the greatest of Nonconformist Divines, Dr. Dale of Birmingham, taught a high idea of the Church and of the Sacraments; and generally there has been a reaction from extreme simplicity of worship and individualism in Church polity. Quite lately a certain tendency to rationalism has been checked, and there has been an evident return to the verities of the Catholic faith.' (*North American Review*, May, 1899, vol. clxviii, p. 545.) Among the Wesleyans Hugh Price Hughes was delighted that his denomination called itself no longer a 'society' but a 'church'. It was due to him that

cies thus represented in many respects the reversal of what Edward Miall, half a century before, had proudly termed the Dissidence of Dissent and the Protestantism of the Protestant Religion. The 'Protestant' emphasis on independence and individuality was yielding to the 'Catholic' emphasis on unity and organization.

5

Is this all that can be said? If we regard the situation from a purely intellectual rather than from a sociological standpoint, and consider the problems with which contemporary thinkers were concerned, we shall possibly conclude that not only England, but the entire West was subject at this time to a reaction, which extended to every province of life and thought, against the spirit of the dying century. In its most obvious aspect it was a reaction against the intellectual simplification, which had reached its climax about the middle of the century when all the problems of science and philosophy had, it was believed, found a simple and definitive solution. Upon the principle of the conservation of energy, or to use the more indefinite terminology of the current materialism, the conservation of force, an entire cosmogony had been erected, of which Herbert Spencer's 'synthetic' philosophy was the most thorough-going statement. Spencer, now an old man, but an indefatigable worker to the last, was still engaged in adding the final stories to his philosophic edifice. But the positive sciences had already raised new problems with which this crude realism was unable to deal. 'The electric theory', Balfour pointed out to a scientific audience at Cambridge, 'analyses matter . . . into something which is not matter at all. . . . Matter is not merely explained, it is explained away.'[1] In short, where the science of 1860 had

the 'district meeting' took the name of 'district synod'. (*Life*, by his daughter, pp. 525–6.) The missions he organized possessed, like the Salvation Army, 'sisters' after the Catholic model, and when in 1892 he decided that the sisters and other lay assistants of the Wesleyan body should from time to time retire from the world to meditate on the eternal verities, 'he refused to designate this retirement by the title of Convention. It was, he said, to be a "Retreat" and caused strong shivers accordingly among certain staunch Protestant sisters.'

[1] *Presidential Address to the British Association*, August 17, 1904. Cf. G. Wyndham to Mrs. Drew, October 30, 1904: '. . . Are you, by chance, following Oliver Lodge's pronouncements? They interest me deeply. He is a sage in the front of modern science. A year and a half ago, he was at the point of saying to me that Christianity and the Church had made Faith unnecessarily hard to thinkers. But at Babraham the other day, after Arthur's address to the British Association, he said suddenly: I begin to see that the Church was right about the Incarnation.' (*Life and Letters of George Wyndham*, by J. W. Mackail and Guy Wyndham, vol. ii, pp. 483–4.)

seen 'things', or rather one single 'thing' always identical with itself, a more modern and more cautious science was content to see only representations, conceptual relations, which afforded no ground for positing a single material substance underlying them. What metaphysical system should be based on this new physics? Two lines of thought lay open to the choice of the English-speaking philosopher.

It might be said that the mind, to make the universe intelligible to itself, had the right to frame any hypothesis it pleased, whose only truth was the degree in which the hypothesis in question made it possible to foretell the succession of phenomena. In a science thus conceived every statement would possess only a fragmentary and provisional truth and be liable to constant revision. It was a positivism less dogmatic than Comte's, an empiricism more subtle than Mill's. This was the new philosophy, Anglo-Saxon, if not English, shortly to be christened pragmatism. Or it might be maintained that between the different diagrams of the universe to which the man of science successively resorts, a real order, a hierarchy, exists, that this order, this hierarchy is the universe itself, and its determination is the province of philosophy. This was the position represented by the Hegelian idealism of Oxford. And as the Hegelian philosophy of the state satisfied those social needs of which we have already spoken, so the Hegelian philosophy of nature promised, when it had been cleared of mistakes and brought up to date, to satisfy the demands of the understanding better than the scientific monism of 1860 had done. And the philosophy of the state and the philosophy of nature together culminated in a philosophy of the spirit, a religious metaphysic.

We must not, however, forget that this reaction against the intellectual simplification of the last generation, a reaction which favoured a revival of the Christian idealism, was accompanied by a victorious attack upon another simplification, the simple Christianity which consisted in the uncritical acceptance of the truth of the Bible and half a century earlier had satisfied the British mind. In a Bible, divinely inspired from the first word to the last, everyone whose heart was pure could find the entire truth of religion. That was the belief, undisturbed by intellectual or ethical misgivings, held by the large number of wealthy middle-class Englishmen of whom John Halifax, Gentleman, is an idealized but

faithful portrait. It was the creed of the heroes of Bible Christianity—brave missionaries, or devout soldiers—Livingstone's
creed and Gordon's. Voltaire's sarcasms, even when in France
they seemed to have shaken for ever the traditional beliefs, had
but shocked Englishmen and confirmed them in their faith. But
now the work of a host of German critics, patient scholars,
reverent even in their doubts, and still claiming to be called
Christians, had buttressed the destructive criticism of the eight-
eenth-century Frenchman. As each generation of critics improved
upon the theories of its predecessor, the student was driven to
ask what in either Testament was left standing. And, since this
criticism was the work of Protestant professors, the infection
spread by a multitude of channels to the English theologians. But
for the devout Protestant what an agony of soul! He based his
religion exclusively on the Bible, and now the Bible was failing
him.

Indeed the most unorthodox theories of German criticism
were now being exceeded by the even more daring theories of
British critics. To study the problem of Christian origins the latter
had made use of the data which the vast empire of Great Britain
placed at their disposal, embracing as it did, a host of peoples at
every stage of civilization. They had sought to give a scientific
account of those primitive beliefs which preceded the great revealed religions, that 'natural religion' which the philosophers of
the eighteenth century had formulated too crudely. Tylor had
inaugurated the study of comparative religion at Oxford in 1871
by his book on *Primitive Civilisation*, and the first volume of
Herbert Spencer's *Principles of Sociology*, published five years later,
had familiarized the public with Tylor's 'animist' view of religion.
In the course of the following decade Tylor's theory had been
rendered obsolete by the sensational discoveries of W. Robertson
Smith[1] and James Fraser.[2] Robertson Smith studied the Semitic
peoples, the Jews in particular, Fraser the classical mythology of
Greece and Rome which he sought to explain by parallels taken
from the religion of savage peoples in every quarter of the globe,
America, Africa, Australia, and Asia. Both discovered a stock of

[1] Article 'Bible' in the *Encyclopædia Britannica*. Speech delivered at a special meeting of
the Commission of Assembly of the Free Church on October 27, 1880, 1880. *Kinship and
Marriage in Early Arabia*, 1885. *Lectures on the Religion of the Semites, First Series*, 1889.
See Black (J. S.) and Chrystal (G. W.), *The Life of William Robertson Smith*, 1921.
[2] *The Golden Bough, a Study in Comparative Religion*, 1890.

ideas, the common possession, it seemed, of primitive man throughout the world. In their opinion, these beliefs threw new light on the Christian doctrine of sacrifice. In its original significance sacrifice had not been an offering made by man to his God to win the Divine Favour. It had been a feast, shared in common with the Deity, at which the God himself often was the food. Thus the essence of the sacrifice was the absorption and incorporation of the Divine Substance into the worshipper's living body. From these premises they concluded that the Supper of the New Testament was merely a survival of the antiquated metaphysic, or to speak more accurately, of the antiquated science and medicine of savages.

When in 1877 Tylor reviewed the first volume of Herbert Spencer's *Principles of Sociology*, he drew the attention of the public to the revolutionary character of the new theory.[1] It must be admitted that, even twenty years later, only a very small number, even of believers, were seriously disturbed by these disquieting studies. For their publication had been contemporary with a revival of metaphysical idealism which is hardly conceivable without a corresponding re-awakening of the need for religion. But since the historic foundations of Christianity seemed to have been undermined, that need sought satisfaction in strange directions, off the beaten path. Some were led by a study of the phenomena of hypnotism and telepathy[2] or even by their investigation of that tenuous matter, the subtle radiations which were the subject of the electro-magnetic theory, to entertain daring hypotheses, and savants of recognized authority, Crooks, Tait, and Sir Oliver Lodge, came to regard spiritualism as something between a branch of experimental science and a religion. Others—civil servants, soldiers, ordinary travellers—had visited India and fallen

---

[1] *Mind*, April, 1877 (vol. ii, p. 142).

[2] Edmund Gurney, *Phantasms of the Living*, 2 vols, 1886. Fred. W. H. Myers, *Science and a Future Life, with other Essays*, 1893. See especially pp. 73–4: 'Man's history in short is as yet in its first chapter, and science has lived as yet but a moment in the brief history of man; yet already, and so to say with the first glance out of our prison windows, we have seen enough to make it tolerably certain that after a few more centuries the number of first-rate discoveries must constantly lessen, while the number of men equipped and eager for discovery will constantly increase. Unless, indeed, some insight is gained into the psychical side of things, some communication realized with intelligences outside our own, some light thrown upon a more than corporeal descent and destiny of man, it would seem that the shells to be picked up on the shore of the ocean of truth will become ever scantier, and the agnostics of the future will gaze forth ever more hopelessly on that gloomy and unvoyageable sea.'

under the spell of the occult wisdom of the East.[1] A Russian adventuress, convicted, moreover, of imposture, had converted Annie Besant, and Mrs. Besant, breaking with Bradlaugh and abandoning her atheistic propaganda, attempted by means of the recently founded Theosophical Society to infuse new life into Brahmanism in the hope that this rejuvenated Brahmanism might in turn regenerate the entire world.[2] But if these eccentric movements were characteristic of the period which gave them birth, they were confined to narrow coteries. The vast majority of those who felt acutely the need of a religious faith continued to look to the old religion in which their parents and themselves had been educated. We are thus brought back to the question, which of the two forms of Christianity which prevailed in England, the Nonconformity of the Sects and Anglicanism, was the more in harmony with the spirit of the age as we have just described it.

6

We cannot hesitate as to the answer. It was not Nonconformity. When the theories of German Biblical criticism penetrated into the centres of Nonconformist theology—and they could not be kept out: even the orthodoxy of the Wesleyans was shaken[3]— the consequences could not fail to be disastrous. For among the Nonconformists the Evangelical creed, the literal acceptance of the Bible, had been universally taught in its most uncompromis-

[1] Arnold Edwin, *The Light of Asia, or the Great Renunciation. Being the Life and teaching of Gautama . . . as told in verse by an Indian Buddhist*, 1879. Ed. 25, 1885. Olcott (Henry Steele), *The Theosophical Society. Address . . . together with the rules of the Society*, 1879. *The Life of Buddha and its Lessons*. A lecture . . . 1880. *A Buddhist Catechism* (its circulation reached its 30th thousand in 1888). *Theosophy; its friends and enemies*, 1881. Sinnett (Alfred Percy), *The Occult World*, 1881; *Esoteric Buddhism*, 1883.

[2] Sinnett (Alfred Percy), *Incidents in the Life of Madame Blavatsky*, 1886. *Annie Besant, An Autobiography*, 1893, ch. xiv, pp. 329 sqq. *The Building of the Cosmos and Other Lectures*, 1894. *Ancient Ideals in Modern Life*, 1900: 'India,' wrote Annie Besant, 'a conquered nation, won by the sword, ruled by the sword, and that sword held in the hand of the dominant factor in the coming world empire. But at the same time her thought, her teaching, her ancient literature translated into the English tongue, which is the most widely spread tongue on the earth, and is fast becoming the world language, which is spreading in every direction, which is talked by the foremost nations of the world. Thus, while politically she is subject, her thought is beginning to dominate the whole of that Western civilization. . . . Her great teachings are becoming assimilated all over the world through this vehicle of a world language which is being made part of our own national life' (pp. 9–11).

[3] W. T. Davison, *The Praises of Israel: An introduction to the Study of the Psalms*, 1893, p. 7: 'I have freely consulted and used very various authorities from Augustine and Calvin to Ewald and Delitzsch, Perowne and Kay, Bäthgen and Schultz, Driver and Cheyne, Kirkpatrick and Robertson Smith.' After defending the application of historical methods to the study of the sacred text, the author concludes (p. 6): 'A fresh reading of the familiar

ing form. Dissenters therefore, when once the infallibility of Scripture had been abandoned, were confronted by the difficulty which faced the Protestant conscience in its most acute form. True, an intellectual basis for the Protestant religion was devised, a new theology, also of German origin, which centred entirely on the person of Christ. Granted that the four Gospels were no more than history books, the work of writers who were ignorant and credulous, fanatical partisans; the application of modern scientific methods had removed this vast mass of ignorance, credulity and prejudice and revealed in its original beauty the authentic portrait of Jesus Christ. If Jesus was indeed Divine, what was to be feared from approaching Him directly, instead of through the medium of a fallible book?[1] But were the masses capable of understanding this purified Christianity, reduced so to speak to one single tenet. The believer was obliged to choose between two methods of approaching Christ. He could read the Bible. But to read the Bible in the light of Protestant higher criticism was beyond the capacity of the ordinary man. He could accept the interpretation of a clerical body. In that case the Churches provided with a priesthood had the advantage over the Churches of private judgment. The Church of Rome reserved to her priests the duty of knowing and explaining the Scriptures. And the Anglican Church, though less uncompromisingly sacerdotal, nevertheless refused to put the Bible into the hands of children unaccompanied by a catechism to safeguard the ignorant reader against extravagance or incredulity.

Nor was this all. However paradoxical it may appear, the conclusions of Robertson Smith and Fraser did not seem irreconcilable with the demands of a Christian apologetic which had deliberately abandoned the position of Evangelical Protestantism. Christian faith might be emperilled by the discovery that the doctrine of the Real Presence of God in the Bread and Wine of the

---

and beloved Psalms may bring here and there a ray of new light, a glimpse of new meaning, a breath of fresh religious inspiration given by the Spirit who of old moved those holy men to write. If fresh interest be awakened, fresh benefit cannot fail to follow' —Joseph Agar Beet, The Immortality of the Soul, A Protest, 1901. The writer's object is to develop views he had already propounded in 1897, in a work entitled The Last Things. On the whole Mr. Beet defends, though with certain reservations, the thesis of 'conditional immortality'.

[1] For the best presentation of this theology see A. M. Fairbairn, The Place of Christ in Modern Theology, 1893. Cf. John Clifford, The Coming Theology; or the Primitive Christian Faith; the Source and Basis of a living and progressive Christian theology. The address from the Chair of the General Baptist Association, held at Burnley, June 23–25, 1891.

Eucharist represented a survival of primitive religion. But, at any rate, it had proved that the doctrine was not an excrescence on the body of Christian doctrine, for which the Catholic Church was responsible. On the contrary, it was Catholicism, not the iconoclastic rigorism of a Calvin or the ethical deism of a Rousseau, which by its insistence on the dogma of the Real Presence had fulfilled the instinctive expectations of mankind. In short, the conclusions of Robertson Smith and Fraser favoured a revival of Catholic 'sacramentalism' at the expense of 'Evangelical Protestantism'. Fraser's work had scarcely appeared before the Anglo-Catholic theologians of the High Church party combined its theories with the Hegelian philosophy which was current at Oxford, and seemed likely to provide Anglican theologians with the metaphysical basis which the contemporary revival of Thomism was providing for the theologians of the Catholic Church.[1]

But if the situation was so favourable to the sacramental varieties of Christianity, why be content with the Anglican Church or, in that Church, with the party which admittedly imitated Catholic practices? Why not go directly to Roman Catholicism? After the storms which had marked the early days of her revival, the Catholic Church in England was becoming a firmly established institution. At Westminster, Manning's place had been taken by Cardinal Vaughan, a man of estimable character and narrow sympathies. He, it was, who laid the foundation stone of the cathedral which English Catholics were preparing to build, as though in defiance, within a mile of the old Anglican Abbey. It was a striking mark of the increased power of the Catholic Church in England, a power shown by the number of conversions she made. 800 or 1,000 a month; this was the rate of progress.

Who were these new converts? Clergymen, noblemen and gentlemen, women of the world: literary, artistic and theatrical circles also provided their quota. Queer subjects, one might think. But Catholicism has always made provision for people of this kind, and her attraction was felt not least by those among the æsthetes of the day whose lives had been most chequered.[2] For

[1] Charles Gore, *The Body of Christ, An Inquiry into the Institution and Doctrine of Holy Communion*, 1901, pp. 12 sqq. Cf. Frank Byron Jevons' *Introduction to the Study of Religion*, 1896, pp. 411 sqq.
[2] Oscar Wilde and his friend, Lord Alfred Douglas; Aubrey Beardsley, Lionel Johnson, Ernest Dowson: Francis Thompson and Henry Harland were born Catholics (George N.

there are many rooms in the spacious mansion of Rome, and one in particular, somewhat retired and comfortably furnished, for artists who have learned that penitence is a pleasure, and a pleasure whose intensity is in proportion to the depth of their falls. On the other hand, the influence of the Catholic Church on the masses was very slight. Nor was she more successful with the middle classes. We must, moreover, inquire whether the conversions were not balanced by the defections.[1] For one Saint George Mivart or Tyrell,[2] whose official excommunication made a stir, how many withdrew in silence from the authority of the Church of Rome?

But the converts came from circles which attract public attention—the conversion of a son of the Primate, the brilliant writer, Robert Hugh Benson, caused a sensation[3]—and it was natural that the Establishment should take alarm. Her apprehensions increased when in 1894 the High Church party conceived the ambitious design of effecting a corporate reunion between the Catholic and Anglican Churches, which would amount to the absorption of the Church of England by the Church of Rome. A plot was hatched between Lord Halifax, the High Church leader, and two French theologians. An attempt was made to prove that Anglican ordinations were sacramentally valid. Then steps were taken at Rome to persuade Leo XIII to seal that opinion with his

Shuster, *The Catholic Spirit in Modern English Literature*, 1922). Holbrook Jackson (*The Eighteen Nineties*, p. 79) remarks that: 'The one who persistently hardened himself against the mystical influences of his period, John Davidson, committed suicide.'

[1] The following statistics are derived from Catholic sources: For the year 1891, 1,357,000 Catholics in England and Wales; 343,000 in Scotland; for the year 1901, 1,500,000 in England and Wales; 433,000 in Scotland. That is to say, in 1891 in England 1 out of every 21 of the population was a Catholic and in Scotland 1 in 12, in Great Britain 1 in 19; in 1901, 1 in 22 in England and Wales, 1 in 10 in Scotland, in Great Britain 1 in 19 as before. When we take into account the importance of the Irish immigration and the fertility of the Irish lower classes, these figures are significant. The statistics of Catholic marriages issued, during the period with which we are concerned, every ten years by the Registrar-General, furnish the following figures. For the period 1861–1870, 79,591 Catholic marriages (45 per thousand of the total number of marriages); 1871–1880, 81,367 (42 per thousand); 1881–1890, 87,991 (43 per thousand); 1891–1900, 97,781 (41 per thousand); 1901–1919, 109,482 (41 per thousand). It is true that since 1911 the proportional increase has been more rapid (47 per thousand in 1914, 52 per thousand in 1919). The Catholic Church in England has nevertheless remained stationary, as may be seen from the estimates published quite recently by two Catholics, Joseph Boubée, *Le Mouvement religieux hors de France* (*Études*, January 20, 1924, vol. cxxxviii, p. 234), and S. W. Poynter, 'The Present Position of Roman Catholicism in England (*Hibbert Journal*, April, 1924, vol. xxii, p. 545).

[2] *Autobiography and Life of George Tyrell*, in two volumes, vol. i, *Autobiography of George Tyrell*, 1861-1864, arranged with supplements by M. D. Petre; vol. ii, *Life of George Tyrell from 1884 to 1909*, 1912.

[3] For the history of his Conversion, see his interesting *Confessions of a Convert*, 1913.

approval and by this action admit that the Anglican clergy possessed the same orders as the Catholic. Leo XIII loved new ideas.
He loved the Anglo-Saxon world. For a moment he was attracted
by the suggestion, and short-sighted Anglo-Catholics could in-
dulge the belief that the day was at hand when the Anglican
Church would cease to be a separate body.[1]

Naturally, the scheme came to nothing. It horrified Cardinal
Vaughan. Was Rome about to inform him that all those Anglican
clergymen, whom he had regarded as Protestant ministers, had
been all the while, though neither he nor they had suspected it,
priests like his own clergy? It horrified the Archbishop of Canterbury, the spiritual head of the Established Church, *papa alterius
orbis*. The Curia discovered in time that it had been deceived as
to the situation by Lord Halifax and the French theologians; a
Papal Bull was issued, positively deciding against Anglican orders,
and for some time, as a result of this ill-conceived attempt, the
Anglo-Catholic wing of the High Church party was under a
cloud. A member of the lower middle class in London, Kensit
by name, the secretary of a society for religious propaganda,
emerged from his obscurity and declared war on Ritualism. He
went from church to church, protesting in loud tones and stirring
up brawls wherever he was informed of the illegal introduction
of some ceremonial novelty, tainted with Romish idolatry. Even
members of the episcopate were not secured by their rank from
these noisy demonstrations.[2] People were shocked by his methods,
but he succeeded in arousing public opinion. Sir William Harcourt, the aged and active leader of the Liberal party, conducted
in the Press and in Parliament a campaign against what he termed
'lawlessness in the National Church'.[3] Then the bishops, of whom
the great majority were moderate Evangelicals,[4] reluctantly took

[1] A. C. Benson, *The Life of Edward White Benson, Sometime Archbishop of Canterbury*,
pp. 589 sqq. *Life and Letters of Mandell Creighton, Sometime Bishop of London*, by his wife,
vol. ii, pp. 176 sqq. J. G. Snead Cox, *The Life of Cardinal Vaughan*, vol. ii, pp. 141 sqq.
[2] *John Kensit: Reformer and Martyr. A Popular Life* by the Rev. John C. Wilcox. See
especially (*Life and Letters of Mandell Creighton*, by his wife, 1904; vol. ii, pp. 287 sqq.) how
Kensit brought about the resignation of Philipps, curate of St. Ethelburga's.
[3] *Lawlessness in the National Church*. Reprinted from *The Times*. By the Right Hon.
Sir William Vernon Harcourt, M.P., 1899 (the letters had been originally published in
1898). Cf. A. G. Gardiner, *The Life of Sir William Harcourt*, 1923, ch. xxv, 'The Battle with
the Bishops', pp. 480 sqq.
[4] With the exception of Creighton, a High Churchman of the old school, a professional
historian, and more of a politician than a spiritual leader, Ingram, a High Churchman of
the new school, militant and given to advertisement and popular propaganda, who had
borrowed the methods of the Salvation Army, preaching in the open air and giving

up the matter. It could not be denied that in strict law the protests were justified and that in ever increasing numbers the churches of the Establishment were departing from its primitive form of worship.[1] The 'Lambeth Opinion', a judgment delivered by the two Archbishops, forbade certain ceremonies, in particular, the use of incense. But what disciplinary powers did the Archbishops possess to enforce their decision? And even had they been disposed to take action, how could they have overcome the general indifference? The public, profoundly uninterested in questions of ritual, received with annoyance these protests against what it regarded as harmless and, on the whole, picturesque ceremonies. Kensit, who had addressed a public meeting at Liverpool, was killed, as he left the hall, by a blow delivered by some fanatic with an iron bar. No one has ever suggested the erection of a monument to this martyr of the Protestant faith.

The position of the Catholic Church had improved; within the Anglican Church, the position of the High Church had improved to the detriment of the Low Church; and the position of the Anglican Church had improved to the detriment of the Nonconformist sects. We may deny that these phenomena represented a genuine and profound religious revival. For the great ages of religion are the ages of heresy, and this revival of the more ecclesiastical types of Christianity was possibly due to the decline of the Christian faith. But this does not alter the fact that within these limits they were genuine, and that in consequence the situation was calculated to encourage the Church of England, as she entered upon her campaign to secure legislation more favourable to her educational interests. And her immediate prospects were further improved by the support of the Catholics. For they also maintained voluntary schools and were even more determined than the Anglicans to preserve their denominational character. It was for the sake of their schools, that the Irish Catholics, after com-

---

sensational missions in the suburbs, and Gore, a High Churchman of the young Oxford school, philosophic and subtle, all the bishops appointed by the Conservative Government were moderate Evangelicals.

[1] Robert Hugh Benson, *Confessions of a Convert*, 1913, p. 70. 'Here, as well as in the three Churches of Mirfield, which we attended, as we liked, on Sunday evenings, I found all kinds of teaching and ceremonial. In one church they would wear elaborate stoles but no vestments, with doctrine to correspond; in another, vestments would be used at services to which the important Protestants did not come; Confession would be referred to in a hasty aside as the "Sacrament of Reconciliation", or taught explicitly only to a favoured few at some small guild service.'

promising the Liberals on the question of Home Rule, betrayed them on the morrow of the election and made terms with the Conservatives on the question of education.[1] Thus circumstances obliged and encouraged the Unionists to adopt in this sphere a 'clerical' policy.

III THE EDUCATION ACT OF 1902

I

The problem which in 1895 faced the victorious party was to satisfy both the educational reformers and the Church of England. Under the existing conditions, the problem could be solved along the lines of Lord Beaconsfield's policy, and Bismarck's policy in Prussia. The educational system must be reformed, but the reform must be conservative and must respect the religious traditions of the country. Seven years later the Unionists would frame and carry the requisite legislation. But we are amazed by the contrast between the magnitude of the achievement and the character of the statesmen whose position in the new Cabinet made them responsible for carrying it through. They were two: a more ill-assorted couple it would be difficult to conceive.

The President of the Privy Council, who, as ex-officio chairman of the Education Committee of the Council, occupied the position of a Minister of Education, was the Duke of Devonshire.[2] He was head of the Cavendish family, one of those noble families, traditionally attached to the Liberal party, which had seized upon the pretext afforded by the Home Rule crisis to break with Gladstone and join the Conservative party, as revived under the title of Unionist. He was the nominal leader of that group of Liberal

[1] Even during the election there is reason to believe that in many British constituencies the Catholics voted for the Conservative candidate in obedience to their Bishops. See *Methodist Times*, July 18, 1895: 'The Duke of Norfolk has been put into the Ministry; Mr. Matthews has been made a Peer of the Realm; and the Roman Catholic Bishops in all parts of the country have issued instructions to their flocks that they are to vote for the clerical candidates. The alliance between Romanism and Conservatism is complete.' A little later, at the election of 1900, the Liberals attributed their defeat in the Scottish constituencies to the loss of the Catholic vote. (J. A. Spender, *The Life of the Right Hon. Sir Henry Campbell-Bannerman*, vol. ii, pp. 294–5.)

[2] For the Duke of Devonshire see Bernard Holland, *The Life of Spencer Compton, eighth Duke of Devonshire*, 2 vols, 1911; also the reminiscences in the *Memoirs of Sir Almeric Fitzroy*, 2 vols, 1925.

Unionists whose policy was dictated by Chamberlain. As leader of his group and a member of the Cabinet, he continued the tradition of those halcyon days of aristocratic Liberalism when the manufacturing and commercial middle class required nothing more from its rulers than a policy of *laisser faire*. He was a past master in the art of laying foundation stones, opening public meetings and delivering, with befitting dignity, speeches written for him on subjects of which he was ignorant. True, we have seen him play an active part in promoting an understanding with Germany, but it was no doubt his German wife who took the initiative in the matter. Melancholy and solemn, he presided over her diplomatic intrigues, as he presided over her social receptions. He was known to cherish only one strong passion—that for his stud of race-horses.

The Vice-President of the Education Committee of the Privy Council, whose duty it was to defend the educational policy of the Government in the House of Commons, while the Duke of Devonshire defended it in the Lords, was a man of very different calibre. Sir John Gorst had been a member fifteen years earlier of that little Fourth Party, whose audacities had done so much to rouse the old Conservative leaders from their slumbers and revive the party by making it democratic. Four men had made up the entire Fourth Party. What had happened to them since? Sir Henry Drummond Wolf had vanished into the diplomatic service; Lord Randolph Churchill had died a failure; Balfour, respectable and universally respected, was the second in command of the Conservative party. And Sir John Gorst had been given this subordinate position in the Cabinet in 1895. Might he not increase its importance by inaugurating that educational policy, at once reforming and traditional, whose principle we have just stated and which was entirely in the spirit of the Fourth Party? This was exactly what he did. Unfortunately, he retained too much of the insubordination which had distinguished the little group with whom he had begun his public life. He assumed towards his colleagues the attitude of an independent statesman, almost of a rebel. He soon found the Duke of Devonshire's somnolent dignity as intolerable, as the Duke found his own headstrong cynicism. He took pleasure in shocking his fellow Conservatives by the most inopportune speeches: 'To jog them up', he would explain. He certainly amused the Opposition without gaining their confidence. Nor did he gain the confidence of the Ministerialists and he certainly did not amuse them.[1]

These were the two men who out of the entire Cabinet were specially responsible for taking the necessary steps to satisfy the demands of public opinion in the matter of education. Those demands were urgent. The Royal Commission which the previous Government had appointed to advise upon the best way to set up a well-organized system of secondary education in England reported in August. The report recommended a complete and systematic reorganization of the government departments and local authorities. On the other hand, four months had not elapsed since the general election when a deputation of the Anglican clergy, headed by the Primate, waited on the Prime Minister and the Duke of Devonshire to demand for the voluntary schools relief from the heavy burden imposed on them by the competition of the board schools.[2] The Cabinet was not slow to act. It ordered the officials of the Education Department to draw up a single Bill which should contain provisions satisfying the demands of both parties.

The Bill, introduced into the House of Commons on March 31, 1896, constituted each county council the supreme educational authority within its area. The council must appoint for that purpose an education committee, the numbers and qualification of whose members were left by the Bill to the choice of the council. The only stipulation laid down was that the majority of the committee must be members of the council. The council, acting through the education committee, was empowered to promote secondary education by making grants to institutions already in existence and founding new ones wherever in its opinion they were needed. The committee was entrusted with the distribution of the grants made by the Government to the free, as well as to the board schools, and in areas where no school board existed to see that the law which rendered attendance at school compulsory was carried out. Not only was the limit of seventeen shillings and sixpence abolished, but an additional grant of four shillings a child was placed at the disposal of the education committee to assist voluntary schools and necessitous board schools. Educational

[1] Those who would like to know what was happening behind the scenes in the Education Department during this period must read (with due reserve) Sir G. Kekewich's slanderous book, *The Education Department and After*, 1920.
[2] November 20, 1895 (*Annual Register*, 1895, p. 196).

institutions were exempted from rates. Finally, two provisions were introduced to give satisfaction to two different sections of public opinion. The extension to twelve of the age of compulsory attendance at school would please the Radicals. And the Catholics and Anglicans, for whose special benefit the clause was inserted, and even the Nonconformists would, it was hoped, be satisfied by the provision that, both in the board schools and in the voluntary schools, if they objected to the instruction demanded by the majority of parents, their children might, in certain specified cases, receive separate religious instruction in the school buildings.

The Bill failed. Obviously it was a clumsy makeshift. Its object was to replace the religious compromise established in 1870 by a compromise more favourable to the Anglican Church. It set up new local authorities which would not only possess a jurisdiction over elementary education, parallel to that of the school boards, but would tend to encroach on the jurisdiction of the latter. On the other hand, since the school boards were not touched, the proposed legislation, far from remedying the existing muddle, would make it worse by the further friction which must result from the creation of an additional authority. What was the explanation of this bungling?—the fact, that however intimate the coalition between the old Conservatives and the Liberal Unionists, it was not a fusion, and that among the latter, Chamberlain's word was law. But Chamberlain, who was no Anglican, in the days of his youthful radicalism had played an active part in securing the statute of 1870. Indeed, if he could have had his way entirely, no religious instruction would have been given in the new schools. Moreover, the Birmingham school board prided itself on the work it had accomplished during the previous twenty-five years, and there can be no doubt that Chamberlain still shared the devotion to the school board, professed by the Liberals of the Opposition. Hence the timidity which marked the Bill. Further difficulties arose when the large towns which possessed no 'county council' expressed their determination not to recognize the authority of the education committees of the councils in whose area they were situated, and demanded education committees of their own. Then the Unionist Cabinet retreated, abandoned for the time the attempt to reorganize the educational system and returned to the policy of the dole. An Act of

1897[1] made an additional grant to the voluntary schools of five shillings, instead of the four shillings fixed by the Bill of 1896. The voluntary schools were not even obliged to purchase this grant by accepting the control of the county councils. Its distribution was entrusted by the Act to associations of the voluntary schools which, of course, would be purely denominational. The Radicals protested, but finally gave way, and were content with securing an Act which by way of compensation provided for grants to poor board schools.[2] The Cabinet estimated that it had made a present of £616,500 to the free schools, and £154,000 to the board schools.

Just then the great struggle broke out within the Anglican Church between the Ritualists and the Protestants, and the position of the Church seemed in consequence to have been temporarily weakened. The passage of a Benefices Bill,[3] which sought to check the abuses of lay patronage by increasing the powers of the bishops, provoked lively protests from the Liberal, or rather from the Protestant, members of the House. Conservative seats were lost or endangered in several by-elections; and these reverses were attributed to the defection of a number of Nonconformists who had voted for the Government in 1895. It was not a propitious juncture for the Anglicans to put forward any further demands. Moreover, the Church of England had won a decided success in the statute of 1897. For some time the Cabinet was not disturbed by Anglican claims and Sir John Gorst, after provoking a scene in the House by a speech in which he enlarged on the inefficiency and deterioration of the voluntary schools,[4] turned his attention to other problems with which his department was equally concerned.

2

An alteration was made in the system under which the grants were allotted to the schools. They were no longer to be deter-

---

[1] 60 Vict., Cap. 5: An Act to provide for a Grant out of the Exchequer in Aid of Voluntary Elementary Schools, and for the Exemption from Rates of those Schools, and to repeal part of Section Nineteen of the Elementary Education Act, 1870 (*Voluntary Schools Act*, 1897).

[2] 60 Vict., Cap. 3, 16: An Act to amend Section Ninety-seven of the Elementary Education Act, 1870 (*Elementary Education Act*, 1897).

[3] 61 & 62 Vict., Cap. 48: An Act to amend the Law relating to the Patronage of Benefices and to their avoidance on Sequestration, and to amend the Pluralities Acts, 1838 and 1886 (*Benefices Act*, 1898).

[4] H. of C., June 17, 1898 (*Parliamentary Debates*, 4th Ser., vol. lix, pp. 596 sqq.).

mined by the marks obtained by each pupil in the final examination, an excessively mechanical arrangement whose effects on
education competent judges unanimously condemned.[1] A system
of pensions was introduced for superannuated teachers in the
elementary schools.[2] In 1899, the school boards were authorized
to establish special schools for defective children.[3] A Bill introduced by a private member, to which Sir John Gorst, acting independently of his colleagues, gave a hearty support which ensured
its passage, extended the age of compulsory attendance at school
to twelve, no exceptions being admitted.[4] And the following year
a further statute permitted the age for leaving school to be raised
to fourteen.[5] By an Act passed in 1898[6] the University of London
became at last a teaching body in the full sense of the term, a
federation of all the institutions for higher education which during
the past century had sprung up at random in the metropolis.
Among these institutions was the Fabian 'School of Economics'.
Sidney Webb, who took an active part in drawing up the Bill of
1898, found himself in regular communication with the Education
Department, a collaboration from which the cause of national
education could not fail to benefit. And, if for the moment Gorst
avoided the question of religious instruction in the schools, he
never ceased to interest himself in the other aspect of the education

[1] For a number of special grants allotted to each school in accordance with the marks
obtained by the pupils in a number of papers set on particular subjects, there was substituted a block grant which the inspector assigned to the school, subject to a right, if he
were dissatisfied with the standard, to reduce it by one shilling as a warning, and if there
were no improvement, to withhold it entirely. For the details of the reform see *The New
Code of Regulations for Day-schools* for the year 1899–1900, also the Codes for the preceding
years which paved the way for the Reform. See further, *The Times*, March 23, 1898,
March 22, 23, 1899, March 16, 29, 1900. H. of C., May, 1900 (*Parliamentary Debates*, 4th
Ser., vol. lxxxii, pp. 596 sqq.). Also in a work entitled *Education in the Nineteenth Century*,
1901, Sir Joshua Fitch's article 'Primary Education in the Nineteenth Century', pp.
48 sqq.
[2] 61 & 62 Vict., Cap. 57: An Act to provide for Superannuation and other Annuities
and Allowances to Elementary School Teachers certificated by the Education Department
(*Elementary School Teachers' (Superannuation) Acts* 1898).
[3] 62 & 63 Vict., Cap. 32: An Act to make better provision for the Elementary Education
of Defective and Epileptic Children in England and Wales (*Elementary Education (Defective
and Epileptic Children) Act*, 1899).
[4] 62 & 63 Vict., Cap. 13: An Act to amend the Law respecting the Employment and
Education of Young Children (*Elementary Education School Attendance Act* (1893) *Amendment Act*, 1899). See Sir John Gorst's speech H. of C., March 1, 1899: *Parl. Deb.*, 4th Ser.,
vol. lxvii, pp. 972 sqq.
[5] 63 & 64 Vict., Cap. 53: An Act to amend the Elementary Education Acts, 1890 to
1893 (*Elementary Education Act*, 1900).
[6] 61 & 62 Vict., Cap. 62: An Act to make further provision with respect to the
University of London (*University of London Act*, 1898).

question, the reorganization of the department and the establishment of a system of secondary education.

He did not, however, repeat the mistake of 1896. He had learned how many difficulties stood in the way of any reorganization of the local authorities. The Science and Arts Department was content to urge these authorities to combine and come to an agreement among themselves, so as to avoid overlapping in the allocation of grants by the Department. But the local bodies showed little readiness to respond to the appeal, and in the large towns an unrelenting war was waged between the Technical Instruction Committee of the County Council and the local School Board.

The Government began by reorganizing the central departments. At the end of 1898, the Duke of Devonshire introduced in the House of Lords two Bills to give effect to recommendations of the Commission on secondary education. The first united the Education Department and the Science and Art Department in a single department to be placed under the control of a responsible minister. For the Science and Art Department had been too long a sort of *imperium in imperio* with no clearly defined functions and its mismanagement had just been condemned after an inquiry by a committee of the Commons. Moreover, the Bill, while refraining from interference with the educational activities of the Charity Commissioners, provided for regular co-operation between the Education Department and the Charity Commission. The second Bill, though it did not establish the advisory council for public education for which the Royal Commission had asked, set up a council, entrusted with the more restricted function of compiling an official register of teachers, and thus bestowing upon them the professional status lacking under the old system of free competition and private initiative.

The introduction of these two Bills at the close of the session was a mere formality. A few months later, a single measure which combined the two Bills of 1898 was introduced in the Lords by the Duke of Devonshire and passed both Houses before the session of 1899 closed.[1] The statute was the first step towards the unification of the government departments which controlled education.

[1] 62 & 63 Vict., Cap. 33: An Act to provide for the establishment of a Board of Education for England and Wales and for matters connected therewith (*Board of Education Act*, 1899).

Although, instead of appointing a Secretary of State with a salary of £5,000, the Government was content to set up a Board of Education, similar to the Board of Agriculture, whose chief would receive a salary of only £2,000, the President of the new Board was nevertheless for all intents and purposes a minister of national education, and both the Education Department and the Science and Arts Department were placed under his authority. If the endowed schools remained under the independent jurisdiction of the Charity Commission, provisions, more definite than those contained in the Bill of the previous autumn, ensured the gradual transference to the Education Department of the Commissioners' educational functions. And the compilation of a register of elementary and secondary teachers was not, as before, entrusted to the uncontrolled discretion of an advisory council, formed for that special purpose, but to the Board of Education itself, assisted by the council.

All this amounted to a considerable measure of reform. But the problem of secondary education remained unsettled. How could it be settled unless the unification of the central departments was followed by the unification of the local authorities? And how could the obstacles be overcome which ever since 1895 had made the latter reform impossible? If the school boards were spared, the Government would lose the support of the Anglicans, who wished to destroy them for reasons wholly unconnected with secondary education, and, while it was plainly out of the question to unify the local administration of the Education Acts on the basis of the school boards, it seemed equally impossible to attempt any unification so long as they remained in existence. Should they then abolish the school boards? Every Dissenter and every Radical in England would be up in arms. Should they at least restrict their powers? Gorst had, it would seem, attempted for several months, in fact until the end of 1899, to solve the problem by friendly agreement between the school boards on the one hand, and the county councils on the other.[1]

[1] Speech at Bradford, January 1899: 'It would be a most unfortunate thing if the board schools, the higher elementary schools, and the schools of science in the large cities were in any way interfered with.' Speech in London, November 17, 1899: 'If only the County Councils and the school boards in every place would come together. . . . What little the Science and Art Department could give to promote such agreements it had offered. . . . The very difficult problem of devising a scheme which would properly supervise the secondary education of the country might be more likely to be solved by the wisdom of these Councils and school boards than by the wisdom of Governments and Parliament.'

Was it the obduracy of the school boards which made him lose heart? Or did the pressure brought to bear on the government departments by the educational reformers, or possibly by the Anglicans, finally prove too strong? This at any rate is certain. From the beginning of 1900 we find the Board of Education the avowed supporter of the County Councils and the open enemy of the school boards.

In February 1899, it was decided that the classes organized by the school boards had no right to grants from the Science and Art Department. The grants were to be confined to those local bodies who came under the terms of the Act of 1899 on technical education, in other words the County Councils. In May, a private establishment in the north of London took legal action to put an end to the competition of certain schools which had been set up by the school board, free schools at which the pupils were even supplied with pencils, paper, and all other requisites for writing and drawing. The plaintiff denied that it was legal under the Act of 1890 to maintain out of the rates any school at which the education given was above the elementary standard. The case had been brought at the instigation of a committee lately formed to combat the school boards. Its chairman was Lord Robert Cecil, the youngest son of Lord Salisbury, and one of the lights of the High Church Party. Among the more prominent members was another Cecil—Evelyn Cecil—who had been quite recently the leader of the moderate opposition on the London school board. On June 8 an auditor of the Local Government Board called Cockerton before whom the case was argued decided in the plaintiff's favour.

Thus, by the beginning of the summer of 1899, the right of the school boards to receive government grants or employ the rates for the maintenance of schools, not in the strictest sense elementary, had been very seriously contested. In February, there had been a departmental decision adverse to the school boards; in June the Government stood entirely aside and left the London school board to fight its own battle before the auditor Cockerton. A month later, the Cabinet introduced in the Commons a new Bill for the promotion of secondary education. It provided that henceforward it should be obligatory, not, as in the past, optional, to devote the whisky money to the maintenance of schools. And the County Councils were empowered to levy for educational purposes a maximum rate of 2d., instead of the 1d. prescribed by the Act of 1889. Both grants and rates might be applied by the Councils to the support, not only of technical, but of secondary education generally. Parliament could not pass before the recess a measure introduced in July. Nevertheless, the Bill was a significant manifesto. The Board of Education proclaimed its intention to make use of the County Councils, not the school boards, to organize secondary education. In fact, from now onwards, in the official publications issued by the Board, the technical education given by the County Councils is termed secondary education.[1] And, on the other hand, a departmental decision forbade the school boards to admit to their evening classes pupils above sixteen years of age.

After Cockerton's adverse decision the London school board, well aware that it would be exposed in future to the attacks of the Board of Education, decided to seek the protection of the courts. It appealed against the Cockerton decision. But the appeal failed, and on December 20, 1900, the Court of Queen's Bench confirmed the decision. And when the school board appealed once more the Court of Appeal confirmed on May 1, 1901, the judgment of the lower court.[2] The board did not carry the matter to the final court of appeal, the House of Lords. It had recognized at last that it had no case. The letter of the Act of 1870 was opposed to its claims. Nor could it supply for the silence of the statute by appealing to the intention of the legislator. There could be no doubt that Parliament in 1870 had contemplated only elementary education. The school board could plead nothing more than the long continued connivance of the public authorities. But, if that

[1] Board of Education, South Kensington, London, S.W. *Directory with regulations for establishing and conducting science and art schools and classes* (From August 1, 1900, to July 31, 1901), 1900, Sect. vii. Also: Secondary Education. Return for every County and County Borough which possesses an Organization for the Promotion of Secondary Education (*Sect. 7 of Directory of Board of Education*) of the Constitution of Such Organization and the date of its Recognition by the Board of Education, April 17, 1901.

[2] It will be as well to explain in somewhat greater detail the three successive decisions or judgments. The arbitrator, Cockerton, had decided that the School Board did not possess the right to apply to a form of education which came under the control of the Science and Arts Department, any portion of the school fund, that is to say, any portion of the funds to which the School Board was entitled under the provisions of the Act. The Court of Queen's Bench did not adopt so extreme an attitude, and merely laid down that the school boards were not entitled to apply to any purposes, other than the support of primary education, that portion, but only that portion, of the school fund, which was furnished by the rates. The Court of Appeal returned to the more radical position and confirmed the Cockerton judgment in its entirety. For a clear statement of the question see the article in *The Times*, May 31, 1901, entitled 'The Cockerton Judgment and After', also for a complete history of the struggle, J. H. Yoxhall's speech (H. of C., March, 1901: *Parliamentary Debates*, 4th Ser., vol. xc, pp. 594 sqq.).

connivance made it difficult to close off-hand all the educational institutions illegally maintained by the London school board and by many school boards in the provinces, it was not a legal argument in their favour, and further legislation was imperative to regularize or alter a situation *de facto* illegal. The reforming activity of the Board of Education was made easier by the intervention at this juncture of the Fabians.

3

In January 1901, one of those tracts was published—the 106th of the series[1]—which constituted their habitual method of propaganda. The anonymous writer, after describing and criticizing the muddle which had arisen and pointing out that, after the Cockerton judgment, it was impossible to 'go on drifting', proceeded to inquire what system should be substituted for the existing system or rather want of system. The principle which must be established was 'that there ought to be, in each district of convenient size, one public educational authority, and one only; responsible for providing and controlling all the education maintained in the district out of public funds, whether it be literary, scientific, commercial, artistic, or technological in type—whether it be, for any of these types, primary, secondary, or university in rank'. What then should it be? The school board?—in that case it would be necessary to extend the system to that third of the kingdom which neither possessed nor wished to possess school boards. It would also be necessary to remodel completely, where it existed, an institution which had grown up at hazard, and, while retaining the old name of school boards, set up entirely new corporations invested with novel functions. But in that case what need was there to go to such trouble and repeat the old mistake of setting up a special elective body to provide for each of the public services? Since the creation of the County Councils it was

[1] Fabian Tract No. 106. *The Education Muddle and the Way Out. A Constructive Criticism of English Educational Machinery.* The Fabian, William Pember Reeves, agent-general of New Zealand in London, gave the Webbs and his friends the assistance of his colonial experience. In a communication made to a congress of teachers he pointed out that his native country possessed a Minister of Education who had under his jurisdiction strong Local Education Boards assisted in turn by district school committees. An Education Institute, which amounted to a union of the teachers recognized by law, was regularly consulted by the Central Department and the Local Boards on all questions affecting national education.

no longer necessary. The school boards, therefore, should be abolished and their functions transferred, as part of a complete educational jurisdiction, to a committee of the County Council. The authority of the education committee should extend not only to the former board schools, but also to the voluntary schools, which should in future be assisted out of the rates, but must in return accept control by inspectors appointed by the Council and the formation of a committee of managers of whom two, at least, should be representatives of the ratepayers. In conclusion the Socialist ideal was categorically affirmed. It was not the object of education to provide the manufacturers with the necessary experts and foremen. 'The democratic ideal in education is not merely that a ladder should be provided, whereby a few students may climb unimpeded from the elementary school to the university. What the national well-being demands, and what we must insist upon, is that every child—dull or clever, rich or poor, should receive all the education requisite for the full development of his faculties. For every child, in every part of the country, at least a "national minimum" of education must be compulsorily provided.'

The tract enjoyed an extensive circulation. Before the end of the year a second, and a very large, edition had become necessary. The manifesto had scarcely been published when Sir John Gorst distributed copies to his fellow ministers to prove to them that the time was ripe to carry out a bold measure of administrative socialism, which would satisfy, at the same time, both the educational reformers and the Anglican clergy. One of the most eminent representatives of British socialism, Sidney Webb, had shown them the way. At a moment when the Boer War was at its height, they would do well to pay attention to the man who in the Socialist camp gave such valuable support to their imperialist policy. It must be admitted that the Bill which Sir John introduced in the House of Commons on May 7—and which in many respects betrayed the direct inspiration of the Fabian Tract—was after all a timid measure. So far as its immediate effect was concerned, it hardly differed from the Bill of 1896. It did no more than pave the way for the transference at some later date to the committees of the County Councils of the powers at present exercised by the school boards. But it sufficiently revealed the Government's ulterior intentions, and therefore aroused the opposition of the Nonconformists and Radicals. For the moment, the Cabinet yielded and was content to carry a Bill, passed without debate, which saved the illegal schools and classes from immediate suppression by continuing the *status quo* for a year.[1]

Should the Government renew the attack in 1902 and, since a timid measure had done nothing to conciliate the Opposition, strike boldly the great blow whose success was assured by their majority of 130 votes, supported, as it would be, by the 80 votes of the Irish Catholics? Acrimonious discussions took place between the members of the Cabinet. 'Gorst', said Balfour, 'sees no difficulties, and the Duke sees nothing else.'[2] Since Sir John was now completely at loggerheads with the Minister, his private secretary, Robert Morant, was employed as a go-between to influence the Duke. He was a High Churchman, who had studied theology at Oxford. He was also an imperialist, who for several years had been the intimate adviser, practically the prime minister, of the King of Siam. A firm believer in the creed of efficiency, he was more than Sir John's subordinate. In the final negotiations he played a decisive part.

After several Cabinet councils, at which, from December onwards, the reform was often endangered by Chamberlain's opposition and Lord Salisbury's timidity, the Bill was at last ready in March. On this occasion also, Gorst, who, besides his quarrel with the Duke of Devonshire, had given serious offence to the Unionist members of the Commons, was set aside, and it was Balfour in person who took charge of the Bill, which he introduced in the House of Commons on March 24, 1902. More than two months passed before the debates began on June 2, the day on which peace was concluded.

4

Little progress had been made with the discussion of the Bill, when on August 8 the session came to an end. In the meanwhile, Lord Salisbury's retirement had occasioned a remodelling of the

---

[1] Edw. VII 1. Cap. 11. An Act for enabling local authorities to empower school boards temporarily to carry on certain schools and for sanctioning certain school board expenses (*Education Act*, 1901).
[2] *Memoirs of Sir Almeric Fitzroy*, vol. i, p. 62. For the discussions which took place in the Cabinet and the details of the intrigue carried on by Sir John Gorst, ibid., v, pp. 62, 63, 66, 67, 69, 72, 73, 74, 80, 81, 82. Cf. Cecil Chesterton, *Gladstonian Ghosts* (1905), p. 16: 'It is often possible to get the Tories to pass good measures without knowing it, as Mr. Webb and Mr. Morant are supposed to have induced them to pass an Education Bill.'

Cabinet. The new President of the Board of Education, Lord Londonderry, was like his predecessor, the Duke of Devonshire, an aristocratic figure-head and with a less imposing personality. The Vice-President who succeeded Sir John Gorst was, on the contrary, a competent official in whose hands lay the actual administration of the department. He was Sir William Anson, one of the two members for Oxford University, and a professional jurist. He did not, however, display in his new office the zeal for reform which had distinguished his predecessor. He left to Balfour, now Prime Minister, the task of defending in debate the Bill he had introduced with an important speech. Shaking off his indolence, Balfour showed himself the untiring and invincible debater he could be when he pleased. In the autumn session, which opened on October 16, he was obliged to have recourse to the closure to finish the debates in both Houses before Christmas. Finally, the new Education Act was passed on December 18. It comprised two distinct reforms.

In the first place it abolished the school boards. Henceforward the 'local education authority' would be the County Council, represented, according to the formula suggested so often during the last few years, by an education committee. The majority of the committee were to be elected by the Council, the remainder appointed by the Council on the nomination of other bodies. The committee would thus represent, besides the voters, certain public bodies of a non-party character. Women were eligible to serve on the committees. As originally draughted, the Bill had been content to empower County Councils to take over at their discretion the functions of the school boards. The Government had wished to placate Chamberlain and the Birmingham group of Liberal Unionists, who were bitterly opposed to the reform. But in July the malcontents had yielded to the majority of the Cabinet and the permission became an obligation. For the purposes of the Act the Councils of the county boroughs were treated as County Councils. This indeed had been the case with the unsuccessful Bills of 1896 and 1899. Moreover, as a further concession to local feeling, boroughs with a population over 10,000 and 'urban districts' with a population over 20,000 were given education committees. The Act, therefore, was not a measure of centralization after the French pattern: had that been the case, every English or Welsh county would have had an education committee whose authority was conterminous with the county area. Within the counties the autonomy of every considerable centre of population was carefully respected. Nevertheless, the old system had received its death blow. England would no longer possess bodies specially elected to administer public education. Moreover, the new education committee did not simply take over the functions hitherto exercised by the school board (the local control of elementary education), and the County Council (the local control of technical education). The word 'technical' does not appear in the new statute. It spoke only of 'elementary' education and of 'higher or non-elementary' education. In consequence, the jurisdiction of the new local authorities embraced the whole of elementary education and secondary education, and even, if they wished, could be extended to include higher education. 'For the first time', wrote Sidney Webb in a triumphant article which he contributed to the *Daily Mail*, 'the Bill definitely includes as a public function education as education—not primary education only, or technical education only, but anything and everything that is education from the kindergarten to the university. This renders the Bill of 1902 epoch-making in the history of English education.'[1]

In the second place, the Bill abolished the distinction, made hitherto, between the schools maintained out of the rates and the voluntary schools belonging to the various denominations and maintained by them. Anglicans and Catholics secured for their schools their share of the rates, to be paid by the education committee. Both classes of school were thus placed under the control of the committee, the schools, known in future as the provided schools—that is to say, the former board schools whose buildings had been provided by the public authority, and the non-provided schools, the voluntary schools, whose buildings 'had not been provided' by the public authority. In what did this control consist in the case of the non-provided schools? To qualify for the grant given by the statute, a voluntary school must be controlled by a board of managers, six in all, four of whom would represent the founders, two the local education authority. The education committee of the County Council or other equivalent body had the right to determine the secular instruction given at the school, and its consent was required for the appointment or dismissal of the teachers,

[1] October 17, 1902.

though it must never be refused on religious grounds. Further, in the course of the debates, a Conservative member of the House of Commons, Colonel Kenyon-Slaney, moved an amendment which in both Houses rekindled the fires of the ritualist controversy. His amendment, which was carried, to protect the schools against the introduction of doctrinal novelties by High Church clergymen, entrusted the board of managers, as we have seen, a mixed body, with the duty of ensuring that the religious teaching was in conformity with the wishes of the original founders. These were the essential provisions of the new statute which saved the denominational schools from decline and eventual extinction by giving them a share in the rates, as well as in grants by the central authority. The amount of these grants was, moreover, twice raised during the discussion of the Bill, so as not to frighten voters by the prospect of too high an increase in the rates. The provision to be made to protect the children's freedom of conscience, the division of the cost of maintaining the buildings between the funds of the voluntary schools and the public purse, and the procedure to be followed in opening new schools were the subject of complicated bargaining between the two parties.

5

Such was the important measure with which the Parliament, elected in 1900, after sitting for thirty months of war inaugurated its labours under the conditions of peace. Regarded from the distance of a quarter of a century it seems no small achievement. It has received the indisputable consecration of stability. Nor has it, despite the prophecies of the Opposition, revived the old denominational feuds. In the large urban centres, the education committees of the County Councils have continued with increased, rather than diminished, energy the excellent work the school boards had accomplished during the previous thirty years. In the country districts, they could not fail to be an improvement on the little sleepy school boards which they succeeded, and their powers were far wider. But the real importance of the new legislation lay in the clauses which dealt with secondary, not with elementary, education. For the first time in England the provision of secondary education was recognized as the duty of the State and was brought under public control. No doubt, the new institutions have preserved many features distinctively British—the intimate co-operation between the local authorities and the governing bodies of the Universities, and the independence within very wide limits of individual headmasters. Nevertheless, England had seen the necessity of copying the Continental, the Prussian example, and providing institutions similar to the French lycées and the German gymnasia.

With what zeal, in this sphere, too, the statute was applied! In the school year immediately preceding its enactment England possessed 341 establishments where education above the elementary standard was given, attended by 27,989 pupils and in receipt from one source or other, under the complicated system which then prevailed, of government grants to the amount of £140,888. Five years later, the number of these establishments had risen to 689, the number of pupils to 66,004, and the grants to £246,220.[1] And during the following years the progress became even more rapid under another Government, which administered the Act on more democratic lines. It was a social revolution of the first magnitude. Throughout the whole of the nineteenth century the sole means by which members of the lower middle class in the towns and country districts could rise in the social scale was by becoming wealthy. It was only for his sons that the successful manufacturer or merchant could hope for an education not picked up at random, that genuinely liberal education which would admit them to the Universities and through the Universities to the polish and refinement which distinguished the upper classes. In future there was no county or town in which the lower middle class was unprovided with secondary schools where for a low fee, or even without payment, their children could receive an education as good as that given to the children of the gentry or the upper middle class.

When we consider all the forces which co-operated to produce the statute of 1902, and on the other hand its permanent success, our first impression will probably be that about the beginning of

[1] See *Board of Education, Statistics of Public Education in England and Wales*, 1903-4-5, 1905-6-7. See the figures for each school year. Number of recognized establishments: 1901-2, 341; 1902-3, 418; 1903-4, 482; 1904-5, 575; 1905-6, 689. Number of pupils earning grants: 1901-2, 27,989; 1902-3, 33,748; 1903-4, 39,066; 1904-5, 51,779; 1905-6, 66,004. Amount of grants: 1901-2, £140,888; 1902-3, £157,220; 1903-4, £175,248; 1904-5, £211,254; 1905-6, £246,220. The number of pupils would be considerably higher, if we took into account all the pupils attending the schools, and not only those earning grants. 1905-6, 65,994 boys; 49,694 girls. Total 115,688.

the new century some legislation of the kind was inevitable. To organize secondary education the British Government could not fail to undertake responsibilities similar to those it had undertaken thirty years earlier to organize elementary education. And the moment it was a question of entrusting the local control of secondary education to one or other of the two authorities, it was inevitable that the County Councils should be preferred to the school boards. That step once taken, the Councils must of necessity take over all the functions hitherto exercised by the school boards. Nevertheless, we cannot avoid the impression that both the introduction and passage of the Act of 1902 were due to a happy chance. If the Liberals had not been turned out in 1895, we do not see how they could have dared to touch the school boards. And if, on the other hand, they had attempted to extend the school boards to the entire country, we do not see how they could have overcome the opposition of the Church of England, allied, as she was, with the Catholics. We can envisage only some unreal solution, some vague compromise.

On the other hand, it is easy to understand why the Conservatives succeeded, where the Liberals must have failed. Did the Conservative ministers perceive the significance of the far-reaching reform they carried through Parliament in 1902? Only in the case of one of them is this at all probable. But Sir John Gorst occupied a subordinate position, and, as we have just seen, when the Cabinet was remodelled in June 1902, he was turned out of the Government on account of his quarrelsome temper and eccentricities of judgment. As for the Cecil faction and their leader, Balfour, they probably saw in the measure only two features— the grant of financial aid to the denominational schools of the Anglican Church and the abolition of the board schools, whose extravagance had long been the object of Tory denunciation.[1]

[1] When Lord Salisbury, shortly after taking office, received a deputation of clergy he took the opportunity to complain of the lavish expenditure of the school boards, some check on which he thought necessary. (*Annual Register*, 1895, p. 196.) And in the speech with which he introduced the Bill in the House of Commons on March 24, 1902, Balfour pointed out as one of the unforeseen results of the Act of 1870 that: 'A strain, or at all events a burden was put upon local finances in School Board areas through the action of a body responsible indeed to the community, so far as regards education, but having no responsibility for the general expenditure, which was, of course, in the hands of the local authority. . . . What on earth should we think of a system which gave to the experts of the Navy and Army, for purposes of national defence, unlimited power of drawing cheques on the National Exchequer? . . . I do not believe that this system of *ad hoc* authority with unlimited rating is one which really has any important experimental endorsement behind it at all.'

And there can be little doubt that the energy which the education committees of the County Councils displayed, as soon as they came into existence, must have disconcerted them considerably. 'I did not realize', Balfour admitted later to an eminent Socialist, 'that the Act would mean more expense and more bureaucracy.' The Bill had been suggested to him and his Tory colleagues by the department, which had found a valuable ally in the person of Sidney Webb. It was Webb whose propaganda had rendered the Liberal experts powerless, and who had contrived through the Press to recommend the Bill to public opinion. That the Bill favoured the Anglican, and even the Catholic Church, would not displease the Webbs. For, faithful in this to the old tradition of the Saint-Simonians, they have always regarded the Catholic type of Christianity as more in harmony with the Socialist ideal than Protestant individualism. Nor was it any objection to the Bill in their eyes that it had been introduced by the Conservatives and was inspired by a Conservative spirit. That was a victory for the disinterested Machiavellianism which was the essence of the Fabian method. At their instigation Tory politicians had introduced into the law of Great Britain without intending, or even being aware of it, an important measure of educational Socialism.

6

The ministers were mistaken as to the permanent significance and value of the new statute, and their mistake secured its passage by a Conservative majority. But by giving a clerical and Tory aspect to a measure, destined to succeed so completely, they aroused a storm of opposition which did much to weaken the position of the party that had now been in office for over seven years. And one member of the Cabinet, at least, was aware of this. Chamberlain was himself a Nonconformist. He had brought over with him to the Tories an entire group, of whom the majority in Birmingham were possibly Dissenters. And the Education Bill, passed at a moment when the reconstitution of the Cabinet in June had weakened his influence, was a further victory within the Government of the old Tories and the Cecils. It was the more complete, because Chamberlain could make no public protest. But while, for the sake of party discipline, he forced himself to allay the fears of his friends in Birmingham, he frankly communicated his true sentiments to the Duke of Devonshire. 'The political future seems to me—an optimist by profession—most gloomy. I told you that your Education Bill would destroy your own party. It has done so. Our best friends are leaving us by scores and hundreds, and they will not come back.'[1]

It was indeed only to be expected that the Dissenters should immediately interpret the Conservative measure as an attack upon themselves. The school boards had been their strongholds, and in their eyes the adoption of all the voluntary schools by the public authority would irrevocably confirm the tyranny of the Anglican clergy in the country districts. On the question of the Boer War their leaders had been divided. Now that the war was over, the moment had arrived to close their ranks against the common enemy at home. To the intense disgust of George Cadbury, whose sole aim in working for the federation of the sects had been to further the cause of religion and assist the evangelization of the country, the National Council of the Free Churches provided an opportune rallying point for the new agitation. The programme of the rebels, which they had already adopted in the spring, was to make the application of the Act impossible by refusing to pay the education rate if it was to be used for the support of the Anglican, as well as the board schools. In Wales, the revolt assumed a more dangerous character. There, only a small minority belonged to the Established Church. The utmost she could claim was that she possessed a larger membership than any of the Dissenting sects taken singly. Now, however, when the sects were federated and the object of a common attack by the Conservatives, they formed, as a federation, the genuine national church of Wales. Lloyd George put himself at the head of the Welsh revolt. In Parliament he led the opposition to the Bill, as Lord Hugh Cecil, one of Lord Salisbury's sons, led the defence; it was a duel between a Baptist and a High Churchman. Outside the House he advised the malcontents. Three Welsh County Councils declared that they would not co-operate in carrying out the Education Act. What purpose, asked Lloyd George, could this rebellion serve? Surely the more sensible course would be to apply the Act in such a way as to defeat its authors' intention. As a lawyer he knew how this could be done. For example, why

[1] Chamberlain to the Duke of Devonshire, September 22, 1902 (*The Life of Spencer Compton, Duke of Devonshire*, by Bernard Holland, vol. ii, p. 284).

should not the Councils make use of the control which the statute gave them over the former 'voluntary' schools, the non-provided schools of the new Act, to choke them out of existence? He could count on the Welsh County Councils. Let them bring the English Councils into line, and he ventured to say that in three years' time the priests would have lived to regret the insolence that had made them demand this Act of Parliament.[1]

Besides resisting the application of the law, the Nonconformists could also work for its repeal. So long as the present Tory majority continued, repeal was impossible; they must, therefore, ensure a Liberal majority at the next election. And not only a Liberal majority, but a majority in which the Nonconformists, still very poorly represented in Parliament, would occupy a position corresponding to their influence. In every constituency they must organize, to use the phrase of one of their number, a Nonconformist *caucus* for the purpose of increasing the Nonconformist representation in the Commons. In this way the difficulty with which the Liberals had been obliged to contend in 1895 would be solved. Then, there had not been sufficient Liberal candidates. They could secure them now on a somewhat lower social level, from the Nonconformist middle class. A by-election was held on July 30 in a Leeds constituency. At five elections in succession the constituency had returned a Conservative and in 1900 the Conservative majority had exceeded 2,000. Now, the Radical candidate was returned. He had fought the election on the single issue of education, and he was a Baptist. In August there was another by-election at Sevenoaks in Kent, one of those rural constituencies of the south where the return of the Conservative seemed a foregone conclusion. He was indeed returned, but his majority was insignificant. The Education Act had been presented to the electors as a measure transferring to their shoulders the burden of the Anglican schools hitherto supported by private charity. Who had made them believe this? Obviously the local Nonconformists. And the Liberal candidate so nearly successful was again a Baptist.

The Liberal statesmen, possibly less interested in the dispute than we should gather from their public speeches, followed the lead given by those groups of Dissenters, who in the constituencies composed the local party organization. The Liberal Imperial-

---

[1] Speech delivered at the seventh National Council of the Evangelical Free Churches at Brighton, March, 1903.

ists, delighted to find a platform on which they could unite with the other section of the party, threw themselves energetically into the campaign. With the solitary exception of Haldane, who was under the direct influence of the Webbs, they violently opposed the Bill, and when Lord Rosebery received a Nonconformist deputation on December 8 his speech, which in thinly disguised language encouraged the Dissenters to disobey the law, was the subject of protests in the Lords.

Throughout the Nonconformist and Radical ranks frenzied excitement prevailed.[1] To read the Liberal newspapers of the day you would imagine that the Cecils were preparing to revive the policy of Laud, if not of Strafford, and that in every village a Nonconformist Hampden was about to rise against their persecution. But what was the truth? The age of the Stuarts was no more than an historical memory, wars of religion a thing of the past. The grievances of which the masses were sensible were of a very different order. When we consider what they were, we can hardly help suspecting, that, if certain Liberal leaders espoused the Nonconformist cause with such ardour, it was because they wished to create a diversion, not only from the internal quarrels which imperilled the unity of the party, but also from the agitation whose history we must now relate, an agitation which threatened to prove equally dangerous to both the traditional parties, the Conservative and the Liberal alike.

[1] It is characteristic of the situation that in the second of two excellent articles contributed to the *Revue de Paris* by M. Ch. V. Langlois ('La Loi Anglaise sur l'Enseignement,' April 1 and 15, 1903, dixième année, Nos. 7 and 8, pp. 498, 805), articles written only a few weeks after the Act was passed, only 3 pages were devoted to the question of secondary education, 18 to the struggle between the Church and the sects.

CHAPTER II

Social Questions: The Birth of the Labour Party

I THE LABOUR MOVEMENT AND THE POLICY OF THE GOVERNMENT

I

EVERY year, since 1868, the parliament of the working class met in one or other of the large towns. The Anglican Churches and Nonconformist chapels of the locality celebrated by religious services the opening of the Congress of British Trade Unions. The mayor of the city, wearing the insignia of office, gave the members a civic welcome. The meetings were attended by Members of Parliament and British or foreign economists who were received with the utmost respect and courtesy. The speeches were usually dignified, the debates methodically conducted under the strict control of the chair, and the delegates concluded the discussions by passing a number of resolutions which reflected every year the feeling that prevailed among the trade unionists. The Congress brought the session to a close by electing a Parliamentary Committee to look after the interests of the working class in the House of Commons during the following year and make arrangements for the ensuing Congress.

The reasonable and orderly spirit which marked the proceedings are the more remarkable when we consider the great and constantly increasing numerical strength of the unions. About the year 1895 a million trade unionists sent delegates to the Congress. And the total membership of the unions of the United Kingdom, including those which were not represented at the Congress, was estimated at one and a half million—that is, say, about a fifth of the entire number of adult male workers. There was nothing like it in any other great nation. Moreover, an estimate of the strength of the working class not confined to a general view of the country as a whole, but distinguishing between the different districts and branches of the national industry yielded even more striking results. In the building trade and among the railwaymen trade unionism was still in its infancy. Of the four million inhabitants of Ireland only 40,000 were members of a union. In the agricultural districts of England trade unions were almost unknown. And in London and in the Midlands their membership was small. Nor was the number of trade unionists very much larger in Yorkshire or in the Welsh coalfield. But there could be no doubt that the day would come when, throughout the entire country, the working men would follow the example set by the workers of certain districts and certain privileged trades. In Lancashire, Durham, and Northumberland the trade unions contained at least a tenth of the entire population, and half the adult male workers.[1] It would be true to say that for the Lancashire cotton spinner or weaver, the miner in Durham or Northumberland, membership of a trade union was in practice compulsory.

Indeed the size of this army of workmen was perhaps the best security that the unions would pursue a prudent policy. In a highly-civilized country there are not a million or a million and a half revolutionaries; and of the British unions, about the year 1895, the most conservative and cautious were precisely those whose membership included the largest proportion of the men employed in the trade. The reason becomes plain, when we consider their members' economic position. The normal wage earned by a mechanic, a metal worker, a cotton spinner, or a miner was thirty shillings or more a week, the week consisting of six, sometimes of only five, working days. Moreover, he had learned to make use of those great co-operative societies of consumers which covered with a network, thicker every year, the manufacturing districts of the Kingdom, and thus had sensibly reduced the cost of living. And for a considerable number of years the family income was increased by the children's labour. In short, current prices had enabled a very large body to come into existence among the British proletariat, able to keep up a standard of living almost as high as that of the middle class. The self-respecting

[1] For all these figures see particularly Sidney and Beatrice Webb, *The History of Trade Unionism*. Revised Ed., 1920, pp. 422 sqq. See also, for the position of the trade unions about the year 1895, Sidney and Beatrice Webb, *Industrial Democracy*, 1897. Also the volumes of the comprehensive inquiry carried out by the Royal Commission appointed in 1891 'to inquire into the questions affecting the relations between employers and employed; the combinations of employers and employed; and the conditions of labour, which have been raised during the recent trade disputes in the United Kingdom; and to report whether legislation can with advantage be directed to the remedy of any evils that may be disclosed and, if so, in what manner.' 1893-4.

workman in the north of England wanted to own his cottage and garden, in Lancashire his piano. His life was insured. If he shared the common English failing and was a gambler, prone to bet too highly on horses and risk his savings too often in unsafe investments, the rapid growth of savings banks proved that he was nevertheless learning the prudence of the middle classes. There were even several trade unions which were themselves mutual benefit societies and attracted members by insuring them against the risks incident to a workman's life, sickness, accidents, a destitute old age. To organize their systems of benefit these unions accumulated enormous funds. An historian of Trade Unionism calculated that during the single year 1889 the receipts of the Amalgamated Society of Engineers amounted to £183,651, the expenditure to £132,642; the receipts of the United Society of Boilermakers and Iron Shipbuilders to £104,513, the expenditure to £56,655; the receipts of the Amalgamated Society of Carpenters and Joiners to £75,069, the expenditure to £39,824.[1] In 1894, the economist and statistician, Robert Giffen, estimated the total yearly income of the British Trade Unions[2] at £1,200,000.

Were the unions opposed to State interference in any shape or form? Certainly not. Perhaps the principal function of the great cotton and coal unions was to see that the Factory Acts were fully carried out in the workshops and mines. But, if we insist on regarding the Factory Acts as a beginning of Socialism, we must admit that contemporary labour leaders were entirely unaware of it. Neither the members of the Parliamentary Committee, with the exception of one or two, nor the tiny group of working men whom the miners had begun to return to Parliament as their representatives, Burt for example and Fenwick, pious Methodists and local preachers, universally respected for their earnestness and virtues, had the least wish to be considered Socialists. They persisted in regarding themselves as the heirs of great Liberal tradition, the sworn foe of protection, Socialism, and war, the tradition of Cobden, Bright, and Gladstone. The leaders of the Liberal party had secured their allegiance and paid their election expenses. And so long as they were at Westminster

---

[1] G. Howell, *Trade Unionism, Old and New*, p. 225.
[2] Representing 871,000 members. *Fourth Report of Royal Commission on Labour, Min. of Ev.: Evidence given by Robert Giffen*, 6,987, 6,988 (p. 480).

regular payments from the party funds enabled these working-class members to appear in the House like respectable citizens of the middle class. A bricklayer, Broadhurst by name, had been appointed in 1880 Under-Secretary of the Board of Trade. And when, in 1893, the Liberal Government instituted a Labour Department, an important place in it was found for the engineer, John Burns. About a hundred working men had been appointed Justices of the Peace while the Liberals were in office between 1892 and 1895.[1] In this way, as members of a capitalist society and the Liberal party the leaders of the proletariat were becoming accustomed to take a share, however modest, in the government of the nation.

2

Conservatives on the Continent admired this self-imposed discipline, this courteous behaviour, this absence of revolutionary bitterness and held them up as an example—especially among the Latin nations, though also among the Teutonic—to their own revolutionary proletariat. But the British capitalists about 1895 did not share the feelings which the spectacle of trade unionism inspired in the foreign observer. All this discretion was accompanied by a power which was becoming formidable. There was good reason to wonder whether the organizations of the working class, even the most conservative, were not silently building up a system of trade union rule which was perhaps one of the causes, if not the chief cause, of the alarming stagnation of industry. It was not surprising that the United States and Germany were outstripping England in the struggle for industrial supremacy. Neither Carnegie nor Krupp had to deal with trade unions.[2]

No doubt the extensive system of benefits which was the boast of certain unions proved that their members were inspired by the spirit of individualism, not of revolution. But on the one hand, many unions, and not the least important, had no system of benefits; for example, the great unions of cotton operatives and miners. And on the other hand, even where it existed, the benefit system of a trade union differed in many respects from the system worked by a friendly society, the typical mutual benefit society.

---

[1] The report of the Parliamentary Committee to the Trades Union Congress of 1893 mentions seventy appointments which had been made since the previous Congress.
[2] W. S. Ashley, *The Tariff Problem*, p. 190.

In the first place, among the other benefits it offered, the union undertook to assist its members during unemployment. And the relief would be given whether the unemployment was involuntary—the result of a depression in trade, or a lock-out by the employer—or a deliberate strike, even a strike called by the union itself. Throughout, the aim of the unions was to secure that the working class should present a united front to the employers— that is to say, all their arrangements implied that a state of war was the normal relation between the two classes, the employers and the men. And whenever that hostility became an open conflict the unions reserved the right to suspend all payment of sickness or accident benefits, even of old age pensions due to their members. For war is war, and the entire funds of a union might be needed to finance the strike.[1] The secretaries of the unions were too anxious to make the best use of the vast sums in their hands to engage in a struggle lightheartedly. Whenever they could they preferred to gain their ends by threatening the employers with a strike, than to make an actual use of the weapon. But when a union took the supreme decision, it was the more serious because it had been so deliberate. The wealth which had made it hesitate so long before declaring war, increased its power of resistance when the contest had once begun. There was not a country in the world where revolutionary catchwords had less power over the organized workers than in England. But the fact remains that in England, as everywhere else, the trade unions were organized for the class war.

Whether put forward continuously or at intervals, urged by silent pressure or open war, what were the claims made by the unions? Obviously, the workers were seeking to improve their conditions of life, to shorten their hours of work, and raise their wages. But we have still to inquire how they proposed to regulate the conditions of labour in order to secure these objects? In the first place, by the systematic restriction of the numbers employed in a particular branch of industry:[2] they either enforced an appren-

[1] George Howell, *Conflicts of Capital and Labour*, 2nd and revised ed., 1890, pp. 477–8. S. and B. Webb, *Industrial Democracy*, pp. 152 sqq.

[2] We base our statements on the evidence collected by Sidney and Beatrice Webb (ibid., pp. 434 sqq.). The book is partly based on the inquiry of the Royal Commission on Labour of 1891, but also on an extensive private investigation, organized by the two authors. It is a work of the highest value, but the reader must not forget that it is a work of apologetic as well as a scientific treatise, and that the facts related by the writers sometimes compel dissent from us to their interpretation. For example, in their

ticeship, extending over a large number of years, on all who wished to enter the trade, or fixed the proportion of children to adults that might be employed by any firm. Sometimes the men even reserved a definite proportion of the vacancies for their own children. The aim avowedly pursued by the vast majority of unions was the transformation of every industry and every trade into a species of guild closed to outside labour. When the employer could no longer use the competition of outside labour to keep down wages, they became, to the great benefit of the workmen, a monopoly price. Employers complained of the damage these methods caused to national industry. In their opinion the workmen had given up the savage method of breaking machinery only to adopt a more complicated, but equally efficacious, procedure. The American or German employer was free to introduce into his factory the plant and process which made it possible to substitute unskilled for skilled labour. But the British employer was faced by the organized opposition of his men. In the engineering trade he could employ only skilled workmen, each of whom would serve only a single machine, whereas his German competitor could employ one unskilled workman to tend three machines at the same time.[1] He had therefore strong grounds for contending as he did, that in the never-ending struggle with the

opinion the unions which limited the number of their members by fixing the number of apprentices represented only two-fifths of the total membership of the unions. This in itself would be a high proportion. But they class under other headings unions such as the Cotton Spinners' and Miners' which by restricting the number of children employed to assist the adult workers, made it difficult to improve the plant, prevented the substitution of unskilled for skilled labour, and had therefore been equally successful in establishing in the industry the monopoly of a close aristocracy of trade unionists. Moreover, they attempt to show that even in the unions which profess to restrict apprenticeship, the regulation could not be carried out, since it was incompatible with the conditions of modern large-scale industry and was in fact becoming obsolete. While fully appreciating the ingenuity of the authors' explanations on this point, it is not easy to avoid the impression that these regulations were still by no means a dead letter, since when the Great War broke out in 1914, the Government, with the entire approval of the Webbs, persuaded the trade union officials to suspend their rules in the interest of national safety.

[1] A. Marshall, *Industry and Trade*, p. 137 n. In chap. viii of their *Industrial Democracy* ('New Processes and Machinery') Sidney and Beatrice Webb attempt to prove that the opposition of labour to machinery was entirely a thing of the past and that the sole concern of the workers was to settle the conditions on which they would permit the employer to install machines. This is quite possible. But if the conditions were such, that the employer could no longer profit by the installation, we must admit that the trade unions at the close of the nineteenth century were still obstructing technical progress. The Webbs practically admit this in the case of the engineers (*History of Trade Unionism*, ed., 1920, p. 7—Cf. S. Webb, 'La Guerre Industrielle en Angleterre', *Revue de Paris*, December 15, 1897, pp. 915–17). Why then is there not a word about the engineers in the chapter to which we have just referred? For the lock-out of the engineers (see below, p. 251) was the outstanding event of the industrial situation when the Webbs' book appeared.

unions he stood for progress, his trade unionist employee for an unprogressive routine.

Nevertheless, in spite of the unintelligent conservatism of labour, machinery continued more or less slowly to make progress, and in many unions the workmen, realizing that the development could not be prevented, had modified their tactics. They left the employer free to engage all the men he wanted, on condition that when the new hands were taken on they should be obliged to join the union, and accept engagement, only if the position of the workers was not rendered harder in consequence, and on the understanding that, if their labour increased the employer's profits, the men's wages should be correspondingly raised. Throughout the country a system of Boards of Conciliation had come into existence—committees on which masters and men were equally represented and which met at regular intervals to revise amicably the conditions of labour. Sometimes the system accepted by both parties was to make the rate of wages dependent on the prices fetched by the manufactured article. That was the case in the iron manufacture of the North of England and in the coalfields of Northumberland and South Wales. It was a system detrimental to the consumer, because it made high prices the common interest of employers and men. And it was inapplicable to branches of industry in which the manufactured article was not sold directly. Moreover, from the workmen's point of view it was open to the objection that it did not automatically correlate wages with profits. The workers in the Lancashire cotton industry had, therefore, devised a more scientific arrangement. The famous Brooklands Agreement, concluded in 1893 between the cotton spinners and their men, after a strike which for twenty weeks had brought the cotton manufacture to a standstill, laid down rules which effected an automatic correspondence between wages and profits, prescribed the methods by which the latter were to be estimated, appointed experts to secure their regular application, and finally, to obviate future strikes, set up a graduated series of committees, with appeal from the lower to the higher, to settle amicably any difficulties which might arise in the interpretation of the agreement.

Why not extend to every branch of industry a system which had worked very well in the Lancashire cotton mills and proved equally successful in other branches of the cotton manufacture,

and thus settle peacefully the conditions of labour throughout the entire country? The idea attracted a number of philanthropists and politicians. It is unlikely that many manufacturers shared their enthusiasm. Though the manufacturers bowed to the inevitable, they would have preferred freedom to increase their profits uncontrolled by their employees. They must have read with considerable uneasiness the evidence given by the president of the Cotton Spinners' Union before the Royal Commission appointed in 1891 to investigate the conditions of labour in Great Britain. 'We look', declared the witness, 'at the general profit that the trade is making; we know the price cotton can be bought at; we know the price that yarn is sold at every day; we know exactly the margin; we know to the hundredth part of a penny what it costs in store; the fixed stock is public property; we know what a sensible and reasonable depreciation is upon the same; and we know that, after we have got our wages out of it and we leave the balance to the employer, he has nothing to make a great noise about.'[1]

3

Such were the misgivings with which about the year 1895 the British employers regarded the methods employed by the oldest and most Conservative Unions, the unions whose respectable and law-abiding officials were the admiration and envy of employers all over the Continent. But their anxiety was increased by the fact that for the past few years the proletariat had been exposed to the influence of a novel agitation. From 1886 onwards a series of great strikes which broke out in London had brought into prominence the names of a few young firebrands, John Burns and Tom Mann among the engineers, and Ben Tillett among the dockers. In 1889 the Socialist parties of Europe celebrated the centenary of the French Revolution by holding in Paris the first congress of what was to be known as 'the Second International'. Did this chronological coincidence fire the youthful imagination of a number of British workers? Among the working class there were those who believed that the centenary of the French Revolution would witness the social revolution in England. Nothing of the sort happened.

[1] Royal Commission on Labour, *Minutes of Evidence Group C*, vol. i, p. 21: Evidence of George Silk. Cf. the words spoken by the secretary of a London Union of Stone Cutters to P. de Rousiers during his inquiry: 'You see, sir, employers are exactly what we make them' (*Le Trade Unionisme en Angleterre*, p. 39).

There was no revolution either that year or in any subsequent year. But a new spirit took possession of the trade unions.

Grades of labour too poor to pay large subscriptions and, until now, too completely crushed by the hardship of their lot to dream of revolt, learnt to organize and form their unions, and it was among the unskilled labour of the metropolis that the strike of 1889 had occurred. The dockers, the unskilled workers on the railways, the gas workers, the seamen, founded unions which from the outset secured a very large membership, and were distinguished by the extremely low subscriptions they demanded from their members and the fact that they were organized exclusively for strikes. Nor were they confined to a particular trade. The National Union of Gas Workers and General Labourers and the General Railway Workers' Union were open to all the unskilled—the 'general' labourers—whatever the workshop in which they were employed. True, this sudden explosion of what was called the new unionism was to some extent a flash in the pan, and by 1895[1] the majority of these unions had lost a very large proportion of their members. Nevertheless, the old unions felt their influence, and their spirit tended to become less aristocratic and less selfish.

Less aristocratic: in 1892, a union so exclusive as the Amalgamated Society of Engineers admitted classes of workmen hitherto ineligible. Less selfish also: hitherto every trade possessed its union, and the most absurd rivalries had occurred between the unions of kindred trades. The formation of confederations of textile workers, engineers and shipbuilders proved that the workers were beginning to look further than the unions of their particular trade. We even remark the beginnings of international federation among the dockers, miners, glaziers and textile workers. All manual workers, whatever their position in the ranks of

[1] Those who remained were probably those who were better paid, and under their influence the unions of the New Unionism fell back into the ways of the Old. See Sidney and Beatrice Webb, *History of Trade Unionism*, 1895, p. 406: 'The Dock, Wharf, and Riverside Labourers' Union now gives Funeral Benefit—usually the first to be added; whilst many of the branches of the National Union of Gas Workers and General Labourers have local benefit funds, and the addition of Accident Benefit by the whole society is under discussion.' Cf. P. de Rousiers' *Le Trade Unionisme en Angleterre*, 1897, p. 184: 'I have already pointed out that the original militant character of the Union (The Dockers' Union) has been modified. Of this the rules actually in force are a sufficient proof. Strike pay plays but a small part and its amount is not even determined. On the other hand the funeral benefit introduced shortly after the foundation of the Union is the subject of detailed regulations. The amount given has been gradually raised, and is now about eight pounds. This is a high figure for a Union in which the subscription is only threepence a week.'

labour, and in every branch of international production, were, it seemed, becoming conscious that they were all members of a single class.

At the same time, the nature of their demands changed. They no longer asked for 'sliding scales' by which wages rose and fell with the fluctuations of market prices or employers' profits. They claimed a fixed living wage which would enable them to live in decent conditions worthy of a free man. That wage, the just wage, was their right, the first charge on industry. When it had been paid, the employer might compensate himself as best he was able, and make whatever profit he could. They also demanded a minimum of leisure, and as a nine hours' day was tending to become the rule throughout the important industries, they began to claim, in accordance with the programme laid down by the Second International, an eight hours' day. These demands were addressed in the first instance to the employer, but in the second place to the State. The old trade unions, declared Burns, were mistaken in their belief that the conditions of labour could be improved by voluntary agreements between masters and men. In fact, the only result of these agreements had been the official ratification by the men's representatives of wage reductions imposed by the employers. It was for the Municipality, the County Council, and Parliament to fix a minimum wage and limit the working day to eight hours. The first success of the new policy was a concession obtained from the Liberal Cabinet. The State in its capacity as an employer of labour set the example to private enterprise by making an eight hours' day the rule in all workshops under the authority of the War Office and the Admiralty, and in all Post Offices. These new demands amounted to a form of Socialism. For they implied that the worker possessed a right to the produce of his labour which must be enforced before any claim by the employer could be entertained. In fact, during the last five or ten years the masses had been influenced by a Socialist movement fully conscious of its aims.[1]

[1] For the Socialist groups in England about 1895, see the annual published from that year onwards under the title: *The Labour Annual, the Year Book for Social and Political Reformers*; the contemporary French work by A. Métin, *Le Socialisme en Angleterre*, 1897; also M. Beer, *Geschichte des Sozialismus in England*, 1913, pp. 440 sqq. (English Translation 1919-20). See further A. W. Humphrey, *A History of Labour Representation*, 1912.

4

In 1884, the year following Karl Marx's death, his disciple Hyndman, after feeling his way for three years, founded the Social Democratic Federation. It had been his intention to found on the basis of Marx's doctrine a political party similar to those 'Labour Parties' which about the same time were springing up in every country of Western Europe in imitation of the German Socialist Party. The group maintained itself in existence with its local branches, its weekly organ *Justice*, and its general council furnished with dictatorial powers. If it had lost William Morris, the poet, and Champion, the ex-soldier whose plans for the organization of an armed revolution had terrified the middle classes, it still possessed a tiny, but compact, staff of officers, in which the intellectuals seemed to outnumber the workers. The books in which Hyndman taught the British public orthodox Marxism found readers. And the works, bristling with Hegelian terminology, which Belfort Bax poured out in regular succession, ran to several editions. Among the members of the 'General Council' the name of Eleanor Aveling, Marx's daughter, possessed the value of a red flag. Nevertheless, the Federation's pedantic fanaticism produced very little effect on the general public. There is something pitiable in the history of a group whose members were never weary of uttering threats, proclaiming the imminence of revolution and declaring their readiness to take control of it, yet had never succeeded, in spite of persistent efforts, and never would succeed, in securing the election of a single candidate. Obviously, neither their doctrine nor their methods answered the needs of the country.

This sour creed, imported from abroad, which refused to set before its adherents an ideal which made appeal to the heart but was content to prove by scientific arguments, or what purported to be such, the approach of a complete upheaval of society, at once violent in its methods, and beneficent in its effects, repelled many of those Englishmen who for the past twenty-five years or more had been approaching Socialism by other routes. In agreement with the Marxists to denounce a social order based on the unhappiness of the majority and the war of all against all, they did not share the Marxian interpretation of history. They did not invite the working classes to use violence. The formula of the class war was absent from their vocabulary. Neither Ruskin, the man whose spirit inspired British Socialism, nor William Morris himself, though he professed a species of anarchist Communism, was in the strict sense a revolutionary. England had passed through two revolutions—the Puritan revolution of the seventeenth century, the industrial revolution of the eighteenth—and their dark shadow still lay over the land. Without recourse to violence, Socialism must teach the nation the art of being good, and happy, the cult of beauty.

About this time, a writer was preaching a philosophy which, though far more crude, was not without obvious connections with that of Morris. He was Robert Blatchford, the editor of a weekly paper called the *Clarion*, and founder of a fellowship called by that name. The titles of his works—*Britain for the British*, *Merrie England*—sufficiently indicate the tone of his propaganda. A former soldier, he was an ardent patriot and the support he gave to the Government during the Boer War, and his call to arms against the German peril a little later, cost him much of his influence with the Socialist masses. But for the moment it was enormous. His books of propaganda enjoyed a very large sale, the *Clarion* had an immense circulation, and equally great was the success of the red vans, the Clarion Vans, which went up and down the country preaching Socialism. The groups he founded did not aspire to become branches of a political party. He made converts to Socialism by bringing happiness into their lives, and made their lives happier by systematically organizing Sunday amusements—cricket, football, bicycle excursions, campings out in the country—a welcome reaction from the rigid Sabbatarianism of the Evangelical middle class. As we have seen, it was about this time that the Puritans of the Sects began to make efforts to establish contact with the masses and to substitute for their old individualist Radicalism a species of Protestant Socialism. May not one of their motives have been to counteract this secularist propaganda? From the warp and woof of such opposing tendencies the temper of a great people is woven. But in any case, neither on the one side nor on the other, was there a trace of the Marxian pedantry and bitterness.

The methods advocated by the Social Democratic Federation were as unattractive to the British public as their creed. What were they? Hyndman and his friends aimed at founding in as many constituencies as possible, a political Socialist party, opposed to the two historic parties, but organized, like them, for the conquest of seats in Parliament. To make that possible a large number of supporters was necessary and a well-replenished party coffer. But in 1895 the supporters of the Federation barely exceeded five thousand. And where could the funds be obtained? The Federation could neither obtain subscriptions from wealthy sympathizers, like the bourgeois parties, nor support a party organization on the paltry subscriptions paid by the 5,000 Social Democrats. Once, during the election of 1885, the Federation had accepted 'Tory gold' to prevent the return of certain Liberal candidates. Since the transaction had been made public and the Liberal candidates returned, the intrigue had served only to discredit the Federation. Nevertheless, it was surely paradoxical that at the very time when the British Marxists were forced to admit their destitution, both numerical and financial, vast working class organizations were in existence whose total membership far exceeded a million, and which out of small subscriptions had accumulated enormous funds. They existed for the class war, to defend the workers' interests against their employers. But their vision was bounded by their trade, they knew nothing of Socialism or, if they had heard of it, the very name frightened them. The ten or twelve working men—secretaries or former secretaries of the great unions—who sat in Parliament had, as we have seen, been adopted by the Liberal party. They constituted its most Radical group and were content to insist that a number of reforms demanded by the working class should be incorporated in the party programme. And these reforms amounted to very little, for the Parliamentary representatives of the working class had accepted the creed of Gladstonian Liberalism. The miners could not even agree to demand for their industry the legal enactment of the eight hours' day. It was a ridiculous situation, and it must continue so long as the hostility persisted between the Socialist party and the Trades Union Congress. It was the latter which possessed the necessary numbers and funds, and was inspired by a genuine class consciousness. If a Labour party were to be founded sufficiently powerful to intimidate the bourgeois parties it must be founded upon the trade unions.

5

The offensive began in 1888 at the annual Trades Union Congress at Bradford. A small body of agitators made use of the opportunity to discuss outside the regular meetings of the Congress the possibility of persuading the unions to support the foundation of a third party, wholly Labour in character. The discussions reached no definite result. But a few months later the proposal won the support of the workers of Scotland. The man who had launched it at the Bradford congress was a Scotchman, named Keir Hardie, a little over thirty years old. At the age of eight he had gone down into the mine and had never attended school. He was a self-educated man. Originally without religious convictions, he had been early converted to a vague Christianity which displayed the influence of Ruskin's religious freethought and the rigid morality of the Scottish Presbyterians. He stood at a by-election against the opposing candidates of the two parties, refusing the advances of the Liberal agents who promised him, if he would withdraw his candidature, a safe seat and an annual income of £300. He obtained only a handful of votes, but his independent action produced a powerful effect. His ardent zeal made him a leader. In a year he had organized a sufficient number of small groups to unite them in a party which called itself the Scottish Labour Party.

In England also, similar local groups were formed, and proved their vitality by their victories at the polls at the general election of 1892. Keir Hardie was returned in one metropolitan constituency, John Burns in another, and John Havelock Wilson at Middlesborough. Ben Tillett almost won a seat. The same year, 120 delegates from different bodies met at Bradford for the purpose of definitively founding a Labour party which should not concern itself with differences of economic theory. Should it be called as one delegate suggested, the Socialist Labour Party? No. That would alarm the very people whose support it was desired to win and, once more, explicitly transform a combination based on the practical interests of its members into a group of political theorists, a party, representing a class, into a party representing an economic creed, a doctrinaire party. For Ben Tillett British Trade Unionism was the best form of Socialism and the best policy for labour. The Continental Socialists were no better than stupid windbags, parrots repeating meaningless phrases. The party was not christened the Socialist Labour party but the Independent Labour Party.[1] Nevertheless, its programme was Socialist. And the men who inaugurated the movement were convinced Socialists. But they were aware that, if they were to gain a footing among the trade unions whose Socialism was unconscious, they must begin by excluding from their programme any features which could in any way suggest religious or political revolution and, for that reason, must avoid the term 'Socialism'.

Keir Hardie was already engaged in a direct and by no means unsuccessful attempt to win the Trades Union Congress to his views. The problem to be solved was the formation of what was called a 'Parliamentary fund' to be maintained out of the subscriptions paid by the members of the unions. It would be used partly to defray the expenses of candidates, partly to provide successful candidates with an adequate salary, so long as they remained in Parliament. The proposal, rejected by an overwhelming majority at the Congress of 1891, met, on the contrary, with a favourable reception the following year and was remitted for examination to the Parliamentary Committee with instructions to prepare a detailed scheme for the next congress. It was drawn up, and a contribution from every union of five shillings for every 100 members proposed. The Congress of 1893 passed a motion accepting the institution of a Parliamentary fund, adopted, by a very small majority, it is true, Keir Hardie's motion that the Labour Members of Parliament should be independent of the Liberal as well as of the Tory party, and refused to give financial assistance to candidates whose programme did not comprise public ownership and control of the means of production, distribution and exchange. At the Congress held the following year at Norwich the question of the Parliamentary fund was not re-introduced, but when a motion was submitted to the Congress in favour of nationalizing the land and mines, Keir Hardie moved the addition of the words 'all the means of production and exchange'. His amendment, supported by Tom Mann and John Burns, was carried by 219 votes to 61, and the result was received

[1] Originally, the title Labour Party was intended to be the exact translation of the Continental title, *Parti Ouvrier*, *Partito Operaio*, and *Partido Obrero*. Albert Métin in his book on *Socialism in England*, published in 1897, speaks of the *Parti Ouvrier* Independent. For the history of the Party, see J. R. MacDonald, *The History of the I.L.P.*, with Notes for Lecturers and Class Readers (undated).

with applause. The Congress proceeded to elect the secretary of the Parliamentary Committee. The retiring secretary, who stood for re-election, was Fenwick the miner, a trade unionist of the old school. He had just succeeded at this very Congress in excluding all mention of the mines from the text of a motion relating to the eight hours' day. There were two other candidates. One was Tom Mann the Socialist. The other was Samuel Woods, the extremely energetic secretary of the National Federation of Miners, who, if not technically a Socialist, was one of the most prominent representatives of the new Unionism. He was trying to unite the miners' unions in common action to secure the eight hours' day. On the first scrutiny Woods was leading and on the second he was elected, Tom Mann retiring from the contest.

We must not imagine a bitter struggle fought amidst wild excitement. Woods declared his regard and friendship for Fenwick. Fenwick congratulated Woods, while giving him a friendly warning that he would find the post of Secretary no light task. But the change which was coming over the outlook of trade unionists was very marked nevertheless. At the election of 1895 the Independent Labour Party put forward 28 candidates. Besides these there were five candidates who represented the Marxist Federation or were not attached to any organization. Together they made up a total of 33 candidates, avowed or unavowed Socialists.

6

To the Conservative Press this incipient Socialism was a very alarming phenomenon. But there were Conservatives who found it a matter for thoughtful reflection and drew auguries by no means unfavourable to the prospects of their party. It was all very well for the optimism which inspired the orthodox political economy to prove that wages were higher in England than in any other country and the hours of labour shorter, and that the position of the British workman was even better than it appeared at first sight owing to the rapid fall in the cost of foodstuffs during the last twenty years. This was true at most of the skilled labourers, the cotton operatives, the miners, the engineers, but even their prosperity was insecure, and the fluctuations of the world market exposed them to a constant risk of unemployment. But what of the unskilled labourers who must find work from day to day in the London docks? And what of the tailors and seamstresses of the East End, so cruelly exploited by what was known as the Sweating System? A statistician, Charles Booth, calculated that one-third of the population of the East End was living in a state of chronic destitution,[1] and he was a Conservative. University settlements were being founded in the slums of the large cities to bring university men into direct contact with the working classes, and the young intellectuals who came to teach the poor something of their knowledge, and learn meanwhile the lessons taught by the spectacle of the slums, did not all belong to the parties of the left. Among them were Conservative philanthropists. At Toynbee Hall in Whitechapel the young Milner had spoken on the social question. The discontent of the masses was evidence of their sufferings, and their sufferings a proof that the hopes entertained by men such as Cobden and Gladstone had not been fulfilled, that economic liberalism had not solved the problem of poverty.[2] Here, if anywhere, was the opportunity for the Conservative party to copy the German model.

The social legislation Bismarck had inaugurated during his two last years in power was without doubt one of the most important

[1] For the figures see Charles Booth, *Life and Labour of the People in London, First Series, Poverty*, vol. i, p. 36. Robert Giffen, giving evidence before the Royal Commission on Labour, estimated that the labourers earning a salary of thirty shillings a week or more were only 17.4 per cent of the working class, and the labourers whose wages did not exceed one pound, 23.6 per cent.

[2] For the economic conditions of the British working-class at the end of the nineteenth century, see the optimistic conclusions of Sir Robert Giffen (*Economic Inquiries and Studies*, ed., 1904, vol. i, pp. 382–399, vol. ii, pp. 79 sqq.), and Arthur L. Bowley, *National Progress since 1882*, 1904 (*Elements of Statistics*, ed. 1, 1907, pp. 33 sqq.). See further the copious evidence received during the inquiry by the Royal Commission on Labour, 1891, and the results of the extensive investigation conducted by Charles Booth and published by him between 1892 and 1897, under the title *Life and Labour of the People in London*, 9 vols. (2nd ed., 17 vols, 1902–3). See also the interesting statistical details collected by the Economic Club under the title *Family Budgets: Being the Income and Expenses of Twenty-eight British Households*, 1891, 1894, 1896 (by Charles Booth, Ernest Ames, and Henry Higgs). It follows humbly, the authors state in their preface, and at some distance, in the footsteps of Le Play. René Lavollée's *Les Classes Ouvrières en Europe, Etudes sur leur Situation Matérielle et Morale*, T. III *Angleterre*, 1896, is an extremely voluminous and useful compilation from the evidence taken by the Royal Commission and other sources, interspersed with the reflections of the author, who had personal knowledge of British conditions. The reader will also consult with profit the contemporary evidence of the French writer, P. de Rousiers, *La Question Ouvrière en Angleterre*, 1895; *Le Trade Unionisme en Angleterre*, 1896 (inquiries conducted on the spot by the author; both works are amply furnished with evidence and give proof of very careful reflection), and the German, Gerhart Schulze-Gävernitz, *Der Grossbetrieb ein wirtschaftlicher und socialer Fortschritt. Eine Studie auf dem Gebiete der Baumwollindustrie*, 1892 (English Translation, 1895). The second part of the third chapter contains interesting and exact details.

political events in the history of contemporary Europe. Bitterly opposed at first by the German Socialists, it had finally won their support, conscious or unconscious, express or tacit, and as the Socialists learnt to make use of the machinery provided by the Imperial Government, without admitting it, sometimes not even to themselves, they dropped revolutionary features of their original Marxism. Moreover, the Emperor William, after his dismissal of Bismarck, had facilitated this reconciliation between the Socialists and the Empire by repealing the extraordinary legislation to which they were subject at his accession. By adopting with an ostentation, almost theatrical, measures which paved the way for an international regulation of labour he had invited Europe to follow the example of Germany. But of all the Conservative parties in Europe, the British was surely in a better position than any other to accept the Imperial invitation. Must not the policy of the Conservative revival, if it were true to the conception enunciated by Disraeli after the Reform Bill of 1867, be one of social reform as well as imperialism? When Disraeli became Prime Minister in 1874 had he not honoured his pledges? And later, had not Lord Salisbury, during the six years of the first Unionist Government, found himself obliged, if he was to keep the support of those Chamberlainite Radicals who had just broken with Gladstone, to pursue a policy of active social reform, inspired by the principles laid down by Disraeli? And now, when there was not only a coalition, but an actual fusion between the Liberal and Conservative Unionists, a Unionist Cabinet of which Chamberlain was a member might be expected to introduce bolder reforms than the Cabinet of 1886.

When we were describing just now the Socialist organizations we made no mention of the Fabian Society. Our reason for the omission will be clear to those who remember what we said of the attitude adopted by that group, or at least by its leaders, both during the Boer War and when the Education Bill of 1902 was being drafted—haughty isolation from every other 'advanced' movement, whether among the Liberals or the Socialists. The Society was exactly contemporary with the Social Democratic Federation; at the end of eleven years the Federation possessed five or six times as many members. But whereas its failure to enlist an army of more than 5,000 Socialists spelled disaster to the Federation, the Fabian Society was content to be a small regiment of 700 or 800, a group of students whose propaganda was intended to influence the intelligentsia rather than the masses. It will be as well to repeat and emphasize in somewhat greater detail the peculiarity of their method. They wished to restate Socialism in the plain prose of a workaday world. They derided the revolutionary romanticism of Karl Marx, the myth of an inevitable catastrophe which should transform in a moment the conditions of human life, and inaugurate a golden age, secure from further revolution. They derided every Utopian dream of an earthly Paradise—the Utopia of William Morris for example—dreams so remote from reality that they could afford no guidance in solving the problems of the world, as it really is. If, however, Socialism represents the evolution of historical forces, and if the modern world is moving towards it by an inevitable law, it must be taking shape already under our eyes, even if we are unaware of what is happening. Therefore, in the opinion of the Fabians, the effective Socialist propaganda must be to convince co-operators, trade unionists, Members of Parliament and members of local bodies that, for a long while already, they had been practising unconsciously a Socialist policy. They would thus be persuaded to envisage deliberately and on principle the aims they were already pursuing under the blind urge of an unreasoned instinct.

Was it then advisable to found an independent Labour party? Keir Hardie's campaign took the Fabians by surprise. Towards the close of 1893 Bernard Shaw, the firebrand of the group, in a magazine article which the Society republished later as one of their tracts, demanded an independent trade-unionist party, a party fund of £30,000 and fifty Labour candidates at the next election.[1] On the other hand, the twelve Fabian delegates who attended the conference at which the Independent Labour Party was formed, insisted that they were present only as 'guests' and finally pronounced the experiment fruitless. Sidney and Beatrice Webb upheld their attitude. They declared themselves fully satisfied with a state of affairs in which, as for instance was the case in Lancashire, the secretary of one trade union might be a

---

[1] 'To your Tents, Oh Israel!' By the Fabian Society (*Fortnightly Review*, November, 1893, vol. lx, pp. 569 sqq.). Also *Fabian Tract No. 49, A Plan of Campaign for Labour*, containing the substance of the Fabian Manifesto entitled 'To Your Tents, Oh Israel!' With practical proposals for Labour Representation. Cf. Edward R. Pease, *The History of the Fabian Society*, pp. 114 sqq., and Ed. Bernstein, *My Years of Exile. Reminiscences of a Socialist*, 1921, p. 227.

Conservative, the secretary of another a Liberal, and in consequence the unions were in a position to exercise direct pressure on both the historic parties.[1] Opposed as they were on principle to Utopias of any kind, and intent on putting before the electorate a programme susceptible of immediate realization, they were content to invite the larger unions, the captains of industry, and the bureaucratic State to conclude a species of concordat. They called upon the workers to abandon all regulations or claims made by their unions which in any way hampered the progress of machinery, and upon the employers to accept in return the principle of a regulation of labour which might even extend to the legal enactment of a minimum wage, and they urged both alike to get rid of their liberal prejudices and submit to the authority of the State whose protection they enjoyed. It was a 'Prussian' rather than a revolutionary programme. Was a Socialist party necessary to carry it out? 'The strong desire of nearly all sections of Trade Unionists for this or that measure of legal enactment . . . does not, for the moment, attach them, as Trade Unionists, to any political party. But it implies that they would be strongly, and even permanently, drawn to any political leader, of whatever party, who shared their faith in the efficacy of the Common Rule, and who convinced them that he had the technical knowledge, the will, and the Parliamentary power to carry into law such proposals for legal regulation, as each trade from time to time definitely demanded.'[2] Who would be this leader? Lord Rosebery? Chamberlain? The Webbs were thinking of both. If in 1895 Chamberlain was to be their man, Sidney and Beatrice Webb were at his service, prepared to give him the support of their zeal, industry and genius.

In fact, the leaders of the Unionist party, impressed by the formation of the Independent Labour Party, were asking them-

[1] *Industrial Democracy*, 1897, p. 259.

[2] Ibid., 1897, p. 539. See a little before on the same page the following contemptuous criticism of orthodox Socialism: 'The Socialist candidates are ready to promise the Trade Unionists a systematic and complete regulation of all the conditions of employment. But they show a lamentable deficiency of technical knowledge of the exact regulations required, and they mingle their proposals with revolutionary Shibboleths, as to the "nationalization of the means of production, distribution and exchange", which the bulk of the Trade Unionists fail even to comprehend.' For the history of the Fabian Society see *Fabian Tracts No. 41, The Fabian Society. What it has done. How it has done it.* A paper by G. Bernard Shaw, 1892. Also Edward R. Pease, *The History of the Fabian Society*, 1916. But the real history of the Fabian Society during the period with which we are concerned does not always agree with the official account.

selves whether it was not, in the first instance at any rate, a menace to the Liberals and when, about the beginning of 1895, they perceived that the defeat of the Liberal Cabinet was imminent, they offered the masses a programme more attractive than the social policy of the Liberals had proved. They would cut at the root of Socialism by inaugurating an era of prudent and moderate social reforms,[1] and to the obsolete Radicalism of the Gladstonians would oppose 'a Constructive policy', 'a policy of social reform combined with the maintenance of individual liberty and resistance to Socialistic schemes'.[2] What was this 'constructive' programme of 'social reform' which however was not 'Socialist'? It was, the Tory speakers replied, the policy of Chamberlain.[3] What then was Chamberlain's social policy, as he put it forward, in expectation of the day when the electorate would once more return the Unionist coalition to power? Again we must refer to the Bismarckian legislation, which provided his model. Bismarck had set up an elaborate system of compulsory insurance against the risks incidental to a workman's life, accident, sickness, disablement, and unprovided old age. The cost of the scheme was borne in some cases by the employers alone, in others shared between the employers and workmen, or between the employers, the workmen and the taxpayer. He had even, it would seem, intended to tackle the problem of unemployment. Unfortunately, he had fallen from power, and none of his successors had the ability to carry out his intention. It must be admitted that Chamberlain's programme, as expounded in his speeches, fell very short of the comprehensiveness which Bismarck had given to his proposals, when, for the first time, he traced the lines of his social policy. Chamberlain did not raise the question of insurance against sickness. He made no reference to unemployment,[4] in spite of the fact that, during the years of industrial depression through which the country had just passed, it had given birth to a lively agitation

[1] Arthur Balfour. Manchester speech, January 16, 1895: 'Social legislation, as I conceive it, is not merely to be distinguished from Socialist legislation, but it is its most direct opposite and its most effective antidote. Socialism will never get possession of the great body of public opinion . . . among the working class or any other class, if those who wield the collective forces of the community show themselves desirous . . . to ameliorate every legitimate grievance and to put Society upon a proper and more solid basis.'
[2] Arthur Balfour. Speech delivered at a meeting of the Primrose League, April 26, 1895.
[3] Arthur Balfour: Manchester speech, January 16, 1895. Sir Henry James: speech at Bow, January 18, 1895.
[4] Curiously enough, the only Unionist speaker to mention unemployment in his election speeches seems to have been Lord Salisbury (speech at Bradford, May 22, 1895).

among the working classes. He produced no comprehensive scheme. He was content to promise the workers compensation for accidents which might befall them in the course of their employment, whether caused by their negligence or not. He promised pensions to deserving workmen compelled by old age to leave their employment.[1] What steps would the Unionist Cabinet take to redeem these promises?

7

Everyone gave Chamberlain the credit for the statute dealing with workmen's accidents, introduced by the Cabinet and passed by Parliament during the session of 1897. Not only did he throw himself wholeheartedly into the debates, not shrinking from a public attack on Lord Londonderry, a powerful mine owner and magnate of the Conservative party, who in the country and in the House of Lords led the opposition to the Bill,[2] but the Bill itself reproduced in every detail the measure he had suggested. The last Liberal Cabinet had passed through the Commons a Bill which considerably extended the employer's liability for accidents to his employees. But the Lords had introduced an amendment authorizing workmen to contract out of its provisions and the Cabinet, regarding the amendment as changing a compulsory measure into one merely permissive, and thereby rendering it a dead letter, had preferred to drop the Bill. Chamberlain persuaded his Conservative colleagues not to be content with merely re-introducing the Bill of 1894, but to introduce a measure embodying a different and a far bolder principle. It was no longer a question of the extent of the employer's liability; the Bill recognized the workman's right to compensation for any accident incurred in the course of his work, whatever its cause. Parliament accepted the bill as drafted by the Government,[3] with only an

[1] See his speech at St. James' Hall, May 23, 1895, also for a complete statement of his programme of social reform his article entitled 'The Labour Question' (*Nineteenth Century*, November, 1892: vol. xxxii, pp. 677 sqq.).

[2] H. of C., July 15, 1897: Chamberlain's speech (*Parliamentary Debates*, 4th Ser., vol. li, p. 211).

[3] 60 & 61 Vict., Cap. 37: An Act to amend the Law with respect to Compensation for Workmen for accidental injuries suffered in the course of their Employment (*Workmen's Compensation Act*, 1897). In a case of disablement the victim was to receive after the first fortnight following the accident, half his wages, the amount paid not to be less than one pound a week. If the accident was fatal, the widow and children of the deceased were to be entitled to his wages for three years, the amount paid not to be less than £150 nor exceeding £300.

unimportant modification introduced by the House of Lords which restricted very slightly the right to compensation.[1]

It mattered little that the British measure did not go so far as the German, and refrained from imposing on employers the obligation to insure as a body against the accidents to which their employees were exposed. Chamberlain expressly declared against compulsory insurance as too bureaucratic to be acceptable to public opinion in Great Britain,[2] and the public seems to have agreed with his point of view. It mattered little that the statute did not apply to all branches of labour, that agricultural labourers, seamen and domestic servants were excluded from its scope, and that to spare the small employer it was applicable only to workshops in which machinery was in use. Nor even did it greatly matter that the Act, like the previous Bill, permitted employers and workmen to contract out of its obligations, and that the House of Lords had removed from the Bill a clause likely to render the permission nugatory.[3] An important principle had been laid down which had been absent from the Liberal measure. On this point at any rate Chamberlain had obviously taken steps to fulfil his promises to the electorate. The measure had been before the house from May to July 1897—that is to say, at the very time when he was extricating himself from the fiasco of the Jameson Raid and, eager as he was to push the Government forward on the path of imperialism, was anxious to secure the goodwill of the masses. He succeeded.

On the question of pensions for aged workmen, his attitude was different. When the Unionists came into power in 1895, two or three years had passed since the attention of the working class had been drawn to the question by Charles Booth, the philanthropist, famous for his inquiries into social conditions. The scheme proposed by Booth was, it is true, completely different from Bismarck's solution. He asserted the right of every man without exception to a pension in old age. Neither workmen nor employers were to contribute. He did not speak of insurance, but of relief.[4] And Chamberlain had obtained the support of a group

[1] H. of L., July 26, 1897 (*Parliamentary Debates*, 4th Ser., vol. li, p. 1006).
[2] H. of C., May 3, 1897, Chamberlain's speech (ibid., vol. xlviii, p. 1467).
[3] H. of L., July 26, 1897 (ibid., vol. li, pp. 1024 sqq.).
[4] Enumeration and Classification of Paupers and State Pensions for the Aged (*Journal for the Royal Statistical Society*, December, 1891; vol. liv, pp. 600 sqq.), also the discussion which follows (ibid., vol. lv, pp. 56 sqq.). Pauperism, a picture, and the Endowment of Old Age, an Argument, 1892. The Aged Poor in England and Wales, 1894. Old Age,

of Members of Parliament, belonging to both parties, for a carefully studied scheme, far more moderate than Booth's proposal, or even Bismarck's law—a system of optional insurance to be assisted by the State—and had again developed his proposals before a Royal Commission, appointed in 1893 to inquire into the question.[1] The Commission, however, had in 1895 reached a purely negative conclusion. It was the same with a Parliamentary Committee appointed in 1896 which reported in 1898.[2] But Booth's proposal suddenly acquired an unexpected importance when the Government of one of the self-governing Colonies passed legislation, based on a principle similiar to that which he had enunciated. In Australasia, democratic communities, in defiance of the prejudices the British had obstinately cherished throughout the nineteenth century, were pursuing a policy at once protectionist and socialist, protecting the workmen of Australia and New Zealand, alike against foreign competition and capitalist exploitation. The New Zealand Old Age Pensions Act,[3] first introduced in 1898 by the Prime Minister, Mr. Seddon, and finally passed towards the end of the summer, granted a pension of £18 a year, that is about seven shillings a week, to every person above the age of sixty-five not in possession of an

Pensions and the Aged Poor, 1899. The proposal had already been suggested by S. A. Barnett, the first Warden of Toynbee Hall, in an article entitled 'Practicable Socialism' (*Nineteenth Century*, April, 1883, vol. xiii, pp. 554 sqq.; see especially p. 577) also by R. P. Hookham, *Outlines of a Scheme for Dealing with Pauperism*, 1879 (Charles Booth, a *Memoir*, 1918, p. 22).

[1] Report of the Royal Commission on the Aged Poor, appointed to consider whether any alterations in the system of Poor Law Relief are desirable, in the case of persons whose destitution is occasioned by incapacity for work resulting from Old Age or whether assistance could otherwise be afforded in these cases (January 7, 1893), vol. i, and vol. ii and iii of *Minutes of Evidence*, 1895. See the account of Booth's scheme in the report and in Booth's own words, p. 69 and p. 575 sqq.; of Chamberlain's by the reporter, p. 76, and by Chamberlain himself, pp. 657 sqq. See especially in Chamberlain's reply to question 12 (p. 97), in which he rejects Booth's proposal. 'It has to my mind one fatal objection and that is that the House of Commons would never provide the money for it. I should not myself think that any statesman or any Government would ever be found in any time that could look forward, to propose additional taxation to the extent of twenty or twenty-four millions a year for such a purpose. . . . I think it would be out of the range of practical politics.' The majority report decisively rejects all the schemes suggested. See *sub finem*. 'The number of aged poor who seek public relief, while still very large, has much lessened in proportion in the last thirty years, although the rate of decrease has greatly diminished in the last decade. . . . The self-reliance and strength of character of the working classes . . . will greatly aid in the solution of the problems of old age poverty, as well as of general pauperism.'

[2] Old Age Pensions Committee, *Report*, June 7, 1898.

[3] For the New Zealand Act and on Australasian Socialism generally see Albert Métin, *Le Socialisme sans doctrines. La question agraire et la question ouvrière en Australie et en Nouvelle-Zélande*, 1901; also André Siegfried, *La Démocratie en Nouvelle-Zélande*, 1904, Chaps. ix. to xiii.

income exceeding £52 or capital exceeding £260. The New Zealand legislation was immediately explained to the British public by the agent-general of the colony in London, the Fabian, W. P. Reeves; and Booth made use of it to push his own scheme. He launched an extensive campaign throughout Great Britain, for which he obtained the support of the trade unions, the co-operative societies, the Nonconformist bodies, twenty-seven Anglican Bishops, and Cardinal Vaughan.[1] Three months had not passed, and his National Committee of Organized Labour for promoting Old Age Pensions for all had scarcely been formed, before Parliament was roused to action. A committee of seventeen members appointed by the House of Commons reported, after a rapid inquiry, in favour of the New Zealand system.[2] A second committee was then appointed to investigate its financial aspects. The report, issued at the beginning of 1900,[3] estimated that, when all deductions had been made—those in receipt of Poor Relief, criminals, lunatics, aliens, those whose income exceeded £10 a week, and others classed as unfit to receive a pension—655,000 British subjects of sixty-five years of age and upwards would receive a pension. If, as proposed, the amount were fixed at seven shillings a week in the towns, five shillings in the country, that is to say at an average of six shillings, the total cost of the scheme to the taxpayers would amount to £10,300,000 in 1901, £12,650,000 in 1911, £15,650,000 in 1921. The movement had been well launched in the traditional English fashion. It enjoyed the support of the working classes. If in any party a statesman, inspired by Fabian principles, was prepared to adopt either Booth's scheme, or the system which had been set up in New Zealand, he would have the country behind him. What was Chamberlain going to do?

He did nothing. At first sight his inaction is surprising. He was universally understood to have given an explicit pledge before the election of 1895 to provide the workers with old age pensions. From the zeal he had displayed in defending the

[1] For this campaign see *Review of Reviews*, April 15, 1899 (Article by F. H. Stead) and *Revue Politique et Parlementaire*, June 10, 1901 (Article by C. Sansas). Frederick Rogers, *Life and Literature. Some Memories of Sixty Years*, 1913, pp. 203 sqq.
[2] Report from the Select Committee on Aged Deserving Poor: together with the proceedings of the Committee. *Minutes of Evidence and Appendix*, July 26, 1899.
[3] Report of the Departmental Committee on the financial aspects of the proposals made by the Select Committee of the House of Commons, of 1899, about the aged deserving poor, January 9, 1900.

Compensation Bill, when it was debated in 1897, one might expect that he would continue to advocate a bold policy of social reform. And surely his imperialism could not fail to be attracted by a reform which had originated in one of those self-governing Colonies whose bonds with the mother country it was his constant endeavour to draw closer. Nevertheless, he did nothing. When George Cadbury held a large public meeting at Birmingham which was attended by 630 delegates representing a body of 300,000 persons, he refused an invitation to be present in an extremely evasive letter. Pressed with questions in the House of Commons, and elsewhere, he explained that the plan he had had in mind was different, a grant to be made by the State to friendly societies which gave old age pensions to their members.[1] If that plan were adopted, assistance would not be given indiscriminately to the deserving and undeserving alike, and State intervention would be confined to the encouragement of thrift. But he took no steps to ensure that even this proposal was adopted by the Government. 'The time', declared the Queen's Speech, 'is not propitious for any domestic reforms which involve a large expenditure.' The explanation was that circumstances had changed since 1897. Not only had the Boer War begun and was proving a heavy financial burden, but Chamberlain, who had recovered from the effects of his initial fiasco and was once more the protagonist of a militant imperialism, no longer felt the need to justify his conversion to Toryism by a programme of social reform. Defy Russia, humiliate France, crush the Boers—that was the way to win a brilliant reputation at home and abroad! This terrible fellow had now something else to think of than old age pensions.

8

If, leaving the Compensation Act out of account, we take the measure of the social reform accomplished by the British Government between the year 1895 when the Unionists came into office and the conclusion of the Boer War in the summer of 1902, what did it amount to? An Act providing, but not enforcing, a

[1] Reply to a deputation from the friendly Society of Oddfellows, Birmingham, May 24 1899. This was indeed a part, but only a part, of the scheme which he had put forward in 1892, itself far less comprehensive than Booth's or even Bismarck's.

method of arbitration in Labour disputes.[1] An Act to consolidate and amend the Factory Acts, which secured in 1901 the approval of the Trades Union Congress.[2] A few statutes of more restricted application protecting particular categories of labour—the seamen in the merchant service, the workers in the cotton industry, railwaymen and shop assistants,[3] also three Acts to protect children.[4] And in 1900, the provisions of the Compensation Act were extended to agricultural labourers.[5] Not a record to boast of: the Cabinet had merely followed the movement of public opinion which for many years past had impelled Parliament without distinction of parties to regulate the conditions of labour with an ever increasing stringency. If among the statutes, passed while the Unionists were in office, which had a bearing on social questions, we look for legislation which reveals the characteristic policy of the Government, we shall find two measures which without being Socialist represented a reaction against the traditional Liberalism of the nineteenth century. One was an Act dealing with Joint Stock Companies. Its object was to restrict the almost unlimited freedom the Companies enjoyed under the Act of

---

[1] 59 & 60 Vict., Cap. 30: An Act to make better provision for the prevention and settlement of Trade Disputes (*Conciliation Act*, 1896).

[2] Edw. 7, Cap. 22: An Act to consolidate with Amendments the Factory and Workshop Acts (*Factory and Workshop Act*, 1901).

[3] 59 & 60 Vict., Cap. 43: An Act to amend the Coal Mines Regulation Act, 1887 (*Coal Miners' Regulation Act*, 1896)—60 & 61 Vict., Cap. 58: An Act to give power to make regulations with respect to Cotton Cloth Factories (*Cotton Cloth Factories Act*, 1897) —62 & 63 Vict., Cap. 21: An Act to provide for seats being supplied for the use of Shop Assistants. 63 & 64 Vict., Cap. 27: An Act for the better Prevention of Accidents on Railways (*Railway Employment [Prevention of Accidents] Act*, 1900). For the circumstances under which an earlier Bill was withdrawn in 1899 under pressure from the Railway Companies, and referred for examination to a Royal Commission, and the action taken by R. Bell, Secretary of the Amalgamated Society of Railway Servants, who arranged that the necessary evidence should be given before the Commission and thus obtained a favourable report, see R. W. Alcock, *Fifty Years of Railway Trade Unionism*, p. 300.

[4] 60 & 61 Vict., Cap. 52: An Act to extend the Age under which the Employment of Young Persons in Dangerous Performances is prohibited (*Dangerous Performances Act*, 1897). 60 & 61 Vict., Cap. 57: An Act to amend the Law for the better Protection of Infant Life (*Infant Life Protection Act*, 1897). 64 Vict., & 1 Edw. 7, Cap. 20: An Act to amend the Law relative to Youthful offenders and for other purposes connected therewith (*Youthful Offenders Act*, 1901).

[5] 63 & 64 Vict., Cap. 22: An Act to extend the benefits of the Workmen's Compensation Act, 1897, to Workmen in Agriculture (*Workmen's Compensation Act*, 1900). See also 59 & 60 Vict., Cap. 41: An Act to amend the Truck Acts. 62 & 63 Vict., Cap. 30: An Act to amend the Inclosure Acts, 1845 to 1882, and the Law relating to Commons and Open Spaces (*Commons Act*, 1899). 62 & 63 Vict., Cap. 44: An Act to empower Local Authorities to advance Money for enabling persons to acquire the ownership of small houses in which they reside (*Small Dwellings Acquisition Act*, 1899). 63 & 64 Vict., Cap. 59: An Act to amend part iii of the Housing of the Working Classes Act, 1890 (*Housing of the Working Classes Act*, 1900).

1862.[1] In future promoters would no longer be able by bogus subscriptions of capital to appropriate, without the knowledge of the public, an excessive share of the profits. The other was an Act dealing with money-lenders,[2] which marked the beginning of a reaction against the repeal in 1854 of the Statutes against Usury, and was bitterly opposed by the Liberal Opposition. Henceforward the law would recognize only 'professional money-lenders' whose operations would be subject to legal regulation. They would be obliged to furnish every borrower with a copy of the terms of the loan. If the rate of interest exceeded 10 per cent, the courts could modify the terms of the contract. Both statutes were examples of paternal legislation, in other words State intervention, to protect the individual against his own imprudence, as a father might protect his child. But in both instances the State protected capitalists against their fellow capitalists, lenders against borrowers, or borrowers against lenders. It did not protect one class against another, the workman against his employer.

If we examine more closely the strictly social legislation introduced and carried by the Conservative Cabinet, we shall detect here and there a desire to oppose the growing demands of labour. The Conciliation Act of 1896 was but the relic of the numerous projects which had been entertained by many Conservative philanthropists, while the great Labour Commission was sitting from 1891 to 1894. Why not regulate disputes between employers and their men and enforce an orderly settlement? Why not compel both parties to form themselves into recognized organizations? Institute a system of arbitration between these two representative bodies, applicable to all disputes and fine whichever of the two refused to accept the decision? But the trade unions had consistently been opposed to accepting financial liability of this nature, and we shall presently see the intense feeling which the question would arouse during the opening years of the twentieth century. The Cabinet had yielded without a struggle and contented itself with an uncontroversial measure providing for optional arbitration. The Factory Act on the other hand had been

[1] 63 & 64 Vict., Cap. 48: An Act to amend the Companies Act (*Companies Act*, 1900). For the Bill and its historic antecedents see an excellent article 'The Reform of Company Law' (*Quarterly Review*, vol. xli, pp. 373 sqq.).

[2] 63 & 64 Vict., Cap. 51: An Act to amend the Law with respect to persons carrying on business as money-lenders (*Money Lenders Act*, 1900). For the abuses which the Act was designed to remedy see Thomas Furrow, *The Moneylender Unmasked*, 1895.

introduced in 1900, before it was passed in its definitive form in 1901. At that time the Boer War necessitated a great effort to furnish the needs of the army, and the Government, acting in concert with the secretaries of the Unions, had broken, both in the State workshops and in private firms engaged on war work, every regulation which hampered production—for instance, the regulations forbidding the employment of women, work during the night and the system of double shifts. Why not legalize, for the future, breaches of the law committed with the tacit consent of the parties interested by empowering the Government to sanction these breaches of the law? But the trade union officials protested, the Bill was hung up, and by the following session the provision which had aroused the workers' hostility had disappeared.[1] On this point, as on some other matters of detail, the Government, when the Bill was finally passed, had yielded to the demands of labour.

In both instances the Government had shown a desire to oppose Socialism, and its intention had been frustrated by the opposition of labour. In another instance, however, the victory lay with the anti-Socialism of the Government and certain contemporary tendencies suffered a decided check. We refer to what was known —by the name which Sidney Webb had made fashionable—as 'municipal Socialism'. Since Parliament had placed the town councils on a democratic basis, they had municipalized one after another a constantly increasing number of public services— water supply, gas, electricity, tramways, markets, public baths, workmen's houses. Politics played very little part in municipal elections, and up to 1895 only an occasional Socialist had been elected here and there to certain town councils. The mayors and the councillors of the large cities were leading citizens, chosen for the most part without any consideration of party, and it was not Socialism, but pride in their municipality which urged them to municipalize every year a greater portion of the productive capital within their jurisdiction, to the delight of the Webbs, who saw in this policy a perfect expression of the Fabian method. For some years past, however, partly, perhaps, because the Webbs drew the attention of the public to the Socialistic character of the

[1] See the Home Secretary's reply to the letter of James Macdonald, Secretary of the London Trades Council, June 7, 1900 (*The Times*, June 11, 1900). Cf. *The Times*' leader of April 14, 1900.

development this municipal Socialism had begun to arouse considerable anxiety in financial and industrial circles. A lengthy controversy had arisen between its defenders and opponents.[1] Its apologists claimed that all these municipal undertakings earned large profits with a corresponding reduction of the rates. Its opponents denied the existence of these large profits, and disputed the calculations which professed to prove them. Otherwise, they asked, how could the rapidly increasing indebtedness of all the British municipalities be explained, and a burden of rates which was becoming insupportable? To these arguments it was replied, that to reduce the entire question to a balance of profit and loss was to take too low a view. The moral and physical welfare of the citizens was well worth pecuniary sacrifice. Which of the two parties was right? One thing, at any rate, became certain, as soon as the country returned in 1895 a Unionist majority. The sympathies of the new Government were with the critics, not with the defenders, of municipal Socialism. Of this, an important problem relating to the administration of the metropolitan area afforded ample proof.

Since 1888, London had possessed a County Council. Except in the City, which retained its old form of government and constituted an enclave within the district administered by the London County Council, the latter possessed the same powers as the other Councils throughout the country—that is to say, it did not possess an extensive jurisdiction. Neither the care of the streets nor the gas and water supply, nor the establishment and maintenance of markets, nor the public health, nor the burials, nor the police of the metropolis was subject to its authority.[2] Were such diverse and important services to be finally abandoned to a medley of unco-ordinated bodies? And if they were to be reorganized, on what principle? Should the powers of the County

[1] On this question of municipal Socialism see Report from the Joint Committee of the House of Lords and the House of Commons on Municipal Trading, 1900. For a defence of the system see Albert Shaw, *Municipal Government in Great Britain*, 1895, also Frederick Dolman, *Municipalities at Work. The Municipal Policy of Six Great Towns and its Influence on their Social Welfare*, 1895. For a criticism, extremely moderate and practical, see Leonard Darwin, *Municipal Trade. The Advantages and Disadvantages resulting from the Substitution of Representative Bodies for Private Proprietors in the Management of Industrial Undertakings*, 1903; also *Municipal Ownership*, Lectures delivered at Harvard University, 1907. But above all, the student should consult C. Hugo's excellent manual, *Stadtverwaltung und Municipal Socialismus in England*, 1897.

[2] For the London County Council and its administration see Fabian Tract No. 61, *The London County Council: What it is and What it does*, February, 1895. See also A. G. Gardiner, *John Benn and the Progressive Movement*, 1925.

Council be enlarged? Or, on the contrary, should the jurisdiction of the Council be left as it had been defined by the statute of 1888, and the administration of the capital made federal, and systematically divided between a number of separate local bodies. The former alternative, the method of centralization, was advocated by the 'Progressive Party', which possessed a majority in the County Council, the party of which Sidney Webb was one of the most active members, and which wished to extend the 'Socialist' experiments in which it had engaged ever since 1888. The latter was advocated by the 'Moderate' party, which constituted the Opposition in the Council and declared itself opposed in principle to municipal Socialism. A Commission appointed in 1890 to examine the question reported in 1894 in favour of an intermediate solution, which combined both principles. On the one hand, the City would lose its independence and be absorbed together with the County Council in a single body whose authority would extend to the whole of London. But, on the other hand, a number of municipalities over whom a mayor would preside would administer particular districts of the metropolis, subject to the control of the new Council. But this was not enough to satisfy the Moderates, whose position was strengthened by the Conservative victory in 1895. Chamberlain spoke in their support.[1] In 1899, the Government introduced and carried a Bill which abolished all the bodies which were still performing a large number of municipal functions within the area of the County of London, and transferred their powers, not to the County Council, but to twenty-eight borough councils administering special areas. The Bill was introduced by Balfour in person, and he presided over the debates with that competence, keenness, and skill in argument with which it amused him to delight and disconcert the House after months of listlessness. The decentralization was in itself a safeguard against the extension to the entire metropolitan district of the methods of municipal Socialism. The wealthy boroughs would not be rated to provide for the needs of districts inhabited by a population of slum dwellers.[2]

[1] Speeches at Stepney, February 6, 1898, at Camberwell, March 1, 1898.
[2] 62 & 63 Vict., Cap. 14: An Act to make better provision for Local Government in London (London Government Act, 1899). For a more detailed history of the Bill, see A. G. Gardiner, John Benn and the Progressive Movement, 1925, chap. xii, xv (pp. 201 sqq., 249 sqq.). When in 1902 it became urgently necessary to place the water supply of London, which had been previously in the hands of eight private companies, under a single control, the Government entrusted it not to the County Council, but to a Board of

In reality, the conditions which obtained in England during the closing years of the century were altogether unlike those which prevailed in Germany when Bismarck successfully applied his system of 'social monarchy'. There, a monarchy founded on divine right and a military aristocracy which was a survival of feudalism, as a result of the historical situation and under the guidance of a great statesman, controlled the development of a mercantile and industrial community of the modern type. Therefore, when the new claims of the proletariat alarmed the manufacturers, the Crown and the aristocracy were in a position to arbitrate between the working class, against whom they afforded the employers the protection of the army, and the wealthy upstarts whom they despised. Provided public order was not disturbed, they were quite willing to come forward as the defenders of labour against these plebeian capitalists. The situation in England was totally different. It was under the banner of the dominant Liberalism that the old aristocracy of landowners, divided, as it was, into two hostile groups, had by sleights of hand, successfully sustained, contrived to retain the leadership of a community more completely industrialized than any other in the world. But could the *tour de force* be maintained permanently? At the very moment when the gentry, almost to a man, were

sixty-six members, of whom only fourteen were elected by the Council, the remainder by the Borough Councils and other bodies (2 Edw. VII, Cap. 41: *Metropolis Water Act*, 1902). For the drafting of the measure see A. G. Gardiner, ibid., chap. xvi, pp. 265 sqq., also *Memorials*, by Lord Long of Wraxall, 1924, p. 135. When the London school board was abolished the division of the new powers entrusted to the local authorities between the County Council and the Borough Councils was the object in 1903 of very lively debates between the Government and the Opposition, which resulted in an elaborate compromise, more favourable to the central authority of the County Council than the Government would have wished (see Edward R. Pease, *The History of the Fabian Society*, pp. 146 sqq. Also below, p. 244). It would be of interest to study in detail the attitude adopted towards municipal Socialism by the Parliament of 1895 without confining ourselves to questions of metropolitan administration. A Distribution of Power Bill which would have enabled a private company to compete in providing electricity with the 'municipal Socialism' of several large towns in the Midlands was thrown out in the two successive sessions of 1898 and 1899. The organized opposition of the municipalities proved too strong. Four Bills of the same nature could be carried in 1900 only after a compromise had been reached with the Association of Municipal Corporations, important restrictions imposed on the companies' powers, and several municipalities excluded from the operation of the Act, the companies being forbidden to furnish current in the area subject to their jurisdiction (E. Garcke, *The Progress of Electrical Enterprise*, 1907, pp. 30 sqq.). But, on the other hand, the Cabinet introduced and carried a Bill which restricted the monopoly of the National Telephone Company and facilitated the competition of the municipalities (62 & 63 Vict., Cap. 38: *Telegraph [Telephonic Communication etc.,] Bill*, 1899). That is to say, the Unionist Government which opposed municipal Socialism when it interfered with capitalist enterprise was not unwilling to play off 'municipal' against 'State' Socialism, and foster the former as a safeguard against nationalization.

leaving the Liberal party, the financiers, merchants, and manufacturers, threatened by the Socialist menace, were also flocking to the Tory camp. At the outset of his career, Chamberlain had done more than any other man to give the Liberal party a Radical and Socialist character; and the movements he had initiated did not cease with his defection. But whether he would or no, he was compelled by his charge of allegiance to play an entirely different rôle in the party he joined, to make of it a party in many respects similar to the Republican party in the United States, the party of progressive capitalism and large-scale industry. No one could be in a worse position to pursue a policy of State Socialism. This is the explanation of the failure of the Cabinet of 1895 to promote social reform. In the sphere of education it copied the German model, though probably without clearly understanding what it was doing. So far as social reform in the stricter sense was concerned, it understood very well the significance of Bismarck's legislation and for that very reason did nothing. And its refusal to take action was encouraged by the apathy which, after ten years of Socialist agitation, suddenly came over the working class on the morrow of the election of 1895.

9

At that election, the candidates of the Independent Labour Party had polled almost 45,000 votes—at first sight, a splendid achievement. That in several constituencies their candidate had contributed to the defeat of the Liberal candidate caused them no misgivings. If they could intimidate the Liberal party, so much the better. But, on the other hand, they were compelled to face the fact that not a single one of their twenty-eight candidates had got into the House. Even Keir Hardie had been defeated. Moreover, the Members of Parliament who, without being Socialists, belonged to the working class had been involved in the Liberal defeat. Before the election, there had been sixteen representatives of the working class in the House of Commons. Now there were only twelve. Hence a feeling of acute resentment against the members of the Independent Labour Party among the leaders of the Unions. It was revealed when, in September, the annual Trades Union Congress met at Cardiff, and adopted two amendments to its constitution, proposed by the Parliamentary Committee to stifle the propaganda of the militant Socialists.

Hitherto, the Congress had comprised two distinct elements. There were the delegates of the trade unions, bodies confined to the members of a particular trade. There were also the delegates of the trade councils which contained representatives of every trade in a particular town. The secretaries of the unions were business men rather than politicians, men with a middle-class outlook taken up with the difficult task of managing the finances of their union. But the local members of the trade councils and their representatives at the Congress were not trade-union secretaries. They were men of a more daring temper, at once more political and more revolutionary than the former. And it was on the trade councils, rather than on the trade unions, that the Socialists relied every year to win the support of the Congress. The committee proposed and carried a motion excluding the councils from the Congress, which would in future be confined to the delegates of the unions.

Up to the present the vote had been taken by a majority of the delegates. But the three large unions whose membership amounted to 100,000 or even 200,000 did not send a proportionate number of delegates. The expense would have been too great. Therefore, when it came to the vote, the small unions possessed an unfair advantage. That, surely, explained the success of the Socialist motions at Belfast and Norwich? The committee proposed that in future the vote at the Congress should be taken in accordance with the membership of the unions represented, not, as hitherto, with the number of delegates. And, finally, the proposal was made that no one should in future take part in the Congress who was not an actual member of a union. This would exclude those former trade unionists who had become politicians, not only a prominent revolutionary like Keir Hardie, but a trade unionist of the old middle-class type such as Broadhurst. But Broadhurst was quite willing to be deprived of his seat, if Keir Hardie lost his. And his sentiments were shared by John Burns, who was abandoning his extreme views, and had been for several months at enmity with the Independent Labour Party, having taken offence, because he had not been offered the leadership. By a trick of procedure, of very doubtful legality, the committee carried all its proposals. The result was immediately evident. In 1894, Keir Hardie had carried his formula of unqualified Socialism by 219 to 61 votes. In 1895, a similar motion was lost by 607,000 to

186,000 votes. When the Parliamentary Committee came up for re-election, Ben Tillett was turned out, and instead of two Socialists on the Committee, there was now only one.

In July of the following year an important international Socialist Congress was held in London. It was the third since the tradition of the first 'International' had been revived in Paris in 1889. Its proceedings were calculated to disgust the leaders of the British Labour movement. Not only was there a scene of disgraceful disorder in which the German and British delegates laboured in vain to compose a violent quarrel between two French groups, but the object of the dispute was unintelligible to the British members of the Congress. The question under discussion was whether the Congress should admit to its membership, besides the Socialists in favour of political action, those soon to be known as the syndicalists, who advocated action by the unions alone and opposed all political action. At first sight it might seem that the problem debated in London as an international question resembled the question discussed a few months earlier at Cardiff. This was not the case. At the London Congress the supporters of political action were the moderates who appealed to the British Unions to give them the assistance of their votes against the partisans of a general strike for the expropriation of the capitalists, whereas the French anarchists, hostile to the democratic State and Parliament, claimed their support in the name of trade unionism. The British delegates could not understand the position, nor had they any wish to understand it. For them France, the Continent generally, was a topsy-turvy world.

The Unions with a large membership—Cotton and Coal—Unions opposed to Socialist theory,[1] anxious to keep the interests of their trade apart from politics and content that any representatives they might return to Parliament should be elected under the official auspices of the Liberal party, dominated the Congress. In 1896 at Edinburgh the Congress refused by 136 to 62 votes to

---

[1] 'Socialism, with its appearance of easy solutions, often attracts well-organized groups, if they are faced by some unsurmountable difficulty—for instance, the plumbers, printers, and all those trades whose members are easy to organize, but in which owing to the operation of inevitable forces conditions are in process of transformation. Socialism is also attractive to unorganized groups, hastily collected, and incapable of obedience to a leader. To the former Socialism appeals as a force capable of supplementing their weakness. To the latter it appeals as the ready-made organization they need to compensate for their own incapacity to organize. In every case, the attraction to Socialism is a sign of inferiority.' (P. de Rousiers, *La Question Ouvrière en Angleterre*, 1895, p. 491.)

submit to a referendum by the unions the question of forming a parliamentary fund by means of special subscriptions. The vote was a definite breach with the Independent Labour Party.[1] The following year, at Birmingham, the Congress by 317,000 to 282,000 votes declined an invitation to take part in an international congress of trade unions. It had become more professional and more insular than it had ever been.

Probably the Government would have been well advised to anticipate the wishes of labour by a bold policy of social reform. And there can be no doubt that, if the employers had taken a reasonable view of the situation, they would have gladly accepted the alliance the moderate trade unionist leaders were only too willing to conclude with them against the revolutionaries. But they were too short-sighted. Unable to brook the control, even of the moderates, and interpreting the sudden slackening of the Socialist offensive as a sign of weakness, they judged the moment opportune to deliver a counter-offensive. We shall see what forms it assumed and what were its results.

II EMPLOYERS' ATTACK AND WORKERS' REVOLT

I

'Formal organizations of employers', so runs the report of the Royal Commission appointed in 1891 to inquire into the relations between employers and men, 'usually make their appearance at a later date than those of the workmen and arise for purposes of joint resistance, when individual employers find themselves too weak to cope with the growing strength of trade unions.'[2] The associated employers lay down the conditions—the same for all— on which they will engage labour, guarantee each other against the risk of a strike, and make all the necessary preparations for joint action, if the association should decide to declare a lock-out. In 1892, there were seventy of these associations. The oldest dated

---

[1] 'In numbers the Independents greatly exceeded the other groups, but after securing a measure of success until 1895, their progress has been suddenly arrested. Today new adherents are rare, they have lost the solitary seat they possessed in the House of Commons, their influence in the municipal councils and other public bodies is nil, they have no standing in the co-operative societies, and their attempt to capture the trade unions has failed hopelessly.' (P. Verhaegen, *Socialistes Anglais*, 1897, pp. 359–60.)

[2] Royal Commission on Labour. *Fifth and Final Report*, 1894. 581, p. 31.

from 1865 and they were rapidly multiplying. Twelve had been founded since the beginning of 1890.[1] Moreover, since the unions had fashioned an organ of collective action in the annual Trades Union Congress, why should not the employers' associations be federated in their turn? The first National Federation was formed in 1873; 'in consequence', as the words of the initial manifesto declare, 'of the extraordinary development, oppressive action, far-reaching, but openly avowed designs, and elaborate organization of the trade unions'.[2] After a few years it ceased to exist. It seems probable that a proposal to revive the Federation of 1873 was discussed among the employers shortly before 1895. But the first sign of their intention at this juncture to oppose a united front to the workers' claims was the foundation of a curious association which, though it originated with the employers, adopted the guise of a workmen's association, genuine or bogus.

The sudden growth of trade unionism, which had reached its height in 1889, was followed by a period of industrial depression and unemployment necessarily unfavourable to the prosperity of the unions. Strikes were fewer and failed more often. But during those hard years the British workman did not display his usual resignation. The revolutionary propaganda, whose progress we have described, was bearing its fruit; the strikes, if fewer and less successful, were more often accompanied by scenes of violence. The Government adopted the novel procedure of sending troops to restore order. On one occasion there was actual bloodshed. The issue was not always a question of wages or hours of work. Often, and more frequently as the century drew to its close, the men contested the employers' right to employ non-unionist labour.[3] Already at the end of the nineteenth century the trade

---

[1] Royal Commission on Labour. *Rules of Associations of Employers and of Employed*, together with introductory memoranda. June, 1892. *Memorandum on the Rules of the Associations of Employers*, pp. 21 sqq. For the Employers' Associations in Lancashire, see the interesting details in P. de Rousiers' *Le Trade Unionisme en Angleterre*, 1897, pp. 316 sqq., and for the Shipowners' Federation and its struggles with the Dockers' Union, ibid., p. 172.

[2] George Howell, *Conflicts of Capital and Labour*, ed. 2, 1890, pp. 392, 399.

[3] The number of workmen directly concerned in disputes as to the employment of non-union men, or turning on other questions in which the principle of trade unionism was involved, after attaining a maximum in 1895, decreased until 1898, when it once more began to increase at the following rate: 1898, 2,215 men concerned; 1899, 5,130; 1900, 19,573; 1901, 11,531; 1902, 25,489 (a little over a fifth of the men who went on strike in the course of the year). For all these figures see the annual publication entitled: *Strikes and Lock-outs*, Board of Trade (*Labour Department*). *Report on Strikes and Lock-outs in the United Kingdom*.

union leaders felt themselves sufficiently powerful to dictate to the entire working class, although in the majority of trades, only a minority of the workers were members of a union. In many cases, therefore, the employers believed that in contesting the authority of the trade union they were defending against an oligarchy, not their own interests alone, but, at the same time, the liberty of the individual labourer. But it was a desperate effort, and if they fought with such obstinate determination it was because they felt the day at hand when all the workmen would be compulsorily enrolled in the unions, and the employer would be at their mercy.

Already, there were many districts completely industrialized, where the employers' sole resource, when the union had declared war upon them, was to introduce labour from outside. They found such labour in the eastern counties—Norfolk and Suffolk— where trade unionism hardly existed. They found it in Ireland, which for a century past had furnished British capitalism with the 'reserve army', to use Marx's phrase, which it needed. The new hands thus engaged were brought by railway and taken to barracks where they were confined, out of reach of the strikers' persuasions and threats, so long as they worked in the factory. But was it impossible to improve on this makeshift? The employers, who with great difficulty had succeeded about 1889 in defeating the revolt of unskilled labour, were asking themselves whether it would not be worth while to form from the ranks of non-unionist labour, a permanent 'reserve', a 'reserve' in the strict sense, ready to come to their assistance the moment they were called up.

The first step was taken by the Shipowners' Federation, as soon as it was founded in September, 1890. This seems, in fact, to have been its founders' primary object. A few weeks after the Employers' Federation, a General Labour Union was formed to organize the labourers emancipated from the tyranny of the unions. A guarantee was given that in yards owned by members of the Federation they would always be engaged in preference to men not enrolled in the Union. When disputes arose with the secretary of the Union the shipowners had recourse to another device. They opened under their direct control Free Labour Registries, to enroll non-union labour which the agents of the Federation often obtained from abroad. One of these Registries was opened in Hull in March, 1893, and it was upon them that the Dockers' Union made war, when in April it declared a strike. The entire working class was in a ferment, and but for the prudence with which John Burns and a few others handled the situation, a general strike would have been declared in London. The strike was finally concluded by a compromise.

Already dissatisfied with the result of their policy, the shipowners were alarmed to discover that the Free Labour Registries had pledged their responsibility too directly. Workmen, enrolled by a Registry and subsequently dismissed, sued the Federation for breach of contract. They, therefore, returned to the device of a union, ostensibly independent of the employers, like a genuine trade union. At this juncture, when a further experiment had failed, a man named M. W. Collison, who had practised wellnigh every trade and had lately founded in London a union for tram and omnibus employees from which he had been expelled in circumstances not very honourable to himself, obtained subscriptions from the employers to found a National Free Labour Association, which professed to embody the determination of a large body of workers to throw off the yoke of the trade unions.[1] The Association, whose members were at the service of the employers in the event of a strike, held its annual Congress at which it published its accounts and its membership. As even its officials admitted, its funds were chiefly derived from the employers' subscriptions. Its membership, if they are to be believed, had at times exceeded 100,000; in fact it seems never to have been greater than 30,000. Moreover, the men supplied by Collison to his patrons were the refuse of the labour market. Their labour was cheap only because it was of such poor quality. The chief use made of the Association by the capitalists and the Conservative Press they controlled was to make the public believe that the workers were beginning to revolt against the unions. The employers did not need the assistance of Collison and his rabble to win, in 1897 and in 1898, two brilliant victories over the working class.

[1] For the foundation of the Free Labour Association, see J. M. Ludlow, 'The National Free Labour Association' (*Economic Review*, January 1895; vol. v, pp. 110 sqq.). Clem. Edwards, 'Free Labour Frauds', a series of articles amply furnished with evidence in the *Critic*, June 18 and 25; July 2, 9, 23; August 13, 1898. Paul Mantoux and Maurice Alfassa, *La Crise de Trade Unionisme*, 1903, pp. 194 sqq. See also P. de Rousiers, *Le Trade Unionisme en Angleterre*, 1897, pp. 353 sqq., and G. H. Perris, *The Industrial History of Modern England*, 1914, pp. 435 sqq.

It was with the Amalgamated Society of Engineers that the first battle was fought. The Society, which had been in existence more than forty-five years, clung to the old methods and contemplated with pride the improvement in the condition of its members brought about by the extensive system of benefits it had organized. In the spring of 1897 the Society possessed a membership of about 92,000 and had accumulated funds amounting to more than £360,000. These splendid results had, it must be admitted, been secured by a series of rules the Society had forced on the employers which had brought to a standstill the development of machinery in this branch of British manufacture. One of these prohibited the employment of unskilled labour which, if used to serve some new machine, might have proved a dangerous competitor to the skilled labour hitherto indispensable. But about the year 1890 the new unionism had shaken this exclusiveness. John Burns and Tom Mann were engineers, and had been sent as their delegates by the Amalgamated Society of Engineers to the Trades Union Congress held at Liverpool in 1890. In 1893 it had admitted to its membership one branch at least of unskilled labour, the 'machine men'. A workman of Socialist tendencies, George Barnes, a candidate of the Independent Labour Party at the General Election, had just been elected Secretary. Was it under the influence of the new ideas that the Society adopted a more aggressive policy, and in 1895 was among the first unions to demand a share in the profits accruing from the recovery of trade in the shape of an increase of wages? 15,000 engineers came out on strike at Belfast and on the Clyde. But after a struggle, lasting three months, their obstinate refusal to lower their demands gave the victory to the employers. It was no doubt this initial success which two years later encouraged them to face a sterner contest.[1]

This time the battle was fought on the question not of wages, but the eight hours' day.[2] Had not the eight hours' day been

[1] For the Amalgamated Society of Engineers on the eve of the great strike of 1897, the admission of the machine men and the struggle on the Clyde, see P. de Rousiers, *Le Trade Unionisme en Angleterre*, pp. 256 sqq.

[2] Nevertheless, we must consider whether this formula, fashionable in Socialist circles, did not conceal a demand for an increase of wages. See P. Verhaegen, *Socialistes Anglais*, 1897, pp. 133 sqq. 'The present strike of engineers originates in a demand . . . that the working day should be reduced to eight hours. The real demand of the engineers was merely that the overtime work, at present almost universal in their workshops, should begin an hour earlier every day.'

ever since 1889 the slogan of Socialists throughout the world? The Newcastle engineers could claim that, at the cost of a strike of six months in 1871, they had been the first among British workers to secure the nine hours' day. The London engineers now demanded a day of eight hours. Two important provincial firms engaged in the manufacture of machinery had already adopted it. At first a hundred London firms accepted the Society's demands. But they were firms of no importance. The large firms refused. Moreover, the employers perceived that, badly organized as they were, they would be fighting against heavy odds, if the struggle remained local; the engineers, assisted by the subscriptions of their comrades still at work in the provinces, would be able to hold out indefinitely. The London manufacturers therefore joined the Employers' Federation, which, as a result of the strike on the Clyde, had been formed in the north towards the end of 1895. To the strike declared by the employees of five London firms, the Employers' Federation replied by decreeing the lock-out of a quarter of the men employed in the industry throughout Great Britain. To this step the Amalgamated Society of Engineers replied in its turn by declaring a general strike wherever the employers' lock-out was enforced. Battle had been joined along the entire front.

But the contest suddenly changed its character. Before the demand for the eight hours' day had been made, a host of minor disputes had arisen in the workshops over the introduction of machinery. Either the men opposed it entirely, if it were likely to have the effect of replacing skilled by unskilled labour; or they demanded that committees of control should be set up in the workshops through which the workers would dictate to the employers the conditions on which they would consent to work the machines. The Employers' Federation was, therefore, not content with refusing the eight hours' day, it attached further conditions to the re-opening of the factories. It demanded that the men should formally accept piece work and the principle of working overtime, abandon every rule which in any way limited the number of apprentices, and repudiate all claim to interfere in the management of the firm. In future, employers would be free to settle the conditions of labour directly with their employees without any intervention by the Society. In other words, the engineers must abandon the principle of collective bargaining which is the foundation of all corporate action. In consequence, the entire world of organized labour was up in arms and came to the assistance of the engineers. The Trade Unions subscribed almost £70,000, the Co-operative Societies more than £2,000. From Australia and New Zealand they received £5,500, from Germany £14,600. The total assistance received by the strikers amounted to £116,000. Fifteen Oxford dons, philanthropists, the German economist Brentano took the side of the men. All to no purpose. An attempt at intervention by the Board of Trade failed. The employers' terms, rejected the first time about the middle of December by an overwhelming majority, and when again brought forward a fortnight later with insignificant modifications[1] rejected a second time by a majority almost as large, were finally accepted on January 28. The strike had lasted over thirty weeks, from beginning to end had thrown 28,000 men out of work, and had resulted in the most serious defeat British trade unionism had received within living memory.[2]

The engineers had not returned to work before another conflict broke out in the South Welsh coalfield. For the past twenty years wages had been fixed by the sliding scale: every two months the average price of coal was calculated in four chief centres of the district and wages adjusted in proportion. The miners had, however, the right to ask for a revision of the arrangement, provided six months' notice were given. On October 1, 1897, they gave the required notice, but the mine owners, who perhaps were elated by the victory the employers were on the point of winning in their struggle with the engineers, did not wait until April 1 before giving notice that on that date they would regard themselves as released from any contract with the men and would re-employ them only on the old terms. The miners refused to yield. Before the middle of April work on the coalfield was at a

---

[1] The text was not actually modified, but to every clause an explanatory note was appended with the object of reassuring the men as to the spirit in which the new regulations would be applied (see for the text of the agreement in its final form the *Labour Gazette*, February, 1898, p. 37).

[2] For the engineers' strike see *Strikes and Lock-outs. Board of Trade (Labour Department) Report on the*, 1897, 1898, pp. lii sqq. *Amalgamated Society of Engineers Notes on the Engineering Trade Lock-out* (1897–8), *with list of contributions from trade and labour councils, trade societies and other sources and general balance sheet.* Also Appendix, Albert Gigot, 'La Grève des Mécaniciens Anglais' (*Correspondent*, March 10, 1898; vol. cxc, pp. 932 sqq.). S. Webb, 'La Guerre Industrielle en Angleterre' (*Revue de Paris*, December 15, 1897, 4me année. Vol. vi, pp. 912 sqq.). In the opinion of A. Marshall (*Industry and Trade*, pp. 137–8) the employers' victory of 1898 had the most excellent results on the engineering industry in Great Britain.

standstill. The mine owners called it a strike, the miners a lock-out. Of the 139,000 miners in South Wales 90,000 were involved. Not a single act of violence was committed. Nevertheless, at the request of the magistrates and owners troops were sent to the district, as though to impress on the miners that the owners had the support of the Government.

By forcing, as they had done, the commencement of the struggle the owners had secured an initial advantage. For everybody knew what they wanted, namely the maintenance of the *status quo*, whereas the miners, taken unawares, were less certain of their ground. Indeed, they had not had the time to agree on a common programme. The majority accepted the principle of the sliding scale and were content to demand that their wages should be raised by a tenth. But in certain respects the system of the sliding scale bore hardly on them. Throughout Britain, and especially in Wales, the coal trade was an export trade, affected by all the fluctuations of prices in the international market. Therefore, since their wages varied with prices, the miners lived by turns in comfort and destitution. How could the evil be cured? The South Welsh miners hesitated between two remedies. Some favoured the adoption of a system which had for a long time been practised by the English miners, and for which they had obtained the approval of the International Miners' Congress held at Berlin in 1894;[1] it consisted in keeping prices high by limiting the supply of coal—that is to say, in a combination of owners and miners against the consumer. The others who were influenced by Socialism and who were very soon, if not the more numerous, at any rate the noisier section, advocated the introduction of a minimum living wage.

The owners rejected all the miners' demands. As always in a mining district, it was a stubborn contest. The miners, who often owned their cottages, who had contributed to the cost of building those little chapels, Methodist, Baptist, or Congregationalist, dotted about all over the countryside, and among whom mining was an hereditary profession, son succeeding father in the pits,

[1] In the teeth of a Socialist motion put forward by the German miners. 'The Congress', ran the motion finally carried, 'is of opinion that the over-production of coal is due to the employment in the mines of unskilled labour, and to the enormous increase in the competition between coal merchants. The Congress, therefore, is of opinion that all nations should make use of every lawful means to limit the supply of coal and endeavour by every means legally permissible to prevent for the future the employment of unskilled labour in the mines.'

had come to regard themselves as joint-owners of the soil and the coal measures beneath it. But they were badly organized. They had not yet learned, like their comrades of the Midlands, Durham, and Northumberland, to form strong and wealthy unions. When the strike began, their funds barely amounted to £10,000. To keep themselves and their families, they were driven to desperate makeshifts. In a district where the entire electorate belonged to the working class, they controlled the boards of guardians,[1] and appear to have made use of their power to maintain themselves out of the poor rate. But the moment arrived, about the end of August, when starvation stared them in the face and they surrendered.

On August 28 an anxious crowd surrounded from early morning the building in which the representatives of the owners and the men were discussing terms. Though the unfortunate men knew that they were beaten they refused to give up hope, and every now and then a comforting rumour went round that the owners were divided, that they were conceding a minimum wage. The afternoon passed, the negotiators separated for their evening meal, and nothing had been settled. Finally, it became known that an agreement had been reached on the basis of 'a variable minimum wage'. It was a clever formula to express the concession which the owners wished to have the appearance of making. It was agreed that whenever the operation of the sliding scale reduced wages to a rate more than $12\frac{1}{2}$ per cent lower than that which had obtained in 1889, the miners would have a right to terminate their contract at six months' notice. But what did this amount to? They possessed the right already, whatever the rate of wages. And had it not been the owners who, by refusing to admit it the previous winter, had acted with flagrant unfairness? Moreover, the system of the sliding scale was maintained without any alteration until 1903. An immediate increase in wages of 5 per cent was a purely formal concession. The miners would have been entitled to it if the operation of the sliding scale had not been interrupted by the strike. And finally,

[1] Since the Local Government Act of 1894 (56 & 57 Vict., Cap. 73) had made the electorate democratic and abolished the plural vote hitherto possessed by those who paid high rates. Precise figures are lacking for South Wales but we can understand how strong the representation of the miners in the local governing bodies must have been, when we discover (F. Willmore, *The Miners' Unions of Durham and Northumberland*, pp. 214–5) that at an election of parish councils held in Durham in 1895, of the 615 members returned, 370 were miners.

they were compelled to give up the monthly holiday hitherto in force in the district. It was known as Mabon's Day. Mabon was the nickname of a labour leader named Abraham, who represented in the House of Commons the Glamorganshire constituency of the Rhondda Valley. It was Mabon who had obtained this holiday for the miners. And on this occasion also it was Mabon who defended the interests of his clients against the owners. In vain he attempted to preserve at least an annual holiday, a last relic of the Mabon's Day they had lost. He was defeated by the owners' obstinate refusal. 'Tell our friends,' ran the message which Abraham communicated the same evening to the Press, 'that this has been a terrible day for us, and it ends with a terrible disappointment for all of us. It has been a fearful fight all day. It was a case of Mabon fighting tooth and nail for his day. It has gone by. You will, boys, do the same as I have had to do today— namely, accept the inevitable, and prepare to organize for better things.'[1]

3

The employers, encouraged by the two victories they had just won in the course of a single year—the first over the engineers, the second over the Welsh miners—now decided to unite their scattered organizations in a single central organization. On November 15, representatives of all, or almost all, branches of the national industry met in London. A peer, Lord Wemyss, took the chair. The meeting decided that it was imperative, in the common interest of employers and men, to take active measures to oppose the weakness Parliament displayed towards the demands of the unions, and the Socialistic tendencies of recent legislation. Why was the working class in a position to dictate terms to Parliament? Because it had learned to organize. The employers in their turn must learn to organize for the defence of freedom, the freedom of employers and men alike. This was the origin of the Employers' Parliamentary Council, which consisted of representatives of the various employers' federations, and such individual employers as the Council should decide to co-opt. At its head was an Executive Committee composed of a President, five Vice-Presidents, and five ordinary members. The Committee

---

[1] *The Times*, September 2, 1898. For the official account of the strike, see *Strikes and Lock-outs of 1898*, Board of Trade (*Labour Department*) *Report on the*, 1899, pp. xlv sqq.

would hold regular meetings, and inform all the members of the Council of any Bill introduced in Parliament which in its opinion affected their interests. The opinion of the members would be obtained and the necessary steps taken to support or oppose the Bill, whenever either course was advised by unanimous agreement of the federation immediately concerned and by two-thirds of the Council.[1] In short, the Council was to become to the employers what the Trades Union Congress was to the working class, and the relation between the Executive Committee and the Council would reproduce that which obtained between the Parliamentary Committee and the Congress.

Among the members of the Executive Committee of the Employers' Council was Sir Henry Vyvian, the representative of the quarry owners. No doubt this prominence was given to that particular body of employers because public attention was focused just then on another labour dispute, of which Lord Penrhyn's slate quarries at Bethesda in North Wales were the scene. Not more than 3,000 men were involved, but the bitterness was intense. And because the battlefield was so restricted, it was easier for the public to grasp on this small scale the aims the leading employers had entertained ever since the election of 1895, which they had regarded as their victory. The quarrymen possessed no union in the strict sense, but they elected a Quarry Committee which claimed, in the event of a dispute with Lord Penrhyn, to represent the men in the same way as the committee of a trade union. Lord Penrhyn refused to recognise the Committee. Because, in obedience to the Committee, they demanded an improvement in the conditions of their work in September, 1896, he discharged a number of men. Their fellow quarrymen espoused their cause and came out on strike. It lasted almost two years, supported by the assistance given by trade unions and by the begging tours which a number of strikers conducted up and down the country, and even in London; in this way, with the help of the *Daily Chronicle*, they collected almost £20,000. After Lord Penrhyn had refused the arbitration of the Board of Trade, the dispute was apparently settled in August, 1898, by a compromise. On the one hand, the quarrymen's right to elect representatives to bring their grievances before Lord Penrhyn or his subordinates was recognized, but on the other hand their demands

[1] *The Times*, November 18; December 17 and 18, 1898.

were to be examined, not by committees composed equally of representatives of both parties, but by the owners' representatives, the officials of the quarry, and in the last instance by the owner himself. It was not long before the struggle broke out afresh. When towards the end of the Boer War, in 1902, a very large number of strikers returned to work, the troops had to be called out to protect them against their comrades still on strike. Opinion in Liberal and democratic circles was finally impressed by the long struggle, and Lloyd George, speaking one day in the Commons, let it be understood that, in his opinion, the State had a right to take over the quarry and work it for the benefit of the nation under more humane conditions that Lord Penrhyn would concede.[1] It was not until the end of 1903 that the last strikers yielded.[2]

The three disputes whose story we have told may be considered as typical. When we consult the statistics for the period with which we are concerned, we find that in each year the victories won by the employers outnumber, often very considerably, the victories of labour. Moreover, between 1894 and 1900 the number of strikes fell from 929 to 648; the number of workers involved also decreased, falling from 257,000 in 1894 to 135,000 in 1900.[3] At first sight these figures are surprising, for they belong to a period when trade was prosperous, a period of increased exports and diminished unemployment, and at that time it was universally believed that those conditions infallibly produce a large increase of strikes. Improvement in trade is accompanied by a rise in prices, and the labourer demands an increase of his wages. But if prices continue to rise, the increase immediately appears insufficient, and the workmen go from strike to strike, always victorious and always dissatisfied. Why did this fail to happen during the five years of prosperity with which the nineteenth century closed? Possibly because there was no general rise in prices sufficient to compensate for the general fall during the previous five years,

[1] H. of C., March 17, 1903 (*Parliamentary Debates*, 4th Ser., vol. cxviii, p. 1674). Cf. H. of C., April 27, 1903. Motion by H. Asquith (ibid., vol. cxxi, pp. 482 sqq.).

[2] For the history of the dispute see W. S. Parry, *The Penrhyn Lock-out, 1900–01. A Statement and an Appeal*, 1902. The work appears to be supported by ample evidence, but it cost the author £500 damages when Lord Penrhyn took proceedings against him.

[3] The annual figures are as follows: Number of strikes: 1894, 929; 1895, 745; 1896, 926; 1897, 864; 1898, 711; 1899, 719; 1900, 648. Number of men directly involved: 1894, 257,314; 1895, 207,239; 1896, 147,950; 1897, 167,543; 1898, 200,769; 1899, 138,058; 1900, 135,145 (*Strikes and Lock-outs. Board of Trade. Report on Strikes and Lock-outs in the United Kingdom*).

and, therefore, in this exceptional instance, the labourer found his position improved by the increase of wages which his employer conceded without the necessity for a strike.[1]

But must we insist at all costs on a purely economic philosophy of history? Why should we refuse to look elsewhere for the explanation of the peaceful attitude displayed by the working class during the five or six years which followed the election of 1895? A wave of imperialism was sweeping over the country, and, as hatred of the foreigner—the German, the Russian, the Frenchman—prevailed over hatred of the domestic enemy, and racial hostility thrust the conflict of classes into the background, the situation became unfavourable to labour agitation. It may surprise us that in 1897 the engineers failed to excite the sentimental pity natural to the British temperament, as on similar

[1] A. L. Bowley (*Statistical Studies: Relating to National Progress in Wealth and Trade since 1882: A Plea for Further Inquiry*, 1904, p. 10) estimates that in the period 1882–1902 wages had risen in the building trade 15 per cent, in the engineering trade 10 per cent, in the printing trade 7 per cent for piece work, in the mercantile marine 20 per cent, in the coal mines 30 per cent, in the cotton industry 10 per cent, whereas in the woollen manufacture they were practically speaking stationary. He adds that the increase had been gradual in every case, with the exception of coalmining, in which the fluctuations of prices had been violent and rapid. He continues (p. 35): 'If we make up a budget of the goods most usually purchased by the working classes, and compare the prices at which they were bought year by year for the last twenty years, we find that such a budget, costing one pound in the period 1898–1902, would have cost nineteen shillings and sixpence in 1893–1897, twenty shillings and sixpence in 1888–1892, and twenty-one shillings and sixpence in 1883–1887. In other words, during the last twenty years, the purchasing power of money has increased about 8 per cent, or what is the same thing, prices have fallen about 8 per cent. Thus whilst the apparent increase of wages was about 30 per cent in that period, the real increase . . . is found to be about 40 per cent.' We have refrained from making use of these figures in our text on account of the arbitrary character of these divisions into periods of five years, particularly during this period. It conceals the fact that the price of coal and of several important articles of food, for example potatoes, lard, mutton, and fish, was at its lowest in 1896—that is to say, immediately before the end of one of A. L. Bowley's five-year periods. This was followed by a rise in prices, so slow however that, on an average, prices from 1898 to 1902 were scarcely higher than they had been between 1893 and 1897. A. C. Pigou (*The Riddle of the Tariff*, 1903) represents the general level of real wages in the United Kingdom by the following figures: 1861, 91; 1871, 100; 1881, 116; 1891, 144; 1901, 165. The same writer (*Protective and Preferential Import Duties*, 1906, pp. 45–6) represents as follows the movement of nominal wages: 1886–1890, 100; 1891–1895, 105.5; 1896–1900, 110.3, and the movement of real wages: 1886–1890, 100; 1891–1895, 109.6; 1896–1900, 119.9. If these figures are correct, the rise of the latter was the more rapid. Charles Rist, in the course of his interesting article on the growth of strikes in France and its significance (*Revue d'Economie Politique*, 1907, pp. 1 sqq.), attributes the decrease in the number of strikes in Great Britain at the close of the nineteenth century to the operation of the recently established Conciliation Boards, which enabled the workers to secure the increase of wages for which they asked, without striking. And the same explanation is suggested in the Board of Trade *Report on Strikes and Lock-outs for the year 1899* (p. xxii). But if Charles Rist had published his article in 1910, instead of 1907, could he still have accepted this explanation? Did the Conciliation Boards prevent a rapid and continuous increase in the number of strikes in Great Britain during the seven or eight years immediately preceding the Great War?

occasions in the past it had been enlisted on behalf of the British workman: it was because the imagination of the middle class, and even of the proletariat, was pre-occupied. The engineers' strike or lock-out began in the middle of the festivities of the Jubilee, ended a few weeks after the occupation of Kiao-Tchau by Germany and the first move of Russia towards Port Arthur, and the Press was full of these events. Nor surely was it without importance that the strike of the South Welsh miners the following year placed the Admiralty in a difficult position, and owing to the lack of steam coal the original programme of the naval manoeuvres could not be carried out; and that, on the other hand, the strike ended just in time to allow the Admiralty to work up public feeling about Fashoda? Must we not conclude that there were a large number, even among the working classes, who regarded the Welsh strikers as traitors?

4

All the symptoms we have related were calculated to dishearten that militant and more or less consciously Socialist section of labour which just before 1895 had shown such assurance and activity. But was the setback a permanent reaction of the community against their propaganda, or merely the temporary success of a class, numerically small, against whom they could organize in the hope of avenging their defeat in the near future? Other signs, of a more encouraging nature, revived their spirits. If the Amalgamated Society of Engineers did not recover from its defeat in 1897, it was not the same with the Welsh miners. Only a month had passed since they ratified the agreement which registered their defeat, when at last they shook off their apathy and for the first time in their history united to form a Union—the South Wales Miners' Federation which began with a membership of 128,000. Moreover, the total membership of the trade unions was increasing every year. Between 1895 and 1901 the increase amounted to more than a third, and in the latter year the number of trade unionists had almost reached 2,000,000.[1] In the ranks of so formidable a host there could not fail to be men who

---

[1] 1895, 1,408,486 members; 1896, 1,495,476; 1897, 1,613,753; 1898, 1,649,461; 1899, 1,803,897; 1900, 1,910,614; 1901, 1,922,780 (*Abstract of Labour Statistics Board of Trade* [*Labour Department*] *Ninth Annual Abstract*, 1901-2, p. 121).

would address themselves to the task of devising a reply to the employers' offensive.

The sole link which united the various unions of the country was the annual Trades Union Congress. But the Congress was nothing more than a deliberative Assembly. The unions represented at the Congress were not bound by the voting. Nor did it possess an executive committee which could take action in the interval between each annual Congress. Steps should be taken to improve the organization of trade unionism. Why not form a general federation of the unions which would be in a position to oppose to the employers' combination a united front of organized labour? Every union would come to the assistance of the union threatened by the employers, and since the latter would not dare to meet this proof of solidarity by declaring a general lock-out, they would inevitably lose any battle in which they were rash enough to engage. At first sight, the scheme might seem a copy of French syndicalism; it was in 1895 that the *Confédération Générale du Travail* had been formed. In reality, nothing could be further from the truth than this comparison. It was the American Federation of Labour which had provided British labour with a model. Far from preparing a general strike to expropriate capital, the object of the proposed Federation, as stated in its manifesto, was to promote industrial peace and by every amicable means, for instance conciliation, mediation, and arbitration or by the establishment of permanent boards, to prevent contests—strikes or lock-outs—between employers and men, or disputes between unions. The proposal had been originally made in 1894 by the Clarion group and had won the passing approval of the Trades Union Congress at Norwich. It was revived in 1897 by the Birmingham Congress, and submitted in 1898 by the Bristol Congress to the examination of a Special Committee. The Federation was at last founded in 1900. It has continued in existence because English foundations do not perish. But it has never contained more than a small minority of the trade unionists. It made the mistake of imposing too strict conditions on the affiliated unions. No Federation was admitted as a member of the General Federation. Every Federation whose affiliated unions wished to join the General Federation must first be dissolved, that the unions which had composed it might enter the Federation as independent units. Naturally the powerful Miners' Federation,

which already contained two-thirds of the miners, refused to
commit suicide that the affiliated associations—some twenty in
all—might be enabled to enter the General Federation; and when
the miners withdrew, the Federation was condemned to
stagnate.[1]

5

The forces of labour could be marshalled by a different method.
Why not revive the proposal which had been accepted in 1893 at
Belfast, to be rejected at Cardiff in 1895? Why not form a party
for political, not economic, action on the basis of the trade unions
and with a Socialist programme? At Edinburgh in 1896 the
Congress passed the motion demanding the nationalization of
the means of production, distribution and exchange only with
considerable modification and refused to re-affirm the motion,
passed three years earlier at Belfast, by which the unions were
invited to adopt the financial measures which would enable
Independent Labour candidates to stand at the next election. But
the following year at Birmingham the Congress once more began
to demand that all the means of production, distribution, and
exchange should be nationalized, and two years later at Plymouth
decided by 546,000 to 434,000 votes to summon a conference to
advise on the best method of increasing the representation of
Labour in the House of Commons.

The Conference was held in London on February 27 and 28,
1900. It was attended by 120 delegates. Representatives of the
various Socialist organizations were present. The trade unions[2]

---

[1] George Howell, *Labour Legislation, Labour Movements, and Labour Leaders*, 1902, p. 455.
S. and B. Webb, *The History of Trade Unionism*, ed. 1920, pp. 554 sqq. Original documents:
Clarion Pamphlet No. 17: Trades Federation, by P. J. King and Robert Blatchford (*Nun-
quam*) 1897. *No. 24: Good and Bad Federation. The Clarion Scheme more fully developed and
explained. Alternative schemes examined, Criticisms of the Clarion scheme answered*. By
P. J. King, 1898. *No. 28: Federation in a Nutshell*, by P. J. King, 1898. *No. 33: Trades'
Federation, The Official Scheme. A Crushing Criticism*, 1899. *Trades' Union Congress Parlia-
mentary Committee. Agenda for Special Congress on Trades' Federation, to be held in St. James'
Hall, Oxford Street, Manchester, on Tuesday, January 24, 1899, and two following days,
commencing on the 1st day at 12 o'clock*. (An enumeration of seven schemes to be examined.)
*The General Federation of Trades Unions. Report of the proceedings of the Special Trades
Federation Congress which was held at St. James' Hall, Manchester, January 24, 25, and 26,
1899. Together with the Rules (as amended) and the List of Delegates. The General Federation
of Trade Unions. Minutes of the first General Council Meeting, held at the Westminster Palace
Hotel on Wednesday, 19 July, 1899*.
[2] For the history of the beginnings of the Labour Party see Paul Mantoux and Maurice
Alfassa, *La Crise du Trade Unionisme*, 1903, pp. 239 sqq. A. W. Humphrey, *A History of*

and even the trade councils, which had been excluded from the Congress in 1895, were represented. That the representation of the working class might be complete the organizers of the conference had invited the Co-operators, but they had refused the invitation. A social democrat proposed the foundation of a party on the principle of the class war and with a programme of unqualified Socialism. His motion was defeated. But, on the other hand, the Conference refused to be content with a mere group of trade unionists, free if they pleased to remain members of the Liberal Party. It therefore decided in favour of a group which, without being committed to a particular economic theory, would nevertheless present in every respect the character of a 'party', politically independent. An ambiguous solution, but cleverly contrived to win the approval of the Trades Union Congress, and in keeping with the tactics the Independent Labour Party had consistently pursued for the past seven years. A committee was elected which took the name of the Labour Representation Committee. It consisted of seven trade unionists, two members of the Independent Labour Party, two members of the Social Democratic Federation and one Fabian. Through their Unions 353,000 Trade Unionists gave their allegiance to the Committee. The Unions agreed to pay a subscription of ten shillings for every 1,000 members. The Secretary of the Committee was a certain James Ramsay MacDonald of whom, until this moment, hardly anyone had heard. He was a man of thirty-four, of a sombre and handsome countenance. The son of a Scotch peasant woman, he had attended an elementary school, and become a school teacher. He had then gone to London to seek a livelihood, where for some time he had lived the hand to mouth existence of the intellectual worker of humble origin. He had been for a time a member of the Fabian Society, where he was remembered as a man not easily influenced. He was one of the founders of the Independent Labour Party. Everything about his past, his obscure origin, the life of destitution he had lived for ten years in London, destined him, one might have imagined, to become a revolutionary. In fact he had the politician's temper and gifts, and the founders of the Labour Representation Committee could not have made a

Labour Representation, 1912, pp. 142 sqq. M. Beer, *Geschichte des Sozialismus in England*, 1913, pp. 476 sqq. Edward R. Pease, *The History of the Fabian Society*, 1916, pp. 148 sqq. Sidney and Beatrice Webb, *The History of Trade Unionism*, ed. 1920, pp. 683 sqq.

better choice. He displayed that blend of moral austerity and practical shrewdness which composes the typical Scot.

It seemed as though the campaign the Independent Labour Party had inaugurated in 1893 was about to bear fruit, and that the policy it advocated was beginning at last to win the decided support of the Unions. But we must not exaggerate the strength of the new movement. No doubt it was a victory for Keir Hardie to have won back John Burns, Hyndman, and the Fabians. But there was no room in a single church for three popes. Once more John Burns' bowler and stiff collar quarrelled with Keir Hardie's trilby and soft shirt, and Burns retired, finding no doubt that a majestic isolation suited his naïve vanity better than any other position. Shortly afterwards, Hyndman and his Social Democrats also left, when they realized that they were not to absorb the Independent Labour Party, but the Independent Labour Party was to absorb them. The Fabians, it is true, remained, but at the meetings of the Committee, instead of collaborating on the same footing as the other members, they adopted the attitude of slightly supercilious and rather stand-offish advisers.[1] Their leaders, Sidney and Beatrice Webb and Bernard Shaw, did everything in their power to discredit the Labour Representation Committee. We have already remarked the ostentatious support and the lavish advice which they gave during the Boer War to the group of Liberal Imperialists. And the war had hardly begun when the Fabian, Sydney Olivier,[2] was appointed by Chamberlain Colonial Secretary in Jamaica.

Indeed, the war was itself detrimental to the Committee. Amid the turmoil, it was not easy for the Committee to make itself heard. At the election of 1900 it put forward only fourteen candidates, obtained very little over 50,000 votes and won only two victories. Keir Hardie was returned for Merthyr Tydvil, John Burns for Battersea. And Burns was attached to the group by a very feeble tie which he would shortly break. The number of trade unionists affiliated to it amounted to no more than 353,000 out of the 1,250,000 represented at the last Congress.

[1] 'For several years after this (1901) the Fabian Society did not greatly concern itself with the Labour Party. I attended the Annual Conferences and took a regular part in the work of the Executive Committee, but my colleagues of the Fabian Society, as a whole, showed little interest in the new body. In a sense, it was not in our line.' (Edward E. Pease, *The History of the Fabian Society*, p. 150.)
[2] Later Lord Olivier, Secretary of State for India in the Labour Government of 1924.

At the end of the first year the paltry budget of the Committee amounted to £342 of receipts, as against £286 of expenditure, that is to say, there was a surplus of £56. On the election it had spent £33.

The vast majority of the trade unionists still regarded the experiment with hostility or indifference. As against the one or two members of the Labour Representation Committee in the new Parliament, there were eight representatives of labour who would have nothing to do with it. In the Congress itself the miners had adopted an attitude of contemptuous hostility to the motion in favour of unqualified Socialism. They had refused to vote on it, disdaining to support or oppose a demonstration which they declared to be meaningless. In 1899 the miners and cotton spinners had voted against the resolution, introduced by the railwaymen, which had resulted in the foundation of the Representation Committee. True, they had been defeated, but at this very Congress of 1899, the Parliamentary Committee, on which the moderates were in a majority, decided to amend the rules of the Congress. The following year, 1900, the Committee submitted to the Congress the following proposals. In the first place, the chairman of the Congress should no longer be appointed by the unions of the town in which it was held, but should be the Chairman of the Parliamentary Committee. The change would prevent a repetition of the scandal which had occurred at Bristol in 1898, when the cabinet maker, James O'Grady,[1] had opened the Congress with a Socialist speech aimed at the moderate policy of the Committee. Secondly, the Parliamentary Committee would determine beforehand the programme of the Congress with power to eliminate all motions which in their opinion were not germane to trade unionism. In this way all strictly Socialist motions would be excluded in advance. By insisting that the vote on these amendments should be taken not by the number of individual delegates present, but by unions, whose vote should be in proportion to their membership—the procedure laid down at the Cardiff Congress in 1895—the moderates secured their adoption. Like the Cardiff Congress of 1895, the Huddersfield Congress of 1900 declared in favour of a bourgeois policy.

A Socialist who wrote about the beginning of 1901 reviewed

[1] Later Sir James O'Grady, Governor of Tasmania.

the situation of Labour and drew the gloomiest auguries.[1] The
Trades Union Congress? Entirely in the hands of a few large
unions, it had lost all influence over trade unionists as a body;
nobody took its futile and muddled debates seriously. The
Parliamentary Committee? It possessed neither the moral
authority nor the necessary funds to compel Parliament to
respect what were presumed to be the wishes of the Congress.
The Labour Representation Committee? It was paralysed by
personal feuds, and by the obvious determination of the trade
union secretaries not to break with the Liberal Party. 'Yet,'
added the writer, 'with a sublime faith, the efforts are continually
repeated, and will one day succeed.' That day would indeed
come, and certainly far sooner than he expected it himself. A
year had not elapsed since the Huddersfield Congress, when a
further defeat suffered by the unions in their struggle with the
employers' federations awoke them from their bourgeois somno-
lence. To understand it, we must first inquire what at the end of
the nineteenth century was the legal position of the trade unions,
against which the employers had declared war.

6

Their legal position was determined by an important statute
passed in 1871.[2] It did not confer on the unions the fictitious
personality which would have given them the legal status of
'corporations'. They were merely declared lawful, and obtained
the right, if they had complied with the necessary formalities of
registration, to prosecute a treasurer who embezzled their funds.
But they were given no right of action against their members for
breach of contract, or for the non-payment of a subscription or
fine. And, on the other hand, their members had no right of
action against the union, if it employed their funds for purposes
which in their opinion were contrary to the statutes. In this
respect a union was on the same footing as a club which, if a
member fails to pay his subscription, can do no more than expel
him, and whose members have no remedy except resignation if
they are dissatisfied with its financial management. But, if in the

---

[1] Henry W. Macrosty, *Trusts and the State. A Sketch of competition*, 1901, p. 244.
[2] 34 & 35 Vict., Cap. 31: An Act to amend the Law relating to Trade Unions (*Trade Union Act*, 1871).

course of a strike ordered by a union, its members were guilty
of illegal acts, had the victim a right of action against the union?
The Act was silent on this point, and its silence had been interpreted to mean that the right did not exist. Indeed, the debates
which had preceded the passing of the Act sufficiently proved that
this had been the intention of Parliament when in 1871 it refused
to 'incorporate' the trade unions, while protecting them against
any fraudulent acts their treasurers might commit. An exorbitant
privilege? Possibly, and indeed silence had seemed the only
method by which it could be conferred. But the defenders of the
unions brought forward the old argument of Adam Smith; they
must be given a privileged position, if they were to be protected
against the intangible 'but constant and uniform combination' of
employers.

The same year, to redress the balance, another Act[1] was passed
which considerably restricted the right to strike. All 'threats' or
acts of 'intimidation', 'molestation' or 'obstruction' were made
punishable by imprisonment. Under 'obstruction' was included
what was known in current parlance as picketing, the posting of
patrols by the strike committee to see that every workman
obeyed the orders of his union. It was made illegal 'persistently'
to 'follow a person', also 'watching or besetting' any building or
its approaches, and the workmen were deprived of the protection
given by a clause in the previous statute of 1859,[2] now repealed,
which had expressly declared it legal to employ peaceable persuasion to induce an individual to enter the union. But these
dispositions were amended or repealed to the advantage of the
workers by a further statute, passed in 1875. In future, the magi-
strate who gave sentence was empowered to inflict a fine instead
of imprisonment. The old terms 'coercion' and 'molestation'
disappeared, and if 'watching and besetting' were still legal
offences, it was enacted that the mere fact of 'attending at or near
the house or place where a person resides or works or happens to
be, in order merely to obtain or communicate information' did
not constitute 'watching or besetting' within the meaning of the
Act: that is to say 'peaceable persuasion' was once more expressly

[1] 34 & 35 Vict., Cap. 32: An Act to amend the Criminal Law relating to Violence,
Threat and Molestation (*Criminal Law Amendment Act* [*Violence*], etc., 1871).
[2] An Act to amend and explain an Act of the Sixth Year of the Reign of King George
the Fourth, to repeal the Laws relating to the Combination of Workmen, and to make
other Provisions in lieu thereof, 1859.

declared to be lawful. And finally, it was laid down that agreements between two or more persons to perform, or to cause another to perform, a particular act in the course of a labour dispute could not be punished as conspiracy, if the act in question did not constitute a crime when committed by a single person.[1]

For many years it seemed that the provisions of the Trade Union Act of 1871 and the Conspiracy and Protection of Property Act of 1875 adequately protected the unions in the exercise of their right to strike. And where the interpretation of the statute of 1875 was doubtful the Courts seemed disposed to interpret the law in the sense most favourable to the unions. For instance, the Act of 1875 mentioned an offence of 'intimidation', without defining its exact nature. The Courts decided in 1891, in the cases of *Gibson v. Lawson* and *Curran v. Treleaven,* that there was 'intimidation' only when the act threatened was of a 'criminal' nature. It was still disputed whether, when this was not the case, civil proceedings, at least, could be taken against the persons who had committed an act of alleged intimidation. It was decided in 1897, in the case of *Allen v. Flood,* that no action could be brought. A dispute had arisen in certain London shipyards between two unions. Two shipwrights, who were members of a union of carpenters, had accepted work which the boilermakers, who as ironworkers belonged to another and a very powerful union, considered that they alone were entitled to undertake. The ironworkers secured the discharge of the two carpenters by threatening the employer with a strike if he refused. The discharged men

---

[1] 38 & 39 Vict., Cap. 86: An Act for amending the Law relating to Conspiracy, and to the Protection of Property and for other purposes (*Conspiracy and Protection of Property Act,* 1875). On the other hand two clauses (*Articles* 4 & 5) of the statute declared a breach of contract criminal—(1) If it deprived a locality of its supply of gas or water; (2) If it endangered life or damaged property. See further 38 & 39 Vict., Cap. 90: An Act to enlarge the powers of County Courts in respect of disputes between Employers and Workmen and to give other Courts a limited civil Jurisdiction in respect of such Disputes (*Employers and Workmen Act,* 1875). The Act extended the competence of the County Courts while restricting the jurisdiction of the Justices of the Peace. Also 39 & 40 Vict., Cap. 22: An Act to amend the Trade Union Act 1871 (*Trade Union Act* [1871] *Amendment Act,* 1876), which defined more precisely the formalities to be fulfilled in founding and registering a union. For the text and significance of this legislation see Sir James Stephen, *History of Criminal Law,* 1883, vol. iii, pp. 222 sqq. Herman Cohen and George Howell, *Trade Union Law and Cases. A Text-book relating to Trade Unions and to Labour,* ed., 1901. Royal Commission on Labour, *Fifth and Final Report,* pp. 157 sqq., Appendix ii: 'Memorandum by Sir Frederick Pollock, on the Law of Trade Combination'. Sidney and Beatrice Webb: *The History of Trade Unionism,* ed. 1920, pp. 275 sqq.; *Industrial Democracy,* 1897, Appendix i, *The Legal Position of Collective Bargaining,* pp. 853 sqq. P. Mantoux et M. Alfassa, *La Crise du Trade Unionisme,* 1903, pp. 5 sqq. 19 sqq. Henry-Emile Barrault, *Le Droit d'Association en Angleterre,* 1908, pp. 63 sqq., 213 sqq.

brought an action against Allen, the local secretary of the union which had boycotted them. On December 14, 1897, the House of Lords in its capacity as the Supreme Court of Appeal decided that the action taken by Allen was not only no crime, it was not even a civil offence.[1]

7

The decision, given at a time when the employers were attacking the Society of Engineers, attracted wide attention. But, though the judgment was a defeat, they did not lose heart, or give up hope of retrieving it in the near future. Even in the case of *Allen v. Flood* the House of Lords had simply reversed an unfavourable decision of the Court of Queen's Bench which had been confirmed on appeal. Moreover the decision had not been unanimous. Of the nine judges trying the issue, three had dissented from the judgment. And the decision would perhaps have been different if the law lords had not considered themselves bound by a judgment they had themselves delivered two years earlier in a case of boycotting by employers. An act which they had pronounced to be lawful when committed by a combination of employers, they could hardly after so brief an interval declare illegal when committed by a trade union. But this employers' boycott, the case of the Mogul Steamship Company, would be forgotten, as the years passed. The normal course of promotion would ensure at some future date a Conservative majority among the law lords. Did not professional judges entertain an instinctive antipathy to all sectional associations? And did not judges who belonged by birth and education to the middle class feel an equally instinctive dislike of anything which in the remotest degree resembled an insurrection of the proletariat? There was, therefore, good reason to hope that the decision of the Courts would be reversed. And that expectation was encouraged by the fact that this latest judgment of the House of Lords ran counter to the spirit of several recent decisions—both in the Flood case and in other cases—which seemed to show a determination of the employers to secure

[1] For the case of *Allen v. Flood* and a history of subsequent legal decisions, see the excellent legal monograph by Jean Fouilland, *Allen v. Flood, Le Boycottage, les listes noires et les autres instruments de contrainte syndicale devant la loi civile. Les deux courants actuels de jurisprudence. Les origines du courant libéral.* 1922. (The author corrects a mistake made by Mantoux and Alfassa.)

an interpretation of the statute of 1875 more favourable to themselves, and a new disposition on the part of the judges to give them a remedy for the grievances of which they complained.

For instance there was the *Temperton v. Russell* case of 1893. The men employed in the building trade at Hull had entered into a joint agreement with several firms. One of these refused to fulfil the conditions of the agreement. When a strike failed to overcome the employers' resistance the men resorted to a boycott and forbade the contractors to provide any more materials to the firm, until their demands had been granted. A contractor named Temperton refused to yield to their threats. He was then boycotted himself, and every builder who bought materials from him was informed that six men would refuse to handle any materials he might deliver. He brought an action and sentence was given against the defendant, Russell, both in the first instance and on appeal.

There was also the case of *Lyons & Sons v. Wilkins*. The employees of Messrs. Lyons had gone on strike. Pickets had been posted at the doors of all the buildings belonging to the firm. They distributed to every employee who entered printed handbills asking the employees who did not belong to the Union to refuse work until the dispute had been settled. They refrained from any act of violence. At most they had, once or twice, trespassed on the premises of the firm. Messrs. Lyons prosecuted one of the men who had employed this method of propaganda, and Wilkins was convicted both in the first instance, and on appeal.

These decisions cast doubt on the accepted interpretation of the Act of 1875. And about the same time the current interpretation of the Trade Union Act of 1871, which was believed to guarantee the Unions against financial liability, was also called in question. We are not referring either to the opinion expressed by several witnesses before the Royal Commission on Labour of 1891 that their liability ought to be established by further legislation,[1] or

---

[1] Royal Commission on Labour, *Fifth and Final Report*, pp. 540–1. The report, signed by a majority of the Commissioners, complained of: 'The inconvenience which may be caused by the existence of associations having, as a matter of fact, very real corporate existence and modes of action, but no legal personality corresponding thereto.' But it refrained from proposing a remedy. Eight members of the Commission (among them the Duke of Devonshire, Sir Michael Hicks-Beach, Leonard M. Courtney, and Sir Frederick Pollock) were content with signing the 'observations' published as an appendix to the report (pp. 115 sqq.) in which it is suggested that associations, whether of workmen or employers, should be permitted to claim the status of a corporation, capable of suing and being sued in the courts.

to the Bill to that effect drafted by the Employers' Parliamentary Council.[1] To demand new legislation was to admit that, as the law stood, the union funds could not be touched. But already, indirect attempts were being made to discover whether, without any change in the law, it might not be possible to obtain damages from the unions for offences committed by their members. In all the cases of which we have just spoken and in others besides, the employers attempted to prosecute not only the workman whose conduct was directly in question, but the officials of his union, sometimes even the union itself. The attempts usually failed, but in one or two instances were partially successful;[2] and the attitude of the courts alarmed, in 1897, Sidney and Beatrice Webb. 'Collective bargaining will become impossible if, whenever trade unionists are warned not to accept employment from a particular firm for any reason whatsoever, the trade union officials can be harassed by writs, costs in damages, and driven into bankruptcy. Unfortunately,' they added, 'the present generation of trade unionists, not excluding the responsible officials, are not alive to the gravity of the legal situation.'[3] In this, the trade unionists and their leaders were typical Englishmen. Englishmen keep their imagination under control and refuse to meet misfortune half-way.

8

In July, 1901, the blow fell. It was a decision of the House of Lords, once more acting as the supreme court of appeal. A year before, a strike had broken out on the lines of the Taff Vale Railway Company. The Company had prosecuted the secretary of the local branch of the union and the secretary of the union on the charge of instigating certain offences the Welsh railwaymen had committed during the strike, and then, in spite of the opinion given by their legal advisers, had tried the experiment of claiming damages directly from the Amalgamated Railway Servants' Society.

[1] For our knowledge of this Bill we are indebted to the very learned work by P. Mantoux and M. Alfassa, La Crise du Trade Unionisme, p. 31. But the employers' Bill cannot belong, as they have dated it, to the year 1897, since the Employers' Council was not founded until the end of 1898.

[2] In the cases of Trollope and Others v. The London Builders' Federation and Others, 1895, and Warnham v. Stone, 1896 (H. Cohen and G. Howell, Trade Union Law Cases, p. 80. Paul Mantoux and Maurice Alfassa, La Crise du Trade Unionisme, p. 21. Sidney and Beatrice Webb, Industrial Democracy, ed. 1, p. 858 n.).

[3] Ibid. , p. 861.

The union officials were taken by surprise, the more so because they did not consider that they had been responsible for the Welsh strike. Though, under the clever guidance of Richard Bell, the Amalgamated Railway Servants' Society had made rapid progress, and could boast of a membership of 62,000, it was, nevertheless, far from possessing the power which the Miners' and Cotton Operatives' Unions wielded in the North. It recognized that the Companies, and possibly, even the public, were disinclined to admit the right of railwaymen to form a union at all.[1] Two unsuccessful strikes in 1898 had cost the Society £18,000 and the ill-humour their failure aroused had led to the resignation of more than 31,000 members.[2] At first, the Society had intended to disavow the strikers, and it was almost with reluctance that it finally decided to support them. Possibly the union's half-hearted attitude encouraged the Railway Company to attack it. The Society replied to the summons by claiming that its name should be omitted from the action on the ground that it was incapable of being sued in court and that any action taken against it was legally invalid. In the first instance the Company won its case. But no one was surprised when the contention of the Society was upheld on appeal, for the statute of 1871 had always been understood by the public to support it. Finally, the case was taken to the Lords. The Lords refused to interpret the silence of the statute by the manifest intention of the legislature and held the Society responsible. The gravity of the decision can be appreciated by the fact that when, in consequence of the judgment of the House of Lords, the case came again before the courts, the Amalgamated Railway Servants' Society was condemned eighteen months later to pay £23,000 damages. In future, the financial strength of the unions would reduce them to impotence; they would be unable to declare or approve a strike without risk of ruin.

And the risk was all the greater because the rights of the strikers would henceforward be more narrowly restricted. It was for their action in picketing that the railwaymen of the Taff Vale Company had been successfully prosecuted by the Company;

---

[1] 'You might as well have a Trade Union or an Amalgamated Society in the Army, where discipline has to be kept at a very high standard, as have it on railways.' Words spoken about 1896 by Sir George Findlay, manager of the London and North Western Railway (Sidney and Beatrice Webb, *History of Trade Unionism*, ed. 2, p. 525).

[2] G. W. Alcock, *Fifty Years of Railway Trade Unionism*, 1922, pp. 298–9.

and it would certainly appear that in this instance the limits of peaceful picketing had been exceeded. But what of the case of *Charnock v. Court*, decided in 1897? A Bradford employer during a strike brought over workmen from Ireland. The union sent two men to the port of Fleetwood, fifty miles away, to persuade the Irish not to break the strike and offer them their fare back to Ireland if they would consent to return. The men were found guilty of watching and besetting in spite of the very careful definition of the offence in the Act of 1875. The workers suspected that the employers had adopted a new method of attack, to challenge in particular cases the weaker unions and obtain legal decisions in their favour on the question of picketing. And there could be no doubt that the employers had won an important success when, a few days after the Taff Vale decision, the House of Lords delivered a judgment in a boycotting case which contradicted the judgment they had given four years before in the case of *Allen v. Flood*.

A wholesale butcher in the suburbs of Belfast, named Leathem, employed non-union labour. The local union of Butchers' Assistants ordered him to discharge these men. On his refusal to comply, he was forbidden, so long as they were still in his employment, to supply one of his Belfast customers, a butcher named Munce, and at the same time, Munce was forbidden to obtain meat from Leathem. Otherwise his men would strike. Moreover a black list was published of all the tradesmen who dealt with Leathem. Leathem brought the matter before the courts and judgment was given in his favour in the first instance, on appeal, and finally on August 5, 1901, by the House of Lords. Had the decision in *Allen v. Flood* been reversed? Not exactly. A judgment given in one case does not reverse a judgment given in another. But the judgment in *Allen v. Flood* had been a pronouncement delivered with the utmost formality after the question had been weighed with more than usual care, and in circumstances which seemed to prove that the House of Lords intended to lay down a general rule which for a long time to come should determine the law in the matter of boycotting by workmen. Now, it would be regarded as having settled only a particular case. In future, the judges would have to decide, whenever a case of boycotting came before them, whether the decision of 1897 or the decision of 1901 was applicable. The unions were placed at the mercy of the judicial bench, and they felt that the judges were becoming increasingly hostile to their claims.[1]

9

The working classes were panic-stricken. At the annual Trades Union Congress, held a month later at Swansea, the leaders of the militant section expressed their fear that not only the funds of the unions but their personal property might be liable to confiscation as a result of the recent decision by the Lords. John Hodge, a steel smelter, told the Congress that he had made over his few possessions to his wife, and advised his comrades to do the same. But the Labour Representation Committee profited by the general alarm. It was only with extreme reluctance that in 1898 the union officials had assented to the policy urged by the advocates of political action, and perhaps had given way only because they expected the experiment to fail. Now, they suddenly realized the mistake they made in welcoming the failure of the Committee to make headway. They had put their trust in the House of Lords, confident that it would rectify any judgments unfavourable to the working class which might be given by a lower court. Had not the Lords in 1897 affirmed the lawfulness of the boycott? Had they not since then, in several instances, put the most liberal interpretation upon the Workmen's Compensation Act of 1897? Now, the event had proved how misplaced their confidence had been. How was it they had failed to understand that these law lords were politicians as well as judges?[2] Three years later, a

[1] Jean Fouilland, *Allen v. Flood*, 1922. Renè Hoffherr, *Le Boycottage devant les cours anglaises*, 1901–1923. R. B. Haldane, 'The Labourer and the Law' (*Century Review*, March, 1903, vol. lxxxiii, pp. 362 sqq.). 'These decisions disclose divergencies of views among distinguished men which make it hopeless for any one to try to say with accuracy or certainty what the law is. Speaking for myself, I should be very sorry to be called on to tell a Trade Union Secretary how he could conduct a strike lawfully. The only answer I could give would be that, having regard to the diverging opinions of the Judges, I did not know.'

[2] 'A legal decision—or more correctly speaking, a semi-political decision' (speech by the President of the Swansea Congress, September, 1901).—Cf. Frederick Harrison, 'The End of Trade Unionism' (*Positivist Review*, September, 1901; vol. ix, p. 181): 'I do not say that these or any judges are prejudiced, but the social and political tone of the time invariably colours the bias of all courts of law. They are constitutionally conservative and see all things through the eyes of Property and Power. I am certain of this—that these cases would not have been decided exactly in this way between 1870 and 1890.' R. B. Haldane, 'The Labourer and the Law' (*Century Review*, March, 1903, vol. lxxxiii, p. 371): 'My own view of the matter, speaking as a plain M.P., is that the law is in a muddled condition, and that this arises not from any want of ability on the part of the great lawyers who have from time to time delivered conflicting opinions about it, but from the circum-

Labour leader pointed out that the Lord Chancellor during his nine years of office had appointed only one judge who was not a member of the Unionist Party.[1] With a judicial bench of that complexion what hope was there of a change in the spirit which animated the judges? It could be effected only by the pressure of a public opinion favourable to the claims of the unions. And in 1901 that public opinion did not exist.

The middle class had declared war upon the unions. Indeed the rumour was current that, if the final decision in the Taff Vale case had been adverse to their interests, a Bill establishing the principle of the unions' financial liability would have been introduced in the Commons at the beginning of the next session.[2] The Press by a large majority approved of the Lords' decision. That this was the attitude of the Conservative Press goes without saying—it was the mouthpiece of the Employers' Federation. *The Times* published a series of articles on *The Crisis in British Industry*[3] in which it denounced, not the methods employed by strikers (the Courts, it was to be presumed, had put a stop to them), but the attempts made by the workmen to reduce their labour without any loss of wages by a deliberate restriction of output. More alarming was the fact that even the Liberal Press spoke with two voices.[4] And, finally, in Parliament Labour was represented by a mere handful of members, even fewer than eight or ten years earlier, whereas on both benches sat a host of manufacturers and business men whose immediate interests were

stances that these have been men of diverging political and economic views. . . . Under such circumstances, judge-made law, and most of our law is judge-made, is apt to produce unsatisfactory results. . . . No one, for example, could say that the views upon the law affecting such questions, of the late Lord Herschell and the late Lord Bramwell had been formed from the same standpoint. It is not a question of one or of the other having been right. It is a question of whether it is desirable to leave to the chances of individual opinion what is really a great question of national policy.'

[1] Labour Representation Committee, Fourth Annual Conference, Bradford, February 4–6, 1904: Speech by John Hodge.

[2] Richard Bell, 'The Status of Trade Unions: The House of Lords' Decision.' (*Clarion*, August 3, 1901.)

[3] *The Times*, November 18, 30; December 3, 14, 16, 24, 26, 27, 30, 1901; January 4, 16, 1902.

[4] *Daily Chronicle*, July 23: The decision of the House of Lords . . . is one of considerable importance to the general body of Trade Unions. . . . The judgment of the Lords of Appeal may be accepted as a practical recognition of the nature and responsible status of the Unions. The extra responsibility thrown on the societies for the acts of their committees and officials will naturally make them more cautious in the future, and less able, whatever they may desire, to back the hasty and injudicious decisions of their local branches.' *The Speaker*, April 10: ' Wisely employed, the Taff Vale Case might . . . be made a most powerful ally in a campaign for compulsory arbitration of Trade Disputes.'

obviously in direct conflict with those of the working class. The Labour Representation Committee was right; if in place of the hundred brewers, manufacturers, and bankers, there had been a hundred Labour members in the House of Commons, the law lords might well have hesitated to upset the interpretation of the law which had been accepted without dispute for twenty years. Threatened in the factory, before the courts, and in the Press, the only hope of trade unionism lay in the ballot box and the Parliamentary representation of Labour.

When the Labour Representation Committee held its second annual conference at Birmingham in February, 1902, it could point to a very considerable increase in the number of workmen affiliated to the movement. Instead of some 350,000 there were already about 450,000. True, the theorists of the Social Democratic Federation had left the party, but their departure had its compensations when Keir Hardie and his friends were doing their utmost to win over the moderate section of trade unionists. For these moderates—led by the Cotton and Mining Unions—were being rapidly converted to the principle of political action. But they were still indisposed to unite with the Labour Representation Committee, and showed an inclination towards independent political organization by individual unions, each union possessing its own election fund and putting forward its own candidates. How were they to be persuaded that the more centralized the political action of labour, the more effective it would be? The new party it was desired to found must be presented not as an instrument for the realization of an economic theory but as a weapon to defend the corporate interests of labour. This had been the consistent policy of the leaders of the Independent Labour Party, which they did but emphasize by founding the Labour Representation Committee. At one of the conferences of the Committee Keir Hardie explained that if the promoters of the conference, 'being Socialists, had insisted that all should be Socialists, there could be no such gathering. . . . They had,' he continued, 'fixed upon a common denominator that, when acting in the House of Commons, they should be neither Socialists, Liberals, nor Tories, but a Labour Party. Let them have done with Liberalism and Toryism and every "ism" that was not Labourism.'[1]

[1] Speech at the Newcastle Conference, February, 1903.

But even when it was admitted that a Labour Party must be formed at the earliest opportunity, the problem had still to be settled of the immediate action to be taken to defend the threatened rights of the unions. The unions might demand a new definition of picketing, since the text of the statute of 1875 was not so clear as had been hitherto believed. The suggestion was even made that since the House of Lords had as yet made no pronouncement on the subject of picketing the unions should put forward a test case and submit it as soon as possible to the Lords, that the actual state of the law might at least be definitely settled. Moreover, a Bill might be drafted declaring that strikers should not be liable to civil prosecution for any action which, by the statute of 1875, was not a criminal offence. But these proposals dealt only with the legal definition of offences committed by strikers. They did not touch the vital question of the unions' financial liability. How were they to escape from the impasse in which they had been placed by the decision of the Lords?

Ramsay MacDonald urged that special legislation should be introduced to quash the new interpretation of the law. The proposal was regarded as inopportune, and he was silenced by his colleagues. Sidney and Beatrice Webb, on the other hand, advised the unions to make the best of the conditions created by the Lords' decision. This too obvious surrender cost them considerable abuse.[1] Robert Blatchford in the *Clarion* declared himself at first in favour of the new interpretation of the law; if it enabled employers to prosecute the men, it equally enabled the men to prosecute the employers.[2] He was supported by Richard Bell of the Railway Servants' Society, but, taken warmly to task by George Barnes of the Engineers,[3] he altered his mind.[4] In trade union headquarters confusion prevailed. The device adopted in the statute of 1871 of keeping silence as to the liability

[1] See their model Bill of six clauses: To amend the Laws relating to Trade Disputes (*Industrial Democracy*, 2nd ed., 1900; introduction p. xxxiv n.). The question of the financial liability of the unions is not touched. They are content to define very carefully the 'acts committed' and 'the agreements, combinations or conspiracies entered into by or on behalf of an association of employers or a trade union', which do not in themselves render their authors liable to prosecution.

[2] 'The Status of Trade Unions: The House of Lords' Decision.' (*Clarion*, August, 3, 1901.)

[3] 'The Status of Trade Unions' (*Clarion*, August 10, 1901): In spite of this, Barnes himself, when a few months later he was questioned by a French investigator, expressed a different opinion and approved the decision of the Lords. (P. Mantoux and M. Alfassa, *La Crise du Trade Unionisme*, pp. 265 sqq.)

[4] *Clarion*, August 10, 1901.

or otherwise of the unions had now been made impossible. But, however desirable it might be from a practical standpoint, would any Parliament commit the legal enormity of enacting in set terms the principle that trade unions were not financially liable for their members' acts? The legislature might be willing to define their liability very strictly and limit it to cases in which the wrongful act was committed at the express orders of the union officials. But that would be a poor compensation for the loss of the privilege the unions had enjoyed for the last twenty years! Or the suggestion might be adopted which was proposed by the wisest brains of the Liberal party, by lawyers such as Asquith, Haldane, and Sir Robert Reid, that the unions should be divided into two associations, each possessing its own funds—one, a society for the defence of its members' interests, the other, a benefit society whose funds could not be made liable for strike damages. But it would be a complicated arrangement, and even if accepted by the unions would involve abandoning the system to which the most important unions attributed their prosperity during the past fifty years—the fusion in a common fund of the strike fund and the benefit fund.

The question was brought before Parliament on May 14, 1902, by a Radical member, who moved that the House should declare legislation necessary, 'to prevent workmen being placed by judge-made law in a position inferior to that intended by Parliament in 1875', and the muddled debate which followed revealed both the weakness of the Government, which could obtain a majority of no more than 29 for the rejection of the motion—203 to 174 votes—and the embarrassment of the Opposition speakers, not one of whom was able to state clearly, what form in his opinion the new measure should take. In fact, so long as the Boer War continued, matters remained, and were bound to remain, at a standstill. The revival of Labour was indeed shown by the fact that several Labour candidates were put forward at by-elections but they were all unsuccessful. The miner, Robert Smillie, stood as a third candidate for Lanarkshire in September, 1901, on the morrow of the Swansea Congress. But what was the position? The Liberal candidate, Cecil Harmsworth, was a near relative of the director of the *Daily Mail*. The most notorious opponents of Liberal Imperialism worked for Smillie. Thus his candidature, which had the support of the *Manchester Guardian*, represented the war against war, rather than the war against capitalism. He was at the bottom of the poll. In January the plans of the Labour Representation Committee were thwarted by the action of Harry Quelch, the Social Democrat, who came forward as a Socialist candidate, prevented any other Labour candidate from standing and was defeated. At this juncture there appeared on the scene the delicate figure of Philip Snowden, with his lame body, sharp profile, and obstinate, clean-shaven chin.[1] No manual labourer he. Before he threw himself into the Socialist agitation, he had been a clerk in the Excise. When in March he stood for Wakefield he was not quite so unsuccessful as his predecessors. But, as the war still continued, he also was the representative of peace at any price, and as such was defeated.

10

Suddenly, with the restoration of peace, the situation changed entirely. The peace was signed on June 1. A few days later a seat became vacant at Clitheroe in Lancashire. It was among the curiosities of Labour representation that hitherto the operatives in the cotton manufacture, unlike the miners, had never attempted to return a representative to Parliament. The seat was hardly vacant when the local branch of the Independent Labour Party invited Philip Snowden to avenge at Clitheroe his defeat at Wakefield. He accepted the invitation. But Ramsay MacDonald intervened. He persuaded Snowden and the Independent Labour Party to alter their tactics and put forward as the candidate, not of the Independent Labour Party alone, but also of the Labour Representation Committee and of all the local Unions and Co-operative Societies, a weaver named Shackleton,[2] a trade unionist of the old school, whose political opinions were not Socialist but Liberal, and who believed that the new Labour party should be nothing more than a group within the Liberal party, defending the professional interests of labour. The Liberals could not find a candidate to oppose him and on August 1 he was returned unopposed.

The trade unions were not slow to grasp the significance of this victory. Nevertheless, it does not appear to have received from the London Press the attention it deserved. The election

[1] He had stood for Parliament already at the election of 1900, and had polled a little over 7,000 votes. This was at Blackburn, where he opposed two Conservative candidates.
[2] Later Sir David (James) Shackleton, K.C.B., Chief Labour Adviser since 1921.

had taken place at a distance from the metropolis, and at a time when the attention of Londoners was engrossed by the King's illness, the Coronation, and the meeting of the Imperial Conference. It was very different with the Woolwich election seven months later.

Towards the end of February, 1903, the seat of Woolwich was declared vacant. The workers at the arsenal composed the bulk of the electorate, and the Unionists regarded the constituency as perfectly safe, since a warlike policy was obviously in the voters' interest. During the past fifteen years the Conservative majority had constantly increased, until in 1900 the Opposition, which since 1892 had been Labour, decided not to contest the seat. Only a year ago Lord Charles Beresford, a jingo of the jingoes, had been returned, again unopposed. On his appointment as Commander of the Channel fleet he resigned his seat. What was the political situation at Woolwich, when he resigned so unexpectedly?

The Unionists, taken by surprise, nominated as their candidate a certain Geoffrey Drage, an entire stranger to the constituency and without one of the qualities which make a good candidate. He was a clever, learned and dull young man, who, because he had been secretary to the Royal Commission on Labour and on the strength of a number of books he had published on the social question, had acquired a vague reputation as a Tory Socialist, though all his books, had anyone taken the trouble to read them, were pleas for individualism.[1] On the other hand, there was no question of putting forward a Liberal candidate. For a long while past the party had ceased to possess an organization at Woolwich. But there was a Labour Committee, which though not affiliated to any larger organization was all the more active within the boundaries of the constituency, and if it had very little money, it chose the right man when it nominated William Crooks.

Of very humble origin—he had been born in a workhouse—Crooks had for many years taken a leading part in the local government of the metropolis. He was a member of the Poplar Board of Guardians, sat on the County Council as a representative of the Progressive majority, and, when Poplar was constituted a borough by the Act of 1899, had been chosen Mayor, the first Labour mayor in London. He was a big, bearded, good-natured

[1] See especially *The Labour Problem*, 1896.

creature, without a trace either of the pedant or the revolutionary in his composition, a former cooper and, as such, a member of a conservative union of the old type. Temperamentally, he was one of those liberal workmen who for the past half-century had been the admiration of the bourgeois parties on the Continent, but had been converted by the Fabian propaganda and the force of circumstances to an advanced policy of social reform, which amounted in practice to Socialism. In London Society he occupied a unique position. He was popular even in the West End, where his jovial plebeian humour delighted the dinner parties of his fellow councillors. He was popular in the borough, his own borough of Poplar, to which he was always very pleased to invite his new friends of the upper and middle class. He shamed them by the spectacle of poverty, so easily forgotten by those who avoid the sight of it, and showed them at the same time by the example of his own popularity, how easy it was to win the affection and confidence of the British lower classes. How are we to classify so sturdy a personality? 'Will Crooks', wrote his friend Chesterton, 'is not a demagogue. He is not even a democrat. He is the demos, he is the real King.'[1]

His election campaign was totally devoid of anything resembling theoretical propaganda. Even the recent decisions of the House of Lords do not seem to have received much attention in the speeches of the candidate and his supporters. Possibly a suppressed resentment had smouldered in the arsenal since the Secretary for War, Brodrick, had refused to receive a deputation from the Labour Protection League and discuss with that body the possibility of establishing a minimum wage.[2] The election was principally fought on the question of free trade. The last budget, which had envisaged a possible prolongation of the war, had imposed a slight duty on imported corn. Crooks came

[1] George Haw, *From Workhouse to Westminster. The Life Story of Will Crooks, M.P.*, 1911, with an introduction by G. K. Chesterton, p. xvii. Cf. p. 15. 'The Labour members, as a class, are not representatives but missiles. . . . Working men are not at all like Mr. Keir Hardie. If it comes to likeness, working men are rather more like the Duke of Devonshire. But they throw Mr. Keir Hardie at the Duke of Devonshire, knowing that he is so curiously shaped as to hurt anything at which he is thrown. . . . A man like Mr. J. R. MacDonald no more suggests a Battersea workman than he suggests a Bedouin or a Russian Grand Duke. These men are not the representatives of the democracy, but the weapons of the democracy. . . . There is really only one modern Labour Member who represents, who symbolizes, and who even remotely suggests the really labouring men of London, and that is Mr. Will Crooks.'

[2] Trades Union Congress. *Annual Report*, 1902, p. 44.

forward as the opponent of dear bread. That he had been a convinced Pro-Boer stood him in good stead now that the struggle was over with all those who were weary of war. As represented by him, the new Labour Party seemed not so much the precursor of a new political programme, as the natural heir of the defunct middle-class Liberalism. The electioneering experts were very doubtful of his prospects. The Conservative majority seemed too large to be destroyed, but the trade unions and the Labour Representation Committee, when they threw themselves heart and soul into the support of their unique candidate, read the signs of the times better than the experts. On March 11, on the balcony of the Town Hall, the returning officer, amid a scene of indescribable enthusiasm, declared him elected by a majority of 8,687 to 5,438.

It was in vain that the Press of the official Opposition laboured to prove—not, as we have just seen, without a certain semblance of truth—that Crooks' victory was a Liberal victory. For the Conservative Press, more clear-sighted, because the party interest which blinded the Liberals opened their eyes, had no difficulty in bringing home to the public the gravity of the event. A fortnight before the election the Labour Representation Committee had held its third annual conference at Newcastle. The membership was found to have increased by 300,000 during the past year, having risen from 450,000 to 750,000, and the Committee had decided to form a party fund to finance elections, to which every member was to contribute a penny a year; had undertaken to pay every Member of Parliament returned under the party's auspices and accepting its whip, a salary of £200 a year; and had drawn up for the first time a list of nine prospective candidates, headed by Crooks. What was the programme of the new party? Its policy, deliberately adopted, and justified by the double victory at Clitheroe and Woolwich, was to present every success at the polls as a harbinger of the triumph, not of a programme or economic creed, but of a class. But the question at once arises whether the appearance of the working class in the political arena was not in itself the first step, even if unconscious, towards the realization of a Socialist programme, and whether Socialism, too abstract as a formal doctrine to make a direct appeal to the masses of Great Britain, was not after all the logic of their unformulated desires.

PART III

THE DECLINE OF THE UNIONIST PARTY

CHAPTER I

Chamberlain and the Programme of Tariff Reform

I THE ANTECEDENTS

I

IN October, 1902, the public was informed that the Colonial Secretary, Joseph Chamberlain, intended, with His Majesty's sanction, to visit South Africa and make a personal study of the situation left by the war. It seemed only reasonable that, six months after the conclusion of the war, he should wish to investigate on the spot the problems which must be solved, if the work of pacification were to be completed. He left on November 26, landed at Durban, visited Pietermaritzburg, Pretoria, Johannesburg, and the Cape, re-embarked on February 25, 1903, and reached Southampton on March 14. Nowhere in England, except in Birmingham, did he receive the enthusiastic welcome he had perhaps expected. Was he losing his hold over the public? He, at any rate, did not think so. On the contrary, he believed himself the victim of a policy forced upon him by colleagues of mediocre ability, and of the organization of the old Conservative party which he had intended to smash for his own advantage but which held him fast in its grip. In spite of the glamour which invested his name, the real weakness of his position had been brought home to him when King Edward chose Balfour to succeed Lord Salisbury as Prime Minister, without even troubling to ask his advice. And how had the aristocratic Cecil connexion managed the business of the country during the past few months? In his absence Parliament had passed the Education Bill which he detested. The Venezuelan embroglio in which Great Britain had become involved at the invitation of the German Foreign Office must have been the more distasteful to him because he knew that the public might very naturally hold responsible for the *fiasco* the statesman who barely five years ago had inaugurated the grandiose policy of Panteutonism. And finally, on landing at Southampton, he was greeted by the news of Will Crooks' election a few days before. It was a serious warning to the Unionist agents that if they wished to secure a third victory at the polls, similar to the triumphs of 1895 and 1900, and rally to the Conservative banner the whole, or even a considerable section, of the working class, they must without further delay find a new slogan. What should it be? Chamberlain had his plans prepared and lost no time in taking the public into his confidence.

On May 15, speaking at a public reception given at the Birmingham Town Hall to welcome him on his return to England, he related the impressions he had received on his travels and asked his audience to realize the magnitude of the Empire to which they belonged. In the United Kingdom there were forty million British subjects; overseas, ten million. But these ten million might one day be forty. Did they want those forty million united with themselves 'closely, intimately, affectionately?' Or were they willing to let these large populations break away, to become each an independent nation? 'The question of trade and commerce is one of the greatest importance. . . . You want an Empire. Do you think it better to cultivate the trade with your own people or to let that go in order that you may keep the trade of those who are your competitors and rivals?'

And a week later in the House of Commons he returned to the same theme.

The question of old age pensions was being debated. Lloyd George seized the opportunity to make Chamberlain the object of one of his most violent diatribes. 'The right hon. Gentleman might have given his engagements to the millionaires of Johannesburg; but the right hon. Gentleman had given earlier engagements to the deserving poor of the United Kingdom, and by those engagements he was bound.'[1] In reply to this direct attack Chamberlain pointed out that even the very limited scheme of old age pensions, which he had had in mind, would cost the country £10,000,000 a year. How could so large a sum be raised? It was an impossibility with the present system of taxation. 'I do not think that the question of old age pensions is a dead question, and I think it may not be impossible to find the funds, but that, no doubt, will involve a review of that fiscal system which I have indicated as necessary and desirable at an early date.'[2] Thus, perhaps unintentionally, Chamberlain imitated the German

[1] H. of C., May 22, 1903 (*Parliamentary Debates*, 4th Ser., vol. cxxii, p. 1549).
[2] H. of C., May 22, 1903 (Ibid., vol. cxxii, p. 1553).

model. He announced his intention to repeat the experiment Bismarck had made so successfully at Berlin twenty-five years before. Like Bismarck, he believed that the way to revive Conservatism was to adopt a policy of social reform, and like him, to combine it with a new fiscal policy of protection.

We can easily imagine the astonishment with which this brief declaration, whose significance escaped none of his hearers, was received by his entire audience, colleagues, supporters or opponents. But, if the sudden outburst took members and journalists by surprise, we must not forget that for many years past the possibility of abandoning the traditional policy of free trade had been openly discussed in many quarters, and that on May 22, 1903, all his hearers should have been prepared for Chamberlain's declaration—the members of the House of Commons by what he had said and done during the past eight years, his fellow ministers by what he had said and done for more than six months. That the reader may be in a position to understand the struggle we are about to describe, we will give a brief account of the events which led up to it.

2

To reach the source of the British movement in favour of a return to protection, we must go back a quarter of a century to those twenty years of industrial depression which marked the decline of the Liberal party. The time had gone by when England, watching, about the year 1848, the revolutions which shook the Governments of the Continent, had believed that free trade was the panoply of social and political order. The time had also gone by, when between 1860 and 1870, France, Italy, Austria, and the German States were at war, and England, keeping her neutrality and remaining at peace, had grown rich, while the other nations were consuming, instead of producing, wealth. It was in 1872 that British exports had reached their maximum, having almost doubled since 1859—£256,257,000 instead of £130,412,000. Even when we take the growth of the population into account and calculate the value of the exports per head, the increase was almost as large—£8 1s. 0d. instead of £4 11s. 2d. Then came the lean years of low prices and diminished trade. In 1879, exports had reached their first minimum of £191,532,000

—£5 11s. 0d. per head of the population. The figure of 1872 had been exceeded—in 1890. In 1894, the year preceding the return of the Unionists to power, exports amounted to only £216,006,000—that is to say, £5 11s. 8d. per head, almost the same figure as in 1879.

It was, therefore, no longer possible to predict under a system of free trade, and, as the inevitable effect of its operation, a continuous and indefinite increase of exports. Nor could it any longer be maintained that the necessary and immediate result of free trade was to enrich every individual in every rank of society, and thus solve the problem of poverty. As we have already seen, this period of depression witnessed an extensive revival of Socialism in Great Britain. But, if Socialism was the natural reaction of the working class to the new economic conditions, might not the employers react after another fashion? The distinctive feature of the new epoch, so unfavourable to British trade, was the fact that the great Continental Powers, who, during the period which followed 1860, had inclined under the influence of England towards free trade, were now following the example of the German Empire and returning to protection. In every case, a market was closed to British imports, a barrier erected behind which new-born industries were maturing in safety for the day when they should be sufficiently strong to invade the British market. Inevitably the question was asked—why not follow the German example?

When the Conservatives took office in 1886, the Government appointed a Royal Commission to inquire into the cause of the depression from which British trade was suffering[1] and at least a minority of the members reported in favour of a return to protection. They asked for a duty of 10 to 15 per cent on manufactured articles imported from abroad and light duties on foodstuffs imported from the Colonies. On the other hand, to conciliate the consumer, who might otherwise take alarm at the prospect of paying higher prices for a certain number of articles, they proposed the abolition of the duties on tea, coffee, and sugar. And some Colonies would benefit by their abolition. These were the measures which, in the opinion of the four members of the Com-

---

[1] *First Report of the Royal Commission appointed to inquire into the Depression of Trade and Industry. Second Report with Minutes of Evidence and Appendix. Third Report, with Minutes of Evidence and Appendix. Final Report, with Minutes of Evidence and Appendix,* 1886.

mission who signed a minority report, must be adopted without delay if British trade were to recover.[1] A year later, at the Annual Congress of the National Union of Conservative Associations, one of the four, Howard Vincent, introduced and carried a resolution demanding a 'speedy reform in the policy of the United Kingdom as regards foreign imports and the influx of indigent foreigners'.[2] Lord Salisbury, in the speech with which he closed the session of the Congress, dismissed in a few non-committal phrases Vincent's motion in favour of protection. In 1890, however, the adoption by the United States of the Mackinley tariff, which set up a very rigorous system of protection, seemed a further blow to the British export trade, and in 1892, on the eve of the General Election, Lord Salisbury admitted that a free trade country, surrounded by nations who practised protection, might find herself obliged to introduce protection as a measure of reprisals, to force her competitors to lower their tariffs.[3] This was the position formerly adopted by the young Disraeli in opposition to Peel. Universal free trade was admitted as the ideal. But one-sided free trade was condemned as absurd. Unqualified free trade was a mistake; the true principle was trade on equal terms, or in the language of its defenders, fair trade.[4]

The Unionists were turned out. When they returned to office in 1895, after an interval of three sessions, there were signs of a recovery in British trade. The imperialist, Henley, published in his *New Review* a series of alarmist articles by an economist, named Williams, in which he insisted on the danger of German competition, but when Williams republished his articles in book form with the title, shortly to become a catchword, *Made in Germany*,[5] he was compelled to admit in the preface that his book was not appearing at the most opportune moment, that a

[1] *Final Report*, pp. xliii sqq., especially pp. lxv sqq.
[2] *The Times*, November 22, 23, 1887.
[3] Speech at Hastings, May 17, 1892.
[4] For the origin of the Fair Trade Movement see W. Farrer Ecroyd, *The Policy of Self-Help. Suggestions towards the Consolidation of the Empire and the Defence of its Industries and Commerce*. T. N. Farrer (Lord Farrer) *Free Trade versus Fair Trade*, 1882 (written from the free-trade standpoint); also two excellent articles in the *Quarterly Review*, July, 1881, 'English Trade and Foreign Competition', also October, 1881, 'Fair Trade and British Labour' (vol. clii, pp. 271 sqq., 552 sqq.).
[5] *Made in Germany*, by Ernest Edwin Williams, 1896. The title of this tract, a title destined to catch on, was an allusion to the mark which goods manufactured in Germany had borne in the British market since the Merchandise Marks Act of 1887 (50 & 51 Vict., Cap. 28) made it illegal for British traders to pass off articles of foreign origin as manufactured in Britain.

recovery of British trade had just set in, and that his was the unpopular part of the skeleton at the feast. In fact, between 1894 and 1896, exports were once more increasing, and, after a very slight setback in the two following years, the increase recommenced. In 1899, the maximum of 1872 was almost reached, and in 1900 the total value of British exports had risen to £291,192,000. In 1901, the amount, £280,022,000, though slightly less than the preceding year, was still far higher than it had been two years before, and in 1902 the total was £283,424,000, very close indeed to that of 1900. Nevertheless, in certain quarters at least, a feeling of anxiety persisted, a lack of confidence in the future.

3

Of course, the increase was not denied, but since the trade of rival nations had made still greater progress during the same period, even if immediate financial interests were secure, patriotic sentiment, the pride of Britain in her economic supremacy, continued to suffer. Moreover, the reassuring figures with which the official statistics supplied the public were susceptible of a different interpretation. The year 1900 had been abnormal; supplies on a large scale had been exported to South Africa for the service of the Army. And when the figures were examined in detail, it was found that there was at least one branch of British industry whose prosperity was colossal and unbroken. For a century the export of British coal had shown a continuous increase. Coal mining had not felt the depression from which so many branches of British industry had suffered between 1872 and 1895, and the amount of coal exported had risen enormously between 1895 and 1900. This huge increase in the coal exports cloaked the stagnation of the textile industries, the cotton industry in particular which was still, as it had always been, England's peculiar boast. And in one important industry—the iron manufacture—there was not merely stagnation, but actual decline. It was explained by the discovery of new iron deposits in Germany and America, the invention of the Bessemer process, which for the past twenty years had made it possible to work abroad certain ores, before unworkable, and finally the powerful organization of the American trusts and German cartels.

This is not the place to relate the series of developments, many of them of a dramatic character, which led up to the formation in the United States on February 25, 1901, of the great trust founded by J. Pierpont Morgan with a capital of $1,150,000, the United States Steel Corporation. The trust had hardly been founded when it created a panic in the City by purchasing the majority of the shares in the Leyland shipping company, which owned sixty-five vessels, representing a total tonnage of 321,000,[1] and thus making it possible to flood the British market with iron and steel, imported in its own steamers. Nor can we relate the origin or describe the working of the innumerable cartels which in Germany combined every branch of industry—the iron manufacture above all—under the joint control of the manufacturers. The regular procedure of all these new combines—trusts or cartels—was as follows. They fixed a price, a fairly high one, for the home market which they made it their business as far as possible to stabilize. They fixed another price for foreign markets, sometimes very low, occasionally even below cost price. The loss was recovered by raising the price in the home market, and the sudden influx of foreign goods sold at prices, impossibly low, ruined the native industry of the country whose markets were thus flooded.[2] The invasion began with pig iron and raw steel; manufactured articles, rails, and machinery followed. The practice became known as dumping. The British iron and steel trade felt its very existence threatened by the iron industry of Germany and the United States.[3] How should the attack be met? By forming

---

[1] F. Hirst, *Monopolies, Trusts and Kartells*, 1905, pp. 138 sqq.

[2] For the export policy of the trusts and cartels (German Empire, United States, Austria-Hungary) see *British and Foreign Trade and Industry, Memoranda, Statistical Tables and Charts*, 1903, pp. 296 sqq. See also the figures contained in the Report of the Tariff Commission, vol. i. *The Iron and Steel Trades*, § 63: 'A firm employing nearly 1,500 hands, writing in February (1904) states that the current price of basic pig iron in Germany was then 58 marks per ton. The lowest cost at which this could be converted into steel joists and beams could not be less than 31 marks per ton. Yet these German joists, costing not less than 89 marks, were being offered f.o.b. Antwerp at 82½ marks per ton, less 2½ per cent discount. The home price in Germany for joists f.o.r. at works, was 105 marks. Similarly, the current price for pig iron at Pittsburg was $13 (54/1); the cost of manufacturing these into billets could not have been less than $6½ (27/1) per ton, making together 81/2. Yet these were being delivered c.i.f. at any British port, at 75/- per ton, making a difference of 6/2 per ton, exclusive of sea freight and land freight from Pittsburg to the American port. The home prices for these billets at Pittsburg was $24 (100/-).'

[3] We should notice the following difference between the American and the German dumping. America exported only a very small portion of its production, whereas the German exports were almost half the total amount produced. See the figures given by the *Report of the Tariff Commission*, vol. i. *The Iron and Steel Trades*, § 1143: '(American) exports in any one year never exceeded 1,154,284 tons and the average of the last five years was 800,000 tons out of an average production of 14,600,000 tons, or less than 6 per cent. It was different in Germany. The average annual production of the last three years

British trusts and cartels? No doubt about this time a large number of amalgamations were effected in the iron and steel trade, in the cotton trade and in many others. But with the possible exception of the vast combine effected by J. & P. Coats in the sewing cotton trade,[1] these amalgamations can hardly be said to have presented the distinctive features of the cartel or trust, namely the formation of a single organization co-extensive with the nation and monopolizing, under a more federal form in Germany, under a more centralized form in the United States, an entire branch of manufacture. Let those sworn to the creed of free trade rejoice, if they would. Let others, more open to the lessons of experience, and impressed by the success of the German and American combinations, lament. The fact was undeniable and its explanation seemed obvious. Trusts and cartels could be organized only under a system of protection.[2] The British manufacturers were fighting in the open and as scattered units a foe

was about 8,700,000 tons, but the exports averaged 3,400,000 tons or 38 per cent of the whole production.'

[1] For the formation of the company J. & P. Coats, Ltd., see H. W. Macrosty, *Trusts and the State*, 1901, pp. 165 sqq. A. Raffalovitch, *Trusts, Cartels, et Syndicats*, ed. 3, 1903, pp. 354 sqq. For the attempt, too simple in its design to be a practicable scheme, made by Sir George Elliot in 1893 to amalgamate the entire coal mining industry of the United Kingdom, see H. W. Macrosty, ibid., p. 178; A. Raffalovitch, ibid., p. 358.

[2] P. de Rousiers wrote in 1898: 'If England shows no instance (of a trust), it is because the artificial conditions required for the formation of a monopoly do not exist. The system of free trade renders impossible any unfair intervention by the State in the interest of the private manufacturer, and the public interest is sufficiently defended by its official guardians to prevent the monopolization of public services by private enterprise without guarantee or compensation.' (*Les Industries Monopolisées aux Etats-Unis*, p. 324.) H. W. Macrosty, in 1901, combats this statement implying as it does the impossibility of trusts in England, and declares it 'completely falsified by recent events.' (*Trusts and the State*, p. 203.) Raffalovitch, however, speaks two years later of conditions in England very much as P. de Rousiers had done in 1898, though his language is more qualified. 'Producers' combinations are easier in countries where protection exists but . . . they are also to be found in England, with, however, this essential difference, that they do not press so hard on the consumer. Lacking the artificial support of a tariff they are more liable to vicissitudes.' (*Trust, Cartels, et Syndicates*, ed. 2. Revised and enlarged, p. 351.) Cf. *Report of Tariff Commission*, vol. I, *The Iron and Steel Trades*, 1904, f. 539: 'If foreign tariffs were lower, I do not think we should dump, to do this you must have a general combination like the Kartell, which we are not likely ever to have in this country.' Ibid., f. 697: 'On the question of the causes of amalgamation in different countries, I believe that many works in Germany would not have existed without a tariff.' Ibid., f. 738: 'I understand that the chief reason for the amalgamation of small concerns always is to prevent excessive home competition, and to regulate the output so as to avoid over-production. Possibly the shutting out of foreign competition by means of a tariff has made it easier for manufacturers to combine.' Vol. iv, *The Engineering Industries*, f. 693: 'The causes of amalgamation in the United States particularly and in Germany as well, have no doubt been greatly strengthened by tariffs, enabling them to fix their prices in their own country, manufacture more largely and compete at lower prices in other markets with their surplus production. The causes of amalgamation have not been operative to any appreciable extent in England. We have no tariff and have little or no cause for these amalgamations.'

secured by strong entrenchments and organized as a disciplined army.

There is, therefore, ample evidence that between 1895, when the Unionists returned to power, and the eve of 1903 the anxiety and discontent on which we have already had occasion to insist continued to be felt. The question was being everywhere asked, why manufacturers and merchants no longer found the ready markets which had been theirs two generations earlier in the golden age of free trade. Possibly the evil was due to the colonial expansion of the great rival powers, for every annexation of colonial territory meant the closing of a market hitherto open to British exports—hence the determination to acquire new colonies or new 'spheres of influence', wherever it was evident that the principle of the open door could not be maintained much longer. Others blamed the rough and ready methods of the British manufacturer, in which he persisted at a time when German manufacture was becoming increasingly scientific—hence the new demand that the British middle class should receive that technical education with which it had fondly believed its native genius could dispense. The manufacturers, charged with a hide-bound conservatism, replied that, if the equipment of their factories lacked the improvements installed by their German competitors, the fault lay with the tyranny and unintelligent routine of the trade unions. They therefore appealed to the courts to assist them to throw off a tyrannical yoke, and in 1901 the House of Lords delivered judgments to make the right to strike ineffective. But when all was said and done, there was a striking difference, affecting many branches of manufacture, between the conditions of British industry on the one hand, and of its two great rivals, American and German industry, on the other. Unlike the former, the latter were protected. Under the protection of their tariffs they had acquired the leading position in the markets of the world. Why not do likewise?

4

Hitherto we have studied only one of the two great branches of national production. What report can we give of the other, which awaits our examination? If the position of industry was doubtful, about agriculture there could be no doubt. It was in an advanced state of decay.

The defenders of protection, attacking the new system introduced by Peel in 1846, had predicted that the fall in the price of agricultural produce would be the ruin of agriculture, and that it was the avowed object of the free traders to bring about that fall. The latter had denied that this was their object and had argued that an increase in the amount of agricultural produce imported from abroad would not necessarily lower prices. Its only effect would be, by facilitating exchange, to encourage the export of manufactured articles. For twenty years their contention had been, or had appeared to be, justified by the event. To be sure, the amount of imported corn increased, and the increase was far in excess of the growth of population. In the five years 1841–1845 sufficient corn was grown to feed 24,000,000 Englishmen, that is to say 89.55 per cent of the population. Thirty years later (1871–1875) the amount of wheat grown in Great Britain was only sufficient to feed 15,600,000, 48 per cent of the population. Yet prices did not fall. They remained at a level which fluctuated between 50/- and 55/- a quarter; only twice towards the beginning of the period did the price of wheat fall below 50/-, and on only five occasions between 1850 and 1860 did it exceed 55/-. Then the fall began. The British agriculturist was accustomed to date his misfortunes from the bad harvest of 1879. But a continuous fall of prices cannot reasonably be explained by bad harvests. Are we to regard this fall, which began about 1875, as merely one instance of the general fall of prices which took place about this time, not only in England but throughout Europe and America, and, explaining it by the increasing scarcity of gold, agree with those who prescribed as a remedy the adoption of bimetallism? The true cause was the enormous increase of cultivation in the United States, Canada and the Argentine, together with the development of railways and the lowering of freights. But in no other country in Western Europe had the fall been so rapid as in England, and the British farmers and landlords, unlike those of France and

[1] After remaining in the neighbourhood of 30/- a quarter during the period 1886-1890 with an exceptional rise to 39/- in 1891, the price of wheat again fell until it reached 22/10 in 1894; rising again to 34/- in 1898, but on the whole remaining below 30/-. Price in 1899: 25/8; 1900, 26/11; 1901, 26/9; 1902, 28/1; 1903, 26/9; In 1901 Continental prices were as follows: France, 35/3; Italy, 45/7; Prussia, 35/3, the Grand Duchy of Baden, 37/10; Bavaria, 38/4; Wurtemburg, 37/3. (*Wholesale prices of Cereals and Flour, in the Second Series of Memoranda, Statistical Tables and Charts, prepared in the Board of Trade with reference to various matters bearing on British and Foreign Trade and Industrial Conditions,* 1904, p. 214.)

Germany, had therefore good reasons to regard themselves as victims of the over-industrialization of the country, at the very time when the manufacturers were beginning to complain.

It was calculated that in the last twenty-five years rents had fallen by half.[1] And since, for several years past, the landlords had been obliged to pay dearer for all manufactured articles, how could they help believing that ruin stared their class in the face? It is true that no marked tendency had shown itself to break up large estates. The death duties which Sir William Harcourt had forced through the Lords in 1894 had not been in operation for a sufficient length of time to produce their revolutionary effects. An income tax which had reached a shilling in the pound, though it caused widespread apprehension, was not crushing. To enter society it was still necessary to buy an estate. In consequence every estate which came on the market found a purchaser. But a new spirit was coming over the landed gentry. As we have already seen, their income was now derived from directorships in large companies and shares of every description, and the outlook of a shareholder is not that of a gentleman farmer. At the opening of the twentieth century, the aged Earl of Leicester, son of the celebrated Coke of Holkham, who from one year's end to the other lived on his model estate supervising its cultivation, seemed the last survivor of an heroic past. Landlords no longer lived in the country to make their money, they visited the country to spend it. How many estates in the Eastern Counties were let, or even sold, at a high figure, not for cultivation, but for sport? On how many were crops raised only for breeding partridges? And how much time could a landlord spend on his estates after a lengthy residence in town, a visit to Paris, Rome, Monte Carlo or Switzerland, followed by a voyage to Egypt or even India?

[1] H. Rider Haggard, *Rural England, being an account of Agricultural and Social Researches carried out in the Years 1901 and 1902*, passim. *The Tariff Commission*, vol. iii. *Report of the Agricultural Committee*, 1902 passim. See also, on the condition of British agriculture at the close of the 19th Century: *First Report of H.M.'s Commissioners appointed to inquire into the subject of Agricultural Depression*, 1894. *Second Report*, 1896. *Final Report*, 1897. The statement in the text that rents had fallen by a half is obviously based on an average; there are cases in which the fall fell short of or exceeded that figure. And the further question arises whether the situation of the landlords was so bad in the North, as it was in the Midlands or the Southern Counties. Rider Haggard's extremely pessimistic conclusions are based on investigations which were not carried further North than Yorkshire. Cf. F. A. Channing's conclusions, *The Truth About Agricultural Depression. An Economic Study of the Evidence of the Royal Commission*, 1897, p. 37. On the other hand the inquiry conducted by the Tariff Commission discloses in the neighbourhood of Glasgow (f. 677) and in the county of Montrose (f. 832) falls of rent almost as great.

The mobility characteristic of modern civilization was taking the landlords from the land.

Had the factors which weakened the position of the land-owners strengthened the farmers'? The fall of rents was not sufficient to compensate for the other difficulties with which they were obliged to contend. Among the most serious of these was the labour crisis, if we can apply the word to a condition which during the last quarter of the century was rapidly becoming permanent. The emigration of labour to the towns was de-populating the country districts. The young girls were leaving. The young men were following them. Only the weaklings and the unenterprising remained behind. No doubt, when trade was depressed, the unemployed came back to the country to find work. But what work were they capable of doing? At best, that of an unskilled labourer. Who could tend and work the horses, look after the cows and milk them? Where could shepherds be found? There remained the old men, attached to their master and their village. When they died, the farmers complained, farming must cease altogether for lack of labour. Even as it was the labourers' behaviour was intolerable; they gave notice at the least remark, and left off work at three o'clock on Saturdays. On Sundays, the farmer with the help of his wife and children was obliged to do, in addition to his usual work, the work which his hands should have performed.

The farmers were furious. To keep their labourers they had yielded all their demands. Had not the wages of the agricultural labourer been raised by a third within the last twenty years, been doubled in the last half century? It was a poor return for the sacrifice, if the labourer whose wages had been increased by 30 per cent furnished an amount of labour 30 per cent less than before. No wonder the farmers looked back, as upon a lost Eden, to the days when they could obtain labour at eight shillings a week, five shillings for an Irishman.[1] But on the other hand, it is obvious that a wage, originally so small, might be raised very considerably, and still be insufficient to satisfy the labourer's needs. According to the farmer his wages were now one pound a week. This was, practically speaking, the wage of an unskilled labourer in the towns. Then why not migrate to the town where, though no doubt there was a risk of destitution, there was also an opportunity

[1] Rider Haggard, *Rural England*, vol. i, p. 404.

to earn high wages, even the possibility of attaining in the end the comfortable circumstances enjoyed by the lower middle class? Moreover, the progress of civilization was rapidly multiplying the occupations open to an agricultural labourer which offered him an assured livelihood. He might become a policeman or a railway servant, or obtain employment in an omnibus or tramway service. Moreover, when the landowners and farmers estimated his wages at one pound a week, they included in their calculation, only too often, a number of perquisites it was customary for a labourer to receive—bacon, potatoes, and beer or cider at seasons of exceptional work. It was only in Scotland and in the northern counties of England that his cash wage reached and occasionally exceeded twenty shillings, everywhere else it was distinctly lower, sometimes even less than fifteen shillings.[1] And since the calculation of the remainder was purely arbitrary, the agricultural labourer could not without indignation compare his wages with those earned by any description of urban labour, with the possible exception of the sweated industries. Besides, the situation cannot be adequately represented by statistics alone. The intelligence of the rural labourer had been aroused. It had been awakened by the propaganda of the first Socialist agitators, however evanescent the unions they had founded in the country had proved. And it had been awakened, even more thoroughly, by the influence of the school, which, moreover, by keeping children from work in the fields until the age of twelve, had contributed to estrange them from it. The agricultural labourers accordingly fled from the country because they could not endure the dismal monotony of the winter and had discovered a way of escape. Like the nobility, they were being swept off the land by the movement of modern civilization.[2]

[1] For the wages of the agricultural labourers see the following official documents: *Royal Commission on Labour, The Agricultural Labourer, Review of the Inquiry carried out in England and Wales, Scotland and Ireland,* in 1892 and 1893, and of the reports of the Assistant Commissioners by William C. Little (Senior Assistant Commissioner), 1894: *Earnings o, Agricultural Labourers (Board of Trade Labour Department) Report* by Mr. Wilson Fox *on the Wage and Earnings of Agricultural Labourers in the United Kingdom, with Statistical Tables and Charts,* 1900. *Memoranda, Statistical Tables, and Charts prepared in the Board of Trade with reference to various matters on British and Foreign Trade and Industrial conditions,* 1903, pp. 210 sqq. Charles Booth, *Family Budgets: Being the Income and expenses of twenty-eight British households,* 1891–4, pp. 896, 48 sqq. See also Rider Haggard's *Rural England* and the *Report* of the Agricultural Committee of the Tariff Commission already mentioned.

[2] The number of agricultural labourers and farm servants, 983,919 at the census of 1881, was 866,543 in 1891 and 689,292 in 1901. On the other hand, the latter decade witnessed an increase in the number of shepherds and farm bailiffs, which more than compensated

The impossibility of obtaining labour, combined with the low price of agricultural produce, spelt the farmers' doom. In the eighteenth century they had replaced, throughout rural England, the yeomen, those peasant proprietors who had been in the seventeenth their country's pride. Now, it seemed, it was their turn to perish. In the towns subordinate posts of every kind were occupied by a host of unsuccessful farmers who had given up farming just in time to escape utter ruin. Those who had managed to keep their heads above water were advising their sons not to stay on the land, and the latter did not need their fathers' warning to perceive that their prospects would be much better in a lawyer's office or bank. The farmers, a class once so progressive, now clinging unintelligently to a traditional routine, did nothing to combat the difficulties of their situation. They took no steps to overcome their instinctive individualism and follow the example set by the Continental peasants, who everywhere were forming co-operative banks and co-operative societies for joint purchase and sale. Every year the arable farms between two and three hundred acres in size were becoming fewer. This was not due to a concentration of property in a few hands, the absorption of small farms in a single large ranch, in which the use of agricultural machinery after the American fashion made it possible to reduce the number of labourers employed. On the contrary, the area of land under cultivation in the United Kingdom had fallen from 8,244,372 acres in 1871 to 5,866,052 acres in 1901[1]—that is to say, over a quarter of the arable land had gone out of cultivation in thirty years. Only in two ways could the land still be made to yield satisfactory returns. Large farms entirely under grass and devoted to stock raising were still profitable.[2] But even the British grazier was beginning to suffer severely from the competition of the frozen meat imported from Australia and New Zealand. And in the neighbourhood of the large towns market gardeners and dairymen found a ready sale for their vegetables and dairy produce.[3] But for several years butter imported from Denmark, Holland and Canada had come on the British market. And the

for the decline of the previous decade. The increase was perhaps due to the increase of pasture at the expense of arable land. (*Board of Agriculture and Fisheries. Report on the Decline of the Agricultural Population of Great Britain, 1881–1906*, 1906, p. 7.)

[1] E. Prothero, *English Farming, Past and Present*, 1912, p. 378.

[2] Between 1871 and 1901 the acreage of pasture rose from 11,367,298 to 15,399,025 acres (idem, ibid.).

[3] F. A. Channing, *The Truth about the Agricultural Depression*, pp. 38 sqq.

foreign butter, though it was not cheaper than the home produce, found a readier sale because its quality was better. Here, as elsewhere, England had lost the technical superiority she had once possessed.

5

For these very serious evils what remedy could be found? The farmers complained that railway transit was too dear, and asked for legislation to compel the companies to carry their produce cheaper. Some of them even wanted the railways nationalized. They also complained that the rates had been raised to an intolerable figure. In some districts they had been doubled since the county councils had been set up in 1888. The Unionists were hardly in office when they attempted to remedy the latter grievance of their supporters in the country. An Act passed in 1896 had reduced by half the rates payable on agricultural land; the relief amounted to an annual gift to the farmers of £1,500,000.[1] But what was it worth, if the rates continued to rise? When they were spent on improving the roads, the increase might be tolerable, but the farmers were indignant when their money was taken to provide the neighbouring town with drainage. Nor were they any better pleased when the new Education Act saddled them with the maintenance of all the voluntary schools, and obliged them to support an additional corps of those detested school teachers whose activities, they were convinced, contributed more than any other factor to the depopulation of the country districts.

Certain Radical politicians attempted to turn the farmers' discontent against the landlords. According to these advisers the cause of the evils from which they suffered was to be sought in the rents, which, in spite of very large reductions, were still excessive,[2] or at any rate, since by the terms of the lease they remained the same for a considerable number of years, were too

---

[1] 59 & 60 Vict., Cap. 16: An Act to amend the Law with respect to the Rating of Occupiers of Agricultural Land in England and for other purposes connected with it (*Agricultural Rates Act*, 1896).

[2] F. A. Channing, speech at Finedon, in 1897: 'The farmers tried to do their duty by the land and the labourers. But the estate and farm accounts showed that landlords did not base rents on twice the farmer's profit, but, in some cases, had taken up to fifty-five times the return the farmers obtained. My analysis, at the Conference, showed that for the years given in the accounts, the average return to the owner was twenty shillings per acre; the average profit to the tenant in the years of depression did not exceed sixpence per acre.' (F. A. Channing, *Midland Politics*, pp. 200-1.)

slow in adjusting themselves to the fall of prices and the rise of wages. If this were the case, should the principles of Henry George's agrarian Socialism, which had made so much stir twenty years before, be adopted, and a campaign inaugurated for the expropriation of the landowners? Or, at least, should a statute be passed extending to Great Britain the legal regulation of rents which had already been enacted for Ireland? Some attempts had been made to legislate on these lines,[1] but they amounted to very little and the farmers do not appear to have demanded any further steps in this direction. Propaganda of this kind made no appeal to them. As always, or almost always, during the past century, they felt that their interests and their landlords' were identical.

A different policy could be followed. The exodus of the country population to the towns might be arrested by a return to the system of peasant proprietorship. This proposal, also, had been originally put forward by a group of Radical politicians, whose recognized leader was Chamberlain's friend, Jesse Collings, and it was now in considerable favour with the Unionist party, of which Collings, like his friend, had become a member. But a statute on these lines passed in 1892[2] had remained a dead letter, and at the beginning of the twentieth century only a handful of Englishmen was even aware of its existence. When all is said and done, landlords and farmers knew only one legislative remedy to check the simultaneous fall of profits and rents. It was a return—avowed or disguised—to the protection of earlier days.

The victory of free trade about 1850 had been won in spite of the agriculturalists' opposition. Throughout the second half of the century the Tory party, under their influence, had maintained an attitude of suppressed hostility to the triumphant free trade. The Tories were too afraid of the manufacturers and urban proletariat to give the farmers much encouragement to demand openly duties on articles of food. For they could not hope for a Parliamentary majority without the support of these two classes. But they secured the passing of a statute designed on the pretext of combating certain contagious diseases to protect the British

[1] 46 & 47 Vict., Cap. 61: An Act for amending the law relating to Agricultural Holdings in England (*Agricultural Holdings [England] Act*, 1883), Cap. 62. *In Scotland* (*Agricultural Holdings [Scotland] Act*, 1883), 58 & 59 Vict., Cap. 27: An Act to extend and amend the provisions of the Agricultural Holdings (England) Act, 1883, so far as they relate to Market Gardens (*Market Gardeners' Compensation Act*, 1895).

[2] 55 & 56 Vict., Cap. 31: An Act to Facilitate the Acquisition of Small Agricultural Holdings (*Small Holdings Act*, 1892).

farmer against the importation of foreign cattle.[1] They proposed a system of bounties on agricultural produce which, without placing any direct restrictions on imports from abroad, would make it easier for the British producer to compete with them. And they further suggested that, by way of a feeler—a first timid experiment—the nominal duty on corn of a shilling a quarter, which had been retained in 1846 and abolished only in 1869 on grounds of principle, might be restored.[2] We shall shortly see how in 1902 the advocates of Agricultural Protection secured from the Unionist Cabinet a concession which went a certain way to gratify their desires.

6

Evidently the time had passed when England felt herself sufficiently strong enough to open her markets without restriction to all comers and defy the competition of the entire world. The question had now arisen whether, if she wished to keep her position in the world market, she would not be well advised to force her foreign rivals by a retaliatory tariff to lower their duties. And there was even a school which maintained that the situation of certain industries, not to mention agriculture, had now become so critical, that the home market must be protected by a tariff against the dumping of foreign goods. In fact, however, the demand for protection had another aspect. The policy was neither cosmopolitan in its inspiration, as free trade had been in the middle of the nineteenth century, nor strictly national, like the old protection. It was imperial. Britain renouncing her former rôle as the world's universal provider would compensate herself for the loss by drawing tighter the economic bonds which linked the different parts of the empire, the mother country, the self-governing and the Crown colonies, the empire of India, and thus forming a market so large that it would be a world in itself and exclusively her own. Its adoption would involve a general re-

[1] 59 & 60 Vict., Cap. 15: An Act to amend the Diseases of Animals Act, 1894 (*Diseases of Animals Act*, 1896); reinforcing 57 & 58 Vict., Cap. 57. An Act to Consolidate the Contagious Diseases (Animals) Acts, 1878 and 1893 (*Diseases of Animals Act*, 1894).

[2] Lord Coventry to H. Rider Haggard: 'I think the Chancellor of the Exchequer might have re-imposed a shilling duty upon wheat without hurting anyone. Until we in England are placed on even terms with the foreigner, agriculture will never flourish again.' (Rider Haggard, *Rural England*, vol. i, p. 365.) Rider Haggard had advocated this step in the *Daily Express* in 1901 (ibid., vol. ii, p. 531).

adaptation to new conditions—no easy task—and private interests might well suffer. But we have already had occasion to depict the character of British imperialism, in many respects more sentimental than economic, and more patriotic than utilitarian. 'It is the business', declared Chamberlain in his great Birmingham speech, 'of British statesmen to do everything they can, *even at some present sacrifice*, to keep the trade of the Colonies with Great Britain; to increase that trade, to promote it, *even if in doing so we lessen somewhat the trade with our foreign competitors.*' The aim of the tariff reformers was to constitute by means of a common tariff system an enormous mercantile community of fifty million, the combined populations of the mother country and the self-governing colonies, or of four hundred million, if all the dependencies of the Empire were included. In comparison with a community so vast, the fifty million Germans, or the hundred million Americans or Russians would weigh light. This was the grandiose scheme Chamberlain's imagination entertained, and which he invited the British nation to carry into effect under his leadership.

It was by no means a novelty. Thirty years before, Disraeli, to whom the historian must constantly refer who would understand the forces at work to revive the Conservative party at the end of the nineteenth century, had made it one of the cardinal features of his programme. Without contesting the right of the British colonies, South Africa, and Australasia to the autonomy they prized so highly, he regretted that, when it was conceded, the grant had not been made part of a comprehensive policy of 'imperial consolidation'. He would have liked an 'imperial tariff', a 'military code' accurately prescribing the conditions of colonial defence and the terms on which, if necessary, a colony would be entitled to obtain military aid from the other colonies, and, finally, the establishment in the mother country of a representative council of some kind to maintain regular and uninterrupted communication between the colonies and the home Government. What had been done to realize this ideal? And was there any suggestion of further steps? The federation of Canada in 1867 had been followed by the federation of Australia in 1900 and there was reason to hope that, as a result of the British victory in South Africa, a federation of the English and Dutch communities might be at last achieved. But it was very questionable

whether, as some had originally hoped, these local federations
could be made the foundation of a political federation of the
entire empire. The transformation of the House of Lords into an
Imperial Chamber, representation of the colonies in the House of
Commons, utilization of the Privy Council as an Imperial
authority—all these suggestions had been examined only to be
rejected.[1] On the other hand, a series of 'Colonial Conferences'
had been held in London at which the Prime Ministers of the
self-governing colonies or their representatives discussed with the
British Government on an equal footing questions which concerned the Empire as a whole. And at the first of these conferences,
which met on the occasion of the Queen's Jubilee in 1887, the
two other questions were discussed which Disraeli had raised in
his speech of 1872, the question of a 'tariff' and the question of a
'military code'.

From that time it became customary to speak not of an imperial
tariff, but of a Zollverein, not of a military code, but of a Kriegsverein. In the speech with which he opened the conference, Lord
Salisbury explained why the time was not ripe for imperial
federation, and hinted that in his opinion it would never arrive.
But before the foundation of the German Empire, the German
states had been united by two bonds, both of which were feasible
in an empire constituted like the British. One was a tariff union
which could be effected as soon as England was willing to renounce a fiscal policy based on the principle of unqualified free
trade. The other was a military union which could be brought
into being immediately. The use of the terms Zollverein and
Kriegsverein, and the invocation of these historical analogies is
eloquent of the extent to which British politicians were obsessed
at this period by the desire to imitate in every sphere what we have
termed the German model.[2]

We must be sure we understand the nature of the two problems.
The Colonies counted on the British Navy to ensure their safety.
The mother country, which, when the Colonial Conference met
in 1887, had just realized that for many years the Navy had been
unduly neglected and had begun a series of budgets providing

[1] For these various suggestions and the difficulties which prevented their adoption, see
Lord Rosebery's speech at Leeds, November 15, 1888.
[2] The term Kriegsverein was as a matter of fact coined by Lord Salisbury as a parallel
to Zollverein; it was not used in Germany. (C. J. Fuchs, *Die Handelspolitik Englands und
seiner Kolonien in den letzen Jahrzenhten* 1893, p. 373. English translation, p. 337.)

for a heavy naval expenditure, asked the colonies whether it was not fair that they should accept their share of the burden. That was the problem of a Kriegsverein. The self-governing colonies had secured the right to establish a customs tariff, and to levy duties, not only on foreign but on British goods. They originally took this step, not for the sake of protection, but solely to obtain revenue. In a new country, where the population is very scattered, customs duties are easier to collect than direct taxes. But very soon they had conceived and carried out the ambitious project of employing their tariffs to foster their new-born industries, and had concluded commercial arrangements with other colonies. The Australian Colonies, for example, had entered into mutual agreements of this kind.[1] On occasion, they had even concluded such agreements with foreign powers—for example, Cape Colony with the Orange Free State and the Transvaal, and Canada with the United States. England could not benefit by any of these commercial treaties. Her system of free trade made it impossible for her to offer any preference to colonial goods. The question was therefore widely asked whether she should not free herself from the bondage of the traditional doctrine, and under the cover of a tariff common to the entire Empire establish a system of mutual preference which would lead eventually to unrestricted free trade between the mother country and her colonies. This was the problem of the Zollverein. One of the three representatives of the Cape Colony in 1887, Jan Hendrick Hofmeyr, asked the conference to deal with both questions at the same time and discuss the feasibility of promoting closer union between the various parts of the British Empire by means of an imperial customs tariff, the revenue derived from such tariff to be devoted to the common defence of the Empire. He estimated at £352,000,000 the total value of the goods imported into the mother country and into the colonies in 1885. He suggested a duty of 2 per cent on these imports. It would bring in a revenue of £7,000,000. which would pay for a very considerable part of the British fleet.[2]

[1] This had been originally prohibited by a statute passed in 1850 (13 & 14 Vict., Cap 59 f. 27) and an Act of Parliament was required to make it legal. It was passed in 1873 (36 & 37 Vict., Cap. 22). See the interesting debate on the Bill in the House of Lords, May 15, 1873 (Parliamentary Debates, 3rd Ser., vol. ccxv, pp. 1908 sqq.). The surviving restrictions imposed on the Australian Governments by the statute of 1873 were repealed in 1895 by 58 Vict., Cap. 3.

[2] Proceedings of the Colonial Conference, 1887, vol. i, p. 465.

The Australian Colonies made a contribution, though a very small one, to imperial defence. But in the matter of the tariff, which alone concerns us at present, the mother country would do nothing to make a solution possible, and the Colonial Conference held at Ottawa in 1894 was content with expressing the wish that 'until the mother country can see her way to enter into a customs arrangement with her Colonies, the Colonies should take steps to conclude such agreements between themselves'.[1] Nevertheless, the problem continued to engage the attention of the Imperialists, and a German economist, writing in 1893, expressed the opinion that the situation demanded a statesman with the necessary intelligence, courage, and practical ability to undertake the task of changing the economic policy of England and effecting the commercial union of the Empire.[2] In 1895 he appeared. He was the new Colonial Secretary, Chamberlain.

If this declaration of May, 1903, caused considerable consternation, it was among those who had forgotten his two first years in office. Before he adopted in 1898 the programme of a great panteutonic alliance and the extension of the Empire by forcible annexation, commercial union between the mother country and her dependencies overseas had been the key-note of his policy. On November 28, 1895, within a few months of taking office, he addressed a despatch to the Colonial Governors calling their attention to the paramount importance of ensuring that British producers and manufacturers should have as large a share as possible of British colonial trade, and asking them to furnish him with a detailed statement, compiled according to a plan drawn up in the Colonial Office, of the loss which in each colony British goods suffered from the competition of foreign imports.[3] The despatch was followed by a public explanation of his pro-

[1] Foster's motion (Report . . . on the Colonial Conference at Ottawa, with the proceedings of the Conference . . . 1894, p. 33). Notice the sentimental character of the appeals made by the various colonies to the mother country to induce her to conclude a tariff union. 'All that they were asking of England,' declared Playford of South Australia (p. 189), was 'to treat her own children a little bit better than she treats foreigners.' Cf. the speech by the Canadian Prime Minister, Foster: 'I just simply want to point out this, that we do not ask Great Britain to make a revolution. . . . Even the slightest action would give new life to the production of grain in the colonies, *and more than that, make a thrill go through any part of the Colonial Empire, that Great Britain, at least, has recognized that her Colonies were to be treated a little better than other countries*' (p. 203).

[2] C. J. Fuchs, *Die Handelspolitik Englands*, p. 312. The author concludes: 'But this must be done very soon, or it will be too late.'

[3] *Despatch from the Secretary for the Colonies to the Governors of Colonies on the question of Trade with the United Kingdom*, November 28, 1895.

gramme in two speeches delivered, the first before the Canada Club on March 25, 1896, the second at the Congress of the Imperial Chambers of Commerce on June 9. Like Lord Salisbury in 1887, he held up to his audience the example of Germany. 'The creation of the German Empire . . . commenced with the union of two of the states which now form that great Empire in a commercial Zollverein. They attracted the other states gradually and were joined by them for commercial purposes. A council, a *Reichsrat*, was formed to deal with those commercial questions. Gradually in these discussions national objects and political interests were introduced and so from starting, as it did, on a purely commercial point and for commercial interests, it developed until it became a bond of unity and the basis of the German Empire.' Chamberlain excluded as Utopian the supposition that the Colonies might agree to adopt unrestricted free trade. And he rejected as unacceptable to the British electorate the suggestion that Britain should impose a light duty on all imports, including foodstuffs and raw materials, the colonies raising by the same amount their tariff on imports not of British origin. But he accepted a Canadian proposal, that a British Zollverein should be set up which should establish free trade between all the members of the Empire, on condition, however, and the proviso was essential to the scheme, that Great Britain agreed to impose light duties on certain foreign imports which competed with staple industries of the colonies, on cereals, meat, wool and sugar. 'I say,' he concluded, 'that such a proposal might commend itself even to an orthodox free trader. It would be the greatest advance that free trade has ever made, since it was first advocated by Mr. Cobden, to extend its doctrines permanently to more than 300,000,000 of the human race.'

In the debate which followed his address to the Chambers of Commerce, it became evident that on these matters the different colonies entertained widely divergent views and any public discussion of the question would undoubtedly be premature. When therefore another Colonial Conference met in London, on the occasion of the Diamond Jubilee of 1897, Chamberlain admitted the difficulty of obtaining the unanimous support of the colonies for a Zollverein on the German plan, and informed the Conference that the Government did not intent to put forward any definite proposals, but merely desired to ascertain the views of the Colonial Governments.[1] But although the ambitious proposals he had apparently entertained the previous year were not brought forward at this Conference, certain questions relating to the trade between the mother country and her colonies pressed for solution. So urgent were they that the Government under pressure from the colonies and supported by a Conservative House of Commons made up its mind to break on two points with the tradition of free trade.

7

As compared with the other British Colonies, in Australasia and South Africa, Canada occupied a unique position. Politically it was subject to the British Crown, and the political bond was reinforced by a profound Canadian patriotism, which refused to entertain the idea of incorporation into the great neighbouring republic of the United States. Nevertheless, incorporation seemed to be dictated by economic arguments not easy to refute. Why should not the five million Canadians, of whom two-thirds were English-speaking, unite in one political body with the 100 million citizens of the United States? Why maintain an artificial frontier, 3,000 miles long, when very often mere chance had determined whether a particular immigrant from England should settle as labourer or cultivator to the north or south of the line, and the population was constantly shifting to and fro across the boundary between the two states? As a result of these special conditions the economic policy of Canada was subject to frequent fluctuations.

Long ago, in 1843, a British Act of Parliament had reduced the duty on Canadian wheat and flour to so low a figure that for practical purposes it ceased to exist.[2] But the step had been taken at a time when England protected its corn against foreign competition. When, in 1846, the corn laws were replaced by a system of unqualified free trade, Canada was automatically deprived of the preference granted three years before. Moreover, she now began, for revenue purposes, to set up a tariff on her frontiers and, abandoning the hope of receiving a preference from England,

[1] Proceedings of a Conference between the Secretary of State for the Colonies and the Premiers of the Self-Governing Colonies at the Colonial Office, London, June and July, 1897, p. 10.
[2] 6 & 7 Vict., Cap. 29: An Act for reducing the Duty on Wheat and Wheat Flour, the Produce of the Province of Canada, imported thence into the United Kingdom.

committed henceforward to free trade, turned towards the United States. In 1854 the Canadian Government, or, rather, the British Government on its behalf, concluded with the States a commercial treaty which remained in force until 1866. It was then broken, not by Canada, but by the States.

Meanwhile, a party had arisen in Canada which avowedly favoured protection as a principle, and this party, the Nationalist party, was returned to power at the general election of 1878. But when the triumphant majority introduced a protectionist tariff in 1879, the question again arose of according a preference to a particular nation. Negotiations for a new commercial treaty were begun with the Government of the United States. They were broken off in 1891 when the McKinley tariff marked the triumph in the States of a policy of the most stringent protection. In Canada an entire party—the Liberals—continued to advocate a commercial arrangement with the United States, amounting eventually to absolute free trade. But in 1897 the McKinley tariff was completed by the Dingley tariff. In future Canadian statesmen could look only to Great Britain. Unfortunately they were faced in this quarter by difficulties of another kind. In the first place England was not in a position to grant Canada any preferential treatment in return for the preference which Canada might grant her, and secondly she had made it impossible to conclude a treaty of commercial reciprocity with one of her dependencies. Canada was faced with a difficulty of international law, if she proposed to grant a preference to British goods, even without asking for any preference in return. A commercial treaty which England had concluded with Belgium in 1862 provided that 'Articles, the produce or manufacture of Belgium, shall not be subject in the British Colonies to other or higher duties than those which are or may be imposed upon similar articles of British origin.' And a similar clause was contained in the commercial treaty concluded in 1865 with the German Zollverein. In virtue of these provisions any preference granted by Canada to Great Britain must be immediately extended to Belgium and Germany. In 1892 the Canadian Parliament demanded the abrogation of the Anglo-Belgian and Anglo-German agreements.[1] Two years later the matter occupied a prominent

---

[1] For the text of the two clauses see *Ottawa Conference, 1894. Despatches from the Secretary of State for the Colonies, on Questions of Trade and Commercial Treaties*, 1895, p. 10.

place in the discussions of the Ottawa Conference.[1] Finally on
April 23, 1897, the Canadian Parliament adopted a 'reciprocal
tariff' which reduced the duties, by an eighth until June 30,
1898, and by a quarter after that date, on goods imported from
any country whose tariff admitted Canadian produce, on the
same terms as those conceded to that country by the reciprocal
tariff. In this way the Government of Ottawa believed they had
evaded the legal difficulty arising out of the treaties of 1862 and
1865 and, without explicit mention of Great Britain, had granted
a preference to the goods of the mother country and one or two
colonies which had adopted free trade.[2] But on May 9, the Belgian
and German Governments declared the Canadian Bill a breach
of the treaties. The colonial representatives, once more meeting
in London, demanded their abrogation and on July 28 the British
Government acceded to their wishes. The treaties, now formally
denounced, expired a year later on July 31, 1898. This was the
first victory of no slight importance which the Imperialists had
won since the Unionists took office three years before. It was
estimated that British trade with Germany and Belgium was
equal in amount to the entire trade between Britain and her
Colonies.[3] Nevertheless, the Government preferred to run the
risk that this valuable trade might be hampered by a retaliatory
tariff, rather than reject the advances of the Canadian Govern-

In the charter of the great company which he founded to develop Rhodesia, Rhodes had
wished to insert a clause providing that duties on British goods should not exceed the
duties imposed in Cape Colony. The Liberals, who were in office at the time, insisted on
an alteration in the wording of the clause, the specification 'British goods' being replaced
by the general term 'imported goods'. (Gilbert Murray, Hammond, and Hirst, *Liberalism
and the Empire*, p. 70.)

[1] Colonial Conference, 1894. *Report* by the Right Hon. the Earl of Jersey, G.C.M.G.,
*on the Colonial Conference at Ottawa, with the proceedings of the Conference and certain Corre-
spondence*, 1894, pp. 24, 27, 29, 82, 150 sqq.

[2] See the reply of the Canadian Premier, Sir Wilfrid Laurier, in May, 1897, to a request
for an explanation by the Colonial Office. It was contented that the Belgian and German
treaties did not apply to Canada, since by 1859 the old province of Canada had been taken
out of the category of the colonies referred to in these treaties by A. T. Galt's declaration
of tariff independence; that in any case while 'Canada had undoubtedly been actuated
by the fact that the mother country was the only nation in a position to enjoy the advantage to be reaped from the minimum tariff, yet it was also true that the offer was made to
the whole world. No favour was extended to any special country and, if Belgium and
Germany could not share, the fault lay with them, since at any moment they could
qualify simply by complying with the conditions; if, however, a different view of the
effect of the treaty bonds was taken by the British authorities, it would be necessary to
ask that "the treaties be denounced in so far as Canada is concerned." ' (O. D. Skelton,
Life and Letters of Sir Wilfrid Laurier, vol. ii, pp. 56-7.)

[3] The Marquis of Ripon to the Governor-General of Canada, the Governors of the
Australasian Colonies (except Western Australia) and the Governor of the Cape, June
28, 1895 (*Ottawa Conference*, 1894, *Despatches*, 1895, p. 12).

ment. The primary motive of the decision was not immediate economic advantage. It was, by tightening the bonds which linked Canada with the mother country, to prevent the Canadian Government from again approaching the United States.

To the south of the States the position of the West Indian Colonies closely resembled that of Canada. Like Canada, these Colonies were politically members of the British Empire; and as in the former cases it seemed strange that they had escaped economic absorption by the United States. But the economic situation of the West Indian Colonies was far more critical than Canada's. For Canada was a large country rich in natural resources of every kind, which entertained from many points of view a reasonable expectation of becoming in the future, by developing her mines and water power, a great industrial nation, and by bringing into cultivation the prairies of the Far West, a great agricultural nation as well. The West Indian Colonies were islands of very small size whose populations of a few hundred thousand depended for their prosperity almost entirely on the sugar plantations. But the cultivation and manufacture of cane sugar in the West Indies were seriously threatened by the measures which protected the sugar industry on the continent of Europe. Not only did the Continental nations protect their markets by a high tariff against the importation of foreign sugar, but France had introduced in 1880 a system, soon imitated by her rivals, of giving export bounties. In consequence of these bounties European beet sugar was sold on the British market below cost price, and the West Indian planters saw themselves in danger of losing in the near future the entire market of the mother country. To satisfy the Colonists the Government suggested a system of mutual free trade, or at least of preference, between the West Indies and Canada. When the plan failed to mature, they sanctioned the conclusion of a commercial treaty between the West Indies and the United States, by which West Indian sugar was admitted into the States free of duty, and in return the West Indian Colonies lowered their tariff on American imports. But the Anglo-Belgian and Anglo-German treaties barred the way and the proposal was dropped. In 1887 the representatives of the West Indies wearied the first Colonial Conference with their importunities.[1]

By the end of the century the situation had become worse. All

[1] *Proceedings of the Colonial Conference*, 1887, vol. i, pp. 386 sqq., 475 sqq.

the great Continental Powers had increased their sugar bounties. The occupation of Cuba and Porto Rico by the United States had further alarmed the sugar-growing colonies. American capital, they feared, would introduce in these two islands, which till now had remained under Spanish rule, the most modern methods of sugar planting and refining; the American Government would grant a preference to their sugar, and thus the ruin of the British colonies would be complete. The island of Jamaica was practically declared bankrupt by the British Government, which employed dictatorial methods to place the finances of the colony on a sound basis, increasing the number of nominated members of the Legislative Council and taking over the railways. It also subsidized the planters and sanctioned the conclusion of a commercial treaty between Jamaica and the United States, the Belgian and German treaties, denounced in 1897, no longer standing in the way.[1] But to save the planters from ruin the Government went further and devised another expedient which was a glaring breach of the principles of free trade.

When France inaugurated the system of export bounties, Mr. Gladstone's ministry had contemplated shortly afterwards calling an international conference to secure the abandonment of the system by common agreement of all the nations. But a free-trade Government had no means of putting pressure on protectionist states, and the plan fell through. Twenty years later conditions were more favourable. The Continental system of fostering exports by bounties, dumping officially organized by the State, had been carried to such lengths that it was in danger of perishing from its own excess. In 1896 and 1897 the Governments of France and Germany had doubled their bounties. Had not the time arrived for these two Governments and the other Continental Powers to consider whether a system, financially ruinous, had not been stultified by its universal adoption? When the United States imposed a duty on European sugar equal in amount to the bounty it received, British India followed the example, and the English Government no doubt judged the moment opportune for reviving the project of a conference to familiarize the public

---

[1] Chamberlain appears at one time to have contemplated granting the planters a bounty of 4d. a gallon on rum imported into the United Kingdom to compensate for the duty of 4d. But the local authorities advised him that the United States would regard the step as a bounty to the sugar industry and he abandoned the idea (*Daily Chronicle*, October 26, 1901).

with the idea of a return to protection. The nations which produced beet sugar were approached by the British Government. As a result of the negotiations the Convention of Brussels was concluded on March 5, 1902. The Convention abolished bounties, and the contracting parties—Germany, Austria, Belgium, France, Holland, and Great Britain—undertook to prohibit the importation of sugar in receipt of a bounty, or, at least, to subject it to a duty equal to or higher than the bounty. To ensure that the agreement would be observed a permanent commission was appointed which would sit at Brussels.[1]

By taking this step England accepted the principle of reprisals. It is true the policy was not adopted for the sake of the British consumer, whose interest lay in taking full advantage of the ruinous competition among the Continental nations, as each strove to sell its sugar cheaper than its rivals. Nor did the Convention protect the British producer. England did not manufacture beet sugar, and those branches of British industry which used sugar as a raw material—for instance, the manufacture of jam and marmalade—had an interest in the continuation of the bounty system. The step had been taken solely in the interest of the sugar colonies, against the immediate interest of the British consumer, and even of the British producer. The problem, which was political, not economic, was to prevent the entrance of the West Indian Colonies—as of Canada a short while before—into a Zollverein not British but Yankee, and moreover, as the stepping-stone to a more complete union.

8

But when in the spring of 1903 Chamberlain demanded tariff reform, he appealed to considerations of another order, of a strictly financial nature. It was, he informed the House of Commons, impossible to spend more money on social reform and in particular to organize a system of workmen's pensions without recourse to the new sources of revenue which a protective tariff on foreign imports would provide. In urging this plea he was only repeating the favourite argument of Conservative

---

[1] What, we wonder, could Richard Jebb have meant when in a work otherwise excellent (*Studies in Colonial Nationalism*, 1905, p. 309) he denounced this convention as a 'marvellous monument of Cobdenite fanaticism'?

financiers who for many years past had been insisting that 'the basis' on which the British system of taxation rested was too narrow and 'must be broadened'. To appreciate their argument we must understand the unique character of British finance.

We are always being told that of all the nations in the world the British are the least attached to principles held as dogmas. The statement, if true at all, requires immediate qualification. In the sphere of finance the British nation has, ever since the middle of the nineteenth century, been attached more strictly than any other to a dogma, the dogma of free trade, which the country, or Parliament on its behalf, has rigorously applied in its annual Budgets. On no account must any duty be imposed on foreign imports to protect home production. All such duties are condemned by the principle of free trade, and for two reasons—in the first place, because they shackle and deflect the natural movement of trade and thus retard the accumulation of national wealth, and in the second place, of their very nature they must throw the Budget into confusion, it being impossible to pursue with consistency at one and the same time two distinct objects of taxation, to provide the necessary revenue, and to foster particular branches of production. It is no doubt true that Great Britain had not totally abolished customs duties. After sixty years of free trade the annual receipts from customs had reached the round sum of £20,000,000. But the duties were levied on tea, coffee and tobacco, and did not protect a single British producer. Moreover, since 'colonial preference' was excluded by the doctrine of free trade, they did not favour the Colonies at the expense of foreign nations. There were indeed duties on alcoholic beverages imported from abroad, but their sole object was to balance the heavy taxes on spirits manufactured in Great Britain. The remainder of the necessary revenue was obtained by direct taxation—Stamp Duties, Land Tax, House Duty, Death Duties, and Income Tax.[1]

The economists who had formulated the principles of this financial policy were moreover obsessed with the desire to economize. They were hostile to war, because it ruined nations

---

[1] For the history of British taxation during the nineteenth century see Sydney Buxton, *Finance and Politics; an Historical Study, 1783 to 1885*, 2 vols, 1888; also for the period when free trade was accepted without question, Sir Stafford H. Northcote, *Twenty Years of Financial Policy. A Summary of the Chief Financial Measures passed between 1842 and 1863 with a table of Budgets*, 1862; and finally for the period with which we are immediately concerned, Bernard Mallet, *British Budgets 1887-88 to 1912-13*, 1913.

while reducing their productive capacity and hostile to State Socialism, because it also ruined the State which adopted it, while sapping the initiative of the individual and thus reducing his capacity as a producer. But the position entirely changed when as a consequence of the Reform Bills of 1867 and 1884 the electorate was considerably extended. The new electors demanded costly measures of social reform. Between 1870 and 1895 the expenditure tabulated in the budget under the heading of the Civil Services was doubled, rising from about £10,000,000 to about £20,000,000, and in particular the expenditure on education increased sevenfold during that period. Before the introduction of compulsory education in 1870 it had barely amounted to £1,500,000, and when the Unionists took office in 1895 it had reached the figure of £10,256,000. And during the same period the change in the international situation had compelled the Government to ask, and Parliament to vote, the sums necessary to maintain a stronger army and navy. The army estimates, which during the latter years of Gladstone's ministry had been kept at a figure of about £15,000,000, had exceeded £19,000,000 during the three last years of Lord Beaconsfield's administration, when the foreign situation had been exceptionally disturbed. After a temporary reduction they had again risen in 1895 almost to the level of 1879. But it was on the naval estimates that the increase was the most striking. Between 1870 and 1880 during the administrations of Gladstone and Lord Beaconsfield the expenditure on the Navy had remained almost stationary at a figure of about £10,000,000. There had followed a series of ambitious programmes of naval construction which had pledged the naval estimates for many years in advance. There was Lord Northbrook's programme in 1884; the naval estimates exceeded £12,000,000 in 1885, £13,000,000 in 1886. There was Lord Spencer's in 1894: the estimates exceeded £17,000,000. In 1895 they approached the figure of £20,000,000, and for the first time exceeded the army estimates. Within fifteen years they had almost doubled.

The total expenditure of the nation, which about 1870 had been £70,000,000, exceeded £80,000,000 in 1878, £90,000,000 in 1891 and £100,000,000 in 1895. What sources of revenue could be tapped to provide for this continuous rise in expenditure? Though universal suffrage had not yet been adopted, the British franchise, since the reform of 1867, and still more since the reform of 1884, had become extremely democratic. Only a small minority of the voters paid direct taxes.[1] Now when it had become impossible to count on the normal increase of receipts to defray the increased expenditure, so long as the Chancellor of the Exchequer refrained from touching the indirect taxes, and was content to ask Parliament to increase the direct taxes paid only by the wealthy, he satisfied the majority of the electorate which did not even notice that the taxation had been raised. The income tax, rendered democratic by a graduated scale of reductions for small incomes, rose from the twopence in the pound to which it had fallen in 1874 to eightpence, which it reached for the first time in 1885 and to which it returned in 1894, never again to be reduced below that level. The system of graduated death duties introduced by Sir William Harcourt in 1894 inflicted a very severe blow on landed proprietors: its effects were, of course, hardly perceptible when the Conservatives took office the following year. A memorandum issued by the Treasury in 1896 showed that in the financial year 1871-2 the direct taxes stood to the indirect in the proportion of 27 to 73, in 1881-1882 of 40 to 60, in 1891-1892 of 44 to 56 and in 1895 of 48 to 52.[2]

The day was at hand when the proportion would be equal, 50 to 50. Liberal financiers were delighted. Sir William Harcourt, who had been Chancellor of the Exchequer in the last Liberal Cabinet, demanded that this equal proportion should be adopted as the fundamental principle on which all future Budgets should be based.[3] And the Liberals could, indeed, argue that the principles of taxation originally laid down by Peel and Gladstone were scrupulously respected, since the system of taxation continued to

[1] On the other hand, the rates directly affected a very large section of the electorate, and while the expenditure of the Central Government increased, the expenses of local government had increased in a very high proportion. The receipts of the local authorities had risen from £42,736,000 in 1874 to £75,938,000 in 1894. The Central Government, however, to relieve the burden of which the ratepayers complained, had assumed a constantly increasing share of the local expenditure. In 1874-5 £19,199,000 was received from the ratepayers, the State providing a subsidy of £1,681,000. Twenty years later in 1894-5 the rates yielded £33,855,000, and the State subsidy amounted to £8,997,000. (See further Etienne Martin, Les impôts directs en Angleterre. Taxes locales et impériales, 1905, p. 125.)
[2] H. of C., April 16, 1896: Sir Michael Hicks-Beach's Speech (Parliamentary Debates, 4th Ser., vol. xxxix, p. 1074); also Memorandum explaining the Basis of some of the Figures which Mr. Chancellor of the Exchequer used . . . relating principally to the Progress of Population, Revenue, and Expenditure, April 30, 1896.
[3] H. of C., May 21, 1897 (Parl. Deb., 4th Ser., vol. xlix, p. 1006).

rest on a small number of indirect taxes of a non-protectionist character supported by the direct taxation. But this does not alter the fact that the resemblance between the Budgets of the closing century and those of the great age of British free trade was merely on the surface. Peel's and Gladstone's Budgets had been governed by the principle that taxation must be kept at the lowest possible figure, so as not to interfere with the natural distribution of wealth. The income tax had been introduced in 1842 by Peel only as a temporary measure to compensate for the decrease of revenue consequent on the abolition of a large number of duties. He hoped that the day would come when the few taxes on articles of consumption which he had retained would suffice, by the increased revenue they brought in, to defray the entire national expenditure and render an income tax unnecessary. And indeed, there was a moment about the year 1870 when the commercial prosperity of Great Britain attained its culmination, and his hope seemed on the verge of realization. The income tax fell from sixpence in the £ in 1871, to fourpence in 1872, threepence in 1873 and twopence in 1874. Was it destined to disappear altogether? With 1876 a movement in the opposite direction began. Not only did the income tax rise continuously after that date, but in 1894 Sir William Harcourt's great Budget inaugurated the era of a financial policy, no longer Liberal, but deliberately Radical, whose aim was not simply to defray the cost of governing the country, but to modify in the process the distribution of wealth.

9

Many a middle-class Englishman who twenty-five years earlier had supported the system of taxation adopted by Peel and Gladstone must have been alarmed at the fashion in which it was now being applied. Already Goschen, a Liberal who had become a Unionist and Chancellor of the Exchequer in Lord Salisbury's first Unionist Cabinet, had asked himself whether it might not be 'better service to the State to increase the number of sources of Revenue, than to attempt to find simplicity. I say,' he continued, 'you have pushed simplicity of taxation up to a point beyond which you cannot carry it without danger.'[1] When the Unionists returned to office in 1895, the same complaints were raised by

[1] H. of C., April 15, 1889 (*Parliamentary Debates*, 3rd Ser., vol. cccxxv, p. 514).

members of their party. The system of taxation, as it was actually applied, placed no check upon expenditure by a House of Commons elected on a democratic basis, and destroyed all sense of financial responsibility in the vast mass of those who were politically responsible for the government of the country. The basis of taxation must be enlarged by increasing the number of taxes and in particular the indirect taxes. The group of Fair Traders preached in the interest of the Treasury a return to Protection. James Lowther demanded the institution of a duty of five shillings a bushel on imported corn, and further duties on articles of foreign manufacture.[1]

Sir Michael Hicks-Beach, the new Chancellor of the Exchequer, admitted that these criticisms were well founded, and that the narrow basis on which British taxation rested might become dangerous in the event of war on a large scale or a serious industrial depression. But he continued to profess allegiance to free trade, and it is not easy to see what steps a free trader could take to enlarge the basis of taxation. During the early session when he was responsible for the Budget, no important war or industrial depression occurred. On the contrary the country witnessed a sudden recovery of trade. Every year there was a large surplus. And finally, the revenue derived from the death duties introduced in 1894 by Sir William Harcourt and scarcely modified since, was so considerable that his task was made still easier. Expenditure was on the increase, especially on the army and navy, but it could be met without increasing the existing taxes or introducing new ones, and it was even found possible to reduce certain taxes. In 1896 and 1897 a few modifications were made in the death duties, and in 1898 the duty on tobacco was slightly reduced. In 1896 some relief was granted to agriculture, and in 1898 the income tax on smaller middle class incomes was reduced. It was not until 1899 that the financial position again gave cause for anxiety. The natural increase of receipts was less than in previous years, and at the same time the Government asked for an additional expenditure of £4,000,000 on the Army and Navy. It was the morrow of Fashoda and imperialism was proving a costly policy. Once more there was a deficit. It was supplied by recourse to three different methods of raising revenue.

[1] H. of C., May 20, 1897 (*Parliamentary Debates*, 4th Ser., vol. xlix, pp. 954 sqq., especially pp. 961–2).

In the first place, the stamp duties were raised in certain cases. This increase of direct taxation was in conformity with the methods which had become traditional during the previous half century. The same could not be said of the second method adopted, the reduction, during peace, of the amount devoted to the sinking fund. Scrupulous observance of the rules hitherto in force might, the Chancellor of the Exchequer argued, be carried too far, at a time when Consols were above 110, and the nation was therefore paying £110 or more to pay off a debt of £100 and when the Savings Bank was investing more and more money in Government securities and thus diminishing the amount available for the private investor, so that the slightest interference with the market on the part of the Treasury would suffice to cause a rise and make the purchase of stock more difficult. In the third place, the duties of wine were raised. Should this last measure be regarded as a first step towards the protection demanded by a group of Unionists? The Chancellor of the Exchequer pointed out that, when the duties on wine were reduced, it had been in the hope that the wine producing countries would in return proportionately reduce their tariff on articles of British manufacture. That expectation had been disappointed, and it was therefore only reasonable to revoke a fruitless concession. That is to say, Sir Michael Hicks-Beach spoke the language used by Lord Salisbury when he advocated a policy of retaliatory tariffs. Nevertheless, the duties on wine were no more protective that those on tobacco, tea, and coffee, and when Sir Howard Vincent attempted to give them a protective character by proposing that the wines of Australia and the Cape should be exempted from the new duties[1] the House of Commons rejected his amendment by 192 to 37 votes.[2]

The South African crisis supervened. Of the financial year 1899–1900, six months were months of war. It became necessary to ask Parliament for additional credits of £23,000,000. The prosperous condition of trade and the excellent yield of the existing taxes provided 5 of these 23 million. There remained a deficit of £18,000,000. To defray the expenditure of the financial year 1900–1901 the Government asked Parliament for £154,000,000. This was £37,000,000 in excess of the revenue

[1] H. of C., April 13, 1899 (*Parliamentary Debates*, 4th Ser., vol. lxix, pp. 1041 sqq.).
[2] H. of C., May 11, 1899 (ibid., 4th Ser., vol. lxxi, pp. 369 sqq.).

from existing sources. To this was added £18,000,000 to cover the deficit of the previous year and £5,000,000 for any unforeseen expenditure which might be found necessary. The Government asked for an additional £60,000,000. Once more the question arose whether it should be obtained by borrowing or taxation. Sir Michael decided to employ both methods. No addition was to be made for the present to the sinking fund; Treasury bonds were to be renewed and a loan of £35,000,000 raised. In levying the new taxes no departure was made from the traditional principles of Peel and Gladstone. They were merely adapted to the needs of an age no longer economical or pacific. The income tax was raised at a stroke from eightpence to one shilling in the pound. The taxes on tea, beer, and spirits were raised, as also was the duty on tobacco, the concessions made to the taxpayers two years before being partly withdrawn. The only measure which in any way presented a protectionist character was an increase of sixpence in the pound in the duty on foreign cigars. The Government disclaimed all intention to innovate. The news from South Africa was good; it was expected that the war would be over in six months, and that normal conditions would be restored before it became necessary to draw up the Budget of 1901. Nevertheless, complaints were heard both in Parliament and in the Press that the Government had not made use of this favourable opportunity to enlarge the basis of taxation by a thoroughgoing reform of the entire system.

The dissatisfaction was more vocal, when it became evident in the following winter that the war would continue, indeed, threatened to prove unending, and the need of money became more pressing—until at last the Chancellor of the Exchequer, it would seem, found himself compelled to do something to satisfy his critics. The estimated receipts for the ensuing financial year were £132,255,000, the estimated expenditure £187,602,000—that is to say, a deficit was expected of £55,347,000. To cover this and provide for the possibility of an unforeseen increase of expenditure the sinking fund was tapped and a loan of £60,000,000 raised. On the other hand, there was a further increase of twopence in the income tax, which was thus raised to one shilling and twopence in the pound. The import duties on sugar, abolished in 1894, were restored, and if the Government denied that the new duties were of a protectionist character and refused to exempt

319

colonial sugar, the fact remained that they had the appearance of a reply to the Continental system of bounties. Moreover a duty of one shilling a ton was imposed on exported coal. No doubt this duty was not, technically speaking, protective. But its object was unquestionably to restrict the export of coal, which was assuming alarming proportions and fed the Continental rivals of the British factories.[1] When the Chancellor, defending the new tax, insisted that it would be paid by the foreign consumer, the group of protectionists loudly applauded; they were delighted to hear him expressing sentiments which were not those of free trade 'It is idle', John Morley declared, 'to deny that Sir James Lowther is much nearer to having a considerable following in the House and the country than he ever had before. If you are going to be militant imperialists free trade goes. That is my firm belief. And the beginning of the job is the Budget which the Chancellor of the Exchequer has introduced.'[2] No doubt the Chancellor was a free trader. But what was the meaning of the plaintive peroration with which he concluded his speech in defence of the budget, if not a feeble protest against the imperialism which made the abandonment of the old healthy finance inevitable? All the better, such was the tenor of his concluding words, if a broadening of the basis of taxation brought home to the public the cost of the policy to which at the election of 1900 it had given its enthusiastic support.[3] The Budget of 1902 seemed to justify Morley's forecast.

---

[1] It also supplied the navies of the Continental powers which in the event of war would be opposed to the British fleet. Goschen, however, first Lord of the Admiralty in 1900, went out of his way to reassure the public on this point: 'I think the House may be interested to know what the percentage of the export of coal to France and Russia is to the total output of the United Kingdom. It is 4 per cent. The coal which went to France and Russia combined in 1899 was 9,000,000 tons.' (H. of C., February 28, 1900: *Parliamentary Debates*, 4th Ser., vol. lxxix, p. 1155.) The *Economist*, however, of January 28, 1905, basing its calculation on the report of the Coal Commission, estimated that: 'Of the output of the special class of coal required for naval purposes one-sixteenth is retained for the Royal Navy, the remainder apparently being for the most past supplied to the navies of other countries.'

[2] H. of C., May 23, 1901 (*Parl. Deb.*, 4th Ser., vol. xciv, pp. 1088-9).

[3] H. of C., April 18, 1901: 'I will not rate the intelligence of my fellow-countrymen so low as to suppose that when they supported and cheered the expenditure' (the cost of the South African War), 'they did not know that they would have to pay the bill. When I remember that among those who supported it were the working classes—the majority of the working classes—and when I also remember that the working classes in many matters set to us all an example of unselfishness, I will not think so ill of them as to imagine that they supported this expenditure with the idea that it should all be put on other shoulders than their own. . . . I can conceive nothing more unfair than that the policy of this country and the increased expenditure it may cause, should be controlled by the voice of the whole of the people and that one class alone should be left to bear the increased burden.' (Ibid., vol. xci, pp. 651-2.)

Introduced at a moment of uncertainty, when everyone felt that peace was imminent, yet the possibility that the Vereeniging negotiations might break down and the war be prolonged could not be excluded, it made provision for a revenue of £147,785,000. The estimated expenditure was £174,609,000. This left a deficit of £26,824,000, and Sir Michael Hicks-Beach proposed to raise a further sum of £18,500,000 to provide for the contingencies of a very doubtful future—that is to say, over £45,000,000 had still to be found. He decided to raise it by a suspension of the sinking fund, a loan of £32,000,000, a further increase of the income tax (one shilling and threepence in the pound instead of one shilling and twopence), an increase of the stamp duty on cheques, and finally a new tax, which aroused a storm of controversy, on imported corn and flour. He refused, it is true, to exempt colonial corn and flour; nevertheless he spoke of the economic relations between the mother country and her colonies in ambiguous terms which the advocates of 'imperial preference' could interpret as favourable to their views.[1] Moreover, the new duty was very light (threepence per hundredweight for corn, fivepence for flour), was in fact only a revival of that nominal duty which Peel's Government had imposed when he abolished the duties on corn and which had not been removed until 1869. In spite of this, it was the object of violent attacks in the House of Commons. The Cobden Club and the Manchester Chamber of Commerce protested against the tax. Equally significant was the approval of Sir Howard Vincent and James Lowther, and the interpretation which Chamberlain appeared to put upon the duty in a speech delivered at Birmingham on May 16. Nor could it be denied that for more than a year the advocates of agricultural protection had been demanding a duty of this description and saw in it a concession of principle. In both camps everything had been done to give the Budget of 1902 the appearance of an initial victory won by the supporters of tariff reform.

[1] H. of C., June 9, 1902 (*Parliamentary Debates*, 4th Ser., vol cix, pp. 165 sqq.).

II CHAMBERLAIN AND HIS OPPONENTS

I

Under these circumstances Chamberlain might well believe in the summer of 1902 that the time was ripe for tariff reform, a return to the system of protection. The sugar convention had just been signed and there was no doubt that it would be ratified by the Unionist majority in the House of Commons. The British Government had found no reason to regret the step taken in 1897, when, to please the Canadians, it had challenged the German Government and denounced the commercial treaty of 1865. For Germany had not dared to take up the challenge and postponed the breach from year to year. And finally, by incorporating in the Budget of 1902 a duty on imported corn, the Government had made it possible to introduce at some future date into the fiscal system of the country, without too violent a shock to public opinion, the principle of 'imperial preference'. The Boer War was over. The policy of a great panteutonic alliance was obviously defunct. Chamberlain had tacitly repudiated it on the occasion of his public quarrel with von Bülow six months earlier. What new programme should the Government adopt which would make an appeal to the masses? Clearly the programme of 'imperial preference', an all-British Zollverein, which had attracted Chamberlain in the years before 1898. The Colonial Conference which was held in London on the occasion of the coronation and sat from June 30 to August 11, provided him with the opportunity he needed to exchange views with the representatives of what he called the 'great nations overseas'.

Unfortunately, very little can be gathered from the brief summary issued as the official report of the Conference.[1] The political relations to be established between the Colonies and the mother country were discussed, but no results were reached. The Conference debated with rather more success the measures which should be adopted to secure the collaboration of the Colonies in the military and naval defence of the Empire. The question of commercial relations was also discussed. What happened was

[1] Colonial Conference, 1902. *Papers relating to a Conference between the Secretary of State for the Colonies and the Prime Ministers of Self-governing Colonies. June and August,* 1902. Cf. in the *Daily Telegraph,* August 12, 1902, a long article containing interesting disclosures of the proceedings at the Conference.

probably this: Chamberlain was defeated by the opposition of the Chancellor of the Exchequer. Sir Michael Hicks-Beach took up in opposition to the Colonial Secretary the position he had himself adopted five or six years before, would accept nothing less than a Zollverein in the strictest sense, based on unqualified free trade within the Empire. This conflicted with the protectionist policy of the self-governing Colonies. Chamberlain could only invite from their representatives offers and expressions of opinion favourable to the establishment of a system of inter-Colonial preference. New Zealand, Cape Colony, and Natal were disposed to follow the example of Canada and grant a preference to British goods, even without reciprocity. But all united in 'respecfully urging on His Majesty's Government the expediency of granting in the United Kingdom preferential treatment to the products and manufactures of the Colonies either by exemption from or reduction of duties now or hereafter imposed'. What were these duties '*now* imposed'? Manufactured goods imported into Great Britain were not subject to duty. The duties in question were those on tea, coffee, cocoa and sugar, also the new duty on corn; a memorandum specially drawn up by the Canadian Cabinet leaves no doubt on the point.

Two or three months later we find Chamberlain attempting in the private deliberations of the Cabinet to win his colleagues to his views. Why not exempt in future Colonial corn, especially Canadian, from the new corn duty? This surely would be the natural reply to the preference Canada had granted in 1897 to articles of British manufacture, and increased in 1900? In July, Sir Michael Hicks-Beach, pleading age and ill health, had followed Lord Salisbury into retirement. The new Chancellor of the Exchequer, David Ritchie, might possibly prove more amenable. If that was Chamberlain's hope, he was quickly undeceived. On November 19 Ritchie distributed among his colleagues at a Cabinet Council a note in which he set out the reasons for which he refused his assent to Chamberlain's proposal.[1] But the Duke of Devonshire slept, Balfour gave a very guarded approval to Ritchie's views, the other Ministers kept silence.[2] Chamberlain

[1] D. Ritchie, speech at Thornton Heath, November 18, 1903.
[2] E. T. Raymond, *Mr. Balfour*, 1920, p. 97. For the manner on which a few weeks later at Johannesburg Chamberlain explained his great scheme to Lord Milner, see an interesting article by Sir Percy Fitzpatrick, 'The Turning Point. Preference and the Empire. A Scrap of History' (*The Times*, November 28, 1924). Cf. *Times' History of the War in South Africa*, vol. vi, p. 87.

was thus encouraged to hope that the day would arrive when with his colleagues' support he would overcome Ritchie's opposition, and thought it wise to let the matter drop for the present. On the 24th, speaking in Parliament in a debate on the sugar question he again expounded the principles on which his imperialism was based, principles of a 'moral' rather than a 'material' nature. 'Are we prepared to say that the pecuniary question and that alone is to decide our policy? Are we to say that we are ready to repudiate the principles of common justice, if it be found that the adoption of these principles may involve us in more or less pecuniary loss?'[1] The following day he sailed for South Africa.

We have already spoken of his return on March 14 of the following year. Before the end of the month he was present at two Cabinet Councils. The Budget was discussed and his colleagues sided with Ritchie against him. The Budget introduced on April 23 was a free-trade Budget. It was also a peace Budget in which for the first time for several years a surplus was expected. The Chancellor of the Exchequer estimated the expenditure at £143,954,000. If the existing taxes were continued, they would produce, he estimated, £154,770,000. He proposed to take fourpence in the pound off the income tax, and abandon the corn duty of 1902, which would thus be proved to have been merely a measure of war finance, not the beginning of a return to protection. The speech which Chamberlain delivered at Birmingham on May 15 possesses its full significance only when it is read in the light of the incidents, secret and public, which had preceded. It was his declaration of war on the colleagues who for the past year had lost no opportunity of making him understand that he was not the Prime Minister.

2

To the Cabinet his declaration came as a thunderbolt. The very day on which he spoke at Birmingham, Balfour had received a protectionist delegation and informed its members that the time was not ripe to bring forward Colonial preference. Harassed by the criticisms of the Liberal opposition, embarrassed by the protests of prominent Unionists, themselves divided, one Minister

---

[1] *Parliamentary Debates*, 4th Ser., vol. cxv, p. 341. (H. of C.)

holding one opinion on the question, another an entirely different point of view, the Ministers were longing for the recess to begin and bring them some respite from their difficulties. Balfour had frankly admitted his inability to 'profess . . . to have concluded convictions upon a thing which he had not got concluded convictions upon'.[1] He had recourse to the usual expedient of a government which finds itself in a difficult position, and ordered the Board of Trade to hold an inquiry into the condition of foreign trade and British industry.

In the very middle of the recess, on September 14, public anxiety was increased by the announcement that the Ministers had all been summoned to London to attend a Cabinet Council. The Council lasted three hours, was adjourned until the next day, and on the 15th the discussion proceeded for a further hour and a half. On September 16 a short pamphlet was published over Balfour's signature. It was entitled *Economic Notes on Insular Free Trade* and its theme was the risks involved in the position of a free-trade country isolated in a protectionist world. On the 17th the resignations of three Ministers were announced. Two were free traders, Ritchie and Lord George Hamilton, the third, to the universal astonishment, was Chamberlain himself. What was the explanation of the mystery?

The matter was soon cleared up by official disclosures. On August 13, the last day of the session, Balfour had submitted to his colleagues a programme which amounted to the acceptance of Chamberlain's. But it had met with such powerful opposition that by common consent the question was left undecided. What correspondence subsequently passed between the Prime Minister and his Colonial Secretary? We know only the long letter Chamberlain wrote to Balfour on September 9, at a moment when the date of the next Cabinet Council had been already fixed. He proposed an arrangement by which each should undertake a particular role, Balfour at the head of the Cabinet, Chamberlain outside it. Balfour accepted it. Its nature was as follows.

Evidently the time was not yet ripe for submitting to the electorate a programme so far-reaching and so revolutionary as Chamberlain's. Such a step would court disaster and, in addition, produce a split in the Conservative party, even before the election. His experience during the past year had shown Chamberlain how

[1] H. of C., June 10, 1903 (*Parliamentary Debates*, 4th Ser., vol. cxxiii, p. 572).

many of his fellow Ministers still clung to free trade, a principle which in the previous fifty years had become one of the most sacred national traditions. And Balfour had even more reason to know how strong was the hold of free trade even upon the Tories. He knew the anger with which his aged uncle, Lord Salisbury, shortly before his death (he had died on August 22) had seen, at a time when three years of war had left the old country in greater need of rest than ever before, this fellow from Birmingham condemn it to a further period of agitation, and imperil the Unionist party itself, which, moreover, should he prove success-ful, would be transformed into a Conservative party of the American or Colonial type, a party of manufacturers and *nouveaux riches*.[1] He saw his cousin, Lord Hugh Cecil, a devout Anglican and an ardent Tory, defending the cause of free trade with a zeal almost worthy of Gladstone. For his own part, he was incapable of such rancour and such zeal. We may even admit that he was not by instinct sympathetic to the dogma of free trade with its implicit cosmopolitanism and enthusiasm for the welfare of mankind. But he was too well versed in political strategy not to perceive the danger to the party involved by the mere existence of these free-trade zealots. Under these circum-stances he must continue to play the part he had played so patiently for eight years, appease, compromise, conciliate. He would drop the policy of Colonial preference, which was dangerous from its very complexity and raised immediately the question of taxing foodstuffs. He would adopt the more restricted programme of 'reprisals'. He would claim for England the right to impose duties on the importation of certain articles of foreign manufacture, that armed with them he might be in a position to negotiate commercial treaties with foreign powers on favourable terms. This, after all, was the policy Lord Salisbury had advocated for years.

When the annual meeting of the Union of Conservative Associations met at Sheffield at the beginning of October, Balfour's cautious language averted an open breach with those Unionists who were still in favour of free trade and, above all, of the free importation of foodstuffs. But he was unable to prevent further

---

[1] For Lord Salisbury's attitude see the correspondence sent to *The Times* between Lord Salisbury, Chamberlain, Asquith, and Sir Michael Hicks-Beach. The writers contradict each other's statements. (*The Times*, March 27, 28, 29, 30, 31, 1905.) See also *Autobiography of Mrs. Asquith*, vol. ii, pp. 62–3.

secessions from his Cabinet. In all, five free traders resigned, the last being the Duke of Devonshire. The Cabinet, as remodelled by Balfour, was more strictly Tory than it had been hitherto; the appointment of Lyttelton as Colonial Secretary strengthened the small clique of the Prime Minister's personal friends. Nevertheless, by giving the post of Chancellor of the Exchequer to Joseph Chamberlain's son, Austen Chamberlain, the Premier showed his intention to maintain relations with the man who, outside the Cabinet, had assumed a role as easy and honourable as Balfour's was difficult and thankless. Chamberlain, free from all ties, and apparently pledging only himself, but sustained by the conviction that he had behind him the vast majority of the Unionist party, traversed the country as the missionary of fiscal imperialism. He was not Prime Minister, the old Tories would not allow it, but he was something more than a Minister.

His programme, as he announced it in an important speech delivered at Glasgow,[1] was simple. A duty of two shillings a quarter would be imposed on foreign corn (with the exception of maize), a duty of the same amount on flour, a duty of 5 per cent on meat and dairy produce (with the exception of bacon), and an average duty of 10 per cent on articles of foreign manufacture. Colonial produce would be exempted from all these duties. Moreover by the way of compensation for so many new duties on food stuffs, he proposed a reduction of three-quarters on the duty on tea, of a half on the duty on sugar, and corresponding reductions of the duties on coffee and cocoa. There was nothing original in this programme, which was borrowed almost verbally from the Fair Traders of 1880.[2] But the time had come when the Fair Traders could rally an entire party to their views, and their propaganda was conducted by the greatest leader of men in England. Under his auspices a Tariff Reform League was founded, the counterpart of that famous Anti-Corn-Law League which in the middle of the nineteenth century had done so much to bring about the triumph of free trade. In December, the League appointed a Tariff Commission to inquire into the condition of the various branches of British production, and it published the information obtained, in a series of scientific reports, all of which,

[1] October 6.
[2] The programme of the Fair Trade League will be found in T. H. Farrar's work (written from the free-trade standpoint), *Free Trade versus Fair Trade*, 1882.

of course, were in favour of a return to protection. When Charles Arthur Pearson, president of the League, who already owned the *Daily Express*, the *Saint James's Gazette* and several provincial newspapers, purchased the *Standard*, the entire Conservative Press was with Chamberlain. He obtained the support of several economists, representatives of the 'historic' school, who had revolted against the dogmatism of the orthodox political economy. Cunningham of Cambridge, Ashley of Birmingham, Hewins and Mackinder of London, and Charles Booth assisted Chamberlain's somewhat raw genius with their more subtle arguments.

Nevertheless, it was Chamberlain's genius that for the new party of tariff reform was the pledge of final victory. Though seventy years of age he threw himself into the struggle with the ardour of a young man, or perhaps with the fevered impatience of an old man who feels that his time is short. On October 6 he opened at Glasgow a campaign of speeches which took him in October to Greenock, Newcastle, Tynemouth, and Liverpool; in November to Cardiff and Newport; in December to Leeds. He had no difficulty in collecting in every place vast and enthusiastic audiences. But when on January 18, 1904, he concluded his campaign by a speech delivered at the Guildhall to an audience of city men, his courteous but chilly reception warned him of the obstacles which stood in the way of his propaganda. Their character must now be examined, and with particular care, because for many years to come they were destined to appear insurmountable.

3

When the Budget was discussed in 1902 a young Unionist, Winston Churchill by name, had united with the Liberals in opposing the reintroduction of the nominal duty on corn. He was the son of that Lord Randolph Churchill whose unconventional brand of Toryism had created such a sensation twenty years before. While still quite young—in 1902 he was only twenty-eight—he had attracted public attention by his exploits in the Sudanese and the South African War. He had entered the House of Commons in 1900, eager to take his share in the party struggle, and succeed where his father had finally failed. So little did he fear political isolation, that he took the first opportunity to criticize his leaders, denounced 'increases of expenditure out of all proportion to the national enrichment', and predicted that to broaden the basis of taxation must inevitably lead to the imposition of heavy duties on bread, meat, and other necessary articles of consumption. He wondered 'what would happen, if the fair trade issue was openly raised by some responsible person of eminence and authority in the country. They would stand once more on all the old battlefields. . . . Party bitterness would be aroused, such as the present generation could furnish no parallel for, except in the brief period of 1885–6.'[1] And he asked himself what would be the effect of this formidable problem on the existing party divisions. The event soon approved the youthful politician's foresight. Even before Chamberlain championed the principle of a duty on foreign corn, the timid innovation made by the Budget of 1902 had excited widespread hostility. Already in May, before the conclusion of peace, the corn duty cost the Conservatives a seat.[2] It apparently played a more important part than the question of the rights of trade unions in bringing about Crooks' return in the following March. It was probably in consequence of the representations of the party agents that the Government abolished the duty in 1903, and Balfour was actuated by similar motives when he refused to introduce duties on foodstuffs into the Conservative programme. The Irish question had brought over to the Government an enormous number of electors in the urban areas. Were they prepared to throw away lightheartedly this host of supporters in an attempt to broaden the basis of taxation by imposing duties on articles of food? To be sure, Chamberlain and his allies pointed out that in countries which had adopted protection the cost of food did not rise in proportion to the protective duties imposed, and therefore that the duties did not fall entirely on the native consumer, but were partly paid by the foreign producer. Indeed, they went further, and argued that since the duty they wished to introduce was exceedingly light, scarcely more than the duty of 1902, it could raise the price of the loaf only by a trifling amount, might perhaps not raise it at all, not even by a halfpenny.[3] Possibly. But in

---

[1] H. of C., April 14, 1902 (*Parliamentary Debates*, 4th Ser., vol. cvi, p. 240).
[2] By-election at Bury, May 10, 1902.
[3] Chamberlain, Liverpool speech, October 28, 1903. W. J. Ashley, *The Tariff Problem*, 1903, pp. 168 sqq.

that case how would the British farmer be protected?[1] And if the contention were true, why did the tariff reformers promise the working man, as a compensation for the increase in the cost of bread, a reduction in the duties on sugar and tea, coffee and cocoa? The use of so lame an argument was itself a proof of the difficulty the exponents of Chamberlain's new programme experienced, when they were faced with the necessity of persuading the democratic electorate of a thoroughly industrialized nation, in which moreover bread formed a greater part of the workman's diet than in any other European country except France. The policy of 'tariff reform' was a return to that policy of dear bread against which Cobden's league had rallied public opinion shortly before the middle of the last century, and once more public opinion rose up against it. Its advocates could not even secure the unanimous support of the Unionist party; indeed, it would seem that the sole object of the tactics devised by Balfour, an unavowed return to protection by a different route, was to prevent sixty or seventy malcontents—known as the Free Fooders, determined opponents of every kind of duty on articles of food—from seceding from the party and thus forcing upon the Government a premature dissolution.

What exactly was the Prime Minister's policy? He disclaimed protection. His object was not like Chamberlain's, to erect a permanent tariff wall between the British Empire and the rest of the world, but simply to place in the hands of the Government a weapon with which to combat the protectionist policy of the foreign powers, and dumping in particular. He claimed for the Government the right to impose duties, if necessary very high or even prohibitive, on particular articles of foreign manufacture whenever they considered that the difficulties of British industry were due to the tariff policy of rival nations. The only way in which their competitors could be compelled to alter their policy was by turning against their own industries the methods of which they had themselves given the example. The moment this object had been attained, the normal condition of free trade would be restored. The Liberals protested against this policy on the ground that it unduly enlarged the authority of the executive at the

[1] W. J. Ashley, *The Tariff Problem*, p. 171: 'The common protectionist teaching that the foreigner pays the duty, stated in that broad and unqualified way, is an immense exaggeration; and it is of course inconsistent with the very purpose of protection.'

expense of the legislature.[1] We may, however, leave this question of constitutional law out of account. The question with which we are more immediately concerned is, whether the industrial situation of the country was sufficiently critical to justify at the bar of public opinion recourse to exceptional measures.

To understand how Chamberlain and his supporters had convinced themselves that this was the case we must know the state of trade at the close of the Boer War.[2] Between 1894 and 1899 the value of British exports had risen from £216,000,000 to £264,492,000. During the first year of the South African War the export trade had been still further stimulated by the needs of the Army, and in 1900 exports had reached the figure of £291,192,000. But in 1901 they had fallen, and the restoration of peace in 1902 had not been followed by the boom in trade which everyone had expected.

Consols, after reaching in 1899 a maximum of 111½, had fallen during the war and in July, 1901, were as low as 91. They had subsequently risen and when peace was concluded had reached 97⅞. But they had again fallen, and to a lower figure than they had ever reached during the war. On September 29, 1903, they were worth only 86⅞. Railway shares had fallen concurrently with the fall in Consols. Did this mean that investments bearing a fixed interest were at a discount, and that the decline in Consols and railway shares favoured the development on industrial concerns which were attracting the capital of the country? On the contrary, the new issues by industrial companies were lower

[1] H. of C., February 2, 1904: Sir Henry Campbell-Bannerman's speech; February 8, 1904: John Morley's speech (*Parliamentary Debates*, 4th Ser., vol. cxxix, pp. 132, 639).

[2] The student should consult the two blue books issued in 1903 and 1904 under the title, *British and Foreign Trade and Industry, Memoranda, Statistical Tables and Charts*, prepared in the Board of Trade with reference to various matters bearing on British and Foreign Trade and Industrial Conditions. The *Annual Register* has published every year since 1901 a supplementary chapter, entitled 'Finance and Trade', relating the economic history of the year. *The Economist*, a weekly review, publishes every year in its January and February numbers a series of articles in which the fluctuations of exchange, the increase or decrease of production in individual branches of industry during the preceding year are methodically studied. For contemporary estimates of the industrial situation see amongst other works, A. C. Pigou, *The Riddle of the Tariff*, 1903; Arthur L. Bowley, *England's Foreign Trade in the Nineteenth Century*, 1905 (representing the standpoint of free trade); W. J. Ashley, *The Tariff Problem*, 1903; Sir Vincent Caillard, *Imperial Fiscal Reform*, 1903 (Protectionist). Contemporary French works: Victor Bérard, *L'impérialisme britannique*, 1900 (a picture very graphic but exaggerated of the 'decline' of Great Britain), also Jacques Bardoux, *Essai d'une Psychologie de l'Angleterre contemporaine. Les Crises belliqueuses*, 1906, ch. ix, 'La Stagnation commerciale et la Guerre', pp. 482 sqq.

by a third than they had been in 1902.[1] In every branch of business the same complaint was heard. Imperialist politicians had promised that, if Lord Milner's progressive administration replaced Kruger's reactionary government in the Transvaal, the change would result in an enormous development of the mines. Not only would the existing mines be worked more profitably, but the discovery of new deposits would transform vast districts into a new Eldorado, and as a result Great Britain would find in the new Colony a market for her rails and locomotives, machinery of every description, and the clothing needed by a more numerous and wealthier population. The forecast was not fulfilled. On the contrary, a crisis prevailed on the Rand which did not provide the expected market for British goods. Nor was it to be found in the Far East, over which hung the cloud of the impending conflict between Japan and Russia. And, if in the American foundries an attempt was being made to limit the output, German dumping assumed larger proportions than ever before.[2] Moreover too many ships had been built during the boom which had ended in 1901, and the Clyde dockyards were in the throes of a crisis which threatened to affect every branch of engineering.[3] The cotton industry suffered severely from a rise in the cost of raw cotton, combined with the constant fluctuations to which prices were exposed. Never before had so little raw cotton been consumed by the industry; and, as in 1892 and 1893, in 1902 and 1903 the Lancashire mills were working at a loss.[4] Unemployment, which had steadily declined between 1894 and 1899, increased every year until 1904.[5]

[1] The fresh issues were only about £110,000,000 as compared with £154,000,000 in 1902, *Annual Register*, 1903 (p. 242).

[2] *The Economist*, January 9, 1904: 'Iron and Steel, 1903.'

[3] *Ann. Reg.*, 1903 (p. 245).

[4] *The Economist*, January 16, 1904: 'The Cotton Trade in 1903.'

[5] The 'index numbers of employment' (the figure for 1900 being taken as 100) are as follows: 1893 and 1894, 95.0; 1895, 96.7; 1896, 99.3; 1897, 99.2; 1898, 99.7; 1899, 100.5; 1900, 100.0; 1901, 99.0; 1902, 98.2; 1903, 97.5; 1904, 95.9 (*Abstract of Labour Statistics. Board of Trade (Labour Department) Eleventh Abstract of Labour Statistics of the United Kingdom*, 1905–6, 1907, p. 2). The percentage of unemployed trade unionists was 5 in 1904; it had been 2.9 in 1900. The same year, the percentage in the building trade was 7.7, in the ship-building trade 14, in the furnishing trade 8.7. There had, it is true, been years in the past when unemployment was greater. For the period before 1895 the 'index numbers of employment' show a minimum of 95 in 1894, 93.1 in 1886, and 91.9 in 1879. Nevertheless, the increase demands explanation. It cannot be accounted for by the sudden demobilization of an army of 200,000, for it began, not with the restoration of peace, but in 1900. Shall we have recourse to a more subtle hypothesis, one might almost say oversubtle, and explain it as entirely due to the growth of population. Only a little more than twenty years had passed since the birth-rate of the United Kingdom had at-

The widespread pessimism with which public opinion regarded the situation was increased at this juncture by the publication of their decennial census returns by the great powers. In the last thirty years the increase of the urban population alone in Germany and in the United States exceeded by 5,750,000 and 7,000,000 respectively the increase of the entire British population, and the increase of the American population during the same period was equal to the population of Great Britain.[1] Unless steps were taken to deal with the new situation, Britain might well appear doomed to be defeated in the near future by her rivals. It was natural to ask whether the recovery of trade which had marked the first five years of Unionist Government was anything but an accidental interruption of a period of stagnation, if not of positive decline, which had begun in 1875. Even the increase of exports in 1900 was called in question; three-fifths of it were explained as due to the increase in the price, not the quantity, of the coal exported. 'It is proverbially unsafe', Professor Ashley wrote in September, 'to prophesy; but it is more probable that the world (and England with it) is about to enter into another period of depression.'[2] 'I think I see,' Chamberlain declared in November, 'and I believe that every man of business sees, symptoms which, if not attended to in time, may lead to danger and disaster.'[3]

tained its maximum, and ever since, as a result of the improvement of the national hygiene, the death-rate had been steadily declining. This involved about the beginning of the twentieth century a sudden influx of labour which industry was unable to absorb (Sir William Beveridge, *Population and Unemployment*, paper read before the Liverpool Congress of the British Association 1923, p. 16). But if this disproportion between the supply and demand of labour had been the cause of the distress from which the working class suffered, it must on the other hand have favoured the capitalist by lowering the cost of labour. But the most characteristic feature of these two or three years of depression was the chorus of complaints raised by the employers. We are, therefore, compelled to admit that on the home market there was a decline in the demand for British goods. Surely the true explanation is the warlike policy of the Government and the sudden increase of taxation.

[1] British and Foreign Trade. Memorandum. Board of Trade: *Memorandum on the Comparative Statistics of Population, Industry and Commerce in the United Kingdom and some leading Foreign Countries*, 1902, pp. 5, 6: 'The conclusion, therefore, would seem to be that the conditions of the manufacturing and industrial predominance of the United Kingdom, and even of its manufactures, and industrial pre-eminence, are becoming different from what they were when the non-agricultural population of every other country in the world was smaller than in our own. Industry and manufactures abroad, particularly in the United States and Germany, have become much bigger things, relatively, than they were. It has long been foreseen that this condition of affairs was likely to come about sooner or later, but the change appears now to be already with us and the developments will need to be closely watched.'

[2] W. J. Ashley, *The Tariff Problem*, p. 56. We must remember that Ashley is pessimistic in regard to the future, not of England alone, but of the entire world, beginning with Germany and the United States. [3] Speech at Cardiff, November 20.

But it soon became clear that the protectionist's pessimism was unfounded. Even in 1902 and 1903, which were undoubtedly years of depression, it could not be denied that the diminished demand in the home market was accompanied by an increase in exports.[1] Their value no doubt had fallen from £291,192,000 to £280,022,000 in 1901. But it rose again to £283,424,000 in 1902 and £290,800,000 in 1903. And the increase was even more rapid when account is taken not only of the value but the quantity of goods exported. From this point of view it was in 1900 that the decline had occurred, and the revival had begun its uninterrupted course in 1901. Towards the end of 1904, and above all in 1905, it was obvious that manufacturers and merchants were no longer complaining, were indeed once more optimistic. With the solitary exception of coal, prices rose and the increase in the value of exports—£300,711,000 in 1904, £329,817,000 in 1905— proved that more goods were being sold abroad and at higher prices. Prosperity hitherto unparalleled prevailed in the cotton trade. Orders poured into the shipyards, and the good effects were felt in every branch of metal working and engineering. Shipbuilders on the Clyde were astonished to discover that a vessel delivered immediately cost less than a vessel whose delivery was promised several months ahead.[2] This was because every one counted on a rise of prices and believed that a period of extraordinary production was beginning, a period marked by a phenomenon of which the cause and even the importance were not as yet understood, a fall in the purchasing power of gold. It was a most unpropitious moment to launch a campaign in favour of protection. The opponents of free trade were calling for a tariff to raise prices on the British market, when prices were beginning to rise without any artificial aid. Without making any pretension to draw a complete picture of the state of British industry when the twentieth century opened, we may glance at a few of the chief branches of the national industry. A few concrete instances

[1] *The Economist*, January 14, 1905, after noticing the increase of exports for the year 1904, adds: 'The curious feature about it is, that this expansion in our overseas business has coincided with a period of more or less pronounced depression in some of our staple industries. The only inference is that our foreign trade, important as it is, constitutes by no means the preponderating influence in determining the state of our industries that it is frequently supposed to do. Though precise statistics to measure the volume of the home trade are lacking, such as are available clearly indicate that it is there that depression has prevailed.'
[2] 'The activity in shipbuilding and the aspect of shipping' (ibid., January 6, 1906).

will enable us to understand better how inopportune was the campaign to which Chamberlain was committed.

4

According to the census of 1901 1,500,000 workers of both sexes, English, Scotch, and Irish, were engaged in the textile industry. It was divided into several branches which differed in the conditions and degree of their prosperity.

We can afford to neglect the silk manufacture. Admittedly, it was rapidly decaying, and in 1901 employed only 39,000 workmen instead of the 131,000 employed half a century before. Its decline was attributed by the protectionists to the impotence of a free-trade country in face of competitors protected by a tariff. Another explanation was that the opening of the Suez Canal and the establishment of direct trade between the United States and the Far East had deprived London of its position as the great emporium for raw silk. But whatever its causes the decay of the industry made it impossible for the grievances of its few remaining employees to affect public opinion. What were 39,000 out of the entire nation? What influence could 14,000 male workers exercise on such a vast electorate?[1]

We can also neglect the linen manufacture. Its condition was a subject of bitter complaint. It was no doubt true that their protective tariffs enabled the great European nations to compete successfully on the home market with linen manufactured in the United Kingdom. The industry further suffered from the decline in the cultivation of flax in Great Britain and the growing use of cotton. If the canvas ordered by the War Office enabled Dundee to maintain its position as the metropolis of the industry, Belfast seemed to be definitely in a state of decline. There were 200,000 fewer spindles at work than in 1870, and since 1891 the number of workers had decreased by a fifth. Nevertheless, the export figures proved that the situation had not yet become altogether critical. Great Britain still kept her supremacy in the manufacture

[1] *Report of the Tariff Commission*, vol. ii, *The Textile Trades*. Part 6, *Evidence on the Silk Industry*. The report estimates the hands employed at 13,859 men and 25,176 women, a total of 39,035. W. Page (*Commerce and Industry*, p. 231), who bases his estimate on the *Annual Report of the Chief Inspector of Factories and Workshops* and the *Statistical Abstracts* for the United Kingdom, gives even lower figures: 8,966 men, 22,589 women, a total of 31,555.

of fine cloth and damask. The loss of the Cuban and Porto-Rican markets as a consequence of the Spanish-American War might not be more than temporary. The export to the United States was still very large, equal to half the total. And if the Italian and Spanish markets had been lost, the trade with Canada had made enormous strides.[1] In short, it could not be denied that, if home consumption had possibly declined and certain markets remained closed, the total export had increased. However, the number of hands employed, if larger than in the silk industry, was very small nevertheless. It did not amount to 109,000.[2]

The woollen manufacture demands closer study. It employed in the United Kingdom some 250,000 workers of both sexes. Here also considerable dissatisfaction prevailed, and the protectionists were able to point out that exports had decreased in value by almost a third since the date, thirty years earlier, when they had exceeded £30,000,000. Between 1898 and 1902 they had remained steady at about £22,000,000. But the free trader could reply that the fall had not been uninterrupted, that on two occasions, in 1889 and in 1895, they had reached the figure of £30,000,000, and since 1902 had once more shown a distinct upward tendency. Moreover, the important question was the relation between the fluctuation in the amount of goods exported and the fluctuation in prices. From this point of view it was significant that the export of woollen yarn had steadily increased in value since 1880, the maximum reached in 1871 had been regularly exceeded since 1885, and tended to reach a value a third higher than that of 1871. The value of cloth exported had fluctuated irregularly without showing any marked decline until 1902 when a steady rise set in. In fact, for some time past, every class of woollen goods had shown an increase with the exception of worsted and, if Bradford was declining, the decline did not necessarily affect Yorkshire as a whole. No doubt the protectionist could reply that the export figures were not a reliable index of the prosperity of an industry, and that on the home market the supply of wool and woollen cloth was unable to keep pace with the

---

[1] *Report of Tariff Commission*, vol. ii, *The Textile Trades*, Part 7, *Flax, Hemp and Jute*, 1905.
[2] *British and Foreign Trade and Industry* (Second Series), *Second Series of Memoranda. Statistical Tables and Charts prepared in the Board of Trade*, 1904, p. 456. The following figures are taken from the census returns: 1881, 143,400; 1891, 134,700; 1901, 108,700. For Ireland, the principal seat of the industry: 1881, 92,650; 1891, 93,150; 1901, 75,100.

demand. The number of factories had decreased, falling from 2,750 in 1885 to 2,379 in 1904. And the number of workers had also diminished by a sixth in ten years.[1] And, finally, whereas imports had doubled during the last thirty years of the century, exports had decreased by a third. But these contentions did not leave the free traders without a rejoinder. They were able to point out that, as compared with the decade 1883–1892, the decade 1893–1902 showed an increase of 25 per cent in the consumption of raw wool. How could this fact be reconciled with a fall in the demand for English produce? Nor had imports increased during the last ten years. If the number of factories was less, it was perhaps because the industry had been concentrated in a smaller number of larger factories. And the decline in the number of hands might well be a temporary consequence of the development of machinery. Moreover, the number of workers employed had slightly increased since 1901. And since there had been a simultaneous increase in exports, there was nothing to justify, even to the Yorkshire public, the sudden and revolutionary change of fiscal policy advocated by Chamberlain.

But of all the branches of the textile industry, the most important, the branch which for a century had represented the industrial supremacy of Great Britain, was the cotton industry. Lancashire had long been the typical example of modern capitalism, and, if it was from Lancashire that Marx had drawn arguments in favour of his revolutionary Communism, it was also in Lancashire that the economists of the free trade school had found their most enthusiastic disciples. The importance of the cotton manufacture at the beginning of the twentieth century can be gauged from the fact that it furnished employment to more than 600,000 inhabitants of the United Kingdom and that the exports of cotton yarn and cloth amounted to over a quarter of the total British exports, representing a value of 73 out of 280 million pounds.[2] No doubt, even in this field the protectionists found reasons for anxiety. Though the number of persons employed in the manufacture was so enormous, it had been declining during the past ten years, falling from 625,000 in 1891 to a bare 609,000 in 1901.[3] The value of yarn exported, after remaining stationary between 1880

[1] *British and Foreign Trade and Industry* (Second Series), 1904, p. 448: 1881, 284,500; 1891, 303,700; 1901, 252,400.
[2] W. J. Ashley, *The Tariff Problem*, p. 60.
[3] *British and Foreign Trade and Industry* (Second Series), 1904, p. 440.

and 1890, had been decreasing steadily and at a fairly rapid rate ever since, and if the value of the cloth exported was still increasing, the rate of increase was becoming slower and more irregular. Nor was this in the least surprising. Every nation in the world, protected by its tariff, was beginning in turn to manufacture cotton yarn and cloth, was attempting to supply its own needs independently of British competition, and exporting every year larger quantities of goods to Great Britain. A solitary branch of the cotton industry, the manufacture of sewing cotton, had been able, thanks to the energetic policy pursued by Messrs. Coates, to keep the monopoly of the world market, but the firm could only break through the tariff barriers which stood in the way of its trade by building factories abroad which, if they continued to increase British capital, took work from the British worker. Was it time to speak of an irretrievable decline? When in 1905 the Tariff Commission issued its report on the cotton industry, it admitted that the three or four previous years were of an 'exceptional' character, and that the crisis from which Lancashire had suffered was due, not to the protection adopted by foreign countries, but to the high prices of raw material, which were the result of a series of bad crops in America. Thus, even on the admission of the Protectionists, the statistics of the last few years, so alarming at first sight, could not be interpreted at their face value. In the opinion of the vast majority of witnesses the home market had not suffered to any appreciable extent from the unfair competition of foreigners, that is to say, from their dumping. It was the general conviction that, except during the periods of depression, more labour had been employed, and wages had risen. And, if many branches of the industry had suffered from the restrictions placed on the export trade, the loss had been made good by the increased prosperity of other branches.[1] As even Chamberlain's followers were obliged to admit, the suggestion of a tariff war with the protectionist nations was universally rejected, and the sudden boom which occurred in 1905 completed the discomfiture of the tariff reformers. The 600,000 employed in the cotton trade remained unshaken in their optimism and attachment to free trade.

[1] *Report of the Tariff Commission*, vol. ii, *The Textile Trades*. Part i, *The Cotton Industry*, 1905, 55, 63, 77, 108.

5

Trade statistics united under the same head the smelting of pig iron and steel and the manufacture of iron and steel goods. It is an unsatisfactory method of classification. For it confuses branches of industry whose interests are not only dissimilar, but divergent and even directly opposed. The 100,000 workers[1] employed in the production of iron and steel were voluble in their complaints. What foundation existed for their grievances? Undoubtedly Great Britain no longer occupied the same position in iron manufacture that she had held twenty years before. About 1880 the steel produced in Britain amounted to a third of the world production, in 1902 it represented a little less than a seventh. Nevertheless, the actual amount had risen from 1,020,000 tons in 1880 to 4,850,000 tons in 1902. But world production increased during the same period at a ratio almost three times as large, from 2,040,000 tons to 31,040,000.[2] No doubt, even if British production had not been positively diminished by the exhaustion of the raw material, no tariff could prevent foreign nations working the vast mass of ore hitherto unworked or unworkable before the discovery of the Bessemer process. The malcontents were not silenced. They alleged that England was directly threatened by a system which made possible the German-American dumping. But this dumping might very well prove a temporary phenomenon. The United States and Germany were suffering from a crisis due to over-production, and, in consequence, both countries were anxious to get rid of their surplus at a low price. When the crisis came to an end, dumping would cease. And further it was arguable that, if dumping was detrimental to the smelting industry by lowering the price of pig iron and steel, it assisted all those branches of manufacture for which pig iron and steel were not the finished article, but raw material. If it was to the interest of the 100,000 men employed in the smelting industry that the price of pig iron and steel should be high, it was to the interest of the 1,200,000 who were employed in Britain in all those branches of manufacture and construction which made use of iron and steel[3] that it should be low. If prices fell, what could the 100,000

[1] England: 85,907; Scotland: 23,263. Total: 109,170. (*British and Foreign Trade and Industry* (Second Series), 1904, p. 475.)
[2] *Report of the Tariff Commission*, vol. i, *The Iron and Steel Trades*, 34–36.
[3] *British and Foreign Trade and Industry* (Second Series), 1904, pp. 476–480.

sufferers do against more than a 1,000,000 who profited by the fall?

To be sure, here also the protectionists found cause for anxiety. They drew the attention of the public to the unquestionable fact that in this branch of industry, as in so many others, Britain had lost her monopoly of production, and the new nations were progressing at a rate which it would be difficult for an old nation to emulate. They complained of the excessive number of pipes, rails, agricultural machines, electric apparatus, and motors of foreign manufacture sold in the British market. Nevertheless, they were compelled to admit that statistics proved Great Britain had contrived to overtake her rivals by selling other goods. The number of machines, railway carriages, and bicycles exported was rapidly increasing. In the ship-building industry she maintained her supremacy. It was estimated that between 1899 and 1903 she had built every year for the foreign market vessels representing a tonnage of 740,000.[1] There was not a nation which did not employ vessels of British construction for the transport of its goods. The number of persons employed in handling iron from the treatment of the ore to the manufacture of tools and machinery of every description, and the construction of ships, rose from 830,000 at the census of 1881 to 971,000 at the census of 1891 and 1,198,000 at the census of 1901.

And, finally, there was a branch of British industry about which there could be no question whether it was declining, stationary, or progressing at a more or less rapid rate. The amazing increase in the amount of coal mined, and the even more amazing growth in the amount exported, was perhaps the most striking feature of the industrial situation in Great Britain at the close of the nineteenth century. About 1860, 60,000,000 tons of coal were mined in Britain; ten years later the amount had doubled, and about 1905 had almost doubled again. The coal mines employed 495,000 men in 1881, 668,000 in 1891, 807,000 in 1901, and

[1] A. L. Bowley, *England's Foreign Trade in the Nineteenth Century*, 1903, p. 120. Cf., p. 119: 'If we exported nothing, the services of our ships (our "invisible exports") would pay for imports to the amount of £90,000,000, and rank us at once as a second-rate trading power with only France, Germany, the United States, Holland, Belgium and Austria ahead.' It must be added that the men-of-war ordered by the Admiralty were a certain source of profit to the shipbuilding trade, automatically protected against foreign competition. The abandonment of the Belleville boilers, of French manufacture, which the Admiralty made use of until 1901 was, whatever the alleged reasons for the change, a measure of disguised protection.

842,000 in 1903.[1] This output of coal was more than sufficient
for the needs of the national manufactures. Coal had become one
of the most important British exports. About 1860 Great Britain
exported some 7,000,000 tons of coal, about 1875 twice the
amount, about 1889 twice as much again—nearly 50,000,000
tons in 1905. In the middle of the nineteenth century coal
represented about a hundredth part of the value of British exports,
at the beginning of the twentieth about a tenth.[2] Not only had
this growth of the export trade been a direct source of revenue
for British capital and labour. It had contributed enormously to
the development of British commerce. Vessels left the ports with
a cargo of coal to return with huge freights of the foodstuffs and
raw material required for the national consumption and industry.

There were therefore nearly 1,000,000 men for whom the
problem of foreign competition was literally non-existent, and
for whom protection meant nothing except a rise in the cost of
living. If economists who belonged to the protectionist school,
or, to speak more accurately, envisaged the economic question
not from a cosmopolitan, but from a purely national standpoint,
found cause for anxiety in the coal industry, they advocated a
species of inverted protection. The extent and quality of her coal
measures had been perhaps the most important factor in the
industrial prosperity of nineteenth-century Britain. But the
supply of coal seemed doomed to inevitable exhaustion within
the next two or three generations. At any rate, the cost of working
the mines would be too great to be profitable. In 1901 a Royal
Commission was appointed to investigate the question.[3] What
steps could be taken meanwhile to delay as long as possible the
extinction of one of the sources of the nation's wealth? British
industry should be given special rights over the coal extracted,
and the export of coal reduced. For that purpose duties should be
imposed not on the import of foreign, but on the export of
British, coal. As we have already seen, the British Government
had taken a step in this direction in the Budget of 1901. But the
measure, which benefited only indirectly and to a very slight
extent the branches of manufacture which used coal, was directly

[1] *British and Foreign Trade and Industry* (Second Series), 1904, p. 470.
[2] Total value of exports in 1900: £352,000,000, value of exported coal: £38,620,000.
This is more than a tenth, but the export of coal decreased during the succeeding years.
[3] *Royal Commission on Coal Supplies. First Report of*, August 5, 1903. *Second Report*,
February 24, 1904. *Final Report*, January 7, 1905.

detrimental to the interests of the powerful group which owned or worked the coal fields.

It was all very well to refute Chamberlain's followers by proving that contrary to the belief suggested by their pessimism exports were increasing. They replied by insisting on the fact that the commercial balance sheet was persistently unfavourable to Great Britain; the value of imports exceeded that of exports and, it would appear, in an increasing proportion.[1] To this the free traders had two replies. In the first place, they argued that account must be taken of all the money earned and brought into the country by the personnel of the merchant service. And that personnel was not limited to the service of the British importer and exporter; half the commerce of the globe was carried on British vessels. Here was an entire world, shipbuilders, shipbrokers, and over 200,000 seamen, whose interests were intimately bound up with free trade. And in the second place, they claimed that the capital lent by Britain to foreign countries and on which those countries paid interests to the British investor should also be taken into account. We have already spoken of this practice in which the protectionists found cause for alarm; British capital, instead of promoting the industries of the nation, went abroad to feed foreign industries. But whether or not it was otherwise injurious to the country's economic interests, the practice had called into being in and around the City a vast society of bankers, bank clerks, stockbrokers, and stockjobbers of every description for whom that German-American peril which alarmed certain manufacturers had no existence. Add to these the 1,000,000 employed in shipbuilding, 1,250,000 workers engaged in the transport service at the ports, and on the roads and railways, for whom the question of foreign competition was equally unreal. When the day of battle came, Chamberlain would find under his command only a few scratch battalions with which to meet all these hostile armies.

It had in fact been a masterstroke of policy on the part of the British free traders when half a century before they had made

[1] See *Memorandum on the Excess of Imports into the United Kingdom* (*British and Foreign Trade and Industry. Memoranda. Statistical Tables and Charts prepared in the Board of Trade*, 1903, pp. 99 sqq.). The excess of imports over exports had even reached such a point by the close of the century that certain protectionists doubted whether the invisible exports were always sufficient to make it up. (*Nineteenth Century*, May, 1899, p. 850, article by J. W. Cross, 'British Trade in 1898. A Warning Note.')

their country a country of absolute free trade, instead of a country mildly protectionist. It is an easy matter to raise a tariff already in existence, and, however slight the duties may be at the outset, to increase them by imperceptible degrees, until they present an almost insuperable barrier to the importation of foreign goods. But where there is no tariff from which to start, it is impossible to begin with one group of interests without coming into conflict with others. The supporters of free trade took fresh heart from the knowledge that public opinion was behind them. They answered meetings with meetings, pamphlets with pamphlets. The Cobden Club awoke from its slumbers. To reach a more popular audience the *Daily News* and the *Daily Chronicle* followed the example of the *Daily Mail*[1] and became halfpenny papers. The occupants of the principal chairs of political economy pronounced that the doctrine of free trade was supported by the principles of their science.[2] To the officials of the Liberal party and the leaders of Nonconformity and trade-unionism[3] free trade was something more than a scientific conclusion. It was a sacred tradition invested with a sentimental and semi-religious halo, like the kindred principles of peace, liberty, and the brotherhood of man. No doubt the young politicians of the Liberal party were aware that free trade had not realized all the expectations of the masses, that the demolition of tariff barriers was not the indispensable and sufficient condition of universal prosperity, that fifty years of free trade had not solved the social problem, and that, if poverty were to be abolished or even reduced, a thorough-going policy of legislative action was indispensable. The official leader of the party, Sir Henry Campbell-Bannerman, was in agreement with this point of view.[4] Nevertheless, many

[1] The *Daily News* from February 15, 1904; the *Daily Chronicle* from February 29 of the same year.

[2] See in *The Times* of August 18, 1903, the manifesto signed by fourteen professors.

[3] *Report of the Tariff Commission*, vol. iv, *The Engineering Industries*, 1909, §. 595: 'Our workmen have not had an opportunity of expressing themselves in any direct way yet, but on the whole they are opposed to anything like protection. They follow the directions of their leaders on political grounds, and the "dear loaf" idea is carefully instilled into them. On the whole, the workmen are open to reason, and the balance would be in favour of protection, taking the whole of the electorate, because a large number are not trade unionists. It is impossible to understand the trade union leaders taking such a firm stand, considering the question of continuity of labour. If you talk to the men individually, they are in favour of protection.'

[4] Speech at Perth, June 5, 1903: 'Twelve million of the people are underfed and on the verge of starvation. . . . We used to hear of a submerged tenth of the population. We now know of a submergeable third. The effect of taxing the food of the people would be to turn the submergeable third into a submerged third.' See also his speech at Newport,

Liberals of the old school nursed the secret hope that Chamberlain's imprudent step would bring about the downfall of that militarist and Socialistic philosophy of State interference which for the past decade had threatened to sweep everything before it; that Herbert Spencer had died in December, 1903, not just too late to escape witnessing the final defeat of his principles, but a little too soon to witness their recovery. Surely the present resembled the period which followed the Crimean War. That had been a difficult war, followed by victory, and the victory had been followed by disillusionment, when its fruits were compared with the cost in wealth and blood. Why should not history repeat itself now? At the next Election might not free trade prove a more powerful cry than Imperialism or Socialism and revive the philosophy of 1860?

6

What meanwhile was the attitude of the group of Liberal Imperialists, the men who at the beginning of 1902 had founded the Liberal League to oppose the National Liberal Federation? Must they not recognize in the programme of 'colonial preference' an article of their own creed? Had not the protagonist of imperialism, Lord Rosebery, spoken, long before Chamberlain adopted the formula, of the necessity for 'a bond of commercial unity' between the different parts of the Empire?[1] Chamberlain might well have hoped that by raising the question of an imperial tariff he would not only prevent a reconciliation between the two factions of the Liberal party, but might even widen the breach between them. It would in fact seem that in May, 1903, Lord Rosebery had hesitated as to the attitude he should adopt.[2] But he quickly made up his mind. In common with the other members of his group, Asquith, Sir Edward Grey, and Haldane, he came to the conclusion that Chamberlain's rash step might

November 30, 1903: 'We are not fanatics. We do not attribute to free trade miraculous powers, or claim for it that it can of itself remove the burden of poverty. We leave panaceas to others. But we don't want England turned once more into a poor man's purgatory.'

[1] Speech at Leeds, October 10, 1888: 'I do not see that you can obtain the great boon of a peaceful Empire, encircling the globe with a bond of commercial unity and peace, without some sacrifice on your part.' What sacrifice? Lord Rosebery did not make his meaning clear. There is in fact nothing in the context which proves that he was thinking of a tariff.

[2] Speech at Burnley, May 19, 1903.

prove disastrous to the imperial unity he desired to consolidate.

What was the aim of the tariff reformers? If we are to believe Chamberlain's words—to make the Empire an economic unit 'self-sufficient and self-contained'. But it was an aim not easy to achieve.

Presumably the advocates of an all-British Zollverein were inclined, more or less vaguely, to regard the United Kingdom and her Colonial dependencies as being from an economic point of view complementary. Great Britain was the town with its offices, counting houses, and factories, the Colonies the country-side which might be given the monopoly of foodstuffs and raw materials needed by the mother country, provided that in return they gave the latter a monopoly of the manufactured articles of which they were in need. For example, why should not a prefer-ence be granted to the wines of the Cape Colony and Australia? The proposal had been made several times in Parliament, when the debate on the Budget called attention to the duties imposed on the importation of foreign wines, a tariff which in obedience to the principles of free trade gave no preference whatever to the Colonial wine grower. And since Chamberlain promised the British consumer a reduction of the duties on tea, coffee and cocoa, why not make a further reduction in favour of Ceylon tea and West Indian coffee? Or again, why not encourage the cultivation of cotton in the British Colonies in Africa—it was beginning to attract attention just at this time[1]—so that one day Lancashire might cease to be dependent on the American crop? There was nothing in these proposals to alarm the British producer; Great Britain had neither vineyards nor plantations of tea, coffee or cotton. But the question of corn was more difficult.

If Chamberlain promised the British consumer a reduction of the duties on tea and coffee, it was to compensate him for the duty which he proposed to place on foreign corn. Should Colonial corn be exempted from the duty, in particular corn from Canada, which during the past decade had become a great corn growing country? If this were Chamberlain's intention, the workers in the great industries and the inhabitants of the large towns would benefit by it. But he seems as far as possible to have evaded the

[1] For the work accomplished by the British Cotton-Growing Association, which succeeded in increasing the growth of cotton within the Empire threefold in a few years, see the interesting debate H. of C., April 5, 1905 (*Parliamentary Debates*, 4th Ser., vol. cxliv, pp. 544 sqq.).

issue; for the free admission of Canadian corn would alienate the agriculturalists, the landlords and farmers, who formed the solid core of the protectionist forces, and who, if they were in favour of making the importation of wheat from Russia, the Argentine and the United States more difficult, had no desire to see the importation of Canadian corn directly encouraged as a result. Thus the conflict of interests between the British and the Colonial producer which had remained hidden, so long as Great Britain remained firmly attached to the principle of free trade, was revealed by the mere proposal to introduce a new system of tariffs.

Moreover, the British Colonies had already to a considerable extent outgrown the stage of a purely agricultural economy. With one exception, all the Australian States had adopted a policy of protection, before the constitution of the Commonwealth in 1900 compelled the single free trade state, New South Wales, to become protectionist like the rest. At the same time, Australia was Socialist, and the working class, which universal suffrage had placed in power, was endeavouring to set up a system of high prices and high wages, to be maintained by the deliberate interference of the legislature, in other words, to make the country a closed commercial unit, 'self-sufficient and self-contained', proudly ignoring the rest of the world, and, in the first place, the rest of the Empire. Canada was endeavouring to develop her mineral resources, iron and coal, and harness her waterfalls, so as to become, like the mighty Republic at her doors, a great industrial as well as a great agricultural country. On the London market complaints were already being heard of the dumping practised by the Canadian iron and steel manufacture. Was there any prospect that the adoption of the proposed tariff would suffice to arrest the fever of industrialism which raged throughout the Empire? That the moment their corn, wool, and wine were granted a preference on the British market, the Colonies would be content to develop their cultivation and renounce the aim of becoming by the advance of industrialization complete and independent nations? In one of his missionary speeches Chamberlain ventured to express this hope,[1] but the passage provoked

[1] Speech at Glasgow, October 6, 1903: 'Canada has been Protective for a long time. The Protective Policy has produced its natural result. The principal industries are there, *and you never get rid of them.*' The industrial development of Canada was still in its infancy. This was even more true of Australia. In South Africa there were practically speaking no

such angry protests in the Colonies that he thought it advisable to suppress it when he re-edited the speech later. The truth must be faced. The Empire was composed not of complementary but of competing economic societies. Along what lines could they reach a harmony of interests acceptable to all parties?

The advocates of 'colonial preference' claimed that their policy, far from doing violence to the natural operation of economic forces, was, so to speak, in the line of historical development. While commerce with foreign nations was becoming more difficult, statistics proved—so Chamberlain and his supporters contended—that as a result of the community of language and customs, commerce between the mother country and her Colonies was steadily increasing in volume: 'trade followed the flag'. British exports to foreign countries had fallen from £195,700,000 in 1872 to £174,300,000 in 1902, a decrease of £21,400,000. During the same period exports to the Colonies had risen from £60,500,000 to £109,000,000, an increase of £48,500,000. And the importance of the trade between Great Britain and her Colonies, especially the self-governing Colonies, became still more evident, when the small size of their populations was taken into account. A German, Dutchman or Belgian bought in 1902 11/8 worth of British goods, a Frenchman 8/- worth, a citizen of the United States 6/3 worth. But a Canadian bought £1.18.4 worth, an Australian £5.5.6 worth, an inhabitant of Cape Colony £6.19.6 worth, a New Zealander £7.5.7 worth, and an inhabitant of Natal £8.0.6 worth.[1] What an encouragement for Britain to send her emigrants to the Colonies! And with what

manufactures. Might not the colonies be asked in the common interest of the Empire ('because we are kinsmen') not to carry their policy of industrialization any further? 'There are many things which you do not now make, many things for which we have a great capacity of production: leave them to us.' For the suppression of the passage in the volume of collected speeches which Chamberlain published at the end of 1903, see John M. Robertson, *Chamberlain, A Study*, 1903, p. 60.

[1] *Birmingham Tariff Committee's Handbook for Speakers* quoted by W. J. Ashley, *The Tariff Problem*, 1903, p. 144: There can be no doubt that sentiment was a factor in promoting trade with the Colonies, as several witnesses admitted in their evidence before the Tariff Commission. See *Report of Tariff Commission*, vol. i, *The Iron and Steel Trades*, § 811: 'The reason why the Colonial markets have expanded so considerably is that we have made a dead set for those markets. . . . We have done it at a very great sacrifice indeed. The tubes have been sold for years and years now, approximately at cost price. . . . The reason why we wish to retain Colonial markets is a sentimental one probably.' Ibid., §. 915: 'Many merchants in Australia prefer to buy English wire. There is a certain amount of sentiment. I believe English wire is better, but for fencing purposes I cannot help thinking that any ordinary wire would do. The consumers in New Zealand believe in English wire. They like to buy English goods and for English goods they are willing to pay higher prices.'

well-founded hope could she look forward to the day when their population, scarcely more than 10,000,000 in 1901, had doubled, quadrupled—even become equal to that of the mother country ! Could nothing be done to stimulate the natural movement of trade, already tending, even without artificial encouragement, to draw closer the commercial ties between Britain and her Colonies? It could be hastened by a system of preferential tariffs. The Colonies were asking for it. As we have already seen, Canada had reduced by a quarter first, then by a third, the duties on goods of British origin. At the conference of 1902 her representatives had declared their willingness to extend the system of preference for British goods and the representatives of Australia, New Zealand, Cape Colony, and Natal had held out hopes that their Colonies would follow the Canadian example.

These arguments were not unanswerable. The question which immediately concerned the British exporter was not how much Canada or Australia, as compared with Germany or the United States, spent annually on the purchase of British goods per head of population; what interested his pocket was the total amount of goods exported to each country. But about 1900 the annual exports to the Colonies amounted to only £102,000,000, whereas the exports to the remainder of the world were worth £252,000,000.[1] Imports told the same tale. The trade within the Empire was very far from amounting even to half the trade with foreign countries. Was it reasonable to push imperial patriotism, the sentiment of racial solidarity, so far as to hamper foreign trade in the hope of stimulating the development of trade with the Colonies? It was already growing of itself, the tariff reformers argued, and it was simply a question of assisting a natural growth. Their opponents questioned the truth of this contention, and denied that it was fair to take as the starting point of comparison the year 1872 when exports to foreign countries reached an exceptionally high figure. When the entire second half of the nineteenth century was taken into account, it would be found that the proportion which trade with the Colonies bore to trade with foreign countries had remained almost invariable.[2] Between 1895

---

[1] Including the re-exports (Sir Robert Giffen, 'The Dream of a British Zollverein', *Economic Inquiries and Studies*, vol. ii, pp. 387 sqq.).

[2] For a good study of this question see Alleyne Ireland, *Tropical Colonization. An Introduction to the Study of the Subject*, 1899, chap. iii, 'Trade and the Flag'. Ireland shows that during the same period the trade between the Colonies and *foreign countries* was increasing

and 1900 the export trade with foreign countries had increased more rapidly than the Colonial trade. Between 1900 and 1903 it declined and then remained stationary; the Colonial trade slowly increased. But, after 1903, to the discomfiture of the tariff reformers, trade with foreign countries expanded rapidly, whereas the growth of trade with the Colonies continued to be slow. What conclusions could be drawn from statistics whose interpretation was so uncertain?

7

The very language used by the tariff reformers was likely to repel those whom they wished to convince. They held out no hope that the adoption of their system would increase the industrial prosperity of the United Kingdom. They asked the country, in return for the 'sacrifice' the Colonies were called upon to make by contributing to imperial defence, to make the corresponding 'sacrifice' which the introduction of a tariff on foreign imports would involve. This was how Chamberlain stated the position in his Birmingham speech on May 15, 1903, and his lieutenants were even more outspoken. The Imperialist, Mackinder, explained that 'the immediate effect of any sudden raising of duties is usually to lessen total production' and raise prices. True, he attempted to reassure his readers by adding that those 'incipient losses are in reality a national investment to bear subsequent fruit'.[1] But another Imperialist, Hewins, went further and maintained that the object of a policy of 'constructive imperialism' should be 'the greater political or social stability, or the greater defensive power of the Empire', not immediate, or even ultimate gain, of a purely economic character.[2] It was certainly honest, but perhaps it was not tactful to present the new policy under so chivalrous an aspect. The nation was uneasily conscious that its

at a more rapid rate than their trade with the mother country. See also in the blue book entitled *British and Foreign Trade and Industry. Memoranda. Statistical Tables and Charts.* 1903: The memorandum (followed by tables and diagrams): *Export Trade of the United Kingdom to Protected and Unprotected Foreign Countries and Colonies* (1850 to 1902).

[1] J. R. Mackinder, *Money Power and Man Power*, 1906, p. 18.

[2] W. A. S. Hewins, *Imperialism and its Probable Effect on the Commercial Policy of the United Kingdom* (1901). Cf. W. J. Ashley, *The Tariff Problem*, p. 189: 'The supreme object of English statesmanship in the period on which we have now entered, should be to obtain as secure a basis as may be for the economic life of the nation, and, if some redistribution of industry should prove to be necessary, to moderate its pace and to confine it as far as possible within the limits of the Empire.'

powers of production and its wealth were no longer increasing, or, at least, no longer increasing so rapidly as in the past. It was for that very reason that so many manufacturers and merchants had been shaken in their allegiance to free trade, and now they heard from Chamberlain and his friends that possibly, even probably, the adoption of tariff reform would not increase their wealth. At this point the programme of 'colonial preference' conflicted with the programme of economic reprisals. It inevitably alienated from the policy of imperial federation those who had been originally attracted by the prospect of a war against foreign protection.

Was it even certain that, if the British accepted the sacrifices, temporary or permanent, which the neo-protectionists demanded, they would at least give satisfaction to the Colonies? So the tariff reformers contended, and in support of their contention pointed to the offers which for several years past had been made by various Colonial Governments. But to what after all did they amount? And what proof had the Colonies given that they were in earnest? Australia, whose promises, to be sure, had been of the vaguest, did nothing. New Zealand raised her tariff against every nation, and was prepared to do no more than exempt British goods from the additional duties. The reduction of a tenth granted by Cape Colony amounted to nothing. At first sight it might seem that Canada had already for several years done more. But it must be admitted that the preference of 25 per cent granted in 1897 was in part illusory. For the tariff had been raised immediately before, so that when compared with the duty hitherto paid, the reduction amounted only to 7.5 per cent.[1] And even the preference subsequently granted had given very little satisfaction on either side of the Atlantic. The Canadian manufacturers were agitating vigorously for an increase in the duties.[2] It was fear of their protests which had induced the Canadian Government to make the request which the British Government granted, that the proceedings at the Colonial Conference of 1902 should be withheld from publication.[3] And the British manufacturers were

[1] J. Davidson, *Commercial Federation and Colonial Trade Policy*, 1900, p. 80.
[2] For their agitation, as also for a general account of the Canadian attitude towards Chamberlain's new policy, see Edwin S. Montagu and Bron Herbert, *Canada and the Empire, an Examination of Trade Preferences*, 1904.
[3] *Colonial Conference, 1902. Correspondence relating to the proposed Publication of the Report of the Proceedings of the Colonial Conference in London in 1902*, 1903.

not much better satisfied. Even a preference of 33 per cent was insufficient—given the distance of some 2,500 miles of sea which separated Great Britain from her Colony—to protect them effectively in the Canadian market against the competition of the Canadian manufacturers and those of the United States.

We have mentioned the United States. Here perhaps was one of the most difficult problems the new imperialism had to face. Among the great protectionist countries whose competition was injuring British trade, the United States was undoubtedly the nation which threatened the gravest danger to her industrial supremacy. Was the remedy a tariff war to be waged conjointly by Britain and Canada against the great American republic? On the one hand, it was very doubtful that a suggestion of this kind would find favour in Canada. We have already seen that Canadian statesmen had been anxious to establish a system of free trade between the two neighbouring countries, and that it was only the hostile attitude of the United States, as expressed by the McKinley and Dingley tariffs, which deterred them from the project. If, at any future time, the American Government were willing to lower her tariff in favour of Canada, she would have no difficulty in detaching her from Great Britain.[1] And, on the other hand, even if it were granted that there was a prospect of obtaining Canadian support for such a policy, it was diametrically opposed to the policy pursued by the British Foreign Office. Great Britain was determined to maintain friendly relations with the United States at whatever cost. At the very moment when Chamberlain inaugurated his new campaign, the British arbitrator had decided a serious dispute as to the frontier between Alaska and British Columbia in favour of the States and against Canada. The decision was very badly received by the Canadian Press, which for the moment was far more excited about the boundary question than about Chamberlain's new programme.[2]

[1] R. B. Haldane, speech at Chertsey, February 3, 1905: 'What would be the relations between the United States and Canada if we adopted a preferential system? The United States would reply to our preference by offering Canada special terms, and Canada would be free to make a choice between this country and the States. That was just the kind of situation in which he saw serious danger to the Imperial bond.'

[2] Richard Jebb, *Studies in Colonial Nationalism*, 1905, pp. 40 sqq. See the article from the *Montreal Gazette* quoted on p. 49: 'The decision of the Alaska Commission is due to the imperial desire to enhance American goodwill, to which many Canadian issues have previously been sacrificed.' Also, on the same page, Sir Wilfrid Laurier's declaration, October 23, 1903: 'Difficult as I conceive the proposition to be, I am of opinion that so long as Canada remains a dependence of the British Crown the present powers we have

But Canada was obliged to accept the position. If from the great panteutonic system of 1898 Germany was henceforward excluded, the dream of a moral alliance with the United States persisted. The pan-anglo-saxonism of which Chamberlain dreamed must be incomplete, unless in one way or another it included the States.

In short, the United States, without being part of the Empire, belonged to what might be called the society of English-speaking nations. And, on the other hand, a portion of the Empire of peculiar importance did not belong to that society. We are not alluding to the host of Crown Colonies, too scattered and inhabited by peoples too uncivilized to cause serious difficulty to the British statesman. We are thinking of British India, that gigantic anomaly within the imperial system, with its ancient and splendid civilization and a population which amounted to three-quarters of the entire population of the Empire. It was not a self-governing Colony, and had no power to establish a protective tariff if it desired to do so. Britain had forced on the country a system of unqualified, or almost unqualified, free trade, which opened the Indian market to the importation of British goods, in particular of cotton yarn and cloth. The Liberal Government of 1892 had allowed the imposition of an import duty. It was so slight that it could hardly be considered protective. Nevertheless, Lancashire was in arms. Indeed the victories which the Unionists won in that county at the election of 1895 were widely attributed to the resentment aroused, and the new Government lost no time in revoking the concession made by its predecessor. Cotton cloth was subjected to the merely nominal import duty of 3.5 per cent, which was balanced by an excise duty of the same amount on native cloth. Cotton yarn would pay no duty whatever. Nevertheless, the native industry flourished. The distance which separated India from Lancashire was in itself an effective protection for the Indian manufacture, labour was cheap, and the raw material grown on the spot. Indian cotton competed successfully with British not only in the local market but throughout the Far East.[1] What could be done to check the growth of this

---

are not sufficient for the maintenance of our right. It is important that we should ask the British Parliament for more extensive powers; so that, if ever we have to deal with matters of a similar nature again, we shall deal with them in our own fashion and according to the best light we have.'

[1] See the figures in W. J. Ashley, *The Tariff Problem*, p. 72.

Indian industrialism which was able to flourish without the artificial aid of a tariff? And what system of colonial preference could be devised which would reconcile the claims of the native industry with those of British imperialism? Should India be given the same right as Canada and Australia to protect her industries by a tariff, even against Britain, on the understanding that certain reductions would then be made in her favour? The British Parliament would not sanction such a solution. Should Britain force on India a system of free trade with herself, of protection against the rest of the world? No Indian interest would be served by such a policy. A blue book, published at the beginning of 1904, admitted that the problem was insoluble.[1] In Chamberlain's system, there was no place for the 300,000,000 inhabitants of British India.

8

What was the radical mistake of economic imperialism as formulated by Chamberlain? It was that its advocates in their impatience to consolidate the British Empire overlooked the difference of structure which distinguished it from Empires such as the German or, if you prefer, the United States, or even the Russian Empire. The creators of German unity had begun by establishing a tariff union, to be followed by a political. Why not copy their example? Because the sentiment of moral solidarity which had enabled the Germans to overcome the obstacles of local particularism rested on the solid foundation, not only of a common language and race, but of geographical contiguity. In the case of the British Empire nothing of the sort existed.

When they originally suggested a Zollverein, the advocates of an economic bond between the mother country and her dependencies had meant a system of absolute free trade within the Empire, a single tariff barrier separating the entire Empire from the rest of the world. It very soon became clear that there was no possibility of realizing a project of this kind, and the term Zollverein was either dropped or given an entirely different meaning. The United Kingdom would continue to admit Colonial goods free of duty, indeed the door would be opened even wider to

[1] *East India (Tariffs) Views of the Government of India on the Question of Preferential Tariffs*. A Letter from the Government of India, in the Finance and Commerce Department, to the Secretary of State, dated Simla, October 22, 1903, in reply to a telegram of August 7 from Lord George Hamilton, 1904.

353

Colonial trade by a reduction in the duties on tea, coffee, and cocoa. On the other hand, a tariff would exclude goods of foreign origin. But the Colonies would retain their individual tariffs, not only against foreign goods, but even against goods of British origin. All that the tariff reformers ventured to hope was that they would reduce their duties on the importation of British goods. But was that hope likely to be realized? Moreover, though the economists of Chamberlain's school claimed that the new tariff had been constructed on a 'scientific basis' the principles on which it rested had not been sufficiently thought out. On the one hand, it was not easy to understand how the tariff could afford equal protection in the British market to States so distant one from another, whose interests were as divergent as their geographical position, and which nobody even proposed to bring under a common code of commercial law or into a single monetary system. And, on the other hand, it was equally difficult to see how the tariff could give satisfaction at the same time to the Colonial Governments and to the British manufacturers and merchants, who desired a tariff as the instrument of a policy of reprisals, which could be lowered at any time in return for mutual concessions, in the interest, not of the Colonial, but of the British producer. The original suggestion of an unconditional Zollverein had been too simple. The system of 'imperial preference' had become so complicated that it was unworkable.

Taken as a whole, the Empire comprised a host of different races, at very different stages of civilization. If only the self-governing Colonies are taken into account, it was a loose agglomeration of nations scattered over the four quarters of the globe. According to the orthodox imperialists they were tending to unite more closely, and the Canadian federation achieved over thirty years earlier, and the Australian federation accomplished three years before were the first signs of a movement whose goal would be the federation of the Empire. In the opinion the Liberal Imperialists, on this point genuinely liberal, this was a complete misreading of the situation. The effect of these partial federations had been to give birth to new nationalities locally united and consciously separate, not only from communities not of Anglo-Saxon race, but from the mother country herself. And this local patriotism had been fostered by the advertisement which these small nations received at every Imperial Conference. Though their population barely exceeded that of Switzerland or Belgium, and their culture was far inferior, the respect with which they were treated in London gave them an importance altogether disproportionate. The Government of the mother country treated them in fact not as dependencies or provinces, but as free allied nations. Why attempt the dangerous experiment of altering the present position? It would be wiser to do everything possible to maintain the delicate balance of complicated factors, the indefinable blend of commercial expediency and sentiment. No one blamed the Unionist Government for using the taxpayers' money to build railways in Uganda, West Africa, and the Sudan, or to link the different parts of the Empire by submarine cables. No one blamed it for denouncing the commercial treaties concluded thirty years earlier with Germany and Belgium, because they were incompatible with the tariffs of the self-governing Colonies. Nor did any one find fault with the statute passed in 1900[1] permitting trustees to invest trust funds in Colonial as well as in British stocks. But why go any further?

Each of these British nations, united with the rest by the moral ties of kinship, must continue to exercise the right of establishing whatever fiscal system it might think fit. Great Britain must remain a free trade country, since free trade suited her commercial position best, but Canada and Australia must not abandon protection, since their economy was based on that principle. There were serious objections to using the over-centralized and too 'Latin' term 'Empire' of so loose a bundle of States. Already several English writers had been attracted by the term Commonwealth, which the historian, James Bryce, had used in a celebrated work to describe the United States of America, and which the Australians had borrowed from him as the official title of their new confederation. 'The name Empire', wrote J. L. Hammond in 1900, 'is charged with associations for which Liberals have little liking, and they would prefer to apply the term 'Commonwealth' for the confederacy of States which makes up the dominions of the Crown.'[2]

When, just before the end of the Boer War, the Liberal

---

[1] 63 & 64 Vict., Cap. 62: An Act to amend the Colonial Stock Acts, 1877 and 1892, and the Trustee Act, 1893 (*Colonial Stock Act*, 1900).

[2] J. L. Hammond, *Colonial and Foreign Policy* (in *Liberalism and the Empire*, 1900, p. 207). Cf. Bernard Shaw, *John Bull's Other Island*, p. xxiv: 'The Federal Union of English-speaking Commonwealths, now theatrically called the Empire.'

League was founded at the beginning of 1902, the Liberal party had seemed split irretrievably into two hostile groups. Almost immediately, they had been obliged to join forces against Balfour's Education Act, and a reconciliation had begun. The united opposition of both sections to the Bill had been forced upon them by the desire to satisfy a powerful section of the public, but they did not yet feel, that in their struggle with the Tories, they were leading a genuinely national movement. It was Chamberlain's rash step which at last unchained a national revolt. Liberal Imperialists and Gladstonian Liberals were now united to defend against the protectionist reaction both material interests and spiritual ideals, a deep-rooted political tradition and a doctrine of progress, the cause of the Empire and the cause of mankind.

CHAPTER II

Other Problems: Resignation of the Cabinet

I SOCIALISTS, NONCONFORMISTS, AND IRISH

I

WHAT would be the verdict of the electorate when the question raised by Chamberlain in 1903 was submitted to its decision? Unionists and Liberals alike believed that the victory would lie with free trade. And within the Unionist party there was no disagreement on this point between Chamberlain and Balfour. But if both knew themselves foredoomed to defeat, the breach was nevertheless profound between the rival leaders of the same party.

By the end of the summer of 1903 Chamberlain had been compelled to recognize that the suddenness of his new programme had taken the country by surprise. He had, therefore, decided that it would be unwise to compel a decision by forcing an election on the issue of tariff reform, and that Balfour as Prime Minister should be allowed to put forward a minimum programme with the object of postponing the crisis, a programme which would placate the large number of Unionists who under no circumstances would hear of duties on food. But this was only a provisional concession, a tactical manoeuvre. He continued to put forward, in entire independence of the Cabinet, his complete programme, and as month followed month, he asked himself with growing impatience whether Balfour's temporizing policy was justified by the results. At the end of 1903 the by-elections were still so indecisive that it was possible to believe that the country was accepting the compromise arranged between the two leaders. But with the opening of the New Year the rout began. Even the agricultural districts refused to accept Chamberlain's bait of higher prices for their produce. And the manufacturing districts, which were supposed to feel most acutely the bad effects of the German dumping, would not listen to the advances made by Balfour. In only nine of the thirty-seven by-elections held between the beginning of 1904 and the end of 1905 was a Conservative returned, and even in these cases the Unionist majorities were enormously diminished. What use was it then to keep on waiting and give the impression of shrinking from the prospect of certain defeat? Would it not be a more manly policy to face an immediate *débâcle*, in the hope that it would one day be reversed? Chamberlain was not slow to reach this conclusion and he made no secret of his opinion. He knew that he had on his side the majority, the overwhelming majority of the Conservative associations; that all those leaders of industry who fifteen years before had left the Liberal party were with him against the tiny band of old-fashioned Tories who after his resignation had taken possession of the Government; that the young Tories themselves endured with reluctance Balfour's over-cautious and too academic policy; that they regarded him as their chief, the one man capable of leading them sooner or later to victory. In August, 1904, Kipling sung his praises in a short poem inspired by the biblical story of Joseph's dream, in which he presented him as one of those supermen who for their very greatness are misunderstood and envied by their fellows.[1]

Nevertheless, Balfour clung to the temporizing tactics on which, though they were obviously discredited, he persisted in pinning his faith. It was no easy matter to govern on these lines with a majority, shaken by the quasi-defection of the Unionist Free Traders and continually reduced by unfavourable by-elections. When the leaders of the Opposition forced a vote on a free trade motion, he secured a majority of no more than 50, instead of the 134 of 1900. And on one occasion he avoided defeat only by ordering his supporters to abstain from voting and allow-

---

[1] 'And Joseph dreamed a dream, and he told it to his brethren; and they hated him yet the more' (*Genesis xxxvii*, 5). It was a short poem of four verses. The last two lines of the third verse, and the fourth verse, are as follows:

'Once on a time there was a man.
Things never yet created things.

A bolt is fallen from the blue,
A wakened realm full circle swings
Where Dothan's dreamer dreams anew
Of vast and far borne harvestings;
And unto him an Empire clings,
That grips the purpose of his plan.
My Lords, how think you of these things?
Once—in our time—is there a man?'

Abroad, Chamberlain gave the same impression of irresistible strength. See Karl Peters, *Mr. Chamberlain's Zollreform und Deutschland*, 1904, p. 1: 'In Great Britain and throughout the British Empire, Chamberlain occupies at present the position of a Dictator. Even if it wished, Balfour's Cabinet could not withstand him, nor could the Liberal Opposition. In England his will is bound to become law.'

ing the motion in favour of free trade to be carried unanimously. Nor could he, without constant recourse to shifts and evasions, explain the fact that he disagreed with Chamberlain on a fundamental question and yet fought in the same political camp. In fact he steadily retreated before his formidable ally. When Chamberlain demanded that the next Imperial Conference should be allowed complete liberty to discuss every aspect of the tariff question, he declared himself willing to consent, provided the conference were held after the next Election and that any programme on which it might agree should not be ratified by Parliament until the electorate had been again consulted. But the Conference was due in 1906—that is to say, before the normal term of dissolution. If the Parliament, returned in 1900, were still in existence in 1906, could the Conference be forbidden to consider Chamberlain's programme? To that question Balfour returned an evasive answer, and his ambiguous language was the more serious, because he had apparently made up his mind not to dissolve before the end of the session of 1906.

Balfour obviously found amusement in the very difficulty of his task; but the entertainment he received from a dialectical feat was not his sole object. It was only to be expected that the Unionist party would fall from power after winning two elections in succession, but he was convinced that by violently thrusting into the programme the issue of protection Chamberlain had committed a very grave blunder. What remained to be done but to gain time and allow a host of other questions to arise in the course of Parliamentary business? Some of these the Government might be able to solve to the satisfaction of the public. There were others for which it had no solution. But could the Liberals do any better? Moreover, it might be possible to commit the opposition to rash promises which, when they took office, they would be expected to fulfil. Chamberlain's policy of all or nothing threatened to transform the Unionists' inevitable defeat into a disaster. To obviate the danger Balfour was doing all he could to confuse the issues, expecting a future victory for his party from the number, complexity, and confusion of the problems to which the Government of the country and Empire gave rise. We will try to convey as clear and distinct a notion as is possible of a situation so chaotic.

2

For the Government and the official Opposition alike the social question was a permanent source of anxiety. And the outlook was the more alarming because the ruling classes, who, for three-quarters of a century, had managed to avert the danger of a class war, were obliged to contemplate the humiliating prospect of its revival in the immediate future. Their apprehensions were fostered by a disquieting phenomenon. At the very time when the working class was showing signs of a revolt against the traditional forms of party government, the leaders of thought were adopting Socialism. H. G. Wells, exploiting in a more philosophic vein the genre invented by Jules Verne, had begun his literary career by fantastic romances in which he seemed to be depicting the coming class war or world capitalism merely for his own and his readers' recreation. His pictures of the future, if we insist on reading into them a didactic purpose, were pessimistic and cynical—without a gleam of hope. But he now became a social reformer, and, in 1902, wrote *Anticipations*, a work inspired throughout by 'Fabian' ideals, in which, sacrificing liberty to efficiency, he attempted to describe, at once bold and cautious in his forecast, what mankind might become, if they organized their work for war or peace, about the year 2,000. *Mankind in the Making*, which appeared two years later, started from the point reached by the former work and discussed the novel problems of social and individual education which must be solved in order to create the ideal citizen of the 'New Republic'. In 1905 Wells published his *Modern Utopia*, in the literal sense a 'dream' of a society from which war and poverty had vanished and in which under the freely accepted leadership of an aristocracy the spirit of service had replaced the incentive of gain. He thus revived the Utopianism—more scientific, to be sure, than it had been in the days of William Morris and his group of aesthetes, but deliberately imaginative—which the Fabians twenty years before had attempted to banish, and with such success that by the end of the nineteenth century they no doubt believed that it had disappeared for many a long day.

Nevertheless it was a Fabian—certainly the most eccentric member of the group—who the same year as the publication of the Wells *Modern Utopia*, the year moreover of the first Russian revolution, dealt British moderation and opportunism a more daring blow. For ten or twelve years past known only as a pioneer of the modern drama whose success was confined to a small coterie of youthful enthusiasts, Bernard Shaw had just achieved celebrity. A lady who moved in the most fashionable circles had seen *John Bull's Other Island*, the witty and profound burlesque he had devoted to the Irish Question. She told King Edward how much she had enjoyed it. The King expressed his desire to see the piece and, since it had been taken off the stage, a special performance was given in the Royal honour. That was sufficient to make Shaw fashionable. It was now a social duty to see all his new plays, and Shaw, as though to prove his independence of this novel audience of the upper middle class which, following the King's example, had flocked to his plays, wrote *Major Barbara*.

The old Evangelicalism founders in ridicule to the beat of a Salvation Army drum. Capitalism is displayed in the glare of its triumphant brutality, stripped of hypocrisy and professing that the sole right in the world is force, the only sin poverty. Fabian cynicism reacting against revolutionary romanticism had made the two Webbs conservative reformers. It was a sign of the times that in this critical year 1905, when social revolution was raging in Eastern Europe, it made Shaw, reacting against what we may call Christian romanticism, a revolutionary, half Nietzchean, half Marxist. For an honest man—and by an 'honest man' is meant a man who sees things as they are—there remained only the choice, if we have read correctly the philosophy of *Major Barbara*, between the might of the employers and the might of the proletariat. A century earlier Wesley had defeated Voltaire. Would he defeat Marx?

The novels of George Gissing, which were destined to enjoy popularity after their author's death, breathed the same fiery indignation against the poverty from which he had died before success arrived. No doubt the most popular of the nineteenth-century novelists, Dickens, had attacked the callousness of the rich and lamented the hard lot of the poor. But his treatment was too sentimental to be revolutionary. His wealthy middle-class reader was always left with the impression that he need only be kindhearted, and his wealth would be forgiven both by Dickens and by the poor. But what a change had come over the spirit of

English literature! A cold, dry light lay over it now; sentiment was rigorously excluded. Arnold Bennett was publishing his first novels and was shortly to produce his masterpieces. *Lumen siccum optima anima.* That society might be seen in its true character, the entrancing mirage, Evangelical and British, of a world in which the poor man can be virtuous and the rich man charitable was rapidly fading. An alliance had been concluded between the intelligentsia and the proletariat. In every country that alliance is dangerous to a social order based on property.

In every other country, no doubt, but in England? Shaw's *Major Barbara* did not even shock his audience. We have only to read the reviews which appeared after the first performance to see that it disappointed those who had come to be amused. The burlesque which opens the piece was all very well, but what could be the meaning of that great tirade of Undershaft's which concludes the drama and contains the entire moral? A critic who reviewed the play for a Socialist organ was almost afraid to understand. 'Of the meaning of Andrew Undershaft's philosophy, I can only guess that it is a call to revolution.'[1] Another critic who evidently had understood was pained. 'It cannot be that the moral, or immoral, of that third act is the advocacy of shooting and active violence. That is not the way to get improved conditions. . . . Our state is not that of Russia.'[2] When the spirit of Continental revolution reaches England, it acts like a shell which explodes in a ploughed field and does no damage. By the ploughed field we do not mean only the self-satisfied and tolerant apathy of the middle class. We are thinking of the vast mass of workers, organized in powerful groups to defend their professional interests, but determined not to put them to the hazard of a perilous struggle, or sacrifice for some vague dream of the future such solid possessions as the moral and religious traditions of their country. While Wells and Shaw were writing, how was that newborn Labour party faring, which we left on the morrow of the Newcastle conference and the election of Will Crooks?

[1] *Clarion*, December 8, 1905: Review by Alex M. Thomson who describes his astonishment: 'When to my soul's dismay, I beheld the Prime Minister boxed up with Sir Oliver Lodge, at the Shavian play, with ex-raiding Premier Jameson in the stalls beneath.'
[2] Ibid., December 29, 1905; article by Sir Oliver Lodge.

3

In June, 1903, the Labour Representation Committee won another election at Barnard's Castle in Yorkshire. For many years past the constituency had returned a Liberal, was indeed practically an appanage of the Pease family. A vacancy having occurred the Committee decided to put up a candidate. They approached Arthur Henderson of the Ironfounders, a representative of the old type of working man and a Wesleyan lay preacher who had worked in the constituency as a very active agent of the Liberal Party and the Pease family. There was a Unionist candidate in the field, and after considerable hesitation the Liberals also put forward a candidate. Henderson was returned at the head of the poll, and the Conservative received more votes than the Liberal. Thus, within less than a year and each time under different conditions, Labour had won three seats, Clitheroe, Woolwich, and Barnard's Castle. Would they win, one after the other, all the working-class constituencies in the Kingdom? In September, Chamberlain's new programme and his noisy campaign in favour of a return to protection had, it seemed, altered the situation.

No doubt the Labour Representation Committee continued to enrol new adherents. When the textile unions had been affiliated, it represented from the beginning of 1904 some 900,000 trade unionists. And when it is remembered that the miners, though they had formed a separate organization, were prepared to contribute to the expenses of Labour candidates in all the colliery districts, it may be admitted that the trade unionists had as a body supported the new policy. But, on the other hand, the leaders of Labour were unanimously opposed to Chamberlain's neoprotectionism. In three successive circulars the Parliamentary Committee of the Trades Union Congress insisted on the necessity of fighting the scourge of tariff reform, as one would combat a deadly disease. If, however, Chamberlain's programme was so dangerous, why not unite with the Liberals to defeat it?

At Norwich in December, 1903, a by-election was held under the same conditions which had obtained at the Barnard's Castle election before Chamberlain's dramatic surprise. Two candidates, a Liberal and a Conservative, were opposed by the Labour candidate, G. H. Roberts. Richard Bell of the railwaymen refused to work for his return, blamed him for splitting the free trade vote, and when he was defeated at the bottom of the poll sent the Liberal a letter of congratulation on a success which had been 'a victory for the cause of progress'. About the same time, Henderson and Shackleton spoke on Liberal platforms. Will Crooks refused to subscribe to the statutes passed at Newcastle, which pledged candidates chosen by the Labour Representation Committee to resign, if they were proved not to have observed strict neutrality between the two bourgeois parties. To satisfy Crooks and his friends the conference which met at Norwich in February, 1904, agreed to alter this clause in the statutes and no longer demand the resignation of those who refused to obey.

Under these circumstances the Independent Labour Party, which, in a sense, constituted the core of the Labour Representation Committee, found itself faced with a difficult problem. There was reason to fear that the Labour Party which would take its share in the debates of the approaching session would no longer be that radically 'independent' party, laying down the law to the two others, which they had dreamed of making it, but a mere group representing professional interests and dependent upon the middle class Liberal Party. How could they prevent the ground gained as a consequence of the Law Lords' decision in 1901 being again lost as a result of the general excitement aroused by the new question Chamberlain had raised? James Ramsay MacDonald and his friends were free traders. If nothing else, the necessities of electioneering compelled them to be so. Up to 1903, since the question of free trade had not yet arisen, it was good strategy to make the most of the differences which divided the old Liberal and the new Labour Party, so as to attract the very large number of workmen in the manufacturing districts who had been accustomed to vote Tory. Now the situation was no longer the same. As a body, the workers were opposed to a policy which meant dear bread, and a candidate who wished to gain their vote could not insist too strongly on free trade. We should, however, slander the leaders of the Independent Labour Party if we ascribed their support of free trade solely to electioneering motives. They were genuinely attached to the doctrine, as to those principles of internationalism and world peace indissolubly bound up with it which constitute one of the most attractive features of the Socialist ideal. But how could they bring home to the electorate at one and the same time the excellence and the inadequacy of the free trade programme, the necessity to oppose Chamberlain and the impracticability of an alliance with the Liberals against him?

Philip Snowden and Ramsay MacDonald agreed with politicians like Morley in the belief that a return to protection would not cure the evils from which the country suffered. But neither would free trade cure them. Besides free trade, State intervention was required, the rational organization of the national means of production—in other words, Socialism. The free trade policy of buying everything—even labour—in the cheapest market was the sheer negation of the Socialism cherished by the members of the Independent Labour Party. After professing their attachment to the system of free imports, they finally left the impression that Socialism was fundamentally more akin to protection than to orthodox free trade. 'Factory Laws, Fair Wages resolutions, Trade Unionism itself are contradictions of the economic creed based on the cheapest market policy. They are all Protection—not the Protection of Mr. Chaplin, the landlord, nor of Mr. Chamberlain, the demagogue, but the Protection of the Socialist, not the protection of tariffs, but the protection of the communal conscience and the communal wisdom imposing itself upon individual conduct.'[1]

For the heads of the Fabian Society, Sidney and Beatrice Webb, opposition to the free traders was easier than for MacDonald or Snowden. Convinced imperialists and looking to a national and militarist state to realize their programme of moderate collectivism, they had never felt anything but contempt for every formula of Liberalism and free trade. The great middle-class hoax which during the first half of the nineteenth century had stifled the Labour movement in its cradle and delayed the rise of Socialism for three-quarters of a century seemed likely to be repeated. Would it succeed a second time? They doubted it. They predicted that a Liberal majority would be returned at the next election, only to make itself immediately ridiculous by its failure to understand the imperial and Socialist demands of the new age, and after muddling for a few years through the current business of govern-

[1] J. R. MacDonald, *The Zollverein and British Industry*, 1903, p. 164. Cf. Philip Snowden, *The Chamberlain Bubble, Facts about the Zollverein, with an Alternative Policy*, 1903, p. 5: 'We are, as a legacy of the mistaken commercial policy of the last hundred years, a nation of manufacturers.'

ment would be compelled to make room for a Conservative Party regenerated by Chamberlain. That was the party to which the future belonged, the only party from which the working class could obtain that measure of social reform which these opportunists regarded as capable of attainment. As for the new Labour Party, although a representative of the Fabian Society sat on its committees and Shaw gave it his public support, they did not believe that it could survive. In fact, as a result of their influence the Fabian Society during the three transitional years which followed the end of the Boer War presented a bizarre spectacle. It published a tract on the tariff question in which the writers, while suggesting a number of measures the State might adopt to draw closer the bond between the mother country and her Colonies and stimulate the growth of trade and industry, refused to decide between the two warring policies and seemed to reserve their bitterest sarcasm for the doctrine of free trade.[1] At the weekly meetings of the Society, Hewins openly defended tariff reform, as advocated by Chamberlain; Hubert Bland spoke about Kipling; Benjamin Kidd developed the principles of his anti-intellectualist psychology and his imperialist philosophy of history; Cecil Chesterton laid 'Gladstonian ghosts'. Graham Wallas, one of the founders, left the society. His retirement was perfectly amicable, he continued to be the friend and admirer of those with whom he had worked throughout his youth: but, as he took an active part in the work of the advanced political groups, he felt himself compromised by the deliberately anti-Liberal attitude the heads of the Fabian Society had adopted.

4

Under these circumstances the Conservatives, when once they had recovered from the panic into which Crooks' election had thrown them, and Chamberlain had launched his campaign for tariff reform, began to ask themselves whether they could not turn the Labour movement to their own advantage. It was dividing the forces of the Opposition. It formed an eddy in the advancing wave of free trade, which when the wave broke, might, perhaps, lessen the violence of the shock. The Trade Union

---

[1] *Fabian Tract No.* 116. *Fabianism and the Fiscal Question. An Alternative Policy.* February, 1904.

Congress condemned in Chamberlain's new programme the policy of dear bread, but on several occasions within the past fifteen years it had adopted resolutions of a protectionist character, and the Unionist Parliament had certainly met the wishes of the working class, when it passed in 1897, an Act prohibiting the importation of goods made in foreign prisons.[1] And if protectionist principles were in truth latent in the Socialist creed, and it was only an accident that the Socialist programme was confused with the programme of free trade, the Conservative Party might surely do much to dissociate the two programmes, by proving to the working class that on the other hand the new policy of fiscal protection went very well with a policy of legal protection of labour. That had once been Disraeli's policy. Since 1895 the Conservatives, securely installed in power, had been too forgetful of his tradition. Their neglect had been punished. Now, however, when their mistake had been brought home to them by the danger which threatened their party, there might yet be time to return to the policy he had advocated, the policy of Bismarck and Prussia.

To be sure the Unionist leaders did not realize at first the necessity for this change of front. We can observe the stages of their gradual conversion to the new policy by following the history of their undecided and inconsistent attitude toward the interpretation of the law laid down by the House of Lords in 1901 and confirmed by subsequent decisions[2] which enormously reduced the rights

[1] 60 & 61 Vict., Cap. 63: An Act to prohibit the Importation of Foreign Prison-made Goods (*Foreign Prison-made Goods' Act*, 1897). The Bill was introduced by Sir Howard Vincent, a Conservative member, who took an active part in the Fair Trade movement. He was supported by several members and among them a representative of the working class, Havelock Wilson. (H. of C., February 25, 1897; *Parliamentary Debates*, 4th Ser., vol. xlvi, p. 987.)

[2] A. The Case of the Denaby and Cadeby Main Collieries. The collieries considered that a strike approved in 1902 by the Union (Yorkshire Miners' Association) contravened the Union statutes and two actions were brought. One was brought by a miner named Howden at the cost of the employers' organization. He asked the court for an injunction prohibiting the Union from using its funds to provide strike pay. Howden won his case in every court and finally in the House of Lords on April 14, 1905. The other was brought by the collieries themselves against the Union. The case was decided in the first instance in their favour, but the decision was reversed by the Court of Appeal on May 19, 1905. At this date the case had not yet been taken to the Lords.

B. The case of the 'Stop Day' in the Welsh coalfields. The Union, South Wales Miners' Federation, had forbidden, once in 1900, four times in 1901, work on certain days in order to limit production in the supposed interest of the industry as a whole. The local collieries demanded damages from the Union to the amount of some £60,000. They lost their case in the first instance, but won it on appeal and finally in the House of Lords on April 14, 1905.

We should also notice three decisions of the Court of Appeal dealing with the case of

of labour and tended to make a strike impossible. In 1903, when Shackleton, the winner of the Clitheroe election, introduced a Bill limiting the unions' financial liability, the Government persuaded the Commons to submit the question to a Royal Commission[1] on which, in the hope of placating the Socialists, they found a place for Sidney Webb. They were disappointed. For the past two years Webb had lost contact with trade unionism. The Trade Union Congress protested against the appointment and ordered all the unions to boycott the commission. It condemned even Shackleton's Bill as too timid, and demanded not the limitation, but the unqualified abolition, of the unions' financial responsibility.

In 1905, the first step was taken to satisfy their demands. The Cabinet, while denouncing the 'extravagance' of the proposal, left the House of Commons free to pass by a majority of 250 to 130 votes the second reading of a Bill which embodied the principle of non-liability.[2] It was a mere affirmation of principle, but significant nevertheless. For the election was approaching, and the members of the House of Commons felt the need to court the vast Labour electorate. The Cabinet was of the same opinion. Two Bills, introduced by the Government, and placed on the Statute Book in 1905, show the same desire to make advances to the labour employed in the important national industries. Both statutes, the first directly, the second indirectly, were intended to remedy the evil of unemployment which, as we have already had occasion to notice, was steadily increasing.

No doubt unemployment was not so serious about 1903 as it had been on several occasions during the previous century. To use Keir Hardie's happy phrase, the situation was a 'semi-crisis' rather than a crisis.[3] But the attitude of the public conscience had changed. In the past there had been an aversion to any form of State interference. Now the country was waiting impatiently for the Government to act. There was a growing tendency to condemn the old Poor Law which treated paupers almost like

non-union labourers deprived of their work and boycotted by the trade unionists. Only one was given in favour of the Union. (Airey v. Weighill and others, February 10, 1905.) The two others were given against it (Giblan v. the National Amalgamated Labourers' Union of Great Britain and Ireland, August 11, 1903. MacIlrea and another v. the United Society of Drillers and Others, February 16, 1905).

[1] H. of C., May 8, 1903 (*Parliamentary Debates*, 4th Ser., vol. cxxii, pp. 204 sqq.).
[2] H. of C., March 10, 1905 (ibid., vol. cxlii, pp. 1054 sqq.).
[3] Keir Hardie, *The Unemployed Problem*, 1904, p. 9.

criminals, and compelled them to submit to confinement in a workhouse as a condition of receiving relief. The promiscuity of the workhouse was demoralizing, and all young persons who once consented to enter it were made permanently unemployable. The worker genuinely unemployed, who had been temporarily deprived of his regular job by an economic crisis, shunned the workhouse, which he could not enter without losing his civil rights and where he must consort with the professional tramp and all those physical or mental defectives constitutionally incapable of doing the work of a normal man. What steps could be taken pending the entire reform of the Poor Law system? Industrial crises could be mitigated by a better organization of public works, a better adjustment between the supply and demand of labour could be effected by instituting official labour bureaux, and something might perhaps be done to bring the British workmen back to the land by afforestation, draining marshes, and settling the unemployed on farm colonies. All those who about this time were in search of remedies for unemployment cherished more or less vague dreams, at once Conservative and Utopian, of a return to the distant days of a 'Merry England' which lived on the produce of its own soil, and in which the balance of society had not been upset by the over-development of industry.[1]

There had been extensive unemployment during the fifteen or twenty years preceding the Unionist Victory of 1895, more indeed than in 1903 and 1904; and attempts had already been made to discover remedies for this social disease. In 1886 Joseph Chamberlain, then President of the Local Government Board in a Liberal Cabinet, had issued a circular calling upon the municipal bodies to organize public works as a means of reducing unemployment. Seven years later, Sir Henry Fowler, occupying the same position in another Liberal Cabinet, had decided that Boards of Guardians were empowered by the Poor Law to purchase land and open workshops to provide work for the unemployed.[2] It was,

[1] J. Keir Hardie, M.P., *The Unemployed Problem, with Suggestions for Solving it*, 1904. Higgs (Miss Mary), *How to Deal with the Unemployed*, 1904. Hobson (J. A.), *Problem of the Unemployed. An Inquiry and an Economic Policy*, 1904. Alden (Percy), *The Unemployed. A National Question*, with a Preface by Sir John Gorst, 1905, reprinted in an enlarged form under the title: *The Unemployable and Unemployed*, by Percy Alden and Edward E. Hayward (1908). Contains a good bibliography. See also: *Report of Special Committee of the House of Lords on Reclamation and Afforestation*, 1902.

[2] For this new policy of the Board and the way in which it was applied, see S. and B. Webb, *The Public Organization of the Labour Market; Being Part II of the Minority Report of the Poor Law Commission*, 1909, pp. 115 sqq.

moreover, at the same period that Charles Booth's extensive and scientific investigation of pauperism in London revealed both the complexity and the gravity of the evil, and several parliamentary committees studied the best methods of dealing with it.[1]

After this, during the first five years of the Unionist Government, unemployment diminished, the pressure of the social problem was less keenly felt, and a wave of aggressive Imperialism swept over the country. Now, however, when there was a recrudescence of unemployment, the country was weary of Imperialism and the trade unions were organized for a political struggle against the employers, the unemployment inevitably gave rise to a formidable agitation. It was particularly formidable in London, where John Burns put himself at its head. He seemed determined to prove that, if he had quarrelled with Ramsay MacDonald and the Labour Representation Committee, his zeal as a social reformer had not cooled. The London County Council made him chairman of a committee appointed to investigate unemployment in the metropolis. He associated himself with Crooks and Keir Hardie in demanding the institution of a Ministry of Labour to deal with the problem.[2] The Government did not accept the suggestion, but already in 1902, even before the agitation had developed, had passed an Act empowering the newly created metropolitan 'boroughs' to establish labour bureaux.[3] Then the President of the Local Government Board, Walter Long, set up in London mixed Committees, composed partly of representatives of the borough councils, partly of representatives of the boards of guardians, and partly of social workers of wide experience. The Committees, which possessed no official status, were to provide work, in so far as private charity supplied the means, for such of the unemployed as in their opinion ought not to come under the Poor Law. Their activities were co-ordinated by a central committee. At the same time Long drew up a Bill, finally passed in 1905, when Gerald Balfour had succeeded him at the Board, which furnished these distress committees with legal powers, authorized them to draw on the rates for a portion of

[1] Report on Agencies and Methods for dealing with the Unemployed, 1893. Select Committee on Distress from Want of Employment. First, second and third Reports, 1895. Final Report, 1896.
[2] Percy Alden, The Unemployed, 1905, p. 13. Alden and Hayward, The Unemployable and Unemployed (1908), p. 10.
[3] 2 Edw. 7, Cap. 13: An Act to authorize the establishment of Labour Bureaux throughout the Metropolis (Labour Bureaux [London] Act, 1902).

their expenditure, and empowered the Government to set up similar committees in the large provincial towns. The new committees were to find employment for the men out of work, and eventually to settle them on farm colonies.[1] By these measures, the Conservative Government initiated the legislation against unemployment which was to be so enormously extended within the next twenty-five years. At the same time yielding to the pressure of labour the Local Government Board authorized the local Poor Law authorities to provide free meals for school children whose parents, though ineligible for poor relief, were found on enquiry to be in circumstances which rendered that assistance necessary. Finally, the Government appointed a Royal Commission to investigate the question of Poor Law Reform in all its aspects.

5

But was there not another remedy for unemployment, a remedy particularly attractive to a Conservative Party which gloried in the patriotic character of its policy? Measures might be taken to reduce the competition of foreign immigrants in the British labour market. At every census the number of aliens domiciled in England was found to have increased—114,000 in 1871, 135,000 in 1881, 219,000 in 1891, and 286,925 in 1901.[2] It did not amount to much when we consider the position in this respect of other European countries about the same date. In Great Britain in 1891 there were 5.8 aliens per thousand of the population. In Germany, Austria, and France the proportions were about the same time—8.8, 17.2, and 29.7 respectively. Nevertheless, the foreign immigration into Great Britain presented features which in a measure explained the public alarm. No one was seriously disturbed by the 18,000 Scandinavians, the 22,000 Frenchmen and the 25,000 Italians, nor even, in spite of the steady growth of anti-German feeling, by the 53,000 Germans. The public was even ready to accept the competition which the Scotch miners had begun to feel from the large number of

---

[1] 5 Edw. 7, Cap. 18: An Act to establish organizations with a view to the provision of Employment or Assistance for Unemployed Workmen in proper cases (*Unemployed Workmen Act*, 1905). Walter Long wanted to obtain Government grants for these new public bodies, but the Chancellor of the Exchequer refused. (*Memoirs of Lord Long of Wraxall*, p. 139.)

[2] *Report of the Royal Commission on Alien Immigration*, 1903, p. 15.

Lithuanian immigrants, Catholic and Protestant. But it was impossible to view with equanimity the vast communities of Jews which had come into existence in London and in a few of the large towns, since the revival of Slavonic anti-semitism had caused a general exodus of Jews to the West.

There were 95,000 Russians and Poles in Great Britain, all, or practically all, Jews who had reached the country within the last twenty years. Of these 95,000, 54,000 had settled in London, where they had formed in the East End a large Jewish town with its peculiar customs, religious rites, and festivals, which were not those observed by Christians, and its own language. The British workmen who retired before the influx denounced the invaders' dubious morality and their greed. Those who voiced their discontent in the Press sought to prove that the application of the extremely strict laws which controlled immigration into the United States had driven back into England the scum of the Russian immigrants. It is, however, very doubtful whether the commercial morality of the East End Jews was worse than that of their native rivals. Their sexual morality, assisted by early marriages, was high. Their sobriety was admitted. In every street they occupied the public houses and brothels closed. It was their insatiable appetite for work which made them formidable. For the Jew no amount of wealth was so great that he would not seek to earn more, no wage so small that he was ashamed to work for it. This trait produced the vast fortunes whose display in Park Lane outraged British traditions, also the mass of sweated labour employed by the tailors, shoemakers and cabinet makers of Whitechapel. In consequence, an unmistakable wave of anti-semitism came over public opinion. The Act of 1900 against usury, of which we have previously spoken, was perhaps the first symptom. Here and there the opposition to the Boer War assumed a distinctly anti-semitic character, as was only to be expected since the pro-Boers refused to see in the war anything but a device of the great capitalists, too frequently Jews, to increase their wealth by facilitating the development of the Rand gold fields. And it was also the anti-semites—though they disclaimed the epithet—who were demanding that the invasion of foreign labour should be legally restricted.[1]

[1] *The Jew in London. A study of Racial Character and Present-Day Conditions, being two essays prepared for the Toynbee Trustees, by* C. Russell, R.A., *and* H. S. Lewis, M.A., *with*

England had once possessed Alien Acts, passed as measures of national defence during the war with revolutionary and imperial France. After the restoration of peace their provisions had been steadily mitigated, until nothing more was required than the production of a passport by the immigrants and a declaration by the captain of the ship of their presence on board.[1] Finally, the requirement of a passport had been removed, and the captain's declaration had been allowed to fall into abeyance. During the period of depression which preceded 1895 a Conservative Government had been struck by the inadequacy of the existing legislation, had appointed in 1886 a Parliamentary Committee to inquire into the question,[2] and from 1890 enforced the declaration of immigrants. But this was not enough to satisfy public opinion. In 1892, and again in 1894, the Trades Union Congress demanded an Act prohibiting the immigration of destitute aliens, and the Conservatives were therefore only meeting the wishes of the unions, when at the beginning of 1896 the Queen's speech announced the intention of taking measures 'against the importation of destitute aliens'. In 1898 the House of Lords debated a Bill to that effect introduced by Lord Hardwicke. Nothing came of it. Prosperity had returned and public attention was occupied in other directions. It returned to the alien question at the close of the Boer War. A Royal Commission of inquiry, appointed in 1902, reported in 1903.[3] To give effect to its recommendations the Government introduced a Bill, which was rejected. But a second Bill introduced in 1905 passed both Houses.[4] A complete reversal of the previous legislation, or rather absence of legislation, the new statute provided that in future immigrants should be allowed to land only at eight British ports specified by the Act; that in these ports officials should be appointed to control their

---

an Introduction by Canon Barnett and a Preface by the Right Hon. James Bryce, 1899. Also Arnold White (an anti-semite), *The Destitute Alien in Great Britain. A Series of Papers Dealing with the subject of Foreign Pauper Immigration. Arranged and edited by* ——, 1892. *The Modern Jew,* 1899.

[1] 6 Will. 4, Cap. 11: An Act for the Registration of Aliens and to repeal an Act passed in the seventh Year of the Reign of His Late Majesty. (*Registration of Aliens' Act,* 1836.)

[2] *Report from the Select Committee on Emigration and Immigration (Foreigners); together with the Proceedings of the Committee, Minutes of Evidence, Appendix and Index,* 1888. A further Report under the same title, 1889. See also: *Board of Trade (Alien Immigration) Reports on the Volume and Effects of Recent Immigration from Eastern Europe into the United Kingdom,* 1834.

[3] *Report of the Royal Commission on Alien Immigration, with Minutes of Evidence and Appendix,* 1903.

[4] 5 Edw. 7, Cap. 13: An Act to amend the Law with regard to aliens (*Aliens' Act,* 1905).

disembarkation and should possess the right to prohibit their landing, subject to an appeal to a court set up for that purpose; that every immigrant should be classed as 'undesirable' who could not prove that he possessed, or was in a position to procure, the means of supporting himself under satisfactory hygienic conditions; and that no alien should be admitted who was a lunatic or mentally defective, subject to any disease or infirmity such as might render him dependent on poor relief, or had been convicted of any crime for which he was liable to extradition. Not only did the statute make it more difficult for foreigners to enter Great Britain; it further empowered the Home Secretary to expel an alien from the country without any form of trial for crime, poverty, or vagrancy, or merely, if he had been proved to be living 'under insanitary conditions due to overcrowding'. For the Cabinet the passage of the Bill was a success of no slight importance, and under the circumstances extremely significant. It amounted to a defeat of that theory of free trade against which Chamberlain had launched an offensive judged with good reason premature.[1] The Cabinet had succeeded in finding a question on which the working classes were naturally protectionist. They were free traders, because a propaganda which went back half a century had accustomed them to regard protection as essentially a policy dictated by the interests of agriculture. But they were fully prepared to protect their wages against the immediate and tangible danger of an invasion of sweated labour. It was a situation which could not fail to embarrass the leaders of the Liberal and even of the Labour parties in so far as they were free traders on grounds of principle or, if you prefer, for sentimental reasons. Moreover, to prevent the immigration of destitute aliens raised the question of the 'right of asylum' of which for three centuries all those on the Continent who were victims of a political or religious persecution had taken advantage; for the persecution which was driving the Jews from Russia was both political and religious. To be sure, the Government introduced into the Bill a number of provisions with the object of allaying the apprehensions of the Opposition on this score. The latter naturally refused to accept

[1] 'England, thanks to the Huguenots, Mr. Cobden, the Slave Trade, the Jews, and an inherent incapacity for taking large views of grave national questions, has been the last country in all the world to question, or even to examine, the doctrine that uninterrupted ingress for men, women, and merchandise of other nations, is essential to, and advantageous to, her national life.' (Arnold White, *The Destitute Alien in Great Britain*, 1892, p. 2.)

them as adequate.[1] But if the Opposition obtained the support of a few Conservative idealists, such as Lord Hugh Cecil, an entire group of Liberal members who represented working-class constituencies, particularly in the east of London, voted for the Bill. Nor was the Liberal defeat retrieved later. The Aliens' Act of 1905 was the foundation stone of an entire edifice of anti-alien measures, which amounted in the end not merely to protection, but absolute prohibition.

These two Acts of 1905, the Unemployed Workmen Act and the Aliens' Act, could be regarded as the first outline of a code of legislation, at once conservative, national, and social—legislation conceived in the spirit of Bismarck, the spirit which in England had inspired Disraeli's policy. Though the cautious and sceptical Balfour possessed nothing of Disraeli's genius, and could not find the right catchwords to win the labouring masses, the fact remains that these two statutes, however timid they might be, were a bid by the Conservative Party for the support of labour, made over the head of the old Liberal Opposition. No one could prophesy the fortunes of the Labour candidates in the approaching election. But the Unionist agents presumably hoped that they would win a sufficient number of successes to divide and weaken the ranks of free trade. Paradoxical as it may appear to-day, the prospect of Labour victories at the polls caused the Cabinet and the Unionist party as a whole far less anxiety than the agitation among the Nonconformists aroused by the passing of the Education Act in 1902, of which we have said nothing since we described its beginnings, but which showed no signs of becoming less violent.

6

The English Dissenters had been ordered by their leaders to refuse payment of the Education Rate. The employment of the rate to maintain Anglican schools violated freedom of conscience. A refusal to pay it became the regular procedure. Usually, after the formal protest of a first refusal, the recalcitrant gave way. But he sometimes preferred to allow his goods to be distrained and sold by auction in the street until a sufficient sum had been obtained to discharge the rate. Occasionally, he even went to

[1] H. of C., July 10, 1905 (*Parliamentary Debates*, 4th Ser., vol. cxlix, pp. 110 sqq.).

prison, and at the end of 1904 we hear of a resister who had been in gaol three times. Between May 31, 1903, when the word of command was given, and the end of December, 1904, 37,296 summonses had been issued for refusal of the rate, 1,504 sales of furniture had been held in the open street, and in eighty cases the resister had been sent to prison.[1] No doubt, if these demonstrations were seriously intended to prevent the statute being enforced, they were ineffectual. But their constant repetition aroused public sympathy and unnerved the Government. In Wales the opposition assumed a more formidable shape. The vast majority of the population was Nonconformist, five-sixths of the Welsh members had voted against the Bill, and at the County Council elections, held in 1904, the Liberals considerably increased their majority. In fact, the body of Nonconformist sects constituted the national religion of Wales, and the Church of England could be regarded as a foreign church. All or almost all the County Councils decided, in May, 1902, not to make payments to any school over which they did not possess entire control, or in which the teachers were obliged to belong to a particular denomination—that is to say, they declined to carry out the new statute. The Board of Education, nonplussed by this general revolt, was content at first to postpone the date on which the Act came into operation until February 1, 1904. It then obtained from Parliament a further statute by which it took the place of the defaulting Councils for the purposes of the Act and deducted the amount due from the grants made to them by the central government.[2] The Councils then had recourse to the administrative tactics suggested by Lloyd George. Unable to defy the law directly, they evaded it by refusing to pay the non-provided schools the grant due under the recent legislation on various pretexts which had nothing to do with religion—for example, that they did not comply with the sanitary conditions prescribed by the law. A bitter struggle was carried on between the Board of Education and the local authorities in Wales.

At the same time a moral question arose in connection with the settlement of the Colonies just annexed in South Africa, which

---

[1] *Annual Register*, 1904, p. 203.

[2] 4 Ed. 7, Cap. 18: An Act to make provision for the case of default on the part of Local Authorities in the performance of their duties as respects elementary Schools, *Education [Local Authority Default] Act*, 1904).

aroused the indignation of humanitarians throughout the country and in particular offended what it had become customary to call 'the Nonconformist Conscience'. Throughout the war the supporters of the Government had promised that as soon as the British controlled the country the gold mines, whose development had been arrested by Kruger's hostility and unfair taxation, would enter upon a period of unexampled prosperity. Peace came, the months passed, and a protracted depression settled upon the goldfield. It was very soon evident that the attempt to persuade the British electorate that the Transvaal would repay the cost of the war must be abandoned. Then the magnates of the industry submitted to the British Cabinet a proposal, which after some hesitation[1] they accepted. They requested permission to import Asiatic labour to supplement British, which was too dear, and native, which was inadequate. An ordinance was issued by the British High Commissioner in South Africa, prescribing the terms of the indentures by which the Chinese labourers bound themselves for a certain number of years, at the expiration of which they would be sent back to China at the expense of the firm which had engaged them. It was this ordinance which aroused the indignation of the British public.

The agitation, it is true, was not dictated solely by humanitarian motives. The British workman who was suffering from unemployment, and saw himself deprived of the opportunity of obtaining on the Rand the work he could not find at home, considered that the Government had betrayed his interests by sanctioning this organized invasion of Chinese labour. It was in vain that the Ministers explained that by the very terms of their indentures the Chinese could perform only unskilled labour, that their importation therefore took work from the Kaffir, not from the British workman, and, indeed, by making it possible to open new mines would in the end increase the demand for British labour. Popular imagination was haunted by the picture of these indefatigable toilers entering the African labour market, men for whom the wage of a shilling a day was ten times the sum they earned in their native country. Australian public opinion was

---

[1] Mrs. Asquith, *Autobiography*, vol. ii, p. 65: 'On the 31st of July, 1905, Milner came to see me. He stayed for two hours. . . . He was . . . pleased with Alfred Lyttelton's work in the Colonial Office on South Africa. He told me how strongly Mr. Chamberlain opposed Chinese Labour, and that had it not been for Alfred's backing, it could never have been carried.'

equally hostile, not from any humanitarian consideration, but because it was obsessed by the yellow peril.[1]

Nevertheless, it was on humanitarian grounds that the British opponents of Chinese labour in the Transvaal based their attack. They were not hypocrites. They were actuated by those mixed motives which escape the analysis even of their subject. The British read the ordinance which was the object of so much criticism. They saw that the Chinese workmen on the Rand would be segregated in special enclosures, known as compounds, which they would not be allowed to leave without special permission, and, in any case, for not more than forty-eight hours, that they would have no right to settle in South Africa by purchasing land, and would be subject to a special penal code of extreme severity. In theory they were entitled to bring their wives. In fact, when at the end of a year there were over 27,000 in the country, the Government was obliged to admit that only two had their wives with them. A tyrannical system. And what hideous vices, unmentionable in the British Press, must prevail in those vast communities which did not contain a single woman! The hour of triumph had come for those Radical politicians and Nonconformist leaders who had risked their popularity by conducting, for almost three years, an active campaign against the Boer War. The war, they had always maintained, had been waged only to serve the interests of a group of financiers, and now, at their demand, Lord Milner was setting up in the Transvaal a system which closely resembled slavery. It is hard to realize at a distance of twenty-five years the warmth which this question of Chinese labour aroused; there were by-elections at which the Opposition gave it greater prominence than they gave even to the question of tariff reform.

Can we then speak of a revival of Dissent, which for so many years past had been thought to be on the decline? The Nonconformists certainly allowed themselves to believe it. Until the end of the Boer War, the attempts made by the National Free

[1] Richard Jebb, *Studies in Colonial Nationalism*, 1905, p. 131: 'The uncompromising hostility of the English Liberal party to the policy of Chinese labour in the Transvaal perhaps may be counted a gain to the Empire, in so far as it has unexpectedly committed the former champions of cosmopolitanism to the principle of national exclusiveness, which is expressed in national politics by the rigorous exclusion of low-wage aliens.' Graham Wallas (*Human Nature in Politics*, p. 107) shows how in the course of an agitation whose professed object was to protect the Chinese against the exploitation to which they were subject, the picture of the Chinaman became itself the object of popular dislike.

Church Council to organize throughout the country a missionary movement, like that which in the eighteenth century had been the glory of Wesleyanism, had been unsuccessful, and Australia which had invited the Council to send missioners had not found in England the preachers it wanted. But they had been found in America, and when Torrey and Alexander after a preaching tour which had taken them round the world, reached London on January 9, 1903, and were given an official reception at Exeter Hall by the leading Nonconformists, it seemed likely that the influence of their mission would be widely felt in Great Britain itself. For four months beginning in November, 1904, a young miner in South Wales named Evan Roberts, a Methodist and a poet, was awakened every night by a vision in which he believed himself in the Presence of God. He began to preach and crowds flocked to hear him. 'Conversions' multiplied; it seemed as though the Welsh 'revival'[1] might spread to the whole of the United Kingdom,[2] and the work of the Free Church Council, which since the struggle over the Education Act had begun, had been too political to please Cadbury would assume once more a purely spiritual character and would in turn spiritualize politics. 'We owe the revival of the eighteenth century', wrote a Nonconformist, 'to the rediscovery of the worth of the individual soul and its personal responsibility. The revival of the twentieth century we shall owe to the discovery of the worth of the entire

[1] For the entire movement see W. T. Stead, *The Torrey-Alexander Mission. The Story of the Men and their Methods*, 1905. *The Story of Gipsy Smith and the Missions of the National Free Church of England*, 1905. *The Revival of the West. A Narrative of Facts.* In his book on Gipsy Smith, W. T. Stead makes a significant observation (p. 132): 'Evan Roberts is a Welshman. Dr. Torrey is from New Jersey. Mr. Alexander is from Tennessee. Gipsy Smith is a Gipsy. Of the four Missioners prominent in this Revival not one is either English or Scot.'

[2] Address of the Conference to the Methodist Societies, 1905: 'Since our last Conference, events have occurred in the religious life of this country which have commanded the attention of the most worldly and sensational sections of the secular Press, and set men who care nothing about religion talking of manifestations of the Spirit of God. What has come to be known as the Welsh Revival has profoundly moved those of our societies which lie within the Principality, bringing in great crowds of new members, and quickening the spiritual life of those who have been for years within our Church. But we rejoice to be assured that this blessed awakening has touched the Saxon as well as the Celt, has shown itself unmistakably in many parts of England, and produced its natural result in the largest increase in membership that we have known for many years, and in the promise of still further increase next year. . . . We rejoice in the spontaneous uprising of a League of Intercession, in which many thousands of our ministers and people are joining. . . . We contemplate these miracles of grace with a mighty longing that they may be seen in every town and village throughout Great Britain. We believe that such an event would solve most of the perplexities over which social reformers sigh, and clear away most of the problems of belief which trouble the serious thinkers of our time.'

man and the responsibilities of the community. Our forefathers were content with a Heaven after death; we demand a Heaven here.'[1]

7

This religious agitation was calculated to cause anxiety to the Unionist leaders, and, if it had indeed been called into being by the Education Act of 1902, the measure had been a political blunder. But the centre of the revival was Wales, and whatever hopes the more enthusiastic Nonconformists might entertain, it was very doubtful whether it would develop with the same intensity in England. When the Welsh revival occurred, Cadbury had just conducted in the *Daily News*, of which at the end of 1904 he became the principal shareholder, an inquiry into the condition of the chief religious denominations in London. The inquiry had lasted from November, 1902, till June, 1903; and, if the Nonconformists could find consolation in the fact that the decline of their sects had been perhaps less marked than that of the Anglican church,[2] the results of the inquiry were none the less disquieting to a sincere Christian. While the population of the area to which the inquiry related had increased by 500,000 in about fifteen years, the number of practising Christians not only failed to show a corresponding increase but had actually fallen by 150,000, and when the entire number of persons who practised some form of Christian worship—Anglicans, Catholics, and Protestants of the Nonconformist bodies—was compared with the total population of the Metropolis, it was found that of every

---

[1] *The Religious Life of London*, ed. Richard Mudie Smith, 1904, p. 13. Cf. *Fabian Tract No. 78. Socialism and the Teaching of Christ*, by Rev. John Clifford, M.A., D.D. *With a bibliography of Christian Socialism and Particulars of existing Christian Socialist Societies*, London, August, 1897. *An address delivered by Dr. John Clifford at the Annual Meeting of the Christian Socialist League, at Westbourne Park Chapel*, February, 1895.

[2] The results of the inquiry were collected in a volume under the title: *The Religious Life of London*, edited by Richard Mudie Smith, 1904. They should be compared with the results of the inquiry which Robertson Nicoll conducted in 1886 by much rougher methods, and which can be found in *The British Weekly. A Journal of Social and Christian Progress*, November 5, 1926, December 3, 10, 17, 1886. Though the population had increased by 500,000, the number of practising Christians had decreased by about 150,000: 140,000 in the Anglican Church, 6,000 among the sects. The Nonconformists found a further source of comfort in the fact that the inquiry revealed the more 'virile' character of their religion. The number of women who attended the Anglican Churches of London in 1903 was almost twice the number of men. The number of women attending Nonconformist places of worship only exceeded the number of men by a fifth. For a brief comparison of the two inquiries see C. Sylvester Horne, *Nonconformity in the Nineteenth Century*, 1907, pp. 157 sqq.

380

hundred inhabitants of London only sixteen were practising Christians.[1] We may, therefore, repeat, on the morrow of the Boer War, what we said when we were writing of the period five or six years before, when the Anglicans believed that the victory was theirs. The characteristic feature of the age was not the irreligion (the term would be too strong) but the religious indifference of the masses. Was the Welsh revival the yeast destined to leaven this lump of apathy? It might well be doubted, and there were reasons for thinking that the popular indifference might be turned, to the advantage of the Conservatives and the Anglican Church, against the Liberals and Nonconformists. The Nonconformist lower middle class was intolerant of the vices prevalent among the lower orders. It knew what patient effort it had cost its members to rise above the level of the masses, and it was doing everything in its power to suppress the drunkenness which was so widespread in England, and too often made the labourer an irregular or careless workman. It had made use of the influence it possessed in the councils of the Liberal party to make legislation against the drink traffic an item of the Liberal programme. On the other hand, the old Tory party, which viewed with an indulgent eye the coarse pleasures that helped the lower classes to endure their poverty cheerfully, had for many years past found it good electioneering tactics to oppose the puritanism of the Radicals on this point, and financially profitable to conclude an alliance with the large breweries which monopolized the drink trade in Great Britain. The alliance had undoubtedly contributed to their victory in 1895. Until the election of 1902, the Unionist Government had been content with doing nothing which could

[1] Total population of the 29 boroughs to which the inquiry extended: 4,536,541. From this figure we must deduct 66,237 in hospitals, workhouses, prisons, etc. We are left with 4,470,304. Number of persons attending some form of religious worship: 1,003,361. But of these 1,003,361, 19 per cent went twice to church on Sunday, and were thus counted twice. The figure must therefore be reduced to 832,058, 16 per cent of the population. The investigator continues: 'The estimate allows, of course, for the inmates of institutions already referred to and includes, in addition, all who are: (1) Too young to go to church; (2) Too old; (3) Too busy; (4) Too sick. Presuming the estimate to be correct, we find that the number of those who could, if they would, go to a place of worship regularly is 2,235,152. This leaves a difference between the ideal and the actual of 1,403,101 persons, or 58 per cent, giving us an actual one out of a possible three.' (Richard Mudie Smith, *The Religious Life of London*, pp. 15–16.) Was it the same in the country? See Rider Haggard's account, based on local evidence, of the attitude of the agricultural labourers of Somersetshire. 'Except in a few instances, the clergy were not popular, and ... the trust and belief in an overruling and personal Providence was dying out of the hearts of the rising generation of villagers. Among their fathers this had been strong and constant, a living factor in their lives.' (*Rural England*, vol. I, p. 228.)

offend the publicans: an Act prohibiting the sale of intoxicants to children[1] was the only step taken to give effect to the report, itself timid, of an important Royal Commission.[2] But now when another election was imminent and the struggle would obviously be stern, the Government found itself obliged to take account of the wishes of the large brewers and distillers who were its paymasters. A decision of the courts that the licences granted by the Justices of the Peace must be renewed each year was a direct threat to their interests.[3] An important statute, passed in 1904[4] in the teeth of the violent opposition of the temperance party, transferred the right to refuse a renewal of expiring licences from individual magistrates to the bench sitting at quarter sessions and prescribed a complicated procedure. Indemnities were granted to publicans whose licences were not renewed, which were to be paid from a compensation fund, to be raised by a tax levied on all publicans and amounting to a species of mutual insurance. Should the Radical party decide to raise this issue at the next election, the Unionists were certain of victory.

The situation may be regarded from another angle. It was over the vast mass of the proletariat as occupying a position below the level of middle-class Nonconformity that Socialism was attempting to establish a hold. The more far-sighted and zealous Nonconformists—Cadbury and his group—perceived the danger, and, therefore, as we have seen, gave their religious activities a markedly social, we might even say a Socialist, character. The secretaries of the unions which had taken control of the new Labour party were usually active members of the Protestant sects. Nevertheless, these religious trade unionists had been forced almost against their will into the Labour movement by the judg-

[1] I Edw. 7, Cap. 27: An Act to Prevent the Sale of Intoxicating Liquors to Children. (*Intoxicating Liquors [Sale to Children] Act*, 1901): We must, however, mention another statute passed in 1898 which is concerned with the drink question (60 & 61 Vict., Cap. 60: An Act to Provide for the Treatment of Habitual Drunkards). It defined 'the criminal Habitual Drunkard', and gave magistrates power to sentence him on summary conviction to be confined in an Inebriate Reformatory.

[2] A Royal Commission appointed to inquire into the operation and administration of the Laws relating to the Sale of Intoxicating Liquors, and to examine and report upon the proposals that may be made for amending the aforesaid Laws in the public interest, due regard being had to the rights of individuals. *First and Second Reports*, 1897. *Third and Fourth Reports*, 1898. *Final Report*, 1899.

[3] See the final decision of the House of Lords, March 20, 1891, in the case of Sharpe *versus* Wakefield, and for the state of the law and its interpretation by the courts, an instructive leader in *The Times*, March 21, 1891.

[4] 4 Edw. 7, Cap. 23: An Act to amend the Licensing Acts 1828 to 1902, in respect to the Extraction of Licences and the Grant of New Licences (*Licensing Act*, 1904).

ment of the law lords which threatened their professional interests. Nor could anything remove the essential incompatibility between the traditional individualism of Protestant Nonconformity and the new doctrine which asserted the right of all men, without exception, to the happiness which under the conditions of modern society the harsh law of competition made the monopoly of a privileged few. It was because they were aware of it that the Conservative party made advances to the working classes over the heads of the middle-class Liberals and Radicals. The higher Anglican clergy seem during the early years of the century to have felt more convinced than ever that this was the policy the situation demanded. They hoped to prove that the Anglican Church, in contrast with a narrow sectarianism, was the Church of the entire nation without distinction of classes. The Unemployed Workmen Bill of 1905 was opposed by leading Conservatives, employers, and even members of the Cabinet. It would perhaps have been defeated, if the Bishops, by giving it their support, had not aroused the politicians from their apathy.

And had the Education Act itself, which evoked the wrath of the Nonconformists, really, as they maintained, stirred the nation to its depths? Even in Wales, where there was every appearance of a national revolt against the statute, many were looking for a compromise. The Bishop of Saint-Asaph proposed a compromise, and Lloyd George was in private negotiation with him. In England, whatever noise the 'passive resisters' made, it could not be denied that in the vast majority of cases the execution of the new statute encountered no resistance. If the farmers were discontented, it was from fear of an increase in the rates, rather than from religious scruples. For four days out of five the religious instruction given in the Anglican schools was purely biblical, and on the one day when the Catechism was taught, unless the teacher happened to be a militant high churchman, there was usually nothing in the instruction given to the children at which a Wesleyan could take offence. Moreover, in the majority of cases the lesson was a farce,[1] and if Sir John Gorst on the Conservative side gave offence to

---

[1] Sir George William Kekewich, *Education Department*, p. 170: 'On his return he (the Inspector) reported that the Catechism was said by heart by all the children, who usually gabbled it together, and that the rest of the religious instruction, almost without exception, was of an undenominational character, such as might be given in any Board School, and that that part of the instruction alone was of any value to the children. He said: If this is what the denominationalists are fighting for, they are fighting for a shadow.'

the Church by expressing the opinion that the religious instruction given in the board schools was of better quality than that given in the denominational,[1] Augustine Birrell on the Liberal side gave equal offence to the Nonconformists by remarking that the contest was being waged above the heads of a host of completely indifferent parents.[2]

London had been omitted from the Act of 1902. In 1903, the Government decided to extend its operation to the metropolis, and, if on an important point they were compelled to yield to the demands of the Opposition and place the schools under the control, not of the borough councils, many of which were Conservative, but of the County Council, a predominantly Radical body, nevertheless the principle laid down in 1902 won a further triumph. The most famous British School Board disappeared and the denominational schools of London were given a share of the rates.[3] But even if parents and voters did not take the battle between the Church and the sects seriously, would not the necessity of altering the Act of 1902 to keep pledges given to the Nonconformist minority create a serious difficulty for the Liberal party when it returned to power? Perhaps even that minority might not persist in its present demands. In 1870, the Nonconformists had opposed the provisions of the Bill passed by Gladstone's Government because they wanted religious instruction to be completely divorced from the secular education given in the elementary schools. Today they regarded the Act of 1870 as the charter of their freedom. Who could say that the day would never come when they would be defending the Act of 1902 against a further aggression by the Anglican Church?

[1] H. of C., June 17, 1898 (*Parliamentary Debates*, 4th Ser., vol. lix, p. 598). Further H. of C., April 1, 1896: 'I did not enumerate the religious difficulty as one which had to be surmounted by Parliament, because the religious difficulty is no difficulty at all in the schools. . . . It is a difficulty which flourishes in Parliament and on the platform' (ibid., vol. xxxix, p. 543).

[2] H. of C., June 14, 1900 (ibid., vol. lxxxiv, pp. 64 sqq.). Cf. H. of C., May 8, 1902, Talbot's speech: 'No doubt, there are schools under the control of the clergy for the simple reason that they are, very often, the only people in the neighbourhood who take any interest in education' (ibid., vol. cvii, p. 1124).

[3] 3 Edw. 7, Cap. 24: An Act to extend and adapt the Education Act, 1902, to London (*Education [London] Act*, 1903).

Ireland was another source of anxiety to the Government. To be sure their difficulties were not to be compared with the difficulty the Irish question had caused the Liberal party twenty years before. On the contrary, on many occasions it seemed that the policy of moderate reform and conciliation which since 1895 the Government had attempted to pursue had proved decidedly successful. It had however been attended with several trying disappointments. The story must be briefly told.[1]

When the Conservatives took office in 1895, they found Ireland sunk in a disillusionment in striking contrast with the revolutionary fervour which ten years before had conferred on Parnell a species of moral dictatorship on the other side of St. George's Channel, a position which had in turn given him a firm hold over the entire Liberal party. Parnell had died in 1891, a year after he had seen his political career ruined in a day as the result of a domestic scandal. At present the Nationalist party was split into fragments. There were first of all the Parnellites, a handful of men who under the leadership of a clever parliamentarian, John Redmond, remained in spite of all anathemas, faithful to the memory of their hero. But even those, the vast majority of the party, who, in obedience to the orders of the Irish hierarchy, had broken with Parnell, were themselves divided, and within the ranks of this 'clerical' party a split would shortly take place between the followers of John Dillon and the even more 'clerical' followers of T. M. Healy. These warring leaders, whatever their

[1] The best work dealing with this period of Irish history as a whole is the excellent work by L. Paul Dubois, *L'Irelande contemporaine et la Question irlandaise*, 1907. (It must, however, be remembered that the writer, though always basing his account on reliable evidence, does not claim to be impartial and writes throughout from the standpoint of Catholicism and the most extreme Irish nationalism.) William O'Brien's book entitled *An Olive Branch in Ireland and its History*, 1910, is a valuable account of the nationalist agitation as seen from within, told by one of the agitators. For the policy of peaceful reform made possible by a reconciliation of the opposing parties see Sir Horace Plunkett, *Ireland in the New Century*, also the Right Hon. the Earl of Dunraven, *The Outlook in Ireland: The Case for Devolution and Conciliation*, 1907. For interesting details, related by a former official, of the more intimate aspect of Irish Government under Arthur Balfour, Gerald Balfour, George Wyndham, and Walter Long, see *Memories: Wise and Unwise*, by the Right Hon. Sir Henry Robinson, 1923 (also by the same author, *Further Memories of Irish Life*, 1924). See also J. W. Mackail and Guy Wyndham, *Life and Letters of George Wyndham*, 1925. And the student will find a picture, conceived in the spirit of mockery and caricature, of the entire Irish movement at the opening of the century in George Moore's trilogy, *Salve*, *Ave*, and *Vale*. (The author when he wrote these volumes was a 'renegade' from the movement.)

intellectual gifts, produced a bad impression on the public by quarrels in which self-interest and self-assertion played too large a part. The intransigence of even the most extreme among them had come to be nothing more than a pose; Parliamentary life had exercised on their revolutionary creed the solvent effect it inevitably produces. They had lost the taste for martyrdom, and were resolved at all costs never to return to prison. Moreover, Home Rule, with which all their hopes seemed bound up, had to all appearance received its death blow when the Liberals failed to secure the assent of the Lords to their Bill of 1893, and the British electorate had ratified the verdict of the Upper House. What had been gained by fifteen years' propaganda? The entire Irish nation was out of humour with politics.

A group of Irishmen, nearly all Protestants and opposed to Home Rule, but animated by a sincere and deep love of their country, believed that this condition of public feeling might be turned to good use. They invited their fellow countrymen to examine their own consciences and ask themselves whether, if some unlooked-for turn of events gave them a separate Parliament in Dublin, the intemperance, indolence, and lack of initiative which made them at present bad workmen, bad farmers, bad men of business, would not make them bad citizens incapable of conducting the affairs of their country decently. They urged them to educate themselves in the duties of citizenship and to begin by a professional education. On these terms alone would they be worthy of the Home Rule for which they were asking, and possibly—that was the *arrière-pensée* of the leaders of the movement—when they had once become rich as the result of their work, and were proud of an Ireland which had achieved prosperity under the existing system of government, they would become as content, as the Scotch and Welsh were now, to be 'united' with the Queen's other subjects under the authority of a single Parliament at Westminster.

Horace Plunkett, a Protestant, though the old Irish family to which he belonged possessed two Catholic branches, led this movement which sought to reconcile the two parties and creeds in the pursuit of a common ideal of economic reform. He watched with admiration the results the Danish farmers had achieved by co-operative agriculture. He was also interested in the Credit Associations organized in Germany upon the Raiffeisen system, and which, to quote Plunkett's own words, 'performed the apparent miracle of giving solvency to a community composed almost entirely of insolvent individuals'.[1] The success which attended his propaganda in the country districts of Ireland was a sign of the times. The movement, begun in 1889, had grown sufficiently five years later to make it possible to found in Dublin an Irish Agricultural Organization Society, of which he was President, to correlate and guide the activities of the local co-operative societies. About the same time, a group of Irishmen connected by ties of every kind with the founders of the Irish Agricultural Society formed another project. They found it deplorable that Ireland, so anxious to be independent of England politically, had allowed her culture to be completely Anglicized. Their programme was not the constitutional, but the intellectual enfranchisement of their country. Yeats, Edward Martyn, George Moore, and Lady Gregory determined to create an Irish theatre in Dublin. To begin with it would be an English-speaking theatre. But these men of letters had already conceived a more ambitious design. Gaelic was still spoken in the West of Ireland. But of the 4,500,000 inhabitants of the island, there were barely 600,000 Gaelic speakers, and little more than 20,000 who could not speak English. Why not teach this dying language to the peasants who were forgetting it, and while teaching it revive all those old customs and festivals, that native poetry, which would invest country life with a new charm, specifically Irish? To carry out this programme the Gaelic League was founded in 1893. The Catholic Nationalists flocked to join it, but the statutes expressly forbade political or religious discussions. The founders of the League, and in particular its president, Douglas Hyde, were Protestants, and the religion of the poet, G. W. Russell, who was the soul of the movement, was a heterodox belief bordering on theosophy.

The movement initiated by Plunkett acquired a new momentum after the general election of 1895, which completed the rout of the Irish-Radical combination. During the recess which followed he called a committee, which therefore took the name of the Recess Committee. Its object was to enable Irishmen of the most widely different shades of opinion to agree on a programme capable of immediate realization. The anti-Parnellites refused to

---

[1] Sir Horace Plunkett, *Ireland in the New Century*, p. 195.

join the Committee, but the head of the Parnellite section, John Redmond, accepted Plunkett's invitation. Redmond had decided to adopt for the present the policy of an understanding with the Tories, in opposition to the anti-Parnellites, whose policy of subservience to the Liberals he denounced as futile. A year later, the work of the Committee resulted in the publication of a report which advised the institution of a new government department, to be assisted by a consultative council, and provided with sufficient funds to make grants for the encouragement of Irish agriculture and industries.[1] The suggestion immediately attracted the new Irish secretary, Gerald Balfour, Arthur Balfour's brother. It was obviously popular with the Irish public. If it proved successful, it would place the Liberal Opposition at home and the official Nationalist party in Ireland in a difficult position: to use a current phrase, it would 'kill Home Rule with kindness'.

Gerald Balfour indeed ended by giving the members of the Recess Committee even more than they had dared to ask. The Queen's speech in February, 1898, declared the Government's intention to introduce a Bill, 'for the organization of a system of local government in Ireland substantially similar to that which, within the last few years, has been established in Great Britain'. The measure provided for the establishment of county councils, district councils, and boards of guardians to administer the Poor Law, elected on a democratic basis after the English model. It was passed after a brief debate by both Houses and without amendments of any importance,[2] so that the following year the Government was able to make use of the new Irish county councils to organize the Department of Agriculture and other Industries and Technical Instruction in Ireland on a plan hitherto foreign to the administration of the country.[3] The Department was assisted by a Council of Agriculture, of whom one-third were nominees

---

[1] Sir Horace Plunkett, *Ireland in the New Century*, chap. viii, pp. 210 sqq.
[2] 61 & 62 Vict., Cap. 37: An Act for amending the Law relating to Local Government in Ireland and for other purposes connected therewith (*Local Government [Ireland] Act*, 1895). For the manner in which the Bill was passed see the interesting details related by Sir Henry Robinson: *Memories: Wise and Unwise*, pp. 125–6.
[3] 62 & 63 Vict., Cap. 50: An Act for establishing a Department of Agriculture and other Industries and Technical Instruction in Ireland; and for other purposes connected therewith (*Agriculture and Technical Instruction [Ireland] Act*, 1899). The Government was authorized to transfer to the new Department by an Order in Council such further administrative functions as it might judge expedient. Those responsible for the statute had taken as their model certain Continental, especially Belgian, institutions (B. Holland, *Imperium et Libertas*, p. 247).

of the Department itself, two-thirds elected by the County Councils. It consisted of two Boards, the Agricultural Board and the Board of Technical Instruction, the majority of whose members were elected by the Council of Agriculture or other representative bodies. Thus in this new branch of the administration a very large place was given to the elective principle. Was this 'to kill Home Rule with kindness', or to give Ireland the first instalment of Home Rule? The spirit in which the Government desired the new legislation to be carried out became evident when Plunkett was appointed vice-president of the Department, and for his secretary was given a certain T. P. Gill, an Irish Nationalist who had formerly taken an active part in executing the revolutionary 'plan of campaign' devised by Parnell and his subordinates.

9

Then the difficulties of the Unionist Government began. Protestant Ulster rose against the new policy. At the general election of 1900 the uncompromising opponents of Home Rule set up a candidate in one of the Dublin constituencies against Plunkett, and were only too pleased when by this manoeuvre they got a Catholic Nationalist elected in his stead. It was, however, very difficult for a Conservative Administration to govern Ireland against the express wishes of these extremists. Lord Salisbury and Balfour took advantage of the rearrangement of the Cabinet which took place in November to get rid of a certain T. W. Russell, the Parliamentary Secretary of the Board of Trade, an Ulster Protestant who, during the Election, had declared war too frankly on the Irish landlords, and to replace Gerald Balfour, as Secretary for Ireland, by George Wyndham. It was only to be expected that the old Protestant party should take alarm when they saw a Conservative Government imperil the traditional system of English domination, and the Government Offices in Dublin invaded by those Irish Catholics whom they regarded as both incompetent and disloyal. And the Conservative party could not fail to be irritated by the anti-patriotic attitude the Irish members displayed so blatantly throughout the Boer War. But a new factor now came into operation which further increased the apprehension felt by the Unionists. It was the movement which William O'Brien had just launched by the foundation in January, 1898, of the United Irish League.

In Ireland the political was complicated by an agrarian question, and, whereas the former had still to be solved, the latter had already received, when the Conservatives took office in 1895, a partial solution. Indeed, two steps had already been taken. On the one hand, Gladstone by his Land Act of 1881[1] had subjected landed property to the principle of dual ownership. Every tenant was given the right to demand that the maximum rent his landlord could ask should be fixed by arbitrators set up by the statute. The Act prescribed that their decision should be revised every fifteen years. And, on the other hand, between 1885 and 1892 the Conservatives had begun a system of land purchase for the benefit of the peasantry.[2] The Ashbourne Acts authorized the Treasury to advance to any landlord willing to sell, the entire purchase price (on an average seventeen and a half times the rent), the amount to be repayable by the purchaser in forty annual payments of 4 per cent of the cost of purchase. And, at the same time, in the poor districts of the West the Government purchased certain large estates under pasture which it divided into arable farms of small size. On these the peasants of the neighbourhood who were starving on plots too tiny to support them were settled.[3] But the co-existence of the two systems—dual ownership and State-assisted land purchase—introduced intolerable consequences.

Even after its reduction by the arbitrators the rent the average Irish tenant was obliged to pay was still higher than the sum the tenant purchasers paid the Treasury for a limited term of years, at the end of which they became owners of the land. Should these tenants be told to wait in patience until the day came when by the gradual operation of the existing laws they could all obtain possession of the land they cultivated? The Treasury granted only a limited amount of credit for land purchase every

---

[1] 44 & 45 Vict., Cap. 49: An Act to further amend the Law relating to the Occupation and Ownership of Land in Ireland and for other purposes relating thereto (*Land Law [Ireland] Act*, 1881).

[2] 48 & 49 Vict., Cap. 73: An Act to provide greater facilities for the Sale of Land to occupying Tenants in Ireland (*Purchase of Land [Ireland] Act*, 1885)—51 & 52 Vict., Cap. 49: An Act further to facilitate the Purchase of Land in Ireland by increasing the amount applicable for that purpose by the Land Commission (*Purchase of Land [Ireland] Amendment Act*, 1888). Further amended by 52 & 53 Vict., Cap. 13.

[3] This was the work of the Congested Districts Board set up by an Act of 1891 (54 & 55 Vict., Cap. 48, sec. 41). The congested districts were those rural districts in which the cultivators were too many for the land under their cultivation. This does not mean that those districts, situated in the West of Ireland, were over-populated in relation to the total area.

year; and, since it had adopted the system of paying the landlords, not in cash, but in Consols, the execution of the agrarian legislation had met with unexpected difficulties. From the beginning of the Boer War Consols had fallen, were quoted at 8 or 9 points below par, and the landlords were no longer willing to be paid with stock which had depreciated. It was estimated that up to the beginning of 1903 the entire number of tenant-owners brought into existence since the legislation had been passed did not amount to 74,000.[1] At this rate a century must pass before the transference of ownership was complete. It was to quicken the pace that William O'Brien founded in 1898 in the west of Ireland his agrarian 'League'. Its programme was the immediate extension to the whole of Ireland of the two principles laid down by the Conservative legislature: the division of the great pasture estates, the purchase of arable land. That disgust for the politician which had favoured the moderate movement inaugurated by Plunkett, favoured O'Brien's revolutionary agitation; he soon saw the branches of his League multiply all over the country. He proved the strength of the forces at his command when the moment came to elect the first County Councillors. Redmond had shared Plunkett's desire that the gentry should be duly represented in the new Councils, but he was faced by the opposition, not so much of the organized Nationalist party, as of O'Brien and his leaguers, who in every district packed the councils with their revolutionary candidates, small shopkeepers, small farmers and petty publicans.[2] O'Brien won a second victory when Parnellites and anti-Parnellites were reconciled in the reunited Nationalist Party led by Redmond. It was a proof that the new agitation had made the

[1] Louis-Paul Dubois, *L'Irlande contemporaine et la Question irlandaise*, p. 267.

[2] *Annual Register*, 1899, p. 210. Ibid., p. 240: 'The landed proprietors did not as a class stand aside from the elections for the new councils, but as a class they were, where they offered themselves, rejected by the electors. In Connaught and Munster together only about a dozen country gentleman were chosen, the fatal objection to their candidature being more probably their Unionist politics than their possession of land.' W. O'Brien, *An Olive Branch*, p. 111: 'The candidates of the United Irish League headed the polls in twenty-six out of the twenty-eight county divisions of Mayo, and in all the vast extent of the county of Cork not a single County Councillor who was not a Nationalist was returned.' Sir Henry Robinson, *Memories: Wise and Unwise*, p. 129: 'In the very remote parts of Mayo and Galway the small farmers were all on the same dead level of poverty, and it was, therefore, difficult to find local candidates for County Councillorships who could pay the expense of journeying to and from the county town to attend meetings of the Council. In such cases the people were represented by local shopkeepers from a distance who knew little about them. In other instances local candidates could not be persuaded to come forward, because they were ashamed to appear before the councils in ragged attire.'

old quarrels out of date. He then launched in good earnest a campaign to compel the landlords to sell their land and cut up their pasture. There was no violence in the strict sense but a refusal to pay rent and the boycotting of every Irishman who rented pasture land were sufficient to paralyse effectively the economic life of the country. After long months of hesitation the Government finally decided to put into force, in six counties, the Crimes Act of 1887, which empowered them to suspend the normal operation of the law. The landlords formed a Land Trust with a capital of £100,000 to prosecute the leaders of the revolutionary movement.[1] In the summer of 1902 it seemed as though Ireland was on the verge of another agrarian war.

10

But it was only seeming. In September the landlords proposed a conference at which representatives of both parties should discuss the question of land purchase in a friendly spirit. Redmond and O'Brien were invited to attend. Both accepted. Redmond's acceptance was not surprising; he had been a member of the Recess Committee and the Conference continued its policy. But O'Brien's acceptance and the fact that the vast majority of the Nationalists approved their leader's decision showed the extent to which the country was weary not only of politicians, but of revolutionaries. And on their side the landlords as a body supported the experiment. The Conference which met in December and was called, after its President, Lord Dunraven, the Dunraven Conference, would not accept the principle of compulsory purchase. But what did it matter that the legislation proposed avoided compulsion if effective measures were taken to make purchase universal? All parties would be satisfied if the State bought the land from the big landlords at a price acceptable to them and paid immediately in cash, and was repaid by the small farmers by a series of annual payments of a figure such that the total sum repaid was less than the cost of purchase. The only sufferer would be the British taxpayer, since the difference would come out of his pocket. But this was perhaps equitable if the Royal Commission appointed in 1894 to investigate the financial relations between Great Britain and Ireland was right in its estimate that Ireland

1 W. O'Brien, *An Olive Branch*, p. 139.

paid every year £2,750,000 more than her fair share of taxation.[1] And it was quite possible that in the end the British taxpayer might benefit, even financially. The reconciliation of classes and the pacification of the country districts would make it possible to save the enormous sums now spent on keeping order in Ireland.

The Government gave the Conference its blessing. The Chief Secretary, who had succeeded Gerald Balfour at the end of 1900, was one of those attractive amateurs by whom England at the end of the nineteenth century, faithful to her aristocratic traditions, still liked to be governed. George Wyndham was proud to trace his descent from French and Irish ancestors. An admirer and translator of the French poets, he was not subject to those anti-Catholic and anti-Celtic prejudices which should have made the descendants of the Roundheads, rather than the descendants of the Cavaliers, the opponents of Irish Home Rule. After a year in his new Office he had obviously made up his mind not to reverse but continue Gerald Balfour's policy by introducing a Land Bill and giving Ireland a Catholic University.[2] He hesitated for a long time before he made up his mind in the spring of 1902 to declare war on the United Irish League, and at the very moment when he began his attack on the League, he introduced a Land Bill, which, though it was thrown out, proved his conciliatory intentions. In 1903, he introduced another Land Bill which passed both Houses, the more easily because public attention was engrossed by Chamberlain's widely-advertised campaign for Tariff Reform.[3]

[1] Royal Commission on the Financial Relations between Great Britain and Ireland. *Final Report* by H.M.'s Commissioners appointed to inquire into the Financial Relations between Great Britain and Ireland. The draft report drawn up by the Chairman of the Commission, H. C. E. Childers, estimated the excess payment at no more than two million and a half (*Draft Report*, p. 293). The final report, while giving the estimate quoted in the text, admits that it could be reduced by 'taking into account as a set-off the special expenditure out of Imperial Revenue in aid of local burdens in Ireland'.

[2] He wrote to a friend on October 26: '. . . I don't like the idea of Ireland, but would work there and could be useful.' (J. W. Mackail and Guy Wyndham, *Life and Letters of George Wyndham*, vol. i, p. 75.) Wilfred Scawen Blunt notes in his diary for November 1: 'He' (George Wyndham) 'had some chance of being shifted to Ireland and he said I must write and tell him what I thought of it if it came to pass. I said the Irish remembered he was Lord Edward Fitzgerald's great-grandson, and it would be something to start on, but would not carry him far.' (*My Diaries*, vol. i, p. 460.) Two months later he wrote to his mother: 'I want to smash the agitation, introduce a Land Bill, get money for a Harbour Fishing policy in the West, and float a Catholic University.' (J. W. Mackail and Guy Wyndham, *Life and Letters of George Wyndham*, vol. i, p. 75.)

[3] 3 Edw. 7, Cap. 37: An Act to amend the Law relating to the occupation and ownership of Land in Ireland and for other purposes relating thereto and to amend the Labourers' (Ireland) Acts (*Irish Land Act*, 1903).

The statute of 1903 provided that the land should no longer be purchased piecemeal by individual tenants, but *en bloc* as entire estates. The purchase price would be paid to the landlords in cash, and no longer as under the Act of 1891 in bonds. The tenant would pay for his land by yearly payments of $3\frac{1}{4}$ per cent to be continued for sixty-eight years. To the purchase price the Treasury added a bounty of 12 per cent. To defray the cost of the scheme, the Treasury provided a larger sum than before, funds which would not be exhausted until all the land in question had been purchased. It undertook to issue land stock to the value of £5,000,000 a year bearing interest at $2\frac{3}{4}$ per cent, the loan (interest and capital) to be secured on the payments due from the tenants.

Inevitably, the Act failed to satisfy everybody. The leaders of the malcontents were Michael Davitt, a former agitator, whose Socialism disliked a law designed to hand over the soil of Ireland to 400,000 peasant proprietors, and John Dillon, whose habitual tactics as a member of the Opposition had been completely checkmated by the policy of conciliation, and who was perhaps annoyed at finding himself thrust into the background behind Redmond and O'Brien. They complained that the new statute did not settle the problem of cutting up the pasture land to which the United Irish League and, later, the Dunraven Conference had attached supreme importance. In fact, the two clauses of the Act of 1903 which dealt with the matter had been introduced only for form's sake, and were never carried out. The malcontents further complained that the tenants were being obliged to pay a higher price than under the previous legislation. But was this because the Act had given the landlords too favourable terms? Was not the true reason the rapid rise in the price of land, the keen competition among the tenants to buy it—that is to say, was it not the very success of the Act which made it difficult to carry out? The demand for land was so heavy that already in 1904 the funds provided by the statute were insufficient to satisfy it. Between November 1, 1903, and March 31, 1906, the number of purchases concluded amounted to 85,638. At this rate the entire soil of Ireland would have changed hands in ten years' time.[1]

In the summer of 1903 I visited Ireland and travelled every-

[1] L. Paul Dubois, *L'Irlande contemporaine et la Question irlandaise*, p. 278.

where up and down the country. I remember the contentment which prevailed everywhere, the warm welcome given to King Edward in August, the sorrowful admissions of former agitators, compelled to live in the obscurity of their villages on the memories of their old struggles, that Irish patriotism had apparently found a new outlet. I remember the satisfaction with which the members of the Department and the Board, Catholic and Protestant, working side by side in perfect friendliness, told me of their successful attempts to teach the Irish on the coast deep-sea fishing and the Irish of the interior bee-keeping and weaving. At the end of the year the Irish Agricultural Organization Society could point to 800 societies founded under its ægis, among them 200 land banks and 360 co-operative dairies. Its total membership was 80,000 representing roughly 400,000 persons. Its operations for the year 1903 represented a sum of £2,000,000.[1]

II

But at this very moment fresh difficulties arose. Wyndham had intended to complete the Land Act of 1903 which had been devised in the interest of the farmer by a Labourers' Act to assist the agricultural labourer by facilitating the purchase by the local authorities of the required sites to build cottages. But the Bill introduced in 1904 was dropped before it reached the Committee stage. Wyndham had also hoped to give the Irish Catholics the University they had desired so long. It had been his intention ever since he had accepted the responsibility for the government of Ireland, and it had been for a long while past Balfour's intention. Relations between the English Conservatives and the Catholic Church were better than they had ever been. The Unionist Party had based their administration of Ireland on the principle of securing, as far as possible, the goodwill of the Catholic hierarchy, and the Bishops had finally adopted a policy of compromise, giving a merely formal support to the Nationalists, and to the Government the willing co-operation it earnestly sought. Was it not time to reward their goodwill by a generous concession? A Royal Commission was appointed in 1901 to inquire into the question. Unfortunately it was obliged to recognize the difficulty of solving the problem without arousing on

[1] Horace Plunkett, *Ireland in the New Century*, p. 192.

one side or the other inflexible opposition.[1] About the middle of
the nineteenth century the Catholics had attempted to found at
their own expense a University whose reputation would throw
into the shade the old Protestant University of Dublin, Trinity
College. Newman had been the first rector. The project had
failed and its sole relic was Dublin University College with a
negligible body of 200 students. Why not revive this College by
giving it a State grant and the same official status as Trinity?
The solution was flatly rejected by the Protestants and abandoned
as impracticable by Wyndham himself. There was also in Ireland
a Royal University, undenominational in character and assisted
by the State, which granted degrees and consisted of three
colleges, where the teaching was also undenominational, at
Belfast, Galway, and Cork. Catholics would have nothing to do
with these colleges because of their undenominational character.
Could not a fourth college be added to the existing three, denominational and Catholic? The Commission had reported in favour
of the suggestion, provided the assent of the hierarchy could be
obtained,[2] and Wyndham had persuaded himself that it would be
given.[3] He was disappointed. The Catholics refused to be satisfied
with a denominational college which formed part of an undenominational University. The Government, therefore, recognized
that on the question of the reform of higher education in Ireland
it had reached an *impasse*, when to its intense annoyance it found
itself outstripped and compromised on another question by the
enthusiasm of those in Ireland who were engaged in carrying
out its policy.

The Land Conference, proud of the rapid success which had
attended its efforts, decided to remodel its constitution and
become a permanent body under the title of the Irish Reform
Association. It would be the task of the Association to examine
what measures remained to be taken to effect a peaceful and amicable solution of the problems still outstanding. Its President was,
as before, Lord Dunraven, a large Irish landowner who at that
time occupied in the public eye the position held by Plunkett ten
years before. Formed in August, 1904, the Association issued on

---

[1] Royal Commission on University Education in Ireland, 1901. *First, Second, Third
Reports and Evidence*, 1902. *Final Report of the Commissioners*, 1903.
[2] Royal Commission on University Education in Ireland, *Final Report*, p. 37.
[3] George Wyndham to Arthur Balfour (J. W. Mackail and Guy Wyndham, *Life and
Letters of George Wyndham*, vol. ii, pp. 467–8).

September 26 a report[1] in which it proposed the institution of an Irish Financial Council, half of whose members should be elected. The Council would manage all purely Irish expenditure and possess the right to pass Bills affecting Ireland alone. In future Parliament might, if it thought fit, delegate further functions to an assembly to be composed of Irish peers and members of the new council. The proposal fell far short of the Home Rule demanded by the Nationalists, but it went far beyond the Agricultural Council of 1899. This programme of 'devolution'[2] aroused the instant alarm of the uncompromising opponents of Home Rule. It alarmed Wyndham, who disavowed the Report two days after it was published. But the disavowal did not save him. A year earlier he had chosen as his under-secretary an Irish Catholic of Nationalist opinions, Sir Antony MacDonnell, who, when he was given the post, was occupying an important position in the Government of India. Sir Antony had encouraged Lord Dunraven's undertaking. If Wyndham were not actually his accomplice, he was at least guilty of gross negligence in allowing a subordinate to pursue a policy of which he disapproved.[3] In March, 1905, he resigned. The old Tories, encouraged by this initial success, attempted to push their advantage further. It was, they maintained, nothing short of a scandal that the Irish representation in Parliament had remained for a century practically the same, both absolutely and proportionally, whereas the population of Ireland was now only a tenth, instead of a third, of the entire population of the United Kingdom.[4] The Government

[1] The programme of the Irish Reform Association is printed in full as an appendix to Lord Dunraven's work, *The Outlook in Ireland: the Case for Devolution and Conciliation,* 1907, pp. 271 sqq.

[2] Programme of August 31: 'While firmly maintaining that the Parliamentary Union between Great Britain and Ireland is essential to the political stability of the Empire, and to the prosperity of the two islands, we believe that such Union is compatible with the devolution to Ireland of a larger measure of local government than she now possesses.' The term was borrowed from Chamberlain, who in 1886, when he had not yet decided to oppose every form or degree of Home Rule, proposed as his aim: 'To relieve the Imperial Parliament by devolution of Irish local business and to set it free for other and more important work.' (*Address* to the electors of West Birmingham, June 11, 1886; *Home Rule and the Irish Question,* by the Right Hon. J. Chamberlain, 1887, p. 131.)

[3] See the debate H. of C., February 22, 1905 (*Parliamentary Debates,* 4th Ser., vol. cxli, pp. 964 sqq.). J. W. Mackail and Guy Wyndham, *Life and Letters of George Wyndham,* vol. ii, pp. 87 sqq. Lord Dunraven, *The Outlook in Ireland,* appendix v, pp. 288 sqq. Sir Henry Robinson, *Memoirs,* pp. 144 sqq., 162-3.

[4] At the census of 1821 the population of Ireland was 6,801,827, the population of the United Kingdom 20,893,584—a proportion of 32.5 per cent. And Ireland returned to the House of Commons 100 out of 658 members. At the census of 1901 the population of

promised to introduce, during the session of 1906, a Redistribution
Bill to bestow additional representatives on constituencies with
an excessive population, take representatives from the small
constituencies, and reduce the representation of Ireland by a fifth,
possibly by a quarter.[1]

Had the policy of conciliation, practised with success on two
occasions since 1895, definitely failed? In the first place we must
remember that in 1905 the question presented hardly more than
an academic interest. For the days of the Tory Government were
numbered. If by a *tour de force* it managed to reach a sixth session
in January, 1906, it would inevitably be cut short by a dissolution.
At the next election the Liberals would be returned and the Irish
question, as it was left by the Unionists, might well prove a
difficult inheritance for their successors. For there could be no
doubt that on the question of denominational teaching in the
schools the Irish sided with the Tories against the Radical Nonconformists. As for free trade, when Redmond voted and ordered
his followers to vote against the Government, he was careful to
explain that he did so only from considerations of Parliamentary
tactics and that on this question the Irish people did not share the
convictions of the English Liberals.[2] The Irish were therefore
likely to prove awkward allies for the Liberals, more awkward
allies than the uncompromising Orangemen of Ulster and Dublin
had been for the Unionists ten years earlier. They would not be
prepared to accept from their hands the half measures which
satisfied them when offered by the Conservatives. They would
be content with nothing less than complete Home Rule. But
everything seemed to show that British public opinion had never
been less ready to grant it. Possibly the Conservative leaders
cherished the hope that the Irish question would provide them
with the means of retrieving their defeat. They were careful not
to break definitively with the new methods inaugurated at
Dublin by Gerald Balfour and George Wyndham. If the latter
resigned, the Lord-Lieutenant, Lord Dudley, who, as everyone
knew, was in sympathy with Lord Dunraven's programme,
remained at his post. And, what was more surprising, Sir Antony

Ireland was 4,443,370, the population of the United Kingdom 41,546,598, a proportion
of 10.69 per cent. And Ireland returned 103 members out of 670.
[1] *Annual Register*, 1905, pp. 193–194. H. of C., July 17, 1905 (*Parliamentary Debates*,
4th Ser., vol. cxlix, pp. 896 sqq.).
[2] H. of C., February 15, 1904 (ibid., vol. cxxix, pp. 1421 sqq.).

MacDonnell, whose indiscretions had occasioned the revolt of the Ulster fanatics and Wyndham's fall, was kept in his position under the new chief secretary, Walter Long.

II THE REVERSAL OF THE ENTENTES

I

In regard to the social, religious and Irish questions we have just discussed, the Unionist leaders, between 1902 and 1905, were watching the currents of public opinion on the alert to detect or imagine favourable omens. But there were other problems which caused the Government unremitting anxiety, all the greater because very often it was not shared by the public. They were problems of foreign policy. Intimately bound up with them were problems of military and naval organization, which during these years occasioned the Government considerable embarrassment, while the Opposition exploited and advertised their difficulties to its profit. We propose however to reserve the study of these problems until the time when, under another Ministry, they received their solution. For the present we will be content to point out the indecision which marked the Government's policy in this sphere, and show how it is to be explained by the uncertain and fluid character of the diplomatic situation.

In the first place there was the question of the Navy. The rule followed at the end of the nineteenth century had been to maintain a Navy equal to the two most powerful foreign navies, actually the French and the Russian. Now, however, the young and formidable German Navy was growing up. To meet the new danger, the Admiralty set to work with feverish haste to reform the entire system of instructions given to officers and men, and concentrated a larger proportion of ships in European waters.[1] But the difficulty began when a rule had to be fixed to determine the normal strength of the fleet in these novel conditions. The Government did not dare to lay down the principle of a Three-Power Standard: the Two-Power Standard was therefore verbally maintained, but every effort was made by a variety of strained interpretations to

[1] *Memorandum* by Lord Selborne, December 10, 1904.

apply it under conditions in which it was in fact no longer applicable.[1]

Then there was the question of the Army. Lord Lansdowne, dismissed as incompetent, had been replaced at the War Office by Brodrick, who worked out a comprehensive scheme of Army reform on the basis of three army corps organized after the German model. But the scheme failed, and Brodrick was replaced by Arnold Foster, whose plans had not been completed when the session came to an end in the summer of 1905. What was the double problem both Secretaries were called upon to solve? In the first place, to provide the country with an Army for home defence to be raised by voluntary enlistment—some even dared to say by conscription—to protect British territory against invasion by a foreign army—actually by a French Army. In the second place, to organize an expeditionary force, ready to be despatched to any point in the Empire which might be threatened, especially to India where a Russian invasion was feared. But was it really France and Russia the politicians now had in view? 'As the problem', declared Balfour on May 11, 1905, 'is a problem of invasion, I am bound to take as the potential invader the great nation which is nearest to us. . . . I need not tell the House that the last thing in the world I regard as possible is an invasion by France, but everybody will agree that in taking a concrete instance, I am obliged, whether I like it or not, to take that

---

[1] H. of C., February 29, 1904. Speech by Pretyman, Financial Secretary to the Admiralty: 'The country had decided to adopt what was known as the "Two-power" standard in its naval policy; and this, in the view of the Admiralty, meant that this country should be able to engage in a naval war with reasonable probability of emerging victorious from a contest with any other two naval Powers. This principle must be broadly applied, not solely to particular units or particular ships. . . . In considering the question of cruisers the Admiralty were not governed solely by the Two-power Standard.' (*Parliamentary Debates*, 4th Ser., vol. cxxx, pp. 1259–1260.) H. of C., March 6, 1905, Pretyman's speech: 'The redistribution of the Fleet depends mainly, if not entirely, upon mobility. . . . Through this mobility we have been able to reduce the number of the less up-to-date ships in all parts of the world. . . . There are two new factors of the greatest importance, and of world-wide operation, the advent of armoured cruisers in considerable numbers, and the invention and use of wireless telegraphy. Dealing with the scheme as a whole, I say it is based on these two factors of general application.' (Ibid., vol. cxlii, p. 437.) H. of L., March 21, 1905, Lord Goschen's speech: 'So long as there were a very few naval Powers, you could say that a Two-power Standard was sufficient. . . . When there is a Power with twelve battleships ready in commission within a few hundred miles of your coasts, that is a factor that has to be considered side by side with your preparations to meet any two Powers.' Lord Selborne's speech: 'I do not advocate, I have never advocated, a Three-power Standard, because I do not think the finances of this country could afford it. . . . But the spirit of the Two-power Standard is not equality. The object is to win. It is reasonable security of victory in a contest with two other Powers.' (Ibid., vol. cxliii, pp. 610, 617.)

country, friendly though it be.' 'As an object-lesson,' said Lord Roberts two months later,[1] 'I shall suppose that we are at war with a perfectly friendly Power, with whom I trust we may ever remain at peace. It is in the East that we have become a Continental Power and taken upon ourselves the responsibilities of such a position, and it is on the supposition of Russian aggression in Afghanistan that an inquiry into our military preparations for war may conveniently be based.' These were utterances marked by the caution natural to a public speaker, at a time when the danger of a French or Russian attack could be mentioned in public with the greater safety, because the eventuality had become more remote. In 1905 the dangers of which Balfour and Lord Roberts spoke already belonged to the past. The peril they had in mind lay in another quarter.

2

We must go back to the time when at the end of 1902 after the Emperor William's visit to London and the joint demonstration made by both fleets on the coast of Venezuela the British Government, yielding to the pressure of public opinion, had morally broken with Germany. When the policy of a German alliance had thus been definitely abandoned, what new policy would take its place? The old policy of 'isolation'? Old it certainly was, in fact antiquated. The last great Englishman who within the past few years had remained faithful to it, Lord Salisbury, had just disappeared from political life. The conclusion of other alliances? 'An isolated Germany', wrote the *Standard* the very day in November when William II reached London, 'would be, not indeed weak, but placed in a very anxious and precarious position. The situation of this country is very different. We can always find allies and it will be the fault of Germany if we ever look for co-operation to Powers that bear her no love.' What Powers? Obviously Russia and France. But a year after the conclusion of the treaty with Japan, which amounted to a British declaration of war against Russia, the suggestion of an understanding between the two Empires was more fantastic than ever. Then with France? In that direction also there was a host of difficulties to be overcome. When Delcassé became Minister of

[1] August 2, 1905.

Foreign Affairs in the spring of 1898, he had wished to negotiate
an amicable settlement of all the colonial questions in dispute
between France and Great Britain. We have seen how he had been
thwarted by the hostile disposition of the Foreign Office. Only
the diversion of the Boer War had prevented further conflicts
between the two Governments arising at some point or another
of their colonial frontiers. In Indo-China Delcassé had conducted
an obstinate struggle against the annexationist policy of the
governor Paul Doumer, which had cost him the enmity of the
colonial group. But with this exception it must be admitted that
owing to the force of circumstances his policy in many respects
markedly resembled that of his predecessor Hanotaux. It was an
unavowed understanding with Germany through the intermediary of Petersburg, an understanding whose existence came to
light wherever the colonial interests of the three countries, France,
Germany and Russia, clashed, in Asia Minor, in China even, and
above all in Morocco.

It was at the beginning of 1900 that the French Government
decided to pursue a policy of active intervention in Morocco.
Advantage would be taken of the Boer War, which had begun
two months before and which seemed likely for a long while to
come, to engross the attention of the British Government. Nevertheless the aims pursued respectively by France and England in
Morocco were diametrically opposed. England did not wish to
see any other Power in occupation of Tangiers or any part of
northern Morocco. Neither, for the moment, did she contemplate
a military occupation of the area on her own account. But by
defending the territorial integrity of the Sultan's territory, and
furnishing him with civil advisers and military instructors to
strengthen his authority over its entire extent, she was attempting
to establish in Morocco a species of moral protectorate. In short,
to use a phrase then fashionable in Paris, she was carrying out a
policy of 'peaceful penetration' (*pénétration pacifique*) identical in
its methods with the policy pursued by France.

When, therefore, peace was concluded in South Africa at the
end of the spring of 1902 the problem of maintaining friendly
relations between France and England seemed at once easier and
more difficult than before.

It seemed easier, because a considerable section of the British
public, delighted to see the country emerge victoriously from the

South African embroglio, was evidently weary of war and by no means disposed to engage in further enterprises. Were they to revive the bickerings with France which had prevailed before 1899 and had seemed the prelude to a war? Was not the moment opportune for a general settlement of the colonial disputes outstanding between the two countries? The campaign conducted in the Chambers of Commerce on behalf of an understanding with France without any *arrière-pensée* of hostility towards Germany and solely in the interest of universal peace, by men such as Lord Avebury and Sir Thomas Barclay, acquired a new momentum. Sir Thomas desired a permanent arbitration treaty with France. Lord Lansdowne listened to his suggestions, and, though still rather sceptical, seemed on the whole to favour them.[1]

Unfortunately the disagreement about Morocco appeared to render for the moment any general settlement of the African problem impracticable. France had concluded an agreement with Italy, and there was a rumour that a similar agreement might shortly be concluded with Spain. If the peace of Vereeniging had been delayed, British diplomacy would perhaps have been taken at a disadvantage. As it was, Britain had her hands free. For several months she adopted in Morocco an attitude frankly hostile to France.

The Franco-Italian agreement, the terms of which had not been made public, but which was nevertheless universally discussed, was the subject of numerous criticisms in the House of Commons during the month of July. Since its object was a change in the *status quo* in the Mediterranean it constituted, according to Sir Charles Dilke, a breach of the Anglo-Italian agreement of 1887, which guaranteed the *status quo*.[2] Bryce disclaimed any wish to contest the Italian claims in Tripoli which according to the current report France had recognized. But he added: 'If Morocco had come into the agreement, it would have been different.'[3] In the opinion of Gibson Bowles, 'the arrangement was an alliance between France and Italy made with the consent of Germany and Spain'.[4] A fortnight later he asked 'whether His Majesty's Government had any information relative to communications

[1] Lord Lansdowne to Sir Thomas Barclay, May 20, 1902 (Sir Thomas Barclay, *Thirty Years' Anglo-French Reminiscences*, 1896–1906, p. 212).

[2] H. of C., July 3, 1902 (*Parliamentary Debates*, 4th Ser., vol. cx, p. 705).

[3] Ibid., p. 729.

[4] Ibid., p. 711.

between the Governments of Italy, France and Spain involving overtures for the establishment between these three Powers of a so-called Latin League for regulating or acting upon the political situation in the Mediterranean; if so, whether . . . the suggested League proposed to include within its action the future of Morocco; and if the communications between the three Powers in question had been submitted to the Government of Russia'.[1] No doubt Bowles was a crank whose effusions no one took seriously. But the historian cannot afford to neglect even extravagant rumours. They are often a reliable indication of the state of public opinion. Obviously a section of the public was apprehensive lest the hostility towards England which prevailed universally on the Continent, instead of remaining as hitherto merely a sentiment, might perhaps be given a political expression and take shape as a diplomatic arrangement. Nevertheless it was not easy for the British Government to oppose the Italian agreement. Could Italy, if not nominally, at least for all practical purposes, an ally, be refused the right to expand in Tripoli? And if she formally disclaimed any purpose to interfere in Morocco, what objection could be raised? In fact several months earlier the Italian Government had obtained British approval of her new policy. But the Franco-Spanish agreement was another matter, if by its terms Morocco was divided into two zones of influence, and the two countries agreed not to admit any British control over Morocco, even on the northern coast. Sagasta was on the eve of submitting the treaty for ratification by the Cortes, when in December he was thrown out of office. He was succeeded by Silvela. The latter had been one of the first Spanish statesmen to declare himself in favour of an arrangement with France for the partition of Morocco. Sagasta had communicated to him the text of the agreement and he had given his approval. Nevertheless, when Silvela became Prime Minister he refused to ask the Cortes to ratify the treaty. He was convinced that the British Government would never consider valid any agreement concluded without its consent and in defiance of its wishes.[2]

[1] H. of C., July 21, 1902 (*Parliamentary Debates*, 4th Ser., vol. cxi, pp. 773–4).
[2] It has been suggested (E. D. Morel, *Ten Years of Secret Diplomacy*, chap. x, 6th ed., p. 50) that Silvela had yielded to British pressure. But we know from the *British Documents on the Origin of the War*, vol. ii, p. 279, that only on February 14, 1903, was the British Ambassador at Madrid informed by Silvela of the French proposals, and of the reasons why he had declined to consider them, his chief objection being his unwillingness to act without the knowledge and approval of England.

The situation therefore remained as before. But not for long. A month before Silvela took office the visit of the Emperor William had occasioned the first outburst of anti-German feeling in England, and on the morrow of his accession to power the joint ultimatum addressed to Venezuela by England and Germany had provoked a further storm of protest. In fact, at the very moment when Spain declined to entertain the French suggestion for fear of provoking England, the British Cabinet, warned by the revolt of public opinion that its attitude towards the German Government must be changed, convinced that it would therefore be necessary to seek alliances or understandings in other directions, and recognizing that within less than a year after the conclusion of the Japanese alliance it would be useless to make advances to Russia, was already turning towards France.

The French election of May, 1902, had completed the over-throw of the Nationalists, and the Republican Party, owing to the circumstances under which its victory had been won, was committed to a policy of anti-militarism and peace. Emile Combes became Prime Minister, Camille Pelletan Minister of Marine. In November he demobilised the Mediterranean fleet. He suspended the construction of four ironclads his predecessor had ordered as part of a naval programme passed by the Chamber. At the same time Russia saw with anxiety the disorder produced in every branch of the navy by the ignorant meddling of the new Minister, as later on, when the *entente* had been con-cluded, the British Admiralty in its turn would be alarmed by this state of chronic insubordination. At this juncture it may very well have contributed to restore friendly relations between the two countries. Evidently the enemy to be feared was no longer the old French Navy, but the rapidly growing navy of Germany.

The return of a majority, frankly pacific, to the French Chamber of Deputies had another result, at first paradoxical; it revived the question of Alsace-Lorraine. Gambetta's advice 'never to speak of it' had been the easier to keep during the last few years, because the attention of the Press had been absorbed by the diplomatic disputes with England. Now however the spokesmen of the peace party—D'Estournelles de Constant, Jean Jaurès— declared that the time had come to break silence. Relations, they maintained, between France and Germany would never become friendly, until the question had been publicly discussed and settled in a conciliatory spirit. Their speeches aroused immediate protest. French patriotism refused to admit any solution except the unconditional return of Alsace to France. And it may be doubted if they were better received in Berlin. For Berlin the Alsace question did not exist. But the incident could not fail to arouse the interest of the British Foreign Office. There was clearly an insurmountable obstacle in the way of an understanding between France and Germany. If, under existing circumstances, an alliance with Russia against Germany was impracticable, it might be worth while attempting, what had so lately seemed impossible, an understanding with France.

At the moment the Egyptian question bulked more largely in the imagination of Frenchmen than the question of Alsace. Instead of continuing to regard it as definitely settled, why not admit that the French claims were juridically well-founded and purchase their surrender by the offer of a splendid compensation.[1] During this very autumn the situation of the young Sultan of Morocco, Abdul Aziz, Britain's protégé, became critical. A formidable rebellion broke out in the north of Morocco led by a claimant to the throne, Bu-Hamara, 'the man of the she-ass'. It was not until the end of December that the Sultan's army was routed, his British advisers MacLean and Harris fled to the coast and the Sultan himself was threatened in his own capital. But already in November, it was known that the Pretender's army was successfully defying the Government some thirty miles from Fez. The question of Morocco assumed a new aspect. If British influence were still to be supreme in Fez and Marrakesh, it might be necessary to despatch an army to the assistance of Abdul Aziz. That however was out of the question. Only six months after the conclusion of peace in South Africa, nobody in England wished to see the country committed to another war. And what after all were the substantial interests of Britain in Morocco? An open door for British imports and the neutrality of Tangiers. Provided these two points were secured by a formal undertaking, why not give France a free hand?

[1] The suggestion of a barter—Egypt for Morocco—was not indeed novel. Hints to that effect may be found scattered here and there in the British Press at the time of the Fashoda crisis. See especially *Westminster Gazette*, October 12, 1898: 'If, it is hinted, France gets Morocco, then she may be prepared to recognize the British occupation of Egypt. So it will go on until in "compensation" for Egypt our neighbours get the whole southern littoral of the Mediterranean or until, in return for concessions, graceful or reluctant, we exact something substantial and have it down in black and white.' *Spectator,*

3

In August, Delcassé, through his ambassador in London, Paul Cambon, submitted to Lord Lansdowne proposals for an eventual partition of Morocco between France and Spain, Tangiers to be excluded from it as an international port. At the same time he made further proposals for a similar partition of 'spheres of influence' between France and England in certain frontier districts of Siam. But England still hoped to keep the whole of Morocco in her 'sphere of influence' through the intermediary of the Sultan. Lord Lansdowne therefore refused to consider Paul Cambon's suggestions. The fact that the French Government was negotiating a treaty with Siam, inconsistent with its proposals to Great Britain made it easier to refuse.[1]

Nor had any negotiations begun when, on November 10, Balfour made the speech at the Guildhall, which we have already spoken, in which he emphatically denied the rumours of an Anglo-German alliance to which the Emperor's visit had given rise. He then proceeded to review the situation in Europe and throughout the world, and warned his audience against supposing that all danger of war had been removed. War, he explained, was still possible in those regions of the globe in which civilized peoples were in contact with uncivilized races. No one either in Paris or London appears to have understood to what he alluded. Such was the indifference of the general public to the questions which were engrossing the attention of every Foreign Office. Nevertheless there can be no doubt that Balfour was referring to Morocco. He wished to warn France of the danger of the peace of the world her Moroccan policy involved.

A month later there was a complete change of front. The Foreign Secretary, Lord Lansdowne, speaking at a banquet on December 12, referred to the rumour which was current that negotiations were proceeding with the French Government for the settlement of all outstanding differences. Though he denied

October 15, 1898: 'If France absorbed Morocco, no Englishman could be solicitous except for the freedom of Tangiers, and there are men among us who go even further than that. We believe that Africa will ultimately be French and English, France ruling in the North and the West, and we in the East and South.' Was an arrangement of this kind in Paul Cambon's mind when he proposed a general settlement of the colonial disputes outstanding between the two nations? On that point we are reduced to guessing. In any case until the end of 1902 the proposal was defeated by the persistent opposition of the Foreign Office.   [1] *British Documents*, vol. ii, pp. 264 sqq.

the report, he was glad that it was in circulation, for it was a proof
that the public agreed with the speaker in desiring a better understanding with France. He proceeded to deal with the question
Balfour had raised in November, the friction likely to occur
between civilized and uncivilized peoples, but he gave it an
entirely different turn. What, asked the speaker, was to be
expected when a people of inferior civilization came into contact
with two Western Powers? It would attempt to play off one
against the other and fool both. Why should the two Governments lend themselves to a trick of this kind instead of settling
the matter like men of business? The general public understood
his reference no better than they had understood Balfour's in
November. Everyone both in England and France was sick of
colonial politics. No one took the least interest in Morocco.
But the speech is perfectly clear today. In scarcely veiled language
Lord Lansdowne informed his audience that negotiations on the
Morocco question were pending, had perhaps actually begun.

Henceforward they proceeded without a break. The rumour of
an Anglo-French bargain in which Morocco and Egypt played a
part had acquired by March sufficient consistency to alarm the
colonial group in Paris. Does the Government really propose,
asked one of their leaders, the deputy Deloncle, to sacrifice our
rights in Egypt? Ribot shared his indignation. Delcassé's only
reply was a shrug of the shoulders.[1] He need not fear exposure.
For knowing the violence of anti-British feeling in Paris and
wishing to avoid the danger of leakage at the Quai d'Orsay, he
conducted the negotiations directly through the French Ambassador in London without the knowledge of his subordinates at
the Foreign Office.

It was on November 25 that Chamberlain sailed for South
Africa. He returned on March 14, 1903. It is therefore possible
that he was absent at the time when the change was effected in
the orientation of British Foreign policy, and it is not very easy to
decide what part he can have played in the matter. We must be
content to recall that at the end of 1901 he had quarrelled with
Germany publicly, and that perhaps the secret negotiations on the
subject of Morocco had begun before November 25.[2] It is also

[1] Chamber of Deputies, March 11, 1903.
[2] There is no allusion to Egypt in *British Documents* before July 7, 1903, when Delcassé
held a long conversation with Lord Lansdowne in London, whose terms the latter
immediately reported to Sir E. Monson (vol. ii, pp. 294 sqq.; esp. p. 297). Lord Cromer

significant that, when he returned in March, the action taken by
Germany in several instances was alarming the business world to
which he was attached by such close ties. In January the news had
been received of a note, couched in identical terms, which the
French and German Governments had despatched to China, and
which apparently amounted to a repudiation of the Anglo-
German agreement of 1900. At the beginning of March Germany
had just concluded a convention with Turkey by which she
obtained the long-desired concession of the Baghdad railway. To
construct it she possessed all the material and engineers she needed.
But she lacked the necessary capital. She borrowed it in Paris and
was attempting to borrow it in London. Balfour and Lord Lansdowne were favourable to the projected loan.[1] But the mere
suggestion of serving the interests of German imperialism in the
Levant was sufficient to provoke an outburst of indignant protest
throughout the Press, whatever its political colour. It is probable
that the campaign was directly encouraged by Chamberlain,
and that it was he who, when the matter was discussed by the
Cabinet, compelled Balfour and Lord Lansdowne to go back on

was also informed, and the news that Delcassé was prepared to make concessions in Egypt
seems to have come as a very welcome surprise. (To Lord Lansdowne, Cairo, July 17,
1903. Vol. ii, p. 298.) How then are we to explain the hardly veiled reference to Morocco
in Lord Lansdowne's speech on December 12, 1902, or the debate which took place in
the Chamber of Deputies on March 11, on the subject of a barter between England and
France of their respective claims in Morocco and Egypt? Or again the rumours current in
Madrid at the beginning of April (*British Documents*, vol. ii, p. 283), or the campaign of
The Times which began in January 1903? As far as the Egyptian aspect of the transaction
is concerned, we would draw the reader's attention to two facts: (1) Sir Sidney Lee in his
biography of King Edward (vol. ii, p. 219) mentions a special mission of a high Egyptian
official, Tigrane Pasha, to London and Paris, to ascertain the terms on which a new settlement of Egyptian finance could be effected. It would be interesting to know its date. (2)
On November 26, 1902, a commercial treaty was signed between the French and
Egyptian Governments. By concluding it the French Government recognized for the
first time, after holding out for twenty years, the situation created at Cairo by the British
occupation. When we attempt to solve the problem, it is difficult to resist the conclusion
that there were negotiations, either unofficial or, if official, not allowed to leave any trace
in the Archives of the Foreign Office.

[1] H. of C., April 8, 1903, Arthur Balfour's speech (*Parliamentary Debates*, 4th Ser., vol.
cxx, pp. 1369 sqq.). See especially p. 1371: 'My Hon. Friend, in the whole course of his
speech, never once, I think, mentioned France. Nevertheless . . . as the House is probably
aware, the German group of financiers and the French group are entirely agreed in their
plans; and I have no doubt whatever that whatever course English financiers may take,
and whatever course the English Government may pursue, sooner or later this great
undertaking will be carried out. . . . Therefore, the point on which H.M.'s Government
will ultimately have to decide, and which the House may safely and wisely take into
consideration, is, whether it is or is not desirable that if this railway connecting the base of
the Mediterranean with the Persian Gulf is to be constructed, British capital and British
interests should be as largely represented in it as the capital and interests of any foreign
power.'

their original decision.[1] Moreover he may well have felt that he
was not the right man to effect the reconciliation with France,
when for three years he had done so much to widen the breach.
And this was perhaps a further inducement for him to concentrate
his efforts on a different question, namely, tariff reform. And
tariff reform was itself a declaration of war against Germany.

At the beginning of May, King Edward visited Paris. The
entente between France and Great Britain is usually dated from
his visit. In reality it was a consequence of the understanding
reached some months before by the two Governments which
wanted only the seal of a public manifestation. What indeed
could be more natural than the Royal visit? King Edward was to
visit the King of Portugal and the King of Italy. Was he to keep
away from French territory, or, if he passed through France, to
avoid a meeting with the head of the French Government? The
feeling of the French towards England was still believed to be so
hostile that the visit seemed a stroke of daring. Originally, at the
beginning of March, it was expected that the President and the
King would meet on the Riviera. Paris, where the Nationalists
were still supreme, seemed too dangerous. It is not yet known
whether the original suggestion of the Royal visit either to the
Riviera or to Paris came from President Loubet or King Edward.
But there can be no doubt that the King was at once attracted by
it.[2] For, though, during the first two years of his reign, he had
been scrupulously faithful to the policy of friendship with
Germany, a Franco-British alliance had been the dream of his
youth and he had frequently been on the worst possible terms
with the Emperor William. It was therefore easier for him than
for many others to enter into the new movement of British
public opinion. From this moment the *entente* between France
and England was his work.

His reception at Paris in May was at first chilly. But it very
quickly became cordial. When he departed for home the ice had

---

[1] H. of C., April 23, 1903, Arthur Balfour's speech (*Parliamentary Debates*, 4th Ser.,
vol. cxxi, p. 221). For the entire episode see the exceedingly well informed chapter in
Edward Mead Earle's *Turkey, The Great Powers and the Baghdad Railway. A Study in
Imperialism*, 1923, p. 182.

[2] See the contradictory accounts by Paul Cambon (interview published in *The Times*,
December 22, 1920, under the heading 'M. Cambon's Farewell', 'A Last Message to
England', 'Entente Secrets', 'The War Crisis', and by Lord Hardinge, who had accom-
panied the King to Paris as the representative of the Foreign Office (speech delivered in
Paris, June 3, 1926, at a banquet of L'Association France—*Grande-Bretagne*).

been broken between the two countries. It was plain that on both sides of the Channel the public were tired of a policy of colonial commitments and anxious to heal old wounds. In July, President Loubet visited London, accompanied by his Minister for Foreign Affairs, and received a warm welcome. In October a pact was signed by which the two Powers undertook to submit to The Hague Tribunal all questions on which no agreement had been reached, provided the vital interests, independence or honour of either country were not involved. It realized the dream cherished since 1900 by a number of British workers for international peace. (Sir Thomas Barclay was at the head of the group.) For a long time their efforts had been frustrated by the opposition of the British Ambassador in Paris and by Lord Salisbury's cynicism.[1] That the Foreign Office now acceded to their wishes was a pledge to the public that the negotiations for a general settlement of outstanding colonial questions would proceed without a hitch. They led in fact to the agreements concluded on April 8, 1904, which completely changed the diplomatic situation in Europe.

4

By the terms of these agreements the question of the New-foundland fisheries, so long a bone of contention between the two Governments, was settled, and on the main point under dispute the British contention prevailed. French fishermen lost the right to dry their fish on that part of the coast known as the French Shore. By way of compensation France received a port on the navigable waters of the Gambia, the Los Islands opposite the Ivory Coast, and an important rectification of her frontier between the Niger and the Chad. In Siam, France and England determined by mutual agreement their respective zones of influence. A condominium was set up in the New Hebrides. England recognized the right of France to establish customs in Madagascar. But of all the agreements the most important was that which was concerned with Egypt and Morocco.

Both countries disclaimed any intention to alter the political status of either country. But France undertook not to interfere in any way with British action in Egypt, and England in return

<hr>

[2] Sir Thomas Barclay, *Thirty Years' Anglo-French Reminiscences* (1876–1906), pp. 199 sqq.

left France entire liberty to intervene in Morocco for the purpose of maintaining peace and assisting her to carry out all necessary administrative, economic, financial and military reforms, in other words to establish herself in Morocco, as England had established herself in Egypt. All questions concerning the Egyptian debt were settled in such a way as to get rid of the French veto on the free disposition, claimed by the Anglo-Egyptian Government, of the funds accumulated in the *Caisse de la Dette*. The signatories undertook to respect both in Egypt and Morocco 'the principle of freedom of commerce', and gave that principle a more precise definition, which, it was agreed, should be maintained without alteration for thirty years. They also undertook not to permit any fortifications to be constructed on the northern coast of Morocco. France promised to conclude an agreement safeguarding Spanish interests in Morocco. And both Governments promised each other their diplomatic support to secure the execution of these provisions. The convention was completed by a secret convention not to be made public for seven years. In case either Government should find itself compelled by the force of circumstances to modify its policy in regard to Egypt or Morocco, in other words to substitute for the occupation a protectorate in the strict sense, both undertook to continue their mutual support on the conditions laid down in the public convention. Moreover Morocco was to be divided into two zones of influence, one French, the other Spanish, and the Northern coast from Melilla to Sebu was to be included in the Spanish zone. We would call attention to the procedure adopted, two simultaneous conventions, one public, the other secret; also to the exact terms in which the secret convention was drawn up. We cannot fail to be reminded of the Anglo-German convention of 1898 on the subject of the Portuguese Colonies. The mark of the Foreign Office is visible throughout.

The treaty was criticized from the imperialist standpoint by the *Morning Post* and the *Saturday Review*,[1] also by Lord Rosebery, who represented it as a humiliation inflicted by France on Great Britain. 'No more one-sided agreement', he declared, 'was ever concluded between two Powers at peace with each other,' and he doubted the wisdom of surrendering Morocco to a great

---

[1] *Morning Post*, April 7, 9, 11, 12, 15; *Saturday Review*, April 16.

military Power.[1] It is not surprising that he should have condemned the abandonment by the Foreign Office of what had
long been, and still was, his policy, an alliance with Germany
directed against France. The *Morning Post* regretted 'this desperate
hurry to make friends with someone,' first with Germany, now
with France; the doctrine of the balance of power demanded that
England, while ready to welcome the advances of all nations,
should make advances to none.[2] For the most part the critics were
fanatical patriots to whom any compromise with a foreign Power
was intolerable. But they were only a small minority even among
the imperialists. The vast majority were delighted to see the
policy of friendship with Germany repudiated in the face of the
entire world. And on the other hand the advocates of peace
received with enthusiasm the atonement made by the very
Cabinet responsible six years before for Fashoda. Thus, a few
dissentient voices apart, the convention was approved by the
imperialists, and the heirs of the Gladstonian tradition welcomed
it with one accord.[3] When, therefore, we read the contemporary
utterances of the Press, we do not find it altogether easy to determine the reasons of the general satisfaction. Was it that the British
were delighted to see the beginning of a new system of alliances,
sufficiently strong to curb German ambition? Or was the agreement popular, simply because it satisfied the deep longing for
peace every Englishman felt since the end of the Boer War? Or
were the two motives indistinguishably blended and were the
British pleased to thwart the German Government by a step
which, no one could deny, was strictly pacific? No doubt the

---

[1] Speech at the Queen's Hall, June 10. British pacifists have lately called attention to this
'prophetic' utterance by Lord Rosebery. And Lloyd George has adopted their interpretation of his words in a speech delivered in the House of Commons on June 25, 1925. That
interpretation, however, forgets (1) That Lord Rosebery was the very reverse of a pacifist, and (2) That his protest was directed against the alleged abandonment of Northern
Morocco to France by the power in occupation of Gibraltar. If he had known of the secret
convention he would have known that his objection was unfounded.

[2] April 15.

[3] Later the British pacifists maintained that they had been deceived, and that had they
known of the secret articles, their judgment would have been different. This, we believe,
is mere quibbling. The secret articles stated what the Convention could not state explicitly,
but the articles published in April, 1904, said enough to inform the public. Cf. *Speaker*,
April 16, 1904: 'We entirely demur to the view that we ought to wince and smart over
every acquisition of France, even if this acquisition cost us nothing. It is to the good, and
not to the harm of mankind, that the great colonizing work in which France is engaged
in North West Africa should be hampered as little as possible. . . . This agreement
liberates the energies of France for the undistracted prosecution of a great scheme of
enlightened and humane colonization, and for that we rejoice.'

Daily Telegraph expressed the public feeling most happily, when it declared its satisfaction that an international agreement of far-reaching importance had been concluded without the inter-mediary of the Wilhelmstrasse. 'Berlin is no longer the diplomatic clearing house of Europe.'[1]

5

If the new system of alliances were to be complete, the Anglo-French *entente* must be followed by an *entente* between England and Russia. In fact for the past ten years there had always been Englishmen in favour of an understanding with Russia, more indeed than those who had advocated an understanding with France.[2] A group of Tories who disliked the turbulence and irreligion of French democracy protested against the absurd Liberal prejudice which set up a moral barrier between England and Russia, detrimental to the true interests of their country. King Edward was the uncle of the Czar Nicholas, and the com-munications he maintained with the Russian Court through the intermediary of the Danish caused the Wilhelmstrasse at his accession more anxiety than the French sympathies with which he had for some time been credited. The Liberal Imperialists,

[1] April 13.
[2] Valentine Chirol, *The Far Eastern Question*, 1896. See especially p. 196 (the last page of the book): 'Unfortunately, in the present mood of French politicians, the governing principle of French policy all over the world seems to be rather to deal a real or imaginary blow at British interests than merely to promote those of France, and such a temper is hard to deal with. There is, however, no sufficient reason at present to believe that Russia is definitely pledged to any such policy.' And he advocates an understanding with Russia, for the partition of Asia. Col. Sir George Sydenham Clarke, *Russia's Past and Present, or The Rise of the Russian Navy*, 1898, p. 186: 'Reflection will show that, even after two centuries of expansion, Russia has not occupied a square yard which is now or has ever been desired by Great Britain. This cannot be said of France, of Germany, or of the United States. . . . No policy is so dangerous as that of drift; no assumption is so gratuitous as that Russia is "our great enemy". To remove the long-standing antagonism between our two nations, and to substitute direct agreement between London and Saint Petersburg for competitive manipulation of the dummy Government at Peking, would be a task worthy of a great statesman, and a powerful guarantee of the peace of the world.' Fred I. Jane's book, *The Imperial Russian Navy, Its Past, Present and Future*, 1899, presents less interest, being the work of an eccentric ultra-reactionary. *Russia*, by Sir Donald Macken-zie Wallace, is more guarded in its conclusions. But the fact that Wallace was a man of strong Russian sympathies and from 1891 to 1899 was foreign editor of *The Times*, may have contributed to the anti-German attitude of the paper. See Count Witte's distinctly caustic estimate of Wallace (*Mémoires*, pp. 119, 120). When 'Calchas', in a series of articles, pleaded for an understanding with Russia, a French publicist, while professing his agree-ment with Calchas, asked why the latter had not dealt with the question of an under-standing between England and France, and it was only after his remarks that 'Calchas' turned his atention to the French question. (See above, p. 124.)

while approving of Chamberlain's hostility to France, were never weary of protesting against his attacks on Russia. What object could be served by gratuitously multiplying the number of one's enemies?[1] In the north of China the rapid advance of Russia towards the open waters of the pacific was astonishing the world. No doubt that advance defeated the policy pursued by Great Britain in China, for it must involve the loss of the preponderant influence she had become accustomed to wield at Pekin for the last half century. But since it was obviously impossible to resist it by force would it not be wise to make the best of it? England could clearly afford to abandon northern Asia to Russia without endangering her own Empire. To understand the attitude of British opinion at this time, we must go back in imagination to the period, already remote, when the power of Russia seemed irresistible and unlimited. In the diplomatic system constituted by France and Russia, Russia was the sun, France the planet. It was therefore natural that the politicians and journalists who about the end of 1901 began to contemplate the possibility of an understanding with Russia and France thought of Russia before they thought of France. If the good understanding maintained between the Courts of Berlin and Petersburg had drawn France into the orbit of German diplomacy, the restoration of friendly relations between London and Petersburg might suffice to pull her French satellite in the same direction.[2]

But we already know the reason why the Foreign Office, when,

[1] H. H. Asquith, speech at Saint Monan's (East Fife), September 9, and at Birmingham, December 16, 1898: Sir Edward Grey, speech at Darlington, September 8, 1898, and in the House of Commons, February 8, 1899 (*Parliamentary Debates*, 4th Ser., vol. lxvi, pp. 231 sqq., especially p. 239). The Russian Ambassador, M. de Staal, wrote as follows to Count Mouraview, February 3–15, 1899: 'The most sympathetic, as also the most politic, speech delivered in the House of Commons was made by Sir Edward Grey on February 8. . . . He criticised certain of the political combinations made by his Government in the Far East and placed in its true light the policy which we are pursuing in those countries. He has no dread of a Russian invasion of China and protests against the absurdity of such fears. The impartial judgment of this statesman understands the expansion of Russian interests in the Pacific, and he is convinced that they are compatible with British interests. In consequence he openly advocates an understanding with Russia in the Far East. Sir Edward Grey's speech deserves to be read in full.' (*Archives of the Russian Embassy* in London.)

[2] A.B.C., etc., 'British Foreign Policy' (*National Review*, November, 1901, vol. xxxviii, p. 357): 'In seeking to close our prolonged contest with Russia, we are desirious of doing something which would be for the advantage of civilization, and should it be effected, it would not be less welcome because it brought us back into friendly relations with France—a country whose history is closely interwoven with our own, and with which we share so many political sentiments. The French are perhaps the only nation which will make sacrifices and run risks for the sake of those who enjoy their friendship. They are capable of sentimental attachment as well as sentimental hatred.'

towards the end of 1902, it suddenly decided to give its policy a
new orientation, began by making overtures to France. It was
because the alliance with Japan, admittedly directed against
Russian encroachments in northern Asia and hardly a year old,
made any understanding with Russia impossible at the moment.
The months passed, and, while the relations between Great
Britain and France were becoming more friendly, the relations
between Russia and Japan, the British ally, were becoming
increasingly strained. There was an open conflict between the
two Empires, each of which sought to control Manchuria and
Korea to the exclusion of its rival. On February 6, 1904, Japan
recalled her Ambassador at Petersburg and hostilities began. It is
possible that the outbreak of the war hastened the conclusion of
the negotiations between England and France.[1] For both the
western Powers, the ally of Japan and the ally of Russia, were
equally determined not to be drawn into the war in the Far East.
England was obliged by her treaty to assist Japan only if she was
attacked by two Powers. Therefore French neutrality dispensed
England from the necessity of war, and the French Government
could justify her neutrality at Petersburg on the plea that it
secured Russia against intervention by the British Navy. Nevertheless, the effect of the *entente cordiale*, sealed by the agreement
of April 8, and which moreover had the air of a deliberate reply
to the commencement of hostilities with Japan, was to make
Russian feeling cooler towards France and more hostile towards
England.

The British Government persisted, however, in the attempt to

---

[1] The opening of the negotiations may have helped to bring about the Duke of Devonshire's resignation in October, 1903. See Count Bernstorff to Count von Bülow, October
12, 1903: 'As I am informed on reliable authority, the rumour of negotiations between
England and France led to the first conflict between the Duke of Devonshire on the one
side and Mr. Balfour and Lord Lansdowne on the other. A lively altercation took place
on the subject, because the Duke regarded the negotiations with apprehension as amounting
in themselves to a breach of treaty obligations. England, he maintained, would be considered by Japan guilty of double dealing, and her prestige would suffer accordingly
throughout the whole of Eastern Asia.' (*Die Grosse Politik*, vol. xix, p. 13.) And it is
evident that already at this date, four months before the outbreak of war, the question of
an Anglo-French *entente* was bound up with the Far Eastern question. Cf. Prince Lichnow-
sky, Berlin, January 8, 1904: 'No one (at Petersburg) seems any longer to count on French
help in a war with Japan. The British Ambassador there speaks quite openly to that effect,
and allows the existence of a comprehensive agreement with France to transpire.' (*Die
Grosse Politik*, vol. xix, p. 20.) Cf. Count Witte's *Mémoires* (French trans., p. 147). But
Witte, who always distorts the truth, almost appears to attribute the inauguration of the
negotiations between England and France to the outbreak of war between Japan and
Russia.

conciliate Russia, while maintaining an attitude of friendly neutrality towards Japan. King Edward was at Copenhagen when the agreement with France was concluded. It was remarked that of the entire diplomatic corps he asked to see only the Ministers of France and Russia.[1] With the Russian Minister, Isvolsky, he held a long conversation of which he requested that a written account should be drawn up to be corrected by himself, and sent to Petersburg. Its purport was the possibility of completing the Anglo-French *entente* by a similar *entente* with Russia.[2] Naturally King Edward's only thought was to prepare for a remote future. So long as the Russo-Japanese war lasted, a diplomatic reconciliation between England and Russia would be out of the question. A curious incident which occurred in the autumn reveals both the obstacles which at this time barred the way to a reconciliation and the efforts the Foreign Office made to surmount them.

On August 21 the Russian fleet left the Baltic on its way to the Far East. It encountered in a fog a fleet of British trawlers fishing on the Dogger Bank in the latitude of Hull. The Russian sailors were seized with panic, mistook these little steamers for Japanese torpedo boats and opened fire. A trawler was sunk, two men were killed, several wounded. A cry of execration arose throughout England. Surely such provocation was sufficient to cause dangerous friction between two nations traditionally hostile? But the British Government took the necessary steps to calm the public excitement and appealed to the good offices of the French Government to close the incident. The matter was submitted to the arbitration of The Hague tribunal, while the Russian fleet proceeded on its way to Chinese waters to be annihilated six months later at Tsichuma.

A report was actually current in England that the fatal mistake of the Russian sailors was due to a warning given to Russia by the German Government that Japanese torpedo boats were waiting in British waters to attack the Russian men-of-war when they arrived in their neighbourhood. Germany, therefore, not

[1] Count von Tattenbach to Count von Bülow, Lisbon, May 2, 1904 (*Die Grosse Politik*, vol. xxi, p. 26). According to the same authority, King Edward, on his return to London, received in audience only the French and Russian ambassadors.

[2] See Sidney Lee's account, *The Times*, July 22, 1921. Sir Sidney Lee had been allowed to make use of the archives of the Russian Embassy in London. Count Isvolsky in his *Mémoires* makes only a brief reference to this conversation (p. 24).

Russia, was in the last instance responsible for the blood which had been shed. It was indeed against Germany, not Russia, that feeling ran high in British naval circles. It is interesting to study from this point of view the effect produced on the imagination of the British public by the opening events of the war.

Although it had not yet won the decisive victory, the young and small Japanese Navy had already given proof of its capacity. In February it had opened hostilities with a brilliant exploit, destroying the Russian squadron in the Far East by a surprise attack without a formal declaration of war. It was a feat worthy of those which had covered the British Navy with renown in the days of Drake or Nelson. It recalled the even more splendid achievement of Admiral Gambier in 1807, when, without declaring war, he captured the entire Danish fleet at Copenhagen, and a saying now became current in the British Navy, of which Admiral Fisher was the author, that the day would arrive when it would be necessary to 'Copenhagen' the German fleet. On February 2, 1905, Arthur Lee, Civil Lord of the Admiralty and in that capacity included in the Ministry, explained in an after-dinner speech that it had been found necessary to alter the distribution of the squadrons to make provision against the new danger which threatened Britain in the North Sea, and that all the necessary arrangements had been made to enable the reserve squadron to be mobilized within a few hours. 'If war', he said in conclusion, 'should unhappily be declared, under existing conditions the British Navy would get its blow in first, before the other side had time even to read in the papers that war had been declared.'[1]

In the British Press Lee's speech was suppressed or officially denied.[2] But it produced an enormous impression in Germany, where it was exploited to the utmost by the pan-German propa-

[1] *The Times*, February 4; see also in the *Daily Chronicle*, the popular organ of the Liberal Imperialists, for February 6, the important article signed 'Coloniensis', congratulating Lee on the language he had used.

If the German fleet had been smashed in October, we should have had peace in Europe for sixty years.

For the subsequent correction of the passage see *The Times*, February 7. See further the speech, a year earlier, of Pretyman, Financial Secretary to the Admiralty: 'If there was one lesson which we might learn from recent events in the Far East, it was the rapidity with which a naval blow might be struck at the commencement of a war.' (*Parliamentary Debates*, 4th Ser., vol. cxxx, p. 1272.)

[2] Under pressure from the German Government, if we are to believe a letter from the Kaiser to Admiral von Tirpitz, February 4, 1905 (Von Tirpitz, *Politische Dokumente*, vol. i, p. 14).

gandists at a moment when the Emperor William by a theatrical gesture was about to take his revenge for the diplomatic victory King Edward had gained at his expense the year before. The gesture which we are about to relate was apparently so sudden that it took the whole of Western Europe by surprise. To understand how it had in reality been planned long before, we must go back to the moment when the Wilhelmstrasse was confronted with the new situation created by the Anglo-French *entente* and the Russo-Japanese War.

6

There can be no doubt that the publication of the agreement of April 8, 1904, and the fact that the *entente cordiale* was accepted so readily by French opinion after years of acute anglophobia, came as an unwelcome surprise to the German Government. But it did not feel itself suddenly condemned to the 'isolation' of which certain English newspapers were already speaking. A new prospect dawned upon Bülow, Holstein and William II. Might not the Russo-Japanese War compensate for the reconciliation between England and France? And must not the effect of that reconciliation be to draw closer than before the bonds which united the imperial courts of Russia and Germany? The Czar, who had always detested the English—'Every Englishman', he used to say, 'is a sheeny,'[1]—loathed them more heartily than ever since England had become the ally of Japan. He liked no better the France of Combes and Jaurès, and naturally held French Radicalism responsible both for the policy of the *entente cordiale* with Russia's traditional foe, and the revival of the revolutionary movement in Russia, which in 1905 would assume formidable proportions. Moreover, a year before, the agreement of Mürzsteg had brought a truce to the rivalry between Russia and Austria in the Balkans. What then prevented the creation of an *entente* or alliance between the three great military Empires against the Liberal nations of the West, France reconciled with Italy and England with France? Are we to conclude that the German Government had abandoned its ambitious project of 1895, a combination of the entire Continent against England? On the contrary, this was the goal it hoped to reach by an indirect

[1] *Memoirs of Count Witte*, French trans., p. 167.

route. For it believed that France and Italy were too weak to resist the pressure which would be brought to bear upon them by the three allied Emperors. Willy-nilly, Italy, the ally of Germany, would remain the ally of Austria. And on the other hand, if Russia could be persuaded to conclude a treaty of alliance with Germany, she would surely be in a position to compel France, whatever her wishes, to enter the second Triple Alliance which would thus be formed to reinforce the first. This was the programme whose elaboration by the Wilhelmstrasse we can watch from the January of 1904 onwards,[1] even before the actual outbreak of the Russo-Japanese War, and before the reconciliation between Great Britain and France had produced its full effects. It was, however, recognized that no steps could profitably be taken until the day arrived when Russia, weakened and alarmed, showed by unmistakable signs that she felt the need of German support. A premature advance would have the opposite effect to what was desired. The Russian Government might well believe that it was a Machiavellian plot to embroil her with France. The right moment seemed to have arrived when, after the bombardment of the Hull trawlers, Russia and England appeared to the superficial observer on the verge of a diplomatic rupture. The draft of a suggested alliance was laid before the Czar and accepted after revision. By its first article the Czar undertook 'to take the necessary steps to communicate the agreement to France and gain her adhesion as an ally'. He wanted, however, to communicate the treaty to France, before it was concluded. The Emperor of Germany rejected a proposal which must necessarily lead to the abandonment of the treaty, and the Czar then refused his signature.[2] Moreover, when the Russian Emperor insisted on this condition, the attitude of the Foreign Office had made it certain that the Dogger Bank affair would not cause a permanent estrangement between England and Russia. Evidently the time was not ripe for the Russo-German alliance desired by Berlin.

[1] See Von Holstein's notes on January 22 and 23, 1904 (*Die Grosse Politik*, vol. xix, pp. 46, 48), with which we should compare the cautious observations made by Baron von Richthofen about the beginning of July (*Die Grosse Politik*, vol. xix, p. 194).

[2] For the entire episode see *Die Grosse Politik* (vol. xix, pp. 301 sqq.): The negotiations were not kept so strictly secret as the German Government would have wished. See Count von Bülow's letter, written from Berlin on November 14, 1904. 'To my observations, Sir Frank Lascelles replied that it was true that *The Times* had adopted a most regrettable attitude towards us and was endeavouring to spread suspicion against us in England. . . . Mr. Chirol was the heart and soul of this campaign. Chirol was convinced that we had concluded a secret agreement with Russia directed against England.'

Germany must wait until further disasters brought Russia to her knees. She must also wait until she had compelled the French to realize their weakness as a military Power. The Morocco question provided the German Emperor with the opportunity he required.

When at the beginning of 1900 France had cast her eyes on Morocco, she had found herself in conflict not only with British, but with German influences. German trade, organized, was making rapid progress. Was there no reason to fear lest, some day or other, Germany would repeat on the coast of Morocco her occupation of Kiau-Chau? But if certain organs of the colonial group in Paris occasionally expressed apprehensions on that score, they were quickly reassured by the favour with which the French enterprise was evidently regarded by the German Government. The latter was applying what had been for many years one of the cardinal principles of its foreign policy, to support against England the colonial ambitions of France. In January, 1903, when, for the first time, there was a rumour of negotiations between France and England on the subject of Morocco, Count von Bülow in a speech delivered in the Reichstag offered France in veiled terms a free hand in Morocco *against England*.[1] Now, however, the negotiations between England and France had been brought to a successful conclusion, and France had secured freedom of action in Morocco from England and *against Germany*. The German Government was obliged to reverse its policy. The method adopted was clever.

The status in Morocco of the subjects of European Powers had been settled by an international convention concluded at Madrid in 1881. Though the agreement of April 8, 1904, expressly provided that no change should be made in the *status quo* in Morocco, it was not easy to deny that it gave France the advantages of a privileged position to the detriment of other Powers. England accepted the position, she was entitled to do so; but France—so Germany contended—could not obtain the same acquiescence

---

[1] January 20, 1903: 'It is my whole-hearted conviction that peaceable and friendly relations between Germany and France are in the interest of both countries, and even that there are a number of matters in which they can co-operate to their mutual advantage.' (*Temps*, January 22, 1903.) Cf. E. Bourgeois and G. Pagès, *Les Origines et las Responsabilités de la Grande Guerre*, p. 202. In 1902 M. Bihourd succeeded the Marquis de Noailles as ambassador at Berlin, and when von Bülow received him in January he made 'very marked advances'. The Chancellor spoke of Morocco, but only to insist that Germany was not in any way concerned. 'Germany', he told M. Bihourd, 'has practically speaking no interests in Morocco, so extremely slight and insignificant are they up to the present. (Bihourd's despatch of January 13.)

from the other signatories of the Madrid Convention without their express consent. France had neglected to ask her consent. Germany, therefore, so far as her interests were concerned, could treat the Anglo-French agreement as non-existent. The decision as to the form her intervention would take she would postpone, until France attempted, with the support of the British representatives, to impose her wishes on the Sultan of Morocco.

Meanwhile the German Government set a high price on its acceptance of the new conditions, favourable to Great Britain, which the agreement of April 8 set up in Egypt. The other Powers were content to signify their unconditional assent. Germany insisted on obtaining valuable privileges for her subjects living in Egypt. If, however, a general agreement on the pattern of the Anglo-French agreement could not be secured, the conclusion of a general arbitration treaty, modelled on the treaty concluded the previous year between France and England, was regarded by the Wilhelmstrasse as a good method of reassuring the latter as to German intentions. The German Government hoped that the question of Tangiers would provoke a conflict between the French and Spaniards, that England would support the Spanish claims and thus perhaps destroy the *entente cordiale* within a few months. For it was ignorant of the secret engagement France had taken in April to surrender the entire northern zone of Morocco to Spanish influence. It was accordingly disappointed when the negotiations between France and Spain, which had dragged on amidst the utmost difficulties ever since the end of 1902, reached in October an agreement, whose terms were kept secret, but which was known to give the Spanish plenipotentiaries complete satisfaction. Finally, towards the end of December, the news reached Berlin that the French Government were sending St.-René Taillandier to Fez to inform the Sultan of the conditions on which France was prepared to give him her support. Then the German Government intervened. Its intervention at this particular moment has been explained by the severe defeats inflicted on the Russians in China (the Fall of Port Arthur on January 1, the battle of Mukden, March 10 to 18). But though the coincidence no doubt served the German policy very well, it is doubtful whether it was anything more than a coincidence. If Germany were to intervene at all, she must do so as soon as St.-René

Taillandier reached Fez in February; and since the preceding April she had made up her mind to intervene, whenever the occasion arose.

7

On March 19 the German papers informed the world that the Kaiser in the course of a cruise he was about to make on the coast of Portugal and in the Mediterranean would visit Tangiers. On March 23 he sailed from Bremen after making a speech whose peaceful language contrasted with the warlike tone which usually marked his utterances. On March 29, after a visit to the King of Portugal at Lisbon, he landed at Tangiers, was welcomed by the applause of the natives, and addressed the French representative in insolent terms. He came, he declared, as a protector of the Sultan's sovereignty and the independence of Morocco. This profession covered the demand that his military instructors, engineers, and merchants should receive special privileges; and by perpetuating the state of anarchy in Morocco, the Emperor kept permanently in his hands a weapon he could employ to put a pressure on France and extort diplomatic concessions. Nevertheless, from the standpoint of international law his attitude was under the circumstances perfectly correct. He disclaimed any intention of conquest, and posed as the defender, not of the interests of German commerce alone, but of the commerce óf every nation, including the British. Lord Lansdowne had decided to sacrifice the commercial expansion of Great Britain in Morocco in the interest of imperial policy as a whole. But the German representative at Tangiers declared that the British colony was extremely indignant that their interests had been surrendered,[1] and that it was with the utmost reluctance that Harris, *The Times*' correspondent in Morocco, who had formerly been among the most active opponents of

---

[1] Count von Bülow to William II, Berlin, March 26, 1905: '. . . Your Majesty will notice that as a result of the declaration the British Colony in Tangiers has decided to erect a triumphal arch in your honour. The gesture is a proof that the position we have taken up is perfectly safe. By the very fact of coming forward as the representative of the commercial equality of all nations, we become the protector of the British mercantile community in Morocco whose interests have been sacrificed by the agreement which the British Government has concluded with France. The British trader is too clear-sighted not to understand what it would mean for him, as for all who are not Frenchmen, if Morocco gradually became a French protectorate like Tunis.' (*Die Grosse Politik*, vol. xx, p. 273.) Cf. Sir C. Hardinge to Sir Edward Grey, August 16, 1900: A report of a conversation between King Edward and the Kaiser (vol. iii, p. 369).

French influence, had obeyed the new instructions he had received from London two years before.[1]

This theatrical gesture in which the Kaiser publicly opposed his veto to Delcassé's policy obtained within a few weeks a complete success, a success which perhaps exceeded even the hopes of the German Government. We are, however, inclined to believe that the reply of Paris and London to the imperial challenge was not altogether what the Germans had expected.

In France Bülow expected, and was prepared to defy, a sudden explosion of patriotic and anti-German feeling. In fact the entire country was panic-stricken. The parties of the left, who, even after Combes' fall two months before, still regarded themselves as representing the vast majority of the nation, advocated a policy of disarmament and peace at any price. They had enthusiastically welcomed the Anglo-French *entente* concluded the year before, as it seemed to close the era of colonial conflicts with Great Britain. They had not expected that it would give rise to new conflicts in other directions. The parties of the right, weak in the constituencies, but still powerful in the diplomatic service, the Navy and the Army, believed that the administration of Camille Pelletan and General André had made France powerless to resist German aggression. And even if the French Army had been as organized as perfectly as the German, it was numerically inferior, and since Russia no longer existed as a military Power, would be obliged to face the entire German Army alone. There was, it was true, the British Army, but since the Boer War it had become the laughing-stock of every staff on the Continent. Moreover, the colonial group—which belonged to the centre rather than the right—regarded the agreement of April 8 with strong disapproval. All its traditions were hostile towards England, and friendly towards Russia, and even Germany possessed numerous friends in this quarter. Three months earlier Delcassé's power had been at its height. He had reconciled France with Italy and with England. Between Russia and England he was an intermediary whose good offices in November had been invaluable. It had even seemed possible that the peace between Russia and Japan might be signed at a conference held in Paris over which he would

[1] Herr von Kühlmann to Count von Bülow, Tangiers, January 9, 1905. (*Die Grosse Politik*, vol. xxi, pp. 244-5.) Cf. Herr von Kühlmann to Count von Bülow, March 19, 1905. (Ibid., p. 261.)

preside.[1] For seven years Minister of Foreign Affairs, a member of five successive Cabinets, he had become accustomed to command as an autocrat, not troubling to consult, or even inform, his colleagues. Suddenly his power crumbled. The Prime Minister, Rouvier, promised the German Government to get rid of him on the earliest opportunity, and he knew that his decision was supported by the vast majority in the Chamber, the Press and throughout the country.

Perhaps the Kaiser and Bülow thought that the British Government would, on the other hand, maintain an attitude of reserve, and British public opinion would even be to a certain extent favourable. Was not Germany defending in Morocco the principle of the 'open door', so dear to the British exporter? But if this had really been their expectation, they were quickly undeceived. Without distinction of party, all those who, whether in Parliament or in the Press, shaped British policy, realized immediately that, if on the surface the struggle was between Berlin and Paris, it was at bottom and in the last instance between Berlin and London. An agreement had been concluded the year before by which England obtained certain concessions in Egypt, and France in Morocco. England had already secured in Egypt all the advantages to which she was entitled by its terms. But Germany refused to allow France to take her compensation in Morocco. If England acquiesced in her action, France would complain that she had been fooled and betrayed by England, and Germany would thus have achieved her real aim, the destruction of the *entente cordiale*.

The entire British Press supported Delcassé against Germany, one is tempted to say, against France. 'The British papers', wrote the German Ambassador Metternich from London, 'are more French than the French.'[2] When in April Delcassé was asked to

---

[1] Count von Bernstorff to Count von Bülow, London, September 6, 1904: 'Since the principal object of the British Government in concluding the *entente cordiale* was to localize the war in the Far East, it might very well be made use of now to end the war by mediation.' (*Die Grosse Politik*, vol. xix, p. 220.) Count von Bülow to Count Speck von Sternburg, the German Ambassador at Washington, Berlin, March 23, 1905: 'Kindly inform the President in the strictest confidence that it has indirectly come to the knowledge of our ambassador in St. Petersburg that the suggestion is under consideration there to entrust the settlement of the Russian entanglements in the Far East to a Congress to be held in Paris.' Count von Bülow, seriously alarmed by the plan, orders the ambassador to do his utmost to arouse President Roosevelt's suspicions on the subject. (Ibid., vol. xix, p. 585.)

[2] Count Metternich to Count von Bülow, March 28, 1905 (ibid., vol. xx, p. 60).

resign, he refused. His position was strengthened by the official announcement of a visit of the British fleet to Brest, a public demonstration that England was supporting France. It was further strengthened, or at least Delcassé thought it was strengthened, by a communication from Lord Lansdowne[1] declaring that, in view of the 'most unreasonable attitude of Germany', it seemed 'not unlikely' that Germany might ask for a port on the Moorish coast; and that England, being 'prepared to join the French Government in offering strong opposition to such a proposal' begged for an opportunity 'of conferring as to steps which might be taken in order to meet it'. Delcassé also enjoyed the support of President Loubet, behind whom we may divine the personal influence of King Edward. The latter, during the second half of April, visited Algiers, and, as he passed through France the President had a long interview with him in the railway carriage which was taking him south. On his return, he spent a week in Paris and at the house of the Marquis de Breteuil had a conversation with Delcassé which lasted an hour. To the entire world he gave the impression that he had stopped in Paris to support the policy of the Quai D'Orsay without consulting the French Prime Minister.

Delcassé, with whom King Edward was in full agreement, disclaimed any intention to slight Germany. He was ready to complete the colonial agreement of 1904 with England, by a similar agreement with Germany. But this was not at all what the German Emperor and his Chancellor wanted. Their avowed object was not to complete, but annul, the Anglo-French agreement, so far as Morocco was concerned, and to make Morocco international. Count von Tattenbach, sent by Germany on a special mission to Morocco, had barely arrived at Fez, when on May 28, the Sultan refused the programme of reform submitted by St.-René Taillandier and demanded that a new programme should be drawn up by a conference of all the Powers which had signed the Madrid convention. The diplomatic representative of England in Morocco, Sir Gerard Augustine Lowther, did not wait for the French reply, but on behalf of England immediately rejected the proposed conference.[2] Meanwhile, the German

---

[1] Marquess of Lansdowne to Sir F. Bertie, April 24, 1905 (*British Documents*, vol. iii, pp. 72 sqq.).

[2] It is interesting to discover that the Foreign office, in taking this decision, acted against the advice of King Edward, who wrote on June 3 (two days before Lord Lansdowne's

Ambassador in Paris redoubled his efforts to secure Delcassé's resignation. Just then the King of Spain was on a visit to the President. Rouvier promised the German Government to dismiss his Foreign Minister the moment the King had left. It was therefore on June 6 that the decisive moment arrived. Delcassé showed Rouvier a despatch from the French Ambassador in London which he interpreted as an offer of armed support from England should the danger of a Franco-German war become imminent.[1]

decision): The Conference seems inevitable and might clear up many things. (*British Documents*, vol. iii, p. 88.)

[1] We were careful in the French edition of this volume to neglect the revelations, too sensational not to be suspect (a proposed treaty of defensive and offensive alliance—a promise to land an army of 100,000 men in Holstein), which appeared in the French Press during the year 1905, and based our account solely on the circumstantial evidence contained in a memorandum written on the very evening of June 6 by a member of the Rouvier Cabinet, M. Chaumié, and published seventeen years later by two of his former colleagues (*Temps*, March 19, 1922). It was in fact worded so cautiously that we see no reason to alter it, after reading the evidence contained in vol. iii, of *British Documents*. The chief document among those submitted by Delcassé to his colleagues on June 6 was apparently an important private letter written by Lord Lansdowne to Paul Cambon, on May 25 (and forwarded by Paul Cambon to Delcassé only on May 29). Taking into consideration the attitude assumed by the German Government in Morocco and in other parts of the world, he referred Cambon to a talk he had had with him on May 17, and urged: 'That the French and British Governments should keep one another fully informed of everything which came to our knowledge, and so far as possible discuss any contingencies by which we might in the course of events find ourselves confronted'; and cited, as an example of the steps which might be taken if the situation became critical, the memorandum drawn up by Lord Lansdowne on April 24, and officially handed by Sir Francis Bertie to Delcassé on April 25. Marquis of Lansdowne to Sir F. Bertie, April 24, 1905. (*British Documents*, vol. iii, p. 72 sqq.) This is undoubtedly the paper to which Chaumié alluded, and which he described accurately enough, when he wrote, on the evening of June 6: 'Delcassé then explained our policy. He informed us that England had made proposals for joint action. He read the text of the last, which, without entering into details, expressed in the plainest terms the British offer of joint action.' Moreover, on June 28, according to Metternich's account, Lord Lansdowne reminded the German Ambassador that: 'In the event, which, however, he regarded as entirely out of the question, of Germany "light-heartedly engaging in a war of unprovoked aggression against France, he could not forecast the extent to which British public opinion would call upon the Government to come to her support."' (*Die Grosse Politik*, vol. xx, p. 63.) Lord Lansdowne's account of the interview (The Marquis of Lansdowne to Mr. Whitehead, June 28, 1905. *British Documents*, vol. iii, p. 103) is summary in the extreme, and contains no mention of this threat. But Sir Edward Grey, who became Foreign Secretary six months later, stated twice—the first time to Metternich, the second to Paul Cambon—that it had been uttered. (Sir Edward Grey to Sir F. Lascelles, January 9, 1906; to Sir F. Bertie, January 31, 1906. *British Documents*, vol. iii, pp. 180, 209.) We cannot fail to perceive the grave import of words like these, spoken at a time of international crisis. So much for the offer of armed assistance. So far as the question of a proposed alliance is concerned, we believe that Raymond Poincaré's mention of: 'A general formula of agreement, rather more indefinite however than that which in 1891 had paved the way for the Franco-Russian Alliance' (*Les Origines de la Guerre*, p. 79), is an allusion to both the documents above quoted, the written memorandum of April, and Lord Lansdowne's conversation with Cambon in May, as anybody will see, who compares the terms used by Lord Lansdowne with those in which the Franco-Russian *entente* of August 9–21, 1892, was formulated. We are even ready to go a step further, and attempt to explain how the rumour of a treaty of alliance came to be spread in Paris by Delcassé's friends. Lord Lansdowne's letter, after the sentence

Rouvier understood it in the same sense, and it was sufficient to redouble his alarm. He believed—mistakenly—that the German Government knew of the offer and that it was for that very reason that it was so insistent in its demand for Delcassé's resignation. He invited his colleagues to choose between their Prime Minister and the Minister for Foreign Affairs. Unanimously they declared against Delcassé, and Rouvier took his place at the Quai d'Orsay. By following the advice of his Chancellor, Count von Bülow, the Emperor William had won the victory. He showed his gratitude by conferring on von Bülow the title of Prince.

8

The entire affair which shared with the concluding phases of the Russo-Japanese War the attention of the civilized world, caused the British Government no slight perplexity. It was many years since the diplomatic situation had been so involved as it was during the summer which followed Delcassé's fall. The Russo-Japanese War ended with the victory of Japan, England's ally, but it was received in England with very mixed feelings. It sealed the decline of British influence in northern China, and the peace was concluded in the United States, where the role of arbitrator was played by President Roosevelt, a friend and admirer of the Emperor William. In Europe a timid France was seeking an accommodation with Germany at all costs. And the meeting between the Kaiser and the Czar at Bjorkoe in Finnish waters

we have quoted, went on to express the wish: 'That there should be full and confidential discussion between the two Governments, not so much in consequence of some acts of unprovoked aggression on the part of another Power, as in anticipation of any complications to be apprehended during the somewhat anxious period through which we are at present passing.' It is interesting to know how Paul Cambon interpreted this sentence, reading it in connection with Lord Lansdowne's allusion to the conversation of May 17. In two anxious letters, he expressed to Delcassé his belief that: *Accepter le conversation, c'est entrer dans le voie d'une entente générale qui constituerait en réalité une alliance* (May 29), and again called Lord Lansdowne's suggestions: *Des ouvertures qui . . . nous menent à l'alliance* (June 1); and he entreated Delcassé to give nothing more than an extremely evasive answer to a proposal which it would be, under the circumstances, most dangerous to encourage: 'You would certainly be followed neither by your colleagues in the Cabinet nor by public opinion, and you would be accused of engineering a war.' It is easy to see how Delcassé may have been led to believe that, but for his fall, there would have been an alliance. For our part, we quite agree, Lord Lansdowne was not thinking of an 'alliance'. The more so, as he must have realized that France was terrified by the mere shadow of the idea. But we cannot, on the other hand, help feeling that Paul Cambon's interpretation of Lord Lansdowne's letter described very accurately what the *entente* would become before long: 'Not an "alliance", perhaps, but something very much like one, a semi-alliance or quasi-alliance, which would, if ever things came to a crisis, inevitably "lead to an alliance".'

seemed to betoken a *rapprochement* between Russia and Germany. How alarmed the Foreign Office would have been, had it known how far the gravity of the meeting exceeded its utmost apprehensions, and could have guessed that William II had just extorted the signature of Nicholas to an alliance, to which the Czar undertook to secure the adhesion of France. On his return, shortly afterwards, to Petersburg, his Ministers' insistence compelled Nicholas to retract his signature. And the German Ministers made even William understand that he had committed a blunder. Nevertheless, for a few days he could believe that he had at last attained the object at which he had been aiming ever since his accession.

Even without knowing the details of the interview, the Foreign Office knew enough to be convinced that Britain could not dispense with military safeguards against Russia. The Viceroy of India, Lord Curzon, who belonged to Chamberlain's school of imperial expansion, had taken advantage of the Russo-Japanese War to despatch an expedition to Tibet and a mission to Afghanistan, thus securing against a Russian invasion what he called the *glacis* of British India. In August, at the very moment when the Russian and Japanese Governments signed the treaty of Portsmouth, the Anglo-Japanese alliance of 1902 was renewed. Not only did England by the terms of the new treaty entrust Japan with the care of her interests in Far Eastern waters, and thus make it possible to strengthen her European squadrons by reducing her squadron in the Pacific. An additional clause was introduced by which Japan guaranteed the Indian frontier against a possible aggressor. The treaty of 1905 was thus more explicitly anti-Russian than the treaty of 1902 had been. Apparently the situation was once more the same as in that year; Great Britain exposed to the danger of a German hegemony on the continent of Europe and obliged to meet it with no other assistance except the Japanese alliance.

Moreover, King Edward and his Ministers were compelled to reckon with another factor. Once the first excitement had passed, the British public seemed no longer to concern itself with the problems which caused the politicians such anxiety. When in July and October the public learnt from sensational revelations in the French Press the offer of armed assistance England had made to France during the previous spring, they were disagreeably surprised, and it was to satisfy public opinion that denials were published in the leading British papers. Since ostensibly it was France which had suffered the humiliation, why not stand aside, instead of taking her part, and treat the incident as a matter which exclusively concerned France and Germany, and in which Britain was merely an onlooker? It was obvious that when the agreement of April 8, 1904, had been concluded, neither the British nor the French public had understood that it involved the risk of war. Ever since the end of the Boer War the entire country felt an intense desire for peace, a desire intensified at present by the conclusion of the Russo-Japanese War and the consequent reopening of markets in the Far East, which, it was hoped, would complete the recovery of trade, already very marked for the past few months. Under these circumstances the dispute between France and Germany seemed an unfortunate episode to be closed as quickly as possible. The universal longing for peace found an eloquent exponent in Thomas Hardy, who, eighteen months after the peace of Vereeniging, published his *Dynasts*, in which under a form partly lyrical, partly dramatic, he tells the story of that cycle of revolution and war which had ushered in the nineteenth century. 'The great historical calamity, or clash of Peoples, artificially brought about some hundred years ago.' Among men of letters a new outlook was beginning to find expression, very different from Kipling's militarism, which before long it would supplant in the public favour.

Does this mean that the party which in the Press, at the Admiralty, at Court, and even in the Cabinet had been advocating for the last three years a coalition against Germany had become in a moment defunct? We have only to read the daily papers and still more the reviews[1] to find it still active, and convinced that its propaganda was more necessary than ever in view of the present

---

[1] See in the *Fortnightly Review* Joseph Conrad's anti-Prussian articles, 'Autocracy and War; How it Struck a Contemporary', by J. A. Spender (July Number). 'French and German Relations,' by Rowland Blennerhasset (August number). 'British Naval Policy and German Aspiration', by Archibald S. Hurd. 'French and German Relations, Reflections on the Aniversary of Sedan', by an anonymous writer, who signs *** (September number). 'France and the Equipoise of Europe', by Perseus (November number), and 'The Foreign Policy of Germany', by *** (December number). In the *Nineteenth Century*, articles by O. Eltzbacher, Austin F. Harrison and Robert Machray on 'The Collapse of Russia' (July number); Archibald S. Hurd, 'The Contest for Sea Power' (August number); Herbert Paul, 'Liberals and Foreign Policy' (November number). In the *Contemporary Review*, the three articles by Dr. E. J. Dillon, entitled 'Foreign Affairs' (July, August and September numbers).

situation, a weak France, a Russia vanquished and without a navy in face of an arrogant and powerful Germany, and the Foreign Office defeated, whether it admitted it or not, by Delcassé's fall. The difficulty was to make an active foreign policy acceptable to a public indifferent and deliberately indifferent. The method employed was that equivocal method (we are not using the term in a depreciatory sense) to which England would remain faithful for many years to come. No lover of peace could condemn the agreement which in 1904, after so much friction in Africa and Asia, had removed all causes of war between France and England. Nor could he object to an attempt to conclude a similar agreement with Russia. The revolution which had just taken place in that country, and the Emperor's announcement of his intention to summon a representative assembly, a 'Duma', did much to remove liberal objections. Russia, of course, would be obliged to renounce any designs of expansion on the Indian frontier, but she would be offered ample compensation in Persia and even in Asia Minor, a bargain similar to that by which England and France bartered Egypt for Morocco. At the very moment when the Japanese alliance was renewed newspapers and reviews were again beginning to advocate an *entente* with Russia. In October, Sir Edward Grey, destined to become Foreign Secretary in the next Liberal Government, gave the suggestion his support.[1]

What were the Ministers doing and thinking meanwhile? George Wyndham, who, as everybody knew, had been the most ardent supporter of the new foreign policy,[2] had just resigned. Chamberlain, who at this period must be regarded as a determined partisan of the anti-German policy, had also left the Cabinet, and his son, Austen Chamberlain, had not yet acquired the standing which only age and experience can confer. On the other hand, it was slowly and only with great reluctance that the Prime

[1] Speech at Arbroath, October 21.
[2] 'He was one of the very few Ministers whose foresight urged on a rather reluctant majority, the conclusion of the Anglo-French *Entente*' (F. T. Raymond, *Mr. Balfour*, p. 129). Nothing is said on this subject in his biography by S. W. Mackail and Guy Wyndham. Cf. Wilfrid Scawen Blunt, *My Diaries, 1888–1914*, vol. i, p. 397, May 28, 1899: '. . . About foreign politics George [Wyndham] says that it is now simply a triangular battle between the Anglo-Saxon race, the German race and the Russian, which shall have the hegemony of the whole world. France he considers gone as a great Power, as much gone as Spain or Austria, but the Emperor William means to be supreme overlord. He is holding his hand for the moment till he can get an efficient Navy, but as soon as this is ready, there will be a coalition against England. He, George, and the young Imperialists are going in for England's overlordship, and they won't stand half measures or economy in pushing it on.'

Minister, Balfour, renounced the hope of maintaining the Anglo-German understanding. Lord Lansdowne was a man without strong personality, ready to accept any suggestion, incapable of initiating any policy of his own. Three years before, his lethargy had yielded to the pressure brought to bear upon him by the Foreign Office, by the Press, and possibly to a certain extent by King Edward. Now perhaps it had once more taken possession of him. On August 12, at so critical a moment—a fortnight before the treaty of Portsmouth, six weeks before the renewal of the Japanese alliance—he retired to his estates in Ireland and his absence, which had not been intended to exceed a month, continued until September 24. Is it surprising that the influence King Edward exercised over British foreign policy increased in proportion to his Minister's indolence? He made it his business to pave the way for a *rapprochement* with Russia. About the middle of September, while Lord Lansdowne was taking his holiday, he attempted, though without success, to arrange that Count Witte, who was returning from America by way of Paris and Berlin, should visit London to discuss the situation with himself.[1] And a rumour circulated among the Foreign Offices that negotiations had actually begun.[2] There was nothing in all this to which Germany could reasonably object. If she chose to take offence and proclaim to the world that her foreign policy to be successful required that England should remain permanently estranged from France and Russia, she would confess her responsibility for the unstable condition of Europe.

We have described the policy which before long the Unionist Government would transmit to a Liberal administration. Nothing would be easier for its successor than to speak the same language, for it was strictly pacific. It remains to inquire what military and naval programme would support this foreign policy. More than three years had passed since the end of the Boer War, and the problem of reorganizing the Army had not yet been solved,

---

[1] *Memoirs of Count Witte*, French trans., pp. 387–8.
[2] See Count von Bernstorff's letters of September 8, 12, 22, 25 (*Die Grosse Politik*, vol. xix, pp. 636, 658, 659, 661). Cf. H. of C., November 27, 1911, Sir Edward Grey's speech 'As far as there are records in the Foreign Office to give me any indication of Lord Lansdowne's intentions, I think he would have desired, had he remained in office, to do something of the same kind with Russia. I do not say they had gone far enough for me to say that he had incurred any responsibility or committed himself in any way: but, as far as I have any indication, that was the direction in which he would have gone.' (*Parliamentary Debates*, 5th Ser., vol. xxxi, p. 58.)

and it was only just beginning to be recognized that the rapid growth of the German Navy would compel the Admiralty to alter entirely the plans it had prepared to meet the eventuality of war. Would the Liberals understand the necessity of dealing with these questions? They certainly would if, in their next Cabinet, Lord Rosebery, Asquith, Grey and Haldane occupied positions corresponding to their talents. But it could be foreseen that the policy of armaments which these statesmen advocated would be opposed tooth and nail by the section which revived the old Gladstonian tradition. To overcome the opposition from their own party the Liberal Imperialists would need Unionist support. And their failure would go far to discredit the Liberal party. How easy it would be to frighten the electorate! If the Unionists knew themselves doomed to be a minority in the next Parliament, they also knew that in every question which concerned the foreign policy of the country they would have the last word.

The year had not closed before Lord Lansdowne won in the Levant a diplomatic victory which went some way to compensate for the many failures of the previous summer. The Sultan had failed to take any steps to carry out a programme of reform submitted to him by the Austrian and Russian Governments. Lord Lansdowne presented a different programme to the Powers, which they accepted. The Sultan refused his consent. To compel him to yield it was decided that a naval demonstration should be made, and Mitylene occupied by an international force. The demonstration was completely successful and the Sultan gave way. But it was noticed that though British, French, Italian, Russian and Austrian men-of-war had taken part in it, Germany was not represented. Had she been isolated? Or rather was she deliberately holding aloof from the concert of the Powers?

9

We must not however imagine that the incident, whatever interest it may have aroused in diplomatic circles, made any considerable impression on the British public. For when the demonstration took place on November 11, their attention was elsewhere. Three days later the Unionist party held its annual congress at Newcastle and passed by an all but unanimous vote a motion in favour of protection which seemed a direct condemnation of the tactics adopted for the past two years by Balfour, and a repudiation of those Conservative free traders with whom he persistently refused to break. On November 21, Chamberlain delivered a speech at the annual congress of Liberal Unionists which amounted to a further declaration of war against Balfour's opportunism. 'You must not', he said, 'ask the majority, be it nine-tenths, or, as I think, ninety-nine hundredths, to sacrifice their convictions to the prejudices of the minority. . . . You must not go into the battle which is impending with blunted swords, merely in order to satisfy the scruples of those who do not wish to fight at all.' Balfour perceived that he must abandon the hope of presiding over a sixth session of the Parliament returned in 1900. On December 4th the Government resigned and the country, without even waiting for the new Liberal Cabinet to be formed, threw itself feverishly into the preparations for the approaching election.

Such was the inglorious fall of the Unionist Cabinet whose advent to power ten years before had been hailed as the dawn of a new epoch in English history. To be sure during its first two years in office, the Cabinet's domestic policy had been unfortunate, its foreign policy involved in the scandal and failure of the Jameson Raid. But after 1898 the imperialism of Chamberlain and his followers, stimulated by the example of the United States, proceeded unchecked. That year witnessed the 'victory' over France at Fashoda, the next the preparation and launching of the attack upon the Boers. The passions aroused by patriotism and conquest were at the service of the Government, and at the general election of 1900 constituted the entire programme of the Unionists. Then came the years of weariness and disillusionment. The long and difficult war against the Boers had opened the eyes of the British Government to the inefficiency of its army, and to the hatred with which England was regarded by almost every country in Europe, and on the other hand a host of difficulties arose at home as a result of the policy pursued by the Cabinet and its supporters. At the end of the nineteenth century a Conservative Government could not retain its popularity, unless it supplemented a policy of diplomatic prestige and military glory by a bold policy of domestic reform in harmony with the traditional institutions of the country. This had been understood by Disraeli and Bismarck. It was not understood by the British imperialists of 1895. In this sphere Chamberlain had disappointed the hopes he had raised. We have seen how the imperialist Cabinet made itself unpopular alike by what it did, or permitted, and what it failed to do. When once the Boer War had been brought to an end, what policy could the Ministry adopt to overcome the discontent of the Nonconformists and the working classes?

At this juncture, the leading statesman of the party attempted a noisy diversion, and, brushing aside the opposition of his more timid colleagues and leaving the Cabinet the better to free his hands, demanded in the interest of the country and the Empire the abandonment of that tradition of free trade which for more than fifty years had seemed a part of the national faith. His campaign had served only to increase the unpopularity of the Government. He was not daunted. He counted upon the difficulties which the Liberal party, even if for the moment victorious at the next election, would experience in reconciling in its administration the imperialists and the enemies of imperialism: he counted on the difficulties, possibly even more serious, with which it would have to contend in the attempt to satisfy the demands of the Irish and the new Labour party. The moment would soon arrive when he could renew the offensive with the weapons of his own choice; and under his leadership, accepted at last, the Unionist Party would conquer. Which of the two was right, Chamberlain, irritated by Balfour's conservative caution, or Balfour who was alarmed by Chamberlain's rashness and considered it imprudent by attacking free trade to provide the warring sections of the Liberal party with a common programme of defence? The future would reply. For the present this was a question of electoral tactics which hardly interested public opinion. Who cared about all these questions, of interest only to political theorists and professional politicians! Who bothered about the baffling problems of foreign policy, about Germany, France and the affairs of the Continent! At this critical moment in European history the 'insular' light-heartedness of the British once again overcame the fears which on so many occasions, during the last three or four years, the London Press had endeavoured to excite. The grand national 'match' between free traders and tariff reformers which Chamberlain had started in 1903 and which ever since had been fought according to the traditional rules of the game was drawing to its close. And it was the more exciting, because everyone took part in it, both as a spectator and a player. Nobody wished or was able to think of anything else.

Index